Historical Dictionaries of Asia, Oceania, and the Middle East

Edited by Jon Woronoff

Asia

1. *Vietnam*, by William J. Duiker. 1989. *Out of print. See No. 27.*
2. *Bangladesh*, 2nd ed., by Craig Baxter and Syedur Rahman. 1996. *Out of print. See No. 48.*
3. *Pakistan*, by Shahid Javed Burki. 1991. *Out of print. See No. 33.*
4. *Jordan*, by Peter Gubser. 1991.
5. *Afghanistan*, by Ludwig W. Adamec. 1991. *Out of print. See No. 47.*
6. *Laos*, by Martin Stuart-Fox and Mary Kooyman. 1992. *Out of print. See No. 35.*
7. *Singapore*, by K. Mulliner and Lian The-Mulliner. 1991.
8. *Israel*, by Bernard Reich. 1992.
9. *Indonesia*, by Robert Cribb. 1992. *Out of print. See No. 51.*
10. *Hong Kong and Macau*, by Elfed Vaughan Roberts, Sum Ngai Ling, and Peter Bradshaw. 1992.
11. *Korea*, by Andrew C. Nahm. 1993. *Out of print. See No. 52.*
12. *Taiwan*, by John F. Copper. 1993. *Out of print. See No. 34.*
13. *Malaysia*, by Amarjit Kaur. 1993. *Out of print. See No. 36.*
14. *Saudi Arabia*, by J. E. Peterson. 1993. *Out of print. See No. 45.*
15. *Myanmar*, by Jan Becka. 1995. *Out of print. See No. 59.*
16. *Iran*, by John H. Lorentz. 1995. *Out of print. See No. 62.*
17. *Yemen*, by Robert D. Burrowes. 1995.
18. *Thailand*, by May Kyi Win and Harold Smith. 1995. *Out of print. See No. 55.*
19. *Mongolia*, by Alan J. K. Sanders. 1996. *Out of print. See No. 42.*
20. *India*, by Surjit Mansingh. 1996. *Out of print. See No. 58.*
21. *Gulf Arab States*, by Malcolm C. Peck. 1996.
22. *Syria*, by David Commins. 1996. *Out of print. See No. 50.*
23. *Palestine*, by Nafez Y. Nazzal and Laila A. Nazzal. 1997.
24. *Philippines*, by Artemio R. Guillermo and May Kyi Win. 1997. *Out of print. See No. 54.*

Oceania

1. *Australia*, by James C. Docherty. 1992. *Out of print. See No. 32.*
2. *Polynesia*, by Robert D. Craig. 1993. *Out of print. See No. 39.*

Historical Dictionary of the People's Republic of China

Second Edition

Lawrence R. Sullivan

Historical Dictionaries of Asia, Oceania, and the Middle East, No. 63

The Scarecrow Press, Inc.
Lanham, Maryland • Toronto • Plymouth, UK
2007

A SCARECROW PRESS, INC.

Published in the United States of America
by Scarecrow Press, Inc.
A wholly owned subsidiary of
The Rowman & Littlefield Publishing Group, Inc.
4501 Forbes Boulevard, Suite 200, Lanham, Maryland 20706
www.scarecrowpress.com

Estover Road
Plymouth PL6 7PY
United Kingdom

British Library Cataloguing in Publication Information Available

Library of Congress Cataloging-in-Publication Data

Sullivan, Lawrence R.
  Historical dictionary of the People's Republic of China / Lawrence R. Sullivan.
  — 2nd ed.
     p. cm. — (Historical dictionaries of Asia, Oceania, and the Middle East ;
No. 63)
  Includes bibliographical references.
  ISBN-13: 978-0-8108-5380-5 (hardcover : alk. paper)
  ISBN-10: 0-8108-5380-9 (hardcover : alk. paper)
  1. China–History–1949–Dictionaries. I. Title.
DS777.55.S835 2007
951.0503–dc22   2006027050

For Liu Junqi and Jin Ling and my wife, Yang Liu.

Contents

Editor's Foreword

The People's Republic of China is one of the world's largest countries geographically and is the world's largest in terms of population: 1.3 billion people. It is strategically located, adjacent to other large and populous countries, and is positioned to dominate Eastern and Southeast Asia. Yet, until recently it was not really a major player in world affairs. Thus, it was surprising to some — although this is probably more their mistake — when its impressive economic growth created not only exciting opportunities for its trade partners but bothersome problems as well. This was exacerbated whenever it flexed its economic muscle or intervened actively politically, and even militarily. Now there is talk of a "China threat." However, this threat need not materialize, and China's contribution could be largely positive. Fostering this positive outcome is perhaps one of the biggest challenges of the 21st century.

Obviously, it would be easier to adapt to China's new role if one knew more about the country and its internal operations. Yet, even decades after China opened its doors to the rest of the world, there is a shortage not so much of information as of understanding. This new edition of the *Historical Dictionary of the People's Republic of China* will be helpful in this respect. Unlike much of the information, it is not hot off the press — here today and gone tomorrow — but rather takes a longer view, going back to the Communist takeover in 1949 (and even earlier) and following a long, convoluted, and sometimes torturous path to the present day. The chronology section of this dictionary traces this path, and it is embedded in a broader, more analytic introduction. The specifics on significant persons, places, events, institutions, and crucial political, economic, social, and cultural aspects are contained in the hundreds of dictionary entries. The bibliography provides further background reading.

The author of this second edition is Lawrence R. Sullivan, who also wrote the first edition. He is an associate professor of political science at Adelphi University and a research associate with a specialization in contemporary Chinese politics at the East Asian Institute, Columbia University. In addition to the many articles he has written and papers he has presented, he is coauthor or coeditor of several books, including *China since Tiananmen: Political, Economic, and Social Conflicts*. The bibliography, also updated, was based on the first edition by Nancy R. Hearst, librarian at the John K. Fairbanks Center for East Asian Research at Harvard University.

Jon Woronoff
Series Editor

Reader's Note

The Romanization used in this dictionary for Chinese terms is the *Hanyu pinyin* system developed in the 1950s and currently used in the People's Republic of China. Names and places of some well-known figures (e.g., Sun Yat-sen) and of terms associated with the Republic of China on Taiwan are, however, written according to the Wade-Giles system of Romanization. Chinese terms generally unknown to the Western reader are italicized, as are all newspaper names and book titles. In Chinese and East Asian culture, generally, the family name comes first preceding the given names. Past and some present leaders in China are listed in alphabetical order along with a more general entry titled "Leaders." Cross-referencing in the dictionary section is done by bolding items on which there are separate entries or indicating them in a *See also*.

Acronyms and Abbreviations

APCs	Agricultural Producers' Cooperatives
ASEAN	Association of Southeast Asian Nations
CAC	Central Advisory Commission
CAS	Chinese Academy of Sciences
CASS	Chinese Academy of Social Sciences
CCP	Chinese Communist Party
CDIC	Central Discipline Inspection Commission
CITIC	China International Trade and Investment Corporation
CPPCC	Chinese People's Political Consultative Conference
CYL	China Youth League
DPRK	Democratic People's Republic of Korea (North Korea)
FDI	Foreign Direct Investment
GDP	Gross Domestic Product
KMT	Kuomintang (Nationalist Party)
MAC	Military Affairs Commission
MAT	Mutual Aid Teams
MOFERT	Ministry of Foreign Economic Relations and Trade
NPC	National People's Congress
PLA	People's Liberation Army
PRC	People's Republic of China
ROC	Republic of China
ROK	Republic of Korea (South Korea)
SAR	Special Administrative Region

SARS	Severe Acute Respiratory Syndrome
SEZ	Special Economic Zone
SOEs	State-Owned Enterprises
TVEs	Township Village Enterprises
WTO	World Trade Organization

Chronology

1644–1911 Qing dynasty, China's last.

1912 The Republic of China is proclaimed with Sun Yat-sen as president who is soon replaced by the warlord, Yuan Shih-k'ai.

1919 **4 May:** The May Fourth Movement breaks out among students and workers in protest against the Chinese government's acceptance of the Versailles Treaty ending World War I, which turned over Chinese territory in Shandong Province formerly under German control to Japan. The movement inaugurates modern Chinese nationalism and gives birth to the CCP in 1921.

1920 Comintern envoys from the new Bolshevik regime in Russia arrive in China.

1921 **July:** The Chinese Communist Party (CCP) is formally organized at a girls' school in the French sector of Shanghai.

Period of the First CCP–KMT United Front and the Chinese Soviet Republic 1924–1931

1924 First United Front between CCP and the Kuomintang (KMT). Additional Soviet aid and advisers sent to China.

1925 Death of Sun Yat-sen.

1927 **April:** Anti-Communist coup in Shanghai is led by Chiang Kaishek, KMT leader and successor to Sun Yat-sen. **November:** Mao Zedong sets up Soviet government in Hunan Province.

1928 Sixth CCP National Party Congress is held in Moscow.

1931 Chinese Soviet Republic established in Jiangxi Province. Japanese occupy Manchuria in "Mukden Incident."

The Yan'an Period: 1935–1946

1934–1935 Communist armies retreat from KMT forces in historic Long March.

1937 Japan invades China proper below the Great Wall. Second United Front (1936–1945) is established between the CCP and the KMT.

1942–1944 First CCP Rectification Campaign.

1945 April: At the Seventh National Party Congress, Mao outlines his plan announced in 1940 for a "New Democracy" based on an alliance of workers, peasants, and bourgeois elements. **August:** War with Japan ends.

The Chinese Civil War: 1946–1949

1946 United States Mission headed by General George C. Marshall is sent to China to mediate KMT–CCP armistice. **May:** Communists issue first Land Reform directive. **August:** United States assists KMT forces to occupy key sites in central, south, and east China.

1947 July: Communists launch major counteroffensive against KMT forces, thus turning the tide of the civil war.

1949 January: Communists occupy Beiping (soon renamed Beijing). **April:** People's Liberation Army (PLA) captures Shanghai. **1 October:** Mao Zedong formally proclaims the founding of the People's Republic of China (PRC). **December:** KMT forces with Chiang Kai-shek flee to Taiwan. Mao Zedong visits the Soviet Union in his first journey outside China.

Period of Economic Reconstruction and Political Consolidation: 1950–1957

1950 Sweden, Denmark, Finland, and Switzerland are the first European nations to recognize China. **February:** Sino–Soviet Pact of

Friendship, Alliance, and Mutual Assistance is signed in Moscow between Mao Zedong and Josef Stalin. **April:** China's Marriage Law is promulgated. **October:** China enters the Korean War.

1950–1952 Land Reform implemented.

1951 February: United Nations (UN) General Assembly condemns China as aggressor in Korea. **May:** Agreement of the Central People's Government and the Local Government of Tibet on Measures for the Liberation of Tibet is signed in Beijing. Mao Zedong's son is killed in Korean War. **October:** The Dalai Lama signifies his support for May agreement on Tibet.

1952 January: "Three-Antis" campaign against corruption, waste, and bureaucratism is launched. **February:** "Five-Antis" campaign against corruption inaugurated. **March:** Zhou Enlai denounces United States for using germ warfare in northeast China. **July:** Land reform completed.

1953 January: Beginning of first Five-Year Plan (1953–1957) of economic growth and development. **February:** Mutual Aid Teams are organized in the Chinese countryside. **March:** Josef Stalin dies. **June:** First census of the PRC is conducted. **July:** Korean War armistice. **December:** CCP Central Committee authorizes formation of Agricultural Producers' Cooperatives (APCs).

1954 Great Britain establishes diplomatic relations with China. **April–August:** Zhou Enlai visits several countries in Europe and Asia. **July:** China agrees to Final Declaration of the Geneva Convention on Indochina. **August:** Massive floods hit Yangtze River valley. **September:** First National People's Congress (NPC) promulgates the Chinese state constitution. State Council is established and Mao Zedong is elected chairman of the PRC. **October:** Soviet Union announces withdrawal of all remaining troops from Chinese territory, including the port of Lüshun.

1955 March: Gao Gang and Rao Shushi are officially purged from CCP in first post-1949 leadership struggle. People's Bank of China completes currency changeover. **May:** Beginning of Hu Feng Affair. **July:** Mao Zedong intervenes to speed up formation of rural APCs. **September:** Anti-counter-revolutionary campaign carried out in CCP. **October:** CCP departments are established for Party central, provincial, and local-level committees that function as administrative organs in the government, thereby ensuring Party control of state economic decision-making. Xinjiang-Uygur Autonomous Region is formally established.

1956 "High tide" of rural cooperativization produces vast increase in number of APCs and with it severe disruption of agricultural production. **February:** Nikita Khrushchev denounces Stalin in "secret speech" at 20th Soviet Communist Party Congress held in Moscow. China issues editorial tepidly endorsing Khrushchev's criticisms. **March:** Model regulations for APCs announced. **April:** Mao calls for stability in his speech "On Ten Major Relationships." **May:** Hundred Flowers policy announced by Lu Dingyi and supported by Mao Zedong. **September:** First session of the CCP Eighth National Party Congress indicates relatively liberal direction in economics and politics. **October:** Anti-Communist revolt breaks out in Hungary. **December:** China issues editorial defending Josef Stalin against attacks by Khrushchev.

1957 **February:** Mao's speech on internal "contradictions among the people" signals greater tolerance of intellectuals and free speech. **May:** Three weeks of free expression by Chinese intellectuals in Hundred Flowers Campaign. **June:** Anti-Rightist Campaign launched against outspoken intellectuals. **August:** CCP cadres sent to countryside for "study." **October:** Soviets launch first space satellite. China and Soviet Union sign nuclear sharing agreement. **November:** Mao Zedong visits Moscow for second and last time.

Period of the Great Leap Forward and Its Aftermath: 1958–1965

1958 **Spring:** Decision to amalgamate APCs. **May:** Second session of the Eighth National Party Congress reverses policies and endorses Maoist radicalism. **August:** Politburo meeting of top leadership at Beidaihe announces formation of people's communes in the countryside. **September:** People's militia is established. **December:** Sixth Plenum of the Eighth Central Committee (CC) held in Wuchang announces retreat on formation of the people's communes. Mao Zedong announces his forthcoming resignation as state chairman (also referred to in later years as president, i.e., head of state) at the 1959 NPC.

1959 **Spring:** Economic stabilization policy is enacted. **March:** Armed revolt in Tibet is suppressed. Dalai Lama flees to India. **April:** Liu Shaoqi appointed as state chairman and Lin Biao as minister of defense. **August:** Eighth Plenum of the Eighth CC in Lushan announces shift in the focus of agricultural decision-making power from the people's communes to the lower-level brigades. Peng Dehuai is dismissed. **September:** Khrushchev stops off in Beijing after visiting United States. **October:** Armed clashes between Chinese and Indian troops break out along the border.

1960 The second Great Leap Forward resumes campaign to send cadres down to the countryside. Food crisis that began in 1959 intensifies. **April:** China and India meet to study problems on their mutual border. **August:** Soviet advisers withdraw from China. **September:** Decentralization of rural decision making to the level of the production team. **December:** Natural disasters in China are the worst in the century affecting one-half of all farmland.

1961 **January:** Ninth Plenum of the Eighth CC announces full retreat on the Great Leap Forward. Rectification of basic-level cadres is announced. **February:** *Hai Rui Dismissed from Office* is staged. **July:** China and North Korea sign the Sino–Korean Treaty of Friendship, Cooperation and Mutual Assistance. **October:** Zhou Enlai attends 22nd Soviet Communist Party Congress and defends Albania, which Soviet leader Nikita Khrushchev had censured. **December:** China's future entry into the UN is deemed an "important question" requiring two-thirds vote.

1962 Beginning of the Socialist Education Movement. **January:** *Hai Rai Dismissed from Office* is published. **March:** Liu Shaoqi emerges as primary leader in period of recovery as liberalization is announced for economic and cultural sectors while drought in China is declared worst in three centuries. **July:** China joins the Soviet Union, Great Britain, the United States, and other nations in signing the Declaration of Neutrality on Laos. **September:** Attack on "modern revisionism" at CCP 10th Plenum of the Eighth CC signals return to more radical Maoist policies. Mao insists "never forget class struggle." **October:** Major offensive by Chinese troops is launched on Indian border. **November:** Long-term economic and trade agreement signed by China and Japan. Ceasefire declared along Sino–Indian border.

1963 April: Directive on political work in the PLA. **May:** China and Vietnam call for struggle against imperialism headed by the United States. "First Ten Points" is drafted by Mao Zedong to promote the Socialist Education Movement. **July:** Sino–Soviet conflict worsens. China supports total destruction worldwide of nuclear weapons. **September:** "Later Ten Points" drafted by Peng Zhen moderates Party line on the Socialist Education Movement. **December:** Zhou Enlai and Foreign Minister Chen Yi visit Africa.

1964 Spring: Political departments are organized in various government ministries and bureaus signaling tighter political control. **June:** Campaign to train "revolutionary successor generation." **August:** China denounces bombing of North Vietnam by the United States. **September:** "Revised Later Ten Points" mark another shift in the Socialist Education Movement. **October:** China tests its first atomic bomb. Khrushchev is overthrown in the Soviet Union.

1965 Escalation of war in Vietnam. **February:** Brief meeting is held in Beijing between Soviet Premier Alexsei Kosygin and Mao Zedong and Liu Shaoqi. **March:** China denounces arrival in Vietnam of United States Marines. **June:** China eliminates all ranks in the PLA. **September:** Lin Biao gives speech calling for worldwide "people's war." Mao's calls for criticism of reactionary intellectuals yields little response. **November:** System of part work and part study is proposed for Chinese schools. The play by Beijing vice-mayor Wu Han, *Hai Rui Dismissed from Office*, is attacked by Yao Wenyuan. Mao moves to Shanghai to organize hard-line radicals. China denounces persecution of indigenous Chinese in Indonesia.

Period of the Cultural Revolution: 1966–1976

1966 March: Attack on "bourgeois authorities" in academic and cultural circles. **April:** Large-scale anti-Chinese riots take place in Jakarta, Indonesia.7 **May:** Mao Zedong writes to Lin Biao calling on PLA to be a "great school"—the so-called May 7 directive explicitly targets "capitalist intellectuals" in schools that legitimizes Red Guard violence against teachers. **16 May:** Circular dissolves first Cultural Revolution Small Group for being insufficiently radical and establishes a new group headed by the leftist Chen Boda. Circular targets "capitalist representatives in the academic, educational, journalist, artist, and publication circles." First big-character poster appears at Peking University. China conducts first thermonuclear test. **June:** Work teams sent into China's universities and middle schools. Liu Shaoqi urges work teams to halt any violence as students at Qinghua University and other institutions attack their teachers and school administrators. **July:** Mao swims the Yangtze River. Work Teams withdrawn from educational institutions. **August:** The 11th Plenum of the Eighth CC replaces Liu Shaoqi with Lin Biao as second in command and heir apparent. Liu is demoted from second to eighth position in the Party hierarchy. Mao Zedong gives "enthusiastic support" to Red Guards whom he greets at a number of huge rallies in Beijing. The Party Center voids Liu Shaoqi's call for restraint as Red Guard violence against teachers, educational authorities, and Party secretaries spreads from Beijing to other major cities as students are given free train tickets to travel anywhere in the country. **September:** *Quotations from Chairman Mao*—the little red book—is published in Shanghai. **October:** Deng Xiaoping is attacked at CCP Central Work Conference.

1967   January: Mao Zedong orders PLA to intervene in Cultural Revolution on the side of the leftists. Outbreak of violence by Red Guards in Shanghai—"January storm"—signals near collapse of authority. **February:** "February Adverse Current" calls for end to Cultural Revolution radicalism. **April:** Deng Xiaoping and Liu Shaoqi are accused of committing "crimes" against the CCP. **July:** Wuhan incident brings China to brink of civil war. **Fall:** Height of factional fighting and violence among Red Guards.

1968   June: Violent clashes break out on railways in Guangxi Autonomous Region supplying military hardware to Vietnam. Cleansing of the Class Ranks campaign targets teachers and educators for struggle. **July:** Mao Zedong attacks Red Guard leaders for excessive factionalism and orders students sent to the countryside. **August:** China denounces Soviet invasion of Czechoslovakia. **September:** Revolutionary Committees set up in all provinces of China. **October:** At the 12th Plenum of the Eighth CC Mao Zedong calls for "getting rid of the stale and taking in the fresh" in the CCP. Army veteran and marshal Zhu De is attacked for purportedly opposing Mao Zedong.

1969 **March:** Sino–Soviet border clashes break out along the Ussuri River. **April:** Ninth Party Congress selects Lin Biao as Mao's official successor and proclaims "victory" of the Cultural Revolution. **June:** Major clashes with Soviet forces break out on border in the Xinjiang Autonomous Region. **September:** Zhou Enlai and Soviet Prime Minister Kosygin meet to discuss border issue. **October:** One of eight model dramas *Taking Tiger Mountain by Strategy* is published. **December:** United States partially lifts trade embargo against China.

1970 **January:** China indicates willingness at talks with the United States in Warsaw, Poland, to discuss substantive issues at a higher level. **March:** Coup d'etat in Cambodia against Prince Norodom Sihanouk. **April:** First Chinese satellite is successfully launched. **August:** Conflict between Mao Zedong and Lin Biao over the reestablishment of the position of state chairman, which Mao opposes. Lin Biao offers his theory of genius. **1 October:** American journalist Edgar Snow is invited to 21st anniversary of PRC as a signal to United States President Richard Nixon. **December:** Radical leftists criticized as Beijing Military Region is reorganized.

1971 **April:** Lin Biao supporters who opposed an instruction of Mao Zedong are subjected to open criticism. American table tennis team visits China. **July:** United States National Security Adviser Dr. Henry Kissinger secretly visits China. **12–13 September:** Lin Biao purportedly attempts to assassinate Mao Zedong and dies in plane crash in Mongolia while fleeing China. **October:** PRC is admitted to the United Nations. **December:** Top CCP leadership learns of proposed trip to China by President Nixon.

1972 **February:** President Nixon makes historic trip to China and signs Shanghai Communiqué. **May:** Purported coup attempt by Lin Biao is revealed to CCP rank-and-file. **June:** Attacks against Zhou Enlai begin. **September:** Japanese Prime Minister Tanaka Kakuei visits China.

1973 **January:** Paris Peace Accords bring end to American involvement in Vietnam War. **February:** United States and China set up liaison offices in respective capitals. **April:** Deng Xiaoping rehabilitated as vice-premier and addresses UN General Assembly. **May:** Veteran CCP leaders purged during early years of the Cultural Revolution are rehabilitated. National economic plan is reviewed. **August:** 10th National Party Congress is held and elects radical worker Wang Hongwen into top leadership post. PLA representation on Central Committee is reduced. **November:** Jiang Qing criticizes Zhou Enlai's handling of foreign affairs. **December:** Mao Zedong warns of civil war in China and proposes appointment of Deng Xiaoping as PLA chief-of-staff. CCP Central Military Affairs Commission rotates regional PLA **commanders.**

1974   January: Criticism of Confucius begins. **July:** In letter to Jiang Qing, Mao criticizes her and warns against engaging in factional activity. **October:** Radical leaders resist appointment of Deng Xiaoping as China's first vice-premier. **November:** Mao orders return to task of economic modernization.

1975   January: Deng Xiaoping is reappointed as CCP vice-chairman and as member of Politburo Standing Committee. **February:** Deng Xiaoping criticizes neglect of production in China's rural and urban economy. **May:** Mao Zedong warns Jiang Qing and three supporters against forming a "Gang of Four." **July:** Deng Xiaoping calls for modernization of the PLA. **October:** First National Conference on Learning from Dazhai (Brigade) in Agriculture is held. **November:** Criticism of Deng Xiaoping by radical faction as Hua Guofeng emerges as national Party leader. **December:** United States President Gerald Ford visits China and meets with Mao Zedong.

Period of Late Maoism: 1976–1977

1976   8 January: Death of Zhou Enlai. **February:** Hua Guofeng appointed acting premier as Deng Xiaoping is criticized. **5 April:** Mass demonstrations break out in memory of Zhou Enlai on Tiananmen Square in Beijing and are suppressed by state militia controlled by radical faction led by Jiang Qing. **7 April:** Deng Xiaoping is suspended from all work. **May:** Pakistan President Zulfiqar Ali Bhutto is last high-ranking foreigner to meet with Mao Zedong. **July:** Zhu De dies. Severe earthquake hits city of Tangshan in Hebei Province. **9 September:** Death of Mao Zedong. **October:** Arrest of the Gang of Four (Jiang Qing, Zhang Chunqiao, Yao Wenyuan, and Wang Hongwen).

December: Second National Conference on Learning from Dazhai in Agriculture is held.

1977   7 February: *People's Daily* editorial lauds the pro-Maoist "two whatevers." **March:** Central Work Conference reaffirms the "two whatevers" supported by Hua Guofeng and Wang Dongxing. Wang Zhen and Chen Yun demand rehabilitation of Deng Xiaoping. **May:** Mao Zedong Memorial Hall completed in Tiananmen Square in Beijing. **July:** Third Plenum of the 10th CC restores Deng Xiaoping to the Politburo Standing Committee. Hua Guofeng is confirmed as Mao's successor. **August:** At Science and Education Work Forum, Deng Xiaoping pushes for major reforms and praises the work of intellectuals. 11th National Party Congress held. **November:** Mao Zedong's Theory of the Three Worlds is lauded as major contribution to Marxism–Leninism.

Period of Reform and Political Transition: 1978–1997

1978   April–June: All-Military Conference on Political Work is held at which Deng Xiaoping criticizes leftists in Party leadership. **12 May:** *People's Daily* editorial "Practice is the Sole Criterion of Truth" attacks leftist ideological orthodoxy. **October:** Democracy Wall movement begins in Beijing. **November:** Central Party Work Conference focuses on debate over the "criterion of truth." Deng Xiaoping gives speech supporting shift of Party work from promoting "class struggle" to socialist modernization. **December:** Third Plenum of the 11th CC inaugurates major reforms in agricultural and economic policies focusing on the "Four Modernizations."

1979   January: Democracy Wall movement peaks in Beijing. **1 January:** Formal establishment of diplomatic relations between United States and China is followed by visit to the United States by Deng Xiaoping. **February:** China invades northern territory of Vietnam. **March:** Chinese forces retreat from Vietnamese territory. At Conference on Guidelines in Theory Work, Deng Xiaoping gives hard-line speech on "Upholding the Four Cardinal Principles." Democracy Wall activist Wei Jingsheng is arrested. **April:** At Central Work Conference, Party conservatives criticize reforms inaugurated by the December 1978 Third Plenum. Three-year period of "readjustment" is proposed.

September: Fourth Plenum of the 11th CC promotes Zhao Ziyang to the Politburo and adds senior cadres to the CCP Central Committee. Agricultural policies are revised.

1980 February: Fifth Plenum of the 11th CC elevates Zhao Ziyang and Hu Yaobang to the Politburo and reestablishes the Party Secretariat as the de facto decision-making body of the Party. Radicals Wang Dongxing, Ji Dengkui, Wu De, and Chen Xilian are removed from Party posts. Liu Shaoqi is posthumously rehabilitated. **April:** Hu Qiaomu attacks Party Propaganda Department. At All-Military Conference on Political Work, Wei Guoqing pushes leftist slogan to "promote proletarian ideology and eliminate bourgeois ideas." Deng Xiaoping refuses to attend the meeting. China is admitted to International Monetary Fund and World Bank. **May:** Deng attacks "feudalism" in the Party but critical elements of the speech are later excised from his *Selected Works*. **June:** Politburo Standing Committee holds special meeting to discuss eliminating "feudalism" from the Party. **July:** Political crisis in Poland. **August:** Enlarged meeting of the Politburo decides to replace Hua Guofeng as premier with the reformist Zhao Ziyang. Proposals are made for a bi-cameral NPC and tri-cameral CCP, complete with checks and balances. Third session of the Fifth NPC allows open debate among delegates over the issue of reforming the political system. Deng Xiaoping endorses fundamental institutional political reform. **September:** Central Secretariat meeting decides to apply flexible and open policies in Guangdong and Fujian provinces. Agricultural Responsibility System is strengthened. Zhao Ziyang replaces Hua Guofeng as premier. **November:** Hu Yaobang is charged with routine work of the Politburo and Deng Xiaoping is put in control of the CCP Central Military Affairs Commission. Gang of Four is put on trial. Hu Qiaomu at Central Work Conference launches "struggle against bourgeois liberalization" while Deng Xiaoping, Zhao Ziyang, and Chen Yun endorse economic retrenchment.

1981 March: Deng Xiaoping mentions the "struggle against bourgeois liberalization" for the first time. State Council calls for diversified agricultural economy. **June:** Sixth Plenum of the 11th CC issues document "Resolution on Certain Questions in the History of our Party since the Establishment of the People's Republic of China," which criticizes excesses in the leadership of Mao Zedong and declares as a disaster the

Cultural Revolution (1966–1976). Hu Yaobang is promoted to Party chairman. **July:** Party conservatives attack Special Economic Zones (SEZs). **August:** Forum on Problems on the Ideological Battlefront is held to launch attacks on "bourgeois liberalization." **December:** At Central Committee discussion meeting Chen Yun criticizes Hu Yaobang's alleged mistakes in economic policy. Chen also asserts a primary role for the state in the economy and opposes any further expansion of the SEZs.

1982 January: CCP Chairman Hu Yaobang calls for utilizing foreign investment in China's economic modernization. Chen Yun asserts that economic planning must remain supreme in the countryside, despite the creation of the Agricultural Responsibility System. **February:** At open forum on Guangdong and Fujian provinces, Hu Yaobang focuses on the problem of corruption. **April:** Politburo meeting discusses "economic crimes" and calls for harsh punishments to be meted out by the Central Discipline Inspection Commission of the CCP. **July:** Enlarged Politburo meeting discusses ways to end life tenure for leaders. China's population passes the one billion mark. **August:** At Seventh Plenum of the 11th CC, Hua Guofeng attacks the slogan "practice is the sole criterion of truth." **September:** At the 12th National Party Congress, the Party chairmanship is abolished and replaced by the weaker post of general secretary. Chairmanship of the Central Military Affairs Commission is strengthened. British Prime Minister Margaret Thatcher visits China to discuss the future of Hong Kong. **December:** Enlarged Politburo meeting emphasizes the importance of raising divergent views at inner-Party meetings.

1983 January: At National Conference on Ideological and Political Work, Hu Yaobang and leftist leader, Deng Liqun, clash over the role of ideology in China's modernization. **March:** At an academic forum at the Central Party School to commemorate the centennial of Karl Marx's death, China's former cultural "czar," Zhou Yang, raises the issues of humanism and alienation in a socialist society. **May:** *Death of a Salesman* by Arthur Miller is staged in Beijing. **October:** Chen Yun calls for purging from the CCP former Red Guards known as the "three categories of people." China is approved as member of the International Atomic Energy Agency. **November:** Enlarged meeting of the Politburo decides to limit the "Antispiritual Pollution Campaign" to the fields of art and literature.

1984 January: Deng Xiaoping tours several southern SEZs and voices support for continued economic reform. Zhao Ziyang visits the United States. **February:** Central forum on the role of SEZs produces "heated" discussion on the policy of opening up to the outside world. **March/April:** Forum convened by the Central Secretariat and the State Council on the SEZs opens 14 more coastal cities to foreign investment. **April:** *People's Daily* calls for a fundamental negation of the Cultural Revolution. United States President Ronald Reagan visits China. **June:** Central Committee Document Number One on agriculture calls for strengthening and improving the Agricultural Responsibility System. Rural surplus laborers are allowed to travel into the cities for "temporary" work. Deng Xiaoping promises "one country, two systems" formula for Hong Kong. **October:** Third Plenum of the 12th CC adopts liberal "Resolution on the Structural Reform of the Economy," marking the beginning of the urban reforms. **December:** Fourth Conference of the All-China Writers' Association in Beijing calls for greater autonomy for writers. China and Great Britain sign an agreement to restore China's sovereignty over Hong Kong on 1 July 1997.

1985 January: CCP and the State Council jointly issue "Ten Policies on Further Enlivening the Rural Economy," calling for expansion of the free rural economy. **March:** National Forum on Science and Technology in Beijing calls for radical changes. Third session of the Sixth NPC takes initial step toward price reform. **May:** Central Military Affairs Commission decides to reduce the size of the army by one quarter by demobilizing up to one million PLA troops and to retire older officers. **June:** Restructuring of the administrative organs of the people's communes is completed. State Council decides to enlarge the Xiamen (Amoy) SEZ. **September:** At National Conference of the CCP, Chen Yun attacks "Resolution on the Structural Reform of the Economy" and criticizes Party members for a loss of Communist ideals.

1986 January: Central Cadres Conference focuses on "instability" in the national economy and criticizes "lax" work among Party organs. **March:** China becomes member of the Asian Development Bank. **April:** Washington agrees to sell high-technology electronic aviation equipment to Chinese military. **June:** At Politburo Standing Committee meeting, Deng Xiaoping gives speech on reform of the political structure and on strengthening legal consciousness. **July:** The first national conference of Chinese lawyers takes place in Beijing. **August:** Shenyang Explosion-Prevention Equipment Factory declares bankruptcy, the first in PRC history. **September:** Sixth Plenum of the 12th CC adopts "Resolution on the Guiding Principles for Construction of Socialist Spiritual Civilization." Zhao Ziyang sets up Political Reform Research Group charged with enacting systemic institutional reforms in China's political system. **October:** Queen Elizabeth visits China. **December:** Student demonstrations break out in Hefei, Anhui Province, and quickly spread to other cities, including Beijing. Deng Xiaoping criticizes Hu Yaobang's handling of liberal intellectuals in the CCP.

1987 January: Enlarged Politburo meeting relieves liberal reformer Hu Yaobang of his duties as general secretary of the CCP. Dissidents Fang Lizhi, Wang Ruowang, and Liu Binyan are expelled from the CCP for allegedly advocating "bourgeois liberalization." **March:** Agreement reached with Portugal on return of Macao to China on 20 December, 1999. **April:** Series of conferences on ideological and political work are convened by leftists to continue criticism of "bourgeois liberalization" as direct CCP control is established over previously semi-independent newspapers and periodicals. **July:** Zhao Ziyang initiates Central Work Conference to discuss comprehensive plan for political reform. **September:** Demonstrations break out in Lhasa, Tibet, in favor of independence. **October:** Seventh Plenum of the 12th CC appoints Zhao Ziyang as general secretary of the CCP and approves the General Program for Political Reform calling for separation of Party and government, creation of an independent judiciary, and a shift in authority within state economic enterprises from CCP committees to professional managers. **October/November:** At 13th National Party Congress, Zhao Ziyang characterizes the current state of China's development as the "primary stage of socialism," thereby allowing for further market reforms. Politburo replaces Party Secretariat as the center of CCP decision making. Party departments established in the mid-1950s are abolished. Li Peng is appointed acting premier.

1988 January: CCP sends condolences to KMT on death of Chiang Ching-kuo, the son of Chiang Kai-shek. **March:** At Second Plenum of the 13th CC, Zhao Ziyang proposes the establishment of a professional civil service and calls for greater internal Party democracy. **March/April:** First session of the Seventh NPC formally approves Li

Peng as premier, Yang Shangkun as president, and Wang Zhen as vice-president. State Statistical Bureau warns of inflation. **July:** *Red Flag* ceases publication and is replaced by *Seeking Truth (Qiushi)*. Li Peng encourages Taiwan to invest in China. **August:** After fierce debates among top leadership at Beidaihe summer retreat, commitment is made to pursue price reform, but the decision is quickly withdrawn after panic buying occurs in the cities. **September:** Third Plenum of the 13th CC calls for emphasis on stabilizing and rectifying the economy, with some leaders calling for greater "centralism." China indicates willingness to normalize relations with the Soviet Union.

1989   February: Petition drive begun in December 1988 by Chinese dissidents seeking amnesty for China's political prisoners. First Soviet state visit since 1959 is followed by visit from United States President George Bush. **15 April:** Death of Hu Yaobang. **22 April:** On official day of mourning for Hu Yaobang, massive crowds of students fill Tiananmen Square. **26 April:** A *People's Daily* editorial, based on a speech by Deng Xiaoping, condemns student demonstrations as "anti-Party, antisocialist turmoil." **May:** At Asian Development Bank meeting in Beijing, Zhao Ziyang speaks positively about the student movement. More than 300 journalists demand freedom of the press. Students initiate a hunger strike that leads to a failed dialogue on nationwide TV between Premier Li Peng and student leaders. Mikhail Gorbachev makes historic visit to Beijing. Martial law is declared. **3–4 June:** PLA troops force their way into Tiananmen Square and outlying parts of the city, killing several hundred and perhaps thousands of students and city residents in Beijing. Killings also occur in Chengdu, Sichuan. **24 June:** Fourth Plenum of the 13th CC votes to strip Zhao Ziyang of all his posts and appoints Jiang Zemin as general secretary of the Party. **November:** Deng Xiaoping resigns as chairman of the CCP Military Affairs Commission, his last official position. **December:** Government of Nicolae Ceauşescu in Romania is overthrown.

1990   January: Two-year economic austerity program is announced as Chinese police are put on alert following the collapse of the Communist government in Romania. Martial law is lifted in Beijing. **March:** At Third session of the Seventh NPC, Li Peng calls for tighter control of "hostile elements." **April:** Jiang Zemin is named chairman of the state Military Affairs Commission. Basic Law for Hong Kong is passed by the Seventh NPC. Li Peng visits the Soviet Union. **June:** In the *People's Daily*, Wang Zhen attacks moderates in the government as "hostile anti-Party forces." **October:** *People's Daily* announces a new campaign against crime and such "liberal" influences as pornography. **December:** Economic blueprint for the Eighth Five-Year Plan stresses stability and self-reliance. Shanghai Stock Exchange starts formal operations with 22 members and 45,000 registered investors and 30 stocks listed.

1991   January/February: Trials are held of leading 1989 democratic movement participants. **March:** At a national meeting on economic reform, Li Peng supports further reforms to decentralize the economy. **April:** Shanghai Mayor Zhu Rongji and head of the State Planning Commission Zou Jiahua are appointed vice-premiers. **May:** New press code encourages journalists to spread Marxism–Leninism. Secret emergency directive is issued to all Party and government offices to guard against hostile forces that seek to overthrow the government. **July:** Jiang Zemin views China's "central political task" to be opposition to Western plots against the country that are dubbed "peaceful evolution." Shenzhen Stock Exchange is inaugurated. **August:** Attempted coup d'etat against Soviet leader Mikhail Gorbachev collapses. **September:** Chen Yun's son, Chen Yuan, draws up document on "Realistic Responses and Strategic Options for China Following the Soviet Union Upheaval." **October:** Internal CCP document accuses the Bush administration of attempting to bring about the collapse of communism through "peaceful evolution."

1992   January: Deng Xiaoping's southern tour (*nanxun*) of Shenzhen SEZ leads to calls for further economic reforms. **February:** The *People's Daily* attacks hard-line views and calls for bolder economic reforms. **March:** Supporters of economic reforms attack conservative attempts to reverse economic reform policies. Finance Minister Wang Bingqian reveals a projected budget deficit of US$3.8 billion for 1992 and announces a 13% increase in military spending. **April:** NPC approves construction of the controversial Three Gorges Dam project on the Yangtze River in central China. **June:** Liberal scholars hold unofficial forum to condemn continuing power of the hardliners in the CCP. More than one million workers are laid off from money-losing state-owned enterprises (SOEs). **August:** Outbreak of strikes by industrial workers. **October:** At the 14th National Party Congress, the principle of a "socialist market economic system" is enshrined for China's future development. Central Advisory Commission (CAC) chaired by Chen Yun is abolished and Yang Shangkun is dropped from Party Central Military Affairs Commission. China Securities Regulatory Commission is established as securities industry watchdog. **November:** Deng Xiaoping gives speech admonishing people to follow the "three don'ts," that is, don't revise the political interpretation of the 1989 military crackdown against the second Beijing Spring, don't tolerate "bourgeois liberalization," and don't replace any more leading leftists.

1993   March: Death of Wang Zhen. CCP General Secretary Jiang Zemin is appointed president of the PRC. **April:** The World Bank announces that China is the world's fastest-growing economy, estimated at 12% a year. State Council issues "Provisional Regulations for Stock Issuance and Trading." **June:** Peasant riots break out in Sichuan Province over taxes and other exorbitant fees. **July:** Qingdao Beer Ltd. is first Chinese company listed on Hong Kong stock exchange. **August:** United States imposes trade sanctions on China and Pakistan, charging Chinese companies with selling missile technology to Pakistan. **October:** Governor Chris Patten of Hong Kong announces that his efforts to get China's approval for democratic political reforms in the colony have failed. **December:** China marks 100th anniversary of birthday of Mao Zedong.

1994   February: Premier Li Peng attends ceremony marking beginning of operations of Daya Bay nuclear power plant near Hong Kong. Last public appearance of Deng Xiaoping. **March:** President of China's Supreme Court reports significant increases in serious crimes—murder, robbery, and rape—and economic crime. Taiwanese tourists in Zhejiang Province are robbed and murdered precipitating a crisis in PRC–Taiwan relations. **May:** Chinese intellectuals call on the government to reappraise the 1989 second Beijing Spring. United States extends Most Favored Nation (MFN) status to China, separating human rights and trade issues. **June:** In the midst of a crisis over North Korea's nuclear program, China's Foreign Ministry urges the North Korean government to desist from "fruitless military conflicts." **July:** China successfully launches satellite from Xichang launch site. PRC Companies Law is enacted. **October:** Confrontation between a United States Navy aircraft carrier battle group and a Chinese submarine occurs in the Yellow Sea. **November:** China and Britain sign agreement on financing a new airport for Hong Kong. Jiang Zemin pays an official goodwill visit to Vietnam, during which accords are reached on economic and trade cooperation and automobile transportation.

1995 February: Beginning of a petition movement by Chinese intellectuals, which continues throughout the spring, seeking political reform, an end to corruption, a reevaluation of the 4 June 1989 crackdown against the second Beijing Spring, and more openness in government. Beijing and Washington reach agreement on protection of intellectual property rights. **March:** China adopts first banking law, the Law on the People's Bank of China. **April:** Death of Chen Yun. Vice-mayor of Beijing commits suicide. **May:** China Construction Bank and Morgan Stanley launch China International Capital Corporation, the first joint venture investment bank in China. **July:** Naturalized American Harry Wu is arrested in central Chinese city of Wuhan for supposed criminal activities involving theft of state secrets. **August:** Russia and China sign agreement on cooperation in border guard issues. **September:** UN Fourth World Conference on Women takes place in Beijing. The Education Law of the PRC goes into effect. **October:** Jiang Zemin and President Bill Clinton hold summit meeting in New York on China's entry into the World Trade Organization (WTO). **November:** Jiang Zemin makes first state visit by China head of state to Republic of Korea. Vietnamese Communist Party General Secretary Do Muoi visits China. **December:** China issues White Paper entitled "The Progress of Human Rights in China."

1996 January: China announces cut of PLA by 500,000 personnel to a total force of 2.5 million. **February:** Accident at Xichang Satellite Launching Center kills eight people when carrier rocket fails. **March:** Taiwan (ROC) conducts first direct election for president in Chinese history as the PRC conducts war games in the Taiwan Straits. **April:** China reduces general level of import tariffs by 35%. **May:** United States announces retaliatory measures against China for alleged intellectual property rights violations. China criticizes Japan for encroaching on its territory in disputed Senakaku/Diaoyu islands. **June:** Premier Li Peng attends Eighth National Congress of the Communist Party of Vietnam. China tests two nuclear devices and buys missile technology from Russia to develop multiple independently targeted reentry vehicle capability. **July:** China conducts last underground nuclear test. Shenyin and Wanguo Securities are created as the biggest shareholding securities houses in China. **August:** China's Institute of Modern Physics announces world's first synthesis and identification of the new nuclei americium (Am)-235. **September:** China signs Comprehensive Nuclear Test Ban Treaty. **November:** Chinese satellite launched in October for technological experiments returns to earth. **December:** *People's Daily* attacks speculative behavior and price manipulation in China's stock market.

Period of the Emergence of China as an Economic Superpower: 1997–2006

1997   January: State Power Corporation inaugurated. **20 February:** Deng Xiaoping dies. **March:** The Dalai Lama visits Taiwan and meets with President Lee Teng-hui. United States Vice-President Al Gore visits China. A bomb explodes on a Beijing bus, apparently set by Uygur separatists. Taiwan civilian aircraft is hijacked to Xiamen. Chongqing becomes provincial-level metropolitan area. China calls for complete adherence to the Comprehensive Nuclear Test Ban Treaty. **April:** President Jiang Zemin visits Russia and emphasizes partnership between the two countries. Xinjiang authorities crack down on Uygur separatists. **May:** French President Jacques Chirac visits China, the first French presidential visit in 14 years. **June:** China's People's Bank prohibits unauthorized flow of bank capital to stock market. **1 July:** Hong Kong reverts to Chinese rule. **August:** China offers US$1 billion in aid to Thailand to counter economic crisis. **September:** "Deng Xiaoping theory" is accepted as the guiding ideology of the CCP at 15th National Party Congress. Premier Li Peng warns Japan against any interference in Taiwan issue. **October:** President Jiang Zemin visits the United States, the first visit by a Chinese president in 12 years where human rights, trade, and nuclear issues are discussed. The Yellow River is successfully dammed at Xiaolangdi. China signs International Covenant on Economic, Social and Cultural Rights. **November:** Emergency circular claims there were serious accidents in key national coal mines with multiple deaths. Chinese dissident Wei Jingsheng is released from prison and travels to United States. Yangtze River is dammed during construction of Three Gorges project.

1998 **March:** Zhu Rongji replaces Li Peng as premier. **April:** Live television broadcast of criminal trials is announced by Supreme Court President Xiao Yang. **May:** Israeli Prime Minister Benjamin Netanyahu visits China. China's Supreme Court sets up reporting center to accept public complaints about corruption as Jiang Zemin calls for guarantees of a basic standard of living. **June:** United States President Bill Clinton visits China and expresses differing views on human rights and Tibet from his Chinese hosts while reaffirming American support for a "one China principle." China's system of housing distribution is replaced by a market-oriented housing system. **July:** Former Beijing Mayor Chen Xitong is sentenced to 16 years in prison on charges of corruption. **August:** Regions along the Yangtze River and the Songhua River in China's northeast experience the worst flooding since 1954. **September:** Puccini's opera *Turandot* is performed in Beijing's imperial palaces. **October:** China signs International Covenant on Civil and Political Rights. **November:** President Jiang Zemin visits Japan, the first Chinese head of state to do so. Large numbers of liberal activists are arrested as China declares it cannot follow the Western model of democracy. The birth of China's first test-tube twins is announced. **December:** Township village heads are elected in Sichuan Province in a pilot program to expand elections. China announces that HIV/AIDS infected people can be found in all of the country's provinces and provincial-level municipalities.

1999 **January:** China's State Council establishes 6,000-man strong anti-smuggling police force. Widespread protests by Chinese farmers break out in Hunan Province. **February:** Vietnam Communist Party leader Le Kha Phieu visits China. **April:** Ten thousand followers of *Falung Gong* take place outside *Zhongnanhai* leadership compound in Beijing. **May:** American military aircraft bomb Chinese embassy in Belgrade during war with Yugoslavia, which is immediately condemned by China and produces crisis in United States–China relations as large student demonstrations break out in Beijing. Cox Commission of United States House of Representatives releases its report that accuses China of stealing nuclear secrets. **June:** China receives World Bank loans for Western Poverty Reduction Project. Scientists successfully clone an embryo of a giant panda. **July:** China condemns Taiwan's

President Lee Teng-hui for referring to cross-straits relations as "state-to-state." The PRC Securities Law comes into effect. **September:** China issues statement pledging to respect the will of East Timorese people who vote for independence from Indonesia. Hu Jintao is appointed vice-chairman of the Central Military Affairs Commission. **October:** China marks 50th anniversary of the PRC with military parades and performance of imperial-era operas. **November:** China launches unmanned satellite into space. The 9,000-ton ferry *Dashun* sinks off the coast of Shandong Province killing over 250 people. **December:** China criticizes United States for supporting Taiwan's entry into UN World Health Organization (WHO).

2000   January: China demands that Japan cease to whitewash past Japanese aggression especially its role in the 1938 Nanjing massacre. **February:** China condemns United States for its 1999 human rights report on China. Beijing police break up demonstration by followers of *Falun Gong* during celebration of Chinese New Year. **March:** China responds to election on Taiwan of Democratic Progressive Party (DPP) leader Chen Shui-bian by reiterating its insistence on a "one-China policy." China announces the manufacture of its first passenger aircraft, the MA-60. **May:** North Korean leader Kim Jong-il visits China. Chinese university students hold an orderly, apolitical demonstration protesting lax security that contributed to murder of female student. Up to 5,000 neighborhood committees in Beijing will be chosen by direct election. **June:** In a shakeup of publicity organs, the director of *People's Daily* is replaced. Emergency water supply projects undergo construction to counter ongoing serious drought in north China. China declares support for Comprehensive Nuclear Test Ban Treaty. **July:** Russian President Vladimir Putin visits China as both countries condemn Washington's proposal for a national missile defense system. A former governor of the Guangxi Autonomous Region is executed for involvement in a massive corruption scheme. China and Vietnam reach accord on land boundary. **August:** Explosions in fireworks factories in Guangdong and Jiangxi provinces kill more than 100 workers. **September:** A coal mine explosion in Guizhou Province kills 162 workers. State Environmental Protection Administration announces pollution stopped worsening in China for the first time in a decade. **October:** China announces launch of three-year "strike-hard campaign" against crime. **November:** Premier Zhu Rongji attends the fourth Association of Southeast Asian Nations

(ASEAN) + 3 Summit in Singapore promoting cooperation among East Asian nations.

2001 **January:** The *Shenzhou*-II experimental aircraft is launched and successfully returns to earth. North Korean leader Kim Jong-il visits China. Transmission of "secret" or "reactionary" information over the Internet in China becomes a capital crime. **April:** Collision between American spy plane and Chinese fighter aircraft leads to the downing of an American plane on Hainan Island and the death of a Chinese pilot, which produces renewed tension in United States–China relations. **June:** State Council unveils rules to reduce government holdings in companies to finance social security funds. **July:** A flash flood at a tin mine in southern Guangxi Autonomous Region kills 81 workers. President Jiang Zemin visits Russia, where a Good-Neighborly Treaty of Friendship and Cooperation is signed. Transmission of "pernicious information" on the Internet is condemned by Jiang Zeming. **September:** Premier Zhu Rongji visits Russia. Following 11 September terrorist attacks in New York and Washington, China joins in international "war on terrorism," which human rights supporters claim leads to suppression of dissident Islamic groups in western China. **October:** China criticizes the action by Pope John Paul II who on 1 October, China's National day, canonizes 120 Chinese Catholic martyrs. **December:** China ascends to WTO membership.

2002 Independent film production is legalized in China. **March:** China sends unmanned *Shenzhou*-III into orbit, which, after encircling the earth 108 times, returns to earth. China and Iran stop providing real-time information to the Comprehensive Test Ban Treaty monitoring group in Vienna. **April:** First fatal crash of Air China plane occurs in Seoul, South Korea. China and South Korea denounce visit by Japanese Prime Minister Junichiro Koizumi to the controversial Yasukuni Shrine, which honors those who died in defense of the emperor, including Class-A war criminals. **June:** Month-long diplomatic standoff between China and South Korea ends as North Korean asylum seekers in diplomatic compounds in Beijing are allowed to leave for South Korea. **July:** PLA delegation visits South Korea to discuss bilateral military exchanges. South Korean banks agree to assist Chinese banks in disposing of bad loans. **October:** Jiang Zemin visits United States President George W. Bush at his Crawford, Texas, ranch. **November:** At the sixth

ASEAN + 3 Summit in Cambodia, Zhu Rongji commits China to regional cooperation. The first known case of SARS is recorded in Guangdong Province. Sixteenth National Party Congress held. Hu Jintao replaces Jiang Zemin as general secretary. **December:** Foreigners are allowed to invest in Class A shares on Chinese stock market. Russian President Vladimir Putin visits China. *Shenzhou*-IV unmanned is launched in the final test flight before a manned launch.

2003   China surpasses the United States as world's largest recipient of Foreign Direct Investment (FDI). Four million families in China own automobiles. **February:** Xinjiang Autonomous Region hit by major earthquake registering 6.8 on the Richter scale leaving 268 people dead. **March:** NPC delegates openly express discontent with large-scale corruption by officials throughout the country. Hu Jintao elected as president of the PRC replacing the retiring Jiang Zemin. Wen Jiabao is elected premier. **April:** China acts as liaison in brokering talks between the United States and North Korea on the nuclear issue on the Korean peninsula. Beijing announces 339 previously undisclosed SARS cases as the city's mayor and the minister of health are dismissed. **May:** Third summit meeting of the Shanghai Cooperation Organization is held in Moscow. **June:** Reservoir of the Three Gorges Dam on the Yangtze River begins filling. Conference on Constitutional Reform held by liberal intellectuals in Shandong Province is followed by arrests and dampening of tolerant policy. **1 July:** Large-scale demonstrations are held in Hong Kong on anniversary of handover to China protesting proposed new security law. South Korean President Roh Moo-Hyun visits China. **August:** First round of six-party talks are held in Beijing between China, the United States, South and North Korea, Russia, and Japan. **15 October:** *Shenzhou*-V is launched from Jiuquan launch center sending China's first astronaut into orbit. **December:** Symposium is held on 30th anniversary of the Third Front construction project. Large-scale gas explosion outside Chongqing kills more than 200 people. China's first civilian passenger plane produced in conjunction with Brazilian aircraft manufacturer.

2004   China is the sixth-largest economy in the world and third largest trading economy as country announces existence of several billionaires. **February:** Plans announced to boost development of China's capital markets. Tighter controls of the Internet introduced. **March:** Protection of human rights and private property incorporated into Chinese state constitution. **April:** Germany's Siemans Corporation drops plans to help construct nuclear enrichment plant in China. Efforts by the United States to bring issue of human rights in China to UN Human Rights Commission fails as most non-European countries support the PRC. Last SARS case reported in China. **May:** State Council announces comprehensive education program to combat HIV/AIDS. China expresses interest in joining international Nuclear Suppliers' Group. China also commits to assist in worldwide reduction of poverty. **June:** Vietnam Premier Phan Van Khai visits China for five days and meets with President Hu Jintao. Eleven Chinese construction workers in Afghanistan are killed by Taliban forces. China develops kit to detect SARS. South Korea overtakes Japan as second largest source of Foreign Direct Investment (FDI) for China after Hong Kong. **July:** On anniversary of Hong Kong handover to China, large-scale demonstrations are held for second year in a row protesting proposed security law. China announces plans to renew assistance to Pakistan in construction of new nuclear facility. China has 87 million Internet users. **August:** Yunnan Province hit by earthquake that leaves four people dead and 594 injured. Chinese universities hit by scandal involving admission examinations. **September:** Jiang Zemin gives up post of chairman of Party Central Military Affairs Commission to President Hu Jintao. **October:** A blast at a coal mine in Henan Province leaves 148 miners dead. A series of international jewel heists hit Shanghai and other cities. In the Shenzhen SEZ, 3,000 workers protest low wages. **November:** A gas explosion at a coal mine in Shaanxi Province kills 166 miners. China and ASEAN agree to create open market encompassing two billion people. After Japan joins the United States in declaring Taiwan part of their mutual "security zone," Chinese nuclear submarine passes through Japanese territorial waters spurring alert by Japanese Self-Defense Forces.

2005   China replaces the United States as Japan's largest trade partner with foreign exchange reserves second in the world only to Japan. **January:** Former General Secretary Zhao Ziyang dies. Direct charter flights between Taiwan and the mainland are secured for upcoming lunar New Year. End to global textile quotas leads to surge in exports from China to the United States. **6 January:** Zhang Yichi, a baby boy, is born as China's 1.3 billionth citizen. **February:** 214 miners are killed by a gas explosion at a mine in Liaoning Province. **March:** More than 400,000 people worldwide, mostly Chinese, sign online petitions to oppose Japan's bid for a permanent seat on the UN Security Council. Hu Jintao is elected chairman of the State Central Military Affairs Commission, fully completing transition of power from Jiang Zemin. NPC passes anti-secession law aimed at Taiwan. **April:** Japanese Prime Minister Koizumi calls on China to ensure the safety of Japanese nationals in China as Chinese protestors hold anti-Japanese rallies in major cities and at Japanese diplomatic compounds. **May:** KMT Chairman Lien Chan arrives in Beijing for meeting with Chinese President Hu Jintao. United States invokes measures to halt textile import surge from China. **July:** An explosion at a coal mine in the western region of the Xinjiang Autonomous Region kills 22 miners. China announces limited currency float for the *yuan* following intense pressure from the United States and the European Union. United States Congress expresses concern over bid by China National Offshore Oil Corporation (CNOOC) for the American oil company Unocal. PLA general declares that China will use nuclear weapons to halt any American interference in possible Chinese assault on Taiwan. Nanjing Automobile of China buys bankrupt British automaker, MG Rover Group. **August:** CNOOC abandons its bid for American Oil Company Unocal. Six-party talks on North Korea reconvene. **September:** North Korea agrees to terminate nuclear weapons program though conditions for implementing agreement remain unclear. **November:** A major pollution spill of benzene into the Songhua River in China's northeast forced the entire city of Harbin with four million residents to shut down its water supply for several days while the top environmental regulator was fired in the wake of the initial cover-up of the chemical spill.

2006 China joins members of the International Atomic Energy Agency (IAEA) in opposing the decision by the government of Iran to renew the enrichment of uranium while China also called on the international community to resolve the dispute by diplomacy. **February:** Former CCP officials publish letter to Chinese leaders criticizing the closing of newspapers and excessive censorship. **March:** Chinese government increases taxes on everything from gas-guzzling vehicles to chopsticks to golf balls in a move to rein in rising use of energy and timber and the widening gap between rich and poor. **April:** President Hu Jintao makes long-awaited state visit to the United States as the U.S. Congress considers imposing 27% tariffs on Chinese imports in reaction to China's policy of undervaluing its currency.

Research Sources

Sources used in preparing this chronology include the following: Kenneth G. Lieberthal and Bruce J. Dickson, *A Research Guide to Central Party and Government Meetings in China, 1949–1986*, Armonk, N.Y.: M. E. Sharpe, Inc., 1989; the annual editions of *China Briefing*, Boulder, Colo.: Westview Press, 1984–1992 and Armonk, N.Y., 1997; Richard Bush, Steven M. Goldstein, William A. Joseph, Anthony J. Kane, John S. Major, and Robert Oxnam, eds., "Quarterly Chronicle and Documentation," *The China Quarterly*, London: School of Oriental and African Studies; Colin Mackerras, *The New Cambridge Handbook of Contemporary China*, Cambridge: Cambridge University Press, 2001; and Franz Schurmann, *Ideology and Organization in Communist China*, Berkeley and Los Angeles: University of California Press, 1966.

Chinese Communist Party Organizations*

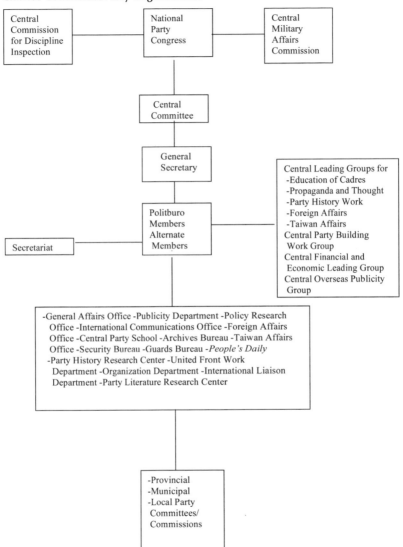

Source: Sullivan, Lawrence R., ed. *China since Tiananmen: Political, Economic, and Social Conflicts.* Armonk, N.Y.: M.E. Sharpe, Inc., 1995. Reprinted with permission. Prepared by Nancy Hearst.

CHINA

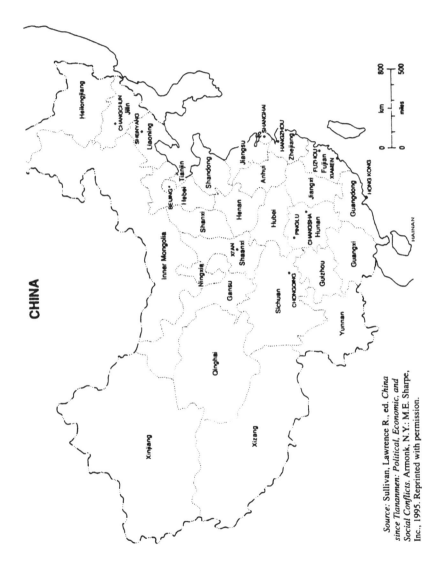

Government of the People's Republic of China*

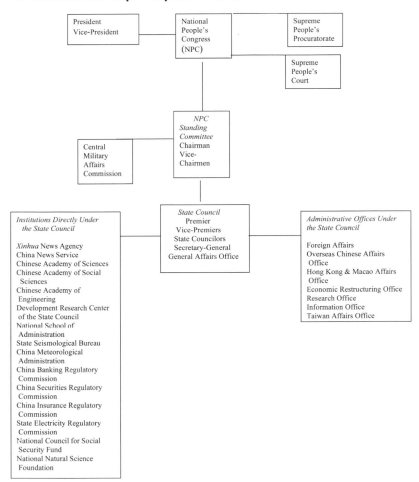

President Vice-President	National People's Congress (NPC)	Supreme People's Procuratorate

Supreme
People's
Court

*NPC
Standing
Committee*
Chairman
Vice-
Chairmen

Central
Military
Affairs
Commission

*Institutions Directly Under
the State Council*

Xinhua News Agency
China News Service
Chinese Academy of Sciences
Chinese Academy of Social
  Sciences
Chinese Academy of
  Engineering
Development Research Center
  of the State Council
National School of
  Administration
State Seismological Bureau
China Meteorological
  Administration
China Banking Regulatory
  Commission
China Securities Regulatory
  Commission
China Insurance Regulatory
  Commission
State Electricity Regulatory
  Commission
National Council for Social
  Security Fund
National Natural Science
  Foundation

State Council
Premier
Vice-Premiers
State Councilors
Secretary-General
General Affairs Office

*Administrative Offices Under
the State Council*

Foreign Affairs
Overseas Chinese Affairs
  Office
Hong Kong & Macao Affairs
  Office
Economic Restructuring Office
Research Office
Information Office
Taiwan Affairs Office

(*continued*)

Commissions

State Development and
Reform Commission
State Commission of
Science, Technology,
and National Defense
State Ethnic Affairs
Commission
State Population and
Family Planning
Commission
People's Bank of China
State Auditing Office
State-Owned Assets
Supervision and
Administration
Commission

State Bureaus Under the Jurisdiction of Ministries and Commissions

State Bureau for Letters
and Calls
State Administration of
Grain
State Tobacco
Monopoly
Administration
State Administration of
Foreign Expert Affairs
State Oceanic
Administration
State Bureau of
Surveying & Mapping
State Postal Bureau
State Administration of
Cultural Heritage
State Administration of
Traditional Chinese
Medicine
State Administration of
Foreign Exchange
State Administration of
Work Safety
State Archives
Administration
National Administration
for the Protection of
State Secrets

Ministries

Agriculture
Civil Affairs
Commerce
Communications
Construction
Culture
Education
Finance
Foreign Affairs
Foreign Trade and
Economic
Cooperation
Health
Information Technology
Justice
Labor and Social
Security
Land and Resources
National Defense
Personnel
Public Security
Railways
Science and Technology
State Security
Supervision
Transportation
Water Resources

Bureaus and Administrations Under the State Council

General Administration
of Customs
State Administration of
Taxation
State Administration for
Industry and
Commerce
General Administration
of Quality Supervision,
Inspection, and
Quarantine
State Environmental
Protections
Administration
General Administration
of Civil Aviation
State Administration of
Radio, Film, and
Television
State General
Administration of Press
and Publication
State Sports General
Administration
National Bureau of
Statistics
State Forestry
Administration
State Food and Drug
Administration
State Administration of
Work Safety
State Intellectual
Property Office
National Tourism
Administration
State Administration for
Religious Affairs
Counselor's Office
under the State
Council
Bureau of
Government Offices
Administration

Introduction

When the Chinese Communist Party (CCP) seized power in October 1949, China was one of the poorest nations in the world. It was so weak that it had been conquered in the late 1930s and early 1940s by its neighbor Japan, a country one-tenth its size. More than five decades later, the People's Republic of China (PRC) is an emerging economic, political, and military superpower with the world's fastest growing economy and largest population (1.3 billion in 2005). A member of the United Nations Security Council since the early 1970s and a nuclear power, China wields enormous influence in the world community. At home, what was once a nation of largely poverty-stricken peasants and urban areas with little-to-no industry has been transformed into an increasingly urbanized society with a growing middle class and an industrial and service sector that leads the world in such industries as steel and textiles and is becoming a major player in computers and telecommunications. All the while, the country has remained under the tight political control of a one-party system dominated by the Chinese Communist Party that, despite periods of intense political conflict and turmoil, governs China with a membership in 2005 of more than 60 million people — the largest single organization on earth.

LAND AND PEOPLE

Geographically, China is located in eastern Asia, bounded by the Pacific Ocean in the east. The fourth largest country in the world behind the Russian Republic, Canada, and the United States, China has an area of 9.6 million km² — fully one-fifteenth of the world's land mass. From cast to west, China's territory extends about 5,200 km; from north to south, it measures 5,500 km. Approximately 98% of China's total land area is situated between latitude 20 and 50 degrees north, the greater part belonging to the temperate and subtropical zones. The PRC is bordered by the Democratic People's Republic of Korea (DPRK) (North Korea) in the northeast; Russia and Mongolia in the north; Kazakhstan, Tajikistan, and Kyrgyzstan in the west; Afghanistan, Bhutan, India, Nepal, and Pakistan in the southwest; and Myanmar (Burma), Laos, and Vietnam in the south. Topographically, China is similar to a gradient staircase, high in the west and low in the east. Mountains, plateaus, and hills account for about 65% of the country's land area, 20% of which is more than 5,000 m above sea level. This region is located primarily in the western Qinghai–Tibet Plateau, the highest and largest plateau on earth. Seven of the world's highest mountains are in China, including the world's highest, Mt. Everest (known in Chinese as *Zhumulangma Feng* and as *Qomolangma*). The terrain in the central part of the country drops to between 2,000 and 1,000 m above sea level; in the east, the terrain is low, generally less than 1,000 m above sea level, where the country's vast farmlands and major cities are located. China has a vast river system that totals 220,000 km in length and consists of three major systems, the Yellow River in the north, the Yangtze in the central part of the country, and the Pearl River in the south. River flow is unevenly distributed, with the highest part lying in the south. The Yangtze (*Changjiang*, "Long River") is the third largest river in the world (after the Amazon and the Nile) and accounts for almost 40% of China's entire water runoff. With a catchments area of 1.8 million km², the Yangtze is also the major water-transport artery in China. The Yellow River, generally considered the cradle of Chinese civilization, is the second longest in China and, in recent years, has been subject to periodic dry-up in its lower reaches. The total volume of water per capita in China is only 3,000 m³, one-fourth of the world's average.

China can be divided into three major physical districts based on the primary elements that affect regional differentiation—geographical position, climatic characteristics, and geological features. About 45% of the country, primarily in the eastern region, consists of a monsoon district that is characterized by a humid and semihumid environment with abundant rainfall. Ninety-five percent of the total population lives here (over 1.1 billion people), and the region contains 90% of the country's farming area. The northwest arid district consists of 30% of the land area, 10% of the total cultivated land, and about 4% of the population.

It is composed of deserts, desert steppe, and steppe and includes the country's major pastoral areas in Inner Mongolia. The third area consists of the Alpine-cold region of Qinghai-Tibet, which constitutes about 30% of the country's land mass and less than 1% of its cultivated land and population.

In terms of cultivatable land, China has more than 320 million acres (or about 130 million hectares). There is only about one-quarter acre per capita of cultivated land in the entire country (in the United States, the comparable figure is two acres per capita). Ninety percent of the cultivated land is concentrated in the eastern region, with 30% of the total in the middle-lower Yellow River region, 21% in the middle-lower Yangtze River region, and 7% in the Pearl River region in the south. In terms of mineral resources, China has one of the world's largest coal reserves (approximately 125 billion short tons), which is the major source of energy for the country and the number one factor in China's growing environmental pollution. Onshore and offshore oil reserves are also substantial, as is natural gas but not sufficient to fulfill China's soaring appetite for energy (in 2005, 10% of the world's total) that has rapidly transformed the nation from a net oil exporter to a major importer of 3.2 million barrels a day in 2005.

At 1.3 billion people in 2005 (up from 1.162 billion in 1994), China has the largest population in the world. By the year 2010, estimates are that the Chinese population will expand to 1.4 billion and in 2025 will reach a peak of 1.48 billion people, since the Chinese government in 2000 set a target of 1.5% population growth rate per year. Currently, China has an average life expectancy of slightly over 70 years, up from 35 years at the time of the establishment of the PRC in 1945. The male:female ratio in 1998 was 51:49, although these figures can vary dramatically in some rural areas, where young males vastly outnumber young females. The geographical distribution of the population is extremely skewed; 95% of the people live in the eastern region of the country with 31% living in urban areas and 69% in the countryside. The metropolitan area of Chongqing, located in the southwestern interior, is the country's largest (32 million people), followed closely by Shanghai on the eastern seaboard with a population of more than 20 million people. The capital of the country is Beijing, which has a population of more than 15 million people. China's most populated province is Sichuan, with a population of over 80 million people. Ninety-two percent of the population is composed of the dominant Han ethnic group, who live in the densely populated eastern region. According to the 2000 census, 8.98% of the population (or 108 million people) belong to one of the 55 officially recognized minority groups. They are concentrated in the thinly populated outlying provinces and regions in the strategically important southwestern and western parts of the country.

Administratively, China is divided into 22 provinces (not including Taiwan), five autonomous regions (Guangxi, Ningxia, Qinghai, Tibet, and Xinjiang), and four centrally administered municipalities (Beijing, Chongqing, Shanghai, and Tianjin). There are 331 prefectures, which include 227 cities at the prefecture level and 2,126 counties, including 437 cities at the county level with 664 cites altogether. More than 160 cities in China have a population exceeding one million people. There are also 91,000 administrative villages, also known as townships (*xiang*), that comprise the basic level of administrative organization in the country, along with 700,000 "natural villages" (*cun*). Between the formation of the PRC in 1949 and 1978, the population distribution was centrally controlled, resulting in very little of the rural-to-urban migration that characterizes most Third World countries. The inauguration of economic reforms in 1978–1979, however, substantially weakened central controls on population mobility and residence, resulting in large migrations of the "floating population" (estimated to be as high as 145 million people in 2000) moving from countryside to city and city to city in search of employment and higher income. This has created a growing problem of housing and social services support in China's increasingly hard-pressed urban areas, especially as government support for a broad range of social services—health care, housing, education, and transportation—has declined. Large cities, such as Beijing, now have upward of 2.5 million unregistered people living in its environs who do not have adequate housing, nutrition, or health care. In addition, rural areas are losing young males at an accelerated rate, thus leaving agricultural production to be increasingly carried out by women and the very old and very young.

HISTORY: IMPERIAL, REPUBLICAN, AND COMMUNIST

When the Chinese Communist Party took power in 1949, it established control over a country with one of the longest continuous histories in the world. Since 221 BC when the first emperor Qin Shihuang unified several warring states, China has remained under a single unified government that survived through a series of imperial dynasties, thus resulting in an empire of cultural and artistic magnificence. During the last dynasty, the Qing (1644–1911), the geographical expanse of the Chinese Empire was substantially larger than the present-day PRC, including, in the 18th century, vast swaths of territory in the west and northeast that in the next century were lost to an expanding Russian Empire. Beginning in the mid-19th century as the Qing dynasty was gradually weakened by growing foreign intrusion following a series of Opium Wars (1839–1842) and massive internal rebellions, such as the pseudo-Christian *Taipings* (1851–1865), the Chinese Empire was reduced in size while foreign interests, including the Japanese, won concession after concession in Chinese territory, including the right to import opium.

The creation of the Republic of China under Sun Yat-sen in 1912 did little to halt the decline. Sun lacked any armed force because military power had devolved into the hands of mostly rapacious warlords with the vast majority of people suffering accordingly. Sun's successor in the Nationalist Party (KMT), Chiang Kai-shek, brought temporary hope when, in 1927, he reunited the country by defeating the northern warlords, and, for a brief period in the late 1920s, China saw a growing economy and relative political stability. Having formed a united front with the small and fledgling CCP, Chiang turned on his Communist allies in 1927, nearly wiping them out and forcing remnant Communist forces to seek refuge in the countryside, where, under Mao Zedong, a Soviet Republic was set up in the rural hinterland of Jiangxi Province. Even as the Japanese increasingly encroached into Manchuria, Chiang remained fixated on the Communists, against whom he launched a series of encirclement campaigns in the early 1930s that forced the CCP into yet another retreat known as the Long March (1934–1935). Thousands of troops set out for the hinterlands of Shaanxi Province in the northwest where the Communists had set up a base in and around the small city of Yan'an. Having survived Chiang's attacks, another united front was secured in the face of Japanese aggression in 1936 and remained in place until the end of World War II. American efforts after the war to broker an agreement between the CCP and the Nationalists came to naught, and in 1946 civil war broke out in which the ill-equipped but highly disciplined Communist forces ultimately prevailed, driving remnant Nationalist forces to the island of Taiwan, where the Republic of China remains in place to this day. The initial years of the PRC witnessed consolidation of CCP control of China as military and political resources were employed to bring large swaths of territory (including Tibet) under CCP direct control. The Communist Party's political support among the peasantry was reinforced by the promotion of Land Reform from 1950 to 1952 and among workers by the socialist transformation of the Chinese economy. Political opponents of the regime, including many Western-educated intellectuals, were subject to severe persecution in a series of political campaigns, such as the "Three Antis" and "Five Antis" in the early 1950s, that often resulted in long periods of imprisonment or execution of the victims. State Party control over the media and all institutions of learning was initiated, and a grassroots structure of "basic units" (*jiben danwei*) and "personal dossiers" (*dang'an*) was put into place. Regional layers of state organization and collective ownership of land gradually gave way to a more highly centralized structure that allowed the CCP to establish control over the economy. Among the Party elite, political differences during this era were largely muted except for one instance when a top regional leader in the northeast, Gao Gang, was purged from the CCP in 1955. Internationally, China aligned itself with the Soviet Union and became embroiled in the three-year war on the Korean peninsula (1950–1953) that ended with an armistice but no peace treaty. Following the death of Soviet leader Josef Stalin in 1953, tensions developed between the new Russian leadership and Mao Zedong, who increasingly accused the former of sinking into revisionism.

While the dramatic attempt by Mao Zedong to make a "great leap" in the Chinese economy from 1958 to 1960 ultimately failed and cost the country the lives of perhaps 20 million people who died in the famine, politically, Mao Zedong suffered very little even as day-to-day economic policy was carried out by Liu Shaoqi, Deng Xiaoping, and other relative pragmatists. In three years of political turmoil and conflict from1966–1968, Mao unleashed rampaging groups of young Red Guards who—egged on by Mao's wife Jiang Qing—persecuted an entire generation of Party and military leaders in an attempt to transform the CCP into a radical leftist organization bent on uninterrupted revolution with Chinese society organized along the lines of Mao Zedong

Thought. Spurred on by a Mao Zedong personality cult that equaled in intensity and irrationality the Stalin cult in the Soviet Union during the 1930s, radical Red Guard factions tore the CCP apart from top to bottom and essentially brought China to the brink of civil war. By 1968, after the Red Guards had become increasingly and destructively factionalized, they were banished to factories and to the countryside to "learn from the workers and peasants," while Mao gradually allowed the CCP to be rebuilt along conventional Leninist lines, although considerable power remained in the hands of the People's Liberation Army (PLA). Following the 1971 assassination attempt against Mao Zedong by Lin Biao, the army gradually retreated from political involvement so that by the 1980s onward it assumed the role of a modern professional military force with little direct role in domestic political affairs.

Following a two-year political interregnum after the death of Mao in September 1976 during which various leftist forces failed to gain control of the country, Deng Xiaoping emerged as China's paramount leader, a position he solidified in December 1978 at the watershed Third Plenum of the 11th CCP Central Committee. During his political maneuvering against Mao's designated successor, Hua Guofeng, Deng embraced both economic and political reform, defending the right of people to write "big character posters" and to exercise their so-called "four big freedoms." The result was an outburst of pro-democratic sentiment with posters covering the Democracy Wall in a western Beijing district, including provocative comments by a former Red Guard named Wei Jingsheng who called on the Party to pursue a Fifth Modernization of political democratization in addition to the official Four Modernizations of agriculture, industry, defense, and science and technology. But once secure in power, Deng quickly reversed course, ordering the closing of the Democracy Wall and the arrest and imprisonment of Wei Jingsheng even as bolder economic reforms were pursued and agreements were reached with the United States on the normalization of relations and with Great Britain on the re-incorporation of Hong Kong into the mainland. Although Deng refused to accept the Party's top position and instead recruited Hu Yaobang as chairman (the Party's last) and then general secretary and Zhao Ziyang as premier, the paramount leader opposed any substantial political reform, a point made abundantly clear when Hu Yaobang was dismissed following student demonstrations in late 1986 and the military crackdown that Deng personally ordered in

June 1989 against an even larger outbreak of pro-democracy demonstrations in Beijing and over 100 other cities. With the appointment of former Shanghai mayor Jiang Zemin in 1989 as the new general secretary and succeeded in 2003 by Hu Jintao—both highly trained technicians with little penchant for political liberalization—China pursued a model of rapid economic growth and social liberalization, including a gradual breakdown of the pervasive "basic unit" (*jiben danwei*) system and the system of rural and urban household registration (*hukou*), all within a framework of strict one-party control.

For most of the Maoist era, China was an antagonist to the West, particularly the United States, intervening in the Korean War (1950–1953) on the side of the North Korean regime of Kim Il-sung and engaging in skirmishes with American allies in the region on the island of Taiwan (which China claims as part of its "one-China" stand) and at least for a time on the side of the North Vietnamese. But even as China developed a modest force of regional and intercontinental nuclear weapons to counter the United States, China's growing conflict with its erstwhile ally, the Soviet Union, with which the country shares the world's longest border, and a changing calculus of international relations by Chinese leaders led the PRC to reach an accommodation with the United States that was highlighted by the high-profile trip to China of U.S. President Richard Nixon in 1972. With the establishment of formal diplomatic relations between the two countries in 1979, Beijing and Washington have sought increasingly closer ties on a range of economic, political, and military issues, including a joint desire to see a non-nuclear Korean peninsula, although the relationship has had its flareups, such as the negative U.S. reaction to the military crackdown in China in June 1989 against pro-democracy demonstrators, the accidental bombing of the Chinese embassy in Belgrade, Serbia, in 1999, and the Chinese downing of an American spy plane off the coast of Hainan Island in April 2001.

On the economic front, the pre- and post-1978–1979 periods in China are as different as night and day. Throughout the 1950s, Mao Zedong and the regime's economic planners replicated the Soviet model of central planning (with some assistance from their Russian allies) with its emphasis on crash industrialization and the socialization of agricultural production. Concerned that economic growth in the mid-1950s was insufficient to dramatically alter China's economic makeup, which remained dominated by agriculture, Mao Zedong in 1958 launched a radical plan of communization in the countryside and an experiment in backyard steel furnaces in the form of the Great Leap Forward that by 1960 produced one of the world's most serious famines. The country gradually recovered in the early 1960s, but Mao became convinced that Party moderates, such as Liu Shaoqi (Mao's first designated successor) and Deng Xiaoping were leading the country down the "capitalist road," and thus from 1966 to his death in 1976, Mao pushed the country into internecine political conflict involving mass mobilization of young Red Guards against the very Party organization upon which Mao relied to rule the country and which ultimately counted Liu Shaoqi as one of its main victims. After an apparent assassination attempt against the chairman in 1971 by his second designated successor (Minister of Defense Lin Biao), the Cultural Revolution gradually sputtered to an end that, in the immediate aftermath of Mao's death in September 1976, led to the arrest and subsequent trial of the chairman's wife, the former Shanghai actress Jiang Qing, and her radical cohorts designated as the "Gang of Four." Although Mao's first official successor, the unremarkable Hua Guofeng, helped carry out the coup against the radical leftovers, Deng Xiaoping, whose life had been protected during the Cultural Revolution by allies in the PLA, beginning in 1978 led the country in a radical direction economically if not politically.

Since 1978–1979, the PRC has followed a package of domestic and foreign policies diametrically opposed to the Maoist era. Whereas the previous era was marked by an economically autarkic policy of "self-reliance" (*zili gengsheng*) that led China to engage in little foreign trade and commerce, under Deng Xiaoping's open-door policy, the PRC welcomed Foreign Direct Investment (FDI), which was initially concentrated in the coastal Special Economic Zones (SEZs), and geared its industrial economy to export in a fashion similar to other Asian economic tigers, such as Taiwan and South Korea. What began with simple electronics and textiles in the 1980s and early 1990s had by the early 2000s expanded into computers, telecommunications, and automobiles, and the PRC has emerged as the world's third largest economy and is predicted to become the world's largest in two to three decades. From 1994 to 2005, China pegged its currency, the *yuan* or *renminbi*, to the U.S. dollar and accumulated dollar holdings in the form of treasury bills of more than US$700 billion. During the earlier period, Mao had disparaged international economic organizations as tools of foreign imperialism, but China in 2001 joined the World Trade Organization (WTO) while also signing the Kyoto Protocol and the Comprehensive Nuclear Test Ban Treaty. With the gradual retirement from the political scene of Deng Xiaoping in the 1990s (he died at 92 in 1997), China's third and fourth generations of leaders from presidents and CCP general secretaries Jiang Zemin (1989–2002) to Hu Jintao (2002/2003–), and premiers Zhu Rongji (1998–2003) to Wen Jiabao (2003–) have put their highly technical training as engineers and scientists to work by concentrating on the country's rapid economic modernization and in science and technology, including several manned space shots, all along maintaining the tight political grip of the Chinese Communist Party. Although political leaders from Deng to the current generation have talked the talk about implementing political reform in China, such as village-level elections, this has not included any significant variation in the CCP dictatorship, especially after crackdowns against pro-democracy students in 1986 and 1989 that cost the political careers of genuine post-Mao reformers, such as Hu Yaobang and Zhao Ziyang. To the extent any demonstrations and open political action is tolerated in China, it comes in the form of state-accepted protests against Japan and the United States, especially over the issue of Taiwan, which, in 2005, remained unresolved—even as an exchange of leaders from the KMT and the mainland hinted at some possibility of rapprochement similar to the 1997 incorporation of Hong Kong back into China as a Special Administrative Region (SAR).

Promulgation of new laws governing everything from the emerging stock and equity markets to copyright infringement and piracy have indicated a greater reliance on legal processes and procedures, while the relatively smooth leadership transition from Jiang Zemin to Hu Jintao was the first case in post-1949 history of a Chinese leader willingly retiring from power. In the economic sphere, China has pursued a policy of converting state-owned enterprises (SOEs) into corporations even as the banking and financial system has remained a major source of funding and debt for an economy in which the state remains the major player. Although the issues of Taiwan and North Korea remain major stumbling blocks in China's relationship with the United States, more and more the two countries have jousted over such mundane matters as intellectual property rights and encryption of Wifi telecommunications technology. Whereas from the 1960s to 1979, China had engaged in a number of confrontations with its neighbors—Sino–Indian War (1962), border clashes with the Soviet Union (1969), and an invasion of its erstwhile ally Vietnam (1979)—by the 1990s and early 2000s, China pursued a policy stressing economic ties and peaceful reconciliation of border and other conflicts with its neighbors (including the establishment of diplomatic ties with the Republic of Korea in 1992 and hosting the six-party talks aimed at creating a nuclear weapons-free Korean peninsula) and has become a major participant in the Association of Southeast Asian Nations (ASEAN). As China's economy has grown, so has its allocation of resources to military modernization. The PLA has benefited from substantial increases in military expenditures to more than US$100 billion in 2005 as China seeks to build a modern air force and blue water navy befitting its great power status. A nuclear power since 1964, China retains a retaliatory nuclear weapons capacity but has made no attempt to match the massive nuclear forces maintained by the United States and Russia, although the PRC reserves the right to deploy force to reincorporate Taiwan into the mainland. In 2008, Beijing will host the International Olympics.

THE DICTIONARY

– A –

"A Q SPIRIT" ("A Q JINGSHEN"). From the 1921 short story by Lu Xun entitled *The True Story of A Q*, this "spirit" refers to the self-deception and fear of the truth that Lu Xun believed was part of China's national character and a major reason for the country's weakness. The story concerns a peasant named A Q, a despicable bastard who repeatedly cheats and is constantly being cheated and yet refuses to admit that he has lost face. He is a perennial optimist, believing that things will turn in his favor, but he is generally disappointed. The 1911 Republican revolution raises great hopes for A Q (and, by implication, for the Chinese people), but the lowly peasant quickly realizes that the new rulers are no different from the previous dynastic overlords. A Q is finally charged with stealing and is sentenced to death, even though in this particular case he is not guilty. The "A Q Spirit" refers to anyone who fears the reality of his own suppression but engages in self-deception by declaring himself a "victor." But it also may refer to those outcasts who see through political and cultural hyperbole and reveal the hidden truths, even when a "new era" under a "new leadership" has been declared. In this sense, the "A Q Spirit" is very subversive of any political authority in China.

Born in 1881 in Zhejiang Province and trained in Japan as a doctor, Lu Xun was modern China's greatest man of letters whose works lashed out at the country's archaic culture and the imperialistic colonization of China. He was also the author of *A Madman's Diary* and *Medicine* and was later venerated by the **Chinese Communist Party** (**CCP**), although some of his works, including *The True Story of A Q*, have been censored or, at times, even banned. Lu Xun died in 1936.

In 2004, a film depicting his life was shot in **Shanghai**. *See also* LITERATURE AND THE ARTS.

"ACT ACCORDING TO PRINCIPLES LAID DOWN" (*"AN JI-DING FANGZHEN BAN"*). This political phrase was propagated in China during the internecine struggle among top **leaders** of the **Chinese Communist Party** (**CCP**) that followed the death of Party Chairman **Mao Zedong** on 9 September 1976. Its intent was to bolster the political forces of Mao's designated successor, **Hua Guofeng**, in his struggle with Mao's widow, **Jiang Qing**, and her radical faction, who were referred to as the **Gang of Four** and were arrested on 6 October 1976. According to the editorials of the CCP official newspaper, the *People's Daily* published at the time: "To 'act according to principles laid down' means to act according to Chairman Mao's proletarian revolutionary line and policies." In practical political terms, this meant that the CCP and the **People's Liberation Army** (**PLA**) should support Hua Guofeng as Mao's successor in line with the chairman's purported statement shortly before his death that with ". . . you [Hua Guofeng] in command, I am at ease" (*ni banshi, wo fangxin*). In a vain attempt to oust Hua Guofeng, the radical faction, led by Jiang Qing, offered the alternative political line that the Party should "act according to past principles." In the arcane language of Chinese political discourse, this was interpreted to mean that because Mao had originally promoted the **Cultural Revolution** (**1966–1976**), the mantle of leadership should pass to the radical faction led by Jiang Qing and not the more pragmatic Hua Guofeng, and, more important, that the radical policies of the Cultural Revolution should be continued.

AFGHANISTAN. As one of 14 nations with which China shares a land border (although only 80 km in length) and a territory that the ancient Silk Road traversed, Afghanistan has figured prominently in the international geopolitical strategy of the **People's Republic of China** (**PRC**). Following the takeover of China by the **Chinese Communist Party** (**CCP**) in 1949, China sent experts into Afghanistan to promote Third World solidarity as part of its overall **foreign policy** goal of countering the interests of the **United States** and the **Soviet Union**. The Sino–Afghan Boundary Agreement signed in 1963 resolved long-standing boundary questions dating back to the colonial era when Afghanistan was embroiled in the "Great Game" of geopolitical intrigue that involved **Russia** and Great Britain. Following the 1979 Soviet invasion of Afghanistan that occurred in the context of the hostile Sino–Soviet Conflict, China denounced the Soviet move bringing it into a closer strategic relationship with the U.S. in opposition to Soviet "hegemony." Like the U.S., China interpreted Soviet actions as part of the broad offensive of the Soviet Union into various strategic areas of the world, including the Middle East, Africa, and Southeast Asia. Whereas before the Afghanistan invasion the U.S., under the administration of President Jimmy Carter (1976–1980), had been reluctant as part of the political fallout over China's invasion of **Vietnam** in 1979 to elevate dramatically the level of U.S.–China cooperation, especially in the military arena, after the Soviet incursion into Afghanistan, Washington quickly assented to significantly broad bilateral military ties. By the early 1980s, the U.S. government, under President Ronald Reagan (1981–1988), supported a coordinated policy with the Chinese to provide weapons and other material to the Afghan rebels known as the Mujahedeen. Throughout the 1980s, China cited the Soviet occupation of Afghanistan as one of the three major obstacles preventing an improvement in Sino–Soviet ties.

Soviet President Mikhail Gorbachev's decision in 1988 to remove all Soviet forces from Afghanistan removed this obstacle, and China openly endorsed the Geneva Agreement on Afghanistan that led to the removal of all Red Army units. The Soviet decision at about the same time to press for the Vietnamese withdrawal from **Cambodia** and to reduce Soviet forces along the Mongolian border with China removed the remaining barriers to improved Sino–Soviet relations that from the late 1980s onward generally prospered, especially on the commercial front.

During the ensuing civil war and factional fighting that wracked Afghanistan throughout the early 1990s, China, like most nations, withdrew from the country, closing its embassy in 1993. With the rise of the Taliban, China maintained limited ties with the insular, orthodox Islamic country, although a Chinese company was involved in the construction of a digital telephone network for the ravaged city of Kabul. But once the Taliban were driven out of power by American air strikes following the 11 September 2001 terror attacks in the U.S. and a new government was installed in Kabul, China supported the **United Nations (UN)** resolution on Afghanistan and quickly reopened its embassy in Kabul in 2002 and sought to renew political and economic ties with the newly installed government of Hamid Karzai by flying in donated computers, clothing, and other aid and pledging to develop friendly exchanges and mutual cooperation between the two countries. In return, Afghanistan expressed its political support for China's long-standing struggle against its own Islamic separatist groups composed largely of the Uygur **minorities** that for several decades have fought to establish an independent "East Turkistan" in the western-most Xinjiang Autonomous Region of the PRC. In 2003, Afghanistan agreed to cooperate with China against four separatist organizations, including the Eastern Turkistan Islamic Movement and the Eastern Turkistan Liberation Organization, which China has labeled as "terrorist organizations," accusing them of receiving millions of dollars in assistance from Osama bin Laden and al-Qaeda in their campaign of bombings and assassinations. In the context of the global struggle against terrorism, China has been anxious to gain international support for its fight against Uygur separatists while international **human rights** groups accuse the PRC of using counterterrorism to punish Uygurs who exercise peaceful dissent. Afghanistan also stood by China by reiterating its support for its "one China" policy on **Taiwan** and joined the PRC and five other regional nations (Iran, Pakistan, Turkmenistan, Tajikistan, and Uzbekistan) in 2004 to strengthen anti-drug interdiction. A practical followup to the Kabul Declaration on Good Neighborly Relations signed in 2002, the Berlin Declaration on Counter-Narcotics was aimed at creating "a security belt around Afghanistan" in reaction to soaring levels of opium production that have exacerbated drug use in China and contributed to its growing HIV/**AIDS** problem. China and Afghanistan also joined in the Central and Western Trade Cooperation Forum that aims at creating a free trade area between China, Russia, Kazakstan, Kyrgystan, Tajikstan, Pakistan, Afghanistan, and Turkey in conjunction with China's 2001 entry into the **World Trade Organization (WTO)**.

China's major economic assistance to the Karzai government in Afghanistan consisted of a pledge in 2002 of US$150 million in direct aid over five years along with forgiving millions of dollars in Afghan debt to China. Major Chinese projects in the country include assisting in the reconstruction of the Kabul state hospital, rebuilding three major highways in north Afghanistan with World Bank funds, and rehabilitating the Parwan irrigation project near Kabul that had been rendered useless by the 23-year devastating civil war. Bilateral **trade** in 2003 hit US$27 million with Chinese-made toys, clothes, and electronics being exchanged for truckloads of Afghan carpets to sell in Chinese cities. In June 2004, China's assistance program in Afghanistan was dealt a severe blow when 11 Chinese construction workers in northern Afghanistan's Kunduz Province were killed as part of the effort by remnant Taliban forces to disrupt any rebuilding activities operating under U.S. influence. China's policy of supporting Afghanistan's reconstruction and peace process involved a willingness on the part of the PRC to accommodate U.S. goals for the region that bring American troops closer to China's western borders. *See also* FOREIGN POLICY.

AFRICA. *See* FOREIGN POLICY.

AGRARIAN REFORM LAW. *See* LAND REFORM.

AGRICULTURAL PRODUCERS' COOPERATIVES (APCs). Established in 1953 out of the **mutual aid teams** and approved in a resolution adopted by the **Chinese People's Political Consultative Conference (CPPCC)**, the APCs emerged as the major organizational structure for China's vast agricultural areas until the late 1950s. The "early stage" APCs that were created in 1953 did not affect the fundamental property rights of the rural **population**, although they did introduce the principle of property amalgamation. By the mid-1950s, about one-third of the rural population had been enlisted in such APCs, theoretically on a "voluntary" basis but often through pressure and coercion sanctioned by the **Chinese Communist Party (CCP)**. Demobilized soldiers from the **People's Liberation Army (PLA)** and Party **cadres** in China's one million villages provided the organizational weapon for enticing villagers to enter the "early stage" APCs where **labor** and land were pooled into a common production effort. In July 1955, despite significant progress in the formation of

APCs, CCP Chairman **Mao Zedong** called for dramatically speeding up the process and demanded that the "early stage" APCs be quickly replaced by "higher stage" cooperatives (also known as brigades) in which land ownership was fully collectivized and amalgamated into one APC per "natural village" (*cun*), although some of the 700,000 plus APCs were expanded to cover the much larger "administrative village" (*xiang*). This organizational transformation meant, in effect, the creation of a unified village **economy**, particularly for the production of basic grains (wet rice in the south and wheat/millet in the north). On average, one APC united about 250 families into a single production unit led by a village CCP member where decisions on the allocation of labor and land were under the direct authority of the Party. The old landlord class who had been dispossessed of its property by the **land reform** (**1950–1952**) and rich peasants became part of the APCs, contributing their labor, land, and capital. According to model "higher stage" APC regulations, "all privately owned land, draft animals, major production materials, such as large-scale farm implements [were to be] turned over to the APC as collective property" (Article 13, APC Regulations). Farmers could retain as private property what they needed for their own livelihood, along with domestic animals and small-scale tools that were needed for individual enterprise. In 1958, the "higher stage" APCs were replaced by the **people's communes** during the **Great Leap Forward** (**1958–1960**). Following the policy shift in 1978–1979 to the **Agricultural Responsibility System**, the socialist system of **agriculture** in China, of which the APCs and the people's communes were the centerpiece, was effectively ended and was replaced by a system of semi-private land ownership.

"AGRICULTURAL RESPONSIBILITY SYSTEM" ("SHENG-CHAN ZIRENZHI"). Instituted in 1978 at the watershed December **Third Plenum of the 11th CCP Central Committee**, this system of organizing **agriculture** replaced the outmoded and highly inefficient rural **people's communes**. The heart of the "responsibility system" is household contracting, technically referred to as "household contracts with fixed levies" (*baogan daohu*) whereby land is parceled out in small plots to individual households on the basis of **labor** power, and output quotas of particular crops are fixed by contracts signed by

Chinese farmers with state purchasing agents. Under this system, land is not formally "owned" by farmers but is leased from the state for a period of 15 years—subsequently extended in 1993 to 20 years and in 2003 to 30 years, although the state retains the right to reclaim land for other purposes. Surplus output above the contracted amount is retained by the individual household for sale on the open market. Initiated in the late 1970s in Anhui Province, one of China's poorest, and later in Sichuan Province, the country's most populated, this system spread to most of China's rural areas, although levels of implementation differed between provinces. Some of the more conservative areas, such as the provinces of Guangxi and Heilongjiang, retained elements of the old socialist model of agricultural production and imprisoned any farmer who dared to dismember the socialist agricultural system.

The impact of the agricultural responsibility system on agricultural production in China was dramatic, especially in the early 1980s. From 1978 to 1983, per capita income more than doubled in the countryside from 133 *yuan* (approximately US$47) to 310 *yuan* (US$105). At the same time, China's rural areas experienced a major boom in housing construction as farmers invested their newfound wealth in new houses, and a dramatic increase in small-scale rural **industry** that absorbed some of the surplus labor freed by the household contract system. Production of basic grains, cotton, and cash crops also increased during the 1978–1995 period, averaging growth rates of 5% per annum.

The shift to the agricultural responsibility system is generally associated with the policy preferences of China's paramount leader, **Deng Xiaoping**, and **Zhao Ziyang**, the **Chinese Communist Party** (**CCP**) general secretary from 1987 to 1989. Zhao experimented with the policy during his tenure as Party secretary in Sichuan Province from 1976 to 1980. Deng Xiaoping supported such a policy even earlier, during the early 1960s after the disastrous **Great Leap Forward** (**1958–1960**). Concerned with the lack of material incentives among China's suffering rural cultivators, Deng and other economically liberal-minded **leaders** in 1962 advocated a similar policy known as "assigning farm output quotas for individual households" (*baochan daohu*). This policy initiative was quickly vetoed, however, by then CCP Chairman **Mao Zedong**, who called for reinstituting socialist agriculture in the wake of the Great Leap disaster. *Baochan daohu* was thus condemned during the **Cultural Revolution (1966–1976)** as a "right-opportunist" concept and "another disguised form of individual undertakings." Not until Mao's death in 1976 did a CCP leader dare revise this judgment, and that leader was Deng Xiaoping. In 1999, the legal definition of China's land system was formally changed in the State constitution by the Ninth **National People's Congress (NPC)** as the responsibility system was replaced with a "dual-operation system characterized by the combination of centralized and decentralized operation based on households working under a contract." In 2003, China promulgated a newly amended Law on Agriculture and put into effect a new Law on Rural Land Contracts that extended the period of guaranteed rights to use the contracted land to 30 years and guaranteed that **women**, whether married or unmarried, were to enjoy equal rights with respect to land distribution. China also issued its "Proposals on Several Policies to Increase Farmers' Incomes" to improve the overall economic livelihood of its food-growing **population**. *See also* "FLOATING POPULATION."

AGRICULTURE. China has 22% of the world's **population** but only 10% of the planet's arable land on which is employed 370 million people to produce as much food as do two million American farmers. China's main crops are rice (for which China is the world's largest producer and consumer), wheat, corn, soybeans, and tuber crops. During the period of Soviet-style central planning from 1953 to 1978, the Chinese government pursued crash industrialization at the expense of agricultural development that in the aftermath of the disastrous **Great Leap Forward (1958–1960)**, in which radical experiments in agricultural production, such as close-planting of rice seedlings and the organization of the countryside into large-scale **people's communes**, led to one of the largest famines in human history. Throughout the period of Soviet-style central planning, the Chinese government pursued the so-called scissors effect of low state prices for agricultural products and high prices for industrial output (consumed by farmers among others) that effectively squeezed about 600 billion *yuan* out of the agricultural sector from 1953 to 1978. But despite the heavy emphasis during this period on local and provincial self-sufficiency in grain production—that effectively ignored comparative advantage within China—there was no impressive improvement in the performance of grain output, which, at 2% growth per annum, lagged behind the mid-1930s in terms of per capita productivity/output per head of population.

Following the adoption of economic reforms in December 1978–1979, agricultural output in China expanded strongly growing in real terms by about 5% per annum from 1978 to 1995. While still retaining the system of **planned purchase and supply**, the Chinese government significantly lifted state procurement prices for 18 major farm products in 1979. By 1985, the number of agricultural products subject to state price control was reduced to 38, a figure that was 30% of the 1980 level. While prices on such products as fish, poultry, and vegetables were liberalized, the Chinese government still maintains pricing and marketing controls over so-called strategic products such as marketable grains (70–80%) and cotton, tobacco, sugar, and silkworms (100%). Ration prices were raised by 68% in 1991 and by a further 45% in 1992, almost eliminating the gap between state grain procurement prices and retail prices. Encouraged by this success, in 1992, the State Council allowed some local governments in China to fully liberalize local grain markets by freeing both procurement and retail prices as a way to reduce the state's fiscal burden generated by high subsidies on grain prices. However, following sharp food price rises at the end of 1993, the government reasserted administrative controls over grain production and marketing through a newly introduced "governor's responsibility system" under which the governor of a province assumed full responsibility for the province's grain **economy**. State procurement by quotas has been substantially reduced to 50 million tons, which represents only 44% of total marketable grain. Responding to market incentives, grain output increased from 283 to 407 million tons from 1977 to 1984 at a rate of 5.3% a year. By 1990, this figure had reached 446 million tons and by 1998 it was 512 million tons. In four of the five subsequent years, total grain production fell so that the figure had dropped to 435 million tons in 2003 but rose again in 2004 to 479 million tons, the largest increase since 1949, but the government does not believe this rate can be sustained into the future.

Although agricultural reform dramatically increased grain output, demand outstripped supply. From 1978 to 1996, China imported an average of 6.5 million metric tons (mt) of grain per year, of which by far the largest share consisted of wheat. Such measures were considered temporary, however, as a major State Council document on "The Grain Issue in China" released in October 1996 asserted that agriculture was still the foundation of the Chinese economy and that the country must continue to be self-sufficient in grains. As of 2004, however, China's agriculture was described by government officials as the "weak link" in the macroeconomy and that grain security was still the "sword of Damocles" hanging over the country's head because in any one year grain production can fluctuate by up to 25 million tons, which, since 1949, has occurred on 11 separate occasions. This sometimes dire situation has been exacerbated by the dramatic rise of agricultural land converted to non-agricultural use at the expense of 70 million farmers who have become landless since 1994. As for food exports, the value in 1980 was US$3 billion, a figure that grew to US$10 billion in 2000.

China's main grain crop is paddy rice grown primarily in the Yangtze River valley and in southeastern China and on the southwestern Yunnan-Guizhou Plateau. Its output accounts for two-fifths of grain output for the country, while wheat, which is grown primarily on the North China Plain, makes up slightly more than one-fifth of the country's total output. Corn is grown in the northwestern, northern, and southwestern provinces, and constitutes one-fourth of total grain output. Soybeans, the basis of the Chinese staple of bean-curd (doufu), are grown on the Northeast China Plain and on the plains along the Yellow and Huai rivers. The main tuber crop in China is sweet potatoes, which are grown throughout the country, but primarily in the Pearl River valley in the south and along the middle and lower reaches of the Yangtze River and in the Sichuan basin. Cash crops include cotton, peanuts, rapeseed, sesame, sugarcane and beets, tea, tobacco, and fruit. Cotton is grown mainly along the moisture-rich Yangtze River valley but also in the arid northwest along the Manas River in the Xinjiang Autonomous Region. Sugarcane and beets are grown in southern China and in the northeast in Heilongjiang, Jilin, and Liaoning provinces. From 1995 to 2000, land under cultivation for grain crops and cotton and tea dropped on average of 3 to 5% while oil-bearing crops, vegetables, and orchards all experienced substantial increases with corn, beans, and tubers remaining relatively constant. Animal husbandry and fishery industries contributed 63.5 million tons and 43.75 million tons, respectively, in 2001.

In 2001, the total area of cultivated land in China was approximately 132.3 million hectares (326 million acres). Based on remote sensing satellite imagery, this figure is dramatically greater than previous estimates of 95 million ha of land under cultivation. Estimates are that China has enough arable land to produce 650 million tons of all grains, enough to feed its projected population of 1.48 billion in 2025 even at currently available levels of agricultural organization and technology. But unlike urban residents who can buy and sell property, there is no market for farmland as it remains distributed based on 30-year contracts and firmly under the control of local authorities, preventing farmers from profiting by selling land rights to other more efficient cultivators. In the absence of secure ownership rights, farmers are often at the mercy of local officials who often utilize obscure clauses in the 1951 Land Law to seize land that has been worked by families back to imperial times, provide meager compensation, and then re-lease the land for major developments and pocket huge profits. Grave concern over the annual loss of arable land to non-agricultural uses led the State Council in 1997 to call for a one-year moratorium on the conversion of arable land to non-agricultural uses while an amendment to the state constitution and the passage of the National Land Management Law in 2004 require adequate compensation for land expropriated or requisitioned. With the decision by the **National People's Congress** (**NPC**) in the same year to recognize property rights, farmers have been legally empowered to resist government-approved land seizures that have often provoked confrontations between local officials and irate tillers resulting in a series of sometimes violent **social protests**. And yet from 1997 to 2004, estimates are that new factories, housing, offices and shopping malls and an explosive growth in golf courses (230 at last count) had consumed about 5% of total arable land. In addition to its cropland, China has approximately 30 million ha of reserve land with grain cultivation potential located largely in northern China provinces such as Heilongjiang. But approximately half of this reserve—15 million ha—would require irrigation in order to become productive. China also has large grassland areas that could be employed more intensely for livestock production although substantial changes toward a more stable form of livestock production would be required to convert these areas into full utilization. Enormous waste in the storage and distribution of agricultural products also plagues the country since each year several dozen million tons of grain, or about 15% of total production, are lost. Returns on growing grain in China remain low, especially when compared to cash crops and other industries. Around 43% of China's agricultural land is irrigated (compared to 59% in **Japan** and 36% in **India**) while China uses 0.28 mt of fertilizer per hectare, second in the world to Japan's 0.31 mt/ha.

Like other nations, China is experimenting with the use of genetically modified crops, including so-called "super rice" that dramatically reduces the need for chemical fertilizers. China is also engaged in transgenetic plant research with 180 different varieties of plants, including tobacco and cotton, developed with virus- and pest-resistant features, although it is still illegal in China to sell what is known as "anti-pest" rice on the open market. Animal cloning is also underway, with much effort concentrated on developing trans-genetic cows that produce high-protein milk. The value of China's output per hectare in 2001 was US$2,181; in comparative terms, this is second highest to Japan among major grain producers, although the value added per worker in China is US$0.3 compared to US$31 in Japan (and US$39 in the **United States**), a reflection of China's still very **labor**-intensive agricultural system in which 50% of the labor force remains in the rural sector. Whereas Canada and the United States lead the world, with 1,642 and 1,484 tractors per thousand workers, respectively, China ranks lowest among major nations, with one tractor per 1,000 workers (compared to six in India), largely because of insufficient agricultural plot size. In domestic terms, China's 370 million farmers—full and part-time—make up half of the nation's work force but contribute only 20% to Gross Domestic Product (GDP); rural labor productivity is one-fifth that of Chinese industrial workers and one-third that of service personnel. Regional disparities in the rural labor force, which between 1995 and 2000 continued to expand, are also very evident with the smallest percentage of farm labor found in Eastern China (approximately 45%) and the largest in Western China (65%) with Central China in the middle with approximately 55%. China's yield per hectare is, on average, higher than the world average on most crops, except soybeans, but China still ranks below the world's leading producers—such as France (wheat), Japan (rice), and the United States (maize). From 1978 to 1995, the agricultural proportion of China's rural economy declined from nearly 70 to 26% while within agriculture the share of crop farming, primarily of grain, declined from 80 to 58% with concomitant increases from 15 to 30% of animal husbandry and 5 to 12% of fishing and forestry.

As Chinese agriculture continues to move away from planning and regional and national self-sufficiency to specialized family farms and away from less profitable (e.g., wheat) to more profitable crops (e.g., citrus), further real gains from the post-1978–1979 liberalization of China's agriculture should be realized. Since 1978, China has moved 200 million people out of poverty—an unprecedented improvement of living conditions in which agriculture has played an important role, although the gap between urban and rural living standards has grown. The ratio of expenditure on food to total living expenditure— Engel's Parameter—has fallen in China from 58% in 1995 to 50% in 2000, indicating that farm families grow enough to feed themselves—the "warm and fed" (*wenbao*) standard—and have enough left over to sell on open markets. While increasing prices for agricultural staples in the 1980s produced dramatic increases in rural incomes, the 1990s undermined those gains as local taxes and fees imposed on farmers soared and the government ended **education** and **health care** benefits and, in 2002, abolished direct taxes on the agricultural population and staple farm crops. Average rural incomes are less than one-third of urban incomes and are growing more slowly.

Sufficient grain supply for the nation is guaranteed by government procurement policies under which the state acquires grain from farmers at a fixed and negotiated price with only a small amount sold at market price. More attractive producer prices would undoubtedly stimulate even greater grain production for domestic consumption and export. Under the 1994 Policies for Agricultural Comprehensive Development, China targeted middle- and low-yield land for an increase in production rate by substantially raising government funding to support agricultural production and cover agricultural operating expenses, although, in percentage terms, these expenditures remained below levels achieved in the late 1970s and early 1980s. Beginning in 1994, China also devoted substantially greater resources to promotion of agricultural **science and technology**, such as widespread adoption of GPS systems for precision mapping of crop yields, use of drop-irrigation under plastic film to cut water consumption in arid regions, and a project for "getting agro-science and technology into each household." Prior to the 1978–1979 market reforms, the state maintained a monopoly over the acquisition of agricultural commodities through the bureaucratically bloated Supply and Marketing Cooperatives that since 1978 have had to adjust their role to an increased market environment.

Real improvements in the living standards of the rural populace remain a major concern of government **leaders**; central bank statistics indicate that total **investment** in agricultural production over the past several years has stagnated while average incomes for farmers in 2004 was US$353, well below their urban counterparts whose average income was 3.2 times higher at over US$1,000. In 1991, 1997, and 2004, high-level policy decisions called for increased emphasis on raising farmers' incomes, a reduction in agricultural taxes (which farmers in China, unlike their urban counterparts, have paid since imperial times), direct payment of subsidies to farmers from the country's grain risk fund, and improvements in agricultural modernization that would raise both farm output and quality. But according to a recent book on the plight of China's farmers (*An Investigation of China's Farmers* [*Zhongguo nongmin diaocha*] by Wu Chuntao and Chen Guidi [translated into English as *Will the Boat Sink the Water? The Life of China's Peasants*], which was subsequently banned) such policies that are decided at the Center are often undone by local CCP bosses who line their own pockets at the farmers' expense by imposing illegal fees and taxes three times the legal amount and by holding back on health, housing, education, and retirement benefits and any compensation funds for land acquisition. Loans for agricultural purposes are often diverted to other areas, especially property speculation on the edges of cities where farms and villages are being cleared away at a cost to production in favor of residential complexes and steel mills with meager compensatory payments to farmers who often fall into long-term arrears.

The most pressing problem confronting agriculture in China is water. This comes in the form of insufficient rainfall in the north and water losses in open irrigation canals and flood-irrigated fields—upward of 60% in the moist areas of the Yangtze River valley and the south. Severe bottlenecks in **transportation** infrastructure, technology, and logistics, such as insufficient harbor capacity and overburdened railroads and roads in many remote areas, pose serious risks in the case of local or regional food shortages. Loss of cropland comes largely from severe flooding and drought that from 1988 to 1995 amounted to 856,000 ha; in 1998 and 2000, China suffered the most severe floods and drought in over a decade. Rising levels of pollution of China's many rivers and lakes have also negatively impacted agriculture, along with advancing desertification and soil degradation. However, in 2001, more than 1 million ha of land were converted into farmland with advances in irrigation. China's family farms instituted under the **Agricultural Responsibility System** are generally too small—averaging 0.46 ha in size—to take advantage of economies of scale and agricultural mechanization so prevalent in Western agriculture. Consolidation of farm structure would improve productivity especially as increasing numbers of rural laborers generate their main income from employment in **township-village enterprises** (**TVEs**).

Prior to its 2001 entry into the **World Trade Organization** (**WTO**), China maintained relatively high **trade** barriers on agriculture many of which were not transparent as international trading in grains was carried out by the highly centralized Cereal, Oil, and Foodstuffs Importing and Exporting Corporation (COFCO). While other sectors of China's trading system were substantially decentralized in the 1980s to literally hundreds of provincial-based foreign trade corporations (FTCs), agriculture remained under tight central control of state agencies, such as COFCO and China's National Textiles Import and Export Corporation (CHINATEX), which handles China's international trade in cotton. With the growth in agricultural trade much slower than the growth of total trade, from 1980 to 1995 the proportion of foodstuffs in China's total exports dropped from nearly 17 to 5%, even as China after a decade and a half of reform became a strong net food exporter. Despite a move to lower average tariffs on agricultural products, China restricted imports through a variety of non-tariff barriers such as quotas, taxes, import licenses, and a state trading monopoly as the country apparently remains committed to the goals of retaining national grain self-sufficiency. China also employed sanitary and pyhtosanitary measures, the latter used to bar imports of American citrus. Although China lacks comparative advantage in land-intensive crops, namely grains, it continues to be a net exporter of rice and coarse grains as well as labor-intensive horticultural products such as vegetables and fruits where China enjoys a comparative advantage. Overall, the volume of farm trade globally will be affected relatively little by China's WTO accession while domestically the decline in the relative importance of agriculture and the gradual increase in the 1990s of domestic agricultural prices to real market levels, is likely to mitigate the liberalization of the agricultural sector post-WTO. The World Bank is forecasting that by 2010 China's net grain imports will increase to 32 million tons, and by 2020 it could reach as high as 57 million tons, all of which is well within the range of fluctuations in the world market. This makes unlikely the scenario advanced by the American economist Lester Brown who has predicted enormous future grain demand on the part of China that could overwhelm world grain supplies. *See also* AGRICULTURAL PRODUCERS' COOPERATIVES (APCs); LAND REFORM.

AIDS. In 1991, China's Minister of Public Health Chen Minzhang issued the first official statement on AIDS in China by announcing that of 300,000 people examined 122 were found to be HIV positive and three to have contracted AIDS. China's first AIDS patients had been reported in 1985 among whom the first death had occurred in 1991. By 1995, about 1,700 cases of HIV infection were reported in China, a 27% increase over 1992. Less than 100 people were reported as having developed AIDS, yet only two million people in China had been tested for the virus. In 1992, it was estimated by the World Health Organization (WHO) that, in fact, more than 10,000 people in China were HIV-positive, information that apparently led China to set up the China Venereal Disease and AIDS Prevention Association in **Beijing** that aimed at mobilizing action to control the spread of the disease. In 1998, to mark World AIDS Day (1 December), China's Ministry of Health announced that HIV-infected people were found in virtually all of China's 31 provinces and provincial-level municipalities with the total number rising from zero in the mid-1980s to 300,000 by 1998, with 184 reported deaths.

By 2004, the spread of the virus had accelerated and in May of that year the Chinese government's State Council warned that despite some moderate efforts at stemming the disease and isolating it to specific and highly vulnerable groups, such as intravenous drug users and prostitutes, AIDS was continuing to spread rapidly, and that "urgent measures" were being adopted to stem its transmission from high-risk groups into the general **population**. While only 107,000 cases have been reported in China, official estimates in 2004 put the number of people as HIV carriers at 840,000 with an additional 80,000 people having tested positive for AIDS and with the number of deaths caused by the disease at 150,000. If strict measures are not taken to stem its annual growth rate of 25%, by 2010, it is estimated China will have 10 million AIDS patients, a situation that would overwhelm China's fledgling **health care system**. In China, statistics on HIV/AIDS are compiled from "sentinel surveillance" sites that carry out HIV tests on persons in targeted groups once or twice a year with estimates in 2003 that 44% of HIV transmission came from injected drug use, 24% from blood donations, 20% from heterosexual transmission, and 11% from men having sex with men. With many prostitutes and drug users apparently ignorant of the disease, only one in nine infected people know they are HIV positive; many infected people, especially prostitutes, keep their condition secret.

The spread of the disease to initially 24 provinces in the mid-1990s and then by 2004 into virtually every province and region in the country reflected the increase in intravenous drug use that began in the 1980s, especially in southwestern Yunnan Province, where most of the first AIDS cases were reported. Areas populated by ethnic **minorities**—Yunnan, Guangxi, and Xinjiang—had particularly high rates of HIV/AIDS infection in 2004, particularly among the Dai and Jinpo minorities. Nationwide, 38% of those people officially registered as HIV/AIDS positive belong to one of China's 55 official ethnic minorities while the fourth highest rate was in Sichuan Province, where 52 ethnic minorities reside with the highest rate occurring among the Yi people, the province's largest minority group. Along with increased use of heroin imported from **Afghanistan** and Myanmar (Burma), sexual transmission has also contributed to the spread of AIDS because of the growth in recent years of prostitution and the involvement of Chinese citizens living along the border with Thailand in that country's thriving sex industry. Other areas reporting elevated infection rates include Guangdong, Henan, Hunan, Guizhou,

Sichuan, Hubei, Anhui, and Shanxi provinces and Beijing and **Shanghai** municipalities. From 2000–2003, the epicenter of the AIDS crisis in China was in Henan Province in central China, where perhaps one million, mostly poor, Chinese were infected with HIV as the result of a profit-driven blood-selling scheme that involved many local officials, none of whom were ever prosecuted. Violent confrontations between AIDS-afflicted residents of villages in Henan Province and authorities have occurred in response to the apparent inability of local officials to deliver promised medical care and drugs.

The incidence of AIDS in China, as in much of Asia and elsewhere, has been surrounded by social and political controversy. Initially, the Chinese government blamed foreigners for the outbreak of AIDS, as conservative, anti-Western elements in the Chinese government linked the disease to China's **open-door policy**. AIDS has also been associated with the small but growing number of homosexuals in China. The first openly gay bar in Beijing was closed down in 1993 because, the government claimed, it posed health risks, particularly the spread of AIDS. Rigorous testing procedures for anyone entering China—including Chinese returning students—were also imposed, provoking protests from frequent travelers (especially Overseas Chinese from **Hong Kong**) when it was discovered that the needles used to draw blood were being reused. Yet, many Chinese doctors and medical professionals quickly realized that AIDS in China was not just a foreign import, and thus they have begun to advocate rational responses to the disease, including an **education** campaign and the construction of the first AIDS hospital in Yunnan Province.

Unfortunately, ignorance of the disease and its transmission is still widespread in China, especially in rural areas. The AIDS hospital constructed in Yunnan had trouble recruiting nurses and other personnel who feared that the disease could be casually transmitted, while, at the same time, many Chinese still associate the disease with foreigners and continue to believe that merely touching an infected person or object can cause infection. Chinese students traveling abroad are told by worrisome parents to wear rubber gloves when touching objects, such as doorknobs. The term for AIDS in Chinese has also been politically charged: *aizibing*—the Chinese transliteration of "AIDS"—is similar in pronunciation to a term that means "loving-capitalism disease." The Chinese government contributed to the air of ignorance and superstition surrounding the disease by initially suppressing open reporting by the media on its transmission, going so far in some cases as to arrest journalists and others who sought to report the spread of the disease. Editors and journalists at the independent and outspoken newspaper *Southern Weekly* (*Nanfang zhoumou*) were fired by management in a move many perceived as tied to its lively and open reporting on Chinese social problems, such as HIV/AIDS, while HIV-positive farmers have petitioned the central government after being met with repressive measures by local authorities. In 2002, China's application to the Global Fund for AIDS was refused on the grounds that the plan failed to develop community participation. Discrimination against HIV-positive individuals in China at the workplace, in housing, in schools, and even in hospitals and clinics has been widely reported.

The Chinese heath-care system also lagged in introducing safety controls: the development of a nationwide blood-testing system was only begun in 1996, and some hospitals reportedly have reused needles to save money. Still, China has participated in several international conferences dealing with AIDS, including the 1994 conference in **Japan**, where, it was warned, Asia would see the largest growth in AIDS cases over the next decade.

By 2004, Chinese government policy executed a nearly 180-degree turn in its approach to the growing AIDS problem. Reflecting the more open and honest approach to medical problems that followed upon the 2002–2003 **SARS** crisis, the May 2004 statement from the State Council on AIDS called for a comprehensive education program on AIDS beginning in China's middle schools and extending to the public display of prevention posters, especially at the burgeoning number of "entertainment venues" that have sprouted throughout major cities and even in rural areas that are considered the epicenter of the AIDS epidemic. Government spending on AIDS was doubled, and several new policies were introduced, including needle exchanges and condom promotion, which, until 2002 in China, could not be publicly advertised. Although the free antiretroviral program introduced in 2003 has had serious problems, the government is moving ahead to expand the number of methadone clinics in China to 1,000 by 2007. Public awareness of AIDS in China remains limited, with 20% of the population in 2003 saying they never heard of the disease and only 13% knowing the three methods of transmission while the social stigma surrounding the disease remains high especially in rural areas.

Local officials have been warned by the State Council that they will be held personally responsible for curbing the disease in their jurisdictions, and that the kind of cover-up that characterized the SARS crisis will not be tolerated—even though in some areas local police have arrested drug users during meetings with local health workers while websites that provide AIDS information over the **Internet** to gay people have been shut down. National and local events in China have also been held on World AIDS day, including a TV appearance by Premier **Wen Jiabao** with an AIDS patient followed by a similar appearance by President **Hu Jintao**. The capacity of China's fragmented health-care system, especially in rural areas, to dispense and monitor the program remains problematic, a situation that has driven many living with HIV/AIDS into an unpredictable world of back street clinics and a booming market of incompletely regulated, experimental remedies. International assistance to China on the AIDS problem has come from many countries, including the American Centers for Disease Control and Prevention that is collaborating with its Chinese counterparts at the national level. By 2003, the situation involving AIDS in China, along with **India** and **Cambodia**, was likened to that of Africa a decade prior, that has since seen its population ravaged by the virus. In 2004, China also signed the Berlin Declaration on Counter-Narcotics with five other Central Asian nations to stem the flow of opium out of post-Taliban Afghanistan that contributed to increased drug use in China.

ALBANIA. *See* SOVIET UNION.

ALL-CHINA FEDERATION OF TRADE UNIONS. *See* TRADE UNIONS.

ALL-CHINA FEDERATION OF WOMEN. Established shortly before the Communist takeover in 1949 as the All-China Democratic Women's Federation, the organization adopted its present name of All-China Federation of Women in September 1957. One of many "mass" organizations used by the **Chinese Communist Party (CCP)** to maintain administrative and political control over various social groups, the Women's Federation is one of the three largest such organizations, the other two being the All-China Federation of **Trade Unions** and the Communist **Youth League (CYL)**. Other smaller "mass" organizations include the All-China Federation of Students, the All-China Federation of **Industry** and Commerce, and the All-China Youth Federation that is supervised by the CYL. Although formally "autonomous," these "mass" organizations are, in reality, under central control, intimately tied to the state and Communist Party apparatus. Based on the original Leninist-Stalinist model of administrative "transmission belts," their primary function, especially during the Maoist era (1949–1976), was to mobilize respective social groups behind policies decided on by Communist Party elites and to promote the political **education** of its members. Policies supported by the Women's Federation include guaranteeing equal pay for equal work, turning "petty housekeeping" into productive work, developing better education for **women** and children, and supporting the state's family planning policies. In helping to enforce the **one-child policy**, the Women's Federation has been accused of contributing to the continuing oppression of women in Chinese society.

With more than 100 million members, the Women's Federation is represented in the **Chinese People's Political Consultative Conference (CPPCC)** and holds annual conferences. During the **Cultural Revolution (1966–1976)**, however, the work of the Women's Federation, as that of all "mass" organizations, was severely disrupted. After 1978, the Women's Federation was reconstituted and headed by Kang Keqing, wife of **People's Liberation Army (PLA)** Marshal **Zhu De**. The Federation's executive committee consists of more than 200 members and includes model workers and nationally prominent women from various fields, such as medicine, **health-care** services, culture, and sports. From 1988 to 1998, the Federation was chaired by **Chen Muhua**, one of the highest-ranking women in the Chinese government and CCP. In the late 1990s and early 2000s, the Federation took a more aggressive stance on a variety of issues relating to Chinese women with an increased focus on pressuring the Chinese government to adopt policies and practices to meet the changing needs of women in the context of the economic reforms and the

open-door policy adopted by the central government since 1978–1979. This includes acting as an advocate for women whose employment ratio under the economic reforms had dropped, who after being laid off from **state-owned enterprises (SOEs)** found it increasingly difficult to find new jobs, who upon graduating from college were shunned in favor of males for state employment, who find it difficult to open their own businesses, and whose rights and benefits as workers were more often encroached upon than their male counterparts by employers.

In addition to pressuring the government to take remedial action on these fronts by improving employment and reemployment policies in favor of women job seekers, the Federation also pushed for establishing a sound **legal system** to guarantee the legitimate rights and interests of women workers. Beginning in 2003, the Federation oversaw a pilot program in select counties of Hebei Province of direct election of representatives to village branches of the women's associations, the basic units of the Federation in rural areas, that were touted as a training ground to prepare women to stand for election in the **village-level elections** instituted in China since 1987. In 2004, the All-China Federation of Women participated in the 11th Global Conference of Women Entrepreneurs held in **Beijing** in cooperation with the newly established China Association of Women Entrepreneurs. The Women's Federation has also become an active member of the International Federation of Women Entrepreneurs, an international non-governmental organization (NGO) of small and medium enterprises that was established in 1993. Another issue on which China's Womens Federation has increasingly acted as an advocate involved calling on the Chinese government to address the growing problem of female suicide in China, especially among young rural women for whom suicide is the leading cause of death. One of the few countries in the world with higher suicides among women than men, China averages 280,000 suicides a year, of which over 150,000 are women. In addition to promoting pilot programs involving crisis hotlines, psychological counseling centers, and shelters for domestically abused females, the Federation has pushed the government to draft a national suicide prevention plan.

In conjunction with operations in China of the **United Nations** International Children's Fund (UNICEF), the Federation has also promoted educational programs for Chinese women subject to the growing problem of female and child human trafficking and Chinese involvement in the sex industry of Southeast Asia. The Federation has also encouraged married Chinese women to report cases of domestic violence, especially the many women who erroneously believe they cannot report their husbands for sexual or domestic abuse. Every year the Federation cites 1,000 "women pace-setters" throughout China for various accomplishments, including, in 2004, a nurse who fought **SARS** and a Chinese woman journalist for her coverage of the war in Iraq. Beginning in 2003, the Federation was headed by **Gu Xiulian** a former minister of the chemical industry.

ALLEY, REWI (1897–1987). A New Zealand–born writer of middleclass background and long-time sympathizer of the **Chinese Communist Party** (**CCP**), Rewi Alley lived in China from 1927 to his death in 1987. As a relief worker for famine and flood victims in the 1930s, Rewi Alley developed a profound compassion for China's poor and indigent **population**. Along with a group of other foreigners, Alley founded the Industrial Cooperative Movement in rural China that established more than 3,000 light industrial cooperatives in villages outside Japanese control during the **Sino–Japanese War (1937–1945)**. He also assisted in training Chinese workers in industrial and agricultural **technology** at the Bailie school in Sandan northwestern Gansu Province, one of China's poorest regions. Although not very political, Rewi Alley protected Communist underground organizers in his **Shanghai** home from Japanese and **Kuomintang** (**KMT**) persecution and maintained contacts with such Chinese luminaries as **Song Qingling** (widow of Sun Yat-sen), **Hu Shi**, and colorful "foreign friends" of China such as Agnes Smedley, George Hatem, and Richard Sorge. After the Communist takeover in 1949, Alley, who was not a Communist, remained in China largely out of a personal desire as a homosexual to avoid returning to his native New Zealand. Working for the Asian Pacific Peace Liaison Committee, a CCP front organization opposed to **United States** policies in Asia, Alley was a prolific writer and also translated Chinese poetry. Unlike some of China's "foreign friends" who during the **Cultural Revolution (1966–1976)** ended up in prison, Alley managed to survive although many of his memoirs, translations, and travelogues were carefully and cautiously edited to fit the CCP party line at any particular time.

"ALWAYS THINKING OF MONEY" (*"YIQIE XIANG QIAN KAN"***).** This phrase was popular during the reform era in the 1980s and 1990s, and was often used by political and economic conservatives to attack China's increasingly commercial **economy** and its social consequences. In orthodox Communist ideology, people should not work for money but "serve the people" and build the socialist state. During the campaign beginning in 1986 to build "**Socialist Spiritual Civilization**," material values were roundly criticized for eroding the social fabric of the country and undermining the "selfless" integrity of the Chinese people. "Always thinking of money" was prima facie evidence that capitalism had penetrated the heart and soul of Chinese society since the economic reforms inaugurated in 1978–1979. Political opponents of **Deng Xiaoping** used the phrase to attack Deng's ideological position that had replaced "distribution according to need" with the less socialist notion of "distribution according to work" (i.e., material incentives).

ANSHAN IRON AND STEEL CORPORATION. A major steel production facility in Liaoning Province in China's northeast in **Manchuria**, the Anshan Iron and Steel Corporation was, for many years, China's largest industrial organization. In the 1990s, the corporation employed upward of 220,000 workers and produced one quarter of China's entire steel output, estimated at 92 million tons in 1991. Like most factories in China after 1949, Anshan became a center of conflict among top **leaders** of the **Chinese Communist Party** (**CCP**) over the proper structure of management and authority. During the early to mid-1950s, the Anshan plant adopted the Soviet model of one-man management in which decision-making authority was invested in a single plant director. This highly centralized authority structure led to the creation of large administrative organs within the facility with direct ties to the Ministry of Metallurgy and other relevant ministries in **Beijing**. This placed the Anshan Party Committee and the facility's workers in an excessively subordinate position, a situation that provoked a radical attempt at industrial reorganization in the late 1950s. Led by the Anshan Party Committee and purportedly supported by the factory's workers, in 1960, the new "charter" of the Anshan Iron and Steel Corporation overturned the Soviet model and instituted a radically new and more decentralized structure of authority that was subsequently idealized by **Mao Zedong**. The charter of the Anshan Corporation has never been published, but, according to Mao Zedong, it contained the five following principles: "give prominence to politics"; "strengthen the leadership of the Party"; "unfold mass movements in a big way"; "promote participation by the proletariat"; and "carry out technical reform." During the **Great Leap Forward** (**1958–1960**), leaders of the Anshan plant were major advocates of the rapid expansion of China's steel production, which led to excessively high targets and ultimately to damage to the country's industrial infrastructure.

Along with the **Baoshan Iron and Steel Complex** and Wuhan Iron and Steel, Anshan is one of China's three steel giants and the country's second largest producer. Following the introduction of industrial reforms in the 1980s, Anshan refashioned itself through corporate reorganization, resource consolidation, capacity expansion, market share enlargement, and competitiveness sharpening. Following the decision of the 15th National Party Congress in 1997 to organize **state-owned enterprises** (**SOEs**) along corporate lines, Anshan was reorganized into the Anshan Iron and Steel Group Corporation (Ansteel or Angang Group) and, in 1997, gained exposure to financial markets with listings of shares in the **stock markets** of both Shenzhen and **Hong Kong**. Composed of two subsidiary steel arms—Angang New Steel and the New Iron and Steel Company, Ltd.—the Angang Group joined its two major rivals in injecting its main and quality steel assets into their listed vehicles. The company also executed a merger with Benxi Iron and Steel Works producing an annual output of 18 million tons as well as forming joint ventures with a leading German steel manufacturer, Thyssen Krupp Stahl AG. The Angang Group has over 40 wholly owned subsidiaries including mines, hospitals, schools, real estate, and property management companies and maintains a 45% stake in Angang New Steel. In 2002, the Group earned 24 billion *yuan* yielding a profit of five billion *yuan* with a main operating profit of nearly 24%. The range of its products extend from cold-rolled steel, thick plate, heavy rail, large section, and wire rod to hot-rolled strips, medium plate, small and medium-sized section, seamless tube, and cold-rolled silicon steel.

ANTI-COUNTER-REVOLUTIONARY CAMPAIGNS. From 1949 to the early 1980s, campaigns of mass mobilization and propaganda that targeted individuals and groups with heavy doses of coercion were a stable feature of Chinese society. Two of these campaigns, the first from 1950–1951 and known as the *Zhengfan* campaign, and the second from 1955–1957 and known as the *Sufan* campaign, targeted so-called counterrevolutionaries (*fan geming*). This label was frequently and arbitrarily attached to any opponent or even critic of the Communist regime. The purpose of the *Zhengfan* campaign was, according to **Chinese Communist Party (CCP)** Chairman **Mao Zedong**, to "wipe out all the bandits, special agents, local tyrants, and other counterrevolutionary elements that bring harm to the people." This included **Kuomintang (KMT)** officials who had not fled to **Taiwan**, along with local landowners and landlords, critics of the new regime, and even businessmen and merchants in China's cities. Altogether, the campaign resulted in the execution of 700,000 to 800,000 people and the imprisonment of several million without the benefit of any legal protection or judicial procedures.

The second campaign, known as *Sufan*, extended from June 1955 to October 1957 and largely spared the general **population**. It was begun ostensibly as an attack on the Marxist literary critic **Hu Feng** and his purported counterrevolutionary clique of writers and **intellectuals** who, in 1953, had criticized CCP policies on **literature and the arts** and who had advocated greater freedom of expression. Ultimately, 81,000 intellectuals were implicated and persecuted. In the wake of the purge of top Party **leaders** Gao Gang and Rao Shushi — the so-called **Gao Gang–Rao Shushi Incident** — the campaign rapidly expanded into an attack on their alleged supporters in the Party and government. Party members and government personnel under suspicion were detained, interrogated, and often obliged to "confess" their past and present political views. Many were sent for "**reform through labor**" (*laodong gaizao*) without the benefit of any judicial proceedings, although some were released in 1956 and received official CCP apologies for having been falsely accused. By the time the campaign came to a close in October 1957, more than

18 million personnel had been pulled into the intense political struggle and 100,000 purported counterrevolutionaries were exposed inside the CCP, the **People's Liberation Army (PLA)**, government organizations and schools, and other public organizations. The nationwide system of the **Public Security Bureau** was a prime target of the campaign as the CCP reasserted control over this potentially politically powerful body.

The announced goal of the *Sufan* campaign was to undermine "**bureaucratism**" among government personnel, to generate greater revolutionary fervor, and to eliminate opponents of the regime that existed within each administrative apparatus. Advocates of the Soviet model of a planned **economy** and of an elaborate administrative bureaucracy were also primary targets. Thus the power of the State Planning Commission, with its many pro-Soviet professionals, was circumscribed, along with the power of industrial managers in **state-owned enterprises (SOEs)**. The number of deaths, injuries, and disappearances during the campaign has never been ascertained. But during the **Hundred Flowers (1956–1957)**, liberal intellectuals proposed that committees be established to review the excesses of such anti-counter-revolutionary campaigns, a proposal that Mao Zedong at times reportedly supported. These committees never became a reality, however, as the relatively open Hundred Flowers was quickly followed by the repressive **Anti Rightist Campaign (1957–1958)**.

ANTI-LIN [BIAO], ANTI-CONFUCIUS CAMPAIGN (1973–1975). One of many mass study campaigns in China that employed contemporary political criticism and historical analogy, the Anti-Lin, Anti-Confucius Campaign followed the death of **Lin Biao** in 1971 and the failure of his purported **Project 571** plan to assassinate **Chinese Communist Party (CCP)** Chairman **Mao Zedong**. Lin Biao and his remnant supporters was one of the major targets of this campaign that was largely carried out in the official Chinese press while the other ostensible target was the ancient sage Confucius (551–479 BC), whose classical writings were subject to scurrilous attacks. In dubbing Lin Biao a "reactionary," one goal of the CCP leadership at this time was to discredit Lin, who, in 1969, at the Ninth National Party Congress had been promoted as Mao Zedong's "closest comrade in arms" and official successor. Despite Lin Biao's intimate ties with Mao and the radical faction led by **Jiang Qing** during the early years of the **Cultural Revolution** (**1966–1976**), it was claimed that Lin Biao had all along been a "**capitalist roader**" (*zouzipai*). He was not progressive but retrogressive, a "reactionary" no different from **Liu Shaoqi** and other victims of the Cultural Revolution whom he himself had persecuted.

The same line of criticism was directed at Confucius (551 BC–479 BC), although any real similarity between the great classical Chinese philosopher and the former Chinese minister of defense requires a great stretch of the imagination. Writing near the end of China's "feudal" period, before the great transformation of China during the Qin dynasty (221 BC–207 BC) into a single empire, Confucius, it was claimed, resisted historical progress and idealized the past. According to the propaganda line of the 1973–1975 campaign, Confucius defended the "slave system" in China, opposed the emerging "landlord class," and even denigrated the role of **women**. The ancient sage was made into a "reactionary" who, along with Lin Biao, was pummeled in China's daily press for almost two years.

Analogy to historiography is a frequent tool of ideological and political struggle in China. Each major faction at this time used the Anti-Lin, Anti-Confucius Campaign to advance its own position. The radical faction, fearing its declining power as the health of Mao Zedong in 1973–1974 worsened, surreptitiously turned the campaign against **Zhou Enlai**, with frequent criticism of the Duke of Zhou, a 12th century BC political figure whose book on rituals Confucius had canonized. The moderate faction, led by **Deng Xiaoping**, who was returned to power in 1973, turned the campaign back against the radicals by claiming that Confucius had resisted promoting scientific research and training **intellectuals**. Deng's foray back into Chinese politics at this time began with his effort to modernize Chinese **science and technology** and to improve the **education** system, efforts that the radicals opposed.

The Anti-Lin, Anti-Confucius Campaign was supposed to involve the Chinese people in a great study campaign. Photographs released by the Chinese government showed poor Chinese farmers engaged in "intense debates" about the historical role of Confucius and factory workers "spontaneously" condemning Lin Biao. In reality, by the mid-1970s, the Chinese **population**, and even its political leadership, was exhausted by political campaigns and there was little popular enthusiasm for it. In early 1975, the Anti-Lin, Anti-Confucius Campaign petered out as the last mass campaign of the Late Maoist era. Following Mao's death in 1976, mass campaigns were generally eliminated from the Chinese political scene.

ANTI-RIGHTIST CAMPAIGN (1957–1958). Aside from the **Cultural Revolution (1966–1976)**, the Anti-Rightist Campaign was the most destructive political campaign in the history of the **People's Republic of China (PRC)**. The targets, labeled as "rightists" (*youpai*), included **intellectuals**, members of China's **democratic parties**, and some **Chinese Communist Party (CCP)** members who had dared to speak out during the earlier **Hundred Flowers (1956-1957)**. Although, in June 1957, CCP Chairman **Mao Zedong** had called on the people to "rectify the Party" and to "express views and speak out freely," those who took Mao up on his offer were quickly subject to persecution in the Anti-Rightist Campaign that lasted for more than a year. Contrary to Mao's expectation that Chinese intellectuals and non-Communist political figures would, if given the chance, freely praise the CCP, these highly articulate groups used their brief period of free expression to excoriate the CCP for its mismanagement of Chinese society and especially for promoting people into prominent positions, including heads of scientific research institutes, on the basis of political loyalty rather than merit. After June 1957, such criticism was labeled as "counterrevolutionary" and more than 500,000 people were punished, ranging from the rather mild penalty of a reduction in pay and rank for "ordinary rightists" (*yiban youpai*) and "middle rightists" (*zhong youpai*), to more severe retributions of dismissal from the Party and from employment and/or sentencing to labor camps to undergo **"thought reform"** (*sixiang gaizao*) and **"reform through labor"** (*laodong gaizao*) for "extreme rightists" (*jiyoupai*). Some of those accused committed suicide and others went mad. In 1959, the State Council and the **Chinese People's Political Consultative Conference (CPPCC)** issued a formal **"reversal of verdicts"** (*pingfan*) of many "rightists" who had been wrongly accused, although most still retained the "rightist" label (also referred to as a "hat"). Attacks on these individuals were renewed during the Cultural Revolution when even more severe punishments were meted out by **Red Guards** and other political thugs against former "rightists." Beginning in 1978, future CCP Chairman **Hu Yaobang** led an effort to rehabilitate the "rightists" once and for all. Most elderly "rightists" had their labels permanently removed as their **personal dossiers** (*dang'an*) containing political accusations were returned to their person. But some "rightists," such as the journalist Chu Anping, have never been officially "rehabilitated," evidently out of deference to CCP patriarch **Deng Xiaoping**, who had been the chief prosecutor of the "rightists" in 1957 at the behest of Mao Zedong and who insisted that the campaign not be fully discredited.

ANTISPIRITUAL POLLUTION CAMPAIGN (1983–1984). This very brief propaganda campaign began in October 1983, during which leftist **leaders** of the **Chinese Communist Party** (**CCP**) tried unsuccessfully to repress certain social trends that they found offensive. Even as the Communist leadership pursued promarket policies in the economic sector, leftist influence in the Party was evident in this propaganda campaign, which stressed ideological orthodoxy in the face of growing foreign social and cultural influence stemming from China's **open-door policy**. Everything from the **Agricultural Responsibility System** to Western-style dress to rock music was targeted for criticism in the Chinese media. As part of the campaign, local **cadres** froze the bank accounts of rich farmers and budding entrepreneurs as both groups were condemned for being influenced by "decadent capitalist ideas and remnant feudal ideas," such as "**always thinking of money**" (*yiqie xiang qian kan*) and for "disregarding the interests of the state and collective." Almost immediately, however, the campaign provoked the united opposition of CCP General Secretary **Hu Yaobang**, Premier **Zhao Ziyang**, and other committed reformers in the CCP leadership who also feared a repeat of the mass mobilization and mass frenzy of the **Cultural Revolution** (**1966–1976**). Although sympathetic to the campaign's denunciation of democracy and its call for ideological orthodoxy, **Deng Xiaoping** bristled at its attack on the **Special Economic Zones** (**SEZs**), the centerpiece of his economic reform program. Concern was also expressed by foreign investors and businessmen that China was reverting to its Maoist past, which was fundamentally antagonistic to the open-door policy and China's integration into the world **economy**.

Thus, after only 28 days, in November 1983, the campaign was effectively restricted to the ideological realm, despite protestations from leftist elements in the Chinese leadership, such as **Deng Liqun** and **Chen Yun** who supported the campaign's basic goals.

APRIL FIFTH MOVEMENT (1976). This crucial political event, also known as the "Tiananmen Incident," marked the beginning of the end for the radical policies of the Maoist dictatorship and the turn to the economic reforms that were inaugurated in 1978–1979. The traditional festival day for "sweeping the graves" (*saomu*), April 5th is when Chinese people pay homage to their ancestors. In 1976, thousands of **Beijing** residents showed up on this day in the massive Tiananmen Square at the city center to honor the recently deceased and highly revered premier of China, **Zhou Enlai**. His death in January earlier that year had been largely ignored by the press, which at the time was under the tight control of **Jiang Qing** and her radical supporters. Wreaths, banners, and slogans were raised to commemorate the beloved Zhou by crowds that grew to more than 100,000 people. Attacks on radical political **leaders** and even **Mao Zedong** were also voiced by demonstrators who chanted "Long Live the People" as a comeback to the chant of "Long Live Chairman Mao" (*Mao zhuxi wansui*) from the **Cultural Revolution (1966–1976)**. These attacks on Mao and his **personality cult** and the radical program provoked the mayor of Beijing, Wu De, to order the crowds to be dispersed. In the melee that followed, hundreds of people were injured and many were arrested and reportedly later executed. The demonstrations were immediately labeled "counterrevolutionary" by the **Chinese Communist Party (CCP)** leadership, which quickly moved to oust **Deng Xiaoping**, whom many of the demonstrators had supported. **Hua Guofeng** was named premier and first vice-chairman of the CCP, which put him into a clear position to succeed the then ailing Mao Zedong.

After the death of Mao Zedong in September 1976, and the subsequent arrest of radical leaders headed by the **Gang of Four** in November 1978, the CCP reversed its official position on the April Fifth Movement. Demonstrators arrested in 1976 were released and calls were made to punish those remaining Party leaders who had authorized executions in the wake of the movement, although this was never done. The April Fifth Movement is considered the precursor to the **Democracy Wall Movement (1978–1979)** and the 1989 second **Beijing Spring** since it marked the first time average Chinese people directly challenged state authority.

ARCHAEOLOGY. Archaeological research in China began as early as the Northern Song dynasty (960–1127 AD) with the cultivation of the epigraphic tradition of collecting, sorting, and studying historical remains. Modern archaeology began in the late 19th and early 20th centuries largely by the efforts of foreign explorers, missionaries, and scholars, such as Sweden's Sven Anders Hedin and Great Britain's Marc Aurel Stein whose surveys and expeditions in China introduced modern archaeological concepts and techniques into the country. Along with the discovery in 1900 of Buddhist-scripture caves at Dunhuang in Gansu Province that dated back to the fourth–14th centuries, major archaeological discoveries included the excavation of human fossil sites—"Peking Man" of *Zhoukoudian*—at the Yangshao settlement in Mianchi County, Henan Province, in 1929 by Johan G. Andersson, a Swedish geologist. Although the **Sino–Japanese War (1937–1945)** and internal political conflict leading up to the **Civil War (1945–1949)** disrupted much archaeological work, important discoveries were made by first-generation Chinese archaeologists such as Li Ji and Liang Siyong (both graduates of Harvard University) including Shang dynasty (16th–11th century BC) royal graves at the Yin Ruins and large numbers of oracle inscriptions either on tortoise shell or animal bones (*jiaguwen*).

Following the establishment of the **People's Republic of China (PRC)** in 1949, an array of organizations and institutes were set up at the national, provincial, and local levels to organize and systematize archaeological research. These included the Institute of Archaeology under the **Chinese Academy of Social Sciences (CASS)**, which after a 12-year hiatus restarted excavation of *Zhoukoudian* and the Yin Ruins. Other relevant organizations included the Paleoanthropology Office under the Institute of Vertebrate Paleontology and Paleoanthropology of the Chinese Academy of Sciences (CAS) and the State Bureau of Cultural Relics (later renamed the State Administration of Cultural Heritage), which supervises nationwide archaeological excavation, museum exhibitions, and the protection of cultural relics through a national ranking system on all cultural relics. Many Chinese universities, including **Beida (Peking University)**, set up archaeological departments with undergraduate and graduate programs that over the decades have turned out highly trained personnel. Three major publications on archaeology (*Cultural Relics*, *Archaeology*, and *Archaeology Journal*) were started and then resumed publication following the disruptions of the **Cultural Revolution (1966–1976)**, along with a plethora of academic studies and monographs, plus 20 specialty newspapers and periodicals put out by research institutes, universities, and publishing houses including the Cultural Relics Publishing House. In 1979, the Chinese Society of Archaeology was established followed by similar organs in the provinces and autonomous regions that in conjunction with the *China Cultural Relics Newspaper* hold an annual appraisal of the top-10 greatest archaeological discoveries in the country. The State Administration of Cultural Heritage oversees national policy on preservation of cultural antiquities in China, which has included drawing up the "China Principles of Archaeology" that enshrine conservation principles and mandate an interdisciplinary management process requiring a master plan for research and sets visitor capacity limits at such sensitive sites as the Buddhist grottos of Mogao at Dunhuang, Gansu Province, where a major restoration and preservation effort of the 492 cave temples has been carried out, with assistance of the Getty Conservation Institute and the Australian Heritage Commission.

Despite the enormous upheaval that characterized the Cultural Revolution, major archaeological discoveries were achieved such as the unearthing of well-preserved bronzes from the 11th century BC. But it was in the 1970s that China experienced its "golden age of archaeology" with such major discoveries as well-preserved tombs near Changsha and, most importantly, the Terra-Cotta Warriors of the Qin dynasty (221–207 BC), which were unearthed in 1974 and 1976 in Shaanxi Province. Although much of the site had over the centuries been looted, archaeologists acted on information provided by local farmers and uncovered three separate pits, the second of which (opened in 1976) contained 1,400 individually crafted warrior figures along with horses and 64 chariots. Surrounding the still unexcavated tomb of Qin Shihuang, China's great but autocratic unifier, the Terra-Cotta Warriors are undoubtedly China's most internationally recognized archaeological treasure. Others include the Buddhist Mogao grottoes, which since 1987 has been listed as a World Heritage Site of the United Nations Educational, Scientific, and Cultural Organization (UNESCO), the imperial tombs of the Ming (1368–1644) and Qing (1644–1911) Dynasties located outside **Beijing**, and lesser-known but historically valuable finds such as the ruins of the imperial palace of the Western Han dynasty (206 BC–23 AD) uncovered outside the city of Xi'an and textiles and lacquer monsters and other works of art from the *Chu* and other cultures (c. 770–221 BC) in the southwest: all of which shed new light on the complex origins and development lines of a highly regionalized Chinese civilization. In addition to modern tools of archaeological research, such as carbon 14 age-measurement data, China has adopted modern modes of archaeological surveying using satellite photos from the **United States** CORONA satellite along with studies of earthquake, hydrology, music, arts, and the history of **architecture**, often in joint investigations with archaeologists from Europe, North America, and **Japan**. In 1993, the Beijing Ancient Capital Cultural Relics Fair took place, the largest such archaeological exhibition ever held in the PRC.

Many archaeological discoveries in China have contributed to a significant rewriting of Chinese and human history, China's contact with the outside world, and the boundaries of Chinese culture with its neighboring states such as **Korea**. Ever since the discovery of "Peking Man," China has weighed in on the complex debate over human origins. Recent discoveries of fossil sites at *Renzi* Cave (*Renzidong*) in Anhui Province show that *homo erectus* may have established itself in China 2.5 million years ago, more than 400,000 years earlier than previously thought, which has led some Chinese scientists to propose human evolution in China as parallel to that already observed in Africa. Although most Western scholars favor an early dispersal of *homo erectus* out of Africa into Asia, *Renzidong* and a half dozen other sites in China dating to between 1.8 million and 800,000 years ago support an "Asian hypothesis," which has energized Chinese scientists and loosened important funding from the Chinese Academy of Sciences and other government agencies. Other archaeological breakthroughs include a 1997 discovery in Shandong Province of what is believed to be the oldest Chinese characters ever written on oracle bones and the oldest inscription on stoneware.

Stone carvings were also recently unearthed from the era of the Eastern Han dynasty (25–220 AD) indicating that Christianity entered China as early as 86 AD, 550 years prior to the Tang dynasty (618–907 AD) when Syrian missionaries are known to have brought Christian doctrine into China. Then there is the case of the 3,000 year-old Cherchen Man mummies, which were discovered in Western China near the city of Ürümqi, Xinjiang Autonomous Region, and whose western, Caucasian features suggest that China's contact with the West occurred during the very beginnings of Chinese civilization. This opened the possibility of Western influence on the origins of Chinese culture while the tombs and ruins of the Koguryo Kingdom (37 BC–668 AD) unearthed in the northeastern provinces of Jilin and Liaoning support contentions by the Chinese that the kingdom considered by Korea (North and South) as its cultural forerunner was, in fact, "an important part of Chinese culture." Such assertions led to immediate, strongly emotional reactions from both North and South Korean spokesmen who accused China of a "serious historical distortion" which they claim was part of a hidden political agenda.

Just as other nations with rich archaeological sites such as Egypt and Iraq have had to deal with the effects of exogenous forces—human and natural—on their cultural relics, China confronts a host of serious assaults including the rash of urbanization and destruction of old urban areas in the name of modernization. Following the Communist takeover in 1949, China cut off foreign involvement in archaeological exploration, citing the role of foreigners in removing relics and antiquities from their original sites to museums and private collections in the West. Frescoes taken from Dunhuang and on view in London, Paris, and Harvard University have been the subject of a repatriation request from the Dunhuang Academy—even as China has reopened its cooperation with foreign investigators in the last two decades. More illicit means of archaeological destructing include the wanton looting of many sites by grave robbers, rural scavengers, and professional smugglers who seek lucrative foreign buyers. China's massive campaign of capital construction, especially highway and road construction, has wrought severe damage to parts of the Great Wall, which spans nine provinces and 100 counties in China and has also suffered from botched efforts at "restoration" by local and largely untrained conservationists. Significant damage has also been incurred at *Zhoukoudian* and to largely unexplored sites of China's southern cultural heritage involving the ancient *Ba* culture in and around the **Three Gorges Dam Project** on the Yangtze River in Central China where unprecedented looting has been met with a tepid government response as local authorities wrangle over which should receive the promised central government funding for relics protection.

Whereas 50 years ago, China had 300 walled cities, by 2004 as a result of China's version of urban renewal, only four were left: Pingyao in Shanxi Province (a 1997 UNESCO World Heritage Site), Xi'an in Shaanxi, Xincheng in Liaoning, and Jingzhou in Hebei. Of China's original 2,000 historic cities, only 100 have survived and only about 20 are preserved in anything comparable to their original state. Although archaeological activists in China have won some notable battles, such as the preservation of the Bund riverfront in **Shanghai** and the famous Nanjing Road shopping street from **Hong Kong** developers, other efforts have failed, such as the belated attempt to protect Dinghai Township in Zhejiang Province and the old city in **Tianjin**. Out of 730 UNESCO World Heritage Sites worldwide, 28 are in China but getting local officials to observe basic rules governing historical conservation has been very difficult as old neighborhoods in the major cities have been relentlessly destroyed in the name of "renovation." In 2002, China passed its Law on the Protection of Cultural Relics, which was subsequently strengthened by vesting ownership of all cultural relics in the state and by prohibiting the sale and permanent export of newly excavated archaeological objects, to stop an increase in looting and illicit sale of antiquities. Documentation of looting in China is carried out by the Beijing Cultural Heritage Protection Research Center, which, in 2005, asked the U.S. to restrict imports of archaeological materials under the Convention on Cultural Property Implementation Act. In 2000, the Chinese government spent millions of dollars at auction buying back treasures looted from Beijing's Summer Palace by British and French troops 140 years ago. The purchase took place after the Chinese State Relics Bureau wrote letters to Sothebys and Christie's Hong Kong protesting the sales. Both houses allowed their sales to proceed and the China Poly Group Corp, a Beijing-based **state-owned enterprise (SOE)** with past ties to the **People's Liberation Army (PLA)**, stepped in to win bids on three of four contested objects—bronze animal heads that once decorated a Zodiac fountain at the Summer Palace.

ARCHITECTURE. China's urban and rural architecture reflects its long history from the imperial era (221 BC–1911 AD) to the period of Western intervention and semi-colonialism in the 19th to early 20th centuries, to the era of Soviet-style planning and Stalinist influence (1949–1978), to the post-1978–1979 reform period of modern and post-modern influences. The imperial era left China with a rich architectural heritage that is reflected in the temples, pagodas, palaces, and extended family homes of the well-to-do as well as the centerpiece of the imperial presence, the Forbidden City in central **Beijing.** Generally speaking, Chinese traditional structures are based on the philosophical principles of balance and symmetry with the main structure of the building serving as the axis for the entire edifice. Secondary structures of residences, temples, and palaces are positioned as two wings on either side to form the main room and yard. Religious buildings are dominated by the Buddhist stupa or pagoda, which takes the form of a storied tower or, more rarely, an upturned bowl. Constructed primarily out of wood, their shape varies from tetragonal, octagon or diagonal with the number of stories varying with each of the buildings. Imperial cities, especially those that periodically served as capitals such as Beijing, Xi'an (Shaanxi Province), and Luoyang (Henan Province), were laid out in a spiritually favorable rectangular pattern typically on north-south and east-west axes and surrounded by a defensive high wall, which, in the case of Beijing, was unfortunately demolished soon after the Communist takeover in 1949, although Xi'an's magnificent wall remains intact. Residences of the wealthy and influential were protected by their own walls, which can also be found, although in less elegant form, in China's villages, where farmers' houses of mud bricks and roots of reed have their own individual protective walls. Roof design plays a key role in traditional architecture exuding deeper spiritual meaning, as in the case of temple roofs with up-curled eaves, reflecting the Buddhist belief that such a design conferred good luck by warding off evil spirits that moved in straight lines.

In Beijing's Forbidden City, the 13 pavilions have ceramic tiles of brilliant yellow, green, and red with intricate designs, almost all of which point in a south-east direction and are dotted with figurines and mythical creatures. Although China's traditional architectural heritage was based on certain basic rules that endured over centuries, thereby producing little temporal variation, regional differences did emerge with the northern architectural tradition comparatively more restrained and sober while that from the south eventually exaggerated curved ornamentation to a high degree.

In traditional and modern times, the positioning and design of buildings is highly influenced by the Daoist cosmological principles of "wind and the water" (*fengshui*), a geomancy system of principles that assesses how buildings in certain areas must be positioned so as not to disturb spiritual aspects of the surrounding landscape. Whether simple farmer residences or a **Hong Kong** skyscraper, ideal forms for particular types of structures are proposed along with carefully arranged spaces and components within a building, all according to time-honored forms that minimize upsetting the fragile balance of the cosmos. While China's accelerated march to modernization and industrial development has led to the demolition of innumerable traditional temples, residences, city walls, and, in some cases, entire towns, scattered examples of old town architecture, such as the highly influential *"Huizhou* style" from the 17th century (with its two-story house plan centered around a courtyard) can still be found even in some big cities, such as Chengdu, Sichuan Province. Perhaps the most famous structure from imperial times is Beijing's Temple of Heaven with its circular mound altar (which served as the site for Ming and Qing dynasty emperors to worship heaven) that was constructed in three tiers with the upper terrace made up of non-concentric rings with the innermost ring consisting of nine fan-shaped slabs and each outer ring consisting of slabs in an increasing multiple of nine—an odd number considered categorically masculine and often found in traditional architectural styles.

China's modern architecture reflects its political and economic history beginning from the mid-19th century onward when, in treaty ports up and down the Chinese coast, European colonial buildings were constructed in concessionary areas carved out of major cities, such as **Shanghai** and **Guangzhou** (**Canton**). Offices, warehouses, churches, and residences of foreign merchants, banks, shipping firms, and missionaries dominated whole streets and neighborhoods with construction of European-inspired buildings in art-deco that like the "stone gate" (*shikumen*) style in Shanghai blended features of East and West, which survived through the 1930s and were left largely intact after the Communist takeover in 1949. During the period of cooperation with the **Soviet Union** in the early 1950s, China adopted many of the features of the brutally functional and wedding-cake Soviet/Stalinist style in everything from factories to exhibition centers to hotels, which followed the identical drab box-like design that is often combined, as in the gigantic Shanghai exhibition hall, with massive spires and towers. Sprouting up in the suburban areas of major Chinese cities were row after row of dormitory-like apartment houses; in the countryside, adobe walls of rural dwellings were replaced with concrete. Perhaps the most emblematic structure of this era is the massive Great Hall of the People located in Tiananmen Square in Beijing, which was built in near-record time during the frenzy of the **Great Leap Forward (1958–1960)** and which remains one of the largest buildings in the world serving as the site for many of the major meetings and conferences convened by the **Chinese Communist Party (CCP)**. Following the death of **Mao Zedong** in September 1976, a mausoleum housing the preserved corpse of the chairman was also constructed in the center of Tiananmen with an architecture purportedly modeled on Washington, D.C.'s, Lincoln Memorial.

Since China opened up to the Western world and a more open **economy** in the late 1970s, there has been a move toward a more "international" look, apparent in the innumerable concrete-and-glass high-rise trophy buildings that dot virtually every major Chinese city. Brighter than their Russian counterparts, these uninspiring and often unattractive structures generally reject any attempt to marry the traditional Chinese form with current needs while putting an enormous premium on gigantic size and monumental postmodern forms often capped off with restaurants resembling flying saucers. Shanghai's Pudong development zone sports some of the most egregious examples of this style with its 101-story World Financial Center (to be completed in 2007), composed of glass and metal following a simple geometric curvature form. The Jin Mao tower, the tallest finished building in China, has an observatory deck on the 88th floor, with the atrium of the Hyatt Hotel starting at the 53rd floor and extending to the 87th floor. Despite a massive glut of office space in Pudong and in most other major skyscrapers in China's major cities, construction of trophy buildings continues unabated with more than 1,000 additional high rises planned for Shanghai alone.

Many of China's most ambitious designs, such as the National Theatre undergoing construction in Beijing near Tiananmen Square and the proposed headquarters of China Central Television, have been done by such notable foreign architects as the French designer Paul Andreu, a situation that has led China's indigenous architects to complain that the country's architectural heritage is being lost in the rush to modernization and international engagement. Andreu's titanium-and-glass design for the National Theatre with its soaring glass dome set like a floating bubble in a lake with an underwater tunnel entrance is said to violate basic "wind and water" geomancy principles. In addition to Shanghai's Grand Theatre designed by the Frenchman Jean-Marie Charpentier with its oriental-industrial architecture, there is the National Museum designed by the Shanghai Architectural Institute in the form of a squat, round building with roof handles resembling a traditional Chinese bronze pot. Major new buildings are also being constructed for the 2008 Olympics to be held in Beijing, such as the central Olympic Stadium, which will take a bird's nest form with crisscrossing steel bars, also of foreign design. Somewhat more elegant designs can be found in less grandiose structures, such as Guangzhou's White Swan Hotel. The Construction Bank of China building in Xiamen, Fujian, features a broad, curving glass curtain wall façade along its southwest side and main entrance that was inspired with a nod to Chinese tradition by the movement of the waves and wind of the nearby ocean.

Mega-size malls, such as the seven-million square foot South China Mall in Dongguan, Guangdong Province, sport a motley combination of copy-cat architecture, including a re-creation of the *Champs-Élysées* and a full-size reproduction of the *Arc de Triomphe* with more than 1,000 stores and shops crammed in a single, colossal five-story structure. New residential buildings in cities, townships, and the wealthier parts of the countryside are dominated by villa-style housing that affords the average Chinese dweller with considerably larger per capita living space than was available in Soviet-era apartments and industrial dormitories. China also plans to build several new central cities from scratch, the largest a 460-km^2 area called Songbei in the northeast that is to be located north of the Songhua River to replace the old section of Harbin and a futuristic design named Lang Fang which is slated for construction 70 km north of Beijing. *See also* CHONGQING; TIANJIN.

ARMED FORCES. *See* "PEOPLE'S LIBERATION ARMY" (PLA).

ASSOCIATION OF SOUTHEAST ASIAN NATIONS (ASEAN). Since the formation of ASEAN in 1967, China's relations with this Southeast Asian economic and political organization, which originally consisted of five member nations (Indonesia, Malaysia, Thailand, Singapore, and the Philippines) has gone through three distinct stages. Throughout the late 1960s and much of the 1970s, the relationship was uneasy and often hostile as the major focus of ASEAN was political, namely to oppose Chinese support for Communist insurgencies in the ASEAN countries that were considered an outgrowth of the relationship of **Beijing** with large and generally suspect Chinese ethnic communities throughout the region. Following China's inauguration of economic reforms in 1978–1979 and promulgation of its **open-door policy**, ASEAN and China experienced a thaw in their relations largely as a result of growing **trade and investment** links and China's shift from an ideologically driven and interventionist **foreign policy** to reliance on formal diplomatic relations. The third stage of normalization began in 1990–1991 with the decision by Singapore, Brunei (which was incorporated into ASEAN in 1994), and Indonesia to restore diplomatic relations with the **People's Republic of China (PRC)**, which was quickly followed by ASEAN's 1991 invitation to China to become a "consultative partner" of the Association.

This relationship led over the next decade and a half to a growing accommodation between ASEAN and China on a variety of economic, political, and diplomatic issues involving trade, South China Sea territorial disputes, and bilateral issues between China and individual ASEAN member states. In 1994, China became a member of the ASEAN Regional Forum—a mechanism for dialogue on regional security issues—and in 1995 China and ASEAN established a separate political consultative forum at the vice-foreign minister level to discuss political-security issues. China became a full dialogue partner of ASEAN in 1996 as part of the ASEAN + 3 arrangement that also includes **Japan** and South **Korea**. In 1997, Beijing was the site of the ASEAN regional forum involving 21 countries, the same year the China-ASEAN Joint Cooperation Committee was set up. ASEAN-China annual summits have been held since the late 1990s, the first of which was held in 1997 in Kuala Lumpur, Malaysia, where the various heads of state issued a joint statement on "ASEAN-China cooperation towards the 21st Century." Despite this increasingly accommodating environment, apprehension toward China's growing regional and international power exists among some ASEAN states, particularly Indonesia, Malaysia, and **Vietnam** (which was admitted to ASEAN in 1995, followed in 1997 by Laos and Myanmar and in 1999 by **Cambodia**). ASEAN has, however, avoided provocative statements or actions toward China as the apprehension of individual states are muted by the Association's emphasis on consensus policy-making known as the "ASEAN way."

ASEAN has rejected hawkish assessments of the "China threat" because of the growing economic, political, and military power of the PRC, and has, instead, embraced a policy of engagement as the only realistic position for dealing with its geographic neighbor whose population of 1.3 billion people dwarfs ASEAN's collective population of 500 million. The major point of conflict between ASEAN and China involves the unresolved territorial dispute in the South China Sea over the Spratly (*Nansha*) and Paracel *(Xisha)* islands. The former is an archipelago of more than 300 uninhabited rock formations sovereignty over which is disputed by the PRC, **Taiwan**, Vietnam, Malaysia, the Philippines, and Brunei. Occupying an important strategic position straddling vital commercial sea lanes linking the Indian and Pacific oceans, the Spratly Islands also encompass valuable fishing grounds and are believed to be rich in oil and gas deposits. In February 1992, China passed the Territorial Law of the Sea by which the PRC claimed sovereignty over almost the entire South China Sea with a proviso giving Beijing the right to forbid passage of foreign warships through the area. In response, ASEAN issued its "Declaration on the South China Sea," which urged all claimants to the islands, including China, to freeze the status quo and shelve the sovereignty dispute. China agreed in principle but in 1994 it dispatched troops to occupy a reef near Vietnam and built oil-drilling platforms in disputed areas and erected a ground satellite station in the Paracels off the coast of Vietnam. In 1995, China occupied Philippine-claimed Mischief Reef near the Palawan Islands; in 1998, they upgraded these Chinese structures to permanent facilities. Tensions between China and the Philippines flared up again in 2000 over multiple intrusions by Chinese fishing vessels into waters claimed by the Philippines in the area of Scarborough Shoal. As a signatory to the 1982 **United Nations (UN)** Law of the Sea, China is bound to resolve such disputes peacefully and has assured ASEAN member states that it would abide by international law to work out overlapping territorial claims. A Code of Conduct for the South China Sea between ASEAN and China would provide for a dispute resolution mechanism and cooperation on marine issues and protection of the area's **environment**.

As for China's growing military power, ASEAN states maintain modern and credible armed forces to act as a deterrent along with defense links to external powers, especially the **United States**, often over the objections of China, which opposes joint military exercises between ASEAN states with countries, such as the U.S. and the United Kingdom, from outside the region. In order to avoid giving China the impression that ASEAN's 10 member countries are ganging up on it, naval visits by Chinese vessels to Thailand, Malaysia, and the Philippines have been carried out with return visits from Thai and Singaporean ships throughout the late 1990s, along with a growth in military diplomacy. China's long-standing land dispute with Vietnam, which contributed to the 1979 Sino–Vietnam War, was also brought to a close by the Treaty on the Land Border signed between the two countries in 2000.

ASEAN–China trade in 2004 totaled US$105 billion and represented a more than 10-fold increase over the US$7.9 billion registered in 1991. This enormous growth averaged more than 20% per annum making ASEAN China's fourth largest trading partner with expectations that total bilateral trade will reach US$200 billion by 2010. Whereas the top five ASEAN exports to China in the early 1990s were, in descending order, oil and fuel, wood, vegetable oil and fats, computer machinery, and electrical equipment, by 2000 the order of importance had changed away from commodities toward manufactured products with computer machinery and electrical equipment rising from 12.4% in 1991 to 38.2% in 2000. ASEAN imports from

China have always been more diversified including textiles and apparel, footwear, vegetable products and food stuffs, and stone/cement/ceramics, as well as electrical equipment, computer/machinery, oil and fuel, cotton, and tobacco. By 2000, nearly half of ASEAN imports from China also consisted of electrical equipment and computers/machinery. Throughout the 1990s, even prior to China's 2001 ascension into the **World Trade Organization (WTO)**, tariff rates fell between ASEAN and China spurring the rapid growth—nearly 20% per annum—in two-way trade.

In 2004, ASEAN and China signed an agreement to form a Free Trade Area (FTA) to take full effect in 2010 that will create an open market of two billion people to compete with the European Union and the U.S. China's entry into the WTO is projected to benefit ASEAN exports of agricultural and natural resources-based products, oil and natural gas, along with electronics to China, while China's exports to ASEAN will see gains in machinery and electrical appliances, optical instruments, **transportation** equipment, metal products, and chemicals. The establishment of Bank of China branches in Indonesia, Singapore, Thailand, and Malaysia has also advanced trade along with plans to build a railway through mainland Southeast Asia into China and a road between Bangkok and Kunming, Yunnan Province. An Agreement on Commercial Navigation on the Lancang–Mekong River was also reached in 2000 between China and ASEAN member states Laos, Myanmar, and Thailand.

Economic links between China and ASEAN have also been enhanced by such actions as the decision of the PRC in 1997–1998 during the height of the Asian financial crisis, which struck hard many ASEAN nations, such as Indonesia, not to devalue its **currency**, thereby preventing China from making gains at the expense of an ailing Southeast Asia. China also offered Thailand a US$1 billion bilateral loan in parallel with the International Monetary Fund (IMF) bailout package at the same time the U.S. rejected such aid. A US$1.5 billion pulp and paper plant to be located in the Malaysian state of Sabah represents China's largest overseas investment. Other areas of China–ASEAN agreement included the formation in 2003 of a China–ASEAN fund to fight **SARS**, along with a multi-million-dollar mutual commitment to rid all of Southeast Asia of drugs by 2015. *See also* ECONOMY; FOREIGN POLICY.

ATOMIC BOMB. On 16 October 1964, China exploded its first nuclear weapon in a desert region of the Xinjiang Autonomous Region in the country's far west. This successful experiment culminated a decade-long effort by the Chinese government to achieve nuclear power status after the **Soviet Union** apparently reneged on an agreement reached in 1957 to provide China with a sample atomic bomb. The day after the 1964 explosion, Premier **Zhou Enlai** pressed for the "complete prohibition and thorough destruction of nuclear weapons," claiming that China's entry into the nuclear club had been "compelled" by the actions of the **United States** and other nuclear powers in the West and that China would never be the first to use nuclear weapons. From 1964 to 1978, China carried out 25 separate nuclear tests involving a variety of weapons to be deployed on bombers and missiles, including a 1966 atmospheric test containing thermonuclear material that, in 1967, was followed by China's explosion of its first hydrogen bomb. In 1969, China's conducted its first underground nuclear test, an event that occurred in the middle of the fractional **Cultural Revolution (1966–1976).**

Despite China's decision in 1983 to join the International Atomic Energy Agency (IAEA), which was finalized in early 1984, China continued to conduct periodic underground tests through the 1990s, despite a moratorium on similar tests by the U.S. and **Russia** and anti-nuclear protests in **Beijing** by the Uygur **minorities** against testing in their native Xinjiang Autonomous Region. In 1986, Premier **Zhao Ziyang** announced that China would cease atmospheric nuclear tests altogether—even as it developed, but did not deploy, a neutron bomb in 1988. In 1992, China acceded to the international Treaty on the Nonproliferation of Nuclear Weapons (NPT), although it continued to carry out underground tests in 1992, 1993, 1994, 1995, and 1996, the latter of which was quickly followed by China's decision to sign the Comprehensive Nuclear Test Ban Treaty after strong protests against such tests were registered by **Japan.** By 1998, Chinese President **Jiang Zemin** declared that China opposed all nuclear testing and would not resume such tests itself with the country effectively suspending its nuclear weapons program since the last test in 1996. Currently, China is a major nuclear power possessing an inventory of nuclear weapons numbering 450 warheads, which is greater in number than Great Britain and France combined.

China's decision to join the nuclear club came in reaction to its participation in the **Korean War (1950–1953)** when it confronted nuclear threats from the U.S. Although **Mao Zedong** dubbed the atomic bomb as a **"paper tiger,"** he and other top **leaders** of the **Chinese Communist Party (CCP)**, such as **Nie Rongzhen**, believed that China could survive in the modern-day world of power politics only by developing and deploying the most advanced weaponry. The American threat near the end of the Korean conflict to use nuclear devices against Chinese targets in **Manchuria** convinced China's leaders that never again should the country be forced to submit to "nuclear blackmail." As early as 1955, Mao Zedong pointed out that "we need the atom bomb. If our nation does not want to be intimidated, we have to have this thing." In 1958, during the second of two **Taiwan Straits Crises**, the Chinese commitment to develop its own nuclear program was further spurred on by the decision of the Soviet Union, under the leadership of Nikita Khrushchev, not to provide China with nuclear secrets. Key scientists involved in China's nuclear program included many trained in the West, such as Qian Sanqianq (the "father of China's atomic bomb") and his wife, He Zehui, and Deng Jiaxian, who had studied in France and the U.S., respectively. In its early stage of development, China was also assisted by the French couple, Frédéric and Irène Joliot-Curie, who helped Qian Sanqiang purchase nuclear instruments in Europe and provided the Chinese physicist with samples of radium salt and by the Soviet Union, where key Chinese physicists, such as **Wang Ganchang**, worked at the Joint Soviet Nuclear Research Center, Dubna, USSR.

China's intercontinental nuclear arsenal consists of single four to five megaton warheads that arm its approximately 18–20 long-range *Dong Feng* ("East Wind")-5/5A missiles, along with the Dong Feng 3/3A, 4, 21/21A, 15, and 11, all of which carry single nuclear warheads ranging from 200–350 kilotons, 15–30 ICBMs in all. China is also in the process of developing the Dong Feng 31 and 41, with ranges of 8,000 to 12,000 km, respectively, and possibly equipped with multiple reentry vehicle or multiple independently targeted reentry vehicle capacity. In the late 1990s, accusations emerged from the U.S. Congress that China had developed two nuclear weapons similar to the American W-70 and W-88 warheads, leading to apparently spurious accusations that the Los

Alamos Chinese American scientist Wen-ho Lee had illicitly supplied China with the weapon's design and that China had stolen nuclear secrets from the U.S. since the late 1970s, accusations that later proved unfounded.

During the 1980s and 1990s, China was periodically accused, primarily by the U.S., of attempting to assist other nations, such as Pakistan and Iran, in developing nuclear weapons from 1965 to 1997, in violation of the NPT, which China had signed in 1992. According to the IAEA, the illicit nuclear programs of Libya and Iran were based on Chinese **technology** provided via Pakistan, a long-time close ally of the **People's Republic of China** (**PRC**). In 1985, China reached an agreement with the U.S. for peaceful nuclear cooperation, which, because of the lack of nonproliferation related certification, was not put into effect. China, on the other hand, demanded that because the two superpowers—the U.S. and the Soviet Union—possessed 95% of the world's nuclear arsenal, it was incumbent on their leaders to take the initiative to stop the arms race. China welcomed the signing of the 1987 Nuclear Forces Agreement as a positive step and, in 1992, issued a major statement at the **United Nations** (**UN**) calling on all nuclear states to follow China in committing themselves not to be the first to use nuclear weapons, in supporting nuclear-free zones, and in observing the principle of the peaceful uses of outer space by ceasing development of space weapons.

Beginning in 1994, China took a more serious approach to nonproliferation issues leading to the inauguration of formal talks with the U.S. In 1996, China promised that it would end all assistance to nuclear plants not under international safeguards, although the American Central Intelligence Agency (CIA) has consistently said that China has not adhered to that promise. In 1997, China promulgated nuclear export controls that were based on a list substantively identical to the trigger list developed and used by the international Nuclear Suppliers Group (NSG), the major multilateral nuclear export group. In the same year, China joined the Zangger Committee, also a nuclear watchdog group that, nevertheless, has weaker enforcement mechanism without IAEA safeguards. And in 1998, China promulgated stronger dual-use controls identical to the NSG and expressed interest in joining the group, which it entered in May 2004, following its 2003 promulgation of a "White Paper on China's Non Proliferation

Policies and Measures" that systematically described the determination and sincerity of the PRC on nonproliferation issues. China was the first among the five nuclear weapons states to ratify the Additional Protocol to Safeguards Agreement in 2002 and has called for modification of the Convention on Physical Protection of Nuclear Materials. China also reached an agreement in the same year with the U.S. for obtaining reciprocal government-to-government assurances that nuclear technology transferred to the other party would not be retransferred to a third country without the consent of the supplier state.

China maintains an elaborate program of dispatching highly trained personnel to other states for training and technical cooperation and has contributed to the development of peaceful uses of nuclear energy in the Asia–Pacific region. As a member of the six-party talks involving the issue of nuclear weapons' development by North **Korea**, China stands for keeping the Korean peninsula free from nuclear weapons. In 2004, China National Nuclear Cooperation (CNNC) signed an agreement with the government of Pakistan to build a second nuclear facility outside the city of Islamabad, which both parties claim is for purely peaceful, civilian purposes—even though Pakistan has yet to cleanse its nuclear establishment of rogue scientists who surreptitiously assisted other nations in developing nuclear programs. Controversial plans of the Siemens Corporation of Germany to export a nuclear enrichment plant to China that could be used to help build nuclear weapons—a claim rejected by the PRC—were dropped in April 2004. In 2005–2006, China joined members of the IAEA in opposing the decision by the government of Iran to renew the enrichment of uranium while calling on the international community to resolve the dispute by diplomacy. *See also* "PEOPLE'S LIBERATION ARMY" (PLA).

AUTOMOBILE INDUSTRY. In 1995, China had approximately 20 million vehicles with the fastest growth occurring among privately owned passenger vehicles, especially in the relatively wealthy urban areas along the coast. Although total vehicle ownership remains low nationwide, major cities such as **Beijing, Shanghai**, and **Guangzhou** (**Canton**) already have high concentrations of ownership of more than a million vehicles per city. Nationwide, there is only one vehicle per 115 people in China compared to one vehicle for every 1.3

people in the **United States**. Fuel efficiency standards are by international comparisons still quite low while the growing vehicle fleet has become a major source of air pollution, especially in urban areas. Recent government plans call for increased fuel efficiency standards on new vehicles and more use of unleaded gasoline and the production of natural gas and hybrid vehicles.

Automobile production in China accelerated at a rapid rate in the post-1978–1979 reform era from 400,000 units in 1985 to over two million in 2000, which is substantially below the overall national production capacity of 2.5 million units. There are more than 100 automobile assembly plants in China and 3,000 spare parts factories, although among the former only four have an annual production volume of more than 100,000 vehicles while overall cost to produce a car in China is 18% greater than in industrialized countries, such as Germany. Productivity by China's two million auto sector employees remains far below international standards while automobile prices are held artificially high by government imposition of fees that constitute up to 20% of vehicle price. Since the 1990s, automobile sales in China have grown 14% annually as four million families in 2003 owned cars with growth rates of one million annually. By 2010, it is estimated that 47 people per 1,000 will have privately owned cars, a rate similar to **Japan** in the 1960s and **Taiwan** and **Korea** in the mid-1980s. Major cities, such as Beijing, have more than 1,000 sales dealers while international automobile shows have been held in Changchun (Jilin Province), where the homemade Red Flag sedan and "**Liberation**" (*Jiefang*) truck were manufactured in the pre-reform era.

The Chinese automobile industry is one of China's most protected industries as imported vehicles confronted a 220% tariff before 1986 that was reduced to 80% in 1997 and 38% in 2000. Foreign joint-venture producers in China include such companies as Volkswagen, Ford, General Motors, and Toyota, whose workers make on average US$1.50 per hour in wages and benefits compared to US$55 an hour for the average American automobile worker. The major domestic automobile companies in China are the Number One Motor Vehicle (the largest manufacturer), Dongfeng, Dazhong, Lifan Group, Shanghai Automotive Industry Corp., and the Chery Automobile Company, which, along with Great Wall Motors, Hafei, and Geely Holding Group, will begin exporting cars to the U.S. in 2007 from plants in

China and Malaysia, following their successful exports to Latin America and Africa. The rapidly growing luxury car market in China is dominated by Audi, Mercedes-Benz, and British Bentley, whose high-end models cost nearly nine million *yuan* (US$1 million).

With China's entry into the **World Trade Organization (WTO)**, the tariffs on imported autos and auto parts are slated in 2006 to drop to 25 and 10%, respectively, while China's protectionist system of quotas and licensing arrangement will be terminated, creating stiff global competition for the country's auto industry. Along with a projected 11% reduction in domestic auto production because of foreign competition, China is likely to experience a concentration of the highly dispersed production system into fewer more high-volume enterprises as companies with annual output of less than 100,000 units will face tough competition on the international market. In 2005, China increased its exposure in the international car market when Nanjing Automobile of China purchased Great Britain's bankrupt M.G. Rover Group. In 2004, Dongfeng Motor Corp announced plans to quadruple production by 2009.

China's automobile industry was the first in the entire country to pilot a defective product recall system, and, in terms of financing, fewer than 10% of all vehicle sales are on credit. China's auto parts exports consist of everything from components for Delphi parking brakes to Johnson Controls seat covers and are exported to countries around the world. The flood of new cars in China has also contributed to a fivefold increase in road deaths over the past two decades; more than 100,000 people were killed in traffic accidents in 2003, roughly two and a half times more deaths than in the U.S. This may reflect the lack of traffic officers who, in 2003, numbered but 200,000 in a country of 1.3 billion. *See also* ENVIRONMENT; INDUSTRY; TRANS-PORTATION.

– B –

BA JIN (1904–2005). Born in Chengdu, Sichuan Province and named Li Feigan, Ba Jin is considered one of the founders of modern Chinese **literature** and has been recognized as a major literary figure since the 1930s. He was a longtime anarchist whose pen name in the Chinese rendition is of the first and last syllables of the Russian anarchists Bakunin (*Ba*) and Kropotkin (*Jin*). His first novel written in France was *Destruction* (*Miewang*), but he is best known for his two trilogies that were written between 1931 and 1940 entitled *Torrent* (*Jiuliu*). The first was titled *Love*, consisting of *Fog* (*Wu*), and *Lightening* (*Dian*) and the second titled *Torrent* (*Jiliu*) consisting of *Family* (*Jia*), *Spring* (*Chun*), and *Autumn* (*Qiu*). Enormously popular among youth of the time, these semiautobiographical novels attack the traditional Chinese family structure and pit youth against age and rising individualism against Confucian orthodoxy. Ba Jin also translated into Chinese the Russian writer Ivan Turgenev's *Fathers and Sons*, and during the **Sino–Japanese War** (**1937–1945**) Ba teamed with the writer **Mao Dun** to produce anti-Japanese propaganda. Beginning in 1949, Ba Jin served in the **National People's Congress** (**NPC**) and subsequently was chairman of the Chinese Writers' Association and vice-chairman of the All-China Federation of Literary and Art Circles. His 14-volume *Collected Works* was published by the People's Literary Press between 1958 and 1962, as Ba Jin also served as the chief editor of several literary publications in the early 1950s, including *Literary and Art Monthly*, *Harvest,* and *Shanghai Literature*.

During the **Cultural Revolution** (**1966–1976**), Ba Jin was branded a "counterrevolutionary" and was forced to work in a labor camp, during which time his wife died after she was denied medical treatment. Ba Jin reappeared in 1977 and resumed his illustrious literary career with the novels *Cold Nights* (*Han ye*) and *Random Thoughts* (*Zaxiang lu*), becoming president of the Chinese PEN Center and acting chairman of the Writers' Association. In 1985, he was inducted as a foreign honorary member of the **United States** National Academy of Arts and Letters and, in 1988, was reelected vice-chairman of the **Chinese People's Political Consultative Conference** (**CPPCC**). A supporter of the 1989 second **Beijing Spring** pro-democracy movement, Ba Jin was criticized by the Chinese government, but was left unharmed. Ba Jin also called for the removal of the corpse of **Mao Zedong** from the mausoleum in Tiananmen Square and the conversion of the building to a museum of the Cultural Revolution. His 100th birthday in 2003 was celebrated across China and included a visit to his bedside by Premier **Wen Jiabao**. His works have been translated into more than 30 foreign languages, while his long memoir entitled *Random Thoughts* published in the 1980s as a reflection on the chaotic turmoil of the Cultural Revolution was reissued following his death at the age of 101.

"BACKYARD STEEL FURNACES" (*"XIAO GAOLU"*). Along with the gigantic **people's communes**, backyard steel furnaces were the most significant product (and one of the biggest disasters) of the **Great Leap Forward (1958–1960)**. The furnaces were a central feature of the Chinese concept of "walking on two legs," that is, of carrying out economic and technological modernization by promoting both relatively capital-intensive, large-scale production units, such as the **Anshan Iron and Steel Corporation**, and relatively labor-intensive, small-scale, and technologically backward production facilities.

The backyard steel furnaces originated in August 1958 when, **Chinese Communist Party** (**CCP**) chairman and prime designer of the Great Leap, **Mao Zedong**, plunged China into an all-out steel production campaign. This campaign was to increase the country's steel output dramatically to a level of 10 million tons, thus putting China well on the road to Mao's declared goal of surpassing British steel production in 15 years. Small, puddling-style furnaces were set up throughout the Chinese countryside and in cities, with the "steel" often smelted out of broken pots, kettles, and other iron implements contributed by the local **population**. At the height of the Great Leap, it was claimed that 49% of China's total steel production came from the backyard furnaces, with the rest supplied by more conventional plants in China's industrial centers in the northeast and **Shanghai**. With tens of millions of rural and urban residents contributing to the steel campaign, the target of 10 million tons was reached. Yet, the costs were enormous because much of the steel from the backyard furnaces proved useless. More importantly, farmers working as much as 24-hour shifts at the furnaces all but ignored the more mundane, and less "heroic," tasks of harvesting crops that were left to rot in the fields.

During the frenzy of the Great Leap, no one among the top CCP leadership dared criticize the backyard furnaces, except for **Peng Dehuai**, who, after visiting the countryside, questioned Mao Zedong about the strategy and was thereafter purged for his impudence. Other **leaders**, such as **Chen Yun**, had lingering doubts but were unwilling to risk their political (and physical) lives by questioning Chairman

Mao Zedong. Yet, in the face of the cold realities, even Mao had to back down, and thus the backyard furnaces were finally shut down in late 1959. By draining crucial **labor** supplies in the countryside, the furnaces contributed to the devastating famine that occurred in the early 1960s, which cost perhaps over 30 million lives and also caused massive deforestation as millions of trees were felled to provide fuel for the furnaces. Following the death of Mao Zedong in 1976, the furnaces were roundly criticized, along with many aspects of the ill-fated Great Leap Forward. *See also* TIAN JIAYING.

BAI HUA (1930–). A writer with the Political Department of the **People's Liberation Army** (**PLA**) in the Wuhan Military Region, Bai Hua was labeled an "anti-socialist element" during the **Anti-Rightist Campaign (1957–1958)** and attacked during the **Cultural Revolution (1966–1976)**. After returning to the army in 1977, he became famous in 1979 at a National Congress of Literature and Art by declaring: "No courage, no breakthrough, no breakthrough, no literature." Bai earned additional distinction by supporting the **Democracy Wall Movement (1978–1979)** and then by proclaiming in a rather direct attack on the Maoist **personality cult** (*geren chongbai*) that "never again should we sing the praises of any savior." In 1979, Bai Hua wrote a screenplay entitled *Unrequited Love,* the story of the frustrated patriotism of an old painter who faces misunderstanding and ill-treatment at the hands of Maoist officials when he returns to China from the **United States**. In 1981, the work was criticized as an example of "**bourgeois liberalization**" while Bai was accused of violating the **Four Cardinal Principles** as the screenplay set off a major political controversy between advocates and opponents of reform in the Chinese government over political control of **literature and the arts**.

Labeled the "Bai Hua Incident," the attack on Bai Hua brought to an end the relatively unrestricted literary freedom during 1979–1980. The promulgation of Central Directive No. 7 by the **Chinese Communist Party** (**CCP**), in 1981, ordered that "artists must support the Four Cardinal Principles" and not "leave people sick at heart when dealing with the Anti-Rightist Campaign or the Cultural Revolution." This created a chill in Chinese literary and artistic circles, although dissident writers and artists were generally treated with a lighter hand than they had been in the 1950s and 1960s. Bai ultimately yielded to the criticism by apologizing for a "lack of balance" in the work and for failing to recognize the power of the Party and the people to overcome obstacles in society. In 1983, Bai was invited by the Ministry of Culture to participate in a conference on film scripts held in **Shanghai**. A few months later, Bai's historical play *The King of Wu's Golden Spear and the King of Yue's Sword* was presented by the **Beijing** People's Arts Theatre even as the work was considered as a veiled criticism of **Mao Zedong** and **Deng Xiaoping**. A member of the All-China Writers' Association, Bai received a national prize for his poetry in 1981 during the height of the criticism directed at his screenplay. In 1988, he visited France and the United States. *See also* CINEMA AND FILM.

BANDUNG CONFERENCE OF AFRO–ASIAN STATES (1955). At this conference of 29 non-aligned African and Asian nations held in Bandung, Indonesia, China's Foreign Minister, **Zhou Enlai**, articulated Chinese policies stressing peaceful coexistence and neutrality toward other Third World nations. Despite China's association with the **Soviet Union** in the Communist bloc, Zhou emphasized China's solidarity with African and Asian nations that were trying to escape the pressures of the different power blocs and to forge an independent, third path to national development and independence. This "spirit" of Bandung led Zhou to propose opening negotiations with the **United States** and to express gestures of friendship to small, non-Communist Asian nations such as the Philippines and Thailand, which feared Chinese support for domestic Communist insurgents. China embraced the Five Principles of Peaceful Coexistence (mutual respect for sovereignty and integrity, non-aggression, non-interference, equality and mutual benefit, and peaceful coexistence) as it tried to appear as first an underdeveloped nation, rather than a Communist state. China also used this opportunity to develop increasingly cordial relations with African nations and with the host country of Indonesia until the 1965 anti-Communist and anti-Chinese coup there effectively terminated relations between the two countries for 25 years. In the 1960s, China's support for peaceful coexistence and neutrality gradually gave way to a more militant and aggressive **foreign policy** articulated by **Mao Zedong** and **Lin Biao**, bringing to an end China's embrace of the Bandung "spirit." *See also* FOREIGN POLICY; VIETNAM.

BANKING AND FINANCE. During the period of China's interaction with the world **economy** in the 1930s and 1940s prior to the rise to power of the **Chinese Communist Party** (**CCP**), the country developed a highly sophisticated banking system composed of domestic and foreign financial institutions. But with the establishment of the **People's Republic of China** (**PRC**) in 1949 and especially the imposition of the **five-year plans** modeled on the Soviet system of central planning in the early 1950s, China's once vibrant system of commercial banks was shattered as virtually all the country's banking functions were taken over by the People's Bank of China. A single, monolithic bank that functioned within the planning system to feed **investment** and operating funds to the growing conglomeration of **state-owned enterprises** (**SOEs**) in accordance with the economic plan, the People's Bank brought the country's rabid inflation rate under control when, in 1955, it began issuing a new "people's **currency**" (*renminbi*, also known as *yuan*) at the rate of 10,000 old to new.

This monolithic system administered through the central Ministry of Finance remained virtually unchanged until the inauguration of the economic reforms in 1978–1979, when the Bank of China was split off from the People's Bank of China and granted authority as the Chinese government's foreign exchange bank to manage international settlements relating to **trade** and non-trade transactions with foreign countries and to handle export and import loans and foreign exchange loans. The bank also issued stocks in foreign currencies and marketable securities. At the same time, the Agricultural Bank of China was also split off. Five years later, in 1983, the State Council adopted a plan to convert the People's Bank of China into the Central Bank and to transfer commercial banking functions to "specialized banks," such as the China Construction Bank, which handled budgetary allocations for infrastructure and capital construction projects. In 1984, industrial and commercial financial transactions were ceded to the Industrial and Commercial Bank of China. In 1987, the Bank of Communications was formally reestablished as the country's first shareholding bank. Throughout the 1980s emerged an array of state-owned, non-bank financial institutions (NBFIs), mainly rural and urban credit cooperatives and trust and investment corporations. The banking and financial system played an increasing role in the Chinese economy as total deposits rose from 427 billion *yuan* in 1985 to 2.3 trillion *yuan* in 1993, and total loans over the same period grew from 590 billion *yuan* to 2.6 trillion *yuan*, a figure five times greater than total government budgetary expenditure. By the mid-1990s, the Chinese government announced a goal of transforming China's banking system to fit the need for increasingly efficient liquidity allocation for the emerging "socialist market economy" by, for example, authorizing the issuance of credit cards by virtually all the major banks including some with foreign stakeholders such as Bank of America. Lending networks for inter-bank borrowing were also set up along with a deregulation of foreign exchange controls over current account transactions. Serious institutional and financial obstacles, however, prevented a fundamental alteration of the system that is still dominated by the four giant state-run banks. In 1995, the **National People's Congress** (**NPC**) adopted China's first real banking laws—the Law on the People's Bank of China and the Commercial Banking Law of China—which were aimed at stabilizing the nation's currency, strengthening bank management, improving government economic control, and ensuring smooth progress in banking system reform. Yet, despite these legal advances, China's banks continued to be hobbled by their primary role in financing the technically bankrupt state-owned enterprises with little or no prospect of repayment and by the lack of independence of banking institutions from political **leaders** at all levels of the CCP apparatus who continued to rely on state-run banks to fund projects without any consideration to their economic value or debt-servicing capacity. Relaxation of banking controls in the early 1990s also led to a flurry of speculative activities by banks in real estate and the emerging **stock markets** in **Shanghai** and the Shenzhen **Special Economic Zone** (**SEZ**) that ended up producing enormous financial losses when monetary controls were re-imposed in late 1993.

The backbone of the Chinese banking system is the four large state-owned, commercial banks: the Agricultural Bank of China, the Bank of China, the Construction Bank of China, and the Industrial and Commercial Bank of China. These massive institutions operate like government agencies, with complicated and multi-tier organizations that extend from their headquarters in **Beijing** to the lowest districts and townships and villages throughout the country. Most of the lending decisions made at the county level and below have little or no oversight from the central office. In 1996, two million people were employed by the nearly 160,000 branches of these banks scattered across the country, supplemented by the national postal system, where savings accounts of depositors are also maintained. There are also three policy banks—the Agricultural Development Bank of China, the Export-Import Bank of China, and the State Development Bank of China—established in 1994 and 11 national share-holding banks and 112 urban commercial banks, such as the Everbright Bank and the Shanghai Pudong Development Bank. Between 1995 and 2005, China's Gross Domestic Product (GDP) more than doubled in size, yet the number of banks in the country remained virtually the same, compared to more than 500 commercial banks in **Japan** and 1,200 in the **United States**. Anywhere from 75 to 90% of all banking assets are held by the four giant state-run banks, whose management and board members are all appointed by the central bank. The only fully privately owned and listed lender is the China Minsheng Bank, which was set up in 1996, sponsored by non-state enterprises. The rate of return on assets for Chinese banks is far lower than in other countries as is their capital/asset ratio. Interest rates remain only partially liberalized with commercial banks sometimes forced to offer de facto negative rates well below potential market rates.

Foreign bank outlets have also been established in 23 cities in China. Beginning in 2002, these institutions were allowed to handle local currency business transactions subject to regional limitation and to participate in inter-bank borrowing and bond trading and purchasing through a national trading and information network. As a result of China's 2001 entry into the **World Trade Organization (WTO)**, by 2007, regional limitations on foreign-funded banks handling local currency business in the entire country will be eliminated as a way to accelerate reform of the domestic banking system. Foreign ownership of Chinese banks is allowed up to the limit of 25% of total asset value, such as occurred in 2005 with the Shenzhen Development Bank, whose major foreign investors include General Electric.

At the provincial level, trust and **investment** companies affiliated with provincial governments or the state banks have emerged. At the local level, in economically vibrant cities, such as Wenzhou, Zhejiang Province, an elaborate system of diverse curb market financing has emerged that, in 2004, drained US$12 billion to US$17 billion from the government-run banking system. This includes everything from legally sanctioned and semi-legal shareholding cooperatives to illegal pawn shops, loan sharks, and Ponzi-type pyramid investment schemes to rotating credit associations that absorb the substantial savings of rural and urban households (estimated at between 30 and 40% of total income) and provide much of the credit to the rapidly expanding non-state sector that, in 2004, made up 40% of all investment. Overall, these several types of non-bank financial institutions are still dwarfed by the state banks with the former possessing only one-fifth the assets of the latter. Although China's more than three million small- and medium-sized enterprises generate about 50% of GDP, they receive only 20% of bank loans that are still reserved for the large-scale state-owned enterprises.

The role of the People's Bank of China is similar to the central banks of other countries. According to the Provisional Regulations on the Administration of Banks passed by the State Council, the People's Bank of China exercises the following power and functions: research and formulation of national guidelines and policies; studying and drafting of financial legislation; formulating basic financial regulations; controlling the issuance of currency, regulating currency circulation, and maintaining currency stability; determining interest rates on deposits and loans and setting the exchange rate for the *renminbi* and foreign currencies; devising the State Credit Plan and exercising centralized control over credit and exercising uniform control over the working capital of the State; controlling foreign exchange, gold and silver, and the state's foreign exchange reserves; examining and approving the establishment, abolition, and merger of the specialized commercial banks and other financial institutions; managing the State treasury and issuing government securities; controlling shares, bonds, and other securities; and participating in international financial activities on behalf of the PRC. The People's Bank of China maintains relations with more than 1,500 banks in more than 150 countries and regions.

In 1995, the independence of the central bank and its many branches from governmental authorities in implementing monetary policy was enhanced by the passage and implementation of the Law of the People's Bank of China, which also ended the bank's direct financing of the government's fiscal debt. In 1997, the People's Bank of China issued a set of provisional rules establishing a board of supervisors to oversee the asset quality and management of state-run commercial banks, including instructions to all commercial banks to form an internal auditing department and prohibiting the unauthorized flow of bank capital to the stock market. In 1998, the People's Bank withdrew from the credit plan, an inflexible form of direct control over credit expansion, and has since relied on high reserve deposits and direct loans to commercial banks for monetary control. And, in 1999, the People's Bank of China announced that the *Renminbi* Administrative Regulation would take effect on 1 May, which, for the first time, would put in place comprehensive legal regulations and standardize policies governing the Chinese currency by defining its legal status, unit, design, and printing and circulation. In 2005, the head of the People's Bank of China was Zhou Xiaochuan (1948–), who has a Ph.D. from **Qinghua University** and was formerly acting director of the State Administration of Foreign Exchange and head of the China Construction Bank.

The major problem that has confronted the Chinese banking and financial system in the post-1978–1979 reform era is the enormous size of non-performing loans (NPLs) by the four major state-run banks, which resulted from years of directed lending under the credit plan and administered interest rates. Effectively uncollectible, these loans are largely to China's more than 100,000 state-owned enterprises whose average debt-to-asset ratio exceeds 80% (consumer loans in China only account for about 6% of the total loans of all financial institutions). Officially, China, in 1999, put the NPL figure at 20% of the total Chinese loan book, four times greater than the international norm of 5%, which is compatible with a viable banking system. Some outside observers, however, believe the NPL figure in China is as high as from 25 to 50% or two trillion *yuan* (US$370 billion), with estimates that 4.5 trillion *yuan* (50% of GDP) would be required to fully recapitalize the 11.3 trillion *yuan* (US$1.58 trillion) in loans held by the entire banking system. By 2004, the percentage of NPLs had dropped to just below 17% after a massive US$170 billion write-off in 1999 and 2000, which was followed in 2003–2004 by a capital infusion into the banking system of US$95 billion from China's US$400 billion in foreign exchange reserves.

These efforts followed upon a largely unsuccessful attempt to manage the NPL problem through debt-equity-swaps (DES) and asset auctions executed by four asset management companies (AMCs) that had been formed and initially financed by the central government's Ministry of Finance and consisted of 19% of the total outstanding loans held by China's four major banks. Accused of illegal practices that cost the government US$800 million, these AMCs had by the end of 2000 disposed of 90 billion *yuan* in bad loans, a mere 6% of the NPLs taken over from the banks. In 2004, another bailout of US$45 billion in foreign exchange reserves was carried out to help shore up the four big banks so that they could sell stock for the first time. Central bank officials promised in 2004 that significant reforms would be pursued to 2007 through a process of first bailing out, then transforming insolvent banks into shareholding companies with shares listed on stock exchanges with strict limits imposed by the Ministry of Finance on the amount of bad loans state-run banks are allowed to write off annually.

Throughout the 1990s and early 2000s, international watchdog agencies, such as Moody's Investor Service, and foreign and domestic observers of the Chinese banking system, continually warned of dire consequences for the Chinese and world economy if the NPL problem was not addressed, especially in light of the role similar banking problems played in the 1997–1998 Asian financial crisis that struck Japan, South **Korea**, and Southeast Asia, where NPL problems were actually less severe than China's. These warnings were made all the more serious as observers considered the possibility of a dramatic slowdown in China's torrid economic growth rate and high domestic savings rates (a staggering 40%) and a possible collapse of the urban real estate "bubble" anyone of which could raise bank NPL levels to 50% of total loan portfolio. The central government has authorized various institutional measures to strengthen macro-economic control and supervision of China's banking system, such as the China Banking Regulatory Commission established in 2003 and the increasingly powerful National Auditing Office, to deal with growing problems of bank fraud in the hundreds of millions of dollars by top-ranking officials at the Industrial and Commercial Bank of China, the mainland's largest lender by assets, and provincial branches of the China Construction Bank. International assistance to address the NPL problem has also been received in the form of US$45 million in equity investments authorized by the Asian Development Bank and a US$1.3 billion deal with a consortium led by Morgan Stanley to dispose of the collateral backing the bad loans.

Critics in and out of China believe these kinds of incremental policies have had little or no effect as they fail to address the problem of moral hazard created by widespread bank bailouts that come without fundamental structural reform of the banking industry and the SOEs. More drastic measures are needed to strengthen banking supervision and accounting standards in line with prudential norms (e.g., ratio of liquid assets to liquid liabilities) rather than government policy goals. Internal constraints, such as the lack of strategic planning, should be rectified with banks allowed more autonomy in credit decisions along with proposals to break up the four giant state-run banks into dozens of regional banks. Without such radical changes, the fundamental flaws in the banking system involving an overly politicized credit approval process, lax corporate governance, redundant branch offices, poor employee performance measures, and lack of institutional transparency will go unaddressed, except in the most egregious cases of employee fraud and embezzlement because Chinese journalists are effectively barred from reporting on the full extent of the banks' troubles. Recent cases of fraud include a branch manager at the Bank of China who, in 2005, fled with US$100 million in cash; accusations of fraud and bribery that led to resignations by two China Construction Bank officials; the arrest of several bank officials from the Industrial and Commercial Bank for forging documents to expedite loans; and accusations of embezzlement and corruption against officials of the Huayin Trust, Dalian Securities firm. These problems are made all the more intractable by the central government's persistent practice of relying on bank funds to prop up domestic equity markets and to stimulate the slowing domestic economy in the early 2000s by credit expansion as the banking system remains the main financial channel underpinning GDP growth in China.

China's policy of maintaining a relatively low value of the *yuan* vis-à-vis the American dollar has also resulted in the expansion of credit that leads to more lending, which continue to flow into overcrowded industrial sectors and infrastructure projects that hold little chance of becoming profitable. If these loans and outstanding obligations by SOEs are treated not as NPLs as defined by the Bank of International Settlements but as indirect borrowing by the state from state-owned banks, then they should properly be included as part of China's overall public debt, which stands between 35 and 40% of GDP, considerably lower than many other countries. (With its banking-led financial structure, China's total loans-to-GDP ratio is 132%, compared to Japan's 310%. The Chinese figure is only 5% less than in the United Kingdom, which is a securities-led financial structure.) China has decided to segregate commercial banking from investment banking that effectively prevents its banks from following their counterparts in Japan and South Korea, which became deeply involved in risky securities trading and underwriting and investment in non-bank financial and productive enterprises that spurred the 1997–1998 Asian financial crisis. Any relaxation of these tight controls is unlikely so as to avoid a repeat of the instability of 1994, when runs on small banks, including the 1998 failure of the Hainan Development Bank, led to government rescue.

Because Chinese banks will never be allowed by the state to fail in a way that hurts depositors, the problems of the banking sector may be somewhat overstated because China's "socialist market economy" operates on principles at odds with an advanced economy of financial capitalism. With US$350 billion in Foreign Direct Investment (FDI) into China from 1992 to 2002, the country can afford to bail out the banks and the SOEs by raising taxes, which, in 2002, constituted only 17% of GDP, partly because of generous tax exemptions granted to the fast-growing new private sector, which generates 20% of total output. In reality, the state is using treasury bonds to recapitalize the big four state banks while resisting calls to channel capital from ailing state companies into productive investments; in the short-run, this would entail factory closures, more layoffs, and **social protests**, which the leadership of the CCP fears most.

In the absence of fundamental bank reform and a cleaning up of bank balance sheets, China was reluctant to take the bold step of appreciating its currency (pegged at 8.28 *yuan*:US$1 from 1994 to 2005) because such a move would have only increased the inflow of speculative "hot money" (estimated at US$300 billion over the past few years) into the banking system from abroad, thereby ratcheting up pressure on banks to expand, rather than contract, new loans into economically unviable projects. Major loans from the Industrial and Commercial Bank of China were used to back the unsolicited bid by the China National Offshore Oil Corporation (CNOOC) to take over the American oil company Unocal that was ultimately abandoned in August 2005. Reorganization of the big four lenders was also improved in 2004 with the China Construction Bank taking the lead in acquiring approval by central authorities to split into two parts—the company group China Construction Bank Group Inc. (CCB Group) and the shareholding company of CCB Corp. into which the China Yangtze Power Co. (CYPC), the listing arm of the **Three Gorges Dam Project**, bought a two billion *yuan* stake. In 2005, the China Construction Bank had more than US$500 billion in assets and a reported profit of US$6 billion.

Future trends in China's banking system include a rapid expansion of the use of credit cards, which were first introduced in 1986 and in 2004 were held by only about 1% of the **population**, although bank cash cards numbering over 700 million are widely used and will also expand. China is also moving toward the adoption of e-commerce under the authority of the China Financial Certification Authority for corporate banking customers and Chinese stock traders and is expanding the role of financial holding groups such as **China International Trust and Investment Corporation** (**CITIC**), Everbright, and Ping'an along with the conversion of the Bank of China and the Construction Bank of China into mixed financial groups. Changes likely to occur over the next decade include: introduction of a deposit insurance scheme for deposit taking in non-bank financial institutions, especially the highly suspect trust and investment corporations; conversion of the *renminbi* into a hard currency floating freely on world markets; greater reliance on open-market operations by the central bank for monetary control; increased foreign investment in not only China's smaller regional banks, such as the Bank of Shanghai, which have fewer resources and expertise, but also offers by the Bank of America and UBS (Europe's largest bank) to buy stakes in the Construction Bank of China and Bank of China, respectively; initial public offering (IPO) listings on both domestic and international capital markets by both the giant state-run banks and smaller regional lenders; the spread of

Chinese bank operations into foreign countries and the inauguration of a large national credit bureau to help banks evaluate loan applications; and the emergence of China as the world's largest market for automated teller machines (ATMs). *See also* INDUSTRY.

BAOSHAN IRON AND STEEL COMPLEX. Located outside **Shanghai**, this huge production facility is one of China's largest steel plants and the major steel-producing component of the Baoshan Iron and Steel Corporation (Baosteel), which, along with the **Anshan Iron and Steel Corporation** and the Wuhan Iron and Steel Corporation, constitute the three largest steel companies in China. The Baoshan plant was begun in the late 1970s as a central component of the grandiose design by then **Chinese Communist Party (CCP)** Chairman **Hua Guofeng** for a "Foreign Leap Forward" in which plans called for completion of several major industrial facilities financed by foreign loans and **investment**, especially from **Japan**. In 1978, in the midst of an overheated **economy** and an impending state budget deficit, and in a political climate in which Hua Guofeng's position as Party chairman was being seriously challenged by the political reemergence of **Deng Xiaoping**, 1,000 joint ventures, including the Baoshan plant, were terminated or put on hold. Not until Japan agreed to provide an extra 300 billion *yuan* in commodity loans was the plant, located near Shanghai's port, completed in the same year.

As the flagship of China's steel industry, Baoshan was blessed with the best managers, imported expensive **technology**, and was allowed to focus on the more profitable products, such as cold-rolled steel and hot-rolled galvanized sheets, leaving low-end products to older rivals with antiquated technology dating from the 1950s and 1960s. More than 200,000 workers have been employed at the plant, which like most **state-owned enterprises (SOEs)**, operated at a loss throughout the 1980s and 1990s but which by 2003 turned a hefty profit of US$1.6 billion as China's demand for steel soared. Production at the plant in 1992 was more than 3.5 million mt and by 2005 production had climbed to 23 million mt as deals with Europe's Arcelor and Japan's Nippon Steel dramatically increased production capacity. China's accelerated annual economic growth rates of 8–10% have produced a voracious appetite for domestic and foreign steel for everything from construction of giant infrastructure, such as the **Three Gorges Dam Project**, to the country's emerging **automobile industry** that turned the steel sector around and made companies like Baoshan enormously profitable.

Like the other major steel producers in China, Baoshan has undergone significant corporate reorganization with a Board of Directors modeled along modern corporate lines and the separation between Baoshan Iron and Steel Co. Ltd. (Baosteel) from its parent company Shanghai Baoshan Iron and Steel Group Corporation. In 2004, Baosteel made a significant public stock offering on the Shanghai **stock exchange** for raising capital though by far the largest stake-holder in the company with non-tradable shares remains the state-owned parent company. Beginning in 2003, the company allocated major capital expenditures to upgrade its production facilities with plans to expand output to 16.5 million tons a year in 2004 (and more than 30 million tons by 2009), making it the world's eighth-largest steel producer. As a result of resource and management consolidation with other formerly independent steel companies, such as Ma'anshan Steel, Baosteel in 2004 had an estimated market value of US$10 billion, which placed it just behind Japan's JFE Holdings and Nippon Steel, POSCO of South **Korea** and Europe's Arcelor. By 2005, Baosteel hopes to become one of the world's top-500 multinationals, although previous plans to offer public shares on foreign stock exchanges in 2000 were scuttled. Baoshan has secured a number of joint iron-ore operations with companies from Brazil and Australia and steel plate joint ventures with Arcelor and Nippon Steel and like other major steel companies in China, it has a number of ancillary businesses including software, property, a chemical company, and trading houses.

BAO TONG (1934–). A close adviser to **Chinese Communist Party (CCP)** General Secretary **Zhao Ziyang**, Bao Tong rose to political prominence in the late 1970s when, as director of the State **Science and Technology** Commission, he drafted speeches for **Deng Xiaoping** on political reform, including proposals for the separation of Party and government. Bao became a member of the CCP Central Committee at the 1987 13th National Party Congress and beginning in 1988 headed the Research Center to Reform the Political Structure. Bao Tong was also the personal secretary to Zhao Ziyang, a political secretary of the

Politburo, and a vice-minister of the State Economic Reform Commission. Accused of conspiring with students against the Chinese state during the 1989 second **Beijing Spring** pro-democracy movement, Bao was arrested after the military crackdown and sentenced to seven years in prison. He was released in May 1996 but kept under constant police surveillance, although this did not prevent him from publishing an article in 2004 in the *Asian Wall Street Journal*, which claimed that during the 1989 pro-democracy movement Deng Xiaoping had overridden the views of General Secretary Zhao Ziyang and many of China's most senior generals who called for a peaceful solution to the political standoff by taking the personal decision to use force. China, Bao claimed, still suffered a fundamental flaw in its political structure where "one man politics" can override all laws and institutions. Bao has also written to the **United Nations (UN)** High Commissioner for **Human Rights** complaining of persistent harassment and intrusions on his personal freedom by the Chinese government's **Public Security Bureau.**

"BAREFOOT DOCTORS" (*"CHIJIAO YISHENG"*). This is an affectionate appellation purportedly used by farmers during the 1960s and early 1970s to refer to **health-care** workers who were given rudimentary training in order to bring basic public health care to China's hinterland. The "barefoot doctors" originated with the "Instructions Concerning Health Work" issued by **Mao Zedong** in June 1965, which advocated bringing medical and health work to the neglected rural areas. The Soviet model of economic and social development adopted by China since 1949 had, in Mao's view, concentrated China's limited resources primarily on the urban areas as policy realms such as health care were dominated by professionals in the Ministry of Public Health who paid inadequate attention to the health needs of China's vast rural **population.** In August 1965, Mao's instruction was picked up by the Hebei Provincial Committee, which proposed training part-peasant, part-medical doctors and one health worker and one midwife for each agricultural production brigade in the province. These individuals were to be trained by medical and health personnel from hospitals at the county (*xian*) level. This policy was quickly endorsed by the Ministry of Public Health but was later dropped after the initiation of the economic reforms in 1978–1979.

"BASIC LINE OF THE PARTY" (*"DANGDE JIBEN LUXIAN"*).
The fundamental parameters for policy in China are set by the "basic line of the Party" as enumerated by the **Chinese Communist Party (CCP)** top **leaders**. From 1949 to 1976, it was Chairman **Mao Zedong**, whose speeches and proclamations constituted the Party's basic line. Beginning in 1978, this task was carried out by **Deng Xiaoping** who in March 1979 promulgated the **Four Cardinal Principles** as the basic line. Specific policies, speeches by other leaders, and general work pursued by CCP **cadres** must conform to the basic line. To do otherwise is to risk ouster from positions of authority. During the Maoist era, deviance from the Party line could even mean purge or possibly physical elimination. Terms of the basic line are expressed in general language and thus can often be used as license to carry out major political struggles. This occurred in the case of Mao Zedong's 1962 statement that "Socialist society covers a considerably long historical period. In the historical period of **socialism**, there are still classes, class contradictions, and **class struggle**. There is the struggle between the socialist road and the capitalist road, and there is the danger of capitalist restoration." This and other general statements on the Communist Party's basic line became the foundation for the political struggles and attacks on top Party leaders, such as **Liu Shaoqi**, during the **Cultural Revolution (1966–1976)**. The Four Cardinal Principles enunciated by Deng Xiaoping were also the basis thereafter for opposing any efforts at substantial political reform in the **People's Republic of China (PRC)**.

"BASIC UNIT" (*"JIBEN DANWEI"*). The matrix of local-level organization in China into which all work and most residential units until recently were structured. The basic unit is a self-sustaining, relatively closed, micro-social system with substantial political, personnel, financial, and social power. Organized geographically and functionally, the basic unit maintains comprehensive control over its members through regulation of basic necessities (housing, food distribution, jobs, and **heath care**), allocation of rewards (job promotions, permission to marry and bear children, and divorce), and discharge of punishments (reductions in salary and housing privileges). Basic units are headed by a unit leader or administrator who, prior to the 1980s, was also the secretary of the Party committee that exists within all basic units. As a result of the preliminary political reforms of the 1980s, non-Party members were allowed to serve as unit **leaders**. Basic units also hold the **personal dossiers** (*dang'an*) that are kept on every urban resident. During the Maoist era (1949–1976), the basic unit was a critical component of China's totalitarian system by monitoring the **population** through the elaborate vertical structure of the **Chinese Communist Party (CCP)** and effectively preventing lateral social organization among the population. Transfer out of a basic unit was rare; for most urbanites their work in the unit was—up until recently—for a lifetime. This not only created enormous tensions among the members of these small societies but also serious rigidities in the allocation of **labor** because some units would have oversupplies and other units deficits, without any method of sharing labor. Permission of the basic unit head was also required under the 1950 **Marriage Law** before couples could legally marry, a power that was often used to reward or punish citizens and, in some cases, to solicit bribes but which, according to the new 1980 Marriage Law, is no longer necessary. Since the economic reforms and market system of the 1980s created greater labor mobility and lateral social organization, it is generally believed that the basic-unit system has weakened and is virtually non-existent for the large **floating population** that has flooded into many of China's major cities. After the government crushed the second **Beijing Spring** in June 1989, many basic units in **Beijing** protected their members from arrest while also surreptitiously documenting the number of deaths and injuries caused by the military crackdown. *See also HUKOU.*

"BEATING, SMASHING, LOOTING, RANSACKING, AND KIDNAPPING" (*"DA, ZA, QIANG, CHAO, ZHUA"*). This phrase captures the random violence and outright thuggish behavior that was committed by **Red Guards** and others during the most violent phases of the **Cultural Revolution (1966–1976)**. Although Red Guards had been admonished by **Mao Zedong** to "struggle by reason," the attacks on Party **cadres** and **leaders** of the **Chinese Communist Party (CCP)** along with teachers, writers, **intellectuals**, and artists, and other targets singled out for persecution, quickly degenerated into wanton acts of violence. Top leaders, such as **Liu Shaoqi**, were placed in cold, dark, isolated cells and submitted to hours of endless interrogation, after which they often collapsed from exhaustion and died. Writers and artists had their hands broken so they could no longer produce "bourgeois art" and, in some cases, were then murdered or driven to suicide. Heavy doses of violence—including cannibalism—were meted out either by small groups of Red Guards or at mass rallies often attended by top leaders within the radical faction, such as **Ye Qun**, the wife of **Lin Biao**. In the countryside, the targets of Red Guard abuse were incarcerated in the notorious "cow sheds," where unsanitary conditions, limited food, and days-into-months of isolation also resulted in death or suicide. **Jiang Qing** and other radical leaders generally encouraged the violence and ordered the **Public Security Bureau** and the **People's Liberation Army** **(PLA)** not to intervene. By 1968, Mao Zedong and other top leaders put a stop to the worst violence, at least in the cities, by sending youth to the countryside and ordering the army to restrain Red Guard rampages.

BEIDA (PEKING UNIVERSITY). One of three premier universities in China, Peking University was established in 1898 as the Imperial University and was renamed Peking University in 1912 after the downfall of the Qing dynasty (1644–1911) and the establishment of the Republic of China (ROC). The **May Fourth Movement** **(1919–1923)**, ushering in modern Chinese nationalism, began at the university under the leadership of prominent Beida professors led by Chen Duxiu (the founder, in 1921, of the **Chinese Communist Party**) and many students. After the Communist seizure of power in 1949, the university was reorganized as part of the nationwide campaign of restructuring higher **education**. It was moved to its current site on the campus of former Yenching University in the western suburbs of China's capital city of **Beijing**. The university was expanded into multidisciplinary programs of **sciences**, technology, humanities, social sciences, management, and education. Ma Yinchu, a renowned professor of economics, was chancellor until his purge in the 1960s, following direct criticism of his views on the need for **population** control by **Mao Zedong**. In 1989, the university had more than 9,000 undergraduates, 3,000 postgraduates, and more than 2,000 faculty members. The university has a modern Physics

Research Center, headed by the world-renowned Nobel laureate physicist Li Zhengdao.

Like all Chinese universities, Beida operates under the direct authority of the Ministry of Education and is subject to political control by the Chinese state. Following the 1989 second **Beijing Spring** pro-democracy movement in which prominent Beida students, such as Wang Dan, assumed leadership positions, the university's president, Ding Shisun, was replaced and the entering freshman class in fall 1989 was required to undergo one year of military training before matriculation while state authorities employed a variety of methods to reestablish closer political control over the student body. Beida students have been uniformly subject to Chinese Communist Party authority as was clearly evident in May 2004, when, on the occasion of the 85th anniversary of the 1919–1923 May Fourth Movement, students were encouraged to enlist in the local chapter of the Communist **Youth League** (**CYL**) and vowed to carry on the May Fourth Spirit of promoting the country's modernization, while the role of the 1919 Movement as the beginning of modern Chinese democracy went unmentioned.

Although political control of the student body has been accomplished since 1989, this did not prevent periodic student actions, such as in May 2000, when more than 1,000 students held an orderly and apolitical midnight march protesting lax university security that had led to the wanton rape and murder of a young female student. The faculty of Beida have also picked up where students left off by taking the lead in challenging the political course of the nation, as the 2004 May Fourth Movement anniversary was seized upon by an outspoken journalism professor who published an essay online attacking the state propaganda department for its "Nazi tactics" in covering up and quashing stories on famine, **corruption**, disease, and other maladies since the Communist takeover in 1949. The author was particularly critical of the state for covering up the starvation of millions in the famine of 1962 that followed upon the **Great Leap Forward** (**1958–1960**) and, more recently, of hiding the 2002–2003 **SARS** epidemic. Following this political outburst, the Personnel Department of the Ministry of Education announced plans to reform the tenure system at Beida and other Chinese universities that would restrict the system of life-long employment to full professors only while associate professors, lecturers, and assistant professors would be subject to contract reviews after 12 years.

Beida's prestige has been maintained by its role in advancing **science and technology**, supporting economic reforms, and making the university a cosmopolitan institution with international ties. In 2004, the university's Neuroscience Research Institute helped develop a method to detect the viral pathogen responsible for SARS. In the same year, the university's Guanghua School of Management signed a tie-up agreement with the Matsushita Corporation of **Japan** to assist in training Chinese high-level managers for the company's operations in the **People's Republic of China (PRC)**. An agreement was also reached with Stanford University that opened its first Asian branch at Beida, whereby Stanford students would study at the Chinese university and take classes from professors from both institutions. As part of China's continuing effort to modernize and professionalize its armed forces, Beida was enlisted as part of a national effort to train military personnel enrolled as university students primarily in programs involving electronic and mechanical engineering. Although not directly involved in an admissions scandal that involved other Chinese universities in August 2004, Beida relies on the national admissions examination that remains shrouded in mystery—even as it is considered the last line of defense for ensuring education equality.

BEIDAIHE CONFERENCE (1958). A crucial meeting of the Communist Party leadership in August 1958, the Beidiahe Conference effectively committed the country to the ill-fated **Great Leap Forward (1958–1960)**. Beidaihe is a summer resort on China's northeast coast where top **leaders** of the **Chinese Communist Party (CCP)** from the **Politburo** retreat every summer in late August for high-level discussions and decisions. At this particular meeting held in mid-August 1958, **Mao Zedong** pushed through his plan to set up the **people's communes** in the Chinese countryside and advocated major increases in domestic steel production through the re-smelting of scrap steel and the infamous **backyard steel furnaces**. In his major speech at the conference, Mao declared that the people's communes contained the "sprouts of communism," and he predicted that this new form of agricultural organization would provide China with a substantial grain surplus. Mao also extravagantly predicted that steel production would increase by millions of tons, such that every village in the country (numbering more than one million in 1958) could build an airport! A substantial expansion of the **people's militia** was also proposed. The Beidaihe Conference represented the peak of Mao's utopian vision. In 2004, the newly elected President **Hu Jintao** announced as an **economy** measure that the Beidaihe summer meetings would no longer be held.

BEIJING. The capital of the **People's Republic of China (PRC)** since 1949, *Beijing* in Chinese means "northern capital." The city became China's relatively permanent capital in 1271 during the Yuan dynasty (1264–1368) and remained so until 1928 when the **Kuomintang (KMT)** government under Chiang Kai-shek designated Nanking (Nanjing) or "southern capital" as the official capital of the Republic of China (ROC). (Nanjing had also briefly served as the Chinese capital during the early phases of the Ming dynasty in the late 14th century). During the Nationalist interregnum (1928–1949), Beijing was renamed *Beiping* meaning "northern peace" (rendered in Wade-Giles Romanization as *Peip'ing*) until the city was restored as the traditional seat of government in September1949 by the Communists, who renamed it Beijing. (Nationalist authorities on Taiwan, however, still refer to the city as Peip'ing). The layout of the city on north-south and east-west axes and its checkerboard streets reflect the traditional cosmology of the Chinese dynastic system. Central Beijing is dominated by the ancient Forbidden City (which is now a museum open to the public) and the giant 440,000 m² Tiananmen Square, which was quadrupled in size in 1958. Beijing was once surrounded, like all Chinese cities, by a high city wall, but that wall was destroyed by the Communist authorities in the 1950s, who considered it a symbol of Chinese **feudalism**, much to the chagrin of local residents and city preservationists.

Beijing municipality (*Beijing shi*) is 10,000 km² in size and includes both urban and rural areas, much of it mountainous and dotted with villages. Administratively, the rural areas are broken down into counties (*xian*) and the urban parts of the city into districts (*qu*) and sub-districts (*fenqu*). Total **population** of the municipality in 2005 was 15.2 million people along with an additional 2.6 million people who were counted as part of China's **floating population**. By 2020, the population of Beijing is expected to surpass 21 million people. In addition to serving as the seat of the central Chinese government, Beijing is a major center of **industry**, including electronics, textiles, chemicals, and steel production. The Capital Iron and Steel Corporation is located in the western part of the city (upwind from the city center) and is one of China's largest such facilities. The *Zhongguan cun* District is the city's center of computer products and businesses. In June 1989, Beijing was one of the major sites of the second **Beijing Spring** pro-democracy movement and the ensuing military crackdown on 3–4 June that occurred in and around Tiananmen Square. Beijing's mayor at the time, **Chen Xitong** (who was subsequently charged with **corruption** and imprisoned) presented a detailed report on "Quelling the Counterrevolutionary Rebellion" to a subsequent meeting of the **National People's Congress (NPC)**. In addition to the incarceration of Chen, the vice-mayor of Beijing, Wang Baosen, committed suicide in 1995 as he, too, faced charges of corruption. In 2005, the mayor of the city was Wang Qishan while the Party secretary was Liu Qi (1942–), who is from Jiangsu Province.

Beginning in the 1980s and 1990s, the city of Beijing increasingly confronted problems associated with urban sprawl and uncontrolled growth that are common to many great metropolises in the world as well as dealing with the **SARS** crisis that hit the city in spring 2003. As the site of the 2008 "green" Olympics when China hopes to put its national achievements and progress on display, Beijing is undergoing a massive transformation aimed at making the city more livable and environmentally friendly. This has included building a series of sewage plants to treat the city's enormous volume of waste water and sludge (1.2 billion tons annually), of which less than 50% was treated in 2003, while at the same time diverting water from a variety of local and far-distant sources to meet the increasing needs of its residents. In 2003, Beijing faced a severe shortage of water supply in its local Miyun and Guanting reservoirs that resulted from a five-year drought and has sought new supply from an emergency project to divert water from Hebei Province and from as far away as Shanxi Province as fees for water usage in the municipality were raised from extremely low levels to reduce consumption that at 300 m^3 per person is still far below the international benchmark of 1,000 m^3 per capita for an area suffering acute water shortage. Predictions are that the city will continue to confront serious water shortfalls until 2010 when, if all goes well with the **South-to-North Water Diversion Project**, ample supplies from the Yangtze River will be made available to Beijing residents.

Equally important has been the city's deteriorating air quality from antiquated factories billowing smoke in the city center, to residential use of coal to heat homes, and from a sharp increase in **automobile** ownership. Periodic heavy smog has disrupted the city's economic life and led at times to partial closure of some city highways. The number of automobiles in the city was more than two million in 2003 with predictions that it will grow another three million in the next few years. Confronted with growing traffic jams and a rush hour that reportedly consumes 11 hours a day, the city government has responded by building a new beltway circling the city known as the Fifth Ring Road and expanding the rail and subway system while also replacing thousands of heavily polluting trucks and taxis with vehicles that meet tougher fuel restrictions. Yet, the inability of the government to handle the problem is demonstrated by the increasing number of illegal and unlicensed taxi cabs that continue to operate despite official restrictions and undoubtedly contribute to the rising number of days with "extremely unhealthy pollution levels" recorded annually in the city.

Beijing has also undergone an enormous construction boom over the past decade that has transformed its urban landscape, sometimes at the expense of its cultural and historical **architecture**. The greatest impact has been on the city's maze of traditional alleyways (*hutong*), 200 of which have disappeared since the Communist takeover in 1949, victims of various spurts of construction from the Great Hall of the People in Tiananmen Square to the Stalinist cinderblock apartment blocs constructed in the 1950s and 1960s to the more recent modern apartment and commercial building spree. Despite the protests and consternation of local residents who fear for the social texture of their lives where traditionally everyone lives side-by-side in close proximity, the transformation continues with 250,000 m² of old houses—including courtyard homes—slated for demolition. In 2003, Beijing was the site of China's first business park, replete with sufficient space for 80 large enterprises while upscale and highly priced apartment buildings (many named after famous sites in New

York, such as the "Upper West Side" and "Park Avenue") continue to be built. Although this benefits the city's new nouveau riche population, it comes at the expense of poorer former residents, whose forceful evictions and meager government compensation have made it impossible for these long-time residents to stay in the central city. Major construction of **transportation**, housing, and sports infrastructure is ongoing, with long-term master plans for the city calling for the creation of a series of suburban satellite towns to ease the population pressure on central Beijing with manufacturing to be concentrated in the eastern sector and high **technology** in the west.

Like other urban and rural areas in China, Beijing is experimenting with a more open form of direct elections to district and county people's congresses that, since 1979, have allowed for multi-candidates. In the wake of the 2002–2003 **SARS** outbreak, which the city ultimately weathered by mobilizing its vast network of residential committees and public health workers, the mayor, Meng Xunong, was ousted amid accusations of initially covering up the crisis in **health care**. His successor, Wang Qishan, promised more transparency in government decision making, especially involving resident relocations, and committed the city to the promise of "putting people first and setting up a practical and clean government" as was also put forth by President **Hu Jintao**. Although the average urban consumer expenditure in Beijing in 2004 remained second behind high-flying **Guangzhou (Canton)**, Beijing citizens were touted as the country's number one user of the **Internet** but the city also ranks as an area with a relatively elevated rate of HIV/**AIDS** infection. A common saying has it that "Beijingers can talk about anything, Cantonese can eat anything, and Shanghainese can do anything." *See also* ARCHITECTURE; BEIJING SPRING.

BEIJING OPERA. *See* PEKING OPERA.

BEIJING SPRING. This term refers to two popular movements for democracy in recent Chinese history: the **Democracy Wall Movement (1978–1979)** and the second Beijing Spring pro-democracy movement from April to June 1989. *Beijing Spring (Beijing zhi qun)* is also the title of one of the major underground periodicals published in the 1978–1979 period.

The second Beijing Spring occurred in April–June 1989, when pro-democracy demonstrations broke out in China's capital city and in about 100 other urban areas. It ended with a massacre in and around Tiananmen Square in **Beijing** and in the city of Chengdu, Sichuan Province on 3–4 June 1989. The immediate cause of this movement was the sudden death of the reformist **Chinese Communist Party (CCP)** leader **Hu Yaobang**, who had lost his position as general secretary of the Communist Party in 1987 but had remained a beacon of hope for students, **intellectuals**, and other social groups that were committed to substantial political reform and liberalization. Hu's death in April 1989 and the rising power of hard-line conservatives, led by Premier **Li Peng**, seemed to spell an end to China's 10 years of reform that had begun in December 1978. Other festering social and economic problems helped generate the outburst of protests during the six-week Beijing Spring, including uncontrolled inflation, growing unemployment, **corruption** among Party **leaders**, and deteriorating conditions on China's college campuses.

At the height of the second Beijing Spring pro-democracy movement in late April and early May 1989, more than a million people filled the streets of the capital in peaceful demonstrations. The demonstrations were initiated largely by college students. But following a stern warning to the demonstrators in a 26 April editorial in the Party mouthpiece, *People's Daily*, and especially after the declaration of a hunger strike by students on 13 May, support quickly mushroomed among a variety of social groups, including intellectuals, newspaper reporters, government employees, urban residents (*shimin*), workers, peasants, and even some military and lower-ranking CCP personnel. Demands ranged from calls for more money for **education**, to government recognition of the movement as "patriotic." Students also demanded that a dialogue be held with the government (which, in fact, occurred on nationwide television), that **Deng Xiaoping** and Li Peng retire, and that there be fundamental institutional changes toward greater democracy, legality, and individual freedoms.

Just as the demonstrations seemed to be winding down and the hunger strike was called off, the government summarily declared martial law on the night of 19 May, opening the way for the **People's Liberation Army (PLA)** to enter the capital, the first time regular army units had entered the city since its **"liberation"** (*jiefang*) in 1949. Yet even the entry of overwhelming military force from the local garrison command in Beijing did not stifle the movement so much as reenergize it, as huge demonstrations occurred on 21 and 23 May. Urban residents and students joined in blocking military vehicles and established a defensive cordon around Tiananmen Square. For more than two weeks, a stalemate ensued as students refused to budge from Tiananmen (although the numbers occupying the increasingly fetid square diminished substantially) and the government, acting on the advice of General Secretary **Zhao Ziyang**, apparently refused to authorize the use of lethal force against the Beijing citizenry. With the Standing Committee of the **Politburo** split evenly between hardliners (Li Peng and **Yao Yilin**) and more moderate leaders (Zhao Ziyang and **Hu Qili**), the role of Deng Xiaoping and the **"revolutionary elders"** (*geming yuanlao*) of **Yang Shangkun**, **Peng Zhen**, **Wang Zhen**, and others was increasingly in favor of deploying force against the demonstrators, who were described in a critical and highly inflammatory report as fomenting "armed counterrevolutionary riots," this despite the overwhelming peaceful nature of all the massive demonstrations.

While Zhao Ziyang attempted to resign his post and was later purged, orders were given from Deng Xiaoping (who still headed the key Central **Military Affairs Commission [MAC]**) to put down the pro-democracy movement with a massive display of lethal force. Moving swiftly with coordinated actions throughout the city on the night of 3 June and the early morning hours of 4 June, elements of the PLA's 27th Army and the People's Armed Police (PAP) moved along Beijing's Chang'an Avenue toward Tiananmen Square with troops firing on student demonstrators and bystanders in and around the Square and in outlying parts of the city, where the highest number of casualties apparently occurred. Upward of 2,000 people were killed in the military assault, although a final count is still unavailable. (Immediately after the crackdown, the Chinese government admitted to only 300 dead, with many of the casualties supposedly occurring among PLA soldiers.) By the morning of 4 June, Tiananmen was "recaptured" by the PLA and the city was put under virtual military occupation that lasted for several weeks. The violence that flared in Chengdu involved PLA troops clearing the city center of student protests. In **Shanghai**, large-scale protests were ended peacefully by the successful efforts of then-Mayor **Jiang Zemin**, although eight people were killed when an express train ran into a human barricade trying to prevent soldiers from entering the city. With movement leaders either killed or on the run—several, including **Wu'er Kaixi**, made it out of the country—this second Beijing Spring came to a rapid halt while the entire movement was denounced in the official press as a "counterrevolutionary rebellion" (*geming baoluan*).

In the years since the crushing of the movement, a heavy police presence in Tiananmen Square has prevented any public display of remembrance for the movement in China; the largest public memorials have occurred in **Hong Kong**, where annual vigils on 4 June have brought out large numbers of the city's usually apolitical residents. Calls by prominent political personages in China, such as **Bao Tong** and Jiang Yanyong (a respected surgeon who exposed China's cover-up of the **SARS** epidemic), for the Chinese government to admit its errors in using military force to crush the demonstrations have yielded no response from authorities.

BETHUNE, NORMAN (1890–1939). A Canadian doctor and prominent surgeon from Montreal, Norman Bethune traveled to China in 1937, after having served with the Republican forces in the Spanish Civil War. Working behind Japanese enemy lines, Bethune brought rudimentary **health care** to many Chinese villages and to Communist soldiers wounded in battle. With very little available medicine, Bethune traveled throughout the Chinese countryside, where he set up mobile medical care units and tended night and day to the sick and wounded. After incurring a self-inflicted cut while operating, Bethune developed septicemia but lacked the necessary antibiotics to cure the disease from which he died in 1939. "In Memory of Norman Bethune," an essay written by **Mao Zedong**, lauds the doctor's selfless contributions to the Chinese people and was standard reading for Chinese children who were encouraged to put aside self-interest so as to "serve the people" (*weirenmin fuwu*).

"BIG-CHARACTER POSTERS" ("*DAZIBAO*"). A primary form of mass communication in China, big-character posters have been generally used for political purposes. First introduced in the **rectification**

campaign of 1942–1944, they were a staple feature during the **Anti-Rightist Campaign (1957–1958)** and especially during the **Cultural Revolution (1966–1976)** and the **Democracy Wall Movement (1978–1979)**. In 1980, the **National People's Congress (NPC)** outlawed "big-character posters" as part of its deletion of the "**four big freedoms**" (*sida ziyou*) from the state constitution in reaction to the growth of democratic forces in Chinese society. Nevertheless, during subsequent periods of political conflict involving the general **population**, "big-character posters" criticizing the regime have appeared on university campuses and at other sites of political protest. Thousands of such posters were mounted during the second **Beijing Spring** from April to June 1989 and have been preserved in a series of volumes on the 1989 Democracy Movement in China.

The popularity of "big-character posters" is in their direct appeal to the general population. Posters are written with Chinese ink brushes that produce large, easy-to-read Chinese-language characters and then are pasted on the network of walls that dominate the landscape in most Chinese cities and villages. During the mass mobilization campaigns directed by the government, such as in 1957–1958, they served the interests of the **Chinese Communist Party (CCP)** political leadership by directly communicating with the general populace, thereby circumventing the official press that, at the popular level, is often ignored or difficult to understand for many Chinese with limited literacy. During the initial stages of the Cultural Revolution, Mao Zedong authored his own "big-character poster" entitled "Bombard the Headquarters" (*paoda silingbu*) to attack his main political rival, **Liu Shaoqi**. In this way, Mao circumvented the CCP Propaganda Department, whose control over the regular channels of communication (newspapers, radio, and television) was purportedly in the hands of Liu's supporters. Mao's action legitimated the use of posters, which quickly became the major tool by which various **Red Guard** factions attacked government officials, **intellectuals**, and one another.

The appearance of "big-character posters" in the 1978–1979 Democracy Wall Movement was initially praised by **Deng Xiaoping** in his struggle at that time with **Hua Guofeng** and members of the radical leftist "**two whatevers**" (*liangge fanshi*) faction. After Deng consolidated power in 1979–1980, however, he quickly turned against the Democracy Wall Movement and persecuted its **leaders**, such as **Wei Jingsheng**, who was arrested in March 1979 for authoring perhaps one of the most famous "big-character posters" in China's recent history on the subject of democracy. In 1980, Deng thus supported abolishing the legal use of the posters that had been recognized in Article 45 of the state constitution of the **People's Republic of China** (**PRC**). Nine years later, during the second Beijing Spring, thousands of "big-character posters" appeared in **Beijing** and many other Chinese cities, some calling for Deng's resignation and quoting his own words on the need for reform. But since the Democracy Movement was crushed in June 1989, few posters have appeared publicly as the strong arm of state control prevents spontaneous political expression.

BIRTH CONTROL. *See* ONE-CHILD POLICY.

BO YIBO (1908–2007). Bo Yibo became a member of the **Chinese Communist Party** (**CCP**) Central Committee in 1945 and was elevated to the **Politburo** in 1956. Throughout the 1950s and early 1960s, he served in various posts dealing with the **economy**, such as minister of finance and the vice-chairman of the State Planning Commission. In 1956, he was appointed an alternate member of the Politburo and a vice-premier. After his purge during the **Cultural Revolution (1966–1976)** resulting from a close relationship to State Chairman **Liu Shaoqi**, Bo was rehabilitated in 1978 and assumed key positions in the government overseeing the economy and in the Party, including vice-premier, state councilor, and vice-minister on the State Commission for Restructuring the Chinese Economy. After playing a major role in Party **rectification campaigns** from 1983 to 1987, Bo joined the **Central Advisory Commission** (**CAC**) as one of its vice-chairmen in nominal "retirement," but reportedly approved of the 1987 removal of **Hu Yaobang** as CCP General Secretary and the military crackdown on the second **Beijing Spring** in June 1989. Bo Yibo's son, Bo Xilai, was appointed mayor of the northeast city of Dalian in 1993, where he has pushed for strong protection of the **environment** through strict enforcement of anti-pollution laws while he also frequently appears on local television to take questions from city residents.

"BOURGEOIS LIBERALIZATION" ("ZICHANJIEJI ZI-YOUHUA").

The catchall term frequently used by the **Chinese Communist Party (CCP)** leadership to criticize the political, social, and cultural values of Western liberalism that Chinese **intellectuals** and young people found attractive in the 1980s and 1990s and that clash with socialist orthodoxy. Despite the greater openness in China since the beginning of the reforms in 1978–1979, elements in the Communist regime fear the inherent attraction of Western notions of individual freedom and democracy that have been decried as "decadent capitalist ideology" and "**always thinking of money**" (*yiqie xiang qian kan*). For many relatively liberal Chinese intellectuals and artists, "bourgeois" ideas involve more profound values, such as respect for scientific knowledge over dogma, greater attention to talent instead of political and personal favoritism, and more independence for academic research and artistic creation—realms that the CCP has controlled since the 1940s. Chinese intellectuals would also like to see greater freedom to explore the verities of the official orthodoxy of **Marxism–Leninism–Mao Zedong Thought** instead of unquestioned obedience.

The regime's opposition to "bourgeois liberalization" began with an attack in the *People's Daily* on 1 January 1979 and peaked in 1986–1987 when a nationwide "anti-bourgeois liberalization" campaign was inaugurated following student demonstrations in **Beijing** and **Shanghai** in late 1986 that culminated in the ouster of CCP General Secretary **Hu Yaobang**. Although official media, such as the *People's Daily*, were full of vitriolic denunciations of Western ideas and cultural values, at schools and universities, the campaign was essentially ignored, even by local CCP personnel who themselves often found "bourgeois liberal" ideas attractive. Following the crackdown against the second **Beijing Spring** in June 1989, criticism of "bourgeois liberalization" was renewed in the media and at schools and colleges, but many intellectuals and students boycotted the campaign. In the early 1990s, the campaign degenerated into an effort by the authorities to punish individuals with foreign friends and contacts. By 1993, however, the regime largely dropped the "anti-bourgeois liberalization" rhetoric and concentrated on the promotion of market **socialism** and other official slogans.

BROADCASTING AND TELEVISION. China currently has only two national-level television stations—China Central Television (CCTV) and China Educational Television (CETV)—both of which are part of the China Broadcasting, Film, and Television Group. CCTV runs 11 channels, including an international channel, and an English-language channel, both of which are available worldwide via satellite and, in May 2005, launched a 24-hour news channel. Provincial-level broadcasters in China, such as the television stations of **Beijing**, Hunan, and the **Shanghai** Media Group, have a national reach and are major outlets for international programming. Television channels in China are government-controlled at the central and provincial level and most domestic programming tends to conservative content such as documentaries, quiz shows, and team competitions, although more programs have emerged from private sources in recent years. Foreign programming includes TV series, movies, animation films, and even such programs as Nickelodeon's "Kids' Choice Awards," whose often outrageous content is toned down for a Chinese youth audience totaling 300 million children under the age of 14. Government approval of foreign programming is required and is bought by China International TV Corporation, which was established in 1992. Encore International is a private company and is one of the largest providers of international programming to the China market while Viacom has a 24-hour MTV channel in Guangdong Province. Hunan TV emerged as a major player in China's media market when, in 1997, the station introduced a satellite channel and introduced such popular shows as "Citadel of Happiness," "Who's the Hero," and the enormously popular "Super Girl" contest that reportedly brought in 400 million viewers. Shanghai Media Group started as a merger of mostly local TV and radio interests and grew to encompass pay television, TV production, home-shopping, music labels, newspapers and magazines, sports teams and arenas, theaters, websites and **Internet** TV ventures. The Shanghai International Television Festival, founded in 1986 and held in conjunction with the Shanghai International Film Festival, is the largest international television-related event in China.

China National Radio is the state-run broadcaster with eight channels while China Radio International (the successor to Radio Peking) broadcasts internationally in 38 languages to more than 60 countries.

Personnel are trained at the Beijing Broadcasting Institute and other such facilities. With the advent of podcasting in China—a **technology** that enables individuals to produce their own songs and videos and upload them to a website—Chinese government control of broadcasting outlets is increasingly challenged by such popular Web sites as Toodou.com operated out of Shanghai. Utilizing free open-source software on the Web that allows anyone with a webcam or Ipod to create his or her own channel of video or audio content, Toodou in 2005 operated 13,000 channels, although it self-censors anything pornographic or critical of the Chinese government.

"BUREAUCRATISM" (*"GUANLIAOZHUYI"*). During the Maoist era (1949–1976), this term was used to characterize the insensitivity and detachment of Party and government personnel from the interests of the general **population**. The unwillingness of Party and state **cadres** to carry out investigations of practical conditions and to explain the policies of the government was a sign of being "divorced from the masses." "Bureaucratism" violated the "**mass line**" and was one of the major targets in the policy advocated by **Mao Zedong** during the **Cultural Revolution (1966–1976)** to have cadres undergo **transfer to lower levels**, where they spent years at **May Seventh Cadre Schools** in the countryside. Democratic critics of the Communist system in China see "bureaucratism" as a major outgrowth of totalitarianism and believe that democratic procedures are the only mechanisms for keeping it in check. In the 1990s and early 2000s, China unveiled three separate plans to streamline its huge government and eliminate overlapping responsibilities that contribute to bureaucratic inefficiency and waste. The latest of these plans, announced in 2004, would create independent regulatory bodies to oversee **banking and finance**, **state-owned enterprises** (**SOEs**) and assets, and the food and drug industries. State companies and the central ministries that support them would be stripped of the power to develop and carry out economic policy. Such proposals can take years to implement and are often watered down by competing factions and the very bureaucratic interests that such plans target to undercut.

"BURNING BOOKS AND BURYING SCHOLARS ALIVE" (*"FENSHU KENGRU"*). This phrase originated with the tyrannical acts of China's first emperor, Qin Shihuang (221–207 BC), who attempted to destroy the original Confucian texts and killed the scholars who had kept alive the ancient sage's teachings. Historically, Emperor Qin was vilified for attempting to destroy the Confucian canon. But during the 1973–1975 **Anti-Lin [Biao], Anti-Confucian Campaign**, the radical leftist faction behind the ideological and political struggle that was aimed at **Zhou Enlai** reversed this traditional historical judgment. They praised Qin Shihuang for playing a progressive role in history by "burning" the Confucian texts that had only confused people and prevented the unification of thought. A practitioner of Legalism, Emperor Qin, it was said, acted properly in eliminating contrary political principles, thereby enabling him to unify several states into a single empire. "Burying the scholars" was also justified by the radicals in that it eliminated supposedly backward-looking **intellectuals** who stood for restoring the old order. With Confucian scholars representing **"feudalism"** and Qin promoting "centralism," in the contemporary version of this struggle, defenders of the former had to be destroyed.

Politically, this phrase and the entire Anti-Lin and Anti-Confucian campaign aimed at justifying in historical terms the radicals' assault on Zhou Enlai and top **leaders** of the **Chinese Communist Party (CCP)** who were returning to power after many years in exile and who were intent on "restoring" the CCP to the status quo prior to the **Cultural Revolution (1966–1976)**. This is an example of how historical allusions are used as frequent tools of debate by various political groups.

– C –

"CADRES" (*"GANBU"*). This generic term refers to all government personnel in China. Party cadres belong to the **Chinese Communist Party (CCP)** and may also hold positions in the **government structure** or the **People's Liberation Army (PLA)**. Non-Party cadres hold positions in the government or army without any responsibilities in the CCP. Cadres have official duties and are paid by the state; not all Party members are cadres because most rank-and-file Party members do not have official positions in either the CCP or the government. Cadres work in both urban and rural areas, although positions in the cities are most prized.

In many ways, the training and discipline instilled in hundreds of thousands of cadres who filled CCP ranks and built and operated its elaborate structure down to the village level were responsible for the rise of the CCP to power in 1949 over its **Kuomintang (KMT)** rivals whose organizational abilities, especially at the grassroots, were marked by enormous **corruption.** During the early years of CCP rule, this army of cadres was responsible for the relatively swift implementation of such crucial policies as **land reform (1950–1952)** in the countryside and the beginnings of industrialization in the cities, along with staffing the urban networks of the "**basic unit**" (*jiben danwei*) system. During the **Cultural Revolution (1966–1976),** cadres were divided into four categories: good; comparatively good; those who had committed serious mistakes but who were not anti-Party, anti-socialist "rightists;" and a small number of anti-Party, anti-socialist "rightists." This categorization was based on whether one supported Chairman **Mao Zedong** and his policies; gave prominence to politics; and had a revolutionary will. Although cadres have been afforded considerable privileges in Chinese society—cheap housing, relatively high wages, and job security—they were frequent targets of political campaigns.

Since the beginning of the economic reforms in 1978–1979, cadres have been more secure from political attack, but their economic security has been threatened by wages that are relatively low in comparison to the private sector, and by the wage stagnation that accompanied the periods of intense inflation in the 1980s and 1990s. Still, many cadres in key positions in government ministries and **state-owned enterprises (SOEs)** have managed to thrive from the economic reforms so much so that, according to polls in China, they are the major beneficiaries of government policy, more than private entrepreneurs, workers, and farmers. Following complaints against corruption in the 1989 second **Beijing Spring**, all cadres were encouraged to return to the selfless and plain-living model of their predecessors. This was followed in a 1996 speech by **Jiang Zemin**, who criticized younger cadres for poor ideological style and a lack of organization and discipline while *People's Daily* urged cadres to integrate Confucian ethics with Marxism so that notions of "self-accomplishment" would lead to improvement in ethical standards. Efforts at regularizing and professionalizing the selection and promotion of cadres in China in the midst of its economic reform and globalization came in the 1995 "Interim Regulations on Selection and Appointment of Party and Government Leading Cadres." *See also* "BUREAUCRATICISM."

CAMBODIA (KAMPUCHEA). Although influenced culturally and religiously primarily by **India**, Cambodia has been the target of Chinese political interests for more than two millennia. During the Yuan dynasty (AD 1260–1368 A.D.), Mongol invaders from China sought to split up the powerful state of Champa that encompassed present-day Cambodia and South **Vietnam**. In the modern era, China has been deeply involved in international conferences and **United Nations** (**UN**) actions affecting the country. During the 1954 Geneva Conference that ended the first Indochina War between France and the Vietminh (i.e., the Vietnamese Communists), China played an active role in ensuring a successful conclusion to the conference by pressuring its Communist allies in Cambodia (the Khmers-Issaraks) to accept the agreement. Following the establishment of diplomatic relations between Cambodia and the **People's Republic of China** (**PRC**) in 1958, China pursued a policy of strict neutrality on Cambodia throughout the late 1950s and early 1960s and courted its non-Communist head of state, Prince Norodom Sihanouk, with frequent reciprocal state visits and generous economic assistance. The presence of a large Chinese immigrant colony in Cambodia reinforced China's attention to its relations with the Southeast Asian nation, which in 1960 led to the signing of a Treaty of Friendship and Non-Aggression, along with several economic agreements. From 1963 onward, Prince Sihanouk visited China almost every year to seek help in convening an international conference that, in the wake of the growing tension between South and North Vietnam and increased **United States** involvement in the region, would guarantee Cambodia's boundaries and neutrality and replace American aid, which the prince had rejected in November 1963. China's own increasing involvement in the Vietnam conflict and the advent of the **Cultural Revolution** (**1966–1976**), however, created severe tensions in Sino–Cambodian relations that, by the late 1960s, verged on a breakdown.

The coup d'état in Cambodia in March 1970 that ousted Prince Sihanouk and installed General Lon Nol, an American ally, fundamentally altered Sino–Cambodian relations. Up to this point, China had differentiated its relations with Cambodia, Laos, and Vietnam, pursuing formal neutrality with the former two and a tenuous alliance with the latter. But from 1970 onward, China spoke of a single, unified "Indochinese war" and increased its influence in all three countries to the detriment of the **Soviet Union** and the U.S., although China refrained from providing direct military assistance to Cambodia's Communist rebels known as the Khmer Rouge. In May 1970, Sihanouk, who—fleeing the Lon Nol coup—had been granted protection in **Beijing**, announced the formation of the Royal Government of National Union of Kampuchea, which China formally recognized, while at the same time denouncing the U.S. troop incursion into Cambodia as a "provocation to the Chinese people." By 1973, after China signed the 1973 Paris Accord ending the American role in the Vietnam War, China returned to themes of "peaceful coexistence" in the region, reiterating its support for Prince Sihanouk and opposing rising Vietnamese "hegemony" in the region. Sihanouk continued to operate out of Beijing, where a National United Front of Kampuchea (FUNK) was established in exile as efforts were made on China's part to bring about reconciliation between Sihanouk and the increasingly powerful Cambodian Khmer Rouge guerrilla forces.

Following the Communist Vietnamese conquest of the South in 1975, China reoriented its policy toward Cambodia to fit, ironically enough, its policy with the U.S. As China acknowledged the desirability of a continuing American presence in Asia, China and the U.S. coordinated their policies vis-à-vis Cambodia, agreeing on the maintenance of a neutral coalition government under Sihanouk, as opposed to a government headed by Lon Nol, the Khmer Rouge, or forces aligned with Vietnam. The triumph of the Khmer Rouge forces in Cambodia and their rapid defeat in December 1978 at the hands of the invading Vietnamese army led to closer U.S.–China coordination in denying the pro-Vietnamese government in Phnom Penh, a UN seat in favor of the anti-Vietnamese coalition (then known as the Coalition Government of Democratic Kampuchea) headed by Prince Sihanouk and in seeking assistance for anti-Vietnamese forces in the Cambodian bush, including the Khmer Rouge. Throughout the

1980s, however, divisions developed in Sino–U.S. strategy toward Cambodia as China showed greater inclination to support the leftist faction in the Coalition Government of Democratic Kampuchea set up in June 1981 that consisted of the Khmer Rouge, led by the notorious Pol Pot (who was considered responsible for the genocidal killings carried out by the Khmer Rouge following their takeover in the 1970s) and Khieu Samphan. Meanwhile, the U.S. favored the non-Communist factions of Prince Sihanouk and Son Sann. In 1988, China agreed to change its position on Cambodia, reducing its support for the Khmer Rouge and embracing a plan that called for a Vietnamese withdrawal and the establishment of a coalition government, including but not dominated by the Khmer Rouge, until elections could be held.

In 1991, a negotiated settlement on Cambodia was reached in Paris, marking the end of 13 years of fighting as China reduced its commitment to the Khmer Rouge and participated in overseeing UN-sponsored elections. In June 1997, reports of the capture of Khmer Rouge leader Pol Pot raised the possibility of placing the notorious leader on trial under UN auspices for crimes against humanity, an action that was opposed by the PRC (a member of the UN Security Council). Wanting to wash its hands of any further intervention in Cambodian affairs, China's Premier **Li Peng** told a high-level delegation from Cambodia in 1997 that even after a coup d'etat was executed by former Khmer Rouge leader Hun Sen, China had no intention of interfering in Cambodia's internal affairs, although it continued to grant Prince Norodom Sihanouk access to medical treatment in Beijing, where he and his family maintained a residence. From the late 1990s onward, China and Cambodia maintained a relationship as "good neighbors" and "good partners," as China supported the goals of the Cambodian government to build political stability and recover economically by providing it with preferential loans and working in concert with Cambodia in the Greater Mekong Sub-region Economic Construction Program, which also includes Laos, Myanmar (Burma), Thailand, and Vietnam. Cambodia, in return, remained a staunch defender of the "one-China policy" pursued by the PRC and expressed its opposition to any form of **Taiwan** independence. Upon the abdication in 2003 of Norodom Sihanouk, the newly installed King Norodom Sihamoni, who had lived in Beijing for years, left China and became Cambodia's first new monarch in 60 years. *See also* ASSOCIATION OF SOUTHEAST ASIAN NATIONS (ASEAN); FOREIGN POLICY.

"CAPITALIST ROADER" (*"ZOUZIPAI"*). A term of opprobrium used in the 1960s by **Mao Zedong** and his supporters among radical **Chinese Communist Party** (**CCP**) factions to label the chairman's opponents. It was used to attack **Liu Shaoqi**, Mao's first designated successor and target of his ideological ire, in the **Cultural Revolution** (**1966–1976**). Labeled "the number one capitalist roader in the Party," Liu did not actually advocate capitalism for China. The same can be said for **Deng Xiaoping**, who was described as the "number two capitalist roader" because both men had argued for more liberal economic policies in the early 1960s than the overwhelming state control pushed by Mao Zedong and leftists. "Capitalist roader" became Mao's ideological cudgel for elevating genuine policy differences over the proper role of the state in agricultural policy into highly charged ideological battles. In this Chinese version of political McCarthyism, Liu Shaoqi and thousands of others in the CCP found it difficult to defend themselves against such hot-button labels, particularly in a society that lacked institutions for rational dialogue. Accusations were equated with the truth, and Mao's imprimatur became the ultimate sanction for the spurious claims that, in advocating a slower pace of agricultural collectivization in the 1950s and 1960s and foreseeing at least a limited role for the market, Liu and other CCP **leaders** were advocating "capitalism."

Mao Zedong first hinted in 1965 that the CCP—the purported vanguard of proletarian class consciousness—was itself infected with "capitalist roaders." At that time, the Central Committee of the CCP issued the document inspired by Mao on "Some Current Problems Raised in the **Socialist Education Movement** in the Rural Areas." Here, it was explicitly noted that "the crux of the Socialist Education Movement is to purge the capitalist roaders in authority within the Party." These purported "capitalist roaders" were, according to the document, not only found among ex-landlords, rich peasants, and other suspect social groups, but also in CCP provincial organizations and even central CCP departments. In the organic metaphors that became so prevalent in ideologically charged CCP documents, these individuals were accused of having "wormed their way into the Party."

"Capitalist roader" was generally dropped from CCP ideological proclamations after the Cultural Revolution and especially after the rise of Deng Xiaoping in 1978 and the inauguration of dramatic economic reforms. Yet, such terminology still finds its way into statements and proclamations by remnant leftist forces in the CCP, such as **Deng Liqun**.

CENSORSHIP (*SHENCHA*). Control of the press, films, and other works of **literature and the arts** has been a central component of the **Chinese Communist Party (CCP)** dictatorship. Beginning in the 1940s and continuing to the early 2000s, the editorials and news reports of the press, especially the *People's Daily*, books and magazines, **cinema and film**, literature and the arts, and **broadcasting and television** have been subject to political control. From the center to the localities, the CCP exercises strict management of the media through its Propaganda Department (recently renamed Publicity Department) and other agencies such as the General Administration of Press and Publication and the State Administration of Radio, Film, and Television, which operate under the direct authority of the State Council.

Three kinds of censorship exist in China. The first is self-censorship, representing conscious efforts by news reporters and writers to remain within the guidelines established by the CCP and to express views consistent with CCP policies. Because policies are subject to sudden and arbitrary change, self-censorship requires constant attention to even the most subtle shift in the **basic line of the Party**. The second form of censorship is the formal system of review for newspapers, books, and cinema and film scripts. Newspapers, such as the *People's Daily*, have set up an elaborate system involving review of draft editorials prior to publication by the chief- and vice-editors as well as by the director of the paper. Editorials and articles by official, un-named "commentators" undergo a continuous process of revision before they are sent to Party and state **leaders** for final review. Party leaders who are assigned responsibility for a certain field, such as **foreign policy**, will review all editorials dealing with the area under their purview. In addition, the central leader in charge of propaganda reviews virtually all editorials and commentaries, while especially important pieces are sent to the CCP general secretary for his final imprimatur. Revisions by the top leader become the standard that all reporters must follow. Editorials, commentators, and straight news items from the *People's Daily* are often republished in other central and lower-level newspapers, creating an enormous uniformity of opinion and message. Following the inauguration of the 1978–1979 economic reforms, the censorship regime was relaxed somewhat by General Secretary **Hu Yaobang**, who, in a 1986 speech, instructed editors that 80% of reporting should focus on achievements in modernization and only 20% on shortcomings. This led some newspapers, most notably the Shanghai-based **World Economic Herald** (*Shijie jingji daobao*) and *Southern Weekend* (*Nanfang zhoubao*) in **Guangzhou (Canton)** to avoid, to a certain degree, the censorial system, although both ultimately faced shutdown and/or major alterations in article content, especially following the June 1989 military crackdown on the second **Beijing Spring**.

The third form of censorship is post-publication review. Authors of editorials or news items that are published and then singled out for **criticism** by top leaders will usually encounter severe repercussions. Books, magazine articles, and films that are initially approved for publication, or somehow get by the censors, are often subject to post-publication censorship by being banned, confiscated, and destroyed with their editors and journalists subject to dismissal, as proved to be the fate of the *World Economic Herald* after 1989 and, more recently, the *Beijing News* in 2005.

Opposition to CCP censorship has been a constant theme in political protests in post-1949 China from the **Hundred Flowers** (**1956–1957**) to the 1989 second Beijing Spring pro-democracy movement. In the mid-1980s, a policy of relative relaxation on censorship was announced by the CCP's **Hu Qili**, who, in a 1984 speech to the National Writers' Congress, decried the political excesses that produce derogatory labels and decrees about what writers should and should not write. But as writers and **intellectuals** began to test the limits, they were reminded by Hu Qili of their "social responsibilities," a thinly veiled warning for them to exercise self-censorship. In 1986, on the 30th anniversary of the Hundred Flowers, the new head of the CCP Propaganda Department, **Zhu Houze**, called for a new

Hundred Flowers in China and was backed up by **Wang Meng**, the newly appointed minister of culture. During the 1989 second Beijing Spring, journalists and reporters joined in the street demonstrations carrying banners reading "Don't Force Us to Lie" and, prompted once again by Hu Qili, they engaged in relatively open reporting throughout the pro-democracy movement. A large group of reporters, led by veteran *People's Daily* director **Hu Jiwei**, also issued a statement during the movement calling for radical changes in CCP press controls. Following the military crackdown on 4 June, television news broadcasters exhibited their disgust with the government action by dressing in black while reporting the news. All these efforts came to naught, however, as protesting newsmen were fired from their positions, and individual reporters with an outspoken reputation, such as **Dai Qing**, were imprisoned.

Throughout the 1990s, the tightly controlled censorship system was reestablished, first under strict control of the military, and then under the authority of a rebuilt CCP propaganda apparatus headed by more conservative leaders, such as Wang Renzhi, **Ding Guan'gen**, and **Zeng Qinglong**. In the initial stages of the **SARS** crisis, from 2002 to early 2003, China's censorship system prevented an open and transparent accounting of the extent of the epidemic until reports surfacing from on-the-scene doctors led to an open admission by the government of the earlier cover-up. But despite the belief that with the replacement of the more hard-line **Jiang Zemin** as general secretary of the CCP by **Hu Jintao** in November 2002, the expectation of relaxed media controls did not transpire even as a policy paper circulated in the high ranks of the CCP called on officials to be more responsive to media requests for information and interviews. In the early months of 2004, journalists who pioneered stories on SARS were imprisoned and transparency proposals were shelved as official prohibitions remained in place against reporting on such stories as the possibility of a reevaluation of China's **currency**, poor job prospects for recent university graduates, suspect business activities of government officials in Anhui Province, and sales at bargain basement prices of state-owned assets. Similar blocks were placed on publication of books on anything to do with official involvement in one-night stands and extra-marital affairs; critics of the state propaganda machinery claimed that it shielded corrupt officials and whitewashed the darkest moments in the nation's history. The major press organ of the Communist **Youth League**, the *China Youth Daily*, was similarly censored for its reporting on abuse of power by local officials in the Shenzhen **Special Economic Zone (SEZ)**, while a newspaper with a liberal slant, the *21st Century Globe Herald*, was closed down and then banned outright in 2004, apparently for such articles as "The death of a radio hostess on a deputy mayor's bed," and "Nanjing Normal University female students were required to dance with officials." A public letter issued in February 2006 by former CCP officials and journalists, including **Li Rui, Hu Jiwei**, and Zhu Houze, denounced recent closings of newspapers, fueling a growing backlash against censorship. In 2005, China topped the list of countries with the most journalists—32—in jail (the seventh year in a row in which China headed the list) for their alleged activities on the **Internet** and for writing articles critical of the CCP that purportedly violated national security laws. *See also* "INTERNAL MATERIALS"; THREE GORGES DAM PROJECT.

CENTRAL ADVISORY COMMISSION (CAC). Established in 1982 and abolished 10 years later at the October 1992 14th National Party Congress, the Central Advisory Commission (*zhongyang guwen weiyuanhui*) was intended as a kind of "halfway" house between full retirement and active service for elderly **leaders** of the **Chinese Communist Party (CCP)**. Following the advent of the economic and political reforms in 1978–1979, the CAC was devised by **Deng Xiaoping** as an institutional arrangement to encourage senior Party and military leaders to give up their positions of authority without a total loss of influence or prestige. Initially, the CAC was composed of more than 170 aged leaders, including Deng Xiaoping as its chair. Commissions were also set up at the provincial level and below to receive elderly local leaders. Although all leaders with more than 40 years of service to the CCP were "qualified" to join the CAC, the intention of Deng Xiaoping was to encourage those older leaders, such as **Chen Yun**, who often opposed reform efforts, to join its ranks. The CAC was designed to end lifelong tenure for Party and government positions in China, a tradition that effectively prevented younger (and presumably more pro-reform) CCP leaders to move up the ranks into positions of authority. Commission members were given the right to "consult" with formal Party and government leaders, and they could even attend Central Committee and **Politburo** meetings, but without exercising a formal vote. In reality, CAC members, such as **Bo Yibo**, continued to intervene in a decisive manner during the high-level decision in January 1987 that forced CCP General Secretary **Hu Yaobang** to step down after student demonstrations broke out in a number of cities. The role of these nominally retired "**revolutionary elders**" (*geming yuanlao*) was also crucial during the 1989 second **Beijing Spring** to produce a consensus among the top leadership to use military force against pro-democracy demonstrators and to demand the ouster of CCP General Secretary **Zhao Ziyang**. For critics of China's authoritarian **government structure**, the experience of the CAC is another example of the weakness of political institutions and rules in a country where "rule by man" prevails over "rule by law."

CENTRAL COMMITTEE OF THE CHINESE COMMUNIST PARTY. *See* CHINESE COMMUNIST PARTY (CCP).

CENTRAL DISCIPLINE INSPECTION COMMISSION (CDIC). The internal disciplinary and watchdog organization of the **Chinese Communist Party** (**CCP**), the CDIC (*zhongyang jilu jiancha weiyuanhui*) was established in 1977, soon after the death of **Mao Zedong** and the purge of the radical leftist faction led by Mao's widow, **Jiang Qing**. The original purpose of the commission was to ferret out CCP members who had risen through the ranks during the **Cultural Revolution (1966–1976)** and, theoretically, to control abuses by Party members of their subordinates and the general populace. In 1982, the power of the CDIC was expanded to include monitoring adherence to Party rules and regulations, the reporting of violations of Party discipline to Party committees, including to the Central Committee, and the ensuring of implementation of Party policies. The reining in of increased **corruption** by Party members evidently brought on by the economic reforms and **open-door policy** was also a major charge of the CDIC.

Initially headed by the relatively conservative Party leader **Chen Yun**, the CDIC quickly degenerated into a political instrument that was used by Chen and other opponents of economic reforms to persecute pro-reform Party members at the provincial level and below. Charges of embezzlement, corruption, bribery, and smuggling were brought against noted Party reformers, who generally regarded the accusations as fabrications. Party members lived in constant fear that CDIC investigators would seize their personal property, calculate its value, and compare this figure to one's salary with any discrepancy leading to formal charges of corruption and disciplinary action on the assumption that the gains were ill-gotten. Although the CDIC and its subordinate organs at the provincial level and below theoretically can bring charges against the highest officials in the CCP, regular Party members are extremely reluctant to report abuses by their superiors out of fear of retribution. As an internal disciplinary organization, the CDIC often protects Party members, especially top officials, from prosecution and punishment by the theoretically independent judiciary system. In that sense, it is widely perceived in China as yet another "special privilege" enjoyed by CCP members.

A system of control was first employed during the 1950s and early 1960s modeled after a similar structure in the Communist Party of the **Soviet Union**. During the Cultural Revolution, however, these organs were abolished and replaced by the "mass" **criticism and self-criticism** (*piping yu ziwopiping*) advocated by Mao Zedong as a method of supervision of the Party that often simply degenerated into political persecution and wanton violence against CCP members and any and all political "enemies." After Mao's death, the CDIC was established to embed the disciplinary function firmly within the CCP hierarchy and to lead the assault on growing problems of corruption that afflicted all levels of the Party. As cases of corruption in the Party mushroomed, the CDIC took the lead in the anti-corruption campaign by issuing a circular in 1990 that urged stricter measures to combat all forms of corruption. The promulgation of the CCP (Trial Implementation) "Regulations on Inner-Party Supervision and the CCP Regulations on Disciplinary Actions" were hailed as measures to strengthen inner-Party democracy and supervision and to safeguard Party unity and solidarity. Among the high-profile cases were the 1996 expulsion from the CCP of senior **Beijing** official Huang Jisheng for bribery and the expulsion in the following year of Beijing Municipal CCP Secretary **Chen Xitong** on charges of corruption that led to his subsequent imprisonment, although some in China believe the charges were trumped up as a payback for Chen's heavy use of coercion in the suppression of the 1989 second **Beijing Spring**. This was followed, in 2000, by the expulsion from all Party and government posts of Cheng Kejie, vice-chairman of the **National People's Congress (NPC)** Standing Committee, again on charges of serious corruption.

In 2004, as the Party leadership reiterated and expanded upon the need to rein in corruption that threatened the very legitimacy of the CCP, the CDIC issued a communiqué that highlighted such problems as officials imposing indiscriminate fees on villagers, law enforcement officials colluding with criminals, managers of **state-owned enterprises (SOEs)** illicitly stripping their companies of assets, officials making personal gains from land sales and building projects, and officials embezzling the wages of migrant workers. Like many pronunciamentos issued by CCP **leaders** in the last decade, this communiqué implored Party members to exercise authority by the law instead of arbitrary, peremptory actions that tend to alienate the general populace. In 2005, the deputy director of the CDIC warned that the CCP could lose power and likely self-destruct unless it eliminated corruption among its ranks. The CDIC also expressed support for the Administrative Approval Law and called on all Party members to support reform of the financial management system, especially the regulation on "separation between revenue and expenditure" as a way to root out pervasive financial corruption. Reform of the personnel system for **cadres** through introduction of a secret ballot system for major personnel appointments was also supported along with fixed tenure for leading Party and government posts and a system to govern resignation by leading cadres. Public bidding for construction projects, transfers of commercial land-use rights, transparent transactions of property rights and government procurements were also reforms endorsed by the CDIC. In 2005, the CDIC was headed by Wu Guanzheng, a member of the CCP **Politburo** Standing Committee.

CENTRAL PARTY SCHOOL. Located in the northwestern suburbs of **Beijing**, the Central Party School (*zhongyang dangxiao*) provides political training and ideological indoctrination for the leadership personnel of the **Chinese Communist Party** (**CCP**), primarily from Party organs below the central level. Students at the Central Party

School come from all over the country for lectures and discussion groups that deal with major policy initiatives, such as the economic reform instituted in 1978–1979, and to improve Party members' basic knowledge of CCP history and Party norms. The system of Party schools was established during the CCP's Yan'an Period (1936–1945) as institutes to indoctrinate the membership in Marxist–Leninist and Maoist ideology. After 1949, Party schools were not only established at the central level but also at the provincial level and below. In recent years, the curriculum of the Party schools has been depoliticized somewhat with the introduction of course work in such fields as Western theories of economics and personnel management. The fundamental ideological purpose of the Central Party School is still very important, however, as every shift in the **basic line of the Party** brings a concomitant change in the curriculum at the Party schools. A center of relatively liberal opinion in the CCP, the Central Party School has been subject to frequent purges and rectifications of its most outspoken members, such as Ruan Ming who was forced to flee to the West.

Throughout the 1990s and into the 2000s, the Central Party School and its provincial and local affiliates emerged as a major think tank and investigative arm of the CCP by conducting numerous surveys of opinions by Party members and the public in accord with the current political line of the leadership. Soon after the 16th National Party Congress in 2002 confronted broad complaints of **corruption** in CCP ranks by committing itself to strengthening the "ruling capabilities of the party," a survey of Party **cadres** above the county level indicated that more than half lacked the ability to "make scientific judgments of a situation" and "had difficulty tackling a complicated situation," as was made most apparent in the 2002–2003 **SARS** crisis. Similar surveys run by the Central Party School showed mass disaffection among Party ranks with a large percentage of cadres more concerned with their individual and family welfare than with service to the people. In addition to managing *Seeking Truth* (*Qiushi*), the primary theoretical journal of the CCP, the Central Party School also publishes *Study Times*, which, in 2003, contained articles advocating political reform. In 2004, the president of the Central Party School was vice president **Zeng Qinglong**, a member of the Standing Committee of the **Politburo**, the Party's highest decision-making body, and head of the Secretariat, who is a reputed protégé of former President **Jiang Zemin**. *See also* LEADERS.

CHAIRMAN OF THE CHINESE COMMUNIST PARTY. *See* CHINESE COMMUNIST PARTY (CCP).

CHEN BODA (1904–1989). Chen Boda served as political secretary and ghost writer to **Mao Zedong** during the Yan'an Period (1936–1945), when he helped shape the chairman's evolving **personality cult** (*geren chongbai*) and the contours of Mao Zedong Thought. In the early 1950s, he was involved in **Chinese Communist Party (CCP)** propaganda work and was vice-president of the Institute of Marxism–Leninism in **Beijing**. In 1956, he was appointed to the **Politburo** and became vice-director of the CCP Propaganda Department and, in 1968, became editor-in-chief of *Red Flag* (*Hongqi*). A radical during the **Cultural Revolution (1966–1976)**, Chen Boda headed the **Cultural Revolution Small Group**, with **Jiang Qing** as deputy head, until he was purged in 1970.

CHEN KAIGE (1952–). A prominent member of China's "Fifth Generation" of filmmakers (so named for their exposure to international cinema), Chen Kaige has produced such sterling classics as *Yellow Earth* (1984)—in conjunction with **Zhang Yimou**—and *Farewell My Concubine* (1993). The former tells the 1939 story of a soldier who goes to a village in the poverty-stricken area of northern Shaanxi Province to collect folk songs. He describes to the local peasants how **women** have been liberated in the nearby Communist redoubt of Yan'an. A local peasant girl, married at the age of 13 to an older man to whom she had been betrothed since infancy, sets out in search of Yan'an, only to be drowned in the process. Ultimately, the local peasants continue to seek salvation from the local gods, rather than **Mao Zedong**, the **People's Liberation Army (PLA)**, or themselves. *Farewell My Concubine* covers a vast swath of Chinese history from the Republican Era (1912–1949) to the **Cultural Revolution (1966–1976)** to the post-Mao period through the eyes of two **Peking Opera** singers. As in the opera, the film is filled with tragedies—of Republican-era **corruption**, the Japanese invasion, Communist oppression, and, lastly, the loss of Peking Opera traditions in the midst of over-commercialization. The film also contains the first explicit treatment of homosexuality in China in this medium. More recent films by Chen Kaige include the highly commercial *Together*, a sentimental story about a talented young violinist, the visually stunning epic *The Emperor and the Assassin* (1999), which traces the driving ambition of Ying Zheng, the King of Qin and China's first emperor Qin Shihuang, to unify seven kingdoms into one magnificent empire, and *The Promise* (2005), a high-profile martial arts film. *See also* CINEMA AND FILM.

CHEN MUHUA (1921–). Along with **Wu Yi** and **Jiang Qing**, Chen Muhua was one of the most senior **women** in the Chinese government and **Chinese Communist Party** (CCP) who served in various posts over a very long period of time. After studying building construction at Communications (*Jiaotong*) University in **Shanghai**, Chen served in the Ministry of Railways and the State Planning Commission and, beginning in 1961, was deputy bureau director of the Foreign Economic Liaison Commission and, in 1973, was elevated to the 10th CCP Central Committee. After the **Cultural Revolution** (**1966–1976**), Chen became a vice-premier in 1978 and served as minister of the State Family Planning Commission from 1981 to 1982, minister of foreign trade and economic relations from 1982 to 1985, and a state councilor from 1985 to 1987. She remained a member of the CCP Central Committee through the 14th National Party Congress in 1997, became president of the People's Bank of China from 1985 to 1988, and served as chair of the **All-China Federation of Women** from 1988 to 1998. *See also* BANKING AND FINANCE.

CHEN XILIAN (1913–1999). Chen Xilian rose to prominence in the Communist armies in the 1920s and 1930s, when he was closely associated with **Lin Biao** and **Liu Bocheng**. Chen became commander of the **Beijing** Military Region in 1974, a member of the Central **Military Affairs Commission** (MAC) in 1977, and served as a vice-premier. He was removed from his post as a **Politburo** member at the 1980 Fifth Plenum of the 11th National Party Congress and was virtually retired by his appointment to the **Central Advisory Commission** in 1982.

CHEN XITONG (1930–). After joining the **Chinese Communist Party (CCP)** in 1949 while a student in Chinese language at prestigious **Beida (Peking University)**, Chen Xitong served in various posts at the municipal and county level in the capital prior to 1979, when he became the vice-mayor of **Beijing**. In 1987, he was promoted to mayor of the city and deputy secretary of the Beijing Municipal CCP, a post he held until 1992. At the national level, he became a member of the CCP Central Committee at the 1982 12th National Party Congress and a member of the **Politburo** in 1992 at the 14th National Party Congress. During the second **Beijing Spring** in May–June 1989, Chen apparently aligned himself with Party hard-liners and, in a detailed official report issued in late June 1989, he defended the military action of 3–4 June 1989. In 1995, Chen was embroiled in a major **corruption** scandal that led to his expulsion from the CCP two years later and a sentence in 1998 of 16 years in prison by the Beijing People's High Court, actions that some observers believe was a payback for his awkward and heavy-handed handling of the second Beijing Spring movement. Chen's appeal to China's Supreme People's Court to reverse charges of accepting expensive gifts was denied. He is one of the highest-ranking officials in China ever to be sentenced by the courts.

CHEN YIZI (1940–). In 1987, Chen Yizi became the director of the Institute for Reform of China's Economic Structure (*zhongguo jingji tizhi gaige yanjiusuo*, abbreviated as *tigaisuo*) under the State Commission for Restructuring the Economy. He also served as the secretary in charge of daily operations of the Political Reform Office (*zhengzhi tizhi gaige bangongshi*, abbreviated as *zhenggaiban*) established by Premier **Zhao Ziyang** in 1986 and was one of Zhao's senior advisers. Accused by the Chinese government of fomenting student unrest during the 1989 second **Beijing Spring**, Chen fled China and thereafter took part in Paris in the formation of the **Front for a Democratic China**. In 2005, Chen headed the Center for Research on Chinese Contemporary History in New York and also served as the chairman of the Preparatory Committee for the New York memorial for Zhao Ziyang following his death in January 2005.

CHEN YONGGUI (1913–1986). After eking out a bare existence in Dazhai, Shanxi Province in the 1940s, Chen Yonggui began his rise to prominence in 1950 by organizing a **mutual aid team** composed of poor peasants. In 1953, during the establishment of **Agricultural Producers' Cooperatives (APCs)**, Chen was criticized for his own radical initiatives as a "supporter of utopian agrarian **socialism**." In 1963, Chen became Party secretary of the **Dazhai Brigade**, which, in 1965, gained national prominence as an example of "**self-reliance**" (*zili gengsheng*). "In Agriculture learn from Dazhai" became a slogan issued by **Mao Zedong** to idealize his vision of socialist **agriculture** in contrast to the more liberal, market-oriented approach of **Deng Xiaoping** and **Liu Shaoqi**.

During the **Cultural Revolution (1966–1976)**, Chen Yonggui came under renewed attack, yet he ended up playing a crucial role assisted by **Red Guards** in establishing the **Revolutionary Committee** for Shanxi Province. In April 1969, Chen was elected to the **Chinese Communist Party (CCP)** Central Committee at the Ninth National Party Congress and in 1971 he became first Party secretary of Xiyang County, Shanxi. In 1973, he was promoted to the CCP **Politburo** and traveled widely throughout China to propagate the Dazhai model. Following the inauguration of the economic reforms in 1978 at the **Third Plenum of the 11th CCP Central Committee**, Chen's political star faded quickly. In 1980 and 1982, he was dropped from all posts in the central leadership.

CHEN YUAN (1945–). Son of **Chen Yun**, China's economic czar and perennial conservative, Chen Yuan was trained as an engineer in the Automatic Control Department at **Qinghua University**. In 1983, he was appointed Party secretary of a West **Beijing** district; in 1984, was elevated to the Standing Committee of the Beijing Municipal Committee; and, in 1988, became a vice-governor of the People's Bank of China. In September 1991, Chen Yuan reportedly joined other members of China's so-called "**prince's faction**" (*taizidang*)—the adult offspring of senior **Chinese Communist Party** officials—in composing a neoconservative document entitled "Realistic Responses and Strategic Choices for China after the **Soviet Union** Upheaval," which called upon China to become an increasingly assertive force in international affairs. Chen steadily moved up the government hierarchy in China even after his father's death in 1995. In 2004, he was appointed governor of the

China Development Bank, the largest of the policy banks in China. *See also* BANKING AND FINANCE.

CHEN YUN (1905–1995). Born Liao Chenyun in a rural county outside **Shanghai**, Chen Yun became active in the early 1920s in the **trade union** movement, along with **Liu Shaoqi**, and joined the **Chinese Communist Party (CCP)** in 1925. He became a member of the CCP Central Committee in 1934 and worked in the Party Organization Department. In the mid-1930s, he was in the **Soviet Union** and in 1937 returned to China, accompanying **Kang Sheng** and Wang Ming (the pro-Soviet figure who vied with **Mao Zedong** for control of the CCP in the 1940s). In 1940, Chen became active in economic issues and worked in **Manchuria**. Throughout the 1950s and early 1960s, he served on the **Politburo** and as a vice-premier in charge of financial and economic affairs. From the mid-1960s to 1976, Chen was a member of the Central Committee but lived in self-imposed exile to avoid the radicalism of Mao Zedong. In the late 1970s, Chen opposed remnant pro-Mao radicals and endorsed the proposals by **Deng Xiaoping** for limited reforms in the **economy**. Throughout the 1980s, however, Chen led the CCP faction that was opposed to wholesale economic liberalization, calling instead for limitations to the market reforms in rural and urban areas and for maintaining a strong role for economic planning. Chen nominally retired from his posts in 1987, but, despite ill health, he nevertheless remained the leading opponent of liberal economic reform and a staunch critic of any and all political reform measures that would undermine the political power of the CCP. Yet, Chen also opposed the arrest of the dissident **Wei Jingsheng** and reportedly was against the decision in June 1989 to employ military force during the second **Beijing Spring**. Chen Yun died in 1995 at the age of 89, while his son, **Chen Yuan**, became a major figure in China's banking sector. As an indication of Chen Yun's status in the CCP pantheon of **leaders**, the two-volume *Selected Works of Chen Yun* was published in 1984.

CHEN ZHILI (1942–). One of the few **women** appointed to a high-level position in the Chinese government as minister of **education** in 1998, Chen Zhili joined the **Chinese Communist Party (CCP)** in 1961 and graduated from Fudan University in 1964, where she majored in Physics. Chen also conducted post-graduate work at the **Shanghai** Institute of Silicate under the Chinese Academy of Sciences (CAS) followed by a stint as a visiting scholar at the University of Pennsylvania's Materials Research Institute. In 1989, she became a deputy Party secretary in the Shanghai CP and in 1997 was elevated to deputy minister of the State Education Commission. A member of the CCP Central Committee since 1987, Chen is most noted for her devotion to the eradication of illiteracy in China. One of only five women to sit on the Central Committee elected at the 16th National Party Congress (2002), Chen is considered a crony of the former General Secretary and President **Jiang Zemin**. In 2004, Chen was promoted to state councilor. *See also* LEADERS.

CHI HAOTIAN (1929–). A full general in the **People's Liberation Army (PLA)**, Chi Haotian ranked as one of China's most important military figures. Starting as a signalman and squad leader when he joined the Red Army in his teens, Chi participated in a number of major military campaigns during the **Civil War (1946–1949)**. During the **Korean War (1950–1953)**, Chi served as a battalion instructor and regimental political officer and in the late 1950s studied at the Infantry School of the PLA. Purged during the **Cultural Revolution (1966–1976)**, Chi Haotian returned to army and political life in the 1970s and became the deputy **political commissar** of the **Beijing** Military Region and served as a leading official at *Liberation Army Daily*, the PLA newspaper. From 1977 to 1982, he was deputy chief-of-staff of the PLA. He became head of the PLA General Staff from 1987 until 1992, when he was appointed minister of defense. A member of the **Chinese Communist Party (CCP)** Central Committee in 1985, Chi Haotian was appointed to the Central **Military Affairs Commission (MAC)** in 1988 and was promoted to the **Politburo** in 1995, when he became vice-chairman of MAC and a state councilor. During the military crackdown on pro-democracy demonstrators during the second **Beijing Spring** on 3–4 June 1989, Chi Haotian commanded PLA troops involved in the operation. Following his retirement, Chi Haotian issued a not-so-subtle criticism of **Jiang Zemin** apparently for holding on to his positions as chairman of both the Party and State MAC until September 2004, long after giving up the position of CCP general secretary and the presidency to **Hu Jintao** in November 2002.

"CHICU." Chinese phrase literally meaning "to eat vinegar" refers to jealousy in affairs of the heart. "You eat vinegar!" is what the comely but innocent bride cries out to her poor husband, racked with jealousy, when he accuses her of flirting with the man in the bicycle shop the day after their wedding. This venerable expression can be traced back to the Tang dynasty (618–904 AD). Emperor Li Shimin, it seems, granted his assistant, a certain Fang Xuanliang, king in a territory known as Liang, a selection of unusually beautiful **women** for his personal disposition. This put Fang in a tricky spot. He was quite sure his wife would look askance at a gift of this kind, so he turned down the offer. But Emperor Li, for reasons of his own, was determined to force the issue. He insisted on pressing these beautiful concubines on his reluctant chief-of-staff. When Fang Xuanliang once again respectfully declined his offer, the emperor asked his own wife if she would have a word with Fang's wife to get her to go along with the idea. Fang's wife, however, was not amused. "Absolutely not!" she cried. The emperor, still unwilling to take no for an answer, tried to "persuade" Madame Fang more directly. He arranged to have a bottle of dark liquid sent to the Fang household, along with a minatory note addressed to Fang's wife. "If you reject my final offer," he warned her, "you might as well drink the 'poisonous' liquid inside this bottle and kill yourself." Fang's wife didn't budge. She was as resolute as ever. Instead, she drank every last drop of the liquid. It turned out not to be "poisonous" at all. It was merely an acid test— of vinegar.

CHINA INTERNATIONAL TRUST AND INVESTMENT CORPORATION (CITIC). A central component of China's **open-door policy**, CITIC was established in 1979 by **Rong Yiren** under the patronage of **Deng Xiaoping** as a state corporation to coordinate national planning and economic goals and to assist foreigners seeking to do business in China. It is a comprehensive conglomerate comprised of production, **technology**, **banking and finance**, **trade and investment**, and service businesses. CITIC set for itself the task of absorbing and utilizing foreign and domestic capital, introducing foreign technology, equipment, and managerial expertise into China and promoting investment in China's infrastructure construction. Immediate priority was given to developing the raw and semi-finished materials industries, transforming the obsolete techniques of domestic enterprises, and fostering overseas investments mainly in the exploitation of those natural resources that China lacked. Numerous new laws, codes, and regulations affecting foreign corporations and employees in China were also enacted. In the bureaucratic organization of the Chinese government, CITIC operates under the direct authority of the State Council and is of the same rank as a state ministry. From this strategic position, CITIC has consistently acted as a powerful force to support the country's opening to the international **economy**. Yet like many state-run entities in China, CITIC has suffered from financial mismanagement, such as in 1994, when it defaulted on a US$30 million loan from foreign interests, and in 1997–1998, when the share price of its **Hong Kong** subsidiary, CITIC Pacific, managed since 1987 by Rong Yiren's son, Rong Zhijian (Larry Yung), was savaged by the 1997–1998 Asian financial crisis (but has since recovered). The CITIC Industrial Bank is one of nine banks in a consortium to help fund the massive **South-to-North Water Diversion Project** that was begun in 2002. In 2004, Larry Yung was listed as one of China's new class of billionaires and is reputed to be one of the richest men in China.

CHINESE ACADEMY OF SOCIAL SCIENCES (CASS). Established in 1977, CASS became China's top think tank on social sciences, comprising more than 30 separate institutes. These include philosophy, **Marxism–Leninism–Mao Zedong Thought**, world **religions**, industrial economics, law, finance and **trade**, minority **literature**, foreign literature, modern history, world economics, politics, and others. In 1982, more than 5,000 researchers, assistants, and translators were employed in the Academy, which also published in excess of 50 journals, including *Social Sciences in China* (*Zhongguo shehui kexue*). CASS initially emerged from the Philosophy and Sociology Department of the Chinese Academy of Sciences (CAS), which was established soon after the Communist seizure of power in 1949. Previous presidents and vice-presidents of CASS included **Hu Qiaomu**, the economist Ma Hong, **Deng Liqun**, and **Yu Guangyuan**, all of whom took part in the intellectual and ideological controversies in the late 1970s and 1980s involving the direction of Chinese economic and political reforms. In 2004, CASS was headed by its President Chen Kuiyuan (former head of the Henan Province CP with extensive political experience in Party affairs in Inner Mongolia) while Li Shenming (a staunch anti-Western **Chinese Communist Party** figure) served as vice-president. Among the CASS research staff in 2001, 53% were professors or associate professors with 60% of those under the age of 45 holding the Ph.D. Most of the funding for CASS comes from the central government, with research projects outlined in conjunction with the development plan contained in the **five-year plans** that govern the Chinese **economy**. During the 1989 second **Beijing Spring** pro-democracy movement, CASS members joined in calling for the ouster of Premier **Li Peng**. After the 4 June military crackdown, key figures in CASS, such as **Su Shaozhi**, Director of its Institute of Marxism–Leninism–Mao Zedong Thought, were forced to resign and/or flee the country. Offices of CASS were occupied by martial law troops for a time, and the academy was thereafter reorganized.

Throughout the 1980s and 1990s and into the early 2000s, CASS adjusted its role to the emerging economic, political, environmental, and international issues confronting China. Several newly established institutes took the lead in providing research and studies to the Party and government leadership and the general public, including, most notably, the Institute of Industrial Economics, the Center for Environment and Development, the Center for Urban Development and Environment, the Institute of Quantitative and Technical Economics, the National Institute of Law, and the Institute of **Taiwan** Studies. With national financial support for projects and publications that has generally increased over the years, CASS engaged in a variety of research projects, ran conferences, took national polls, and published annual studies such as the *Social Bluebook*, which provides a rich collection of social and economic statistics on all aspects of Chinese society and economy and the country's **environment**. The institute also issued works on China's entry into the international economy, such as *China's Path under the Shadow of Globalization*, published in 1999.

In most cases, CASS work adheres to the **basic line of the Party** as was evident in a 2004 symposium marking the 100th birthday of the late **Deng Xiaoping**, which lauded his theoretical contributions to Marxism–Leninism–Mao Zedong Thought. The same is true when

CASS delves into the issue of cross-strait relations with Taiwan, which, in keeping with CCP statements on the issue, condemns any move toward independence by the island and simply reiterates the mainland's boilerplate position on resolving the conflict. On other less-sensitive issues, however, CASS researchers and publications, while not directly challenging the central government, provide an evidentiary basis for questioning the consequence of some of its policies. One CASS survey in 2004 found that the income gap between individuals in China's cities and those in rural areas was one of the largest in the world, with city dwellers earning more than three times the income of their rural counterparts, which, when factoring in differences in non-monetized social services, such as medical insurance and **education**, grew to five to six times larger. Coming on the heels of an independently published book titled *An Investigation of China's Farmers* that reported similar findings, government **leaders** were apparently shocked by the poverty and harshness of life in China's hinterland compared to life in its booming cities.

Although some CASS-conducted surveys and polls provided welcome news for government leaders, such as a 2004 finding that one-fifth of the country's **population** of 1.3 billion is categorized as middle class (with incomes between US$18,000 and US$36,000), other studies offered less sanguine results, such as a 2003 poll of urban dwellers who indicated that the biggest beneficiary of the post-1978–1979 economic reforms were not private entrepreneurs but CCP officials and **cadres** and that the biggest "social contradiction" in China was unemployment followed by **corruption** and the clash of interests between officials and citizens. The Institute of Russian, East European, and Central Studies at the Academy has also been instrumental in helping the central leadership develop its **foreign policy** toward those crucial nations.

CASS researchers have also not been shy about questioning the benefits of major government-infrastructure programs, especially the ongoing construction of major dams and water control projects such as the **Three Gorges Dam Project**. While researchers from the Center for Environment and Development at a CASS-organized forum on hydropower construction repeated standard policy statements on the economic benefits of these huge projects, numerous negative consequences were also cited, such as the threat to bio-diversity. More importantly, the same forum took direct aim at the opaque decision-making process in China's hydropower sector, criticizing the utilization of false and incomplete evaluations, which boast instant economic revenue and ignore future negative effects of the gigantic projects. The same forum also called for substantial alteration of decision-making procedures by bringing in independent experts and subjecting construction plans to public scrutiny and holding officials who make wrong decisions accountable. The impact of CASS research, polls, and publications on government policy is hard to gauge, but its work as a government-funded organization indicates that even in China's one-party state a degree of openness and honest debate exists, at least in academic circles. CASS maintains academic exchange agreements with 44 countries worldwide dispatching visiting scholars for long-term overseas studies.

CHINESE COMMUNIST PARTY (CCP). The CCP is the "vanguard" of the Chinese Communist movement that began in 1921 and since 1949 has been the ruling party of the **People's Republic of China (PRC)**.

HISTORY, 1921–1949: The CCP was founded in July 1921 in **Shanghai** in a French-run girls' school. The decision to form a Communist Party in China was in response to domestic and international developments. Among these were the failure of the Chinese Republic, founded in 1912, to solve the internal political crisis fomented by powerful warlords and the Republican government's inability to prevent the post-World War I Versailles Conference from transferring Chinese national territory in Shandong Province (the birthplace of Confucius) from German to Japanese control. The 1917 Bolshevik Revolution in Russia also had a profound effect on Chinese **intellectuals**, led by two professors from **Beida (Peking University)**, Chen Duxiu and Li Dazhao, who gathered in 1921 to create an alternative model of political and state power.

The Leninist-party model was considered a "modern" institutional structure with the capacity to mobilize society's resources but without the debilitating weaknesses of Western parliamentary democracy. What began as a small and rather ineffectual group of intellectuals and a few workers whose numbers grew from a mere 57 members at the 1921 First National Party Congress to 123 at the 1922 Second National Party Congress and 432 at the 1923 Third National Party Congress, mass membership rapidly expanded in 1925–1926 to an organization of between 10,000 and 18,000 members. This stemmed in part from the First **United Front (1924–1927)** that was established by the CCP, under pressure from the **Soviet Union**, with the **Kuomintang (KMT)** led by Chiang Kai-shek. In April 1927, however, Chiang turned on his erstwhile Communist allies and effectively destroyed the urban apparatus of the CCP, forcing remnant CCP forces to shift operations to the countryside. Although the Party retained the basic organizational structure established in the 1920s, changes were instituted to reflect the Communists' new rural constituency and its increasingly military orientation. The system of "Party core groups" (*dang hexin xiaozu*) was set up to ensure tight Party control of army units and various "mass" organizations. In the Communists' main redoubt in the 1930s—rural Jiangxi Province—a Soviet form of political organization was adopted, and **land reform** policies were vigorously pursued. During the **Long March (1934–1935)**, at an enlarged **Politburo** meeting, it was decided to "establish **Mao Zedong** in the leading position of the Red Army and the Party Center." Steps were also taken to avoid independent power bailiwicks from emerging in the Red Army as a hierarchical structure of military–political committees and CCP political departments was established to ensure Party control over the military.

By 1938, the Communist Party structure of the war years was completed at the Sixth Plenum of the Sixth National Party Congress held in the new Communist stronghold in Yan'an in rural Shaanxi Province. Ad hoc decision making was formally ended as Party rules established clear lines of authority. The Central Committee (originally termed the Central Executive Committee) was reaffirmed as the highest organ in political and organizational matters (except during periodic Party congresses), and standing committees were subordinated to their respective Party committees, reversing a decision made in 1927 during the height of the CCP's fight for survival that had concentrated extraordinary power in the hands of the executive body. The apex of the CCP was the Politburo, the Secretariat, and a Central Bureau and central sub-bureaus. The latter two directed Party activities through a vertically organized structure of Party committees established at the region, prefecture, county, city, district, and branch (*zhibu*) levels. Six departments—Organization, Propaganda, War Mobilization, Popular Movements, United Front, and the Secretariat—were established at the central level with branches of each extending below. Overall, the Organization Department (*zuzhibu*) and Secretariat (*shujichu*) emerged as the most powerful apparatus for directing a membership that grew from 40,000 members to more than 800,000 between 1928 and 1942.

During a **rectification campaign** in 1942–1944, an even more elaborate organizational structure was created. This included a Central Committee Office, a Party Committee for Managing Organs Directly Subordinate to the Central Committee, and the highly secretive Central Investigation Department and the Social Affairs Department—the CCP's secret police. These were charged with investigating the loyalty of **cadres** and ferreting out purported Nationalist "spies." Under the influence of **Kang Sheng**, this internal security apparatus carried out the first major internal Party purge, which Mao Zedong ultimately terminated because of excessive killings and cadre suicides. Finally, Mao Zedong's position as Party Chairman (which he had assumed at the 1938 Sixth Party Plenum) was further enhanced by a March 1943 decision giving him the authority to "make final decisions regarding all problems discussed by the [three member] Central Secretariat." With the promulgation of the Mao **personality cult** (*geren chongbai*), the CCP and the great leader were now virtually indistinguishable. Yet, in upholding the supremacy of the Party committees over individual **leaders** in a 1948 speech, Mao presaged the forthcoming clash between charismatic and institutional authority that would eventually divide the CCP.

THE CHINESE COMMUNIST PARTY IN POWER, 1949–2005: The CCP emerged from the **Civil War (1946–1949)** with an elaborate organization that quickly imposed its network of organizational control over the entire country. From the central to the county level, there were six central and four sub-central bureaus, 24 provincial committees, 17 regional committees, and 134 city and 218 area committees. Total Party membership in 1950 was 4.5 million (up from 3 million in 1948), with 80,000 full-time cadres forming the CCP's organizational core. As the CCP's role rapidly shifted from wartime mobilization during both the Civil War and the **Korean War (1950–1953)**, the need for professionally trained cadres increased dramatically. Meanwhile, the illiterate Party veterans of the wars against the Japanese and Nationalists were now confronted with their own political obsolescence. Party rectifications in the early 1950s thus squeezed out 670,000 rural, uneducated members, while 910,000 more well-educated members were recruited into a Party whose membership continued to expand to 6.2 million by 1953.

Party organization also reflected the imperatives of economic growth and control over the burgeoning state bureaucracy. In 1953, the CCP Central Committee ordered that all laws and regulations dealing with state and government affairs be initiated and drafted by the Central Committee and then implemented by the State Council. Party secretaries were also empowered to take charge of directing and supervising their counterparts in the state apparatus. Leading Party figures also assumed the top positions in the government in order to ensure CCP domination. In 1955, five new Central Committee departments—Industry, **Finance** and **Trade**, Communication and **Transportation**, Political–Legal, and **Agriculture**—were also established. In the mid-1950s, "Party core groups" made up of four or five Party members who held senior posts in the government were extended throughout the administrative system (down to the bureau level) and emerged as the real centers of decision-making authority in the government. This was in addition to the Party "unit affairs committees" (*jiguan dangwei*), which were elected by CCP members working in the relevant government bodies but which exercised little decision-making authority, focusing instead on such tasks as Party recruitment and directing ideological study. Control over government appointments and the training of technical cadres, however, was decentralized, with a concomitant reduction in the authority of the CCP Organization Department. Although Mao Zedong evidently supported such changes, he showed increasing impatience with the highly deliberative process of decision making that emerged with the CCP's shift to economic management. In July 1955, Mao thus upset the gradualist approach to organizing **Agricultural Producers' Cooperatives** (**APCs**) by announcing a "socialist upsurge" in the Chinese countryside that coincided with a growth in Party membership from 9 million in 1955 to 13 million by the beginning of the **Great Leap Forward** (**1958–1960**).

From 1955 onward, the issue of procedural and "collective leadership" (*jit lingdao*) versus Mao's impulsive and individualistic leadership style increasingly divided the CCP. While Mao's enormous charisma allowed him to prevail in most political standoffs, elliptical criticism of the chairman was expressed by relatively liberal CCP leaders, such as An Ziwen, head of the Organization Department, who extolled the Party committees, including the Central Committee, as the final sovereign body. Chinese proponents of the principle of institutionalization of authority were strengthened by the emphasis on the principle of "collective leadership" in the **Soviet Union** that followed the death of **Josef Stalin** and were evidently able to win significant concessions from the chairman at the pivotal 1956 first session of the national **Eighth National Party Congress**. In addition to deleting "Mao Zedong Thought" from the Party constitution, the Congress authorized a more collective top leadership with the appointment of five vice-chairmen, the promulgation of a prohibition against leader cults, and a renewed emphasis in CCP decision making on such procedures as periodic congresses with utilization of pre-set formal agenda.

Yet, Mao was still able to circumvent the formal Party apparatus with his personal charisma and the support of local Party secretaries—the "little Maos"—who evidently admired his decisive leadership. Thus, without formal Central Committee or Politburo approval, Mao personally ordered the wide-open **Hundred Flowers** (**1956–1957**). Speaking prior to a planned Party plenum, Mao exhorted subordinates to "relay and implement" his proposals without formal authorization. "Being the first secretary, I will take charge of ideological work," Mao arrogantly asserted. Then during the debate over the proposed Great Leap Forward, Mao showed his contempt for institutional procedure by authorizing the formation of the first **people's communes** before formal Politburo approval while Mao also personally countermanded central decisions on grain deliveries and production quotas. When **Peng Dehuai** responded at the 1959 **Lushan Conference** by voicing surprisingly mild criticisms of the chairman's leadership style during the Leap, Mao countered by purging Peng and launching a campaign against "rightist opportunism." This action effectively silenced the entire organization and evidently created a basis for Mao's later decision to launch the **Cultural Revolution** (**1966–1976**). The relatively open and semi-legal model of the Party's decision-making structure outlined at the 1956 Eighth National Congress was now effectively defunct.

Following the collapse of the Great Leap Forward and Mao's retreat to the so-called second front of decision making, CCP propaganda organs revived the Eighth National Party Congress model. Throughout the early 1960s, "regularization" of Party decision-making through majority rule in Party committees was reemphasized. A "moderate" leadership style was also advocated in place of the "tyrannical way" (*badao*) that the Party intellectual **Deng Tuo** had criticized in a **Beijing** newspaper. In an obvious reference to the cavalier purge of Peng Dehuai, the right of every Party member to voice his or her views was defended, and Mao's tendency to rely on personal oral orders to set policy was indirectly criticized. With Party membership at 17 million in 1961, central authorities also emphasized the recruitment of well-educated cadres. The increasingly leftward trend of the rural **Socialist Education Movement (1962–1966)**, however, effectively prevented the full substitution of expertise over "redness" in CCP ranks.

In the early to mid-1960s, Mao re-entered the political fray intent on eliminating political obstruction of his renewed effort to attempt yet another Great Leap Forward. Detaching himself from central Party leaders, the chairman mobilized youthful **Red Guards** to attack veteran cadres whom Mao accused of being **capitalist roaders** (*zouzipai*). As Party ranks were decimated at all organizational levels, Mao supported the establishment of alternative political bodies to replace the Leninist structures of the CCP. **Revolutionary Committees** and Party "groups" (*zu*) replaced the regular structure of Party committees throughout the Cultural Revolution—even as Party ranks swelled to 22 million by 1969. At the April 1969 Ninth National Party Congress, the unprecedented action was taken of naming Mao's successor—**Lin Biao**—in the new Party constitution. Yet, even as the last Revolutionary Committees were established in the provinces, Mao became convinced that "rebuilding the Party" was necessary to avoid civil war and national chaos, and so, throughout the early 1970s, the CCP's conventional structure of Party committees was gradually reestablished. Veteran cadres who had been vilified during the Cultural Revolution were rehabilitated, and Party members who had been recruited during the mass campaigns were gradually ferreted out.

Mao's death in 1976 brought an end to mass campaigns, and, in 1978, **Deng Xiaoping** called for bringing about further Party reform. In August 1980, Deng Xiaoping promised to "institutionalize democracy" by strengthening the **legal system** and restraining political leaders from exercising absolutist authority. Criticizing the "patriarchal system" in the CCP and the influence of "**feudalism**" on Party leaders, Deng promised a more open and responsible CCP that would never again make the errors of the Maoist era. In 1985, at the Fourth and Fifth plenums of the 12th CCP Central Committee, a policy of putting younger and better-educated people into senior positions was effected as 20% of leaders resigned from the Central Committee and six new members were elected to the Politburo, including **Tian Jiyun, Li Peng, Qiao Shi**, and **Yao Yilin**. Yet, as criticism of Deng's own leadership by democratic dissidents mounted in the early 1980s and problems emerged in China's economic reforms, major political reform of the CCP was effectively tabled as Deng Xiaoping exercised decisive leadership over the CCP, despite the absence of a formal position of authority. With his own mini personality cult, Deng's reputed contribution to the theoretical realm of **Marxism–Leninism–Mao Zedong Thought** was elevated to new heights but with a pro-reform bent. Throughout the period of economic reforms pushed by Deng, Party membership continued to grow from 35 million in 1977 to 48 million by the time of the second **Beijing Spring** in 1989. Despite the crackdown on Chinese society that followed the events of June 1989, Party membership continued to climb in the 1990s and early 2000s to reach 66 million in 2002.

ORGANIZATIONAL STRUCTURE: The organizational structure of the CCP is based on the fundamental Leninist principles of **democratic-centralism**. Theoretically, authority inheres in the National Party Congress (originally held on an annual basis but since 1997 convened every five years and generally composed of almost 2,000 delegates from all realms of the apparatus) and, when not in session, the Central Committee, which, in turn, selects as its executive organ the Politburo, which was first established in April–May 1927 at the Fifth National Party Congress and which, in 2004, had 24 members. In reality, the Politburo and its executive organ of a Standing Committee, which, in 2005, was composed of nine members, usually exercise final decision-making authority. Since the abolition of the position of chairman at the 12th National Party Congress in 1982, the top executive position in the CCP is the general secretary; from 1989 to 2002, the position was filled by **Jiang Zemin**, whom Deng Xiaoping appointed as the "core" of the "third generation of leadership." **Hu Jintao** replaced Jiang in November 2002 and has been anointed, along with Premier **Wen Jiabao**, as the "fourth generation" (*disidai*) of CCP leaders. Other key central bodies include the Central **Military Affairs Committee** (MAC) (which ensures CCP control of the **People's Liberation Army [PLA]**), the **Central Discipline Inspection Commission** (CDIC), the **Central Advisory Commission** (CAC) a body established in 1987 (and abolished in 1992) for semi-retired leaders, and the all-powerful Secretariat, which prepares reports for top leaders and controls key appointments throughout the apparatus. Formal departments of the CCP include: the United Front Work Department (for work with non-Communist groups); International Liaison Department (for maintaining ties with foreign Communist parties); Propaganda Department (recently renamed Publicity Department); General Affairs Office; Policy Research Office; Security Bureau; Guards Bureau; International Communication Office; Organization Department; Party Literature Research Center; Foreign Affairs Office; Party History Research Center; Archives Bureau; **Taiwan** Affairs Office; *People's Daily*; and the **Central Party School**. Several informal "central leading groups" to deal with problems of finance, Party building, propaganda and thought, and so on have also been established under the direct authority of the Politburo.

The CCP structure at the provincial, municipal, prefecture, and local levels is similar to its central organization. A vast organizational web of various "Party core groups" are also maintained in mass organizations, government bodies, and army units to ensure CCP control of Chinese society. Proposals to separate Party and state organs were inaugurated by Premier **Zhao Ziyang** in the mid-1980s that called for the abolition of the "Party core groups" and the Party departments in government organizations and a concomitant reduction in the authority of Party secretaries in **state-owned enterprises** (SOEs) and universities. After the military crackdown in 1989, however, the role of both the "core groups" and the Party secretaries was reinvigorated, returning the CCP to a more dominant role in social and political life that has been sustained into the 1990s and early 2000s as Party leaders have sought to maintain and even strengthen the crucial grassroots organs of the CCP while the level of **education** among its expanding membership has increased correspondingly in the last decade. The 190 members of the Central Committee of the CCP chosen at the October 1993 14th National Party Congress had an average age of 57 years, 8% of whom were female, 11% were from various **minorities**, and 84% consisted of college graduates. Figures for the 1997 15th and 2002 16th National Party congresses showed similar patterns, although the number of **women** in the 198-member Central Committee was reduced to five with only one woman, **Wu Yi**, serving in the Politburo.

Following the transfer of leadership from Jiang Zemin in 2002 to Hu Jintao, the new "fourth generation" leaders have repeated many of the old saws of Chinese Communist Party doctrine while also attempting to adapt the CCP to China's increasingly dynamic and semiprivate **economy**. Like his predecessors, General Secretary Hu Jintao has repeated many of the axioms of post-Mao CCP doctrine, including his opposition to a personality cult and support for "collective leadership" by the Party's top leaders. Although lip service was given to making the CCP, including its top decision-making bodies of the Politburo and Standing Committee, more transparent and accessible to public scrutiny (with calls to have the agendas of both bodies publicized), little in the way of real institutional reform of the CCP has occurred, except for constant harping on the necessity of Party members to maintain "self-discipline" and cultivate their "moral conduct" while staid ideological concepts, such as the "Three Represents" originally propounded by Jiang Zemin and the "three close tos" (i.e., being close to reality, to life, and to the masses) are hammered away by Party propagandists in what are still incessantly long-winded speeches and essays in Party journals. The cancellation by Hu Jintao of the annual retreat by top leaders to the seaside resort of **Beidaihe** was touted as a major step forward in reducing the CCP's insular decision-making process, although others interpreted this action as further consolidation of political decision making and an overall reduction in the give-and-take of policy discussion that these retreats often incurred.

Confronted with the increasingly intractable problem of **corruption** by Party cadres at all levels of the apparatus, a new system of internal Party inspection and reporting that was to apply to all Party members, including the highest leaders, was introduced in 2004 as a way to bring such errant behavior under control and improve the Party's ability to rule while also making more information available to all CCP members. "Provisional Regulations on the Open Selection of Leading Cadres of the Party and Government" and a "Decision on Strengthening the Building of the Party's Ability to Govern" were also promulgated, along with calls to solicit views from the public that some CCP leaders, such as Bo Xilai (Party secretary of Dalian Municipality and the son of elder CCP leader **Bo Yibo**), evidently took to heart. But without any significant alteration of the Leninist structure of democratic-centralism and of the centrally controlled appointment system run by the CCP Secretariat, which ensure a top-down authority structure, such proposals evidently had little-to-no effect because lower-ranking members were loathe to question or challenge their superiors while the perennial problem of putting "the party secretary in command" and equating the CCP with all public power continued unabated, sapping the institution of any modicum of democratic life or principles. Although Jiang Zemin may have been the last strongman of the CCP, the increasingly unwieldy organization of over 60 million members evidently demands that there be one person at the top in authority. In 2005, that man was Hu Jintao, who, on several occasions, rejected any move on China's part to a Western-style political system and continued the process begun under Jiang Zemin to purge Party organs of any genuine debate or political contestation.

In the 2002 to 2003 leadership transition, all of the top personnel decisions were made by just two men, Jiang Zemin and Li Peng, with virtually all power residing in their protegés, Hu Jintao, Wen Jiabao, Wu Bangguo, **Zeng Qinglong**, and **Luo Gan**, while at the provincial level, political consolidation proceeded with most chairs of the Provincial People's Congresses held by the provincial Party secretary, a complete turnaround from 1987, when virtually all of these posts were held by persons other than the Party secretary or provincial governor. Important decisions in the CCP are still reached through uncontested procedures that draw on a unity of interests and a unitarian principle, which continue to inform the top leadership's political perspective and lead them to reject any form of open or contested political power.

Although real institutional and organizational changes did not occur in the CCP, the Party did reposition itself toward the changing social and economic characteristics of Chinese society undergoing substantial economic reform and growing prosperity. In 1997, at the 15th National Party Congress, General Secretary Jiang Zemin called for introducing corporate organizational structures into state-owned enterprises. Substantive changes were also subsequently proposed to the 1982 constitution that calls on the CCP to protect **human rights** and property rights and to improve the system of land acquisitions ensuring adequate compensation for property owners while also committing the CCP to establishing a national social security system. The phrase "martial law" was also replaced by the more conventional "state of emergency," which the constitution grants power to the State Council to invoke. The CCP also maintains its own Webpage at Chinatoday.com, which was established in 1997 and contains a wealth of official information. *See also* CENTRAL PARTY SCHOOL.

CHINESE PEOPLE'S POLITICAL CONSULTATIVE CONFERENCE (CPPCC). This "consultative" body was established by the **Chinese Communist Party** (**CCP**) in 1949 and is composed of both Communist and non-Communist members, with national and local committees representing various groups and organizations. A **United Front** organization, the initial CPPCC (*zhongguo renmin zhengzhi xieshang huiyi*) consisted of 600 delegates and united all "patriotic" forces in China that had opposed the **Kuomintang** (**KMT**), including many non-Communists, making the conference more broadly "representative" of the Chinese nation than the CCP. According to an official chronology, the meeting in September 1949 "acted on behalf of the **National People's Congress** (**NPC**)" (which did not formally convene until 1954) and declared the establishment of the **People's Republic of China** (**PRC**). It also designated **Beijing** (renamed from Beiping) as the nation's capital and adopted the **Common Program**, which served as China's provisional constitution until a permanent document was adopted in 1954. From 1949 to September 1954, the CPPCC functioned as the parliamentary body of the PRC by passing a resolution in 1953 approving the formation of the **Agricultural Producers' Cooperatives** (**APCs**) and by continuing to retain as delegates representatives from many of China's **democratic parties** and the "mass" organizations, such as the All-China Federation of **Trade Unions** and the **All-China Federation of Women**, as well as key members from China's **minorities**, including the **Dalai Lama**. Considered a crucial institution in the plan for a **New Democracy** in China enunciated by **Mao Zedong**, the CPPCC was eclipsed by the establishment of the First NPC in 1954, which effectively eliminated the official role of the CPPCC as an organ of national power and reduced its function to "rallying" the various nationalities and democratic parties behind the CCP cause. This, in effect, transformed the CPPCC into a "transmission belt" of the CCP, denying it any real political autonomy.

During periods of political relaxation in China, however, non-Communist CPPCC members were relatively outspoken in their criticisms of Communist policies. This occurred during the **Hundred Flowers (1956–1957)** and in the more tolerant political atmosphere of the early 1980s, when CPPCC meetings involved real debate over issues of the national **economy**, **education**, and **corruption**. The body also took the lead in trying to ameliorate relations with **Taiwan** by, for example, sending messages of condolence to the KMT Central Committee on the death of the Nationalist leader Chiang Ching-kuo in 1987. Since the 1989 crackdown against the second **Beijing Spring** pro-democracy movement, however, the CPPCC has generally ceased to be a source of policy opposition, although, in 1992, there were a number of abstentions from a resolution authorizing construction of the **Three Gorges Dam Project** on the Yangtze River. While serving as chair in the early 1990s, **Li Ruihuan** sought to continue the contestory momentum of the CPPCC, but his efforts were dismissed as "interference" by **Jiang Zemin** and **Li Peng** with the consequence that the organization became increasingly subservient.

As China pursued its policy of economic reform beginning in 1978–1979, the CPPCC accommodated itself to these changes by drafting delegates from both the state-owned and private sectors into its leadership structure. In 2003, the 10th CPPCC included 33 members from **state-owned enterprises** (SOEs) and 65 members from China's fledging private sector. This included Xu Guanju a prestigious private entrepreneur from Zhejiang Province, who, as president of a large chemical firm and one of China's few billionaires, was elected vice-chairman of the CPPCC provincial committee. CPPCC delegates were also called upon by Chairman **Jia Qinglin** (a member of the **Politburo** Standing Committee) in 2003 to contribute in the fight against **SARS** and to join in the fight against corruption and for a clean government, a major policy position advanced by President **Hu Jintao**.

CHONGQING. Located in southwestern China on a promontory on the north bank of the Yangtze River and at the confluence with the Jialing River, Chongqing Municipality (*Chongqing shi*) is the world's largest metropolitan region with a **population** of over 32 million people. Formerly part of Sichuan Province, Chongqing was granted provincial-level status in 1997 as a municipal region similar to **Beijing**, **Shanghai**, and **Tianjin**. The municipality includes all of eastern Sichuan counties down river, where most of the population lives over hundreds of square km of farmland. The urban area has a registered population of around 6.14 million people, making it the third largest in China, with an additional four million unregistered migrants. The total urban population is expected to grow to 10 million in the next decade. Chongqing is a main commercial and **transportation** center for Sichuan Province and is the destination for most of the bulk transport that passes through the **Three Gorges Dam Project** undergoing construction 600 km downriver.

The capital of the State of *Ba* in the Fourth century BC, Chongqing (then known as *Yuzhou*) was known for producing great warriors who fought off, but ultimately failed, to defeat the encroaching armies of the Qin dynasty (221–207 BC) that conquered the region. During the Southern Song dynasty (1127–1279 AD), the city's name was changed to *Chongqing*—meaning "double celebration"—and became a center of **trade** for goods from Sichuan and the Tibetan hinterland, including hides and furs, hemp, salt, copper, and iron. Under the Qifu Agreement of 1890, Chongqing, like many river port cities in China, was open to foreign trade, including a massive influx in opium that was grown under warlord control in southwest China. Surrounded by a 30-m wall in the 1920s and 1930s, the city's population grew to 600,000 but lacked its own water supply as 10,000 to 20,000 coolies carried water daily to shops and houses through the steep and narrow lanes of the city. With massive urban reconstruction undertaken in the last two decades, the city's famed staircase streets and alleyways have virtually disappeared along with much of the old city wall. The former city gate at Chaotianmen at the tip of the promontory overlooking the harbor has been rebuilt into a plaza park. In 1939, during the **Sino–Japanese War** (**1937–1945**), the Nationalist government of China moved its capital from Nanking (Nanjing) to Chongqing (then rendered as Chungking), making it a frequent target of Japanese bombing that fortunately was often thwarted by the area's notoriously foggy weather, which probably saved the city from complete devastation.

An interior city, Chongqing and Sichuan Province were the recipients of industrial development during the construction of the **Third Front** promoted during the late 1950s and 1960s. Currently, Chongqing is the main industrial center of southwest China with iron and steel production facilities, along with the largest aluminum smelter and motorcycle plants in China. Landlocked and surrounded by mountains, Chongqing suffers from the worst air pollution in China and has been rated one of the top three polluted urban areas in the world. Construction of a monorail and the introduction of LPG-fueled public buses are designed to reduce the spewing of toxins into the humid air while a series of water-treatment plants is being built in and around the city to stem the flow of untreated waste into the expanding and relatively stagnant waters of the Three Gorges Reservoir. In December 2003, an explosion in a natural gas field in Kai County of Chongqing Municipality took nearly 200 lives, one of China's most severe industrial accidents in recent years. This was followed in 2004 by the outbreak of massive **social protests** in Wanzhou, part of Chongqing Municipality, when 80,000 workers and unemployed **labor** confronted thousands of police and paramilitary units after a relatively minor incident involving a local porter and an official of a local taxation bureau that quickly escalated into a clash between the underprivileged and officialdom. From 1999–2002, the Party secretary of Chongqing Municipality was He Guoqiang, a major figure in China's chemical and petroleum sector who had also served as governor of Fujian Province, and who was replaced in 2003 in Chongqing by Huang Zhendong (1941–), who is from Jiangsu Province and is a former minister of communications in the national government.

CINEMA AND FILM. While the origin of Chinese cinema can be traced back to the Han dynasty (202 BC–220 AD) with its trotting horse lamps and paper shadow plays, the first modern film was made in 1905, *The Battle of Dingjunshan*, a recording of a **Peking Opera**. Chinese cinema came of age under the influence of Western cinema in the 1920s and 1930s with films that were heavily left-wing in content. Centered in **Shanghai**, the Chinese film industry produced a string of films by such notable directors as Cai Chusheng, Cheng Bugao, Sun Yu, and Wu Yonggang, including *Love of the Working Class*, *Spring Silkworms*, *Goddess*, *Midnight Song*, *The Big Road*, and *Moon and Clouds Over the Eight Thousand Mile*, all of which have been ranked as some of China's greatest films in the 20th Century. China's queen of the silent film industry in the 1930s was Ruan Lingyu star of Wu Yonggang's *Goddess* (*Shennu*), the story of a prostitute who wants the best for her son. Ruan died in 1935 at the early age of 24, but her work, now preserved, is still revered by generations of Chinese filmgoers.

After World War II, the film industry quickly reestablished itself in Shanghai with a slew of films that showed the disillusionment with Chiang Kai-shek's **Kuomintang** (**KMT**), including *Myriad of Lights*, *San Mao*, and *The Spring River Flows East*, which depicted the struggle of ordinary Chinese during the **Sino–Japanese War** (**1937–1945**). Major film companies of this era included the Lianhua Production Company and the Wenhua Film Company, which, in 1948, produced *Springtime in a Small Town* by director Fei Mu, which many consider the best Chinese film of all time.

Following the rise to power in 1949 of the **Chinese Communist Party** (**CCP**), Chinese cinema, like all artistic endeavors, was subject to highly centralized control, including heavy doses of political and social **censorship** (*shencha*) with many Chinese filmmakers sent to the USSR to learn the Soviet art form of propaganda. In 1950, the Performing Art Research Institute was set up under the Film Bureau of the Ministry of Culture by the director Yuan Muzhi following a tour of Soviet film institutes to serve as the major training ground for actors and directors that in 1956 was renamed the **Beijing** Film Academy. In the immediate aftermath of the Communist takeover, such films as *The Biography of Wu Xun* (which portrayed the life of a 19th-century folk hero who was devoted to the promotion of free **educa-**

tion for peasant children) sustained earlier artistic and cinematographic traditions. But following the attack on *Wu Xun* by **Mao Zedong**, who criticized the director, Sun Yu, as insufficiently critical of Chinese "**feudalism**," over the course of the next two and a half decades Chinese cinema took on an increasingly politicized and propagandist flavor as most films adhered to the regime's policy of "revolutionary realism." Such works as *Lin Zexu* (the 1959 portrayal of China's subjugation by the West in the mid-19th century Opium Wars), *Women's Detachment* (1961), *The First Sino–Japanese War* (1963), and *Slaves* (1963), achieved none of the standards set by the Shanghai film industry in the 1930s but dominated the industry because of their ideological and political acceptability. Throughout this era, filmmaking was under the strict and rigid control of government-controlled film studios, including the Beijing Film Academy, the August First Film Studio of the **People's Republic of China** (**PRC**), and the China Film Group Corporation. Despite the controls, over 600 films were made from 1949 to 1966, especially during the relative thaw of the **Hundred Flowers (1956–1957)** by such prominent filmmakers as Xie Jin, whose work includes *The Red Detachment of Women* (1961) and *Two Stage Sisters* (1965). During the **Cultural Revolution (1966–1976)**, only five films—*The Red Detachment of Women*, *The White-Haired Girl*, *Taking Tiger Mountain by Strategy*, *Sand Village*, and *Seaport*—were screened in China, and major film training facilities were virtually shut down from 1966 to 1972.

Following the inauguration of the 1978–1979 economic reform program, the Chinese film **industry** gradually recovered as control and censorship was transferred in 1986 from the Ministry of Culture to the newly formed Ministry of Radio, Cinema, and Television that, in 1998, became the State Administration of Radio, Film, and Television. As was the case with "wound literature," many films depicted the emotional traumas left by the Cultural Revolution, such as Xie Jin's *Hibiscus Town* (1986) and Tian Zhuangzhuang's *The Blue Kite* (1993). With the emergence in the 1980s and 1990s of the "Fifth Generation" of young filmmakers—so named for their exposure to international filmmakers from Europe, such as Francois Truffaut and Jean-Luc Godard—Chinese films gained increasing international recognition and frequent run-ins with censorial authorities. Most from this generation, including **Chen Kaige** and **Zhang Yimou**, were graduates of the Beijing Film Academy that reopened following the Cultural Revolution. Along with a number of middle-aged filmmakers, they created a "Chinese New Wave" of filmmaking that, while using historical events and story-line, explored subtle psychological themes, such as the conflict between the ideological orthodoxy of the past with its resistance to change and the craving for human freedom and love. Among the most notable films of this genre were *One and Eight* (1983), *Yellow Earth* (1984), *Red Sorghum* (1986), *King of Children* (1987), *Farewell My Concubine* (1993), and *The Big Parade* (1986), in which the camera and directorial work of Zhang Yimou and Chen Kaige was evidently inspired by Italian Neo-Realism and reflected a respect for the traditional rural culture, into which many of them had been sent during the Cultural Revolution. Also of interest to this new generation were the "marginal cultures" of **minorities** that exist in China's border regions of Inner Mongolia and **Tibet** and were the subject for such respective documentary-like films as *On the Hunting Ground* (1984); *Sacrificed Youth* (1985), which portrays the Dai minority people as sexually liberated; and *Horse Thief* (1986), which features traditional Tibetans and was directed by Tian Zhuangzhuang, whose gritty realism was also on display in *The Blue Kite*. Other Fifth Generation directors included Wu Tianming, Huang Jianxin, Wu Ziniu, Hu Mei, and Zhou Xiaowen, who, like their colleagues, saw their movement end in 1989 with the military crackdown against the second **Beijing Spring**, as many directors went into self-imposed exile abroad.

Official censorship of films in China is carried out through the state-controlled studio system, of which Beijing, Shanghai, Xi'an, and Guangxi Province are the most prominent and by the National Film Bureau in Beijing that examines each and every script. Although some films with explicit political satire manage to make it past the censors, such as *The Black Cannon Incident* (1986), which took on the prevalence of "**bureaucratism**" in Chinese society, other films, such as *Blind Shaft* (2003), a story of illegal mines that have thrived in China in recent years, have been shot on location without government approval. Many prominent films—*The Blue Kite*, *Yellow Earth*, and *Beijing Bicycle* (2001)—were banned in China, although this did not prevent their receiving international acclaim, such as Zhang Yimou's *Judou*, which, in 1990, was nominated for the Best

Foreign Film Oscar in the **United States**. China's relationship with the international film community has gone through rapid changes from the government's biting critique in 1974 of the Italian director Michelangelo Antonioni for his film *China*, in which Chinese life was portrayed as backward and insular, to China's decision in 1986 to allow filming of *The Last Emperor* in Beijing's Forbidden City and to the First Shanghai International Film Festival involving 30 countries held in 1993. Although outright propaganda films were reduced in number and found it harder and harder to compete in the increasingly competitive commercial environment of the film industry, propaganda set pieces, such as the 1990 production of *Jiao Yulu* (a famous **cadre** martyr), were produced as part of the regime's anti-**corruption** campaign.

In the 1990s, the studio system in China began to break down as more and more Chinese films were financed from **Hong Kong, Taiwan**, and other foreign sources, and the Chinese film industry became increasingly commercialized with key financing roles played by the government-run China Film Group, which oversees the production of from 100 to 250 films a year. In this context, the "Sixth Generation" of more commercially adept filmmakers in China emerged, whose works, with their sweeping themes of gritty urban life, played out by grungy malcontents, whose lines more often than not spouted homegrown obscenities, backed by hard-rock music, contrasted with the fixation on history and heroic characters of emperors and concubines preferred by the Fifth Generation. Major Sixth Generation works include *The Days* (1993), replete with Jimi Hendrix's "Purple Haze"; *Beijing Bastards* (1993), with its home-grown punk; *Frozen* (1996), a rare look at the avant-garde world of Beijing; and *Xiao Wu* (1997), with its pickpocket and karaoke girl characters, and *Platform* (2000), both by Jia Zhangke, who, in 1995, founded China's first independent film production group. Other Sixth Generation films include *I Love You, Green Tea, Spicy Love Soup, Cry Woman, Man Yan, Weekend Plot, Eyes of a Beauty, Suzhou River, East Palace, West Palace, Shanghai Dreams*, and Jia Zhangke's *Unknown Pleasures* and *The World*, all of which have been entered in international film festivals. *Me and Dad*, a film produced by the Supreme Concept Cultural Development Co., was the first fully independent Chinese film since 1949, while in February 2002 the National Film Bureau passed a law allowing independent companies to make films on their own, such as *Frozen* by *Beijing Bicycle*'s Wang Xiaoshuai.

Adapting to the new forces of commercialization and market forces—appealing to the public and doing well at the box office—Fifth Generation filmmakers responded with Hollywood-style, big-budget works like Zhang Yimou's *Hero* and Chen Kaige's epic *The Emperor and the Assassin*, which, like the equally blockbuster-style *The Emperor's Shadow*, took as the major story line the highly contentious role of emperor Qin Shihuang in uniting China in 221 BC. Similar commercial ventures included Chen Kaige's sentimental story about a talented young violinist called *Together* and *Blue Kite*-director Tian Zhuangzhuang's remake of the 1948 classic *Springtime in a Small Town*. Sharply reduced government funding has led the state-run studios to concentrate on so-called "main melody films," that is, works with "patriotic" and other themes, such as *Opium War*, a 1996 remake of *Lin Zexu*, that did well at the Chinese box office but was virtually ignored abroad. In 1999, China chose *Lover's Grief over the Yellow River* as its official submission to the American Academy Awards for Best Foreign Language Film, but the work attracted little attention from American critics and audiences—even though it was a box-office hit in China. Beijing Film Studio became involved in a number of joint commercial ventures, including the 1999 box-office hit *Be There or Be Square* about the lives of mainland China's new immigrants to the United States.

Top-rated domestic films in China perennially consist of works largely unknown and generally unreleased in the West (*The Magnificent Birth* in 1999, *Liu Tianhua* in 2000, and *Life Show* in 2001 and *Big Shot's Funeral* in 2002) while Chinese films in receipt of prestigious foreign awards, such as the 1994 Cannes Grand Jury Prize recipient *To Live* by Zhang Yimou and the 2001 Berlin Film Festival winner *Beijing Bicycle*, receive little box-office attention in China if they are not outright banned. *The Story of Qiu Ju* (1992) by Zhang Yimou won popular audiences in the West and was awarded the Golden Rooster, China's equivalent of the Oscar for the best movie. A New Documentary Movement has also grown in the Chinese film world with such internationally acclaimed productions as the nine-hour tale of deindustrialization entitled *Tie Xi Qu* ("West of the Tracks") and *Out of Phoenix Bridge* by the woman director

Li Hong, who relates the story of four rural **women** seeking employment in Beijing.

Domestically, foreign films continue to draw huge crowds in Chinese theaters, a situation that, in 1994, led the Chinese government to issue its "Regulations on the Management of Films" which mandated that theaters allocate two-thirds of showing time to Chinese-made films. In 1999, the Hong Kong Chinese film star Jackie Chan replaced Arnold Schwarzenegger and Sylvester Stallone as the favorite foreign movie star among Chinese high school students in five coastal cities, while Hollywood films specifically tailored to the Chinese market, such as Disney's *Mulan*, crashed at the box office and were vilified in the Chinese press. Recent foreign-made films on politically sensitive topics, such as *Seven Years in Tibet* and *Red Corner*, received withering criticism from the Chinese government, although its attempts to intimidate international film festivals from screening these works largely failed. Chinese films have confronted their own political problems, such as in 1999, when, despite his earlier political problems in China, Zhang Yimou saw two of his films that had passed Chinese censors, *Not One Less* and *My Mother and Father*, rejected as "propaganda" by the Cannes screening committee. Political events, such as the 1999 bombing of the Chinese embassy in Belgrade, have affected viewership of foreign films in China although an active underground DVD market makes many foreign films available for home watching. The highest-grossing foreign film in China was *Titanic* (US$40 million), but with high taxes and government monopoly over distribution, Hollywood cannot rely on China for a huge revenue stream and it ranks well below other countries in Asia.

In both domestic and foreign-made films with a Chinese theme, female actors, especially Gong Li and Joan Chen, have generally outshone their male counterparts. Debuting in *Red Sorghum*, the beautiful Gong Li starred in several films by Zhang Yimou, including *Shanghai Triad* (1995) that won the star international attention for her defiant sensuousness roiled under her silk dresses. The equally vivacious Joan Chen starred in *The Last Emperor* by Bernardo Bertolucci and in American TV shows but has also entered the director's chair with her Chinese-made film *Xiu Xiu: The Sent Down Girl*, a portrayal of the trials and tribulations of a young woman sent to the Tibetan highlands in western Sichuan Province during the Cultural Revolution whose efforts to return to the provincial capital of Chengdu by offering men of influence her sexual favors ends in abandonment and ultimately suicide. Other prominent films by women in China include Peng Xiaolian's *Three Women* (1987), *My Classmate and I* (1987), and her award-winning *Shanghai Women* (2002) and Sun Zhou's *Zhou Yu's Train* starting Gong Li. The crucial role of Chinese women in the country's history has also been the storyline of such films as 1997's *The Soong's Sisters* directed by Mable Cheung, which follows the lives of Song Ailing and her two younger sisters **Song Qingling** (wife of Republican leader Sun Yat-sen) and Song Meiling (wife of Sun's successor Chiang Kai-shek) against the backdrop of China's historical panorama from 1900 to 1949. Tragic events in the recent past, especially the Cultural Revolution, are also frequent plot lines, such as the 2002 production of *Balzac and the Little Chinese Seamstress* by Dai Sijie, which tells the story of a young intellectual banished to the countryside, where he falls in love with a tailor's daughter, and *Electric Shadows* (2005), which portrays the power of cinema to overcome the trauma of persecution and abandonment. The multinational production of *Crouching Tiger, Hidden Dragon* with a Taiwan director and many Chinese actors (Jet Li, Zhang Ziyi, and Maggie Cheung) achieved massive success in Western box offices but bombed in China because it was seen as pandering to foreign tastes. In early 2006, the State Administration of Radio, Film, and Television canceled a showing of the Japanese-produced *Memoirs of a Geisha* because of concerns that the public might react negatively to a movie featuring Zhang Ziyi and Gong Li as geishas, whom many Chinese consider to be prostitutes. The major film festivals in China are the Shanghai International Film Festival, which, in 2002, screened 410 films from 47 countries, and the China International Children's Film Festival, held annually in July.

CIVIL WAR (1946–1949). This four-year conflict led to the defeat of **Kuomintang (KMT)** military forces by the Chinese Communist armies and the establishment of the **People's Republic of China (PRC)** in 1949. Following the defeat of the Japanese in the Asian–Pacific War in 1945, the KMT and **Chinese Communist Party (CCP)** engaged in peace talks, some brokered by the **United States**, even as the two sides carried out an undeclared war.

From August 1945 to June 1946, KMT military units (which outnumbered Communist forces three to one) were transported by U.S. aircraft and retook strategic cities in central, south, and east China, while the Communist forces entered **Manchuria**, where they were provided with substantial stocks of Japanese weapons by the occupying forces of the **Soviet Union**. During this period, American negotiators led by General George C. Marshall, attempted to mediate the KMT–CCP conflict, but this effort ultimately failed as neither the Communists nor the KMT invested much trust in the U.S. From late 1946 to mid-1947, fighting became more intense as the KMT captured the Communist wartime capital of Yan'an, while Communist forces engaged in mobile warfare and mobilized sympathizers among students and **intellectuals** in Chinese cities where KMT **corruption** was rampant and its political repression was growing. In July 1947, the Communists launched a counteroffensive that lasted a year and led to a virtual Communist encirclement of KMT forces in the northeast and in central China. At this point, CCP and KMT forces were basically equal in terms of manpower and weaponry. Hyperinflation in Chinese cities continued to alienate the urban **population**, while CCP underground organizers promoted the CCP line of "peace, democracy, and unity." By late 1948, KMT troops were defeated in two significant battles in Manchuria and central China, as more and more KMT units led by their officers defected to the Communist side. A last-ditch peace initiative by the KMT was turned down by the Communists, who inflicted a major defeat on the Nationalists at the battle of the Huaihai in January, which led to the capture of the cities of **Tianjin** and Beiping (**Beijing**), followed in April and May by the fall of Nanjing (the Nationalists' capital) and **Shanghai**, respectively. In December 1949, remnant KMT forces fled to the island of **Taiwan**. Throughout the war, the KMT was hampered by its corruption, economic mismanagement, and the unwillingness of its leader, Chiang Kai-shek, to delegate authority to military commanders, many of whom worked at cross purposes.

"CLASS LABELS" ("*JIEJI CHENGFEN*"). Politically and ideologically defined, class labels were assigned to all Chinese by the **Chinese Communist Party** (CCP) based on their family lineage that existed prior to the Communist takeover in 1949. Several categories or labels were widely employed: "bad" labels included "capitalist," "landlord," and "rich peasant"; "good" labels were **cadres**," "factory workers," "revolutionary soldier," "revolutionary martyr," and "poor and lower middle peasant." The importance of class labels in China was especially evident during the **Cultural Revolution (1966–1976)**, when such designations determined whether a young person could become a **Red Guard** (restricted to those from families of "revolutionary cadres" [pre-1949 CCP only], "revolutionary military men," "revolutionary martyrs," "factory workers," and "poor and lower middle peasants") or, more importantly, whether a person became a target of Red Guard violence (former "rightists," "reactionaries," "bad elements," "counterrevolutionaries," "rich peasants," "landlords," or "capitalists"). That class background was the overriding factor in the Cultural Revolution was evidenced by the couplet pasted up by Red Guards everywhere which read that "the son of the heroic father is a warrior; the son of the reactionary father is a rotten egg."

The category of "intellectual" has, at different times in the history of the **People's Republic of China (PRC)**, been "bad," especially during the Cultural Revolution, when educators, poets, and artists were frequently singled out for attack. At other times, **intellectuals** were designated "good," namely since 1978, when it was officially declared that they were part of the working class. For years, one's class label affected such opportunities as school, employment, and promotions, plus the possibility of joining the CCP. Most importantly, class labels were instrumental in determining whether an individual became a target in the many political campaigns that occurred in China during the Maoist era (1949–1976). Class labels could only be changed across generations. Offspring from a family with a mixture of "good" and "bad" class labels—to wit, the father is a "worker" and the mother is a "capitalist"—were generally assigned the latter.

"CLASS STRUGGLE" (*"JIEJI DOUZHENG"*). The core of Chinese Communist ideology is composed of **Marxism–Leninism–Mao Zedong Thought** in which class struggle was, until recently, a central value. The goal of class struggle during the Maoist era (1949–1976) in China was to introduce proletarian values into the entire society and create a modern industrial society that would form the basis for the Marxist utopia of a classless social order. Class struggle occurred domestically between capitalists and the workers and peasants, and internationally between **imperialism** and **socialism**. In the early stages of **Chinese Communist Party (CCP)** rule in the 1950s, the domestic class struggle led by the Party was directed at landlords and other so-called bad elements and "counterrevolutionaries" who opposed the establishment of the socialist state. The leading force of international imperialism, the **United States**, was also the target of the international class struggle that the Chinese government promoted throughout the 1950s and 1960s until the rapprochement between China and the U.S. in the early 1970s.

In the Maoist perspective, class struggle in China was a perpetual feature of Chinese society after the completion of the socialist revolution and even occurred within the CCP—the vanguard of the proletariat. It is for this reason that in the early 1960s, Mao warned "never to forget class struggle" and went so far as to sanction attacks against so-called **capitalist roaders** (*zouzipai*) in the CCP during the **Cultural Revolution (1966–1976)** when class struggle degenerated into factional infighting and power struggles among contending leadership groups. Yet, even Mao adjusted his views regarding the intensity of class struggle depending on the political situation. Thus, during the **Sino–Japanese War (1937–1945)**, Mao had called for limiting class struggle to "big bourgeoisie" and "compradors" opposed to China's independence, while forming alliances with national bourgeoisie and other non-proletarian class elements who were willing to fight Japanese imperialism. From the perspective of less-radical **leaders** in the CCP, class struggle should have ended with the completion of **land reform (1950–1953)** and the socialist transformation of the **economy** in the late 1950s and early 1960s. In the absence of a true capitalist class, the regime should have concentrated solely on developing the economy and the notion of class struggle in the CCP should have been regarded as heretical. Although this perspective lost out to Maoist radicalism during the Cultural Revolution, it regained prominence after Mao's death in 1976 as references to class struggle in China gradually all but disappeared from official propaganda. Hard-line ideologues in the CCP, however, still periodically raise the issue of class struggle against a re-emergent capitalist class that has been fostered by the economic reforms pursued since

1978–1979 and against ideas of "**bourgeois liberalization**" imported from the West.

"**CLEANSING OF THE CLASS RANKS**" ("*QINGLI JIEJI DUIWU YUNDONG*"). This was one of the many mass movements launched in 1968 during the **Cultural Revolution (1966–1976)** that aimed at purging the **Chinese Communist Party (CCP)** and **Red Guard** organizations of purported "class enemies who have sneaked into the revolutionary organization." The campaign officially targeted "stubborn bourgeois power holders" (i.e., still unrepentant and perhaps silent supporters of **Liu Shaoqi**, the primary target of the Cultural Revolution); "renegades and spies" (a catchall category of individuals who were accused of being in the service of the **Kuomintang** and/or American "imperialists"); and "landlords, rich peasants, reactionaries, bad elements, and rightists who had not been well reformed" (i.e., individuals, especially teachers, who were accused of not fully embracing the Maoist cause). Both class origin and political performance were the criteria for being targeted in this campaign. Overall, the campaign aimed at "cleansing" the newly formed **Revolutionary Committees** and other "mass organizations" of people who did not fit the radical prescriptions for political allegiance offered by **Jiang Qing** and the radicals. These various organizations had emerged in the political vacuum created during the Cultural Revolution because of the organizational disintegration of the CCP, but were often staffed with individuals of various political stripes, ideological persuasions, and factional allegiances, in addition to administrative incompetents and opportunists. The entire movement quickly degenerated into political retributions and mutual recriminations by one faction against another in the turmoil and chaos of the period.

COLLECTIVIZATION OF AGRICULTURE. *See* AGRICULTURAL PRODUCERS' COOPERATIVES (APCs); AGRICULTURE; "PEOPLE'S COMMUNES."

"**COMMON PROGRAM**" ("*GONGTONG GANGLING*"). Inaugurated in September 1949, the Common Program was passed by the first session of the **Chinese People's Political Consultative Conference (CPPCC)**. This meeting was held in Beiping (soon renamed

Beijing) on the eve of the victory in the **Civil War (1946–1949)** by the **People's Liberation Army (PLA)** against the **Kuomintang (KMT)**. The full title of the approved document drafted by the **Chinese Communist Party (CCP)** was known as the "Common Program of the Chinese People's Political Consultative Conference" (*zhongguo renmin zhengzhi xieshang huiyi gongtong gangling*) and was presented to the conference by **Zhou Enlai**. Although various non-Communist "**democratic parties** and people's organizations" purportedly contributed to its drafting, the document was clearly based on the **basic line of the Party** for the "transition period" that had been decided at the March 1949 Second Plenum of the Seventh Central Committee. The Common Program contained seven chapters and 60 articles that evidently were not significantly amended or altered by the rubber-stamp CPPCC.

The basic purpose of the Common Program was to lay out the broad national goals of the new government consistent with the doctrine of **New Democracy** enunciated by **Mao Zedong**. Specifically, it "summarized the experiences of China's new democratic revolution and clearly stipulated that the **People's Republic of China (PRC)** was a country led by the working class." It also declared China to be a "people's democratic dictatorship founded on the worker-peasant alliance." In the spirit of the New Democracy's **United Front** policies, the program emphasized unifying China's various classes and **minorities** and "stipulated the election rights and powers of citizens and their political freedoms." Yet, as a harbinger of the harsh persecution of **intellectuals** and other social groups that would soon follow, the program singled out "reactionary elements, feudal landlords, and bureaucratic capitalists"—catchall categories in which almost anyone could be arbitrarily placed—as targets of the new dictatorship. Despite the relatively moderate tone of the Common Program, especially in comparison to later CCP policies, this document marked the inexorable path of the PRC to class warfare and political persecution that would peak in the **Anti-Rightist Campaign (1957–1958)** and the **Cultural Revolution (1966–1976)**. The program also signaled the clear intention of the Chinese Communists to create a unified and powerful state structure. After years of warlords and civil war, the program promised a "unified military force, composed of the PLA and the People's **Public Security Bureau**." It also committed the new government to establishing state control over the **economy** and "integrating" different sectors of the economy, such as **agriculture**, **industry**, and **transportation**. During the first five years of the PRC, the Common Program served as a "temporary constitution" until it was formally replaced by the PRC State Constitution adopted in 1954 by the **National People's Congress** (**NPC**).

COMMUNE. *See* "PEOPLE'S COMMUNES."

CONTINUING REVOLUTION. *See* "UNINTERRUPTED REVOLUTION."

CONSTITUTIONS. *See* CHINESE COMMUNIST PARTY (CCP); GOVERNMENT STRUCTURE.

CORRUPTION. A by-product of the economic reforms introduced in China beginning in1978–1979, corruption by government officials and Party **cadres** emerged as a major issue in the 1989 second **Beijing Spring** pro-democracy movement. The **Chinese Communist Party** (**CCP**) had won power in 1949 in part because of its opposition to, and political exploitation of, the enormous corruption of the ruling **Kuomintang** (**KMT**). Despite the reputation of the Maoist era (1949–1976) as relatively corrupt-free, the crucial role of the Party and state agencies in productive and commercial activities (so called "agency production" [*jiguan shengchan*]) sowed the seeds of the post-reform eruption of official corruption that by the 1980s probably surpassed that of its Nationalist predecessors. A frequent target of both popular discontent and criticism, delegates to the **National People's Congress** (**NPC**) were often the recipients of petitions and complaints from local farmers irate over land seizures, police abuse, and inaction on the part of local officials. In a 2003 survey of urban residents by the **Chinese Academy of Social Sciences** (**CASS**), China's top think tank, corruption was listed as the second biggest "social contradiction" in China after unemployment. At the March 2003 NPC, a large number of delegates openly expressed their discontent with corruption at the high levels, especially in the courts.

Bribery, smuggling, nepotism, eating and drinking at public expense, and outright embezzlement are the primary forms of corruption that span from local policemen and clerks in government offices to the highest **leaders** (and their offspring) in the CCP. "Official profiteering" (*guandao*) is undoubtedly the worst form of such corruption in which an official and/or his or her family members buy scarce commodities or raw materials at low, state-fixed prices and then sell them on the open, private market at huge markups. Such corruption was made possible by the existence of a dual-price system, that is, low official state prices (for raw materials, such as coal and food) and high free-market prices for the same items. Lavish lifestyles by high officials result from such corruption: the import of Mercedes-Benz automobiles, the construction of expensive apartments and hotels in major cities for exclusive use by officials, and the sending of their offspring abroad ostensibly for **education**. Managerial corruption has also become rampant as a result of reforms in **state-owned enterprises** (**SOEs**) that have allowed managers to convert their greater "autonomous power" (*zizhuquan*) into "self-enriching power" (*zifuquan*) by illicitly siphoning off factory assets into their own hands while workers go unpaid for months, often provoking major **social protests**. The buying and selling of official "receipts" to pad expense accounts and the scalping of tickets for **transportation** and entertainment events are smaller, yet no less virulent aspects of this corruption.

Despite prosecution of some high-level officials on charges of corruption in the early 1980s, Yang Yibang the vice-minister of the Chemical Industry as one case in point, by 1983, the **Central Discipline Inspection Commission** (**CDIC**), the main disciplinary body of the CCP, announced that economic crimes, including smuggling, graft, bribery, speculation, and fraud, had reached a record high since the founding of the **People's Republic of China** (**PRC**) in 1949 and that any CCP member who takes bribes, however small, would be expelled.

During the 1989 second Beijing Spring, popular discontent was directed at the corruption of the political leaders and their families, including the sons of then CCP General Secretary **Zhao Ziyang**. One of the reasons that the former CCP General Secretary **Hu Yaobang** had lost his position in 1987 was because of his insistence that all top political leaders, such as **Hu Qiaomu** (whose son was accused of embezzlement), take a strong stand against corruption among family members. After 1989, major anticorruption campaigns were launched by CCP political leaders, and several officials were executed on charges of corruption. Yet, despite the Party's effort to respond to the popular outcry, corruption remained a serious and even growing problem with deleterious effects on China's reform program. In 1993, for example, fraud cost the Agricultural Bank of China a loss of US$10 million. Corruption is also linked to the growth of mafia-style organized **crime**, led by traditional Chinese gangs, such as the Triads. In some places, these gangs have taken over local Chinese government and police organs and have even directed organized crime activities abroad, including in New York's Chinatown, and on the high seas, where Chinese pirates have raided commercial shipping. The smuggling of stolen cars from **Hong Kong** and even New York to clients within the Chinese government and the police is now part of the pervasive system of corruption in China.

Warnings that corruption might bring down the Communist Party were voiced by the press and even by **Deng Xiaoping** and President **Jiang Zemin**, who, in 1995, authorized a major anticorruption drive. Aimed at eliminating widespread graft in the CCP, this campaign included among its victims several business executives, including two **women**, who were sentenced to death, and Wang Baosen, a vice-mayor of **Beijing**, who, while under official investigation, committed suicide, a clear indication of the extent and seriousness of the investigation. But some in China saw this and other prosecutions as an example of "sacrificing the pawn to save the general," that is, as an attempt to protect more senior officials in the Beijing municipal government. The most serious cases of fraud occurred in China's **banking and finance** sectors, where billions of *yuan* were embezzled from the Industrial and Commercial Bank of China, the country's largest lender, and the China Construction Bank whose Sichuan Province deputy manager allegedly used bank funds to support eight mistresses.

In 1990, the Chinese government passed the Administrative Procedure Law that granted ordinary citizens the right to sue government officials for corruption or exercise of illegal, arbitrary power. This led to a rash of petitions submitted to government agencies and to NPC delegates from aggrieved parties but with the petitioners who often travel to Beijing sent home or incarcerated on charges of "trouble-

CRIME AND THE LEGAL SYSTEM • 137

making" and "provoking instability." The 1997 Criminal Law contained a strong anti-corruption provision but with an additional provision that exempted employees in collective enterprises. With the central government generally reluctant to act against poorly paid local officials, corruption has continued unabated, which many consider a symptom of China's growing divide between rich and poor, along with the inherent problems of overseeing the transition of state-owned enterprises to a share-holding system that on numerous occasions provoked **labor** strikes and other forms of potentially violent social protests. Although political leaders in Beijing continue to decry official corruption and portray themselves as selfless, anti-corruption crusaders, local anti-corruption whistle-blowers risk being denounced as provoking "political instability" and playing into the hands of "hostile Western forces" and "dissidents overseas," as occurred in 2004 with an outspoken Fujian Province county-level official who was disciplined for his anti-corruption efforts and subsequently himself charged with corruption. Adding to the problem is the creation by local communities and employers of so-called Security Protection Personnel who operate outside the **Public Security Bureau** to maintain order and protect buildings but who also collect "sanitation fees" from workers and members of the **floating population** in return for doing nothing. *See also* HE QINGLIAN; "PRINCE'S FACTION."

COUNTERREVOLUTIONARY. *See* ANTI-COUNTER-REVOLUTIONARY CAMPAIGNS.

CRIME AND THE LEGAL SYSTEM. During the Maoist era in China (1949–1976) when Chinese society was subject to nearly absolute totalitarian control and a puritanical social code, crime rates and criminal activity were virtually unknown. During the **Cultural Revolution (1966–1976)**, however, a great deal of politically inspired thuggery and violence occurred with the consent of the top **leaders** of the **Chinese Communist Party (CCP)**, including **Mao Zedong**. Following the adoption of the economic reforms in 1978–1979 and the loosening of social controls historically enforced by the "**basic unit**" (*jiben danwei*) system, criminal activity of all sorts reappeared in China prompting the government to pass China's first Criminal Law in 1979. Starting in the 1980s, crime grew at very rapid rates and accelerated in the 1990s into the early 2000s as economic prosperity combined with growing gaps between rich and poor. Reflecting China's transformation into a modern society governed increasingly by market forces, many of the new crimes were economic, involving attempts at making a fast *yuan* through such illegal activity as manipulation of share prices and stock-rigging schemes on China's fledging **stock markets** in the Shenzhen **Special Economic Zone (SEZ)** and in **Shanghai**. Direct-marketing scams and elaborate pyramid selling schemes, which often involved such reputable groups as financially pressed but technologically sophisticated college students, grew in number, often taking advantage of those segments of the **population** that had not yet adapted to the increasingly cash-based **economy**. Fraud involving credit cards, letters of credit, and other financial instruments that raked off huge sums of money demonstrated a level of professionalism and high-tech finesse beyond the capabilities of police authorities to match.

Vast numbers of people in China left behind by the economic prosperity of the last two decades, especially from rural areas, have often turned to such crimes as child selling, human trafficking, drug dealing, large-scale train robberies, and even piracy as the only escape from the grinding poverty that still afflicts interior, village China. Theft of China's rich collection of antiquities scattered throughout the country in largely unguarded areas have also risen with many of the perpetrators of this and other such crimes citing their activities as the only recourse to pay off the loan sharks and other financial schemers who often prey on unsuspecting and destitute rural people. For similar reasons, China has witnessed a huge increase in prostitution, illegal gambling, and heroin trafficking in southwestern regions close to the poppy fields of Myanmar (Burma) and **Afghanistan**, all of which have emerged as major growth industries during the years of economic reform.

Groups especially prone to become involved in criminal activity include the vast number of migrant workers who make up China's **floating population** and individuals involved in secret societies and clan organizations long repressed in Maoist China, which have reemerged and often morphed into gang-land and mafia-like organizations. The latter are especially prevalent in China's mushrooming drug trade involving heroin and other outlawed substances with a level of national and international organization that has often defied police interdiction. Even the perpetrators of less serious crimes, such as the selling of fake train tickets and cigarettes, have often displayed a high level of organization with ample uses of sophisticated **technology** and finance that spans several provinces and involves international players. China has even become a target of international jewel thieves from abroad, who carried out a series of heists in Shanghai and other cities in late 2004. Kidnapping, blackmail, gun running, and protection rackets—all features of classic mafia and gang-land operations—now afflict many parts of the country—especially in the more prosperous areas of the south. Although overall crime rates in China are still low by world standards, dramatic increases occurred throughout the 1990s—especially in personal injury cases, robbery, gang violence, fraud, smuggling, and counterfeiting, this according to statistics compiled by China's **Public Security Bureau.**

The greatest threat by crime to China's social stability has undoubtedly come from the dramatic increase in murder and mayhem that has struck both rural and urban China in the past decade. Although China does not consolidate national figures on such crimes, cities especially hard hit by rapid increases in crime, such as Shenzhen, saw the overall crime rate rise in 2003 by nearly 60% and the murder and assault rate by nearly 40%. In addition to gang-land and drug-related killings that have accompanied the reemergence of a Chinese mafia, the country has also witnessed a spate of the most heinous crimes, especially notorious serial murders of adults and children, which, in the world's worst-known case, involved a man from Henan Province who confessed to 65 separate murders from 2001 to 2003. While business tycoons—domestic and foreign—and members of the country's nouveau riche have often been targeted for killing and/or hostage taking by distraught former business associates or estranged spouses, young **women**, from college students to waitresses to prostitutes, have increasingly become the victim of violent crime from rape to some of the country's most grisly murders involving bodily dismemberment, often by outspoken misogynics. No less shocking to China's generally conservative social order, was the spate of attacks in 2004 on middle, primary, and even kindergarten school children, along with assaults by teachers on students and vice-versa, often arising from sexual harassment. Killings and assaults by family members have also grown, with children killing their parents and parents killing children, largely out of economic and psychological duress in the country's increasingly competitive environment. As the divorce rate in China has risen, so have revenge assaults and murders by former spouses and close relatives while increasingly alienated and nihilistic young people turn to wanton acts of assault and violence on unsuspecting victims in **Internet** cafés and on college campuses. As control of many remote rural areas has shifted from increasingly lax local CCP organs to more traditional clans, internecine warfare and violence have reemerged with authorities apparently incapable of stopping such outbreaks. Altogether, in 2003, there were 3.95 million cases of crime reported for the entire country.

The reaction of Chinese authorities to rising crime rates that have unsettled the nation has been very high-profile with liberal usage of capital punishment and other harsh measures that often involve trampling on the very **human rights** and newly enacted legal procedures China has vowed to "safeguard and protect." Although China refuses to release figures on the number of people executed annually, estimates from such foreign sources as Amnesty International put the figure at between 10,000 and 15,000 annually for a variety of crimes including not just murder and rape but many economic, non-violent crimes, such as fraud, embezzlement, and counterfeiting. Lesser forms of punishment include death sentence with reprieve, life imprisonment, imprisonment for varying periods, and supervision. In 1982, provisions were added to the Chinese legal code to punish criminals who did great damage to the national economy. In 1989, following the crackdown on the second **Beijing Spring** pro-democracy movement, the government began a campaign against the "six evils" of narcotics, prostitution, pornography, gambling, superstition, and the buying and selling of women. As a reaction to the explosion of drug use, a 1990 National Narcotics Control Commission was set up to strengthen the fight against drug peddling and addiction. This was followed in 1996 by passage of a new Criminal Procedure Law that expanded a criminal defendant's right to counsel and sought to create a more independent judiciary less subject to political interference by the very power-holders who are often parties to legal disputes. Despite the commitment of China's top leadership to creating the "rule of law," defendants in Chinese criminal proceedings face innumerable obstacles, including an extremely high conviction rate (over 99%), indictment of excessively aggressive defense lawyers, and rulings often by unseen CCP-dominated political and legal committees for whom political considerations can be as important as the law. Appellate courts in China are also reluctant to overturn any lower court decision that might damage its relationship with prosecutors and police. With the passage of a 1989 statute entitling people to sue the state, more Chinese are demanding their legal rights, including giving suspects the right to have a lawyer present during interrogation, while, at the same time, the public continues to pressure the government to maintain "social stability" by halting the steady rise in crime if need be by forced confession, all of which makes any effort to create an adversarial process in the legal system difficult to achieve as protection of the authority of the government supersedes protection of suspects. And yet judges trained at the National Judges College in **Beijing** have been introduced to the modern theory of law: that the courts are impartial and defendants are innocent until proven guilty.

In 1998, CCP General Secretary **Jiang Zemin** announced a major anti-smuggling campaign with formation of a 6,000-member national police force to suppress all forms of domestic and international smuggling that, in some cases, led to the arrest of senior custom officials. This was followed in 2000 by a decision to launch a three-year nationwide "strike hard"(*yanda*) campaign aimed at all sorts of criminals from petty thieves to serial killers to organized crime figures and even leading officials. While often at a technological disadvantage to the increasing professionalism of their criminal prey, Chinese police have adopted up-to-date investigative methods, such as DNA data banks, to track down serious criminals, such as rapists and murderers. Also, they are cooperating with national and international law enforcement networks with international organs, such as the **Association of Southeast Asian Nations (ASEAN)**, especially to fight transnational organized crime and drug dealing. Although gun possession in China remains uncommon, Chinese police in recent years have become increasingly involved in shootouts with individual criminals and organized gangs who have secured weapons by the underground network of gunrunning that now afflicts the country. China has also been hit by a series of explosions in cities, such as Beijing (1997), Changsha, Hunan Province (1999), and in Tiananmen Square (2000) that may have been the work of Islamic separatist groups or just deranged individuals. *See also* CORRUPTION; HE QINGLIAN.

"CRITICISM AND SELF-CRITICISM" (*PIPING YU ZIWOPI-PING*"). This was originally a Leninist concept introduced into the Russian Bolshevik Party organization to ensure that members abided by the policies of the leadership. Individuals on the wrong side of policy and/or power struggles were forced to submit to criticism from others and to criticize themselves. During the 1930s and 1940s in China, the **Chinese Communist Party (CCP)** adopted the same method to impose control over Party members who wavered from the **basic line of the Party**. Criticism and self-criticism were harsh and often resulted in purges and even executions. In theory, although criticism and self-criticism were to be comprehensive within the Party and to involve even top **leaders**. The focus was on Party members who support the wrong side in the interminable ideological and power struggles that have marked CCP history.

CUI JIAN (1961–). A member of China's Korean minority **population**, Cui Jian has been one of China's most popular and often controversial pop singers with a particular appeal to Chinese youth. In 1986, his first song, *Penniless*, swept the country just at the time when rock and roll was entering China, where it appealed as an art form known for rebellion and idealism. During the 1989 second **Beijing Spring**, Cui's provocative song "Nothing to My Name" ("Yiwu suoyou") was highly popular among the student demonstrations for its independent message with anti-government overtones. Cui soon faded from the spotlight but in 2002 and 2004, he made a dramatic return by sponsoring huge outdoor music festivals in such out-of-the-way places as the mountains of Yunnan Province and in the desert of the Ningxia-Hui Autonomous Region located in western China.

CULT OF MAO. *See* PERSONALITY CULT.

CULTURAL REVOLUTION (1966–1976). Perhaps the seminal political event of post-1949 Chinese Communist history, the "Great

Proletarian Cultural Revolution" (*wuchanjieji wenhua dageming*), as it was officially called, represented the personal crusade by **Mao Zedong** and his radical supporters to purge the **Chinese Communist Party** (**CCP**) of their political and ideological opponents. The primary target of this power struggle was Mao's first designated successor, State Chairman **Liu Shaoqi**, whom Mao accused of "**revisionism**" and of being a "**capitalist roader**" (*zouzipai*). The ensuing battle between the Maoist-radical faction in the CCP, which included the chairman's wife, **Jiang Qing** and a reluctant **Zhou Enlai**, and the moderate faction led by Liu and composed of **Deng Xiaoping, Peng Zhen**, and many other top CCP **leaders**, brought China to the brink of a civil war. Although the Cultural Revolution officially began in August 1966 when the CCP Central Committee narrowly approved a resolution calling for a complete revolution in Chinese society, politics, and culture, it was the 7 May 1966 directive by Mao Zedong to **Lin Biao** calling on the **People's Liberation Army** (**PLA**) to become a "great school" in learning and applying Mao Zedong Thought that constituted the first political blow in this monumental struggle, which began by targeting **intellectuals** and especially teachers at some of the country's most elite institutions, such as **Qinghua University**. This was followed on 16 May 1966 when the CCP **Politburo** announced its decision to set up the **Cultural Revolution Small Group**, which was empowered to carry out attacks on "all representatives of the bourgeoisie who have infiltrated the Party, government, and cultural world."

Declaring that "under heaven all is chaos," Mao Zedong relied on the frenzied adulation of **Red Guards** whose organization he sanctioned with a series of eight mass rallies beginning in **Beijing** on 18 August, 1966. For Mao, the Cultural Revolution was an ideological crusade to reinvigorate the Chinese revolution, train a new generation of "revolutionary fighters," and radically alter Chinese culture by Red Guard attacks on traditional culture denounced in the ideological ferment of the day as the **four olds**. Beginning in late July and August 1966, especially after the withdrawal of **work teams** from universities and middle schools in Beijing and a Central Committee order to the **Public Security Bureau** not to interfere in the student movement, violence by young Red Guards against teachers, educators, and Party secretaries escalated with over 100 individuals dying from torture and assaults in one Beijing district during a two-week period alone when the targets of the campaign were forced to wear dunce caps and boards hung around their necks carrying labels. The violence spread from Beijing to **Shanghai** and many other cities as Red Guards were given free train tickets to travel all over the country. From late 1966 to early 1967, factories and educational institutions were thrown into turmoil as the Red Guards assaulted so-called class enemies and even engaged in open-pitched battles among different factions. Senior officials targeted by Red Guards at the behest of Mao and his radical supporters were often abused and humiliated in front of crowds, their heads shaven with paint splashed on their faces, and insulting slogans hung around their necks (such as "member of the black gang" or "reactionary academic authority"), all the time forced to assume the "jet plane style" (*zuo feiji*) with lowered heads, bent bodies, and arms raised backward for hours at a time. Peasants and workers held endless sessions studying Mao's teachings while anyone dubbed "anti-social" was publicly denounced and even executed by a bullet to the back of the head. Western music and art were also targeted as artists and musicians drawn to Western cultural forms were persecuted and their instruments and artistic creations wantonly destroyed. However, the piano and violin were saved single-handedly by China's world-renowned pianist Yin Chengzong, who, in the heat of the attacks, rolled out a piano onto Tiananmen Square and played revolutionary odes to Mao Zedong, which served as a signal to stop beating up on pianists and violinists.

By mid-1967, Mao ordered in the PLA to stabilize production and social order and in 1968 after the Chinese government issued an urgent cable demanding an end to violent clashes on Chinese railways, where military materials bound for **Vietnam** were seized by contending Red Guard factions, the chairman criticized their indulgence in armed struggle. By December 1968, Mao ordered the rambunctious Red Guards to be "sent down" (*xiaxiang*) to the countryside for "reeducation" by the poor and lower middle peasants. While the appointment of Lin Biao as the sole vice-chairman of the CCP in April 1969 at the Ninth National Party Congress apparently signified the political triumph of the pro-Cultural Revolution faction, which included **Chen Boda** and **Kang Sheng,** by August 1970 at the Second Plenum of the Ninth Central Committee Lin Biao's political star had quickly faded as Mao apparently began to question Lin's loyalty, leading the erstwhile successor to allegedly attempt an assassination of Mao Zedong on 12 September 1971 that subsequently led to Lin's death in an airplane crash as he and his immediate family attempted to flee China. By 1973, the Cultural Revolution was effectively spent and yet at the August 10th National Party Congress Mao's protégé, **Wang Hongwen**, insisted that a series of Cultural Revolutions would recur. Although the Cultural Revolution did not officially end until Mao Zedong's death in 1976, during its last years China was effectively under military rule.

Mao Zedong's goals of "cleansing" the CCP were successful, at least temporarily. Liu Shaoqi was purged from the Party and, in 1969, died in a small prison cell. Deng Xiaoping—the "second **capitalist roader**" (*zouzipai*)—lost his positions of power, but was protected from physical harm by sympathetic military commanders. Other targets of Mao's ire were hounded and criticized, but most top leaders, such as **Yang Shangkun, Bo Yibo**, and others, survived the ordeal and returned to power after Mao's death. Besides enormous economic disruption in China's factories and some agricultural areas, the Cultural Revolution also caused the deaths of more than two million people, including many scholars, teachers, scientists, and artists who were sometimes killed by their own students. Since 1978, the Cultural Revolution has been roundly condemned by the CCP leadership and Cultural Revolution changes in **education** and political institutions, such as the **Revolutionary Committees**, have been completely abandoned, although the long-term impact of this political upheaval remains in the form of deep fissures in the social fabric and widespread mutual distrust. A privately funded museum recounting the chaos and human costs of the Cultural Revolution was built in Shantou, Guangdong Province, by the city's former mayor. *See also* "CLEANSING OF THE CLASS RANKS."

CULTURAL REVOLUTION SMALL GROUP. There were two such "Cultural Revolution Small Groups" during the **Cultural Revolution (1966–1976)**. The first was headed by Beijing Mayor **Peng Zhen** and was disbanded on 16 May 1966 for its refusal to engage in the political struggle promoted by Mao against **Liu Shaoqi** and other top **leaders** of the **Chinese Communist Party** (CCP). A second Cultural

Revolution Small Group was then established on the same day and headed by Mao confidant **Chen Boda** and included major radical leaders, such as **Jiang Qing**, **Kang Sheng**, **Yao Wenyuan**, and others. The group operated directly under the Standing Committee of the **Politburo** and was responsible for leading the Cultural Revolution. In August 1966, Jiang Qing was declared the first deputy to Chen Boda in the Cultural Revolution Small Group, which, by the 1970s, was disbanded as the Cultural Revolution began to wind down.

CURRENCY. China's currency is the *yuan* also known as the *renminbi* ("people's currency"), which in 2005 was a semi-convertible currency valued at 8.277 to the American dollar. Following the hyperinflation that afflicted China during the later years of rule by the **Kuomintang (KMT)**, the **Chinese Communist Party (CCP)** on coming to power stabilized the currency. In March 1955, the People's Bank issued a new "people's currency" at the rate of 10,000 old to new *yuan*, completing the changeover by June of the same year. Throughout the era of Soviet-style central economic planning (1953–1978), the setting of prices for basic commodities and consumer goods by the State Planning Commission and reliance on a rationing system for staples led to little or no inflation as internationally China maintained a fixed exchange rate system while its currency was nonconvertible on foreign markets and heavily overvalued. A small black market for the Chinese currency existed in **Hong Kong** that, in the 1970s, developed into an illegal curbside market in major Chinese cities following the opening to tourists and foreign business. In the 1980s, China ran a dual exchange rate system with a different rate set for foreign tourists and businessmen who used so-called Foreign Exchange Certificates (FECs), for which a healthy black market in major cities also developed that produced major gaps between swap and official rates. In 1990, following the establishment of the **Shanghai** Securities Exchange—the first securities exchange on the mainland since 1949—China announced a major currency devaluation of almost 10%, bringing its currency more in line with true market value and in 1994 pegged its currency at 8.277 to the **United States** dollar while dropping the FECs, thereby combining swap and official exchange rates. After several bouts of inflation (which peaked in 1994 at 21%), on 1 December 1996, China made its currency effectively account convertible, meaning that all receipts and payments arising from international trade could be converted although Foreign Direct Investment (FDI), foreign loans, and the trading of securities remained under firm Chinese government control. During the 1997–1998 Asian financial crisis, China resisted any further devaluation thereby avoiding gains in **trade and investment** at the expense of its Asian neighbors—even as its own exports languished and the country experienced substantial deflation as the domestic market was flooded with goods originally designed for export. This policy position was made possible by the country's relatively low debt service ratio (measured by total debt payments as a proportion of the exports of goods and services), which, from 1990 to 1997, was below 12%. By 1998, China had accumulated foreign exchange reserves of US$145 billion, enough to finance 11 months of imports as the debt service ratio gradually declined over the decade reaching 8.6% by 1998.

By 2004, as China's trade surplus with the U.S. grew to more than US$160 billion in 2004, the *yuan*:dollar peg became enormously distorted, which the Chinese government maintained by purchasing US$20 billion in dollars and other foreign currencies each month to prevent the *yuan* from rising in value. Internationally, China was able to limit trading in its currency because of strict state controls on the movement of the *yuan* in and out of the country, which made any settling of contracts on the *yuan* outside of China very difficult while the country also avoided the infusion of "hot money" that can feed domestic inflation and lead to the kind of currency collapses experienced by Thailand and South **Korea** during the 1997–1998 Asian financial collapse. In response to pressure mounted from the U.S., the European Union, and the International Monetary Fund (IMF), China in 2004 announced that the *yuan* would be pegged to a basket of various currencies but that it would not be permitted to rise or fall more than 0.3% a day against the U.S. dollar. China had long resisted removing the peg as an infringement on its national sovereignty despite estimates that its currency was undervalued by as much as 40%, which had led to threats in the U.S. Congress to impose 27% tariffs on all Chinese imports if China failed to let its currency float more freely. Although the slight appreciation of the *yuan* in 2004 was largely symbolic and too meager to make a difference in global trade, there are fears that if the Chinese currency appreciates markedly, some manufacturers would be forced to raise prices or shift production to other low-cost regions, such as Southeast Asia or **India**.

– D –

DAI QING (1941–). Trained as a missile engineer, Dai Qing is the adopted daughter of **People's Liberation Army (PLA)** Marshal **Ye Jianying**. As a "child of the party," Dai Qing was accorded special schooling throughout her youth, followed by secret service training in the PLA. A **Red Guard** during the **Cultural Revolution (1966–1976)**, Dai Qing had a brief stint in the military security services after which she took a job as a journalist at the *Enlightenment Daily* (the major publication for Chinese **intellectuals**). She quickly became known for her investigative reporting on the persecution of intellectuals in the history of the **Chinese Communist Party (CCP)**, including the infamous cases of **Wang Shiwei**, Liang Shuming, and Chu Anping, all victims of Party purges in the 1940s and 1950s. Dai Qing is a strong advocate of press freedom and protection of China's increasingly fragile **environment**, and has collected documents from many scientists and economists who, over the years, have opposed construction of the giant **Three Gorges Dam Project** on the Yangtze River in Central China. In 1989, Dai Qing was imprisoned for several months following the military crackdown on the second **Beijing Spring** while authorities placed a ban on her book of essays on the Three Gorges entitled *Yangtze! Yangtze!* citing its alleged contributions to the political "turmoil." Subsequently released, Dai Qing traveled extensively abroad and was a Nieman Fellow at Harvard University and a fellow at the Freedom Forum, School of Journalism of Columbia University. She was also a recipient of the Goldman Environmental Foundation Award in 1993.

Despite her outspoken views, Dai Qing does not describe herself as a "dissident" and favors gradual, institutional change over mass movements and demonstrations that she believes inevitably lead to violence and political degeneration. Dai Qing continues to reside in China and, in 2003, contracted 5,000 *mu* (*mu* = 0.0667 hectares) of uninhabited hilly land in the outer suburbs of **Beijing**, on which a pilot tree-planting program was begun. The account by Dai Qing of her controversial role in the second Beijing Spring in 1989 and of her time spent in the Qingcheng prison for high-profile political prisoners in China was published in 2004 under the title of *Tiananmen Follies: Prison Memoirs and Other Writings*. Other recent works include *Piquant Essays* and (in Chinese) *My Four Fathers*.

DAI XIAOLONG (1944–). A graduate of China's Central Institute of Finance and Banking, Dai Xiaolong joined the **Chinese Communist Party** (**CCP**) in 1973 and was appointed vice-governor and then governor of the People's Bank of China—the central bank of China—where he served for over seven years. A strong advocate of reform in China's system of **banking and finance**, Dai promoted cuts in China's interest rates as a measure to stimulate domestic consumer spending while he also advocated the decision by China to prevent devaluation of the national **currency** in the midst of the 1997–1998 Asian financial crisis. Dai Xiaolong was an alternate member of the 14th CCP Central Committee (1992–1997) and a full member of the 15th (1977–2002) CCP Central Committee. In 2003, Dai was appointed the mayor and Party secretary of **Tianjin**, one of four provincial-level municipalities in China, where one of the few "second tier," share-holding banks below the giant four state banks was set up with a mix of private, state-owned, and foreign-invested companies. *See also* LEADERS.

DALAI LAMA (1935–). The spiritual and temporal leader of Lamaism in **Tibet**, the current Dalai Lama is the 14th reincarnation of the first Dalai Lama who was initially proclaimed during China's Ming dynasty (1368–1644) by the Mongolian ruler Altan Khan. The word *"Dalai"* is Mongolian for "sea" and *"Lama"* is Tibetan for "wise master." Tibetans, however, refer to him as *Yeshe Norbu* (the "Wish-Fulfilling Gem"); the short form is *Kundun*, meaning "the presence." Beginning in the 18th century, China began to intervene in Tibetan affairs by installing the Dalai Lama and will undoubtedly insist on selecting the next Dalai Lama after the death of the current holder of the position.

Born at Amdo to a Tibetan peasant family and named Lhamo Thondup, the current Dalai Lama (also known as Tenzin Gyatso) was chosen as the reincarnation of the Buddha of Compassion when he identified the previous Dalai Lama's possessions "as his own" and was enthroned in 1940 at the age of five. In the immediate aftermath of the Communist takeover of China in 1949, the Dalai Lama attempted to achieve political reconciliation with the new **leaders** of the **People's Republic of China (PRC)**, when, in 1951, he consented to the 17-Article Agreement of the Central People's Government and the Local Government of Tibet on Measures for the Liberation of Tibet. In 1954, the Dalai Lama made a trip to **Beijing**; in 1955, he was appointed the chairman of the Preparatory Committee for the Tibetan Autonomous Region. By the late 1950s, however, tensions began to quickly boil over and, in 1959, following rumors that the Chinese would kidnap or kill the Dalai Lama, a revolt broke out in the Tibetan capital of Lhasa and the Dalai Lama fled Tibet for Dharamshala in northern **India**, where he resides to this day. While the Dalai Lama was replaced as chair of the Preparatory Committee by the Panchen Lama (the second holiest "living Buddha" in Tibet) who stayed behind in China, as a gesture of goodwill by the Chinese government the Dalai Lama remained as a vice-chairman of the **National People's Congress (NPC)** until 1964.

After reestablishing direct contacts with the Dalai Lama in 1979, China, by the mid-1980s, indicated to his representatives that the Dalai Lama was welcome to "return as a Chinese citizen" as long as he and his followers upheld China's unity, although it also appeared that he would be forced to reside in Beijing and not in Tibet. In 1987, the Dalai Lama reacted to demonstrations by monks and violence on the part of authorities in Lhasa by calling for the designation of Tibet as a "zone of peace." His five-point peace plan proposed to the Chinese government called for: demilitarization of Tibet; an end to Chinese **(Han)** immigration into Tibet; respect for **human rights** in Tibet; a halt to the production and testing of nuclear weapons in Tibet; and negotiation on the future status of Tibet. But following more riots in Lhasa in 1988 and, especially in March 1989, when the worst violence since 1959 broke out, including attacks on the local Han population, China declared martial law in Tibet.

Emboldened by the outbreak of democratic sentiment in the May–June 1989 second **Beijing Spring**, the Dalai Lama began to openly advocate "Tibet independence." Combined with the awarding of the 1989 Nobel Peace Prize to the Dalai Lama, this shut the door to his return to China since Chinese authorities condemned the awarding of the prize although in 2003 China claimed the Dalai Lama had rejected a Chinese invitation to return to Tibet in 1989 to attend the funeral of the then Panchen Lama, an invitation the Dalai Lama says never occurred. After a subsequent official reception given the Dalai Lama in the **United States** in 1993 by President Bill Clinton, dialogue between Beijing and the Dalai Lama that had begun in 1979 was broken off. China became particularly enraged in 1995 when the Dalai Lama named a Tibetan boy as the reincarnation of the Panchen Lama. China held a lottery to choose a different boy, and the Dalai Lama's choice has never been seen in public.

By the late 1990s, as the crackdown by Chinese authorities in Tibet increased dramatically, the Dalai Lama visited **Taiwan**, where his meeting with President Lee Teng-hui was denounced by China as a "collusion of splitists." The Dalai Lama gradually retreated from the demand for "Tibet independence" and, instead, asked that China grant Tibet "genuine autonomy." In 2002, he sent two delegations to Beijing to push for opening negotiations that were renewed later that year. The new leadership in China headed by President **Hu Jintao**, who earlier served as Party secretary in Tibet during the period of martial law, has said the door was open for the Dalai Lama's return to China once he accepts his status as a Chinese citizen, openly admits his wrongdoing for his previous support for "Tibet independence," and declares that Taiwan is also part of China. The Dalai Lama has refused an invitation from Taiwan's president Chen Shui-bian for a return visit. Although perennially shunned by leaders of most European and Asian nations, the Dalai Lama has been received by American Presidents Bill Clinton and George W. Bush. The Dalai Lama also frequently meets with prominent scientists to discuss his long-standing interest in **science and technology**, including such theories as quantum mechanics and cosmology. Top priority is given by the Dalai Lama to the preservation of Tibet's Buddhist traditions and its natural **environment**, both of which have suffered under mass in-migration of Han people and development plans, such as the construction of large-scale dams that have eroded Tibet's pristine landscape. The Dalai Lama's short reign in Tibet prior to his escape in 1959 is portrayed in two Western-made movies, *Seven Years in Tibet* and *Kundun*.

DAQING OILFIELD. Located in China's northeastern province of Heilongjiang (Black Dragon River), the Daqing oil field has been a major petroleum producer for the country and a subject of considerable political adulation and controversy. The development of the field began in the early 1960s—reportedly against the earlier advice of Soviet oil specialists in China—and production was rapidly increased to replace the loss of oil imports from the **Soviet Union** as a result of the outbreak of the Sino–Soviet Conflict. By 1963, 69% of all oil pumped in China came from Daqing, a situation that prompted **Mao Zedong** to inaugurate a campaign to glorify the achievements of the field's workers and the egalitarian political line of the local **Chinese Communist Party** (**CCP**) leadership that, Mao argued, explained Daqing's enormous success. Daqing was held up as a model of "more, faster, better, and more economical," a phrase that had been used in the late 1950s to promote the ill-fated **Great Leap Forward** (**1958–1960**). Along with the **Dazhai Brigade** that Mao also idealized in **agriculture,** Daqing became the subject of a propaganda campaign promulgating economic **self-reliance** (*zili gengsheng*) and the critical role of ideology in motivating workers to produce. Under the banner of "in industry learn from Daqing," it was said that the "Daqing spirit is the revolutionary spirit of the proletariat" and that the "Daqing people know profoundly the great significance of developing the revolutionary tradition of hard struggle and self-reliance." As a result, the oil field became a favorite site for visits and junkets by government personnel. In the meantime, Daqing CCP **leaders** Yu Qiuli, Kang Shien, and Gu Mu, rose to prominence as key economic advisors to Mao Zedong throughout the **Cultural Revolution** (**1966–1976**).

In 1977, the National Conference on Learning from Daqing in Industry was held in **Beijing** but with the relatively quick downfall of then Party Chairman **Hua Guofeng** and the inauguration of economic reforms in 1978–1979, the Daqing model was quickly eclipsed. The oil field's rapid increase in production probably stemmed less from politics and revolutionary zeal and more from the utilization of a water extraction technique that maximized recovery at the early stages of a field's production, but led to later dramatic reductions. As China opened new and more productive fields offshore and in the Central Asian interior around the Tarim basin in the Xinjiang Autonomous Region, in 1995, it announced plans to invest 100 billion *yuan* ($13 billion) in the petroleum sector by 2000, including refitting Daqing as concerns emerged over the field's possible depletion of recoverable reserves. Flooding in the Songhua River valley in 1998 endangered the Daqing oil fields, which are protected by a special dike system that spared it major destruction.

Following the call in 1997 by CCP leaders for **state-owned enterprises (SOEs)** to reorganize along corporate lines, Daqing was put under the ownership of PetroChina Ltd. whose parent company is China National Petroleum Corp (CNPC), China's largest oil production company. Like all large-scale SOEs in China, Daqing is part of a huge corporate conglomerate that includes ancillary production facilities such as the Daqing Refining & Chemical Corporation and of many subsidiaries such as the Daqing Petroleum Administration Bureau. Through the early 2000s, Daqing remained the country's largest oil producer providing one-third of its annual output. As depletion of the oil field's reserves continued, plans were announced in 2004 (and later reversed) to draw down its output since the prospect of expanding its reserves through introduction of new technologies remained murky. Plans were also announced to repair some of the enormous damage to the local ecology of marshlands that the field's rapid development and overexploitation have wrought. Daqing is the proposed terminus site for a 2,419-kilometer pipeline to carry crude oil from Siberian fields in **Russia** to China. *See also* ENERGY; TRANSPORTATION.

DAZHAI BRIGADE. Located in the poor mountainous region of Shanxi Province in northwestern China, the Dazhai Brigade was hailed by **Mao Zedong** as a model of socialist production in the countryside. Like the **Daqing Oilfield**, Dazhai was the subject of a nationwide campaign in the 1960s and 1970s that promoted the concept of **self-reliance** (*zili gengsheng*) and praised the role of socialist ideology and egalitarianism in "transforming nature" and dramatically increasing production. "In **agriculture**, learn from Dazhai" became the guiding nationwide slogan that hailed the brigade as a "new socialist village." Dazhai reportedly doubled the per-unit yield and gross output and at the same time made considerable progress in forestry and animal husbandry. "Revolutionary spirit" and "revolutionary vigor," it was claimed, were the deciding factors in leading the peasants to "give priority to the interests of the whole" and to adhere to "socialist principles of distribution" in which **work points** and income were allocated on a basis that, although not strictly egalitarian, allowed for only small differentials in compensation. Self-assessment and public discussion were the reputed means used to determine the allocation of work points that ultimately affected income distribution in the Chinese countryside. Brigade members who worked overtime received additional points, but not enough to lead to dramatic differences in wealth. Collective **labor** gangs in Dazhai were touted for digging a vast array of irrigation ditches and for terracing fields up steep mountainsides that made possible the dramatic increases in agricultural production.

The leader of Dazhai, a nearly illiterate peasant named **Chen Yonggui**, was elevated to national prominence and ultimately became a member of the **Politburo** of the **Chinese Communist Party (CCP)** and a vice-premier until his rude dismissal from these posts in 1980 and 1982, respectively. Mao Zedong's purpose in promoting Dazhai was clear. After the disastrous **Great Leap Forward (1958–1960)**, the **people's commune** and brigade as the highest forms of "socialist" organization in the countryside yielded their decision-making authority to the lower level and the less socialized **production team**. In championing Dazhai in the early 1960s, Mao made a concerted effort to overturn the reversion to the production team and to renew the advance to a more socialist system in the countryside that, he believed, was firmly opposed by Party **leaders** such as **Deng Xiaoping** and **Liu Shaoqi**. Once the **Cultural Revolution (1966–1976)** broke out, however, Dazhai receded into the background, although in the mid-1970s a Dazhai-type commune was briefly touted as another agricultural model and in 1976 the Second National Conference on Learning from Dazhai in Agriculture was held in **Beijing**. By 1978, the introduction of the **Agricultural Responsibility System**—the polar opposite of the Dazhai model—buried any memory of Dazhai, while recent government studies show that, contrary to its assertions of self-reliance, the Dazhai Brigade had actually received large infusions of state funds, thereby assisting its reputed increases in production. *See also* "PRODUCTION BRIGADE."

DEMOCRACY WALL MOVEMENT (1978–1979). The first of the post-Mao movements for democracy in China, this short-lived but intensely popular movement centered on a high brick wall located on Chang'an Avenue in the Xidan District of **Beijing**. For more than a year, **big-character posters** (*dazibao*) were plastered on the wall, evidently with the initial support of key **leaders** of the **Chinese Communist Party** (**CCP**) committed to changing the political direction and leadership in China. The first of many posters was by the poet Huang Xiang and appeared in March 1978. Many of the posters initially focused their attacks on the leftist mayor of Beijing and **Politburo** member Wu De, who was summarily dismissed as first secretary of the Beijing Party Committee in October 1978. Other themes on the wall posters called for a **"reversal of verdicts"** (*pingfan*) on the **April Fifth Movement** (**1976**) in Tiananmen Square, which had led to the purge of **Deng Xiaoping** and the rise of **Jiang Qing** and the radical leftist **Gang of Four**. Condemnation of **Mao Zedong** for his purge of popular political leaders, such as **People's Liberation Army** (**PLA**) Marshal **Peng Dehuai**; attacks on ideological orthodoxy; and advocacy of democracy, **human rights**, and rule by law were all central themes on Democracy Wall posters.

The Democracy Wall movement peaked in late 1978 at the time Deng Xiaoping was making his political comeback at the important **Third Plenum of the 11th CCP Central Committee**. Locked in a titanic political struggle for control of the Chinese state with the leftist **"two whatevers"** (*liangge fanshi*) faction, Deng, it is widely believed, countenanced and even encouraged the proliferation of wall posters that largely supported his political position. At the same time, activists in the poster campaign, such as **Wei Jingsheng**, began to expand their activities to include organization of study groups and dissident organizations such as the Enlightenment Society and the China Human Rights Alliance. After Deng Xiaoping consolidated his political position at the December 1978 Third Plenum, his need for the Democracy Wall movement quickly evaporated, and so the screws were gradually tightened against the wall and the democratic activists. Activities at the wall (which since 1979 has been covered with commercial advertisements) were banned, and Wei Jingsheng and other prominent leaders were arrested, tried, and imprisoned. In December 1982, the possibility of another such movement was quashed when the CCP eliminated from the state constitution the so-called **"four big freedoms"** (*sida ziyou*) that had guaranteed Chinese citizens the right to speak out, air views fully, hold great debates, and put up wall posters. Now the leadership, firmly under the control of Deng Xiaoping, stressed "stability" and "unity" and opposed any further expression of democratic ideas. *See also* BEIJING SPRING.

"DEMOCRATIC-CENTRALISM" (*"MINZHU JIZHONGZHI"*). Democratic-centralism is a model of organizational structure and decision making employed by Communist parties throughout the world. In the **Chinese Communist Party (CCP)**, it is described as the "basic principle of the proletarian party," providing a "dialectical unity of democracy and centralism." In theory, it both ensures widespread participation of all Party members in decision making and "iron discipline," that is, obedience to central commands.

Lenin developed democratic centralism during the early years of the underground Bolshevik Party in **Russia**. It figured prominently in Lenin's major writings on Party organization where he contrasted this principle of decision making and discipline to the opposite extremes of "bureaucratic centralism" and "anarchism" that purportedly infected other opposition political movements. Democratic-centralism reflected Lenin's deep fear of "spontaneity" in Russian political life, while promising the organization and planning necessary to seize and maintain political power. Democratic-centralism has four essential features as outlined in the rules of the former Communist Party of the **Soviet Union** and in the CCP: all leading bodies are elected; Party bodies must report periodically to their organizations and to higher bodies; the minority is subordinate to the majority; and decisions of higher bodies are obligatory for lower bodies. In theory, democratic centralism allows for substantial debate on policy issues (though within the general guidelines of the official ideology and the **basic line of the Party**) before formal decisions are taken. After decisions are reached, however, strict discipline (what Lenin called "iron discipline") must be followed by all Party members in implementing the decisions of the "majority." Formally adopted as the organizational doctrine of the CCP at the Second National Party Congress in 1922, democratic-centralism remains the central organizational principle of the CCP even as the Party adopted its post-1978–1979 economic reforms and the **open-door policy**.

DEMOCRATIC PARTIES (*MINZHU DANGPAI*). Also known as satellite parties, the democratic parties (*minzhu dangpai*) in China have existed since 1949, reflecting the **united front** strategy pursued by the **Chinese Communist Party** (**CCP**) in its rise to power. As part of his 1945 theory of **New Democracy**, Party Chairman **Mao Zedong** promised that China would be a multiparty state reflecting its multiclass character. As an underdeveloped nation making the transition, in Marxist terminology, from **feudalism** to capitalism, a number of classes existed that besides the minuscule proletariat class were potential allies of the CCP. In addition to the peasantry, the largest potential ally was among the bourgeoisie, a class Mao divided into two component parts: "big bourgeoisie" and "national bourgeoisie." Many in this bifurcated bourgeoisie were considered allies of the Communists, especially in the nationalist cause to defeat the Japanese and oust the **Kuomintang** (**KMT**), although the political influence of these classes even before 1949 was minimal. From 1949 onward, China, like some Eastern European Communist nations, such as Czechoslovakia, permitted the continued existence of non-Communist parties, at least in name.

There are eight democratic parties in China: Democratic League, Revolutionary Committee of the Kuomintang, National Construction Association, September Third Society (*Jiusan*), Association for Promoting Democracy, the Peasants' and Workers' Democratic Party, the *Zhi Gong Dang*, and the **Taiwan** Democratic Self-Government League. Altogether their membership is no more than a few hundred thousand in a country of 1.3 billion people. In reality, these organizations are not political parties in the conventional sense, but closer to interest groups and professional associations. Their major role in contemporary China is educational, as many such parties run schools and do consulting work for enterprises. Fielding candidates in elections for people's congresses is but a relatively minor function.

The Democratic League is the largest of the democratic parties and is composed of approximately 50,000 members, mostly **intellectuals**. In the 1940s, it was ostensibly a middle-of-the-road party that largely inclined toward the Communists out of disgust with the **corruption** and repression of the KMT. (In 1946, after a Democratic League press conference, the poet and KMT critic Wen Yiduo was gunned down after criticizing KMT corruption.) The League was formally dissolved by the Nationalist government, but reconstituted itself in **Hong Kong** in 1948 and then was reestablished as a political party in the mainland after the CCP seized power in October 1949. The Revolutionary Committee of the Kuomintang began with disaffected elements of the KMT, particularly individuals opposed to Chiang Kaishek. From 1927 to 1949, it existed as an underground organization, with its agents working in the KMT apparatus, where they engaged in intelligence work and sabotage. In Hong Kong, Madame **Song Qingling** was honorary chairman and Li Jishen chairman, a man who despite having brutally crushed a Communist uprising in Canton in 1927, was courted in the 1940s by the CCP. After 1949, Li became a leading figure of the democratic parties, constantly luring KMT defectors from Taiwan. The National Construction Association was formed in the mid-1940s to serve as a mediating force between the CCP and the KMT in the run-up to the **Civil War (1946–1949)**. Its major constituency was the business community that was disaffected with KMT policies. The *Jiusan* or September Third Society formed from a tiny leftist academic group in 1945 and is composed solely of intellectuals. The Association for Promoting Democracy was formed in 1946 and is made up primarily of school teachers. The Peasants' and Workers' Party, formerly known as the Third Party, is an organization that tried to bring about a cease-fire between the CCP and the KMT in the Civil War. Despite its name, its primary constituency is **health care** professionals.

After the Chinese Communist seizure of power in 1949, the democratic parties were put under the United Front Department of the CCP, which was maintained as a bridge to non-CCP groups. Financed by the Chinese government, these "parties" were immediately purged of members considered antagonistic to the Communist government and reorganized in a fashion to ensure their subservience to the CCP. They were represented in the **Chinese People's Political Consultative Conference** (CPPCC), which after 1954 lacked any real decision-making authority. Members of the democratic parties were obliged to participate in many early CCP propaganda campaigns, such as the **Resist America, Aid Korea Campaign**, and often became victims of CCP-led purges, such as the **Five Antis**.

In 1957, however, the role of the democratic parties changed fundamentally as Mao Zedong and other Party **leaders** encouraged the democratic parties to join in the **Hundred Flowers (1956–1957)** and voice criticism of the CCP. Through newspapers still controlled by the democratic parties (such as *Enlightenment Daily*, which at the time was an organ of the Democratic League), a bevy of criticism was directed at the CCP, and proposals were aired for radical political change. Accusations were directed at the Communists for trying to control the entire society through their systematic apparatus of "Party core groups" (*dang hexin xiaozu*), for carrying out "**thought reform**" (*sixiang gaizao*) against the bourgeoisie and intellectuals, for preventing the creation of a true independent **legal system**, and for being arrogant and never listening to advice. Universities, it was proposed, should be freed from CCP control; the CPPCC should be given real power in the state; and political decision making should be more open. After a few weeks of such criticism, Mao Zedong and more conservative elements in the CCP had had enough and many members of the democratic parties were forced to recant, while others suffered greater humiliations.

From 1958 to 1978, the Democratic parties were effectively suffocated as their independent newspapers, such as the *Enlightenment Daily*, were put under direct CCP control. During the **Cultural Revolution (1966–1976)**, many members of the democratic parties suffered all forms of persecution, although, ironically, membership in these organizations acted as something of a political cover as **Red Guards** directed their ire largely at the CCP apparatus. Following the death of Mao Zedong in 1976, an effort was made to revive the democratic parties, though much of the membership by then consisted of the elderly who were fearful of ever again voicing independent views. Nevertheless, at the height of the political reform in the mid- to late 1980s, some members of the democratic parties once again took up social causes, such as opposition to the massive **Three Gorges Dam Project**, which was led by *Jiusan* member **Qian Jiaju**. Still, these parties are largely window dressing to claims by the CCP that China has a multi-party system allowing for political pluralism, a claim that is blatantly false since the democratic parties are still virtually powerless.

DENG LIQUN (1914–). From **Mao Zedong's** native province of Hunan, Deng Liqun worked in the early 1950s in the Xinjiang Autonomous

Region, where he assisted **Wang Zhen** in putting down Muslim resistance to Communist rule. Later, he served as secretary to **Liu Shaoqi** and for that Deng was purged in the **Cultural Revolution (1966–1976)**. In 1975, Deng Liqun returned to political life and served on the State Council and, in 1978, was appointed as vice-president of the **Chinese Academy of Social Sciences (CASS)**. In the early 1980s, he headed the Policy Research Office of the Central Party Secretariat (*zhongyang shujichu yanjiushi*), from where Deng Liqun mobilized internal **Chinese Communist Party (CCP)** opposition to market reforms. He was also a member of the Central Commission for Guiding Party Consolidation and from 1982 to 1985 was director of the CCP Propaganda Department. Following the June 1989 second **Beijing Spring**, Deng Liqun emerged as a major "leftist" opponent of political reform and an outspoken critic of "**bourgeois liberalization**" in the CCP and among **intellectuals**.

Following his retirement, Deng Liqun continued to use his position as one of China's most outspoken defenders of Maoist traditions to lambaste economic and political decisions of the country's top **leaders**. In the late1990s and early 2000s, Deng published a series of very critical open letters that while censored by the state-run media made their way onto the **Internet**. One attacked the decision of the CCP to admit private entrepreneurs into the Party saying this violated both Marxist theory and the Party constitution. Deng was particularly critical of General Secretary **Jiang Zemin** whom Deng argued should be expelled from the Party as an "enemy of the people" for having allowed the income gap to grow in Chinese society and for tolerating the massive increase in **corruption**. In Deng's orthodox view, the privatization of state assets meant that the workers no longer belonged to the state but were salaried employees subject to capitalist exploitation. Deng and other petitioners to the central government also called for a resuscitation of Maoist ideals including raising the nation's guard against the "sugar-coated bullets"—a classic Maoist phrase—of Western liberalism and individualism. Despite his leftist credentials, Deng Liqun was one of the few top leaders to leave a wreath at the 2005 funeral of former CCP General Secretary **Zhao Ziyang**, who was ousted in the immediate aftermath of the second Beijing Spring.

DENG PUFANG (1944–). The eldest son of China's former paramount leader, **Deng Xiaoping**, Deng Pufang graduated from the Physics Department at **Beida (Peking University)**. In 1968, during the **Cultural Revolution (1966–1976)**, he was reportedly thrown from a window and crippled by **Red Guards**. Throughout the 1980s and early 1990s, he served in various national and international organizations for disabled persons and in 2003 received the **Human Rights** Award from the **United Nations (UN)** for his role since 1988 as president of the China Disabled Persons' Federation. Deng has also served as deputy director of the Coordinating Committee on the Work of Handicapped People under China's State Council and was an alternate member of the **Chinese Communist Party (CCP)** Central Committee at the 14th (1992–1997) and 15th (1997–2002) Central Committees. In 1990, China passed the Law on the Protection of Handicapped People that along with the work of Deng Pufang has helped in the rehabilitation of more than eight million handicapped people in China.

DENG RONG (1950–). The third and youngest daughter of **Deng Xiaoping** and his wife Zhuo Lin, Deng Rong (nicknamed "Mao Mao") entered Jiangxi Medical School in 1972 as a "worker-peasant-soldier student" while her father was still in exile during the **Cultural Revolution (1966–1976)**. When Deng Xiaoping first returned to power between 1973 and 1975 and then again in 1997 after a second brief purge, Deng Rong was transferred to **Beijing** Medical College. She graduated in 1977 and was assigned to work in the General Political Department of the **People's Liberation Army (PLA)**. She was posted to the Chinese Embassy in Washington for four years. Thereafter, she became her father's secretary and, as his health declined prior to his death in 1997, when his hearing and speaking became difficult for him, she served as both his ears and mouth. In the 1990s, Deng Rong published two books on her father, both translated into English and several other foreign languages, *My Father Deng Xiaoping* and *Deng Xiaoping and the Cultural Revolution: A Daughter Recalls the Critical Years*. While the former depicted the initial period of Deng Xiaoping's life, the latter describes in rich detail the travails of the entire Deng family during the Cultural Revolution. But neither book addresses the role of Deng Xiaoping in 1989, when, as China's paramount leader, he ordered the military crackdown on the second **Beijing Spring** pro-democracy movement.

DENG TUO (1912–1966). One of the premier journalists in the **Chinese Communist Party (CCP)**, along with **Hu Jiwei** and **Liu Binyan**, Deng Tuo was a veteran Communist who, during the **Sino–Japanese War (1937–1945)**, was editor of *Resistance News* (*Kangdi bao*), a major CCP-run newspaper, established in the "white" areas behind Japanese lines. After 1949, Deng Tuo was quickly promoted to editor-in-chief of *People's Daily*, under the CCP Central Committee, and was a major contributor to *Study* (*Xuexi*), the primary theoretical journal of the CCP from 1950 to 1958. Deng also served as head of the Propaganda Department of the **Beijing** Municipal Committee and was a close associate of the city's mayor, **Peng Zhen**. A very learned man, a polished poet, and a traditional calligrapher, Deng Tuo wrote such scathing essays in the late 1950s as "Discard 'The Politics of Simpletons'." Using the pseudonym Ma Nancun, Deng also wrote two columns, under the general title of "Evening Chats at Yanshan" and "Notes from a **Three Family Village**," that were later criticized by **Jiang Qing**, **Yao Wenyuan**, and other leftist **leaders** in the CCP as an attack on **Mao Zedong** and the policies of the **Great Leap Forward (1958–1960)**. Mao personally criticized Deng Tuo in the late 1950s for allegedly running a "dead" newspaper at the *People's Daily* because of Deng's apparent refusal to support Mao's grandiose and ultimately catastrophic plans during the Great Leap Forward. Relieved of his post at *People's Daily*, Deng Tuo edited the journal *Frontline* (*Qianxian*) until he was purged during the **Cultural Revolution (1966–1976)**. Persecuted by **Red Guards**, Deng committed suicide in May 1966 and was posthumously "rehabilitated" (*pingfan*) 12 years later in 1979.

DENG XIAOPING (1904–1997). Born in Sichuan Province, Deng Xiaoping was the eldest son of a landowner. In 1920, he traveled as a work-study student to France where he joined a Chinese socialist youth organization. Upon returning to China, he entered the **Chinese Communist Party (CCP)** in 1924 and assumed his first position as an instructor at the Xi'an Military and Political Academy, established under the auspices of the warlord Feng Yuxiang. In 1929, he helped organize Communist military forces in the southwestern province of Guangxi and became a **political commissar** serving in the First **Field Army** during the **Long March (1934–1935)**. Deng was elected a member of the CCP Central Committee in 1945 at the Seventh National Party Congress and during the **Civil War (1946–1949)** he served as political commissar taking part in the decisive Crossing the Yangtze River and Huaihai battles. Following the "**liberation**" (*jiefang*) in 1949, Deng held several posts in southwest China and, in 1952, was appointed a vice-premier and, in 1954, the CCP secretary-general. After playing a major role in drafting the 1954 State Constitution, in 1956, he became a member of the **Politburo** Standing Committee and head of the Party Secretariat. He also served as vice-chairman of the National Defense Council and minister of finance and was the sixth ranking member of the CCP hierarchy. Like many top CCP **leaders**, Deng Xiaoping was condemned in the **Cultural Revolution (1966–1976)**, allegedly for having previously criticized the **personality cult** (*geren chongbai*) of **Mao Zedong** and having advocated relatively "liberal" agricultural policies, which earned him the label of "the second biggest **capitalist roader**" (*zouzipai*) in China after the disgraced President **Liu Shaoqi**. A harsh critic of **Jiang Qing** and the radicals for their leftist reforms in **education, literature and the arts**, and **agriculture**, Deng was eventually stripped of all Party and government posts and, along with members of his family, was exiled to a remote area in Jiangxi Province, where Deng worked in a tractor factory as a fitter. Following the death in 1971 of **Lin Biao**, the officially designated successor to Mao Zedong, Deng Xiaoping reappeared in 1973 as a vice-premier. In 1975, he was reappointed to the Politburo Standing Committee, only to be dropped from all his Party, government, and military posts in 1976, following the **April Fifth Movement** demonstrations in Tiananmen Square, which were crushed on orders of the **Gang of Four**. Deng Xiaoping reappeared for a second time in July 1977 and assumed all previous posts, plus that of **People's Liberation Army** chief-of-staff. In 1981, he became chairman of the Central **Military Affairs Commission (MAC)**. In November 1987, he formally "retired" from all posts, except the chairmanship of the Central Military Commission, a post that he finally relinquished in 1989.

Throughout the crucial period of economic reform and political crises, Deng remained the paramount leader of the CCP as indicated by his key role in sanctioning the crackdown on pro-democracy demonstrators in June 1989 during the second **Beijing Spring** and in making his historic "southern tour" (*nanxun*) in 1992 to stave off conservative attempts to reverse his 1978–1979 economic reforms. In 1993, Deng again defended his economic reform program in a Five-Point Opinion on Reform that called for further "emancipation of the mind," "speeding up the pace of reform," "strengthening the unity of leading bodies," "eliminating **bureaucratism** and **corruption**," and bringing about "the integration between political reform and economic reform." In 1995, rumors spread inside and outside of China that Deng Xiaoping was gravely ill, provoking speculation of a succession crisis. Noted for his love of playing bridge, Deng Xiaoping died on 20 February 1997 at the age of 92. In 1983, *The Selected Works of Deng Xiaoping* was published. In 1999, "Deng Xiaoping Theory" was incorporated into the state constitution. *See also* Deng Rong.

DENG YINGCHAO (1903–1992). Wife of **Zhou Enlai**, Deng Yingchao joined the Communist movement in China very early in life and became quite active in **Chinese Communist Party (CCP)** policy toward **women**. Her political role preceded her marriage to Zhou Enlai, although undoubtedly this union facilitated her position in the CCP hierarchy. Deng Yingchao was drawn to political involvement during the **May Fourth Movement (1919–1923)** and joined the CCP in 1925, heading the Party's Women's Department in the city of **Tianjin**, and, in the same year, she married Zhou Enlai. After serving in the Jiangxi Soviet, Deng Yingchao was one of the few women to participate in the epic **Long March (1934–1935)**. During the period of the Second **United Front (1937–1945)** with the **Kuomintang (KMT)**, she joined her husband in carrying out a liaison role with Nationalist **leaders** in Chungking (now rendered as **Chongqing**), the Nationalists' wartime base in Sichuan Province. In 1949, she was appointed to head the **All-China Federation of Women**, a post she would hold until the 1970s, and she participated in drafting the first **Marriage Law** that was adopted in 1950. In the mid-1950s, she became a member of the Standing Committee of the

National People's Congress (NPC) and was appointed to the CCP Central Committee, where she played a crucial role in formulating Party policy on women. Following her husband's death in 1976, she was elected to the CCP **Politburo** in December 1978; in 1985, she resigned from her Politburo and Central Committee positions. One of the revered Party **"revolutionary elders"** (*geming yuanlao*), Deng reportedly agreed to the use of force, in June 1989, to put down the second **Beijing Spring** pro-democracy movement—even though she reportedly showed signs of personal angst over the killing of young people.

"DICTATORSHIP OF THE PROLETARIAT" (*"WUCHAN JIEJI ZHUANZHENG"*). In the Marxist–Leninist system that governs China's post-1949 politics, the **Chinese Communist Party** (CCP) maintains its dictatorship in the name of the proletariat over other "classes" (bourgeoisie, landlords, rentiers) in the period of **socialism** that, in theory, precedes the "final" historical stage of "communism." Marx had originally foreseen a very short, transitional socialist period in which such a dictatorship by the proletariat was necessary to eliminate from the state and society the remnant capitalist influence in politics, economics, and culture. In the relatively "backward" conditions confronting the Bolsheviks in **Russia** after the 1917 October Revolution, Lenin then expanded "socialism" and the period of the dictatorship of the proletariat into a much longer historical stage, during which the proletariat's struggle with the still-vibrant bourgeoisie would require a more intense struggle with the full weight of state power under Communist Party control being directed at the capitalist classes. Throughout this period, the restoration of capitalism would be a constant threat and the Communist Party could use any means necessary to destroy the capitalists' social, economic, and political power. In effect, Lenin's elaboration of Marx laid the ideological foundations for the extended period of the Soviet state dictatorship that did not end until the collapse of the **Soviet Union** in 1991.

China fully adopted this Leninist perspective after 1949. Although the degree of dictatorship exercised against the "capitalist classes" in China varied in intensity, China's merchants, businessmen, and incipient entrepreneurs were frequent targets of political persecution in Marxist–Leninist garb beginning in 1949 and extending into the

1990s. In the early 1950s, indigenous capitalists had their industrial/commercial and personal property seized with little or no compensation, and, along with their family members, they were frequently killed or driven to suicide, all in the name of promoting "socialism." The same was true for rural landlords and peasants. During the mid-1960s, attacks against virtually all forms of private property were intensified by the **Red Guards**, acting on edicts and instructions from **Mao Zedong** and the radical leftist faction led by **Jiang Qing**. Mao, in particular, emphasized the interminable struggle between "the two roads of capitalism and socialism" and used this to justify the harshest measures against private interests in the society. Following the chairman's death in 1976, radical faction **leaders**, such as **Zhang Chunqiao**, took up the cause of the "dictatorship of the proletariat" to block the reappearance of Party leaders, such as **Deng Xiaoping**, who opposed the radical and anti-development policies of the Jiang Qing group. In this formulation, the "dictatorship of the proletariat" was no longer directed at "capitalist classes" in Chinese society, because they had largely disappeared years earlier, but rather at proponents of economic reform within the CCP who, following Mao's death, were now poised to return to positions of political leadership. With Deng Xiaoping's return to power in 1978, the "dictatorship of the proletariat" was no longer used in attacks against senior Party leaders. Yet the term is still employed to justify the suppression of social democratic forces, such as those that promoted the 1989 second **Beijing Spring** pro-democracy movement. *See also* LAND REFORM.

DING GUAN'GEN (1929–). Trained as a railway engineer in the early 1950s, Ding Guan'gen served from 1952 to 1983 as a technician in various bureaus of the Ministry of Communication and the Ministry of Railways. In 1983, he was appointed deputy secretary-general of the **National People's Congress** (**NPC**) Standing Committee. In 1985, he became minister of railways. In 1987, Ding was appointed to the **Chinese Communist Party** (**CCP**) Central Committee and became an alternate member of the **Politburo**. In 1988, he was appointed as a vice-minister of the State Planning Commission but was forced to resign as minister of railways as a result of three major train accidents. In 1989, he became a member of the powerful

Secretariat of the CCP Central Committee, where he generally sided with conservative **leaders** on propaganda issues and against further economic and political reform and, in 1990, was made head of the **United Front** Department of the CCP. A member of the CCP Central Committee from 1982 to 1997, Ding Guan'gen was promoted in 1992 to the CCP Politburo and made head of the Propaganda Department (later renamed the Publicity Department) until 2002, where he helped shape policy on communications and the **Internet**.

DONG FURENG (1927–2004). Trained in the early 1950s in Marxist economics at the Moscow State Institute of Economics, Dong Fureng joined the Institute of Economics under the Chinese Academy of Sciences (CAS) and in 1978 became deputy-director of the Institute, which had become part of the newly formed **Chinese Academy of Social Sciences (CASS)**. In 1982, he was identified as the vice-president of the Graduate School under CASS. In 1985, he became the director of the academy's Institute of Economics and a consultant to the World Bank. In 1988, he was a delegate to the **National People's Congress (NPC)** from Zhejiang Province and a member of its Standing Committee. Just prior to his death in 2004, Dong Fureng was instrumental in altering China's 2003 Law on Rural Land Contracts, which, for the first time, granted farmers long-term, guaranteed rights to use their contracted land. He also penned a major article in the same year on China's post-**SARS** economic adjustments that analyzed the impact of the epidemic on the country's industrial structure, **Internet** information **economy**, and private sector micro-economy.

– E –

ECONOMY. In 2005, China's economy was the world's fourth largest, surpassing Great Britain and France, with a Gross Domestic Product (GDP) of around US$2.25 trillion (US$8.5 trillion by purchasing power parity [ppp]) and a growth rate of 9.9% while per capita income was US$1,700 (US$6,200 ppp). In terms of **trade**, in the same year China became the world's third most active trading nation behind the **United States** and Germany but ahead of **Japan** with a trade surplus of US$32 billion, a figure that rose substantially in 2005 to more than US$100 billion, with total trade volume (exports and imports) of US$1.4 trillion. This represented a more than five-fold increase from 1995 when China's total trade was US$289 billion. China's share of the world's output of goods and services doubled between 1991 and 2003 to 12.7% behind Europe's 15.7% and the U.S.'s 21%.

The history of China's economy following the 1949 takeover of the country by the **Chinese Communist Party** (**CCP**) is divided into two distinct periods. From the introduction of the first **five-year plan** in 1953 until the adoption of economic reforms in 1978–1979, China's economy followed, with some notable exceptions, the Soviet model of central economic planning whereby production and **investment** decisions, prices, and **labor** allocation were decided by the State and administered through a hierarchical system of vertically organized ministries with overall coordination in the hands of the State Planning Commission. **Industry** and **agriculture** were fully socialized with the economic structure overwhelmingly composed of the primary and secondary sectors with little or no tertiary or service sector to economic activity. Allocation of basic necessities for food, shelter, and **health care** was by administrative means through a rationing system linked to place of employment with little to no cash economy. Real GDP during the 1953–1979 period expanded on average at a rate of 6.2% with the fastest growth occurring in the heavily subsidized sector of heavy industry (11.37% annually) followed by light industry (7.83%) and agriculture (4.33%). Although real gross capital fixed formation averaged 11.43% growth and capital stock 5.93% growth, real personal consumption grew by only 4.99%, 2.96% per capita. Price increases averaged less than 1% annually, but exports and imports grew on average by 10.98 and 10.27%, respectively.

The second period of economic reform began in 1978–1979 and has been characterized by introduction of market forces into the allocation of goods, labor, foreign exchange, housing, and capital. The creation of new, non-state-owned modes of economic organization for production dominated the agricultural and service sectors while industry, particularly heavy industry, remained highly influenced by State power and direct ownership through **state-owned enterprises** (**SOEs**). In the countryside, **township-village enter-**

prises (**TVEs**) emerged as the primary form of light industrial production while the **open-door policy** allowed for more foreign involvement in China's economy through joint ventures and high levels of Foreign Direct Investment (FDI). With the devolution of economic decision-making power increasingly into the hands of provincial and local governments away from the central ministries and the State Planning Commission, which itself was abolished in 2003, enterprises gained more autonomy and became more professional in their management. In 1986, the **National People's Congress** (**NPC**) approved China's first Bankruptcy Law for trial implementation and in the same year a company in Shenyang, Liaoning Province, declared bankruptcy, the first case in the history of the **People's Republic of China** (**PRC**). In 1993, the CCP gave its imprimatur to a fundamental change in the country's economic structure when, at the Third Plenum of the 14th CCP Central Committee, a decision to establish a "socialist market economic structure" was adopted along with a commitment to change the traditional concepts of the planned economy.

Growth rates in the 1979 to 2000 period averaged 9.62% with an average 8.24% increase in real GDP per capita and average increases of 7.41, 11.23, and 11.10% for agriculture, light industry, and heavy industry, respectively. Real personal consumption grew, on average, by 9.04% (7.70% per capita); real gross fixed capital formation grew by 10.90% (only slightly below the average for the central planning era) and capital stock expanded by 9.82% (a figure above the average for the 1953–1979 period). China experienced relatively slow growth in the mid-1990s as it struggled with the effects of a frenzy of construction that reached its peak in 1993. This was followed by renewed growth rates that were largely unaffected by the 1997–1998 Asian financial crisis and the 2002–2003 **SARS** crisis. By 2003, China's investment share of GDP approached 45%, the highest in the world. Capital stock grew 15.8% but the average productivity of all capital plunged 6.7% as new factories and other facilities were poorly utilized. Inflation averaged 6.11%, although, for the first time in history, the PRC experienced very rapid inflation rates, such as in 1988, when a decision by the **Politburo** to allow prices for most commodities to be set by the market led to panic buying and accelerated price increases leading the State Council to reimpose some controls even as exports and imports grew at average rates of 14.83 and 13.53%, respectively.

Since the early 1980s, China's primary industry has been outstripped by rapid growth rates in the secondary and tertiary sectors, although the primary sector still employs more than 300 million people, a number slightly larger than the secondary and tertiary sectors combined. Whereas, in 1979, the state-owned sector controlled 78% of the gross value of industrial production, by 2000, that figure had shrunk to 24% with concomitant expansion of individual and private ownership that, by 2001, accounted for more than 65% making the country no longer a "shortage" economy as it shifted from a seller's to a buyer's market. Although the growth in per capita income has pulled the country out of the ranks of the world's poor developing countries, huge gaps remain between urban and rural areas with income in the former 3.2 times the size of the latter where annual per capita income in 2004 was a paltry US$353.

Although 10% of the **population** of 1.3 billion remain officially below the poverty line (approximately 130 million people) and consumed only 2.4% of total household income in 2001, the highest 10% of the population consumed 30.4% of household income in 1998 and controlled 40% of the assets for a Gini Index of 40, one of the highest in the world. These trends continued through the early 2000s as 10% of the entire population—urban and rural—still remained below the poverty line, whose absolute numbers, in 2003, grew by 800,000, despite a 9% economic growth rate. Overall economic activity in China in 2003 and early 2004 was largely unaffected by the SARS crisis; only a slight drop in average economic growth from 9.6 to 7.9% occurred in one quarter.

Economic reform in China also brought about substantial changes in the country's economic and investment structure. The most profound change occurred in the agricultural sector, which shrank from 31.8% of the economy in 1981 to 15.2% in 2001, while just the reverse was true for the service sector, which grew from 21.8% of the economy in 1981 to 33.6% in 2001. Industry's share in the economy grew slightly in the reform period from 46.4 to 51.1% though manufacturing dropped from 38.5% in 1981 to 35.4% in 2001. In the early phases of the reform era, agricultural production surged by 5.2% a year from 1981 to 1991 but has since slowed down averaging less than 4% growth from 1991 to 2001. Industry and its manufacturing component, on the other hand, surged 11.1 and 12.6%, respectively, from 1981 to 1991 and grew at even faster rates of 12.6 and 11.6%, respectively, from 1991 to 2001. Steel remains the lifeblood of China's economy; it is used in everything from bridges to ships to the **automobile industry**, making the country the largest producer and consumer of steel (and cement) in the world. Production of steel doubled from 1999 to 2003 and iron imports grew by an even larger amount over the same period. By 2005, 80% of the world's clocks and watches, 50% of cameras, 30% of microwave ovens, 25% of washing machines, and 20% of refrigerators worldwide were "made in China." Ports in southern China handle as many containers a year as in all the U.S. China continues to import huge amounts of raw materials and heavy-duty construction equipment and commercial aircraft from multinationals, such as Caterpillar, Komatsu, Boeing, and Airbus. Services also experienced rapid economic growth, averaging 12.6% from 1981 to 1991, but slowing down to around 8% growth from 1991 to 2001.

Current revenue to the Chinese government dropped from 24% of GDP in 1981 to 17% in 2001 as China continued to retain a relatively low tax base consisting primarily of value-added, consumption, and business taxes with only 7% of the tax take coming in the form of personal income taxes, which, in the early 2000s, left the national budget with increasing deficits. China's national savings rate of 40% remains one of the highest in the world as Chinese consumers confront mounting uncertainties about social security, pensions, and **education** costs. Regional differences in China, which were almost non-existent during the 1953–1979 period of central planning, have grown dramatically during the reform era with a gap of six-to-one or even eight-to-one in per capita income between the wealthiest and poorest regions, although all regions of China—coastal and inland— have experienced positive economic growth, at rapid but different rates, from 1981 to 2001.

Unlike the 1953–1979 era of Soviet-style central planning, China's economy has a growing private sector that in 2000 contributed more than one trillion *yuan* of gross output value from more than one million mostly small-scale, private limited enterprises. Like most developed countries, China is also increasingly dependent on consumer demand and spending for continued growth with private enterprises becoming a dominant force in the tertiary sector. As people's living standards continue to improve in both urban and rural areas, Chinese consumer spending on housing, communications and electronic products, automobiles, and even holiday travel abroad is a major component of the macroeconomy, as retail sales hit 3.8 trillion *yuan* in 2001, with increases to 2003 averaging 10%.

Economic reform in China has also led to the rapid growth of a domestic real estate market as most restrictions on urban property ownership were lifted in the 1980s and Chinese citizens were allowed to own their own homes and developers gained rights to prime land in the country's largest cities. The China Land Development Association was established in 1993 to serve the growing real estate business while government programs have also been designed to promote consumer credit, lower interest rates, and increase the wages and welfare benefits of civil servants. They did so in order to bolster domestic demand among increasingly middle-class consumers, especially in urban areas, where overheated property speculation caused a surge in housing prices and a drain on disposable income. By 2004, the real estate market in China had grown to annual sales of US$130 billion, constituting nearly 20% of total fixed investment and raising fears of a potential real estate and capital construction "bubble." Such concerns led the central government to pursue more contractive policies by imposing new taxes and restrictions on property transactions, increasing bank reserve requirements, and reducing expenditures on construction of steel plants, highways, and skyscrapers

Weak household consumer demand is still a major problem, however, especially in rural areas, where income and credit growth has not kept up with the urban sector and where health insurance and general welfare benefits are less available and cut into household income. But with farmers now spending less than 50% of their household income on food, in an increasingly cash-oriented rural economy, more is left for housing, communications, and telecommunications purchases. Total consumption in China peaked in 2000 at 10.4% of the national economy dropping to 8.07% in 2001, resulting in significant deflationary pressure in the economy. This spurred the central government to pursue an active policy of fiscal stimulus, especially in capital construction, which was also fed by an inflow of FDI and "hot money" speculation. In 2003, these expansionary policies fed fears of overheating of the Chinese economy with investment expanding too fast and credit growing too quickly while consumer spending lagged.

In line with the official slogan by President **Hu Jintao** of "putting people first" (*yiren weiben*) renewed emphasis has been given to providing special dispensations to farmers whose incomes have remained stagnant despite the nation's rapid economic growth, to the **floating population** of rural migrants in urban areas, and to the estimated 130 million Chinese living below the official poverty line. China is also engaged in reducing agricultural taxes, setting up employment programs, and creating a more comprehensive social security system, as well as improving rural health care and education. Regional imbalances are being addressed by such large-scale programs as the Western Poverty Reduction Project, which is being assisted by the World Bank and is directed at the 10 relatively poor western provinces and regions. The enormous wealth gap that Chinese economists such as **He Qinglian** warn has led to 15% of the population controlling 85% of the wealth must also be addressed to avoid potential instability and national upheaval. In 2004, there were 10 known billionaires in China, including Larry Yung, the son of **Rong Yiren**, and head of **China International Trust and Investment Corporation (CITIC)** Pacific Group, with an estimated personal wealth of US$1.5 billion, Huang Guangyu, founder of Gome, China's largest electronics dealer, and Xu Rongmao chairman of the Shimao Real Estate Group. Many of China's richest people have made their fortunes in real estate or **banking and finance**, retailing, or in **Internet** companies, while few were primarily in manufacturing. Under a **World Trade Organization (WTO)** provision in early 2005 eliminating textile quotas, China expanded its grip on the world textile market, especially such items as socks, belts, buttons, neckties, and bras, whose production is concentrated in a number of specialized production cities (e.g., Datang, known as "sock city" in Guangdong Province) in the southeast. Other cities, such as Wenzhou, Zhejiang Province, and Dongguan, Guangdong Province, are trying to capture more high-value-added products by establishing research and development zones and self-styled Silicon and Laser valleys appealing to fiber-optic, electronic, and pharmaceutical companies.

Research centers set up in **Beijing** and **Shanghai** by multinationals, such as Microsoft, Oracle, IBM, and Intel, are aimed at tapping the country's enormous talent bank of engineers and scientists, making China a major research base in East Asia with overall spending on scientific research doubling from 0.6% of GDP in 1992 to 1.3% in 2003. In 2004, 40% of investment was undertaken by the private sector double that of a decade previous.

Cumulative FDI into China at the end of 2001 amounted to US$395.47 billion. In 2003, China replaced the U.S. as the largest worldwide recipient of FDI, taking in US$53 billion. Foreign operations in China are governed by the Income Tax Law Concerning Joint Ventures with Chinese and Foreign Investment (1980), the Law on Enterprises Operated Exclusively with Foreign Capital (1986), the Civil Procedure Law of the PRC (1991), and the Contract Law of the PRC (1999). China has largely welcomed multinational companies and foreign investment, especially by overseas Chinese from Southeast Asia, in most sectors of its economy though international concerns persist regarding China's protection of intellectual property rights. In a break with the past, **stock markets** in Shanghai and Shenzhen allow foreign investors to buy *yuan*-denominated Class-A shares, along with Class B shares, which have been open to foreign investors for years and carry no ownership rights. The State Administration of Foreign Exchange has also made it easier for institutions to transfer money out of and into China, though the government still bans its citizens from buying stocks abroad to prevent an exodus of the foreign reserves it uses to maintain the relatively low international value of its **currency**.

Although China's international debt obligations expanded from US$5 billion in 1981 to US$240 billion in 2005, its reserves, including gold, jumped from US$48 billion in 1991 (1981 NA) to US$795 billion in 2005 with an annual debt service of US$20 billion in 2001, slightly less than half of which is private. In 1998, China established its first large foreign trade group, China General Technology Holding Ltd. By 2004, China utilized its substantial capital holdings to purchase a number of foreign assets, including a controlling stake in South Korea's Ssangyong Motor Company and Canada's giant Noranda mining company, and in IBM's PC division, which was bought by the Chinese computer firm Lenovo. By 2005, China's overall volume of foreign investment abroad in the form of mergers, acquisitions, and other deals exceeded US$50 billion with annual growth rates of 36%.

According to the 11th Five-Year Plan (2006–2010), the major objective of national economic development in China is to maintain fast and stable economic growth and support the "building of a harmonious society" by reducing the growing gap between rich and poor and eliminating the "contradictions" that have led in recent years to the outbreak of **social protests**. By 2020, China's real GDP is slated to rise to 36 trillion *yuan* (US$4.5 trillion in US$ 2001 prices) and US$3,400 real GDP per capita with structural changes continuing to expand the tertiary sector to nearly 50% of the macro-economy with the primary and secondary sectors shrinking to 45.2 and 7.5%, respectively. In 2004, China displaced the U.S. as the dominant market and price setter in the international economy for copper, iron ore, aluminum, platinum, and other commodities. By 2025, it is estimated that China will account for 30–40% of global metal consumption as per capita consumption in China moves to the global average. By 2035, if current trends continue, China will eclipse the U.S. as the world's largest economy. *See also* "AGRICULTURAL RESPONSIBILITY SYSTEM"; BANKING AND FINANCE; FOREIGN POLICY; TRANSPORTATION.

EDUCATION. The commitment to education in post-1949 China by the **Chinese Communist Party** (**CCP**) began in 1951 with the Decision of the Reform of the Education System. During the First **five-year plan** (**1953–1957**), the educational system in China was based on the Soviet model and emphasized technical training to fill the new positions created by the crash industrialization program. Primary schooling during this period was for six years in urban areas and three to four years in the countryside. Although primary schooling was not compulsory, national enrollments increased from 25 million in 1953 to 86 million in 1958. Secondary schooling during the same period consisted of six-year junior and senior middle schools focusing on general academic training, though these schools were largely restricted to urban areas. There were also vocational schools and polytechnic schools. The latter were half-work, half-study schools that prepared students for work in **industry** and **agriculture**. Enrollment in secondary schools grew from two million in 1953 to more than nine million in 1958. Higher education consisted of comprehensive universities with full-time students and polytechnic universities, such as **Qinghua University**, which is often referred to as "China's MIT." Admission to universities was based on demanding entrance examinations conducted nationwide. Many Chinese university students also studied in the **Soviet Union**. Overall enrollment in higher education grew from 110,000 in 1950 to 800,000 in 1959.

During the **Great Leap Forward (1958–1960)** and the **Cultural Revolution (1966–1976)**, various educational experiments were attempted, usually with dire results. During the Leap, vocational and polytechnic education was expanded at enormous rates, with an emphasis on half-work, half-study and heavy doses of political education. Following the abolition of college entrance examinations in June 1966, many schools and universities in China became scenes of violence and factional strife among **Red Guards** that was often aimed at teachers, educational administrators, and Party **cadres** who ended up being beaten to death in what was officially lauded as "revolutionary actions." While violence broke out on university campuses, the most severe and pointless violence occurred at middle schools in **Beijing**, **Shanghai**, and **Guangzhou (Canton)**, especially such institutions as the Foreign Languages College and the Middle School of Qinghua University, which were attended by the offspring of high-level cadres, who became some of the most aggressive and violent **leaders** of the Red Guards. With schools closed from late 1966 to 1968, teachers and school administrators became open targets and were condemned as "pigs" and "poisonous snakes" by Red Guards and were organized into "ox-ghost and snake-demon teams" (*niugui sheshen dui*), where they were forced to do dirty work, such as clean toilets, and could be insulted or beaten at any time. Among those killed were Bian Zhongyun, the vice-principal of the Girls Middle School attached to Beijing Normal University who died on 5 August 1966 as the first victim of Red Guard violence, and Zhang Furen, a Chinese language teacher of the Middle School attached to the Beijing Foreign Languages College. More than 40 institutions in Beijing alone experienced similar violence, directed against everyone from school janitors to the "class directors" (*banzhu ren*), whose job it was to discipline students, to the school head and even to officials in the Beijing City Education Bureau; many educational personnel preferred suicide to beatings. Even as most Red Guards were sent into the countryside in 1968, teachers were targeted once again in the **Cleansing of the Class Ranks** campaign.

When schools were gradually reopened in the early 1970s, the average length for primary and secondary education was reduced from 12 to 9 years in the cities and to 7 years in the countryside. Most youth entered the workforce—urban and rural—at the age of 15 or 16, while students planning to attend the universities that had reopened were required to engage in "practical" work for two to three years before admission. In 1970, all universities reopened as students were admitted on the basis of "nominations" from their work units that stressed political reliability and appropriate class background. Educational administration was given over to **Revolutionary Committees** at the expense of professional educators—which saved the central government money but produced poor-quality students.

After the death of **Mao Zedong** in 1976, the Chinese educational system underwent a major readjustment to fit the nation's goal of modernization especially in **science and technology**. In 1977, the government restored the system of competitive examinations for university admission, and at the primary and secondary levels in urban areas it revived "key-point schools" (*zhongdian xuexiao*). Condemned by radical Maoists as "elitist," these schools received special government funds and the best-trained teachers for the brightest students. Previously taboo subjects such as art, classical music, and philosophy were added to secondary and university curricula while the role of political-ideological studies was for a time significantly downgraded. In the mid-1980s, all school-age children were required to attend at least nine years of school as government funding for education was increased to more than US$40 billion per year. With regulations for the awarding of the academic degrees of bachelor, masters, and doctoral degrees passed by the **National People's Congress** (**NPC**) in 1980, university admissions rose dramatically and Party-state control of curricula and student life was significantly reduced as university administrators under a "presidential responsibility system" were freed from direct political controls. In 1983, China conferred doctoral degrees on the first batch of postgraduate research students trained in the country by its own educators. With the appointment of

Li Peng as minister in charge of the State Education Commission in 1985, all ministers in the central government possessed university degrees as the government issued its Decision on the Reform of the Educational System, which called for education to be geared to the modernization program. While the same document urged universal basic education and overall educational improvements, university students were also increasingly required to contribute financially to their education.

Following the crackdown on the second **Beijing Spring** in 1989, the flow of university students interested in studying abroad increased significantly while only about one quarter of the more than 65,000 Chinese students overseas had returned by 1990. At centers of university student protests during the pro-democracy movement, such as **Beida (Peking University)**, political education and controls were reestablished following the crackdown as curricula with "western" biases were significantly altered. At the same time, the allure of opportunities in the **economy** drew increasing numbers of students and teachers away from education and into the market, raising questions about the future quality of Chinese education. State spending on education remained flat and, as a result, China's goal of achieving universal, compulsory education was not achieved.

From 1949 to 1985, 4.73 million students graduated from Chinese colleges or universities, 22 times the number from 1912 to 1947. China currently ranks 60th among 122 nations in the proportion of people over 25 years of age who have received higher or secondary education. Overall spending on education in China has perennially fallen below the world average of 4.2% of the Gross Domestic Product (GDP). In 1993, China's State Council decreed that education spending would reach 4% by 2000 with a concomitant commitment in 1997 of 130 million *yuan* to spread compulsory education in poverty-stricken areas and among **minorities**. By 2003, however, funds earmarked for education actually fell with less than 10% of China's education funds coming from the central government with the remainder provided by local authorities that have often imposed sizable tuition fees on students for the nine years of compulsory education. Even as China encouraged private **investment** in education, many school children, especially in the countryside and, in most cases, young girls, have been forced to abandon schooling for work, while poor areas also are increasingly unable to attract qualified teachers because of low pay and better opportunities in the cities. In 1992, 33 million children of school age (about one in five) were not attending school while rural school children generally left school at 13 or 14 years of age in order to take up paid work while many rural teachers, having secured their jobs through personal connections with less than adequate training, offer low quality instruction. The high student dropout rate was largely a function of the high fees charged by schools, which, in 2004, the government claimed it would ban as illegal, thereby safeguarding poor students' rights to compulsory education. In 1986, the newly adopted Law on Compulsory Education stipulated that nine-year compulsory education should be achieved throughout the entire country while in1995 the Education Law was passed. By 2004, nine-year compulsory education had become a reality in areas hosting 92% of the country's **population** with illiteracy rates among youth and adults brought down to less than 5%. Still, 327 counties in China do not enforce compulsory education with 60 counties, mostly in rural areas and the west, failing to promote full primary education, a situation that led the government in 2003 to give strategic priority to education in rural areas and the western provinces, such as **Tibet**, where only 78% of children attend primary school compared to the nationwide average of 90%. Schools have also instituted higher tuition that in poor rural areas can consume substantial portions of family income, forcing one or both parents to become migrant workers and join China's growing **floating population**. By 2008, 85% of all children in the country's mountainous west will achieve secondary schooling while by 2015 China claims it will achieve the goals laid out by the World Education Forum that include free and compulsory primary education for all children, a goal that was also incorporated in the 1996 Long-term Development Plan for Education to 2010 issued by the State Education Commission.

High school enrollment in China grew rapidly in the 1990s and early 2000s with the national rate reaching 17% in 2004 and a targeted goal of 20% in the coming years. The same dramatic growth rates occurred with university enrollment, which, during the period of 1995 to 2005, expanded from one million to nearly five million undergraduates and from 50,000 to more than 300,000 graduates. Although only 1.4% of the college-age population attended university in 1978, that figure grew to 20% in 2005 as state funding for higher education grew from US$4 to US$10 billion annually. In engineering alone, China is producing 442,000 undergraduates a year along with 48,000 graduates and 8,000 doctorates, with many of the new graduates slated for employment in the growing infrastructure of research and development laboratories set up in China by both foreign and domestic companies. There were 750,000 researchers in China in 2004, operating with a budget of US$60 billion spent by the country on research and development in such new fields as bio- and nano-technology. In 2004, the top three universities in China were, in order of priority, Qinghua, Beida, and Nanjing, followed by Fudan, Zhejiang, University of Science and Technology, Communications (*Jiaotong*), Nankai, Beijing Normal, and People's (*Renmin*) universities. Chinese students also continued to matriculate abroad with 62,000 studying in the **United States** in 2004, although the number of Chinese students seeking to study in the U.S. at graduate schools fell off by 45% because of competition from Europe, Australia, and other nations and tougher American visa requirements following the 11 September 2001 terrorist attacks.

Prior to 1978, when university-level education was substantially smaller, graduates were assured of a job through the government-controlled **labor** allocation system. But as the number of graduates has expanded and the allocation system has been gradually dismantled, many of China's 2.12 million annual college graduates have found it increasingly difficult to secure jobs. This has been especially true in the coastal cities and among graduates of third-tier schools that hand out meaningless degrees. On the other hand, the country faces a serious shortfall in both high school and college-level teachers—especially in rural areas and the remote interior regions—that began with a mass exodus in 1992, as teachers left their profession because of low salaries and poor social status. In 2004, university enrollment for the fall semester was frozen thereby denying 400,000 prospective students from attending college. And while matriculating students often complain of the overly theoretical content of course curricula, Chinese leaders such as former President **Jiang Zemin** have frequently called on educators to strengthen the teaching of patriotism, national integrity, and Chinese history. In 2000, the country inaugurated a campaign at the primary and middle school level to inculcate students with "honesty and credibility" and such ideological morals as patriotism, culture, and collectivism to counter the increasingly self-interested student orientation fostered by the economic reforms and loosening social controls.

China has also slated for growth the number of foreign students by announcing plans for transforming 100 universities, such as Shanghai's Communications University, into world-class research institutions with many of the faculty lured back from posts in the U.S. Although foreign students matriculating at major universities, such as Peking University and Qinghua, constitute less than 3% of the student body, the country has also looked to expanding foreign-funded education along with cooperative agreements with foreign companies such as Microsoft to develop educational software and train software engineers. Online courses on the **Internet** and education websites have been introduced while a major expansion of education for senior citizens at special schools and universities has been pushed for retired civil servants and other retirees. Despite commitments from education leaders in China to "guarantee academic freedom" especially at universities, Chinese students are not encouraged to challenge authority or received wisdom.

EIGHTH NATIONAL PARTY CONGRESS (1956 and 1958). With an unprecedented first and second session, the Eight National Party Congress was a watershed meeting in the history of the **Chinese Communist Party (CCP)**. Held in September 1956 in the immediate aftermath of the "secret speech" on the "crimes of the Stalinist era" by Soviet leader Nikita Khrushchev at the 20th National Congress of the Communist Party of the **Soviet Union (CPSU)**, the first session signaled dramatic changes in China's political and economic policies that set the stage for intra-elite conflicts that ultimately led to the **Cultural Revolution (1966–1976)**. More than 1,000 delegates attended the 12-day first session of the Congress, theoretically representing the 10 million members of the CCP. A new Party constitution was adopted and a new Central Committee was chosen. Forty-five reports—an unprecedented number—were presented by top CCP **leaders**. The Congress also decided on the contours of the Second **Five-Year Plan**.

The Congress took a conciliatory attitude toward **class struggle** and declared that "the question of who will win in the struggle between

socialism and capitalism in our country has now been decided." In effect, this statement suggested that the mass movements and struggle campaigns that had marked the early 1950s would be phased out. During the Congress, the party leadership also suggested moderation in its treatment of **intellectuals** and in economic policies as the intensive drives in **industry** and **agriculture** launched in 1955 largely by pronunciamentos from **Mao Zedong** were slowed down. According to a report to the Congress by **Chen Yun**, CCP policies would be "prudent and practical," with an emphasis on the kind of gradual change that reflected the concept of "balanced" development laid out by Mao Zedong in his 1956 speech **"On Ten Major Relationships"** (*shida guanxi*). The Congress also called for greater stress on "democracy," which was taken to mean more decentralization of authority in the elaborate administrative apparatus established by the CCP since 1949 and greater tolerance for initiatives at the lower levels.

Organizationally, the first session of the Eighth National Party Congress introduced several changes in the CCP, some substantive and some merely cosmetic. The former included the creation of a Standing Committee (consisting of seven members) to the top decision-making body of the **Politburo** and the formation of a Secretariat (headed by a general secretary) to carry out the leadership's decisions. Five vice-chairmen were also appointed to assist CCP Chairman Mao Zedong in the formulation and execution of policy. In effect, these changes diluted the highly concentrated power structure of the CCP, as decision-making authority was divided between the Secretariat and the Politburo (which Mao Zedong himself labeled the "first" and "second fronts," respectively). The size of the Central Committee was also expanded to almost 100 members, thereby making it an even more unwieldy body. In a move to standardize the top policy-making bodies of the CCP, the many ad hoc commissions that reported to the Central Committee were also abolished.

During the Eighth National Party Congress, Party chairman Mao Zedong was generally on the political defensive. Presenting a short opening and closing address, Mao saw references to his "Thought" dropped from the Party constitution and his policies for "rapid advance" (*maojin*) in the **economy** replaced by the gradualist approach championed by Chen Yun. Explicit criticism of the **"personality cult"** (*geren chongbai*) was also written into Party documents but whether Mao genuinely endorsed this and other policy initiatives is unknown though his April 1956 speech "On the Ten Major Relationships" had seemed to endorse this strategy. But within six months of the Congress, Mao was to assert a more radical line claiming that development could not occur without more intense "struggle."

In May 1958, an extraordinary second session of the Eighth National Party Congress was held, which approved a fundamentally different policy line. Unlike the low profile adopted at the first session, Mao dominated the Second Session by delivering five separate speeches and won strong support for his strategy to bring about a **Great Leap Forward** in the Chinese economy and to pursue a more radical line in agricultural development. Unlike the moderate line of the first session, which had declared the primary contradiction in China to be between "[economic] backwardness and development," this second session put a harder-edge spin on this formulation by announcing that "proletarian versus bourgeois and socialist versus capitalist roads" were now the primary contradictions in the country. Internationally, the hard line continued as Mao, prompted by the stress on international Communist unity at the November 1957 Moscow Party Conference, positively appraised the possible results of a nuclear war. It is generally agreed that the outbreak of the **Hungarian Revolution** in October1956 helped shift the political landscape in China from the moderation of the September 1956 first session to the hard-line May 1958 second session.

"ELIMINATE THE FOUR PESTS" (*"CHU SIHAI"*). In the mid-1950s as part of its National Program for the Development of **Agriculture**, the **Chinese Communist Party** (**CCP**) took on the task of ridding urban and rural China of vermin and other threats to public health. Prior to the CCP takeover of power in 1949, the garbage and filth in China's cities and villages were breeding grounds for animals and insects that carried serious infectious diseases and brought illnesses and suffering to the general **population**. The "four pests" targeted for total extinction in a 12-year period beginning in 1956 included rats, flies, mosquitoes, and sparrows, the latter apparently because they ate grain in the fields (in 1960, bed bugs replaced sparrows as the preferred target for extinction). The mobilization of millions of people in the campaign succeeded over the years in virtually eliminating these creatures from much of the country and dealing a blow to such widespread infectious diseases as schistosomiasis or snail fever. Young and old alike were trained in various procedures to rid their surroundings of these vermin. The unfortunate sparrows were targeted by the widespread and highly accurate use of slingshots by youngsters, resulting in an especially devastating impact on the bird population. Combined with the effects of free **health care** and drugs and national campaigns to wipe out certain diseases, there was a concomitant benefit to the public health as rats, flies, and mosquitoes were generally eliminated, at least in the cities. Since 1978, however, the general increase in wealth has combined with less-stringent efforts at "pest control," thus bringing about a reappearance of vermin, although the public health system is better prepared today to deal with the problems of carriers of infectious diseases in a more conventional manner. As a result of government neglect of the rural health care system and a breakdown in the periodic health campaigns that characterized the 1950s and 1960s, however, some infectious diseases have made a comeback, such as snail fever, which, in the Dongting Lake region of Hunan Province, now infects upward to 80% of the population, especially the poor, who are often unable to afford the medicines for counteracting the disease.

"EMANCIPATION OF THE MIND." *See* "PRACTICE IS THE SOLE CRITERION OF TRUTH."

ENERGY. China currently consumes about 10% of the world's energy and is the second largest energy consumer in the world at 1.5 billion tons coal equivalent (BTCE) following the **United States**. In 2004, China was the world's largest consumer of coal (1.5 billion tons, 30% of the world total) and the second biggest consumer of oil (6.7 million barrels a day) and of electric power with overall generating capacity of 385 million kW and another 130 million kW under construction. Although China also produces about 10% of the world's energy, making it theoretically self-sufficient, major problems in energy resource location, distribution, pricing, and usage has made China increasingly dependent on energy imports (6% per annum) as energy shortages plague the country, afflicting 21 provinces in 2004. Chinese demand for imported oil, which, in 2005, came to 3.2 million barrels a day, is necessary in order to match supply with ever-increasing demand produced by China's annual Gross Domestic Product (GDP) growth rate of over 9%. Demand for total energy in China doubled between the inauguration of economic reforms in 1978–1979 and 1994 and is expected to double again between 1994 and 2006 and redouble by 2015 to reach a level of 2.2 BTCE and 6 BTCE in 2020. Quintupling its current demand, China is expected to pass the U.S. in total oil consumption by 2030. By far, the largest energy consumer in China is **industry** at around 65% with the chemical, iron and steel, nonferrous metals, and the cement and building material industries as the largest consumers. Commercial and residential buildings in China consume 20% of total energy while **transportation** uses only 10% and **agriculture** 5%.

China's domestic energy supply is composed almost entirely of coal, which at 73% makes up the bulk of China's primary energy consumption that is expected to peak in 2015 at 77%. China is both the largest consumer and producer of coal in the world (1.42 billion tons in 2002). While official Chinese statistics showed a decline in coal production and consumption in the late 1990s, coal use began climbing again in 2002–2003 by nearly 8%. By 2020, China's capacity to generate electricity from coal, which, in 2004, was burned by 67% of the country's power plants, is slated to triple over the 2000 figure, but its use is continually hampered by the discrepancy between the location of most coal reserves in the north and northwestern provinces while the **population** and biggest consumers live primarily in the south. Coal also severely pollutes the **environment**, a problem that has become increasingly high-profile in China with the growth of an urban middle class that increasingly demands clean household fuels, such as electricity and natural gas. In 2002, China's recoverable coal reserves were estimated at 125.2 billion short tons with annual coal production of 1.52 billion tons and consumption of 1.42 billion tons leaving China with a coal surplus that because of railway bottlenecks and other distribution problems often end up being stockpiled near mines and/or rail heads. As China's booming **economy** has produced increasing demand for electric power (which despite its enormous expansion left the country in 2004 with a shortfall of 20 million kW), coal prices have risen nationwide and spurred the reopening of many small, decrepit underground mines in Shanxi and Hebei provinces, the center of the country's coal mining industry. Rapid growth in production has yielded profits and tax revenues especially for cash-strapped local governments, but it has also led to a rash of mine explosions and other mishaps that despite the creation of a State Administration of Work Safety Bureau have produced a surge in deaths (over 4,000 in 2004) and injuries among miners.

From 6.48 million tons of crude oil in 1963 to 160 million tons in 2003, China is the world's fifth largest oil producer. Although China managed to achieve oil self-sufficiency in the 1960s and 1970s from the rapid development of domestic sources, such as the **Daqing oilfield**, by 1993 China's rapid economic growth combined with stagnation in domestic oil production made the country into a net importer. In 2003, its imports of 800,000 barrels a day quickly expanded to 3.2 million in 2005, making China the world's second-largest consumer of petroleum products, surpassing **Japan**. By 2015, China is projected to consume 12.8 million barrels of oil a day with net imports of 9.5 million. Natural gas production constitutes around 3% of national energy consumption that was used primarily as a feedstock for fertilizer plants until 1997 when the completion of the Shaanxi-Beijing natural gas pipeline shifted use to electricity production and household cooking and heating. Proven oil reserves are mostly offshore in the East China Sea and in the far western regions of the Tarim, Turpan-Hami, and Junggar basins in western China, where they are now undergoing rapid development in energy boomtowns, such as Korla, Xinjiang Province. Altogether, the reserves in these areas were estimated in 2003 at 18.3 billion barrels. Oil production in the same year was 3.54 million barrels with consumption at 5.56 million barrels, requiring 1.9 billion barrels from imports, mainly from Indonesia. Through the state-owned China National Petroleum Corporation (CNPC) along with China Petroleum and Chemical (SINOPEC), and China Offshore National Oil Corporation (CNOOC), the country is currently involved in acquiring foreign oil concessions in Angola, Azerbaijan, Iran, Kazakhstan, Mauritania, Peru, Sudan, and Venezuela, which, in 2005, gave it worldwide control 300,000 to 400,000 barrels of oil production a day. Most proven oil reserves are still located in China and controlled by the giant PetroChina Corporation, the seventh largest oil corporation in the world with a market value in 2004 of US$94.5 billion. Although a proposed pipeline to bring oil from Siberia to China in a US$140 billion plan was apparently terminated, **Russia** has promised to increase its shipment of oil to China by rail. With China's crude oil refining capacity at 4.5 million barrels a day, the country is able to import raw crude as it continues to subsidize the price of gasoline nationwide. Natural gas reserves (located largely in western and north-central China) are estimated at 53.3 trillion cubic feet while natural gas production in 2002 was 1.15 trillion ft^3. China plans to expand the consumption of natural gas as a substitute for coal by embarking on a major expansion of its gas infrastructure, including construction of the "West-to-East" pipeline from the Xinjiang Autonomous Region to **Shanghai**. Other pipelines connect the Ordos gas field in Inner Mongolia to **Beijing** while China is proposing a link into the Russian natural gas grid in Siberia to supply it and South **Korea**. China has also joined with **India** to pursue large stakes in the Yukos oil company that the Russian government confiscated in 2004 and at the same time has pursued exploration of oil and gas fields off-shore in an area subject to dispute with Japan.

With only two on-line nuclear power plants, one outside Shanghai and the other at Daya Bay outside **Hong Kong**, only 2% of China's energy needs are met from nuclear power. China plans to quadruple capacity by 2010 to 8.7 gigawatts (1 GW = 1,000 megawatts) aided by construction of five additional plants, one in Jiangsu Province with the assistance of Russia. China has enormous hydropower potential with thousands of fast-flowing rivers from steep runoffs from the Himalayan Plateau and heavy rainfall in South and Central China that have been harnessed by 80,000 water control projects (mostly small-scale) constructed since 1949, which, in 2004, provided 21% of the nation's total power capacity, a figure that is slated to increase to 24% by 2020 as such projects as the **Three Gorges Dam Project** on the Yangtze River and the Ertan Power Station on the Yalong River come on-line. As China has embraced the model of sustainable development with its emphasis on renewable energy resources, plans are also afoot to draw on wind, solar, and geothermal power and to develop hybrid and hydrogen-driven engines for its rapidly expanding **automobile industry**. But currently less than 1% of energy comes from these diverse sources as the regions of high solar and wind generation are far from the country's heavily populated areas. Pilot solar and wind projects are ongoing in such places as Gansu Province, **Tibet**, and Inner Mongolia (where a wind farm of 96 turbines is slated to become the largest in Asia by 2008) in conjunction with joint ventures, such as the German–Chinese solar collector plant in Jinan, the largest such project in the world. In 2004, China drafted a Renewable Energy Promotion Law and has joined the European Wind Energy Association and Greenpeace in their "Wind Force 12" project with plans to grow by 50 to 75% a year so that by 2020 wind will generate 200,000 MW of electricity with fully 10% of all energy in China coming from renewable sources, including small hydroelectric dams. Characteristic of many relatively underdeveloped countries with a large percentage of its population in the rural sector, China relies on biomass consisting of biogas, crop stalks, and straw as a major form of renewable energy in the rural sector, where overall consumption is dramatically lower than in its urban counterpart.

Electricity generation and distribution in China has gone through two waves of ongoing reform with the emergence of independent power producers in the 1990s followed by the introduction of corporate management and policy-making functions. The Ministry of Power Industry, which had managed the electrical grid in the period of Soviet central planning from 1953 to 1978–1979, was dismantled in 1997 with its assets transferred to the vertically integrated State Power Corporation of China, which currently manages the nationwide power network and inter-regional power transmission. In 2002, the Corporation was itself divested of most of its generating assets and split into five independent power generating entities (Huaneng Group, Datan, Huadian, Guodian Power, and China Power Investment Group) and two power distribution companies, all of which was part of a plan to create a system of large regional grids that are under enormous pressure to develop new power-generating facilities to claim market share. Electricity prices are regulated by the State Electric Power Regulatory Commission, which sets rates for both industry (26 cents per kilowatt hour) and households. Lacking a high voltage transmission infrastructure and poor interconnection between regional and provincial grids, major parts of the country continue to suffer from periodic black- and brownouts because of inadequate generation and distribution capacity. In 2004, 24 provinces and municipalities experienced blackouts, especially during the summer when the State Electric Power Regulatory Commission reports dramatic rises in electrical demand with major urban areas, such as Shanghai, experiencing a shortage of four million kilowatts. Thermal plants produce 76% of China's total electricity (1.31 trillion kWh in 2001) largely by the burning of coal (86%) and petroleum (11%) with less than 1% burning natural gas. China has built no oil-burning thermal plants in the last decade, saving this resource for other domestic uses. In 2004, China's end-expenditure of energy was 13% of GDP, a figure double that in the U.S. while energy consumption per 10,000 *yuan* of GDP is 10 times that of Japan and 3.4 times the world average, indicating enormous wastes and inefficiencies that China plans to sharply reduce by 2010 through the gradual elimination of price subsidies. The unit energy consumption for 33 major products, such as steel, is 46% higher than the international average.

According to the 10th and 11th **Five-Year Plans** (2001–2005 and 2006–2010, respectively), China will shift its focus from expansion of energy production, the centerpiece of all China's five year plans since 1980, to an emphasis on the production of clean energy by a massive technological upgrading of the energy industry along with energy efficiency incentives to industry and other users. This will include construction of a more efficient national electricity grid with more market reforms in the power industry, where prices of all energy resources, except coal, are fixed or partially fixed by the state. China's heavy reliance on cheap **labor** and high consumption of energy and minerals is slated to last no more than 15 to 20 years necessitating dramatic improvements in energy efficiency by lowering the dependency on coal and imports of mineral resources, improving industrial efficiency, and completing price liberalization. Enormous regional imbalances will continue to exist, however, between the energy-rich eastern, coastal regions and the energy-deficient western, thinly populated regions while increasing public pressure, including major **social protests**, has been brought against construction of power plants on farmland and proposed construction of hydropower stations on such scenic waterways as the free-flowing Nu River in western China.

The major state organs involved in China's energy, including pricing, are the State Development and Reform Commission

(SDRC) whose Department of Basic Industries assesses and approves major energy projects; the State Electric Power Regulatory Commission, which engages in regulatory oversight of the industry; the State Price Bureau (also under the SDRC), which sets prices for electricity, oil, and natural gas; the State Economic and Trade Commission (SETC) under the State Council, which screens **investment** projects and sets and enforces technological standards; the State Environmental Protection Administration (SEPA), which sets enterprise emission standards in conjunction with local governments and the SDRC and SETC; and the Ministry of Foreign Trade and Economic Cooperation (MOFTEC), which screens projects involving foreign investment. For coal, the main state organs are as follows: the China National Coal Corporation (formerly the Ministry of Coal and Industry), which owns the largest state-owned mines; the China Local Coal Mines Development Corporation, which oversees the generally small-scale, nonstate owned mines run by **township-village enterprises (TVEs)**; and the China National Coal Import and Export Corporation, the primary Chinese partner for foreign investors. Research organs such as the Energy Research Institute under the State Development and Reform Commission have also been established to provide decision makers with comprehensive data and policy papers to assist energy planning.

Until the 1990s, China adopted a strategy emphasizing self-sufficiency in the development of its energy industry and so little effort was made to attract foreign investment. The only exception to this trend came in 1985 when China began to allow limited foreign participation in its offshore oil exploration and development largely in the South China Sea. With soaring energy demand and stagnant domestic oil production in the 1990s, China relaxed restrictions on foreign involvement in the oil and other energy sectors to the point that, in the early 2000s, foreign investment in the power industry became responsible for about 10% of total output. Foreign investment is particularly important in construction of the country's system of large regional grids, thermal and hydropower stations, offshore oil production, and nuclear power plant upgrades and construction. Overall, however, the domestic energy market continues to benefit from all sorts of government protection including import quotas and licenses along with high tariffs on imported energy products with imports of crude oil still under the monopolistic control of three state trading companies: China National Chemicals Import and Export Corporation (SINOCHEM), China United Petrochemical Corporation (UNIPEC), and China United Petroleum Corporation (CHINAOIL). While the role of these government-owned entities is not likely to undergo significant alteration as a result of China's accession to the **World Trade Organization (WTO)**, import quotas and licenses for energy products will be abolished by 2008 with tariffs on processed oil and fuel scheduled to drop to 6% from the present 9%.

China looms as the single largest source of new energy demand in the world for the next two decades and will undoubtedly have a profound effect on world energy markets, especially as it seeks to establish free trade agreements with major oil-producing Persian Gulf states. China's search for secure energy supplies has produced conflicts over natural gas development in the East China Sea and access to oil resources from Russia and has also shaped China's **foreign policy** with neighboring states. In 2004, China announced a US$700 million oil development program with Kazakhstan and will spend US$3 billion on a new pipeline from Atasu to the Xinjiang Autonomous Region. China National Petroleum Corporation has also acquired several oil refineries in Algeria and will purchase US$20 billion of liquefied natural gas (LNG) from Iran, the largest LNG contract in the world. China Offshore National Oil Corporation submitted an unsolicited bid of US$18.5 billion (abandoned in August 2005) for the American Unocal Corporation. Although China's effort to purchase a medium-sized oil company in Russia was blocked by the Russian government, plans are in place to build a rail connection from eastern Russia to the seaport of Dalian for transporting oil as China continues to develop corporate relationships with Russian energy companies. With world oil prices undergoing upward pressure in 2004–2005, China launched a major effort to develop a strategic oil reserve on the coast of Zhejiang Province that, in the event of a cutoff of foreign supplies, can meet domestic demand for at least three months. *See also* TRANSPORTATION.

ENTERPRISE REFORM. *See* STATE-OWNED ENTERPRISES (SOEs).

ENVIRONMENT. During the Maoist era (1949 to 1976), China's environment suffered enormous degradation in terms of deforestation, loss of wetlands and grasslands to massive land reclamation projects under the "grain first" policy, and considerable increases in water and air pollution from the crash industrialization programs characteristic of the Soviet-style planned **economy** and the **Great Leap Forward (1958–1960)**. Following the inauguration of economic reforms in 1978–1979, environmental degradation continued and, in some cases, even accelerated with the more rapid economic development that has transformed China into the world's fourth largest economy. At the same time, growing problems of air and water pollution along with ancillary environmental problems such as accelerating desertification have led to a growing awareness among the government and general **population** of the need to curb destruction to China's increasingly fragile environment, which, beginning in the late 1990s, led to a series of "green" policy initiatives on a variety of policy fronts. Economically, pollution and environmental degradation in China cost the equivalent of 8% to 10% of the Gross Domestic Product (GDP) annually due to crop and fishery losses, factory closings, and increased **health care**.

Air pollution is perhaps China's most serious environmental problem, stemming from the large-scale burning of coal for domestic and industrial purposes by over 2,000 coal-fired plants and from the continued use of coal burners instead of natural gas to heat homes along with the explosive growth in **automobiles**, which are now the largest source of air pollution in urban areas. In 2005, China ranked second in the world behind the **United States** in CO_2 emissions (although only roughly one-eighth of those per capita in the U.S.), a figure that is slated to grow from 2000 to 2030 by an amount equal to the increase for the entire industrialized world. China is already the world's greatest contributor to methane greenhouse gas (largely from livestock and wet rice paddies), while the country is responsible for two-thirds of the sulfur dioxides emitted in Asia (22 million tons in 2004) that, along with mercury and black carbon, have gravitated as far as the west coast of the U.S. With the dramatic rise in its production of refrigerators, China has also increased its contribution to worldwide emission of chlorofluorocarbons (CFCs) and halons and is the world's largest source of nonnatural emissions of mercury amounting to 540 tons released into the air annually. Among China's major urban areas, **Chongqing** is the country's most polluted city because of high-sulfur-content coal burned for fuel and highly acidic rain. Overall, 16 of the 20 most polluted cities in the world are located in China, leading to an estimated 400,000 deaths in the country annually from cancer, diabetes, and pulmonary diseases. Estimates are that air pollution levels in China could quadruple within 15 years if the country does not curb its rapid growth in **energy** consumption and automobile use.

Other areas suffering from serious dioxide and acid rain pollution include the provinces of Hebei, Henan, Hunan, Shaanxi, Gansu, Guizhou, Sichuan, Inner Mongolia, and Shanxi, China's most polluted province where coal mines and processing and cement plants have turned provincial cities such as Linfen (population four million) into some of the dirtiest and unhealthiest places on earth. Other heavily polluted cities include Yangquan (Shanxi), Datong (Shanxi), Shizuishan (Ningxia-Hui Autonomous Region), Sanmenxia (Henan), Jinchang (Gansu), Shijiazhuang (Hebei), Xianyang (Shaanxi), Zhuzhou (Hunan), and Luoyang (Henan), while one-third of all agricultural land in China is afflicted by acid rain. In 1995, more than 88 cities in China that were monitored for sulfur dioxide exceeded World Health Organization (WHO) guidelines with some having as much as ten times the recommended levels. A resident of **Beijing**, where an explosive growth in automobiles burning leaded fuel has occurred in the last decade, is subject to about seven times the annual level of total suspended particulates as a resident of Los Angeles and eight times the level of sulfur dioxide, as the average Chinese auto emits about four more times air pollution than its Los Angeles counterpart. Nor does China's air pollution respect international borders as on certain days almost 25% of the particulate matter clotting the skies above Los Angeles can be traced back to China which could eventually account for roughly one-third of California's air pollution. On the flip side, cities in China that are singled out as models of environmental protection include Fuzhou, (Fujian), Dalian (Shandong), Haikou (Hainan Island), Guilin (Guizhou), and Zhuhai (Guangdong), where local environments are all rated as "comfortable." The China Environmental Monitoring Center regularly evaluates air quality in 47 cities and employs a five-tier system for rating air (and water) pollution: Grade I = "excellent"; Grade II = "fairly good"; Grade III = "slightly polluted"; Grade IV = "poor"; and Grade V = "hazardous." In 2004, 142 out of 240 cities monitored recorded air quality of Grade II or better, an increase of 7.9% over 2003.

Pollution of China's 8,000 plus rivers and waterways, numerous lakes, and sea pollution is the second most severe problem confronting the country's environment. China has 2.8 trillion cubic meters of fresh water annually, which places it fourth in the world in terms of total fresh water sources. But as a result of rapid economic growth, industrialization, and urbanization, along with inadequate infrastructure **investment** in sewage treatment plants and inadequate management capacity, China suffers from widespread problems of water scarcity and pollution throughout the country with an estimated 60 billion tons of polluted water produced annually. In 2002, water quality at 41% of monitoring stations along China's rivers failed to meet the nation's lowest standards of Grade V. Water shortages in 2004 plagued 400 out of China's more than 660 cities, including major metropolitan areas, such as Beijing and **Tianjin**, where drawdown of underground water resources is rapidly accelerating. Per capita access to water resources in China is 2,140 cubic meters (31% of the world average), which by 2030 is expected to drop to 1,700 cubic meters, an annual shortfall of 53 trillion gallons. Below market pricing of water throughout China leads to enormous waste with the country using four times the world average to produce every 10,000 *yuan* of GDP. China's annual output of household sewage is largely untreated, as approximately 700 million people drink water contaminated with human and animal waste with many cities imposing frequent water-use restrictions, particularly after pollution spills from chemical and other highly polluting industries. Some municipalities, such as Beijing, have raised water use rates to discourage waste. But with pricing and rights allocation of water largely controlled by the Ministry of Water Resources, preference is given to maintaining low water prices and insuring easy access for **agriculture** and **industry**.

Interior lakes and rivers in such provinces as Qinghai in China's western region, along with the Yellow and Huai rivers, have suffered partial or complete dry-up in recent years because of declines in annual precipitation. The many sources of water pollution include 21 billion tons of annual household sewage, of which only 25% is treated; agricultural runoff from nitrogen fertilizers, of which China is now the world's largest consumer, along with livestock and poultry wastes; and a variety of heavy metals (such as lead, mercury, synthetic ammonia, and cadmium), all of which are spewed into rivers and lakes by generally unregulated industries, particularly refineries, tanneries, paper pulp mills, scrap yards, and smelters. Urban sewage has surpassed industrial wastes as China's biggest source of water pollution; of the 2,418 projects designed for water pollution control, only 777 had been completed by 2004. The target of treating 45% of urban discharge in the 10th **Five-Year Plan** (2001–2005) has evidently not been achieved. Of the seven major rivers and their tributaries in China, less than 30% of the sections have water-quality standards from Grade I to III, while 41% of the sections have water quality worse than Grade V, "hazardous." The Hai River, running through the densely populated Beijing–Tianjin region, is the country's most polluted, closely followed by the Liao River in Liaoning Province and the Huai River in eastern China—even though all three waterways have been targeted for major clean-up efforts by the State Environmental Protection Administration (SEPA). The Yangtze River is the least polluted, while the Yellow River has fallen to its lowest level in 50 years making it an inland river for much of the dry season in north China, as one-third of its 16 original aquatic species confront imminent extinction from pollutants that amount to 4.2 billion m^3 a year. In 2005, a major pollution spill of benzene into the Songhua River forced the entire northeastern city of Harbin with 4 million residents to shut down its water supply for several days and the top environmental regulator was fired in the wake of the initial cover-up of the chemical spill. Three quarters of China's lakes are eutrophicated or polluted by nitrogen and phosphorous, largely attributed to fertilizers and soap wastes, which have fed algae blooms and weeds in the country's biggest lakes, such as Taihu (Jiangsu and Zhejiang), Dianchi (Yunnan), and Caohu (Anhui). Along China's coasts, heavily polluted seas are found in the East China Sea and the Bohai Gulf off the provinces of Jiangsu and Zhejiang and the city of **Shanghai** all of which suffer periodic bouts of red tide and other forms of pollution that cause losses to China's fishing industry of 230 million *yuan* annually.

The issue of environmental protection in China did not gain national attention until 1973 when the first Environmental Protection National Conference was held in Beijing. In 1979, the **National People's Congress** (NPC) committed itself to annual reviews of China's environmental conditions and established an Environment and Resources Protection Committee to oversee the nation's environmental conditions and policies. From the 1980s to the early 2000s, a series of laws were passed to strengthen environmental regulation: Seas and Ocean Environmental Law (1982), Water Pollution and Control Law (1984), Air Pollution and Control Law (1987), Environmental Protection Law (1989), Water and Soil Protection Act (1991), and the Environmental Impact Assessment Law (2003).

Enforcement was advanced in 1983 by the creation of a State Environmental Protection Commission (SEPC, later elevated to ministerial rank and renamed the State Environmental Protection Administration, SEPA), with more than 70,000 local offices established throughout the country to monitor pollution problems. In 1993, SEPA publicized the names of 3,000 Chinese enterprises held responsible for 60% of annual industrial pollutants in the country and rapidly became known as the "richest" government bureau because of its well-known inclination to impose heavy fines on violators. Overall enforcement remained weak, however, as SEPA often lacked the authority to enforce its orders directly leaving that critical function to local governments that are often reluctant to impose fines on the very state-owned operations that provide jobs and revenue into the local economy, a situation that led some observers to dismiss SEPA as a "toothless tiger." In a high-profile case in 2005, however, SEPA took on the powerful Three Gorges Corporation, which manages the **Three Gorges Dam Project** and other hydroelectric facilities, forcing the corporation to file environmental impact statements before beginning construction of two power plants while 30 other large projects in 13 provinces, including plans for 13 cascade dams on the pristine Nu River in western China, were also ordered temporarily halted for failure to meet environmental standards.

A State Oceanic Administration (SOA) has also been established in China to oversee the country's ports and monitor its offshore sea resources while major universities, such as People's University in

Beijing, have established schools of environment and natural resources to supply the trained personnel to staff government agencies. Many non-governmental organizations (NGOs) have also sprung up in recent years to promote environmental **education** and biodiversity and have frequently criticized government policy, going so far as to utilize legal means in attempts to block environmentally destructive projects. In 1994, China spent 0.8% of its GDP on environmental protection, a figure that by 2003 had increased to 1.3%, putting it just short of the 1.5 to 2.0% that is needed for a serious effort to control pollution. This problem is exacerbated by the general weakness of the SEPA enforcement mechanisms due to its very small central staff (300 in 2003) and inadequate budget of US$9 billion that was included in the 10th Five-Year Plan (2001–2005) but was never fully expended. Internationally, China has participated in international conferences focusing on the environment, including the **United Nations** (**UN**) Conference on Environment and Development ("Earth Summit") in Rio de Janeiro in 1992, where Premier **Li Peng** proposed that developed countries bear greater responsibility for protecting the environment than those less developed. In the run up to the 1995 Berlin Climate-Control Conference, China sided with the mostly "southern" developing nations that demanded that more steps be taken by the "northern" developed nations to restrict carbon dioxide emissions into the atmosphere. China has also joined in regional forums for addressing common pollution problems in Asia, hosted the International Forum on Integrated Water Management in 2004, promoted World Water Day (March 22), and in May 1998 signed the Kyoto Protocol, under provisions that, as an underdeveloped nation, it was free from any mandatory controls on emissions. Foreign companies, such as France's waste-management company, Onyx, have also been contracted to help clean up China's environment by carrying out such crucial functions as waste disposal. During 2001–2020, it is estimated that China accommodated 20–30 million environmental refugees fleeing highly polluted regions for urban areas with access to clean water, a development that potentially contributed to increasing problems of **social protests** and unrest. In 2003, the Chinese minister of SEPA, Xie Zhenhua, was awarded the Sasakawa Environmental Prize by the UN for his work in committing the **People's Republic of China** (**PRC**) to a program of sustainable development and helping to make environmental protection one of China's basic national policies.

In the late 1990s and early 2000s, China took dramatically stronger actions on air pollution as a result of the continued deterioration of air quality in major cities, such as in Beijing, where, in 1998, the municipal government adopted 19 emergency anti-air pollution measures. As part of its plan to reduce overall sulfur dioxide emissions by 20% in 2005 compared to 2000, the government has pursued a number of policies including orders to coal-fired plants—responsible for one-third of China's total emissions of 6.6 million metric tons in 2003—to install emissions controls in such cities as Beijing and Shanghai. Restrictions on motorcycle tail gas pollution to European II standards, investment in non-polluting fuel-cell bus **technology** and hybrid automobiles, higher tariffs for electricity to reduce waste and excessive demand, are, unfortunately, counteracted by the continued construction of coal-fired plants to overcome persistent electricity shortages and the restarting of some of the dirtiest outdated plants, this despite a massive program of "clean" hydropower development such as the massive Three Gorges Dam Project on the Yangtze River. In late 2004, air pollution in Beijing was so bad that a French aerobatic show had to be cancelled because the city's air quality was rated "hazardous," a situation that accelerated efforts to drive the dirtiest polluters out of the city in anticipation of the 2008 Olympics. Major clean-up efforts directed at such highly polluted waterways as the Huai River and its many tributaries have also often floundered because of inadequate funding and resistance from local governments and huge industrial companies that are often in alliance with political authorities. China also reports sharp decreases in marine fisheries, principally due to over-fishing and the effects of ocean pollution near its shores. Land reduction, wetland loss, and desertification have also intensified as industrial development zones and real estate speculation consume more and more farmland. Acid rain in China in 2004 fell on more than 90% of the cities located in the "Acid Rain Control Zone" in the country's southeastern provinces of Guangdong, Guizhou, Jiangxi, and Fujian. Areas of the north and northeast have also been hit since 1999 by increasingly frequent and ferocious forest fires, such as the 1987 and 1988 gigantic fires in Heilongjiang Province and Inner Mongolia, due to drought and over-logging.

The willingness of the local authorities in China to sacrifice the environment for the sake of economic development is a major cause of the country's continued environmental degradation and increased rates in respiratory diseases and related cancers. This has led some top environmental officials in China to urge a complete rethinking of economic policies, warning that growth cannot go on in the same way without severe damage to natural resources, and that China must adopt a new "circular economy" (i.e., recycling) model to ensure sustainability of economic growth and environmental health. As a result of such policies, in 2000, SEPA announced that the nationwide pollution situation had stopped worsening for the first time in decades; in 2004, it took tougher actions against polluters and companies that failed to file environmental-impact assessments. Calls were also issued for greater public participation in environmental protection by popular input to newspapers and media that have taken to exposing the most egregious polluters. Growing environmental awareness has produced an increasing number of public rifts with the government by increasingly active environmental NGOs, such as the Green Earth Volunteers, which from 2003 to 2005 collected petition signatures opposing planned construction of dams on the Nu River in Yunnan Province, one of the last pristine and free-flowing rivers in China and the location of a UNESCO World Heritage Site. Joining in the opposition to a plan that would entail construction of 13 separate dams were SEPA and the **Chinese Academy of Social Sciences (CASS)**, which invoked the Environmental Impact Assessment Law to demand public hearings on the proposed project. In other cases, local residents have resorted to more direct measures to halt major polluters and disruptive mega-projects, including sometimes-violent social protests. In response, the government issued an Action Plan in 2004, which foresees renewable and environmentally friendly energy sources accounting for 10% of the nation's total installed electricity generation by 2010 while excise taxes have been imposed on products, such as single-use plastic bags, that contribute to pollution in such relatively isolated regions as **Tibet**. China ratified the Stockholm Convention in 2003, which commits the country to eliminating the production, distribution, and use of persistent organic pollutants (POP), such as DDT, Chlordane, and Mirex. Chinese "green labels"—presenting the sun, hill, lake, and 10 circles—are attached to consumer goods that pass quality and production tests and are considered environmentally friendly.

Chinese cities are also encouraged to vie for the status of "garden city" by reducing their air pollutants by 15% annually. China has also begun to produce environmentally friendly products, such as photovoltaic panels for electricity generation, solar hot water systems, soil substitutes for building roofs, and concrete building blocks filled with insulating foam. China's long-term goal is to create a "green" economy, which some believe can only be achieved by imposing stiff taxes on fuel and other major sources of air and water pollution and by democratizing China's political system to ensure popular input and oversight. China is also toying with the concept of "Green GDP," which measures the country's economy (US$1.3 trillion in 2003) by subtracting the costs of environmental damages and recovery that, in 2004, was estimated at 18% and with the "Earth Index" system, which employs social and environmental indices, along with GDP, to evaluate development.

EPSTEIN, ISRAEL (1915–2005). Born in Warsaw during the period of Russian control of eastern Poland, Israel Epstein was a journalist, author, and sometime propagandist for Communism in China who, in the 1940s, conducted in-depth interviews with **Mao Zedong**. An editor of *China Today* (formerly *China Reconstructs*), an English-language Chinese news magazine, Mr. Epstein also translated the sayings and writings of Mao and **Deng Xiaoping**. During a five-year stay in the **United States**, he authored several books on China, including *The Unfinished Revolution in China* and *Woman in World History*, a biography of **Song Qingling**, with whom he worked during World War II in **Hong Kong**. Returning to China in 1951, Israel Epstein conducted annual conversations with Mao but was still persecuted and imprisoned for five years during the **Cultural Revolution (1966–1976)** for supposedly plotting against **Zhou Enlai**, who ultimately arranged for his release in 1973. Israel Epstein is buried in the Babaoshan Cemetery for Revolutionaries in **Beijing**.

– F –

FALUN GONG. See QIGONG.

FAMINE. *See* "GREAT LEAP FORWARD" (1958–1960).

FANG LIZHI (1936–). An astrophysicist by training and one of China's most eminent scientists who taught at the University of **Science and Technology** in Hefei, Anhui Province, Fang Lizhi was, during his tenure in China, a constant critic of the **Chinese Communist Party (CCP)** dictatorship. Fang was denounced by the Party leadership for allegedly instigating student demonstrations in late 1986 that resulted in the removal of **Hu Yaobang** as CCP general secretary. Purged from the CCP in January 1987, Fang wrote an open letter to **Deng Xiaoping** in January 1989 in which he called for amnesty for all political prisoners, particularly **Wei Jingsheng**, China's most famous dissident. After the June 1989 crackdown against the second **Beijing Spring**, Fang and his wife sought refuge in the American Embassy in **Beijing**; one year later, they were allowed to leave China for the West. He currently resides in the **United States** and teaches physics at the University of Arizona. In 2004, Fang resigned from the Western-based Human Rights in China in a dispute over the composition of its leadership.

"FANSHEN." This Chinese term literally means to "turn over the body." During the **land reform** (**1950–1952**), it came to mean to "shake off the feudal yoke"—that is, the willingness of the peasant and working classes to overthrow the ruling classes that had exploited and suppressed them. In concrete terms, *fanshen* meant that previously landless or land-poor classes had gained land, livestock, farm implements, and even houses in a massive seizure of property that was later reversed by the socialization of the means of production in the countryside and cities advanced by the **Chinese Communist Party (CCP)**. *Fanshen* also implies a change in worldview, an abolition of superstition, and empowerment of the poorest and most dispossessed elements in society, including **women**. This aspect of *fanshen*, however, may be more a product of CCP propaganda than representative of a real change in consciousness, though, in recent years, **labor** activists have begun invoking the term in their often-fruitless struggles to establish independent **trade unions** in Chinese industrial facilities domestic and foreign alike.

"FEBRUARY ADVERSE CURRENT" (*"ERYUE NILIU"*) (1967). This phrase was concocted by the radical faction in the **Cultural**

Revolution (1966–1976) to describe the conservative reaction led by **Tan Zhenlin**, which appeared in February 1967 in opposition against the "January Storm," the most violent phase of **Red Guard** action against **cadres** of the Party and government. The most radical **Rebel Faction** (*zaofanpai*) of Red Guards, who, in January 1967, "seized power" at provincial levels and below, not only physically abused Party and government officials, but also attempted to establish new political structures based on the Paris Commune as originally described by Karl Marx. **Mao Zedong** rejected these power seizures as a sham and, to the consternation of many Red Guards, he vetoed the Paris Commune model, opting instead for the less radical political structure of **Revolutionary Committees**. Meeting in February 1967, top Party officials detected ambivalence on Mao's part and protested that the Cultural Revolution was targeting the entire Party membership, irrespective of revolutionary experience or ideological purity. Fearing for their own lives, these same officials convinced Mao to restrict the targets of attack to only a "small handful of **capitalist roaders**" (*zouzipai*) in the **Chinese Communist Party** (**CCP**). The vast majority of cadres were declared to be "good or very good." Efforts to spare CCP leader **Liu Shaoqi**, whom Mao had designated the "number one authority in the Party taking the capitalist road," did not, however, succeed. Radical groups denounced the "February Adverse Current" but were never able to overcome the strictures against attacking virtually all government and Party cadres, many of whom joined the Revolutionary Committees.

FEI XIAOTONG (1910–2005). Born in Jiangsu Province and one of China's most prominent social anthropologists, Fei Xiaotong studied at **Qinghua University** and London University and worked at Harvard University in the mid-1940s. He was chairman of the China Democratic League, one of the small **democratic parties** that sought a political alternative to **Kuomintang** (**KMT**) rule. He published several books on Chinese rural life and **minorities**, particularly concerning Yunnan Province in China's southwest. Appointed to several government agencies after the Communist takeover in 1949, including the Central Institute for Nationalities, Fei was denounced as a "rightist" during the **Anti-Rightist Campaign (1957–1958)** while during the **Cultural Revolution (1966–1976)** his research papers were destroyed. Sent to the countryside as a farm laborer, Fei returned to **Beijing** in 1972, where he was politically rehabilitated later in the decade and served as a court judge in the 1980 trial of the **Gang of Four**. In 1986, Fei accompanied then Party leader **Hu Yaobang** on a trip to the West.

"FEUDALISM" (*"FENGJIANZHUYI"***).** One of the major historical stages in the Marxist view of history, "feudalism" has proved to be a difficult concept for the Chinese Communists to incorporate into their periodization of Chinese history. Karl Marx's remarks on feudalism are scattered throughout his works as part of his overall analysis of capitalist development and are generally ambiguous in meaning. Friedrich Engels, however, focused on the self-sufficient nature of the feudal **economy**, with its orientation to immediate consumption of "small commodity production" by the producer and the lord, without consideration for a market. For both Marx and Engels, the means of "exploitation" under feudalism combined economic and political instruments in an almost indistinguishable form to ensure expropriation of "surplus" production by the peasantry. But the political-military apparatus of the state was of a more limited and circumscribed form geographically and institutionally in comparison to the subsequent development of the state under capitalism.

In the history of the **Chinese Communist Party (CCP)**, the concept of feudalism and its political usage has varied. From 1921–1949, the CCP was profoundly affected by the Leninist-Stalinist notion that political and economic power in China was in the hands of backward "feudal forces" and "feudal remnants" personified by warlords and militarists, against whom the revolution was directed. The revolution, in other words, was primarily an "anti-feudal" and "anti-imperialist" struggle led by the working and peasant classes, in alliance with the relatively "weak" Chinese bourgeoisie, against "feudal and medieval methods of exploitation." This contrasted with the Trotskyist view that downplayed the "feudal" character of China, emphasizing instead the role of a powerful bourgeoisie and the leading role of the proletariat in the campaign to destroy a fairly well-developed capitalist system that relied on foreign **imperialism**.

Mao Zedong essentially adopted the Stalinist view of China as "feudal" and "semi-feudal." In his speech on **New Democracy**,

Mao declared that China had been "feudal" from the Zhou (1122 BC–256 BC) and Qin (221 BC–207 BC) dynasties until the intrusion of capitalism and imperialism in the mid-19th century, which transformed the country and culture into a "semi-feudal" one. In 1949, Mao declared the Communist revolution to be a victory over "imperialism, feudalism, and bureaucratic capitalism." As the major social prop of "feudalism," the landed gentry were expropriated during **land reform (1950–1952)**. Yet as "feudal forces" were eliminated, Mao claimed that new capitalist forces had arisen that increasingly emerged as the target of Mao's political ire, especially during the **Cultural Revolution (1966–1976)**. "Feudalism" thus gradually waned in importance in Mao's political-ideological discourse. In the post-Mao period, however, "feudalism" once again became a catchall term that represented China's political and economic backwardness. The dangers of "capitalism" in the CCP that had been stressed by Mao were replaced by the purported presence of "feudal" attitudes toward authority among CCP **leaders**. Mao's patriarchal leadership style was considered a "feudal remnant," and in calling for an amelioration of authority relationships in the CCP, **Deng Xiaoping** and other reform-minded leaders attacked "feudalism." In this sense, Chinese feudalism refers not to the economic formation defined by Marx to describe medieval Europe, but to an imperial autocratic system in China that stretched from the Qin dynasty to the Stalinist–Maoist state and to ideological despotism of both thought and culture. Since 1978, feudalism has also been used in economic terms to describe the small commodity economy that the economic reforms have begun fundamentally to transform. Politically, the concept of "feudalism" has been used by proponents of political reform to criticize the traditional leadership style among old-line Communist **cadres** and outworn practices in the CCP, such as lifelong tenure for cadres.

"FIELD ARMY" (*"YEZHAN JUN"*). The field army system was established as a basic organizing unit of Communist military forces in 1948, just prior to the takeover of China in 1949. Organizationally, a field army consisted of several armies, corps, divisions, and regiments. Designation of field armies was by location and included the Northwest (First) Field Army, Southwest (Second) Field Army, the

Eastern China (Third) Field Army, the Central Plains (Fourth) Field Army, and the Northern (Fifth) Field Army, which all together made up the **People's Liberation Army (PLA)**. These were later given numerical designations as the First, Second, Third, and Fourth Field Armies, respectively, while the Northern China (Fifth) Field Army was put under the direct command of the General Headquarters of the PLA. The transfer of personnel, including officers, between field armies was very rare and loyalty in the military was primarily to one's particular field army. **Leaders** who rose to high military or political positions generally promoted associates from their respective field armies. Thus during his political ascendancy in the 1960s, **Lin Biao** promoted officers from his Fourth Field Army. When Lin Biao disappeared from the political scene in 1971, Fourth Field Army military personnel also lost many positions of influence. In this sense, the Chinese military is still not a fully unified military organization though recent reforms in the 1990s have aimed at creating a more modern military organizational structure. Military regions differ organizationally from the Field Army system.

FIFTH MODERNIZATION. In addition to the **Four Modernizations** advocated by **leaders** of the **Chinese Communist Party (CCP)**, a Fifth Modernization, namely democracy, was also proposed in the late 1970s by the political dissident **Wei Jingsheng**, and even by political reformers in the CCP. In January 1979, for instance, the *People's Daily*, the official organ of the CCP Central Committee, stated that "the four modernizations must be accompanied by political democratization." In a similar vein, the constitutional expert **Yu Haocheng** stated that "without democracy there can be no modernization." The most forceful statement, however, came from the **Democracy Wall Movement (1978–1979)** dissident Wei Jingsheng, who used this phrase as a title for a **big-character poster**, in which he asserted that the CCP's program for Four Modernizations was viable only when accompanied by necessary political reforms toward democracy. This poster spurred a torrent of criticism toward the CCP and its leadership that ultimately led to Wei's arrest in 1979 and the shutting down of Democracy Wall in early 1980.

FINANCE. *See* BANKING AND FINANCE.

"FIVE-ANTIS CAMPAIGN" (*"WUFAN YUNDONG"*). This campaign of mass mobilization was launched in 1952, soon after the **Three-Antis Campaign** (*sanfan yundong*). It targeted the owners of private property and industrial capital that the **Chinese Communist Party (CCP)** had not yet abolished. Ostensibly, the campaign aimed at eliminating bribery, tax evasion, theft of state property, cheating on government contracts, and theft of state economic intelligence. In reality, the campaign's purpose was to increase the government's taxes on the private sector, which had actually flourished in the first two years of Communist rule, with growth rates of over 11% per annum. The government also claimed that private business had sold useless products to Chinese military forces during the **Korean War (1950–1953)**. As in the Three-Antis and **land reform (1950–1952)**, the masses were mobilized to denounce purported offenders. Specially trained CCP **cadres** also extorted confessions from businessmen who were forced to engage in so-called **criticism and self-criticism** (*piping yu ziwo piping*). For some of these individuals, the pressure was too great and many suicides were reported as bankruptcies also mushroomed. Thus, in mid-1952, the campaign was softened as the majority of private businessmen were declared to be "basically law-abiding." However, the campaign significantly weakened the urban private sector so that by 1957 it could be completely socialized. Not until the 1980s would the CCP allow for the existence of private enterprise.

"FIVE BLACK CATEGORIES" (*"HEI WULEI"*). Originally "Four Black Categories," this phrase refers to anyone from a family of "landlords, rich peasants, counterrevolutionaries, and/or bad elements," plus anyone fired from his job or disciplined by his organization. In the first two years of the **Cultural Revolution (1966–1976)**, members of the Five Black Categories were frequent targets of **Red Guard** violence and persecution. It was once said that people from the "Five Black Categories" were so evil they were not allowed to donate their blood because it lacked revolutionary character. Over the course of the Cultural Revolution, the radical leadership led by **Mao Zedong** and the **Cultural Revolution Small Group** mobilized support among these dispossessed groups and directed their animosity toward the regular **Chinese Communist Party (CCP)** organization, which was the target of Mao's ire. By emphasizing that "political performance," not "class origin," determines one's class status, people from the Five Black Categories joined the most radical **Rebel Faction** (*zaofanpai*) of the Red Guards in their political movement. Ultimately, the designation itself was abolished.

"FIVE GOOD WOMEN" (*"WU HAO FUNÜ"*). Social models to guide the behavior of individuals and groups in China were a staple of **Chinese Communist Party** (**CCP**) propaganda that, for decades, aimed to mold the social order. These emerged in the absence of a well-developed **legal system** and as surrogates for the moral vacuum left by direct assaults on Confucianism, Christianity, and other moral norms because of their antagonism to **Marxism–Leninism–Mao Zedong Thought**. In the early 1950s, Chinese **women** were urged to adhere to the model of the "five good women." These were women who "made good arrangements for the livelihood of the family, kept good relations with neighbors, brought up children well, did well at encouraging the workers in production, work, and studies, and were [themselves] good in studies." Despite the "revolutionary" goals of the CCP, these standards were socially conservative and envisioned a role for women squarely within the family and generally subservient to men, "the workers in production." In 1957, the strictures were changed to emphasize women's role in performing "cleaning and hygienic work" at home. Women living in China's rural areas were given a different spin on the "five goods" by also being encouraged to "cherish the [agricultural] cooperative" and to "show respect for one's mother-in-law." As mother-in-law versus daughter-in-law relations in China are often quite tense, the Party's propaganda on this matter aimed at achieving a measure of social peace within the rural family.

"FIVE RED CATEGORIES" (*"HONG WULEI"*). This phrase refers to children of "poor and lower middle peasants, workers, revolutionary army men, revolutionary martyrs, and revolutionary **cadres**." These were for many years the five "good" **class labels** in China. During the **Cultural Revolution** (**1966–1976**), students from these five categories, and especially the latter three, used their politically privileged positions to come to the defense of the established Party apparatus that increasingly was the target of purges directed by **Mao Zedong**. In this sense, "five red category" offspring served as a conservative force during the Cultural Revolution, thus making them a primary target of the leftist Maoist forces, which mobilized "**Five Black Categories**" offspring against the establishment **Chinese Communist Party (CCP)**. Throughout the Cultural Revolution, students from these "good" families argued that "class origin" (*chusheng*) should determine one's "class status" (*chengfen*), which, in turn, defined one's political standing in the Cultural Revolution and in the revolutionary ranks of **Red Guards**. In line with this "theory of class origin," it was said "If one's father is revolutionary, then his son is a hero; and if one's father is reactionary, his son is a rotten egg." Initially, membership in Red Guard groups was restricted to students with "good" class backgrounds, while students from Five Black Categories backgrounds were singled out for persecution and were even murdered on the basis of information the Red Guards had gleaned from **personal dossiers** (*dang'an*). But as Mao Zedong emphasized the role of "performance" and "thought" over "class background," the **Rebel Faction** (*zaofanpai*) of the Red Guards mushroomed from all social groups, including the Five Black Categories. Among the children from "bad" family backgrounds, Mao Zedong discovered a potent political force to mobilize against CCP **leaders** whom he was intent on purging. As it turned out, however, factional struggles between competing Red Guard groups led to the most violent phases of the Cultural Revolution in 1967–1968, leading to Mao's decision in 1968 to carry out a "**transfer to lower levels**" (*xiafang*) of Red Guards to the countryside.

FIVE-YEAR PLAN (FYP). Like the former **Soviet Union**, China organized its planned **economy** around a series of five-year plans that began in 1953 and continued into the 1990s and early 2000s. The underlying theory of the planned economy is that, contrary to the free market forces of capitalism, a socialist economy plans the production of goods, prices, and distribution. The "irrationality" of capitalism whereby the "chaotic" market dictates production, prices, and distribution is replaced by a "rational," planned approach that, in both the former Soviet Union and China, emphasized rapid heavy industrial production, low agricultural prices, and few consumer goods. Expenditures on **education**, cultural activities, and the military were also part of the five-year plan's budgetary outlays. The First Five-Year Plan extended from 1953 to 1957 when total industrial output was planned to increase by 98%, **agriculture** by 24%, and retail sales by 80%. These targets were reportedly "over-fulfilled," though the reliability of the statistics can be questioned. The Second Five-Year Plan, which began in 1958, originally aimed for modest increases in economic growth over the First Five-Year Plan. This generated considerable controversy within top levels of the **Chinese Communist Party (CCP)** as **Mao Zedong** opposed targets as excessively "conservative." The result was considerable revision of the Second Five-Year Plan in mid-stream, especially during the **Great Leap Forward (1958–1960)**. This plan, in effect, was not completed until 1965. However, from 1961 to 1965, China shifted to yearly planning in order to deal with the economic disruptions brought on by the Great Leap, including a massive famine in rural areas.

The Third Five-Year Plan did not begin until 1966 and it too was disrupted during the **Cultural Revolution (1966–1976)** and was never really completed. Following the death of Mao Zedong in 1976, the implementation of the five-year plans was afforded greater regularity with fewer mid-course corrections and disruptions. And despite China's move to economic reform since 1978–1979, the five-year plans are still employed, though the degree of state control over the economy, especially over agriculture and light **industry**, has been reduced. Still, the continued ownership of heavy industrial facilities by the state allows for a significant, though not comprehensive, role for the economic plan. The Sixth (1981–1985), Seventh (1986–1990), Eighth (1991–1995), Ninth (1996–2000), and 10th (2001–2005) and the extraordinary Ten-Year Program (1991–2000) set overall macroeconomic and demographic goals for the country, including economic and **population** growth rates in accord with the model of sustainable development (Ninth FYP), allocated resources to the state-owned sector, which, in 2004, constituted 70% of the Gross Domestic Product (GDP), and budgeted key projects, such as the Jilin Chemical Industry Group (Eighth FYP), the **Three Gorges Dam Project** (Ninth FYP), and extension and construction of subways in 10 major cities, including **Beijing, Guangzhou (Canton)**, Nanjing, Qingdao, **Shanghai**, Shenyang, Shenzhen, and **Tianjin** (10th FYP).

In 2003, the government eliminated the State Development Planning Commission, the agency long entrusted with carrying out the five-year plan as part of a large-scale effort to streamline its economic planning apparatus to be more in tune with an increasingly market-oriented economy. This was followed, in 2004, by a decision to change the title of the traditional five-year plan to "five-year program" and to increase public participation in the drafting process by contracting research projects of major economic and social issues to non-governmental institutes and to encourage the public to voice their opinions on developmental strategy. A decision was also made to break from the long-standing practice of setting similar policy goals for various areas of the country to a process of drafting regional developmental programs along with an experimental effort at drafting county-level development programs. Commissions for Regional Development and Reform invited tenders nationwide, in 2004, from domestic enterprises and universities and institutes and even international organizations for the 11th Five-Year Program (2006–2010) through websites on the **Internet** and other forums for making the entire decision-making process more transparent and less likely to entail major errors. *See also* "AGRICULTURAL RESPONSIBILITY SYSTEM"; GOVERNMENT STRUCTURE; STATE-OWNED ENTERPRISES (SOEs).

"FLOATING POPULATION" (*"LIUDONG RENKOU"*). Defined in the 2000 census as migrants who move between provinces or counties and reside at their destinations for six months or more, China's floating **population** numbered 79 million people. If intra-county migrants (66 million people) are added to this figure the floating population in 2000 numbered 145 million. A product of the agricultural reforms inaugurated since 1978–1979 that freed up millions of surplus agricultural workers, the floating population in China can also be defined as the number of migrants without local household registration status or *hukou*. Since 1958, the **people's communes** had effectively tied people to their workplace with no chance for mobility. As the rural population expanded and **agriculture** was subjected to growing efficiencies and mechanization, significant surplus **labor** emerged in the countryside. In 1982, in the first census since the introduction of economic reforms, China's floating population (interprovince and intercounty only) was estimated at around seven million and by 1990 it had reached nearly 22 million, this in response to a 1984 edict by the State Council granting agricultural workers permission to leave the land.

Moving into cities and towns, the floating population became a primary labor force in local industries, especially construction, but also placed enormous strains on China's still underdeveloped urban infrastructure. Because these laborers were assigned the household registration of their rural parentage (inherited through the mother and extremely difficult to alter), they have not enjoyed access to the various amenities of urban registration, such as **education**, free **health care**, housing, and the right to be permanently employed in **state-owned enterprises** (**SOEs**) with their **iron rice bowl** (*tiefanwan*). The most popular destinations of transient workers is the large and relatively prosperous cities and provinces such as **Beijing** (2.6 million), **Shanghai** (4.4 million), and Guangdong (21 million), though floating populations are found in virtually every province and major city in China. In 2000, Sichuan Province, China's most populated province was one of the major sources of transient workers, especially to the Xinjiang Autonomous Region where temporary workers are critical during the cotton harvest season. Much less educated than permanent urban residents, these transient workers have become something of a disruptive force as their movements have placed enormous pressure on China's antiquated **transportation** system while their ramshackle dwellings in many major cities have become serious eyesores.

In 2004, it was reported that members of the floating population accounted for 80% of urban **crime**, especially juvenile delinquency and was a major factor in the burgeoning number of **social protests**. Transient workers also have a reputation, however, as generally compliant and low-wage labor, valued by upstart industries and new entrepreneurs. The overwhelming percentage of the floating population is male and quite young; and many remit their earnings to family members still residing in rural villages where their children—referred to as *liushou* ("left behind")—often spend years with only infrequent visits from their parents. Only 5% or so of the floating population are vagrants, criminals, and prostitutes as most transient workers cite "looking for manual labor or business" as their primary reason for leaving their rural abodes. In the 1990s, rapid industrial expansion especially along the coastal regions made China a world factory, drawing more and more migrants, first from surrounding rural areas and then from remote interior regions. In addition, the migration process is highly influenced by migration networks that over the past 20 years have emerged in different parts of the country as social relationships have formed between employers and migrant workers who exchange information on job availability and wages.

Chinese government authorities have feared that the floating population could become a politically destabilizing force, as apparently occurred during the 1989 second **Beijing Spring**. Concerns that a vast army of floating laborers would descend on the area in and around the **Three Gorges Dam Project** also prompted Chinese authorities to strengthen public security controls in the construction zone. In many cities, transient workers have been subject to arbitrary arrest and extra-judicial detention under a system set up in 1982 that has never been enshrined in law and that violates several constitutional guarantees, including one requiring adherence to certain judicial procedures when people are detained. In many cases, detainees are summarily returned to their home villages only to return to the cities where the cat-and-mouse game with local authorities is begun anew; in more extreme cases, detainees have been subject to brutal treatment at the hands of authorities resulting in death.

In 1991, the Ministry of Agriculture issued an urgent circular that urged rapid advances in the development of **township-village enterprises** (**TVEs**) in order to stem the flow of redundant laborers into the coastal regions. But as the flow of workers continued unabated, drastic reforms were introduced in 2004 to the detainee holding and deportation system for workers who lacked required residency, employment, and hometown permits. The Ministry of Public Security also began issuing temporary residence cards to migrants to monitor their movements and control their overall numbers in such cities as Shanghai, where the number of migrants (4.4 million) constitutes nearly 25% of the city's total population. This is the highest such figure in the nation, followed by Guangdong Province (24%) and Beijing (19%). The floating population is also the target of a new national super ID electronic card that will store vital information and indicate a person's household registration. The floating population has presented China with major public health-care problems especially involving the spread of HIV/**AIDS** and the 2002–2003 **SARS** virus outbreak, which led to dramatic reductions in income for transient workers who fled the cities at the height of the epidemic and returned to their rural abodes.

The floating population has also been generally unable to take part in the embryonic system of **village-level elections** that have become increasingly widespread in recent years. In 2003 and 2004, the Chinese government assisted migrants in retrieving overdue wages (estimated at 100 billion *yuan*) from their temporary employers, most often construction firms, who often withhold payment for months and even years while also docking worker salaries for days missed due to medical or family emergencies. China's State Council has also promulgated its "Notice on Properly Carrying Out the Work of Managing and Serving Rural Migrant Workers in Urban Areas" as a way to manage issues of employment, defaulted payment, schooling of their children, and job training while the 1994 Labor Law requires the prompt payment of wages. *See also* CRIME AND THE LEGAL SYSTEM; TRADE UNIONS.

FOREIGN POLICY. Since the establishment of the **People's Republic of China** (**PRC**) in 1949, Chinese foreign policy has been guided by a set of principles and pragmatic interests that reflect the country's status in the world as a great nation with a long, unbroken history and a large, but relatively poor **population**. China is famous for upholding the standard of principle in the world arena that draws mainly from three sources: traditional Chinese thinking, which conceives of a world of universal harmony; the humiliating experience in its modern history, especially during the 19th and first half of the 20th centuries, which have led China to long for a fair and reasonable world order; and the influence of **Marxism–Leninism–Mao Zedong Thought**, which advocates a world free of aggression and exploitation of capitalism, **imperialism**, and hegemony. From the 1950s to the present, China has advocated its Five Principles of Peaceful Coexistence (mutual respect for sovereignty and integrity, non-aggression, non-interference, equality and mutual benefit, and peaceful coexistence), all along emphasizing its "peaceful rise" and "peaceful development," and has called for establishing a fair and reasonable political and economic world order with no use of force or threat of force in international relations. All nations, big or small, strong or weak, rich or poor, are, China believes, equal in international affairs, and China will always side with the developing countries and never seek hegemony or superpower status.

China has also consistently advocated the principle of state sovereignty and mutual respect for territorial integrity, which is a reflection of its long-standing view that **Taiwan** is an integral part of China along with other territories on its periphery, primarily **Tibet** and the Xinjiang Autonomous Region in the far west. Recovery of **Hong Kong** and Macao were major goals of Chinese foreign policy that were achieved with the reincorporation of the former into the mainland in 1997, followed by the latter in 1999. Although China has more or less stuck to the same principles since 1949, the country's foreign policy posture and decisions have gone through a number of twists and turns in reaction to external and internal developments.

In the immediate aftermath of the Communist revolution, China became embroiled in a diplomatic row with the **United States** that led **Chinese Communist Party** (**CCP**) Chairman **Mao Zedong** to declare that China would "lean to one side" in its foreign relations, namely in alliance with the **Soviet Union** against the West as Mao made the first of two visits to the USSR to meet with **Josef Stalin** in late 1949. China's decision to enter the **Korean War** in October 1950 and engage American forces threw relations with the U.S. into the deep freeze that would last until the late 1960s. The U.S. decision to sign a defense treaty with Taiwan prevented the island's reincorporation into the Chinese state and ensured that the issue of sovereignty and territorial integrity would remain a prime concern of Chinese foreign policy over the next several decades. Despite the decision of the U.S. and its allies in Asia and Europe to withhold diplomatic recognition from the PRC, 19 countries formally recognized China between 1949 and 1951, including **India**, Pakistan, Indonesia, the Soviet Union and its allies in Eastern Europe, and a few European nations with independent tendencies, such as Finland, Denmark, Switzerland, and Sweden. And, despite China's decision to enter the Korean War, China used its diplomatic card by playing a prominent role in the 1954 Geneva talks to settle the Franco–**Vietnam** War in the same year that the PRC won diplomatic recognition from Great

Britain and the Netherlands. China also played a high-profile role, led by **Zhou Enlai**, in the **Bandung Conference of Afro–Asian States** (**1955**) in Indonesia.

In 1957, Mao Zedong made a second trip to the Soviet Union to engage its new post-Stalin leadership in the run-up to the second of two **Taiwan Straits Crises** in 1958, but, by 1959, Soviet leader Nikita Khrushchev began withdrawing Russian experts from China, marking the start of the 25-year long Sino–Soviet Conflict. China became increasingly critical of the Soviet idea of "peaceful coexistence," and despite its own invocation of the same phrase on occasion, the PRC launched into an increasingly aggressive foreign policy posture that led to the outbreak of the **Sino–Indian War** (**1962**) and China's protest of U.S. bombing of North Vietnam in 1964 when China declared that an attack on North Vietnam would be equivalent to an attack on China. Buoyed by its first test of an **atomic bomb** in 1964, followed two years later by the test of its first thermonuclear device, China continued to push a radical foreign policy line even as it won diplomatic recognition in the same year from a major European power, France. During the **Cultural Revolution (1966–1976)**, China offered virtual bibles for revolutionaries throughout the world from Europe to Latin America in such works as the *Quotations from Chairman Mao* and statements by Minister of Defense **Lin Biao** about the rural areas of the world surrounding and ultimately destroying the more developed urban areas. China also provided covert aid to revolutionary movements in Indonesia, Thailand, southern Africa, and to the emerging Khmer Rouge movement in **Cambodia**. With the military coup and crackdown against the pro-China Indonesian Communist Party (PKI) in 1965 and the outbreak of hostilities in Vietnam with increased American intervention, China began to retreat from its forward position on promoting revolution abroad, especially because the internecine violence of the Cultural Revolution intensified and military clashes occurred with Soviet forces along its northern border near the Ussuri River in 1969.

With China's gradual reduction of direct support for the North Vietnamese military, the U.S. signaled the possibility of a change in the two-decade diplomatic freeze between the two countries by partially removing elements of its trade embargo against the PRC. In 1970, China signaled a willingness to discuss substantive issues with the

U.S. at a higher diplomatic level, and, in 1971, U.S. National Security Advisor Dr. Henry Kissinger met secretly with Zhou Enlai in July, setting the stage for the visit to China by President Richard Nixon in February 1972. In 1971, China regained its seat in the **United Nations** (**UN**) and won recognition over the course of the next several years from nations throughout Africa, the Middle East, Latin America, and Europe. By 1979, when full diplomatic relations were restored with Washington, the PRC was recognized by 121 nations and 161 nations by 1999, including Israel, South **Korea**, and South Africa. In 1980, China was admitted to the International Monetary Fund (IMF) and the World Bank. In 1983, it was approved as a member of the International Atomic Energy Agency (IAEA) and it joined the Asian Development Bank in 1986. Diplomatic relations with the Soviet Union were normalized in 1986, after a recurrence of border clashes, and also with Vietnam in 1983, four years after the outbreak of the Sino–Vietnamese War in 1979, the last time China was engaged in armed conflict.

In the aftermath of the collapse of the Soviet Union in 1991, China established diplomatic relations with all of the former Soviet republics and has sought to counter U.S. attempts to shape a unipolar world, stressing instead a multipolar international system in which the PRC will leave its mark on a number of relevant international issues near its borders and in the Asia–Pacific region, where its prime national interests are at stake. But **Beijing** has also reached out to nations beyond its immediate regional concerns, including Israel, which China's foreign minister visited in 1992 with return visits to China by the Israeli president and prime minister. In general, China favors bilateral rather than multilateral channels to deal with international issues, such as the South China Sea territorial issue, as it often perceives multilateral international mechanisms as serving the interests of the dominant powers. But as China assumed a more active role in the UN in the mid- to late 1990s, it has subsequently shown more interest in participating in multilateral political activities, such as the Asia–European Summit, the Northeast Asian **Association of Southeast Asian Nations** (**ASEAN**) dialogue, and the six-party talks on eliminating nuclear weapons from the Korean peninsula. China strongly condemned the 1999 NATO bombing of Yugoslavia, which it perceived as a violation of state sovereignty, but China also issued a statement that pledged to respect the will of the East Timorese people to vote for independence from Indonesia. In 2002, China joined **Russia**, France, Germany, and other nations in opposing the American invasion of Iraq, although it did endorse UN Resolution 1441 that sent weapons inspectors into Iraq and UN Resolution 1511 on the transition to Iraqi sovereignty. The continuing Taiwan issue prevents China from abandoning its 19th century notion of the absolute supremacy of state sovereignty and has led to disputes with nations that continue to supply Taiwan with military equipment—as occurred in 1981, when China demoted its diplomatic relations with The Netherlands after the Dutch government sold Taiwan two submarines.

Since 1997, China has pursued its "New Security Concept" that continues to emphasize the Five Principles of Peaceful Coexistence. Although some disputes, such as the South China Sea issue, remain unresolved, China has declared its willingness to put aside such conflicts for the time being and seek common ground by establishing "partnerships" or "strategic partnerships" with most of the powers along China's periphery. In 2003, China issued a "European Union [EU] Policy Paper," which outlined plans for bilateral cooperation for the next five years in politics, economics, military, science, and culture. While China sees the European Union as becoming its largest trading partner, the document also insists on an EU commitment to the one-China policy. Staging a Global Conference on Scaling Up Poverty Reduction in **Shanghai** in May 2004, China committed itself to assist worldwide efforts at poverty reduction in such nations as Bangladesh and Brazil and joined with India and Brazil in opposing developed countries at the 2004 Cancun conference of the **World Trade Organization** (**WTO**). The same year witnessed China's "charm offensive" as newly appointed President **Hu Jintao** and Premier **Wen Jiabao** visited a host of countries in Southeast Asia, Africa, and Europe, where China pledged itself to a "foreign policy of peace" and common prosperity, calling for greater democracy in international relations and less "hegemony and power politics," all of which is backed up by the country's increasing economic power. Following the disastrous *tsunami* that hit Southeast and South Asia in early 2005, China broke with its past inward-looking tradition by offering US$63 million in aid, one of its largest pledges of international relief.

China seems increasingly committed to abide by international rules and norms and to making its foreign policy decisions more transparent. In the early 2000s, as China's **economy** continued to experience robust growth, the need to secure reliable sources of commodities from iron ore to oil to copper has become an increasingly important factor in shaping its foreign and security policy. This has not only affected its foreign policy vis-à-vis crucial neighbors such as Russia and **Japan** but also more far off areas such as in Latin America where China struck major **trade and investment** deals in such countries as Argentina and Venezuela and announced plans for a "strategic partnership" with Brazil which has emerged as a major supplier to China of iron ore, soybeans, coffee, and airplane parts. In Africa, China deployed 4,000 troops to the Sudan to protect a Chinese investment in an oil pipeline and promised the entire continent that it would boost two-way trade to US$30 billion by 2005. China also pushed for regional political and economic groupings it could dominate, such as the proposed East Asia Community that would cut out the U.S. and create a global bloc to rival the EU. Despite international condemnation of the government of Uzbekistan for its harsh military crackdown against a prison break and an antigovernment rally that evidently resulted in several hundred deaths in 2005, the PRC welcomed Uzbek President Islam A. Karimov for a state visit soon after the outbreak of violence. In terms of international covenants, in 1993 China joined the World Intellectual Property Organization and has stated that it would abide by the Missile Control Technology Regime.

The dominant organ in the implementation of China's foreign policy is the Ministry of Foreign Affairs, which was established immediately after the CCP takeover in 1949. Each area of foreign relations divided either geographically or functionally is overseen by a vice-minister or assistant minister. Regionally oriented departments of the ministry include Africa, the Americas and Oceania, Asia, the Middle East, Russia and Eastern Europe, Western Europe, and Taiwan with functional departments for administration, **cadres**, consular affairs, finance, information, international laws and treaties, international organizations and affairs, personnel, protocol, training and **education**, and translation. During the height of the Cultural Revolution, China recalled all but one of its ambassadors (Egypt) and the ministry practically ceased functioning as little or no training of personnel occurred. Since the early 1970s, the foreign affairs establishment has been rebuilt with personnel recruited from such specialized training programs as the ministry's own Foreign Affairs College, the College of International Relations, Beijing Foreign Languages Institute, and international studies departments at various universities. Specialists from other ministries serve in China's many embassies and consulates with military attachés from the Ministry of Defense, commercial officers from the Ministry of Foreign Trade and Economic Cooperation (MOFTEC), and cultural affairs personnel from the Ministry of Culture and the Ministry of Education. Diplomacy and defense policies of the PRC have traditionally been very secretive with overall coordination by the CCP Leading Group on National Security and with foreign policy initiatives taken by the top Party leadership at the expense of the foreign minister who in 2005 was not even a member of the **Politburo** Standing Committee. In 1999, the Ministry of Foreign Affairs moved toward more transparency by opening up a new, modern international media center where biweekly press conferences are held with simultaneous translation and where according to foreign journalists hard questions are asked and real answers are provided. Senior foreign affairs officials also invite journalists for off-the-record background briefings before release of major policy documents or after major bilateral summits, all of which represents a dramatic departure for a nation once known for its secrecy in foreign affairs. China has also relied on "people-to-people" diplomacy through such organizations as the Chinese People's' Association for Friendship with Foreign Countries and the Chinese People's Institute of Foreign Affairs. In 2005, the foreign minister of China was Li Zhaoxing (1940–), a graduate of **Beida (Peking University)** and former ambassador to the United States. *See also* AFGHANISTAN; INDIA.

"FOUR BIG FREEDOMS" (*"SIDA ZIYOU"*). Also known as the "four bigs" (*sida*), these "freedoms" refer to the writing of **big-character posters** (*dazibao*), holding great debates, airing one's views, and "contending in a big way." These "freedoms" were first mentioned in the late 1950s and were extensively employed during the **Cultural Revolution (1966–1976)** by **Red Guards** in their assaults on the **Chinese Communist Party (CCP)** apparatus. In 1966, the "four big freedoms" allowed for open debate and enabled the general **population** to "clarify correct views, criticize wrong views, and expose all ghosts and monsters" (i.e., opponents of CCP Chairman **Mao Zedong**). In 1975, near the end of the Cultural Revolution, the "four bigs" were incorporated into the state constitution of China. According to the *People's Daily* (20 January 1975), this was to allow for "new forms of carrying on socialist revolution created by the masses of the people . . . and [to] ensure the masses the right to use these forms." During the **Democracy Wall Movement (1978–1979)**, big-character posters and the open airing of views were extensively used by social reform forces in support of the return to power of **Deng Xiaoping** and of political and economic reforms away from the leftist radicalism that had dominated since the outbreak of the Cultural Revolution. But once Deng Xiaoping was securely installed in power, Democracy Wall was closed down and the "four big freedoms" were eliminated from the state constitution in 1982 and derided by Deng Xiaoping as a vestige of the Cultural Revolution and a threat to political "stability."

"FOUR CARDINAL PRINCIPLES" (*"SIXIANG JIBEN YUANZE"*). These "principles" of the **Chinese Communist Party (CCP)** are aimed at rigidly defining the limits of dissent and protest in Chinese society in the post-Mao era. They were enunciated by **Deng Xiaoping** in February and March 1979 at a forum on the principles for the Party's theoretical work that followed the suppression of the **Democracy Wall Movement (1978–1979)** by the CCP. The principles call on all Chinese to "uphold the socialist road; uphold the dictatorship of the proletariat; uphold the leadership of the CCP; and uphold **Marxism–Leninism–Mao Zedong Thought**." Overall, they provide hard-line, orthodox **leaders** in the Communist Party with an ideological carte blanche to persecute any individual, including Party members, who advocates significant political reform and **human rights**.

Since 1979, China's leaders have periodically invoked the Four Cardinal Principles to justify political repression and cultural conservatism. Although always cited in the press and cultural circles as official ideology even during times of greater relaxation and openness, the government's reliance on these "principles" has been especially pronounced during periods of retreat from political reform. This was true during the **Antispiritual Pollution Campaign (1983–1984)** and the subsequent attack on **"bourgeois liberalization"** that followed the dismissal of **Hu Yaobang** as CCP general secretary in 1987. Individuals close to Deng Xiaoping claimed that he considered removing the principles from the state constitution and having them limited to the more strict Party constitution, a move that was effectively thwarted by the outbreak of the second **Beijing Spring** in May–June 1989, which effectively strengthened conservative elements in the CCP. As a result, the four "principles" were a central feature of Communist orthodoxy after the June 1989 military crackdown against the pro-democracy movement.

From the orthodox Chinese Communist point of view, "upholding **socialism** and the CCP's dictatorship" are essential to combat the penetration of Western pro-capitalist and democratic ideas into China. Similar to 19th-century Chinese conservatives who attempted to "use" (*yong*) Western **science and technology** while maintaining the essence, or "body" (*ti*) of traditional Chinese culture, the Chinese leadership, beginning in 1978–1979, introduced modern economic principles and technology while trying to avoid the culturally and politically liberalizing influences of the outside world. The contradictions intensified when the Communist Party exhorted its members to "liberate their thought" (*jiefang sixiang*) from the "evil" leftist influences of the radical **Gang of Four**. Contrary to the intention of orthodox leaders, such pronouncements seemingly encouraged learning from the democratic capitalist world, which is why Deng Xiaoping had a difficult time differentiating "bourgeois liberalization" from "liberation of thought."

Official CCP documents thus warn Party members against being influenced by "the wave of capitalist ideas on freedom" and "capitalist standards of morality and **literature and the arts**." One document complained that "in the Party there are certain comrades who not only do not recognize the dangers of this wave, but even go so far as to encourage more of it." Such warnings were undoubtedly aimed at supporters of Hu Yaobang and the relatively liberal Party members at universities and research institutes, such as the **Chinese Academy of Social Sciences (CASS)**, where support for dramatic political change in the direction of democratic liberalism is its strongest. Even before the spring 1989 demonstrations, Chinese Communist leaders expressed alarm over the active role some Party members were taking in street demonstrations and other popular protests. Once Party members applied their considerable organizational skills to mobilizing the **population** for political change, it was obvious that the old guard's grip on power would be seriously threatened. *See also* SOCIALIST EDUCATION MOVEMENT (1962–1966).

FOUR CLEANS. *See* SOCIALIST EDUCATION MOVEMENT (1962–1966).

FOUR MODERNIZATIONS. Modernization of **agriculture**, **industry**, defense, and **science and technology** by the year 2000 was the goal of **Chinese Communist Party (CCP)** announced at the Fourth **National People's Congress (NPC)** in January 1975 when the phrase was first put forth by **Zhou Enlai.** It was not until the watershed **Third Plenum of the 11th CCP Central Committee** in December 1978, however, that the leadership united fully behind these goals and introduced the economic reform policies, the **open-door policy**, and changes in the **education** system to make such a radical transformation of Chinese society and **economy** possible. A central element of the pursuit of the Four Modernizations was a substantial turnover of CCP **cadres** from those skilled in politics and ideological struggle to a more professionally trained corps. This was achieved through an elaborate process of cadre retirement throughout the 1980s and the recruitment of college-educated personnel into CCP ranks. Although slow in the beginning, by 1985, the CCP had carried out a substantial alteration of its ranks, creating a "third" and then "fourth generation" of younger **leaders** with the professional training necessary to achieve the Four Modernizations. On the national level, the average age of ministers and vice-ministers dropped, in 1985, from 65 to 59 years of age, while the number of ordinary **cadres** in the central state ministries with a college education grew from 38% to 50%, a process that continued throughout the 1990s into the 2000s. Similar changes were also effected at the provincial and local levels of the CCP in pursuit of modernization.

"FOUR OLDS" (*"SIJIU"*). This refers to so-called old ideas, old culture, old customs, and old habits in China that were a target of the

Red Guards during the **Cultural Revolution (1966–1976)**. The so-called exploiting classes in China had, it was said, imposed cultural attitudes and customs on the consciousness of the common people that the radical leadership was seeking to eradicate. In the late 1960s, Red Guards attacked all aspects of the traditional cultural realm by destroying books by classical philosophers, such as Confucius and Mencius, trashing temples, and defacing artwork at traditional Buddhist and Taoist religious sites. Particularly hard hit were religious sites populated by **minorities**, such as in **Tibet**, where more than 10,000 temples were destroyed and many monks killed. Also targeted were the libraries and collections of teachers and **intellectuals** that were often burned. Major historical sites in **Beijing**, however, were largely spared, as **Zhou Enlai** personally ordered the **People's Liberation Army (PLA)** to protect the ancient Forbidden City and other major cultural sites in the capital.

FRONT FOR A DEMOCRATIC CHINA. Following the military crackdown in June 1989 on the second **Beijing Spring** pro-democracy movement, exiled Chinese students and democratic **leaders** met in France and established the Front (or Federation) for a Democratic China. This marked the end of the belief by older **intellectuals** that the **Chinese Communist Party (CCP)** could be reformed from within. Political change in China, it was now believed, could only be affected by the establishment of an organization independent of the Party. The establishment of the Front also marked the first time that older dissident intellectuals, such as **Liu Binyan**, **Su Shaozhi**, and **Yan Jiaqi**, cooperated with younger students, such as **Wu'er Kaixi** and Shen Tong, whose actions until then had been relatively independent. The immediate goal of the Front was to establish a multi-party system in China, even though its founders explicitly denied it was a political party. Violence was abjured as a means of effecting political change toward democratization that would instead come about as a result of economic growth and the emergence of a middle class. Annual meetings of the Front were held in Paris, where appeals were made to the Chinese government to engage in a dialogue to resolve China's political problems. In 1995, the chairman of the Front was **Wan Runnan**, while, in the late 1990s, the Front was largely supplanted by the Free China

Movement, an umbrella organization for 35 separate groups committed to the cause of democracy for China.

– G –

"GANG OF FOUR" (*"SIREN BANG"*). This group consisted of the major radical political **leaders** during the **Cultural Revolution (1966–1976)** and included **Jiang Qing** (the wife of **Chinese Communist Party (CCP)** Chairman **Mao Zedong**), **Zhang Chunqiao** (the **Shanghai** political leader), **Wang Hongwen** (an industrial worker promoted to political prominence by Mao Zedong), and **Yao Wenyuan** (a polemical literary critic and confidante of Madame Mao). The group itself never used the term "Gang of Four" during the Cultural Revolution, but it became popular after the arrest of its members in October 1976 following the death of Mao. The appellation was reportedly first used by Mao when he warned his wife, Jiang Qing, not to form a "Gang of Four." After the arrest of its members, the "Gang" was accused of usurping the leadership of the CCP and attempting to "seize power" through unlawful factional activities. Despite the promotion by the "Gang of Four" of radical politics, opponents claimed that they represented the "bourgeoisie" inside the CCP. A nationwide campaign to criticize the "Gang of Four" and its network of supporters began in 1977 and continued into the early 1980s. All four members of the so-called Gang were tried in 1980 for "crimes" involving the innumerable deaths during the Cultural Revolution. Jiang Qing and Zhang Chunqiao were both sentenced to death (with a two-year reprieve) and Yao Wenyuan and Wang Hongwen were given lighter sentences because of their apparent contrition. Political dissidents in China claim that by blaming the Cultural Revolution on the "Gang" and on the recently deceased Mao Zedong, CCP leaders avoided confronting the systemic flaws in China's autocratic political system. During the propaganda campaign against the Gang, urban residents were known to buy four crabs at their seafood markets, one a female, as representations of the four leaders. By 2005, three of the four members of the "Gang" had died, Jiang Qing by suicide in Qincheng Prison in 1991, Wang Hongwen in 1992, and

Zhang Chunqiao in 2005; Yao Wenyuan was released from prison in 1996 and continues to live in Shanghai.

GAO GANG-RAO SHUSHI INCIDENT. This incident involved the first major factional struggle and purge in the post-1949 **Chinese Communist Party (CCP)** leadership. As the major Party figure in northeast China, Gao Gang, in 1953, proposed that the chairmanship of the CCP be rotated among the top **leaders** rather than held solely by **Mao Zedong**. Rebuffed by Mao, Gao began to engage in clandestine appeals to potential supporters, including **Zhu De** and **Peng Dehuai**, but to no avail. Despite the fact that Mao Zedong and Gao Gang were in agreement on many policies for China, and that Gao was one of the few upfront supporters of the chairman on the decision to enter the **Korean War (1950–1953)**, Mao, supported by **Deng Xiaoping**, decided to move against Gao, ousting him from his leadership position in 1955. Gao subsequently committed suicide. Rao Shushi, a senior Party leader in **Shanghai**, was implicated in the affair, though very little evidence was ever publicized, indicating that Rao Shushi had actively joined Gao Gang's "conspiracy." In all likelihood, the purge of Rao Shushi reflected fundamental differences among top CCP leaders over economic and financial issues that had emerged in the early 1950s. Following the purge of Gao and Rao, extensive criticism was launched against Party leaders who supposedly violated principles of the "collective leadership" *(jiti lingdao)* and who prevented the normal operation of Party committees. Although these criticisms were nominally aimed at Gao and Rao, some Western observers have suggested that they were actually directed at Mao for fostering his **personality cult** *(geren chongbai)*, which would come to the fore over the next decade.

GENERAL LINE FOR THE TRANSITION PERIOD. This refers to the set of policies adopted by the **Chinese Communist Party (CCP)** in the period from 1949 to the completion of the socialist transformation of the **economy** in the 1950s. In 1949, China's situation was similar to that of **Russia** in 1917 in that capitalism was underdeveloped; thus the transition to **socialism** would take much longer than Karl Marx had originally envisioned. This required a relatively long "transition period" that would entail the takeover of **industry, agriculture,**

and commerce by the state (i.e., the so-called socialization of the means of production). In urban areas, according to official CCP decisions, this was to occur in a step-by-step manner and without coercion as China's captains of industry and commerce would, during the first stage of socialization, be "encouraged . . . to move toward the direction of state capitalism," that is, capitalism with considerable state intervention, but still capitalism, not socialism (i.e., outright state ownership). Industry and commerce would then, during the second stage, be transformed into a socialism characterized by state-run and cooperative commerce. In rural areas, the "transition" would occur in three stages, as agriculture would move from **mutual aid teams** to the "semi-socialist" **Agricultural Producers' Cooperatives (APCs)**, and finally to state farms, where the state would be the legal owner of the land. The moderate pace of "socialization" proposed under this policy rubric of the "transition" was generally abandoned in the mid-1950s as CCP Chairman **Mao Zedong** pushed for rapid "socialization" of industrial and commercial property and an equally rapid pace of agricultural cooperativization that was then quickly followed, in 1958, by the ill-fated **people's communes** of the equally ill-fated **Great Leap Forward (1958–1960)**.

GENERAL SECRETARY OF THE CCP. *See* CHINESE COMMUNIST PARTY (CCP).

"GOING THROUGH THE BACK DOOR" (*"ZOU HOUMEN"*). This means to seek certain personal gains or objectives by making use of "connections" (*guanxi*) with people in responsible positions. These "connections" are usually personal and were frequently used to get favorable treatment in the allocation of rationed goods and commodities to obtain an urban household registration (*hukou*) or to gain entry into prestigious schools and universities. "Going through the back door" is perhaps the most blatant form of **corruption** in China, although the growth of the market **economy** since 1978–1979 has perhaps reduced its importance since "connections" have been replaced by "money" as the new grease of corruption.

GOVERNMENT STRUCTURE. The government or state structure of China is highly complex. Since 1949, it has undergone significant institutional revisions (most recently in 1998) that have reflected changes in **Chinese Communist Party (CCP)** policies. The state structure parallels and significantly overlaps with the organizational structure of the CCP, which retains ultimate authority in the Chinese political system. Under the principle of interlocking institutions, Party **leaders** serve in various state positions of authority at the central level and below. The highest organ of state power is the **National People's Congress (NPC)**, a "legislative" body with a five-year term that authorizes all state laws and produces the state constitution. The members of the NPC elect as its executive body the NPC Standing Committee, which is headed by a chairman and several vice-chairmen and a secretary-general who serve a maximum of two five-year terms and oversee the State Central **Military Affairs Commission (MAC)** and the General Affairs Office, the Legislative Work Committee, and the Budget Committee. The NPC also elects a State Council composed of the premier (**Wen Jiabao** in 2005) vice-premiers, state councilors, a secretary-general, and the various ministers. Below the NPC is a subordinate structure of people's congresses at the provincial, autonomous region, municipality, prefecture, county, and township levels to which delegates are elected in generally noncompetitive elections governed by the Elector Law of the **People's Republic of China (PRC)**, which was promulgated in 1953. The NPC also oversees the Supreme People's Court and all subordinate courts and the Supreme People's Procuratorate, which heads the **Procuracy**, China's prosecutorial arm. In 1980, the Organic Law of the Local People's Congresses and Local People's Government was promulgated under which the posts of provincial governors and mayors were restored after the destruction to the government structure wrought during the **Cultural Revolution (1966–1976)**. This was followed in 1994 by the NPC adoption of China's first Budget Law, which prevented regional governments from incurring a budget deficit. The State Council administers the state-run sectors of the **economy** and society through an elaborate structure of ministries, commissions, administrative offices, institutions, and bureaus, which, in 1998, were subject to a major reform and consolidation that largely dismantled the old ministerial system that had emerged during the era of Soviet-style central planning and created an administrative structure in accord with the economic reforms inaugurated since 1978–1979. As a result of the reform, there are 31 ministries and commissions (down from 40) and a variety of administrative offices and bureaus. The General Affairs Office of the State Council is responsible for assisting leaders of the Council in dealing with routine work by preparing meetings and drafting or reviewing documents and is divided into four bureaus and two departments.

The ministries are Agriculture, Civil Affairs, Commerce, Communications, Construction, Culture, **Education**, **Finance**, Foreign Affairs, Foreign **Trade** and Economic Cooperation, Health, Information Technology, Justice, **Labor** and Social Security, Land and Resources, National Defense, Personnel, Public Security, Railways, **Science and Technology**, State Security, Supervision, **Transportation**, and Water Resources. Seven commissions function as macro-control departments of the State Council: State Development and Reform, Science, Technology, and Industry for National Defense, Ethnic Affairs, Population and Family Planning, People's Bank of China, National Auditing Office, and State-Owned Assets Supervision and Administration. Bureaus and administrations under the State Council include General Administration of Customs, State Administration of Taxation, State Administration for Industry and Commerce, General Administration of Quality Supervision, Inspection, and Quarantine, State Environmental Protection Administration (SEPA), General Administration of Civil Aviation of China, State Administration of Radio, Film, and Television, State General Administration of Press and Publication, State General Administration of Sports, National Bureau of Statistics, State Forestry Administration, State Food and Drug Supervision Administration, State Administration of Work Safety, State Intellectual Property Office, National Tourism Administration, State Administration for Religious Affairs, Counselors' Office under the State Council, and Government Offices Administration. Administrative offices under the State Council include Foreign Affairs, Overseas Chinese Affairs, **Taiwan** Affairs, **Hong Kong** & Macao Affairs, Legislative Affairs, Economic Restructuring, Information, and Research.

Institutions directed by the State Council are the **New China News Agency** (**Xinhua**), China News Service, Chinese Academy of Sciences (CAS), **Chinese Academy of Social Sciences** (**CASS**), Chinese Academy of Engineering, Development Research Center, National School of Administration, China Seismological Bureau, China Meteorological Administration, China Banking Regulatory Commission, China Securities Regulatory Commission, China Insurance Regulatory Commission, State Electricity Regulatory Commission, National Council for Social Security Fund, and the National Natural Science Foundation. There are also a number of State bureaus under the jurisdiction of the ministries and commissions, such as the State Bureau for Letters and Calls and the State Administration of Cultural Heritage.

Several of the old-line ministries, such as the Ministry of Railways, are organized and run along highly centralized and militarized lines while others, such as the Ministry of Health and the State Environmental Protection Administration, have traditionally had little enforcement power, especially at the crucial local level. Institutes such as the State Key Laboratory of Information Security, located in **Beijing**, play important roles in China's ongoing effort to master high-level problems of encryption and computer language management. Major reports and documents are published by the government in the tri-monthly *State Council Bulletin (Guowuyuan gongbao)*, which also prints directives, notices, and agreements signed with foreign countries while also registering approval of the central government to local government actions. *See also* PRESIDENT OF THE PEOPLE'S REPUBLIC OF CHINA.

"GREAT LEAP FORWARD" (*"DA YUEJIN"*) (1958–1960). A radical attempt to overcome China's economic backwardness and achieve the stage of "communism" in one fell swoop through mass mobilization, the Great Leap Forward was a bold plan devised largely by **Mao Zedong** at the August 1958 **Beidaihe Conference** that ultimately produced a major economic and demographic disaster. The basic strategy of the leap was to rely on the creative enthusiasm of the masses and the country's nearly unlimited manpower to substitute for the severe lack of capital goods in bringing about dramatic increases in the production of both **agriculture** and **industry** and thereby to free China from excessive dependence on the **Soviet Union**. The unemployed wcre to be put to work and the already employed were driven to work harder, all under military discipline, so that China could break out of the limitations of its economic backwardness. The modern sector of the **economy**—steel plants and other industries built over the past years by the **Kuomintang (KMT)**, the Japanese, and the Communists—would join with the traditional sector of the economy composed of labor-intensive, small-scale production to make a gigantic leap in production. Referred to as "walking on two legs," this policy in the industrial sector was to lead to dramatic increases in steel production by conventional factories and by the **backyard steel furnaces** developed largely in the countryside at a great expense to agricultural production. In agriculture, the major mechanism for increasing production was organizational through the elevation of the basic production and accounting unit in the countryside to the **people's communes**. By 1959, 26,000 communes had been established, with an average of 2,000 households or approximately 10,000 people. In addition to radically altering the allocation of **labor** for agricultural production, the communes served as local government and Party organs that took over virtually all administrative functions in the countryside. As a labor-saving device some communes also set up canteens for collective eating and encouraged farmers to contribute their pots, pans, and other iron materials to the backyard steel furnace campaign.

The Great Leap Forward ultimately failed for a variety of reasons. Excessive demands on urban and rural laborers by Party **cadres** produced an exhausted labor force that was unable to keep up with the pace of work demanded by the production goals established by the **Chinese Communist Party (CCP)** leadership. In addition, Maoist experiments in the countryside—the backyard steel furnaces, the close planting of rice, and deep plowing, which were designed to increase production dramatically—generated, instead, massive reductions in food output, which ultimately led to a rural famine that cost upward of 30 million lives. These manmade disasters were exacerbated in 1959 by serious flooding and drought. Economically, the "Three Bitter Years" (1960–1962) followed the Great Leap Forward, while politically it produced deep divisions in the CCP leadership that ultimately led to the **Cultural Revolution (1966–1976)**. *See also* LUSHAN PLENUM.

GU XIULIAN (1936–). A **cadre** in the **public security bureau** from Liaoning Province in China's northeast, Gu Xiulian was also trained as a metallurgical engineer and served in the Ministry of Textile Industry from 1964–1969. A vice-minister of the State Planning Commission from 1973–1982, she was elected to the **Chinese Communist Party** (**CCP**) Central Committee at the 1982 12th National Party Congress and became Party secretary and governor of Jiangsu Province in 1983. From 1989 to 1998, Gu served as the minister of chemical industry in the central government and, in 2003, was elected president of the **All-China Federation of Women**.

GUANGZHOU (CANTON). The capital of Guangdong Province, Guangzhou is situated on the estuary of the Pear River and is the fifth largest city in China with a **population** in 2005 of 12.2 million people in the Guangzhou metropolitan area (*Guangzhou shi*), of whom eight million live in the urban area. Its international name is "Canton," which originated as a French-language corruption of the Cantonese pronunciation of *Guangdong*. The Chinese abbreviation for the city is *Sui* with a number of nicknames including "city of five rams" (*wuyangcheng*)—so named for the five gods astride goats who with five ears of corn descended from heaven to save the city from starvation—and the "city of flowers" (*huacheng*) as the city's famous flora grow year-round in its semitropical environment. The metropolitan area is divided into 10 administrative districts, including the four districts of the old city, such as Li Wan, with its heavily shaded island of Sha Mian, which, leased to foreigners in the pre-1949 period, contains clusters of European-style buildings, and the newly developed district of Tian He, which has emerged as a center of computer products and businesses. With a Gross Domestic Product (GDP) per capita income in 2003 of 38,568 *yuan* ($4,660), Guangzhou was ranked eighth among China's 672 cities.

First built in 214 BC and originally named *Panyu*, the city became the capital of the Nanyue kingdom, which was annexed into the **Han** dynasty (206 BC–221 AD) in 111 BC. Sacked by Arabs and Persians in 758 AD, the city became a major trading port during the Tang dynasty (618–907 AD) and is the site of the Huaisheng Mosque, the oldest in China. An object of foreign interest in the early 16th century when Portuguese traders won a **trade** monopoly, which was broken in the 17th and 18th centuries by the British and Dutch, the city became the site of a trading post of the British East India Company that sought lucrative trade in tea, porcelain, and silk. Under what became known as the "Canton System" in the 18th century, foreign trade was restricted by the Qianlong Emperor to a small district in the city that included the illegal importation of Indian opium that in 1839 imperial High Commissioner Lin Zexu attempted to halt leading to the nefarious Opium Wars. Under the terms of the "unequal" Treaty of Nanking (1842), Guangzhou was one of five treaty ports opened up to the unfettered opium trade that by the 20th century afflicted approximately one out of every 10 Chinese.

As a seat of the *Guang* Prefecture—hence the name *Guangzhou* (literally "capital of *Guang*")—this did not become the official name of the city until 1918 when a major modernization project was begun of road construction and pulling down the old city wall. Unlike most major cities in China with their north–south/east–west axes of city streets and thoroughfares that exude central authority and celestial order, Guangzhou is a maze of incoherent streets and lanes filled with traffic and commotion. From the mid-19th century onward, the city became a hotbed of political radicalism and opposition spawning individuals from Hong Xiuquan—the charismatic leader of the pseudo-Christian *Taipings* in the 1850s to Sun Yat-sen the founder of the **Kuomintang (KMT)**. The site of a Peasant Training Institute, where **Mao Zedong** once taught, and the Whampoa Military Academy, Guangzhou witnessed the brief establishment of a commune in 1927. From 1938 to the end of World War II, it was occupied by Japanese troops. Conquered by Communist troops under the leadership of **Lin Biao** in the Chinese **Civil War (1946–1949)**, Guangzhou was largely ignored by central policies during the Maoist era (1949–1976) but emerged as a center of market-oriented reforms from 1978–1979 onward.

The central hub of **transportation**, trade, and **banking and finance** in South China, Guangzhou has become the site of numerous industries, including steel, paper mills, textiles, machinery, bicycles, and most recently **automobiles**, in a number of joint ventures, beginning in 1985 with Chinese companies, such as *Dongfeng* ("East Wind") Automotive that, by 2010, will produce 1.3 million units. These developments were accompanied by an infrastructure spending spree beginning in 1997 that was part of the city's larger ambition to reclaim its traditional role as south China's economic and commercial hub from nearby **Hong Kong**. Guangzhou is the southern terminus point of the Guangzhou–Wuhan railway and since 1957 the city has been the site of the Chinese Export Commodities Fair held twice a year in spring and autumn that for years was one of China's few outlets to the global **economy**. From 1980 to 1993, the GDP of Guangzhou increased on average by 14% a year and, in 1990, the city boasted a total GDP of 31.9 billion *yuan* about 64 and 43% of **Beijing** and **Shanghai**, respectively. With the construction of automobile and engine plants by Nissan, Toyota, and Honda, Guangzhou, in 2004, was the third largest car production center in China behind Shanghai and Jilin Province. With its Nansha Development Zone, Guangzhou has also attracted **investment** from South **Korea** including plans for a joint-venture car terminal to be built by Nippon Yusen Kaisha Line, the world's largest ocean-going car carrier by volume.

In 2004, Guangzhou also opened up the state-of-the-art *Baiyun* ("White Cloud") International Airport, which is the hub of China's largest airline, China Southern Airlines. Hit by the 2002–2003 **SARS** crisis that led public health authorities to kill thousands of civet cats (a delicacy in Cantonese cuisine that also includes snakes and cockroaches), Guangzhou has one of China's more successful newspaper dailies, the *Guangzhou Daily* (circulation one million), the official mouthpiece of the Guangzhou CP Committee, which was hit by a financial scandal in 2003. In 2004, Guangzhou authorities carried out a crackdown against the many illicit **Internet** bars that had sprung up in the city, especially close to schools. The local Cantonese cuisine includes such rare delicacies as civet cats and snakes leading to the popular view that the people of Guangzhou "will eat anything." *See also* ARCHITECTURE.

GUO MORUO (1892–1978). Trained in classical Chinese language and educated in **Japan** at Kyushu University, Guo Moruo emerged as one of China's leading Communist **intellectuals**. Appointed a vice-premier in 1949, Guo headed the All-China Federation of Literary and Art Circles from 1949 to 1966 and was a member of the All-China Writers' Association from 1953 to 1966. In the late 1950s, Guo also served on the State Planning Commission. Author of many books on China's ancient history, he was a member of the **Chinese Communist Party** (CCP) Central Committee from 1969 until his death in 1978.

– H –

HAI RUI DISMISSED FROM OFFICE (HAI RUI BAGUAN). A play written by the vice-mayor of **Beijing** named **Wu Han** and first staged in 1961, it describes the role of a 16th century Ming dynasty (1368–1644) official who criticized the emperor for his harsh treatment and over-taxation of the peasantry. Hai Rui was described as a "good and upright" official who was "consistent in words" and "was respected and loved by the broad masses of people" but was summarily dismissed after having "upbraided" the emperor. Written soon after the disastrous **Great Leap Forward (1958–1960)** and the purge of **Peng Dehuai** who had criticized the Leap for its devastating impact on China's peasantry, the play was attacked in 1965 as "an anti-Party poisonous weed" by leftist **leaders** aligned with **Jiang Qing**, the wife of **Chinese Communist Party** (CCP) Chairman **Mao Zedong**, as the opening salvo in the **Cultural Revolution (1966–1976)**. *Hai Rui Dismissed from Office*, it was said, was an elliptical attack on Chairman Mao Zedong and his policies, and therefore "counterrevolutionary." Wu Han was purged and along with him the entire Beijing Party Committee led by **Peng Zhen**. Wu Han denied the charge and, indeed, **intellectuals** in China have since maintained that the play was never interpreted as an elliptical attack on Mao. Wu Han died at the hands of **Red Guards** in 1969. In 1978–1979, following the inauguration of China's economic reforms and a general loosening of ideological controls, the play was restaged.

HAN. This is the dominant ethnic group in China that incorporates about 92% of the entire **population** of 1.3 billion people. The non-minority Chinese people refer to themselves as the Han ethnicity (*Han minzu*) after the name of the highly esteemed Han dynasty (202 BC–AD 222) that followed the chaos of the Qin dynasty (221–207 BC) and created a stable, aristocratic social order that spread Chinese influence far and wide. Han people first distinguished themselves from the "barbarians" of Inner Asia. The Han were often weaker militarily than their "barbarian" neighbors and thus sought refuge in superior social institutions and feelings of cultural superiority. Those who most vigorously opposed assimilation by the Chinese (Han) migrated away and stubbornly developed their own autonomous civilizations, such as the Vietnamese. National **minorities** within China, such as the Zhuang and Manchu, have been highly Sinicized in terms of language and culture, but still distinguish themselves from the Han.

HAN DONGFANG (1963–). A railway worker in the Fengtai Locomotive Maintenance Section in **Beijing**, Han Dongfang emerged as a prominent **human rights** and working-class activist in the wake of the 1989 second **Beijing Spring** pro-democracy movement. Along with other workers, Han Dongfang organized the Beijing Workers Autonomous Federation on the eve of the declaration of martial law in China's capital city. This was one of the few independent **labor** organizations established in China since the Communist takeover in 1949. Turning himself in to the police soon after the June 1989 military crackdown in Beijing, Han Dongfang was labeled a "counter-revolutionary" and, in 1990, was incarcerated in a police hospital with a stomach ailment. He was subsequently released for medical reasons and was treated in the **United States**. Unable to return to China proper on orders of the central government, he resides in **Hong Kong**, where he is director of the Hong Kong-based *China Labor Bulletin*. In the aftermath of several serious underground mine accidents in China in 2003 that led to the deaths of 1,600 miners, Han Dongfang pointed to the role of market reforms in increasing the dangers of underground mining as rising prices for coal encouraged mining companies to open up smaller illegal mines, which are more dangerous than the larger mines run directly by the Chinese government.

Han Dongfang's early life provides few clues to his later rebellion. His given name, *Dongfang*, translates as the "east," and is from the first line of China's martial tune, *The East is Red*, indicating his parents' initial devotion to the Communist cause. In the 1980s, Han was trained in the Public Security Soldiers Corps (*gong'an bing*) and was a guard at a prison labor camp near Beijing, where he received positive evaluations until he challenged the widespread **corruption** among the officer corps at the camp. This rebellious act cost Han his membership in the **Chinese Communist Party (CCP)**. Thereafter, Han became an assistant librarian at Beijing Teacher's College, where he read Western and Chinese works voraciously. Han then joined the maintenance team at the Beijing railway yard, where he gradually evolved into a political and labor activist, protesting the compliant submission of the official **trade unions** to CCP dictates.

HE DONGCHANG (1923–). Trained as an aeronautical engineer, He Dongchang was the **Chinese Communist Party (CCP)** secretary of **Qinghua University** in the 1950s and director of the Department of Engineering Physics. Branded a "counterrevolutionary" in the **Cultural Revolution (1966–1976)**, he returned to public life in 1978 and was appointed to the **Central Discipline Inspection Commission (CDIC)** and became a vice-president of Qinghua. In 1982, he was appointed minister of education and became a member of the CCP Central Committee. In 1986, he headed the State Education Commission. In 1987, he was appointed to the presidium of the CCP 13th National Party Congress and, in 1988, he became a member of the National Academic Degrees Committee. He Dongchang was a frequent critic of excessive "Westernization" in Chinese **education**.

HE JINGZHI (1924–). A leftist writer who joined the **Chinese Communist Party (CCP)** in 1941 after traveling to the Communist redoubt in Yan'an, He Jingzhi graduated from the Lu Xun Art and Literature Academy in 1942 and worked in the Art Troupe of the same academy from 1943 to 1945. In 1945, he wrote the libretto with Ding Yi for the revolutionary opera *White-Haired Girl (Baimao nü)*, for which he received the Stalin Literary and Art Award in 1951. He Jingzhi worked in various literary and theater jobs during the 1950s and 1960s, including deputy director of the Arts Department of *People's Daily* from 1964–1966. Condemned as a "counterrevolutionary," He Jingzhi disappeared during the **Cultural Revolution (1966–1976)** but returned to serve as vice-minister of culture from 1978 to 1982 and as vice-chairman of the All-China Writers' Association and deputy director of the CCP Propaganda Department from 1980 to 1987. Following the military crackdown in June 1989 on the second **Beijing Spring**, He Jingzhi was appointed minister of culture but was replaced in 1992. *See also* LITERATURE AND THE ARTS.

HE QINGLIAN (1956–). Born in Shaoyang, Hunan Province, He Qinglian is the author of several articles and books on China's **economy** and **population**, most notably the 1997 work entitled *China's*

Pitfall (*Zhongguo de xiejing*), which documented a number of the country's economic ills produced by the post-1978–1979 economic reforms. Sent as a teenager to work in the countryside on a railway construction site, she later studied history at Hunan Normal University and economics at Fudan University in **Shanghai** and then relocated in Shenzhen, one of China's **Special Economic Zones (SEZs)**, where she worked in the publicity department of the Shenzhen Municipal Party Committee. As a reporter for *Shenzhen Legal Daily*, she authored *China's Pitfall*, which ultimately sold more than 200,000 copies. It was described by a close adviser to President **Jiang Zemin** as a "masterpiece." Following an article that denounced the growing gap between rich and poor in China, He Qinglian lost her journalist position at *Shenzhen Legal Daily* as part of an ideological campaign in 2000 directed against "liberals and rightists." In 2002, she emigrated to the **United States**.

HE XIN (1949–). A college dropout, He Xin joined the **Chinese Academy of Social Sciences (CASS)** and, in 1982, became a research fellow at its Institute of Modern Chinese History. A constant critic of the excessive attraction to "Westernization" among many Chinese **intellectuals**, he emerged as the intellectual darling of China's conservative leadership, especially after the military crackdown against the second **Beijing Spring** in June 1989. He Xin is also a specialist in Chinese fine arts and has written several books on Chinese cultural history and Western philosophers, such as Sir Francis Bacon. He Xin is often criticized by more Westernized and democratically oriented intellectuals as a defender of China's totalitarian system. In the 1990s, he wrote a major piece on China's military strategy that called for taking a tough line against the **United States** and warned against any accommodation to American imperial designs.

HEALTH CARE. Since the founding of the **People's Republic of China (PRC)** in October 1949, China's health-care system has gone through a profound transformation that has had a dramatic impact on the health and medical welfare of the Chinese people. In 1949, the **Chinese Communist Party (CCP)** inherited what, by all accounts, was a woefully inadequate system and infrastructure of health care: only 33,000 nurses and 363,000 physicians were practicing in a country of more than 400 million people, with most of the meager 3,670 medical and health institutions located in the more well-off urban areas. Life expectancy was a mere 35 years, and the country was frequently ravaged by infectious and parasitic diseases, including tuberculosis, hepatitis, malaria, cholera, plague, typhoid, scarlet fever, and dysentery.

Responsibility for improving health care in China was given in 1949 to the Ministry of Public Health, which quickly set about establishing a national system that emphasized a preventive rather than curative approach to meeting the medical needs of China's **population**. Basic health care was provided in urban and rural areas through a three-tiered system, from **barefoot doctors** at the lowest tier in the countryside working out of village medical centers to township health centers as the second tier, which functioned primarily as outpatient clinics with assistant doctors serving as the most qualified members of the staff to the third and highest tier of county-level hospitals, where senior doctors dealt with the most seriously ill patients. This system was supplemented by a network of industrial and state enterprise hospitals and clinics that were primarily responsible for addressing the health needs of the country's growing army of workers and administrative personnel in China's pervasive **basic unit** (*jiben danwei*) system. "Patriotic health campaigns" modeled on other CCP-run mass campaigns were also a centerpiece of the government's approach to mobilizing the population to improve environmental sanitation and hygiene along with attacking certain chronic rural diseases such as schistosomiasis or snail fever.

The impact of these policies along with a rapid expansion of medical personnel that by 1985 numbered 637,000 nurses and 1.4 million physicians and 436,000 physician assistants operating out of more than 200,000 medical and health institutions was dramatic. While highly infectious diseases, such as cholera, malaria, and typhoid, were all but eliminated by the 1960s, a remarkable increase in life expectancy from 35 to 69 years was achieved by the mid-1980s, though substantial differences between rural and urban areas persisted, with the crude death rate in rural areas of 1.6 per 1,000 people (substantially higher than in urban areas, where there was a greater concentration of senior physicians). Mass inoculations of children also successfully controlled the incidence of measles, polio, diphtheria cough, and epidemic encephalitis; infant mortality fell from 200 per live births in 1952 to 34 in 1982. Despite the fact that the country's population has tripled since 1949 (from 400 million-plus to 1.3 billion in 2005), the number of hospital beds per 1,000 persons grew from 0.15 in 1949 to 2.35 in 1997.

China's health-care system was dramatically affected by the profound social, political, and economic transformation that followed upon the introduction of reforms in 1978–1979 by **Deng Xiaoping** and other CCP **leaders**. In the countryside, the elaborate two-tiered structure of barefoot doctors and township-level clinics and health facilities offering comprehensive and free medical care was all but dismantled by the elimination of the collective welfare system that was a centerpiece of the socialist system of **people's communes**. Since the 1980s, fee-for-service has dominated the rural health care system, making access to doctors and prescription drugs highly dependent on the income of the individual person or their family; this has caused most township health facilities to record a net drop in usage. In the poorest areas of China's countryside, health care became increasingly problematic as access to medical facilities became all but impossible for 15% of the population in backward areas, such as **Tibet** and western China, that have a health status comparable to the least developed nations in the world. The central government virtually withdrew from the rural world, handing the financial responsibility for funding health care to cash-strapped local governments that have proven to be ill-prepared to meet even the most basic health needs of the vast rural population who must often become part of the **floating population** of migrant workers in order to earn enough money to pay for increasingly onerous medical and prescription drug costs. University-trained physicians make up only 1% to 20% of doctors in county hospitals, where most personnel have had "middle education" or lower equivalent. In March 1998, the Ministry of Health established two policies aimed at closing the gap separating the urban and rural health systems by requiring all medical students to work for one year in rural health facilities.

Similar changes have also transpired in the urban areas, where access to health care is highly dependent on a person's place of employment, with well-off state and collective enterprises still able to afford to provide health care for their employees. Workers in financially strapped units have experienced a dramatic drop in their access to care, making them more dependent on individual and/or family income to fill the breach. Under the new system adopted by the Chinese government, government workers are covered by a work-related health insurance system known as the Government Employee Health Insurance (*gongfei yiliao*). Employees in state-run and collective enterprises of the **economy** are covered by the Labor Health Insurance (*laobao yiliao*) and "urban collective medical schemes" (*chengshi hezuo yiliao*). As for the unemployed and self-employed, there is as yet no national system of private insurance, leaving approximately one half of China's urban population without any type of health insurance, a figure that rises to 79% in rural areas. With more and more administrative and budgetary authority in China decentralized from **Beijing** to the provincial and county levels of administration, health-care benefits and infrastructure have become increasingly dependent on a region's overall economic vitality; the wealthier provinces and counties take in sufficient revenue to support and improve on the existing system while the poorer areas face increasingly tight and inadequate budgets. Reforms introduced in the 1980s and 1990s have forced hospitals and clinics to meet more of their own expenditures through high-cost medication and prescription drug fees and to rely less on government-generated revenues, while the introduction of a co-payment system has placed more of the economic burden on consumers whose average health bill as outpatients has grown eightfold from 1990 to 2000, with average inpatient fees rising from US$57 to US$376 over the same period. Chinese hospitals have also taken to lengthening patient stays to about three times the average in the **United States** and to offering lucrative medical procedures such as cosmetic plastic surgery for "wannabe" beauty queens, all as a way to maximize their revenue intake. Overprescription of certain drugs, such as the antibiotics gentamycin and streptomycin, has reportedly led to serious drug complications, including a 30% increase in deafness among urban children.

Overall, available health care and services continue to grow in China's urban areas, while the countryside has witnessed an absolute decline in both personnel and facilities with a predictable deterioration of the health status of the rural poor among whom infectious diseases such as tuberculosis and HIV/**AIDS** have experienced dramatic increases along with a rise in infant mortality rates. This state of affairs led the central government to propose in 1996 that local governments in rural areas support the creation of a rural collective medical care schemes akin to the one that existed in the 1960s and 1970s but without significant financial contributions from the central government. At the same time, with access to modern health care facilities on the decline, more and more Chinese, especially in poorer rural areas, have been drawn to more traditional Chinese remedies, including an offshoot of traditional breathing exercises (*qigong*) known as the *Falun Gong*, this despite the government's crackdown on its activities. Stories of **corruption** and malfeasance at both state-run and newly established private hospitals and clinics fill the Chinese press and has led to a dramatic rise in lawsuits and media scandals aimed at what many see as a fragmented and dysfunctional health care system that is rife with profit-driven low-quality service, where, for instance, ambulances in Beijing will not accept a person who has suffered a heart attack until 10,000 *yuan* (US$1,250) is handed over. Many rural hospitals require hefty deposits from patients prior to their admission. Illegal manufacture of drugs and baby formula have also taken their toll on poor areas, such as the tragedy that afflicted Fuyang, Anhui Province, in 2004, when babies who had been fed bad formula developed "big head disease" and resulted in several deaths.

In 1994, Chinese health officials declared that smoking was one of the major causes of death in China and, in 1996, banned smoking in indoor public places in Beijing. China also conducted the largest polio immunization campaign in history in the 1990s. In 2005, China announced a campaign to vaccinate its entire population of domestic birds to stem an outbreak of avian flu. During the 2002–2003 **SARS** crisis, growing concerns over the inadequacy of China's public health system led to new policy initiatives, such as government guarantees of free care for anyone showing symptoms of the deadly disease. But with health-care costs soaring as China experiences a shift from infectious diseases that could be addressed by the preventive approach of the 1949–1978 era to diseases more characteristic of the industrial world—cancer, cerebrovascular and heart disease that require a curative approach along with a more conventional and less-politicized approach to the treatment of mental illness—the pressure on China's government to come up with a comprehensive and coherent health-care insurance program has increased. In 1996, under a government-inaugurated plan entitled "A Decision of Health Care Reform and

Development" pilot projects in 30 cities focused on the delivery of "integrated care" with general practitioners playing a key role in these projects that are designed to shift the urban insurance system from enterprise-based to city-wide risk pooling to deal with the approximately 24% of urban residents who suffer from some kind of chronic disease. These kind of reforms are made even more difficult to implement by major demographic changes as China is undergoing rapid growth in its elderly population to more than 130 million people above the age of 65, which not only places increased burdens on the medical infrastructure but also entails huge financial pressure on the underfunded retirement and pension systems—especially those of cash-starved **state-owned enterprises** (**SOEs**) and collective enterprises that are no longer economically viable. Overall, China's total health care budget is only 1% of the world's medical spending in a country with 20% of the planet's population. Medical research in China is carried out at hospitals, research institutes, such as the Chinese Academy of Medical Sciences, and even by the **People's Liberation Army** (**PLA**), and has included such advanced procedures as stem cell injection to treat leukemia and other devastating diseases. Oversight of China's growing domestic pharmaceutical industry is carried out by the State Food and Drug Supervision Administration.

In the international health arena, China has become a major player in the world pharmaceutical market. Estimates are that, by 2020, the country will rank second to the U.S. with projected revenues of US$60 billion. Opening up of China's domestic pharmaceutical market was ensured by its 2001 entry into the **World Trade Organization** (**WTO**) while China's own domestic pharmaceutical industry has experienced rapid growth with total output in 2001 of nearly US$600 million *yuan*. Chinese pharmaceutical exports include a wide array of traditional herbal remedies, most prominently the drug artemisinin (a compound based on sweet wormwood (*qinghaosu*) that was isolated and developed by Chinese military researchers in 1965), which world health agencies recommended in 2004 as the primary treatment for malaria, replacing the more conventional quinine derivatives. China has hosted a variety of international health conferences, including a joint meeting and workshop with the March of Dimes in October 2004 on Maternal and Child Health Genetics in China in the 21st century. China has also been a major recipient of international assistance in the health arena, including substantial funding from the World Bank to the Basic Health Services Project, a central government program aimed at improving health care in China's poorest rural areas. Similar international assistance was also provided to ensure medical and low-cost drug access for the 1.3 million people in China who annually contract tuberculosis.

In 2005, the minister of health was Gao Qiang (1944–), a highly trained economist who took over the Ministry of Health in the wake of the outbreak and subsequent cover-up of the SARS crisis, replacing Zhang Wenkang who despite his work at the prestigious PLA Second Medical University from 1962 to 1990 was forced to resign after downplaying the severity of the epidemic. *See also* ENVIRONMENT; SCIENCE AND TECHNOLOGY.

HONG KONG. Governed under the Qing dynasty (1644–1911) as part of Xin'an County, the island of Hong Kong was occupied by Great Britain in 1841 and was ceded in perpetuity as a crown territory by the "unequal" Treaty of Nanking (1842) that followed the First Opium War (1839–1842). A nexus of free trade in East Asia, the territory of Hong Kong expanded onto the Kowloon Peninsula under the 1860 convention of **Beijing** that ended the Second Opium War (1856–1858) and expanded into the New Territories in 1890 by a 99-year lease that terminated on 30 June 1997. In 1916, the **population** of the crown territory was 530,000 and rapidly expanded to 1.6 million in 1941 only to shrink back to 600,000 as a result of brutal Japanese rule during World War II. Following the takeover of the Chinese mainland by forces of the **Chinese Communist Party** (**CCP**) in 1949, many foreign firms relocated from **Shanghai** to Hong Kong, transforming the island into a major manufacturing center. During the **Cultural Revolution** (**1966–1976**), leftist forces in the colony became infatuated with Maoist revolutionary ideology, leading to a violent **labor** movement that led to terrorist incidents, including bombings. In 1974, with the Cultural Revolution winding down on the mainland, the Hong Kong government moved to eliminate pervasive **corruption** among civil servants and government officials that ultimately led to one of the most well-run administrations in East Asia. Following the affirmation of the **United Nations** (**UN**) supporting the claims of the **People's Republic of China** (**PRC**) to Hong Kong and

Macao, talks between Great Britain and China commenced in 1982 aimed at incorporation of the crown colony back into China. The last British governor of the island, Chris Patten, introduced a measure of democratic reforms into the political system of Hong Kong, provoking Chinese ire; however, negotiations between British Prime Minister Margaret Thatcher and **Deng Xiaoping** led to the 1984 Sino–British Joint Declaration on the Question of Hong Kong whereby the colony would be reincorporated into the PRC as a Special Administrative Region (SAR) under the rubric of Deng's formulation of "**one country, two systems**."

On 1 July 1997, Great Britain handed Hong Kong over to the PRC. The sitting Legislative Council, elected under Chris Patten's reforms, was replaced by the Provisional Legislative Council that was elected by a selection committee whose members were appointed by the PRC. Many of the changes were purely symbolic, as public offices after 1 July 1997 flew flags of the PRC and the Hong Kong SAR while the Union Jack flew only outside the British Consulate-General and other British premises. In addition, the portrait of Queen Elizabeth II disappeared from banknotes, postage stamps, and public offices, although, as of 2005, many pre-1997 coins and some banknotes were still in circulation. The "Royal" title was dropped from almost all organizations that had been granted it, with the exception of the Royal Hong Kong Yacht Club. All references to the "Crown" were replaced by references to the "State," and barristers who had been appointed Queen's Counsel were now known as senior counsel. Public holidays were changed, with the Queen's Official Birthday and other British-inspired occasions replaced by PRC National Day (1 October) and Hong Kong SAR Establishment Day (1 July). In other respects, many things remained unchanged: The new SAR remained a separate jurisdiction, continuing to use English Common Law; the border with the mainland continued to be patrolled as before; Hong Kong remained a separate customs territory with its own currency and with freer **trade** with the rest of the world than with the mainland; and Hong Kong retained most immigration controls to foreign countries except politically related visa applications. Similarly, Hong Kong SAR passport holders had easier access to countries in Europe and North America, than mainland citizens. Citizens in mainland China can—as before and after 1997—only apply for a visa to Hong

Kong from the PRC Government, while many former colonial citizens can still use British National (overseas) passports. In addition, English remains the official language and is still taught in all schools. However, many (but not all) schools also now teach in Cantonese, and textbooks are written in both Chinese and in parallel in English. Hong Kong continues to have more political freedoms than mainland China, including freedom of the press (though this became vulnerable to self-**censorship**) and freedom of expression. And Hong Kong, unlike mainland China, continues to drive on the left side of the road, although telephone companies stopped installing British Standard BS 6312 telephone sockets in Hong Kong.

The miniconstitution that China drafted for Hong Kong before Britain handed over the colony in 1997, known as the Basic Law of the Hong Kong Special Administrative Region of the People's Republic of China, was passed by the Seventh **National People's Congress (NPC)** in April 1990 and was promulgated by President **Yang Shangkun** to take effect on 1 July 1997, when China regained sovereignty. The Basic Law is the implementing instrument of the SAR and carries the force of law for the next 50 years.

Institutionally, the Basic Law called for the creation of a powerful chief executive, which was outlined in January 1996 by the Preparatory Committee of the Hong Kong Special Administrative Region (HKSAR) and was chaired by China's Foreign Minister **Qian Qichen**. In December 1996, the Selection Committee for the First Government of the HKSAR (composed of 800 mostly well-off, pro-China members) chose Tung Chee-hwa as the first chief executive with the power to both enforce the laws passed by the Hong Kong Legislature and implement directives issued by the Chinese central government in **Beijing**. Although Article 45 of the Basic Law indicated that the chief executive will ultimately be elected by universal suffrage, the Chinese government retains the power of veto, thereby ensuring that the chief executive will be subservient to Beijing's policies. A new Legislative Council (LEGCO) was also established as a provisional legislature that consists of 60 members, 40 of whom are nominated by functional constituencies composed largely of business elites with pro-China sympathies and with only 18 seats (later expanded to 30) subject to direct election by geographical constituencies. The judiciary consists of a Court of Final Appeal, a High Court, and district courts with judges appointed by the SAR chief executive. Originally, it was agreed that a judge from another common law jurisdiction would sit on the Court of Final Appeal for the entire judicial term, but this was later reduced to one half-term per year, a decision made over the objections of the pre-1997 Legislative Council in Hong Kong. The establishment of the Hong Kong Court of Final Appeal was regarded as a vital legal measure to ensure the colony's freedom after 1997.

At midnight on 1 July 1997, the Hong Kong Special Administrative Region was inaugurated with the official handover attended by a range of British and Chinese dignitaries, most notably Prince Charles and President **Jiang Zemin**. Two months prior to the handover, the Chinese-government-in-waiting proposed changes to the civil law that would prohibit political groups from having links with or accepting advice from foreign organizations and would ban members from soliciting funds from abroad. Political parties would also have to obtain approval from the authorities to operate and police would have the power to refuse applications for political protests. Despite this and other such warnings against memorial commemorations of the 4 June 1989 crackdown on the second **Beijing Spring**, however, there was little in the way of conflict between Hong Kong and the mainland, since no major attempt was made by China to curtail civil liberties in the former British colony.

The first dust-up involving Beijing and Hong Kong occurred in January 1999 when the Court of Final Appeal overturned retroactive legislation passed in July 1997, which took back the right of abode to mainland children of Hong Kong parents. Instead, the court ruled that mainland children born to Hong Kong permanent residents had the right of abode in the territory, no matter whether their parents were married or were residents at the time the children were born. With the potential for increased **population** pressure roiling some critics of the ruling, intense controversy was provoked, which was only brought to an end when mainland authorities overruled the court's decision. In 2000, further controversy erupted when the deputy director of the Chinese government's Liaison Office in Hong Kong issued a statement declaring that the notoriously independent Hong Kong media had the responsibility and duty to uphold the country's "reunification and territorial integrity" and should neither disseminate nor advocate **Taiwan** independent views, a decision that led a number of journalists to quit their jobs at major Hong Kong newspapers, such as the *South China Morning Post*. But by far the biggest political brouhaha broke out over the attempt in 2003 by the SAR administration of Tung Chee-hwa to put into place a National Security Law that is required under Article 23 of the Basic Law. The two measures that caused the most disquiet and ultimately led to the largest mass demonstrations in July of 2003 and of 2004 in the notoriously apolitical city, were the creation of an offense of "subversion" and possession of "state secrets" for which there is no guidance in English Common Law—the foundation of Hong Kong's **legal system**—and a grant of power to the SAR to "proscribe" organizations with any violation of the law carrying a maximum sentence of life imprisonment.

Adding insult to injury was the decision of the SAR administration to enact and complete the new law in only nine months' time—an apparent violation of a government requirement that the drafting of major legislation be carried out over a 16-month period. Because of its tight schedule, the government did not produce a White Paper on the proposed law, preventing ample time for public consultation that was limited to pro-government business groups, especially because the drafting process came amidst Hong Kong's three-month subjection to the **SARS** virus. Following a mass demonstration on 1 July 2003 of one-half million people—one-tenth of the entire population of Hong Kong—the apparent plan of the government to cram through the legislation was dealt irreparable damage when the head of the pro-government Liberal Party resigned from the SAR executive council and called for deferring a second reading of the bill in the legislature, thereby effectively killing it. In the wake of the defeat, two key aids to Chief Executive Tung Chee-hwa resigned. All of this came in the midst of a worsening **economy** and other accumulated sources of grievance against the SAR administration, including rising unemployment, the dishonesty of the SAR Financial Secretary, and the irritating manner of the recently resigned Security Chief, Regina Ip. Opposition from the local Roman Catholic Church over fears that the new security law could be used to limit religious freedom and a more widespread concern that the law might harm Hong Kong's reputation as a free-wheeling hub of international finance was also a factor in bringing an end to attempts at rolling back fundamental freedoms involving the flow of information—even as China offered a new **trade deal** with Hong Kong that further reduced tariffs on imports from the former British colony.

One year later, yet another large-scale demonstration was held on 1 July 2004—the seventh anniversary of Hong Kong's handover to China—demanding universal suffrage and greater democracy, which led the Chinese government in Beijing to denounce opposition leaders in Hong Kong as "clowns" and "traitors" and of "opposing the leadership of the Communist Party and subverting the central government." *Wen Wei Po*, a Beijing-controlled newspaper in Hong Kong, also warned that China's central government had the power to dissolve Hong Kong's legislature, a thinly veiled threat that Beijing could take direct control if things got out of hand politically. Despite growing concerns about the prospects for political freedom in the face of such statements out of Beijing and in the wake of an unprecedented show of force by the Chinese military since the 1997 reversion with a visit to Hong Kong harbor by eight **People's Liberation Army (PLA)** warships, the pro-democracy parties in Hong Kong failed to make dramatic gains in the September 2004 LEGCO elections when their candidates managed to win only 18 of the 30 seats up for direct election, this despite a record turnout of 55% of voters. The results were tainted, however, by charges of aggressive interference in the electoral process by the central government in Beijing—including its arrest while in China of a Democratic Party candidate on charges of solicitation—and an alleged "marriage of convenience" with local gangsters who allegedly intimidated three radio hosts who had aired anti-China views and subsequently resigned their positions. Included in the newly elected legislators was a well-known local activist who has called on China to release political prisoners and to "reverse the verdict on the 4 June 1989" suppression of the second Beijing Spring pro-democracy movement. In early 2005, following rumors that Tung Chee-hwa would seek retirement in the midst of growing unpopularity with his leadership and policies that alienated Hong Kong's powerful business classes, Tung stepped down after eight years in the position and was replaced as acting chief executive by then chief secretary and long-time civil servant Sir Donald Tsang Yam-kuen. The chief executive is chosen by the 800-

member Selection Committee of Beijing loyalists (with plans to expand the committee to 1,600 members) because the NPC Standing Committee has barred universal suffrage and direct election of the chief executive in 2007. The term may be reduced from five to two years by the Standing Committee of the NPC, which has demonstrated an increasing tendency to intervene in Hong Kong political affairs and to limit the transition to full democracy.

Despite language in the Basic Law that calls for an eventual move to universal suffrage, the NPC Standing Committee ruled in April 2004 that Hong Kong's chief executive would have to obtain committee approval before submitting any electoral reform bills to the local legislature and that certain seats in the LEGCO would not be subject to direct election. If Tung Chee-hwa's successor serves a two-year term, the next successor will be elected for five years in 2007 by the current Electoral Committee, leaving no chance for direct elections until at least 2012. But if Mr. Tsang is allowed to serve a five-year term, elections could be held as early as 2010. The Basic Law makes it clear that the Standing Committee of the NPC has essentially complete discretion to decide how the Basic Law is interpreted. The democracy movement in Hong Kong has also pushed for one-person, one-vote elections, along with broader social legislation, including the introduction of a minimum wage and regulations on housing costs that have led Hong Kong tycoons to seek redress from the Chinese government. The pro-government Liberal Party relies mainly on the support of the city's business tycoons and, in 2003, removed from its platform support for greater democratization in Hong Kong.

HU FENG AFFAIR. This refers to the attacks on the Marxist literary critic Hu Feng by the **Chinese Communist Party (CCP)** in the mid-1950s. Hu Feng was a longtime supporter of the Communist movement in China, who, soon after 1949, challenged CCP and Maoist orthodoxy on the role of **literature and the arts** in a revolutionary society. A leader in many of the mass organizations established for writers and artists by the CCP, Hu Feng argued that the Party should show greater tolerance for the independent views expressed in literature. In so doing, Hu Feng challenged the principle laid out in the 1942 Yan'an Talks on Literature and Art, in which **Mao Zedong** asserted that literature and art should serve the interests of politics. "Art for art's sake" was denounced by Mao in favor of the socialist realist principle that writers and artists should portray the lives of workers and peasants in idealistic, utopian terms. Denouncing Hu Feng as anti-Marxist and anti-Party, the CCP launched a massive nationwide campaign that encompassed thousands of literary figures and led to systematic persecution of **intellectuals** in a fashion that anticipated the **Anti-Rightist Campaign (1957–1958)** and the **Cultural Revolution (1966–1976)**. Hu Feng was arrested and incarcerated for many years. He died in 1985 in an insane asylum.

HU JINTAO (1942–). A native of Anhui Province, one of China's poorest regions, Hu Jintao graduated from **Qinghua University**, China's premier technical institution, with a degree in water conservancy and engineering. Largely unaffected by the **Cultural Revolution (1966–1976)**, Hu worked at the Liujia Gorge Engineering Bureau under the Ministry of Water Conservancy and for five years (1969–1974) worked in the ministry's Fourth Engineering Bureau. During his long service in the remote and relatively poor Gansu Province from 1968 to 1982, Hu became active in the Communist **Youth League** and, in 1980, was appointed the first secretary of the Gansu Provincial CP and, from 1982 to 1985, headed the Communist Youth League. From 1985 to 1988, he was first secretary of the Guizhou Provincial **Chinese Communist Party (CCP)**, the youngest person ever to achieve such a high position in the Party, where he consistently fought to alleviate the province's high poverty levels. In 1988, Hu became secretary of the **Tibet** Party Committee and gained recognition by promoting the region's economic growth while taking a very hard-line stance against Tibetan dissident and separatist groups. Appointed as the youngest member to the **Politburo** in 1992, Hu headed the **Central Party School** in 1993 and became vice-president of the **People's Republic of China (PRC)** in 1998. Following the phased retirement of **Jiang Zemin**, Hu Jintao became general secretary of the CCP in 2002 and in 2003 **president of the People's Republic of China**. In September 2004, Hu Jintao assumed the last of the three major posts in China as he succeeded Jiang Zemin as chairman of the Central **Military Affairs Commission (MAC)**, making Hu Jintao China's commander-in-chief and head of the country's 2.5 million **People's Liberation Army (PLA)**.

Hu Jintao has promoted domestic policies that focus on improving the living condition of China's less well off **population** in rural and western areas while pursuing a peaceful **foreign policy** abroad. In his frequent travels around the country, he has encouraged local **leaders** to give more consideration to the plight of ordinary citizens by "putting people first" and to confront the growing income gap in China between rich and poor by building a "harmonious society." Hu has also supported an increasingly vigorous campaign to root out endemic **corruption** while giving mostly lip-service to any real move toward substantial political reform. Along with Vice-President **Zeng Qinglong**, Hu has promoted a "smokeless war" against "liberal elements" in the news media, the legal profession, and religious groups that the two leaders claim threaten the Party's hold on power and are supported by the **United States**. Contrary to the individual leadership style of **Mao Zedong**, **Deng Xiaoping**, and **Jiang Zemin**, Hu Jintao emphasizes collective decision making by submitting his proposed speeches, travels, and major meetings to a formal vote of the Politburo. On **Taiwan**, Hu indicated in 2003 that China would adhere to the basic principles of "peaceful reunification" and "**one country, two systems**" but that it also vehemently opposes any separatist activity in the name of an "independent Taiwan." Peaceful, trade-oriented relations with **Russia** have also been espoused while, in reaction, to calls by American President George W. Bush for "pure and whole" liberty in China, Hu responded by asserting that the "Chinese people know how to cherish and develop the socialist democracy that best suits the real conditions of China" as he categorically ruled out any move toward a multi-party system. As PRC President, Hu Jintao has toured Russia, Europe, Asia, Australia, and Latin America where he has often signed long-term commercial and **trade** agreements and stressed peaceful relations including China's opposition to the U.S. invasion of Iraq. On 26 December 2003, Hu Jintao gave the keynote speech on the 110th anniversary of the birth of Mao Zedong.

HU JIWEI (1916–). One of China's most prominent journalists, Hu Jiwei, in 1954, became deputy editor and, in 1958, deputy editor-in-chief of the *People's Daily*, the official organ of the **Chinese Communist Party** (**CCP**) Central Committee. Hu disappeared during the

Cultural Revolution (1966–1976), but returned as director of the *People's Daily* in 1982 as a staunch advocate of press reform and liberalization. Hu voluntarily resigned from his position in protest over the **Anti-Spiritual Pollution Campaign (1983–1984)**. Hu Jiwei was a strong supporter of the reformist political ideas of CCP General Secretary, **Hu Yaobang**, whose sudden death in April 1989 set off the student demonstrations that culminated in the June 1989 crackdown on the second **Beijing Spring**. During the demonstrations, Hu Jiwei was criticized for soliciting signatures of delegates to the **National People's Congress** (NPC) to call for the convening of a special meeting to rescind the declaration of martial law and to dismiss Premier **Li Peng**. Stripped of his post as a member of the Standing Committee of the NPC, Hu Jiwei operated in relative freedom after 1989 taking advantage of various opportunities to join with other retired senior **cadres** in asking CCP **leaders** to restore freedom to former General Secretary **Zhao Ziyang** who remained under house arrest and to advocate media legislation and greater press freedom in China. Following the death of Zhao in January 2005, Hu Jiwei, despite being over 90 years old, wrote to China's central authorities appealing for a public memorial meeting to rehabilitate the late leader and to hold a solemn memorial assembly. Hu has also taken various opportunities over the past 15 years to advocate press freedom and, in February 2006, co-authored a public letter with **Li Rui** and **Zhu Houze** to China's leaders protesting the closing of newspapers and excessive **censorship** (*shencha*).

HU QIAOMU (1912–1992). From a politically prominent family of wealthy landowners, Hu Qiaomu joined the **Chinese Communist Party** (CCP) in 1935, working with Jiang Nanxiang in the fields of journalism and propaganda in **Shanghai** and Shaanxi Province. In 1945, Hu succeeded **Chen Boda** as personal secretary to **Mao Zedong**, and, in 1949, he founded and briefly headed the **New China News Agency** (**Xinhua**) and became director, in 1950, of the *People's Daily*. The top CCP official in charge of journalism, Hu wrote the definitive book on Party history entitled *Thirty Years of the CCP*, of which three million copies were distributed. In 1956, Hu became a member of the CCP Central Committee and deputy director of the Party Propaganda Department from where he promoted the publication of the controversial play *Hai Rui Dismissed from Office* by **Wu Han**, the criticism of which launched the **Cultural Revolution (1966–1976)**. Dismissed as Mao's secretary in 1962, Hu was publicly berated by **Red Guards** and denounced by Mao's wife **Jiang Qing**, with whom he had been on bad terms since 1950. Hu Qiaomu reappeared in 1974 as a member of the Party Secretariat and the CCP Central Committee and during the campaign directed against **Deng Xiaoping** in 1976 orchestrated by the leftist **Gang of Four** Hu confessed his errors and was extremely critical of Deng. Following the reemergence of Deng in 1978, Hu's political recovery would be slow. In 1982, he became honorary president of the **Chinese Academy of Social Sciences** (**CASS**), where he played a prominent role in the discussions of humanism and alienation in a socialist society. Hu Qiaomu nominally retired from his positions in November 1987 and served as honorary head of the Shakespeare Research Society until his death in 1992. In the mid-1980s, Hu Qiaomu's son was arrested on **corruption** charges, but was later released after the dismissal of **Hu Yaobang** in 1987.

HU QILI (1929–). A graduate of **Beida (Peking University)** in physics and an activist in the All-China Students' Federation and Communist **Youth League** (**CYL**), Hu Qili was branded as a follower of **Liu Shaoqi** during the **Cultural Revolution** (**1966–1976**) and was subsequently purged. He returned in the mid-1970s as a county Party secretary in the Ningxia-Hui Autonomous Region and then as a vice-president of **Qinghua University**. In the early 1980s, he became the mayor of **Tianjin**, director of the General Office of the **Chinese Communist Party** (**CCP**) and a member of the **Politburo** and head of the Party Secretariat. In 1985, Hu was put in charge of the Propaganda and Ideological Work Leading Group under the CCP Central Committee. During the 1989 second **Beijing Spring**, Hu Qili as a member of the Standing Committee of the Politburo sided with General Secretary **Zhao Ziyang** in opposing the declaration of martial law. With the decision by **Deng Xiaoping** and other Party "**revolutionary elders**" (*geming yuanlao*) to deploy lethal force on 3–4 June, Hu was removed from the Politburo and his other posts for also having allowed journalists relatively free rein during the pro-democracy demonstrations. Hu Qili reemerged in April 1990 at a meeting of the **National People's Congress** (NPC) and, in 1993, became the minister of electronics industry and, in 1996, deputy head of the State Leading Group for Information. In 1998, Hu was appointed chairman of the **Song Qingling** Foundation, which was established in 1983 as a children's assistance program.

HU SHI [HU SHIH] (1891–1962). One of China's most prominent liberal **intellectuals**, Hu Shi was a disciple of John Dewey and a major promoter of vernacular Chinese literature in the 1920s. He attended Cornell and Columbia universities, studying at the latter under Dewey and writing his doctoral dissertation on pragmatic tendencies in ancient Chinese thought. Hu Shi was an enthusiastic advocate of experimentalism and a sometime critic of the **Kuomintang** (**KMT**). Hu was Nationalist China's ambassador to the **United States** from 1938 to 1942 and later became president of the Academic Sinica in **Taiwan**, where he died in 1962.

HU YAOBANG (1915–1989). Born in Hunan Province, Hu Yaobang became a Red Army soldier at the age of 15 and, in 1933, engaged in youth work for the central Party leadership in the Jiangxi Soviet. During the **Civil War** (**1946–1949**), he served in the Political Department of the Second **Field Army** and later in the Southwest China Military and Administrative Council, both of which were dominated by **Deng Xiaoping**. From 1957 to 1964, he headed the recently reorganized Communist **Youth League** and, in 1956, was elevated to the **Chinese Communist Party** (**CCP**) Central Committee and served briefly as Party Secretary of the Shaanxi Provincial CP. Like many moderate **leaders**, Hu was attacked during the **Cultural Revolution** (**1966–1976**) and did not reappear until 1972. In 1977, Hu was restored as a member of the CCP Central Committee and became director of its Organization Department. In 1978, he was elevated to the **Politburo** and headed the CCP Propaganda Department and in 1980 became general secretary of the Secretariat. He was appointed the third and last chairman of the CCP and served until this position was eliminated in 1982. Hu remained general secretary, where he led the effort to rehabilitate millions of people, including the future premier **Zhu Rongji**, who had been persecuted in the Maoist era, and he promoted economic reform policies coining the phrase "individual business is glorious." Hu was forced to resign as general secretary in 1987 after coming under fire from Party conservatives, who accused him of allowing **"bourgeois liberalization"** to spread unchecked, which had reputedly led to student demonstrations in late 1986. Hu Yaobang's death in April 1989 sparked the second **Beijing Spring** student pro-democracy movement that culminated in the June 1989 military crackdown. Although Hu's name was rarely mentioned in the Chinese media after 1989, in 2005, the top CCP leadership, led by **Hu Jintao**, decided to officially rehabilitate Hu Yaobang on the 90th anniversary of his birth, despite the fear of some hardliners that such a move could risk giving people the idea that circumstances surrounding the 1989 demonstrations could now be open for discussion and thereby provoke renewed political turmoil. Hu Yaobang is buried in Jiangxi Province, in the Gongqingcheng cemetery, the site of frequent visitation by Chinese leaders and 300,000 people annually.

HUA GUOFENG (1921–). From an extremely poor peasant family, Hua Guofeng joined the Communist Red Army at the age of 15 and, in 1949, became a county Party secretary in Hunan Province, the home province of Chairman **Mao Zedong**. After overseeing the rapid formation of **Agricultural Producers' Cooperatives (APCs)** as Party Secretary of Xiangtan County, Hua was appointed, on Mao Zedong's personal recommendation, as Hunan Party secretary and during the **Cultural Revolution (1966–1976)** headed the province's **Revolutionary Committee**. After supporting construction of a mausoleum in Hunan for Mao Zedong's first wife, Yang Kaihui, Hua was transferred to **Beijing** and headed a special group to investigate the **Lin Biao** affair. Appointed to the **Politburo** in 1973 and minister of public security in 1975, Hua became premier in 1976 and was personally designated by Mao to succeed him as Party chairman, a post Hua assumed in October 1976 following Mao's death. Hua was replaced in September 1982 at the 12th National Party Congress but retained his position on the **Chinese Communist Party (CCP)** Central Committee. Hua's inscription (in gold) still adorns the Mao Zedong Memorial Hall (*Mao Zedong jinian tang*) in Tiananmen Square. Since his dismissal, little has been heard of Hua Guofeng in or outside of China.

HUKOU. The household registration system in China was adopted in the 1950s and provides a system of control over **population** movement and residence by restricting the rural population to villages and townships in the countryside where, up until the 1990s, they were solely dependent on their own **labor** for their livelihood. Nonagricultural or urban registration is the most prized since it carries various amenities, such as access to **education**, free **health care**, grain rations, and housing. Transfer of rural to urban registry was for most Chinese virtually impossible. Since the inauguration of the economic reforms in 1978–1979 and the growth of the **floating population**, the *hukou* system has gradually broken down as large numbers of rural migrants have settled in Chinese cities without a transfer of registry while urban residents have relied more and more on the market for grain supplies and adequate health care. In the 1990s, the city of **Shanghai** many of whose nearly 10 million residents were born elsewhere began the concept of a "blue card" for qualified migrant workers, giving them full access to housing and city services. The capital city of **Beijing** introduced similar reforms in 2003, by granting urban registration to rural residents of its 14 satellite towns and 33 outlying zones and by giving automatic urban registration to children born to rural mothers in the capital and to rural students in the city's higher vocational schools. Nationally, incremental reforms of the *hukou* system were introduced in 2001 that allowed rural workers to apply for a temporary residence permit for smaller towns and midsize cities, a significant step toward creating a truly national labor market in China that the registration system had, since its inauguration, effectively prevented. This was followed, in 2002, by a decision at the 16th National Congress of the **Chinese Communist Party** (**CCP**) to eventually drop the residency permit system that, in 2005, led to an experimental program in 11 provinces to abolish all legal distinctions between urban and rural residents. Local governments under the experimental system will allow peasants to register as urban residents and to have the same rights to housing, education, health care, and social security. China has also dropped its custody and repatriation or vagrancy law under which migrant workers were summarily rounded up, detained, and returned to their home villages. Some metropolitan areas, however, still deny urban registration to most of the floating population working within their midst believing that household registration is their last defense against being inundated by millions of jobless and homeless people. On the other hand, rural people may be reluctant to take out permanent urban registration, which would deny them their right to have two children as city dwellers must abide by the official **one-child policy**. Foreigners working in major urban areas have also been granted all the privileges attached to urban *hukou* status by the introduction of the country's first "green card" system.

HUMAN RIGHTS. The military crackdown on the second **Beijing Spring**, in June 1989, brought human rights issues involving the **People's Republic of China** (**PRC**) to the forefront in its international diplomacy. Prior to 1989, the PRC was not a major focus of international human rights violations because most worldwide attention was devoted to the **Soviet Union** and such nations as South Africa and Iran. Since 1989, however, issues involving the applicability to the PRC of "universal" standards of human rights has been a subject of both Chinese and foreign, primarily American, commentary. PRC policies in **Tibet** are also central to the human rights issue which China, while adopting much of the rhetoric of international human rights, rejects the frequent complaints against its treatment of Tibetans by other countries, particularly the **United States**.

As a member of the **United Nations** (**UN**), the PRC professes "respect" for the Universal Declaration of Human Rights, a document that is not legally binding on its signatories but sets out a minimum standard of human rights protection. The PRC has signed all three of the human rights treaties that carry real teeth in their implementation: the International Convention on Economic, Social, and Cultural Rights (1997); the International Convention on Civil and Political Rights (1998); and the Convention against Torture and Other Cruel, Inhuman, or Degrading Treatment or Punishment (2001), the latter of which China assisted in drafting. Altogether, China had by 2004 incorporated 21 international conventions on human rights. In 1989, the PRC was criticized for its report to the UN Committee against Torture for failing to provide sufficient details on practical measures taken by the government to stop torture, compensate victims, and punish perpetrators. In 1998 and 1999, respectively, China was visited by the UN High Commissioner for Human Rights, Mary Robinson, and a team of UN personnel and independent China experts to assess its obligations under UN covenants. In 2001, Mary Robinson also urged China to abolish the country's nation-wide system of **labor** reform camps.

Beginning in 1993, China took part in international human rights meetings, especially the UN World Conference on Human Rights held in Vienna in June, where the PRC endorsed the UN's commitment to human rights, but also expressed opposition to those countries that "impose their values" on others. The PRC signed the final Vienna document that paid lip service to the "universality" of human rights, but left the implementation to individual countries and also reaffirmed the right to development and other collective rights. In March 1994, a draft resolution criticizing the PRC before the UN's Commission on Human Rights, consisting of 53 UN member states, was tabled. In this resolution, which was narrowly defeated, the PRC was criticized for its treatment of dissidents, reports of torture, arbitrary arrests, unfair trials, and the situation in Tibet. Since 1990, China has successfully defeated U.S.-led attempts to put it on the agenda of the UN human rights session on 11 separate occasions, including the last effort in April 2004, when most European nations supported the U.S. while such countries as the Republic of **Korea**, Mexico, and Argentina—all of which have growing economic ties with China—abstained as China invoked controversial American actions in Iraq involving alleged torture of detainees to successfully defeat the American-led effort.

In 1991, the PRC responded to its critics by issuing its first White Paper titled "The Human Rights Situation in China." This document argued for collective rights, particularly the "right to subsistence" for the Chinese people and various cultural and labor rights. The paper also contained a riposte to critics of China's practice of prison labor, which the naturalized Chinese–American Harry Wu had extensively documented, as well as its policies toward Tibet. This was followed, in 1997, when, at the 15th National Party Congress of the **Chinese Communist Party** (**CCP**), the topic of human rights was, for the first time, included in the major political report to the delegates, promoting it from a theme in international publicity work to a major subject in domestic construction. In 2000, the Information Office of the State Council released another White Paper entitled "Fifty Years of Progress in China's Human Rights." In 2004, a proposed amendment—the first of its kind—to the state constitution was adopted that clearly stipulates that "the state respects and safeguards human rights." Although China's official statements on human rights continued to emphasize the commitment of the government to provide for the collective interests of the Chinese people in terms of economic subsistence, **health care**, and development and addressing such problems as the rapid spread of **SARS** and HIV/**AIDS**, civil and legal concepts of human rights prominent in the Western model have also been given increasing attention. This includes guaranteeing the right of the **population** to legally obtain private property and new rules limiting the authority of police to jail suspects without trial or to arrest itinerants without residence permits. China also claims that it has taken firm action against authorities for extorting confessions by torture, abusive use of weapons by police, and redressing the grievances of people kept under extended detention even as the UN rapporteur on torture after a 2005 visit to China following 10 years of negotiation claimed such abuse was widespread, leading him to call on China to overhaul its criminal laws, grant more power to judges, and abolish labor camps that are operated by security forces with little oversight. A number of human rights organizations have been formed in China with government approval, such as the China Society for Human Rights Studies (publisher of the magazine *Human Rights*), China Human Rights Research Society, and the Human Rights Institution under the **Chinese Academy of Social Sciences (CASS)**. China also continues to engage in bilateral dialogues with other nations on the issue of human rights, where the growing international economic prowess of the PRC has provided it with enormous leverage to encourage countries to refrain from publicly criticizing China's human rights record.

International critics of China, such as Human Rights in China, accuse the PRC of cracking down on Christian groups, **Internet** dissidents, ethnic **minorities**, especially in Tibet, organizers of non-CCP political parties (such as the China Rights Party and the China Democracy Party), and advocates of farmers and other dispossessed groups seeking to bring lawsuits against the government. In 2004, the Chinese government also detained a journalist and researcher in *The New York Times* **Beijing** bureau for supposedly leaking state secrets abroad and brought similar charges against foreign permanent residents accused of industrial espionage and bribery. China responded to its critics by pointing to its publication of bibles in the country, the right of citizens to petition the government and bring human rights abuses to the attention of the media, and expanded religious freedoms for Christians, Buddhists, Muslims, and followers of the *Falun Gong*. In 2004, China, under pressure from the U.S., released a number of political prisoners—a term China rejects—but arrested and detained individuals involved in protests against the government for its treatment of minorities, especially in Tibet, and its lack of adequate compensation and redress to families—the "Tiananmen Mothers"—who lost members during the June 1989 military crackdown against the second **Beijing Spring**.

According to Amnesty International, China, like the former **Soviet Union**, utilizes psychiatric hospitals to intern political dissidents who are said to suffer from such illnesses as "political monomania," which is not an internationally recognized medical term. China has also been accused of mistreating victims of HIV/**AIDS**, imposing the death penalty on victimless crimes (such as using the Internet to spread "state secrets"), tolerating political interference in judicial determinations, and continued widespread abuse of administrative detention introduced in 1957. In 2004, China announced the creation of an electronic super ID card for all the country's citizens containing information on chips that authorities anywhere can access, thereby making it easier for the government to track dissidents. China's record on human rights is expected to undergo increased international scrutiny in the run-up to the 2008 Beijing Olympics.

HUNDRED FLOWERS (1956–1957). The term generally used to describe the off-and-on policy of the **Chinese Communist Party (CCP)** in allowing greater intellectual freedom and expression, Hundred Flowers is taken from the ancient Zhou dynasty (1122–225 BC) slogan of "let a hundred flowers bloom, let a hundred schools of thought contend" and is also referred to as "double hundred." The CCP was most emphatic in tolerating liberal opinion in 1956–1957, the period most closely associated with the term. This policy switch was a reaction to the outbreak of the **Hungarian Revolution (1956)** and grew out of a concern by top Chinese **leaders** that the policy of the CCP toward **intellectuals** had been highly flawed, especially its treatment of writers and scientists.

In January 1956, **Zhou Enlai** called for "bringing the existing powers of the intelligentsia into play" and, in May 1956, **Mao Zedong** joined other leaders, such as **Lu Dingyi**, in endorsing "freedom of independent thinking" and "freedom to criticize." Although intellectuals were initially reluctant to voice criticisms, Mao's February 1957 call for greater openness as a tonic for strengthening the vitality of the CCP and his advocacy of pluralism as an end in itself seemed to allay the intelligentsia's fears. Thus, when, in April 1957, the Party called on non-Communist intellectuals to participate in another of its **rectification campaigns**, a flood of criticism ensued, especially from leaders of the **democratic parties**. But Mao had expected non-Communist intellectuals to shower the CCP with praise for its many accomplishments in uniting the country and developing the **economy**; instead, such abuses as "**bureaucratism**," CCP domination of the government and of intellectual affairs, the Sino–Soviet alliance, and "Party sectarianism" were singled out for criticism often through the popular medium of **big-character posters** (*dazibao*). Proposals were also aired for free elections to **trade unions** and other non-state groups while criticism was voiced of the CCP's elaborate structure of administrative control. Concerned with the intensity of the criticism, the *People's Daily* in early June 1957 denounced the Party's antagonists, which ushered in the notorious **Anti-Rightist Campaign (1957–1958)**.

Since 1957, the Hundred Flowers has been the subject of considerable debate in and outside of China. For many, the Hundred Flowers smacked of a devious trap set by Mao Zedong to ferret out the Party's critics. Others, however, suggest that Mao was genuinely committed to liberalization but was frightened by the intensity of the intelligentsia's attacks and concerned that the CCP might go the way of Hungary and experience an anti-Communist uprising. In 1961–1962, yet another Hundred Flowers period was inaugurated in the midst of China's recovery from the devastating effects of the **Great Leap Forward (1958–1960)**. This time, however, few intellectuals dared to speak out openly as the only criticism came in the form of elliptical historical allusions, such as the 1961 play *Hai Rui Dismissed from Office* by **Wu Han**, in which the author apparently targeted Mao's abusive treatment of the peasantry.

HUNGARIAN REVOLUTION (1956). The Hungarian Uprising in October 1956 had a dramatic impact on China. Internationally, the Chinese were clearly concerned about the erosion of cohesion in the "socialist camp" and thus expressed their strong support for the "leading role" of the **Soviet Union** in the international Communist movement. On a visit to the USSR at the height of the crisis, **Zhou Enlai** encouraged Soviet leader Nikita Khrushchev to intervene and remove the leadership of the renegade Hungarian Communist Party.

Domestically, Hungary also influenced **leaders** of the **Chinese Communist Party (CCP)**, especially **Mao Zedong**. Clearly impressed and worried by this popular revolt against a sitting Communist Party, Mao Zedong implemented various policies to stifle any replication in China of the events in Hungary. Although Chinese **intellectuals** and students were aware of developments in Hungary, there appeared very little desire on their part to engage in the same kind of opposition to the newly established CCP regime as reaction to Hungary on Chinese campuses was relatively low-key. Nevertheless, the fear of Mao Zedong that a similar revolt could break out in China shaped his political position throughout the late 1950s. As opposed to the Leninist principles of **democratic-centralism** upheld by **Liu Shaoqi** and **Deng Xiaoping**, Mao advocated greater "democracy" and external rectification of the CCP by intellectuals in the **Hundred Flowers (1956–1957)**. Although Liu and Deng believed in inner Party democracy—that is, criticism and debate within the CCP—Mao believed that criticism from the outside would relieve tensions in Chinese society and prevent an outburst of opposition such as had occurred in Eastern Europe. To Mao's dismay, however, Chinese intellectuals issued forth with a torrent of criticism that led the chairman to brand his intellectual critics as members of a Chinese version of the Petofi Club that had initiated the anti-Communist movement in Hungary. Thereafter, the **Anti-Rightist Campaign (1957–1958)** cracked down on CCP critics.

– I –

IMPERIALISM (*DIGUOZHUYI***).** The overthrow of "imperialism"— foreign influence and control in China—was a major goal of the Chinese Communist revolution. Influenced by Lenin's theory on the role of imperialism in the international capitalist system, Chinese Communist **leaders** linked their domestic enemies of rural gentry and "bureaucratic capitalists" to the presence in China of foreign powers from Europe, America, and **Japan**. The triumph of the **Chinese Communist Party** (**CCP**) in 1949 was hailed as part of the collapse of the international imperialist order and the victory of **socialism** over capitalism on an international scale. Yet even as China contributed to the eventual destruction of international imperialism, socialism was still engaged in a life-and-death struggle with imperialism, which, after 1949, was represented primarily by the largest and most powerful capitalist nation, the **United States**. Thus China considered such struggles as the **Korean War** (**1950–1953**) and the **Vietnam** War (**1965–1975**) as integral parts of the U.S. effort to halt the world revolution. From 1949 to the late 1970s, denunciation of "American imperialism" was a stable of Chinese polemics with songs and slogans—"down with American imperialism" (*dadao Meiguo diguozhuyi*)—memorized by Chinese schoolchildren and adults alike. Beginning with the visit to China in 1972 by U.S. President Richard Nixon and the establishment of formal diplomatic relations between the two countries in 1979, however, such rhetoric gradually disappeared from the Chinese political scene. As the conflict with the **Soviet Union** heated up in the 1970s and 1980s, the USSR was condemned as "social imperialist," a suggestion by China that the once-socialist country had essentially become an imperialist one. The Sino–Soviet rapprochement in the late 1980s and China's integration into the world order and global **economy** reduced its use of this rhetoric, though China continues to denounce what it terms the "neo-imperialism" pursued by the U.S. in its unilateralist policies, such as the 2003 invasion of Iraq, which, as a member of the **United Nations** (**UN**) Security Council, China opposed. Yet, by joining the **World Trade Organization** (**WTO**) in 2001, Chinese leaders were accused by some leftist scholars in China of being too soft on the U.S. as they declared that the country had become a "lapdog of U.S. imperialism."

INDIA. China's relations with India since 1949 ranged from benign warmth in the 1950s through war and protracted tension, largely over unresolved border issues in the 1960s and 1970s, to rapprochement in the 1980s, and a renewal of tension, followed by readjustment on the part of both countries in the 1990s and early 2000s. The post-Cold War era that accompanied the demise of the **Soviet Union** provided new opportunities for the two states—one communist and the other democratic—to move in the direction of a "productive relationship." But tensions continued over issues regarding their mutual 4,000-km border in the Himalayas, India's sheltering of the **Dalai Lama** since his escape from **Tibet** in 1959, and the outbreak of the India–Pakistan nuclear arms race in the late 1990s—even as China and India relied on frequent diplomatic contacts, growing **trade** and military ties to move their relationship onto a more stable and amicable basis.

China–India relations got off to a good start following the accession to power of the **Chinese Communist Party** (CCP) in 1949, when, under Indian Prime Minister Jawaharlal Nehru, India was not only among the first non-Communist nations to recognize the **People's Republic of China** (PRC) but also consistently backed China's membership to the **United Nations** (UN). Even as China forcibly occupied Tibet in 1950, India offered little protest and, in 1954, warmly greeted Premier **Zhou Enlai** on a state visit when the two countries (following the slogan of *"Hindi-Chini bhai-bhai*, Indians and Chinese are brothers") signed off on the Five Principles of Peaceful Coexistence, known as the Panchshila. Following a return visit to China by Prime Minister Nehru in 1954, the two countries invoked the "spirit" of the 1955 **Bandung Conference of Afro–Asian States** for engaging a host of international political, economic, and military issues.

However, whereas China signed border agreements with India's neighbors, such as **Afghanistan** and Burma (now Myanmar), no such agreement was reached with India, and, in the late 1950s, tensions between the two countries emerged as increasingly frequent border skirmishes, which began in 1959, ultimately led to the **Sino–Indian War** (1962), in which **People's Liberation Army** (PLA) forces decisively defeated their Indian counterparts. At the same time, China refused publicly to recognize Kashmir's accession to India, reversing a position taken by Zhou Enlai in 1956, while China also concluded a border agreement with India's prime nemesis Pakistan in May 1962. During India and Pakistan's 1965 war, China refused, however, to intervene on Pakistan's side, providing only words of support and limited military hardware. This was followed in 1966 by the efforts of Indian Prime Minister Indira Gandhi's government to normalize relations with China, which, in 1976, culminated in the two countries re-establishing diplomatic relations. Following a high-profile visit in 1981 to India by Chinese Foreign Minister Huang Hua, a series of talks on a wide-ranging set of issues was inaugurated by the two countries over the next several years, leading to a bilateral trade agreement in 1984 and a visit by Indian Prime Minister Rajiv Gandhi to China in 1988—the first by an Indian prime minister in 34 years—followed, in 1991, by a return visit to India by Chinese Premier **Li Peng**. Confidence building measures (CBMS) were agreed to by both sides and, in 1993, following Prime Minister Narsimha Rao's official visit to China, the two countries agreed to maintain peace and stability along the "line of actual control" (LAC) that temporarily separates their two borders in the absence of a final border agreement that, by 2004, had still not been achieved. In 1996, President **Jiang Zemin** visited India and expressed China's willingness to freeze existing border disputes while signing off on a series of measures to promote mutual cooperation, including undertaking CBMS on military issues.

But this warming of ties was given a significant setback in 1998, when, in the aftermath of India's Pokhran II series of five nuclear tests, Indian leaders cited their perception of China as "potential threat number one" as a main reason for its actions that ran counter to the principles of non-proliferation espoused by the Chinese. Over the course of the next two years, efforts were made by both sides to put bilateral relations back on track with ministerial trips in 2000 and 2002, when India backtracked on its claim of a "potential threat" from China as representatives from the two countries held their first security dialogue. During a visit to China by the Indian president, both sides reiterated their traditional friendship and common commitment to enhanced economic ties and mutual combating of terrorism and agreed to work toward a settlement of their mutual border problems. In 2002, direct flights between China and India were inaugurated while China pressured both India and Pakistan to resolve the issue of Kashmir in a peaceful manner as China reiterated its traditional position of "neutrality" on the territory's future. Although India expressed concern over Chinese assistance to Pakistan in its nuclear weapons program, China insisted its aid to Pakistan was purely for peaceful purposes and is fully monitored by the International Atomic Energy Agency (IAEA).

Both China and India oppose unilateral actions by the **United States**, including the 2003 military action against Iraq, and have expressed concern over growing American military presence in former Soviet republics, such as Uzbekistan and Kazakhstan. This is why both countries are evidently receptive to the proposals by Russian President Vladimir Putin to create a "strategic triangle" of **Russia**, China, and India to counter the expanding military presence of the U.S. in the region. During his 2003 visit to China, Indian Prime Minister Atal Behari Vajpayee signed a declaration on principles for relations and comprehensive cooperation between China and India that reiterated the Five Principles of Peaceful Coexistence.

Among the issues dividing China and India are the latter's claim to sovereignty over the Himalayan kingdom of Sikkim, which borders China, and continued Indian sheltering of the Dalai Lama and the Karmapa Lama (the third most esteemed figure in Tibetan Buddhism), who, at the age of 14 in 2000, fled Tibet for the Dalai Lama's refuge in Dharamshala, India. Although India has reiterated its position recognizing Tibet as sovereign territory of the PRC and promised China that it will not tolerate any "anti-China" activities by the Dalai Lama or the 100,000 Tibetan refugees on Indian soil, China has still not formally recognized Sikkim as part of India, following the decision of the kingdom to become India's 22nd state in 1975, though China has agreed to open up border trade through Sikkim's territory. On the long-simmering India–China border issue, the PRC continues to occupy the 38,000-km^2 Aksai Chin chunk of Kashmir, through which it built a strategic highway linking Tibet with the Xinjiang Autonomous Region. To the east, India, in turn, occupies the nearly 90,000 km^2 of Arunachal Pradesh claimed by China but which India elevated from a union territory to a state following renewed border clashes with China in 1986. China's construction of roads and a railway into Tibet from Qinghai Province are viewed by some Indians as part of a grand Chinese design to "surround" India that includes increased military ties to Myanmar and Pakistan supplementing the forward positioning of the PLA in Tibet, including possible nuclear missile emplacements. China and India continue to conduct their Joint Working Group on the China–India Border Issue against a backdrop of India declaring, contrary to 1998, that China "is not a threat." Although there have been periodic Chinese intrusions across the LAC, in 2005, China and India agreed to resolve the border issue in the near future. China and India also signed on, in 2003, as dialogue partners to the **Association of Southeast Asian Nations (ASEAN)** and both signed its Treaty of Amity and Cooperation renouncing war as a means to settle disputes among signatory countries. The year 2003 also witnessed the two countries engaging in their first-ever joint naval exercises in a sign of lessening tensions even as India sought to expand its naval power by purchasing an aircraft carrier from Russia. China has also indicated that it may endorse India's bid to become a permanent member of the UN Security Council.

As China and India sought to defuse their territorial, political, and military differences in the early 2000s, issues involving economic ties and trade took center stage. With more than a fifth of global manufacturing done in China and India, whose two economies combined rival the size of the U.S., trade between the two countries expanded from a mere US$5 billion in 2002 to US$14 billion in 2005. Much of the trade consists of primary or low-value added products, including iron ore, plastics, marine products, organic chemicals, coal-coke, and electronic goods, but with increased focus on spurring synergetic trade between China's highly developed computer hardware and India's sophisticated and broad-based software industry. In 2001, the Chinese Software Company Huawei Technologies set up a research and development center in Bangalore India, the center of the country's thriving software sector, while India's software giants Infosys Technologies and Tata Group set up shop in **Shanghai**.

Despite India's continued concern with becoming a target for cheaply produced Chinese goods since opening its domestic market in 1991, the two countries formally launched talks in 2004 to study the feasibility of signing a bilateral Free Trade Agreement as China overtook **Japan** in 2001 as the number one destination for Indian exports and China overtook Japan as the primary source of imports into India from East Asia. In 2003, the two countries set up a compact Joint Study Group composed of officials and economists to examine the potential complementarities between the two countries in expanded trade and economic cooperation and China promised to invest US$500 million in the Indian **economy**. "Learn from China" is the new mantra in Indian business with increased focus on higher growth and greater attention to attracting Foreign Direct Investment (FDI), where India fell woefully behind China with a mere US$3.4 billion in 2002, compared to China's US$52.7 billion. Regional growth plans include the Kunming Initiative, which is designed to bring together southeastern China, northeastern India, Myanmar, and Bangladesh. India and China have also joined together to meet their increasing demands for **energy**. *See also* FOREIGN POLICY.

INDUSTRY. The industrial sector of China's **economy** consists of heavy industry, **transportation**, electronics and telecommunications, aeronautics and astronautics, and light industry and textiles. In 2001, the industrial sector composed 51.1% of the Chinese economy with **agriculture** and services contributing 15.2% and 33.6%, respectively. Manufacturing alone accounted for 35.4% of all economic activity in China for the same year, which represented an increase over the 32.7% figure for 1991 but a slight drop from the 38.5% level in 1981, which followed the inauguration of economic reforms in 1978–1979.

Following the takeover of China by the **Chinese Communist Party** (CCP) in 1949, the Chinese government sought a rapid development of China's backward industrial sector based on the Soviet model of central economic planning and crash industrialization. Metallurgical, mining and **energy** industries, airplane and **automobile** production, and new industries, including petrochemicals, computers, telecommunications equipment, instruments and meters, and aeronautics were built up from almost nothing and centered around a system of **state-owned industries** (SOEs). Despite China's position as a significant textile exporter in 1950, light industry and textiles received very low priority under the Soviet-type central planning system so that by 1970 China accounted for less than 14% of total textile exports originating in developing economies. From the inauguration of economic reforms in 1978–1979 to 1999, Chinese industry, including a revised light industrial sector, increased production at an average rate of 11%, a figure roughly equal to average growth rates during the period of the Soviet-type planned economy. In 2000 and 2001, these rates dropped to 9.6% and 8.7%, respectively, although industry continued to outpace growth rates in agriculture and services, which registered 2.4%, 2.8%, 7.8%, and 7.4% increases, respectively. From 1978 to 1999, 3.5 billion *yuan* of industrial value was added in China, a more than tenfold increase.

The pace of industrialization in the reform period was accelerated by China's decision to break with the autarkic model of "**self-reliance**" (*zili gengsheng*) from the 1953–1979 era of **five-year plans** through the introduction of Foreign Direct Investment (FDI) and opening to the outside world. In 1979, 78% of industry in China was state-owned and 22% collectively owned largely by local governments. By 2000, the state-owned sector had dropped to 24% and the collective to 14% with individual and a variety of other types of ownership, including share-holding enterprises, accounting for 6% and 56%, respectively. Despite these changes in ownership patterns, Chinese industry is still subject to considerable government direction at the hands of the State Development and Reform Commission, the State Economic and Trade Commission, the ministries of Commerce, Construction, Foreign Trade and Economic Cooperation, Information Technology, Land and Resources, Railways, and **Science and Technology** along with the State Administration of Industry and Commerce and other regulatory organizations and bureaus. Industry employs approximately 25% of the Chinese **labor** force that in 2000 totaled over 700 million workers. The hardest-hit region in China since the inauguration of reforms has been the industrial heartland of the northeast, where large numbers of industrial state-owned enterprises (SOEs) were shut down in the 1990s resulting in high unemployment and pension fund defaults, which, in 2003, led Premier **Wen Jiabao** to announce a broad effort to achieve greater balance in growth between regions and to remove the last vestiges of state planning.

Heavy industry in China includes iron and steel, petrochemicals and chemicals, machinery and machine tools, and energy. Long considered the pillar of its national economy, China's steel industry is the world's largest, producing 277 million tons in 2004 (more than the **United States** and **Japan** combined) with projections of 310 million tons of output by 2010. There are 66 separate steel companies in China and more than 4,000 individual producers of various steel products with a total capitalization of US$41 billion (compared to US$50 billion for Japan and US$11 billion for the U.S.) and with the pace of spending on new steel mills accelerating. Large iron and steel enterprises are distributed in Anshan (Liaoning Province), Taiyuan (Shanxi Province), Baotou (Inner Mongolia), **Beijing**, Nanjing, **Shanghai**, **Tianjin**, Wuhan (Hubei Province), and Panzhihua (Sichuan Province), the last a **Third Front** project. The largest steel production facility in China is the **Baoshan Iron and Steel Complex** (Baosteel) located in Shanghai, which, in 2005, produced 23 million tons while a total of 13 producers had production capacity in excess of five million tons, though production in many facilities, such as Nanjing Steel, was hampered by periodic electricity shortages. In 2003, total capital **investment** in the steel industry amounted to 133 billion *yuan*, largely by small private companies, which represented an 89% increase over the previous year pushed by the continued rapid growth in China's major steel consumers: construction (57%); machine building (11.3%); light industry (8.21%) and automobile production (4.22%). Some 1,400 different varieties of steel are produced in China, including high-class steel, such as cold-rolled steel plates and steel sheets, zinc-plated steel plates, and steel pipes and tubes, with total consumption in China doubling that of the U.S. despite the fact its economy is only one-eighth the size. Although China has more than 40 billion tons of proven iron ore reserves, its voracious appetite for iron made the country the largest importer of ore in the world in 2004—outstripping Japan—as China purchased 150 million tons, much of it from Australia, which constituted 30% of world iron ore trade volume. China also imported huge amounts of scrap steel from the U.S. and neighboring countries, such as Mongolia, where the Chinese demand for scrap has become a major industry.

In 2004, a consensus developed among Chinese **leaders** that over-investment in steel, along with cement and the building boom in real estate, threatened to derail China's overall economic growth, leading policy makers to order a halt in the construction of new steel facilities, such as a 10 billion-*yuan* plant planned for Changzhou Municipality in Jiangsu Province, and to end tax rebates for import of equipment for steel construction projects. Rationalization of China's highly fragmented and decentralized steel industry was sought with planned mergers between major producers, such as Benxi Steel and **Anshan Iron and Steel Corporation**, with hopes of reducing China's relatively high steel prices that continue to subsidize small, inefficient producers. Foreign investment in China's steel industry has come from Japan (Nippon Steel Corp.), Europe (Arcelor), and **Korea** (Posco) while such companies as Jinan Iron and Steel raised capital on China's **stock markets** with Class-A share offerings with Baosteel considering an international stock listing.

The chemical and petrochemical industry in China includes chemical extraction, production of fertilizers, pesticides, basic inorganic and organic raw materials, synthetic fiber monomers and rubber, photosensitive materials, rubber products, plastics, polymers, ethane, ethylene, synthetic resin, and chemicals for household and pharmaceutical use. China is a world leader in production of synthetic ammonia, chemical fertilizer, sulphuric acid, soda ash, and rubber tires. while its petrochemical sector is the most profitable industry in the country. Shanghai, Beijing, Tianjin, Dalian, and Shenyang are China's most important chemical industry bases. China is self-reliant in chemical and petrochemical production, which, in 2003, accounted for 970 billion *yuan* in production, 10% of the country's Gross Domestic Product (GDP), with a projected growth rate of 4%. The core SOEs in China's chemical industry are National Bluestar Corp. and China Haohua Chemical Industrial Corp., which, in 2004, merged into the China Chemical Industry Corp., which is projected to control 40% of the domestic industry. Other major chemical companies include China Petroleum and Chemical Group (SINOPEC) and PetroChina, though overall the industry remains highly fragmented with hundreds of small producers scattered around the country. This makes many of China's chemical products, especially petrochemicals and plastics, relatively high priced and subject to intense competition especially after China reduced tariffs as a result of its 2001 entry into the **World Trade Organization** (**WTO**). Major international investors in China's chemical industry include Proctor and Gamble, Unilever, and Hubei C-Bons (**Hong Kong**), which, along with their Chinese counterparts, have tried to tackle the dramatic increases in the production of fake chemical products in China and a rash of accidents in the chemical industry, including 30 deaths in April 2004 from chemical leaks of waste chlorine and hydrogen cyanide gas because of lax safety procedures and outdated equipment. China maintains 350 chemical industry research institutes that act as a magnet for future foreign investment.

The machine tool and machine-building industry in China ranked second in profits in 2003, behind petrochemicals, and in 2002 its output value rose 25%, which led China's machine-tool industry to surpass Germany as the world's largest. More than 50% of the profits in China's machine-building industry came from the rapidly growing automotive sector along with such long-term projects requiring major heavy equipment and machinery purchases as the **Three Gorges Dam Project**. In addition to farm machinery, engineering instruments and meters, heavy mining machinery, and electrical engineering equipment, China's machine-tool sector is capable of providing Chinese industries with large blast furnaces, continuous slab and billet casters, electricity generators, coal mining and oil drilling equipment, and chemical plants. China's machine tool sector is, like steel and chemicals, highly fragmented with over 600 separate producers, though only a handful of companies have sales exceeding US$50 million. The largest single machine-tool producer in China is the Shenyang Machine Tool Company that, over a 50-year period, supplied more than 450,000 machines to China's manufacturing industries and is a publicly traded company listed on the Shenzhen stock market. Machine-tool production in private enterprises and joint ventures in China is equal to or even greater than their state-owned counterparts. Although China still relies on foreign suppliers from Germany, Switzerland, and Japan for high-end machine tools, Chinese producers have become a major international supplier of basic equipment, such as grinders, lathes, automated boring and dye machines, capturing market share from mid-markets rivals based mostly in the Republic of Korea and **Taiwan**.

China's aeronautics and astronautic industry was established in the 1950s with Xi'an, Shanghai, Shenyang, Chengdu, and Harbin as the centers of production and research on both civilian and military aircraft. The *Yun* 7 airliner was produced by the Xi'an Aircraft Corporation as the major type used for medium and short domestic flights in China while Xi'an in a 20-year joint venture with Boeing has supplied nearly 3,000 vertical fins for the B-737. In 1992, China National Aero-Technology Import and Export Corporation (CATIC) entered into an agreement with McDonnell Douglas to co-produce 40 MD-80 and MD-90 aircraft for China's "trunk" routes, but the number of aircraft to be built in China was reduced to 20 in

1994. Chengdu Aircraft Corporation, founded in 1958, produced the J-7/F-7 fighter for the **People's Liberation Army (PLA)** and, in 1991, began production of the FC-1 fighter, which is intended as a replacement for the aging J-7. In December 2003, the 50-seat ERJ145 regional turbofan passenger jet rolled off the production line in a joint venture between Hafei Aviation Industry Group in China and Brazil's Embraer aircraft maker. Hafei is also slated to begin production of the advanced EC-120 Humming-Bird helicopter in conjunction with European and Singapore manufacturers. China's astronautic industry has developed carrier rockets and launched all kinds of satellites and is a world leader in satellite research.

Telecommunications, electronic information, and the computer industry are among the fastest growing sectors in the entire Chinese economy as the country's 1.3 billion people are being gradually integrated into a national telephone and telecommunications network that, by 1997, was the second-largest telephone network in the world. In 2003, the number of fixed telephone users in China reached 260 million subscribers, 62 million more than in 2002 while the number of mobile phone (*dageda*) users grew to 300 million. Together, the users generated 220 billion text messages, more than the rest of the world combined. But although 60 to 80% of citizens in Beijing and Shanghai have a mobile phone, many administrative villages in the rural areas, particularly the poorest ones, lack even one fixed telephone, which is why, in 2004, China launched its Telephone Service in Each Village Project. Investment in the telecommunications sector was US$20 billion in 2003 making China both the largest and fastest-growing telecommunications market in the world. With 21 out of every 100 people in China having fixed phones and/or mobile phones—numbers considerably less than in most developed countries—the potential for future growth in this sector is immense, which is why virtually all major international wireless companies are vying for a share of the lucrative Chinese market. The dominant players in China's wireless market remain China Mobile (a subsidiary of China Telecom), with 66% of subscribers on its GSM network, and the state-owned China Unicom. Although China announced in 1999 that China Telecom would be restructured into four companies—China Telecom Group (handling mainly fixed lines), Chinese Mobile Telecom Group, China Paging Telecom Group, and China Satellite Telecom Group—the Chinese government has been very protective of its domestic industry, with attempts to dictate its own Wifi technology, which was subsequently abandoned, and requirements that foreign vendors manufacture their equipment in China. In response, Lucent opened a third-generation (3G) research and development facility in 2003 in Nanjing, with its main manufacturing facility in Qingdao, Shandong Province, while Motorola has manufacturing centers in Tianjin and Hangzhou employing 12,000 workers. China-made program-controlled telephone exchanges are now competitive on the global market. In 2005, the largest handset producer in the Asia–Pacific Region was located in Tianjin. With 10,000 engineers employed, Huawei Technologies is China's first international player in the communications business with its product line expanding from telephone exchange equipment to fiber-optic networks, mobile telephone technology, and data routing systems.

The computer industry has become the leading factor in promoting the growth of electronic and information technology (IT) in China. In 2004, according to the Ministry of Information Technology, China produced 30 million units and recorded 454 billion *yuan* in sales, a 65% jump from 2003 as office networks including online negotiation, online **education**, and e-commerce were developed, especially in response to the 2002–2003 **SARS** crisis, along with expansion of **Internet** portals. China is slated to become the largest information technology market in the world in five years, including the burgeoning software industry, which has over 8,000 individual companies with exports in 2004 of US$2 billion and a growing synergetic relationship with software companies in **India**. China imports 80% of the semiconductor chips it needs even though imports face a stiff 17% value-added tax (VAT) which is designed to encourage its own domestic industry and foreign investment. While a simmering dispute with the U.S. on computer chips has emerged, American companies such as Intel and Dell have responded with plans to build 19 new chip test and assembly plants in China, while, in 2004, the Chinese company Lenovo, the country's largest producer of personal commuters, purchased IBM's PC business. Concerns remain over the commitment of China to protection of intellectual property, but with its growing synergetic relationship with Indian software companies, China hopes to net US$30 billion from software sales by the end of 2005 when China is expected to become the second largest market for PCs in the world. Supercomputing is also being seized upon by the Chinese government to help speed the nation's transition from low-cost manufacturing to becoming a more powerful force in the world economy. China has 14 supercomputers among the top 500, ranking the country fourth in the world.

The light and textile industry in China involves 40-odd sectors from clothing to food industry to paper pulp production to leather making, diamond polishing, and jewelry making, altogether 300,000 separate products. In 2003, light industry ranked third in overall profit margins with more than one trillion *yuan* in added value. Although garment exports of 62 billion *yuan*, in 2002, remained a major source of China's foreign exchange earnings, increased production and sales in this crucial sector have also been driven by brisk consumer spending within China by an increasingly acquisitive middle class that is said to number 100 million people. Other sectors of light industry, which also registered substantial growth rates in 2003–2004, include the plastics industry, furniture production (in which, in 2004, China ranked fourth in the world), cigarette lighters (in which China controls 80% of the world market), leather making (with leather products from more than 16,000 producers constituting 20% of total export volume of light industry in 2003, staying at first place for the third consecutive year), paper pulp production, and electrical appliances. The latter includes refrigerators, microwaves, lighting equipment, and air conditioners that are produced by new upstart companies such as Kelong, Konka, Little Swan, and Haier, which, in 2005, bid to acquire the U.S. firm Maytag. Light industrial production in China remains concentrated in the coastal provinces of Jiangsu, Zhejiang, and Guangdong especially in such manufacturing centers as the city of Wenzhou, Zhejiang Province, where production was valued at 100 billion *yuan* in 2003.

Sectors experiencing an absolute decline in production and sales included such mainstays of China's light industry as bicycles, which confronted changing modes of inner city **transportation** and increased competition from producers in Japan and Taiwan. During its heyday in the 1960s, Shanghai's Forever Bicycle Company employed 6,000 people and produced three million units a year, but the company's workforce and production have been halved in recent years. Although, in 1994, China became the world's largest clothing exporter, from the mid-1980s onward, textiles and clothing have dropped as a percentage of manufactured exports, indicating greater diversification in China's export mix. Long dominated by state-owned enterprises, textiles and clothing are increasingly produced by **township-village enterprises** (**TVEs**) as the state has gradually withdrawn capital from textile manufacturing establishments and is considering abandoning the export quota allocation system run by the China Textile Import and Export Corporation. *See also* SPACE PROGRAM.

INTELLECTUALS (*ZHISHIFENZI*). The word "intellectual" in China refers to anyone with a high school or college **education**, as well as to white-collar and professional workers, a group that altogether comprises approximately 5% of the entire **population**. Compared with the former **Soviet Union**, intellectuals constitute a smaller percentage of the entire population but possess a strong sense of common identity.

The history of modern China since 1949 has created a peculiar dilemma for intellectuals who have been captive to a regime that needs and demands their services but which repudiates the independent ideas they are equipped to supply. Over the years, the **Chinese Communist Party** (**CCP**) has built up and maintained its political power through absolute control over ideology and thought. Before and after it took power in 1949, the CCP singled out Chinese intellectuals and journalists who championed independent thought and advocated freedom of speech and made them targets of persecution. The 1942–1944 Yan'an Rectification campaign, the 1953–1955 campaign known as the **Hu Feng Affair**, and the **Anti-Rightist Campaign (1957–1958)** prosecuted by **Deng Xiaoping**, were all launched to establish ideological control over intellectuals inside and outside the Party. These brutal campaigns targeted specific "example" intellectuals, but were intended to persecute hundreds of thousands of others.

In the 1940s and 1950s, the CCP needed the services of its educated elite to achieve and consolidate its rule over China. Intellectuals were needed not only for the prosaic tasks of administration of the bureaucracies of government and business (which required literacy), but also for ideological work to buttress the legitimacy of the regime. The source of abiding tension in CCP-intellectual relations, which continued into the 1990s and early 2000s, is that on the one hand the CCP must rely on the social prestige and creative talents of the intellectuals to articulate its policies and motivate the public, while on the other hand, as a Leninist party the CCP inherently distrusts intellectuals as insubordinate and divisive and as potential rivals to political legitimacy. Thus, the CCP has gone to extraordinary lengths (even greater than its counterpart in the former Soviet Union) to win over China's intellectuals to the subordinate propaganda role desired by its **leaders**.

The period from the 1942–1944 Rectification Campaign to the Anti-Rightist Campaign was crucial in establishing CCP hegemony over intellectuals. Drawn to the Communist redoubt in Yan'an during the late 1930s and early 1940s, many Chinese intellectuals joined the Communists out of genuine patriotic loyalty and a commitment to the **New Democracy** that CCP Chairman **Mao Zedong** had promised in January 1940. Yet, despite Mao's promise of a "new culture" and a "new democratic republic" that so attracted the intellectuals who gravitated to Yan'an, political reality consisted of a Party dictatorship that increasingly drew on the experiences and methods of Stalinist Russia where intellectuals were subordinated to the will of the Party leadership. During the Yan'an period, this involved a variety of methods that ranged from public "education campaigns," to the establishment of direct administrative Party control and **censorship** (*shencha*) of the press, to a more brutal campaign known as the "rescue movement" whereby many intellectuals were persecuted and liquidated: "killing one to scare the hundred."

In the initial years of the **People's Republic of China (PRC)**, intellectuals were once again courted by the Party leadership as a crucial component in its plans to develop the Chinese **economy** and advance the country's very backward **science and technology** sector. In June 1949, the major newspaper for intellectuals, *Englightenment Daily (Guangming ribao)* began publication, and a number of non-Communist intellectuals were recruited as delegates to the **Chinese People's Political Consultative Conference (CPPCC)**. Within a few years, however, intellectuals were once again the target of a Communist Party that was acutely sensitive to any criticism from educated circles. This time the targets were Hu Feng and Liang Shuming. Hu Feng, an early critic of the CCP's **"thought reform"** (*sixiang gaizao*) efforts in the 1940s, was attacked from 1953 to 1955 as the reputed leader of the "Hu Feng Anti-Party Clique." Opposed to the arbitrary imposition on writers of a predetermined Communist worldview, Hu Feng appealed to the CCP Central Committee for a more flexible approach to Chinese **literature and the arts**, only to be attacked and subsequently arrested as a symbol of resistance to Party authority. The second target was Liang Shuming, China's "last Confucian," who, in 1953, publicly berated Mao Zedong by citing his own alternative model of rural reconstruction and gradual development that directly challenged the chairman's support for Soviet-style central planning with its emphasis on heavy industry and urban modernization at the expense of the rural areas. Mao's chilling public vilification of both Hu Feng and Liang Shuming led to a nationwide campaign in 1954–1955 against writers and intellectuals who still believed, despite the 1942–1944 Rectification Campaign, that some measure of autonomy and independent thought would be possible under the new regime. They were wrong.

Two years later, in 1957, following the outburst of criticism by intellectuals against the CCP, which had been sanctioned by Mao Zedong's call for a **Hundred Flowers**, the Anti-Rightist Campaign was launched. Hundreds of thousands of educated people throughout the country were affected and, in many cases, either killed or exiled for years to remote areas. The case of *Enlightenment Daily* editor Chu Anping was emblematic of the sharp conflicts that emerged between a regime intent on controlling ideology and intellectuals who considered "thought" their special preserve and independent contribution to society. Intensive criticism, public denunciations, and **criticism and self-criticism** (*piping yu ziwopiping*) and "confessions" were the primary mechanisms for subordinating intellectuals to the will of the Communist leadership and preempting their challenge to Party ideology. During the **Cultural Revolution (1966–1976)**, the persecution of intellectuals continued, this time under the frenzied attacks by **Red Guards**, who condemned intellectuals as the "stinking ninth category" (*choulaojiu*). Intellectuals have been a favorite target in China because of the traditional role that the educated elite has played throughout more than 2,000 years of dynastic history.

Since 1978, intellectuals have been treated more leniently as they are now considered part of the "working class." However, intellectual dissidents in the **Democracy Wall Movement (1978–1979)** and the

1989 second **Beijing Spring** pro-democracy movement were singled out for harsh criticism and persecution by CCP leaders who are terribly frightened by the slightest hint of opposition from educated personages whom the average Chinese still deeply admire. In 1990, President **Jiang Zemin** reaffirmed the crucial role of intellectuals in China's modernization but warned against the influence of Western bourgeois values and "national nihilism." At that time, Chinese intellectuals largely focused on issues involving the **economy** and international affairs while all but ignoring issues of political reform as the CCP combined rapid economic growth with tight political control centered on CCP domination of the political system. In this context, such issues as public order in a market society, government as a public organ, and the logic of the market economy and the concept of the state were the main topics of liberal intellectuals such as Liu Junning, He Jiadong, Hu Angang, and Zhang Shuguang, who generally avoided any possible confrontation with authorities and often served as official advisors. Chinese intellectuals were also enamored of openly nationalistic tracts, especially the widely popular and generally anti-Western work titled *China Can Say No* (*Zhongguo keyi shuo bu*) by Song Qiang, Zhang Zangzang, and Qiao Bian and *China Can Still Say No* (*Zhongguo haishi neng shuo bu*) also by Song Qiang and others in 1996.

In the aftermath of the 2002–2003 **SARS** crisis, which revealed fatal flaws in China's communication and political structures, intellectuals and journalists were allowed increased freedom to once again discuss political reform and ponder far-reaching revisions to the constitution, including calls for the separation of the CCP and state that had been raised in the late 1980s by **Zhao Ziyang,** only to be suppressed following the June 1989 crackdown. Intellectuals also spoke out on various international issues by calling on both China and **Japan** to move beyond the legacy of World War II in their bilateral relations to pursue mutual long-term interests. Following a conference held in Qingdao, Shandong Province, in June 2003 on constitutional reform, such free-wheeling efforts were quickly halted as the CCP Propaganda Department ordered all Party organizations, research institutes, and universities to avoid the "three unmentionables" of political reform, multi-party elections, and a reevaluation of the official position on 4 June 1989. While hopes were expressed that the new leadership of President **Hu Jintao** and Premier **Wen Jiabao** would allow for somewhat greater leeway for intellectuals to address issues of political and constitutional reform, by late 2003 and into 2004, the detention of prominent intellectuals such as the social critic Liu Xiaobo and the prominent writer Yu Jie ended these hopes for the immediate future though the advent of the **Internet** has provided intellectuals with an outlet for exchanging information and circulating petitions. And while the All-China Journalists Association had adopted a code of ethics in 1991 that emphasized the importance of truthful reporting and condemned all forms of falsehood, Chinese journalists, such as **He Qinglian**, continued to confront state intrusion and prohibition of coverage on a series of issues including the increasing frequency and violence of **social protests**.

"INTERNAL MATERIALS" (*"NEIBU ZILIAO"*). The Chinese state and **Chinese Communist Party** (**CCP**) bureaucracies rely heavily on printed material that is not for public consumption. The largest of the circulated "internal materials" is called *Reference News (Cankao xiaoxi)*, which contains a collection of wire-service translations from the foreign media, such as Reuters and *The New York Times*. Introduced in the late 1950s by the **New China News Agency** (**Xinhua**) to keep the Chinese leadership informed of developments outside the country, this publication was originally limited to top-ranking **cadres**, but, in recent years, has become widely available to state employees and university students. It reportedly has a circulation of 11 million, far more than the largest "public" newspaper, the *People's Daily*. Distributed through the mail, this publication is "internal" (i.e., restricted) in name only. Less widely available is *Reference Information (Cankao ziliao)*, which, also controlled by Xinhua, publishes translated articles from abroad but is more comprehensive than the *Peoples Daily*. The next most restricted material is the *Internal Reference (Neibu cankao)*, which contains sensitive reports prepared by Xinhua reporters on domestic and international events. It is limited in its distribution to state and Party ministerial (*bu*) personnel. *Internal Reports (Neibu wengao)* and *Internal Situation (Neibu qingyang)* are two additional sets of reports that are prepared for perusal by China's top leadership. The most restricted materials are so-called red-headed reference (*hongtou cankao*) and hand-copied documents that are limited in distribution to the top political leadership. Books and magazines in China also frequently carry the "internal" classification, but access is not severely restricted.

INTERNET. China permitted the establishment of commercial Internet accounts in 1995. Since then, usage in the country has multiplied from near zero in 1996 to 111 million users in 2005, and the number grows at double-digit rates every year. Along with 135,000 registered websites in China and approximately four million blogs, China is the second largest Internet user in the world after the **United States** and surpassing **Japan** with international bandwidth capacity of 136,000 megabits per second.

The development of the Internet infrastructure in China commenced in academic and scientific circles with the first computer network set up in 1987 as the China Academic Network (CANET). Other academic networks soon sprang up, including the network of the Institute of High Energy Physics and the China Education and Research Network, although as a result of U.S. government restrictions on socialist countries China had no direct connection to the Internet. In 1994, during the Sino–American Federation of Scientific and Technological Cooperation, the first Chinese network directly connected to the Internet became active when the National Computing Facilities of China project opened up a dedicated circuit to the Internet through the Sprint Corporation. ChinaNet was set up as the first commercial network in May 1995. In 1998, competition was allowed but with new companies forced to connect with China Telecom for traffic outside China. By 2001, nine networks received approval from the State Council to offer Internet services that, by 2005, included major shares in the lucrative Chinese market by Microsoft, Yahoo, and Google.

With 90% of the websites in the more developed, largely coastal provinces and urban areas of China, there is a significant regional digital divide in China as Internet users tend to be more affluent and better-educated people. Estimates are that one in four Internet users in China are online gamers many working for so-called gaming factories where young Chinese are paid by more affluent online gamers in South **Korea** and the U.S. to work their way up to the higher levels of games such as War of Warcraft and EverQuest. China's leading

Internet portals are Sohu.com, Netease.com, and Sina.com—the largest portal website in China—while other Chinese Internet companies include Tencent, an instant messaging provider, Shanda Networking, a leading online game operator, and Baidu, a Chinese search engine with minority **investment** from Google. "Legendary" and *"Chuangqi"* are the most profitable online games in China, which, in 2003, made Shanda's owner, Chen Tianqiao, a billionaire at the age of 30 and earned him status as a delegate to the 15th National Party Congress of the **Chinese Communist Party (CCP)**. Unlike the traditional media outlets in China—newspapers, radio, and television—Internet companies in China are privately owned with boards of directors from the U. S. and other Western nations. Among the 500 key enterprises in China, 99% have access to the Internet and 84% have launched their own websites that receive customer orders, allowing for online purchasing and marketing. There are also more than 11,000 governmental sites, although most of them are one-way mirrors with insufficient interactivity which is why, in 2004, less than 10% of the sites recorded frequent usage.

Prior to 2002, China's Internet café business was characterized by back alley, seedy outlets with a fly-by-night quality because many of them were subject to constant government scrutiny and frequent shutdowns. But following a tragic arson incident at a 24-hour-a-day cyber café in the Technology University district of **Beijing**, China's Internet café business went through a process of gentrification as outlets moved into more attractive quarters in upscale shopping malls and retail centers. In 2004, the number of operating Internet cafés was estimated at 135,000, and home dial-up service in China is a rarity in a country where the ubiquitous cell phone is the chosen platform. Government oversight of the Internet is in the hands of the China Internet Network Information Center (CNNIC) under the Ministry of Information Technology and with supplementary regulatory roles played by, among others, the Ministry of Public Security, which ensures the Internet does not leak state secrets, the Ministry of State Security, which decodes traffic on the Internet, the Public Information and Internet Security Supervision Bureau, which ensures Internet Communications Protocol (ICP) conforms to government content guidelines, the State Administration of Radio, Film, and Television, which manages Internet access through cable, and the State Administration for Industry and Commerce, which registers e-commerce websites and grants advertising licenses.

The Internet represents a two-edged sword **technology** in China, where its capacity to bring China into the Information Revolution is offset by its capacity to undermine the political power of the CCP by creating a civil society and modes of social communication outside direct state control. The development of the Internet and text messaging is seen by some observers as capable of bringing immense changes to China's authoritarian regime such as occurred in 2003 when 300 million cell phone users helped to expose the national coverup of the **SARS** epidemic. In 2005, text messaging was used to organize anti-Japan online petitions and to report on numerous **social protests** that broke out in various parts of the country and were virtually ignored by state-run media. But the Chinese government has proved very adept and sophisticated at maintaining effective political control over these media by an elaborate architecture of Internet Protocol (IP)-blocking and a content-filtering system that can monitor and delete e-mail and text messages that contain key words (e.g., "democracy") or phrases ("Tiananmen massacre") that authorities consider suspicious before they reach customers. Beginning with the introduction of commercial Internet usage in China in 1995, the Chinese government issued a series of regulations aimed at controlling Internet content and punishing its violators. As the regulatory framework evolved, the Chinese government shifted responsibility for oversight and control from the **Public Security Bureau** to the Internet service providers themselves, a task facilitated by the top-down nature of China's Internet architecture that includes only nine government-owned gateways that connect to the international Internet. Among the thousands of foreign websites blocked by the Chinese government are news, educational, government (e.g., **Taiwan**), Chinese ex-patriot dissidents and pro-democracy groups, religious organizations, and even health sites dealing with issues such as HIV/**AIDS**. Of greatest concern to Chinese authorities is the capacity of Chinese citizens to use Blogs (e.g., Blogchina.com), bulletin boards, and text messaging to address issues of social justice, **corruption**, or migrant labor or to employ webcams for provocative photos and ironic commentary about sexuality. Individuals and units are therefore banned by a 1997 law from using the Internet to create, replicate, retrieve, or transmit information such as "inciting to resist or violate the [state] Constitution or laws." Individuals accused of violating the rules—so-called "cyber dissidents"—have been subject to long periods of detention and, in some cases, charged with "subverting state power" and sentenced to prison terms. All Internet users must register with local authorities within 30 days of signing up with an Internet Service Provider (ISP) while customers at Internet cafés in **Shanghai** are required to use electronic identification swipe cards that allow administrators to track their Internet use.

Estimates are that China employs upward of 50,000 Internet police to monitor users who might visit politically sensitive sites and to carry out daily inspections of short-message service providers in order to kill off discussion threads on Internet bulletin boards. Microsoft, Yahoo, and Google have all agreed to help the Chinese government censor speech on the Web and, in one case, supply information that helped the government track down and convict a political dissident although China claims its laws governing the Internet are no different from those found in Western democracies, including the United States. The Chinese government has also set up an Illegal and Harmful Content Reporting Center in 2004 for people to complain about lewd and pornographic information on the Internet or anything illegal. Whereas use of the Internet to make online complaints to the government was strictly banned during the tenure of President **Jiang Zemin**, his successor, **Hu Jintao**, approved the creation in 2004 of two sites—China Petition Network (www.chinacomplaint.com) and Media Supervision of China (www.yuluncn.com)—which allow Chinese citizens to alert CCP **leaders** to issues involving social stability, popular opinion, and official corruption.

INVESTMENT. *See* TRADE AND INVESTMENT.

"IRON RICE BOWL" (*"TIEFANWAN"*). A generic term in Chinese used to refer to job security for industrial workers and Party and state **cadres** under the socialist system. From 1949 until the inauguration of the economic reforms in 1978–1979, wages in China were low and consumer goods were few, but workers in the **state-owned enterprises** (**SOEs**) in the industrial sector and the government bureaucracies had total job security. In addition, housing was provided, along with free **health care** and **education**. Over the years, however, the number of workers and their dependents at industrial facilities, such as the **Baoshan Iron and Steel Complex** in **Shanghai**, increased dramatically without commensurate increases in productivity. The "iron rice bowl" ultimately became a metaphor for inefficient and lackadaisical workers, bloated employment rolls, and inflated bureaucracies that ultimately led the **Chinese Communist Party (CCP)** leadership in 1978–1979 to inaugurate economic reforms. The loss of the "iron rice bowl" has been a hallmark of the reforms, though the number of workers who have lost their guaranteed jobs has been relatively small. In many large state-run industrial facilities, jobs are still guaranteed and layoffs and outright firings are few. Fear of massive layoffs and subsequent **social protests** that might ensue has prevented China from carrying out the complete privatization of industry, a process that will undoubtedly accelerate with China's 2001 accession into the **World Trade Organization (WTO)**.

"IT DOESN'T MATTER IF THE CAT IS BLACK OR WHITE, AS LONG AS IT CATCHES MICE" (*"BUGUAN HEIMAO BAIMAO, ZHUAZHU LAOSHU JIUSHI HAOMAO"*). This phrase was used by China's paramount leader **Deng Xiaoping** to justify the package of economic reforms initiated in 1978–1979. Emblematic of Deng's pragmatic approach to policy making, the phrase was first used by Deng in the early 1960s to inaugurate moderate reforms in the agricultural sector, an initiative immediately squashed by **Mao Zedong**. In its original form of an old folk saying from Deng's home province of Sichuan, the cat was "yellow," not "white," but the political meaning was obvious: leftist economic ideas did not work and thus should be replaced by more moderate policies that allowed for some role for the market and economic incentives. In the early 1960s, Deng first uttered the phrase—taken from his old military comrade, **Liu Bocheng**—in suggesting that a "household contract system" (*baochan daohu*) be adopted in the countryside to replace the ill-fated **people's communes** that were hastily set up during the **Great Leap Forward (1958–1960)**. "In deciding on the best production system," Deng asserted on 7 July 1962, "we might have to embrace the attitude of adopting whichever method develops agricultural production most easily and rapidly and whichever method the masses desire most." On hearing that the chairman of the **Chinese Communist Party (CCP)**, Mao Zedong, took the exact opposite view arguing that China's peasants opposed such a system and supported rural **socialism**, Deng quickly withdrew the suggestion, though he was still persecuted during the **Cultural Revolution (1966–1976)** for its utterance as evidence of his "capitalist" leanings. Not until after Mao's death in 1976, did Deng resuscitate the phrase and promote the pragmatic policies it encompassed.

– J –

JAPAN. Following the end of World War II in 1945 and the establishment of the **People's Republic of China (PRC)** in 1949, relations between China and Japan—political, economic, and cultural—were virtually nonexistent. Throughout China's imperial era (221 BC–1911 AD), China and Japan had an extensive economic interaction that provided the basis for a productive period of cultural exchange with Japan accumulating a wealth of knowledge from China as well as adopting the Chinese writing system, learning from China's advanced technical expertise, and emulating China's political institutions. The Japanese phrase *dobun doshu* ("same script, same race") acknowledged Japan's extensive cultural debt to China, though there were long periods when the two societies had little to no contact, for instance between the 10th and 14th centuries, and episodes of conflict over peripheral territories such as **Taiwan** and **Korea**. Japanese aggression against China beginning with the Marco Polo Bridge Incident in 1937 and culminating in the 1938 Nanjing Massacre carried out by Japanese troops against civilians and years of brutal occupation of the mainland, left an indelible stain on Chinese–Japanese ties that continue to this day with controversies over Japan's refusal to issue a written apology for the war and frequent visits by Japanese prime ministers and government officials to the Yakusuni Shrine where Class-A Japanese war criminals are interred among the war dead. Revelations about Japan's conscription of young Chinese **women** as prostitutes ("comfort women") for Japanese troops; whitewashing of Japanese aggression against China in Japanese textbooks approved by the Ministry of Education; and continued revelations concerning Japanese use of biological warfare experiments in China during the war and recent discoveries of Japanese wartime chemical ordinance continue as major irritants to China–Japan bilateral ties.

Japan's anti-Communist alliance with the **United States** in the immediate aftermath of China's Communist revolution left little room for China and Japan to restore their historically close relations though some **trade** did manage to take place from 1950 to the establishment of diplomatic relations in 1972. Following the end of the **Korean War (1950–1953)**, trade between China and Japan grew to US$150 million by 1956. In 1953 and 1956, despite their lack of formal ties, China and Japan called for an exchange of resident trade missions with provision of diplomatic privileges to trade representatives. But with the accession of the intensely anti-Communist Japanese Prime Minister Kishi Nobusuke in 1957, even these limited exchanges took a nose dive that did not recover until the1960s when Chinese Premier **Zhou Enlai** introduced the concept of "friendship trade" whereby trade would be carried out with "friendly companies" (i.e., pro-China firms) in Japan, a number that quickly expanded from 11 in 1960 to 190 by 1962 when the two countries signed the Liao–Takasaki Memorandum on Trade. With the invitation to China of a senior statesman from Japan's long-time ruling Liberal Democratic Party (LDP), Zhou and his Japanese counterpart worked out an agreement explicitly geared to eventual normalization of economic and diplomatic relations as China's demand for Japanese imports soared. While China–Japan relations suffered another temporary setback in 1964 with the election in Japan of the fiercely anti-China candidate Sato Eisaku as prime minister and the subsequent outbreak in China of the **Cultural Revolution (1966–1976)**, the 1972 visit to China by U.S. President Richard Nixon opened the door to full China–Japan normalization that was secured in September 1972 and was followed in 1978 by the Treaty of Peace and Friendship.

Immediately after the 1972 normalization and with the accession in Japan of the distinctively pro-China Prime Minister Tanaka Kakuei who visited China in 1972, the two countries set about solidifying their relationship especially involving trade matters. With the establishment of the Japan–China Economic Association, increases in private-level economic ties were enhanced as Japan removed all existing restrictions on Export–Import Bank financing for China as the first wholesale Japanese manufacturing plant was built in China in late 1972. Several agreements were also signed between the two countries on tariff reduction, civil aviation, maritime **transportation**, and fisheries. Between 1972 and 1975, bilateral trade tripled reaching a total of US$3.8 billion, with Japan exporting steel, machinery, chemicals, and synthetic fibers to China, which, in return, exported crude oil, foodstuffs, minerals, and other primary products to Japan. The world oil crisis in 1973 led Japan to become increasingly interested in the development of China's oil resources and, in 1978, on the heals of the second global oil crisis, China and Japan signed a Long-Term Trade Agreement covering the period from 1978 to 1985. In 1981, Japan promised US$1.3 billion in financial aid to China, including additional monies for completion of the **Baoshan Iron and Steel Complex** in **Shanghai**.

By 1993, China was Japan's second largest trading partner just behind the U.S. as China's exports to Japan gradually shifted from primary products to more **labor**-intensive products such as textiles and clothing. Throughout the 1990s, China became a major outlet for Japanese Foreign Direct Investment (FDI) totaling US$10 billion though with China's increased diversification of its export markets Japan's importance as a trading partner to China began to recede. Japan was the world's first country to provide bilateral aid to the PRC that, over the years, expanded to four major yen loan packages (including one immediately following the 1989 military crackdown against the second **Beijing Spring**). As the Chinese **economy** experienced robust growth, Japan gradually reduced and ultimately eliminated direct aid especially as China began to compete directly with Japanese producers and lure jobs from Japan to the Chinese mainland. In 2002, Japan poured US$4.2 billion into factories and other operations in China; such companies as Hitachi, Fuji Film, NEC, and Sharp drew not only on cheaper Chinese labor but the often-superior quality of Chinese engineers. Japan actively supported Chinese entry into the World Bank and the International Monetary Fund (IMF) and was a primary sponsor of China's 2001 entry into the **World Trade Organization (WTO)**. By 2003, bilateral trade between the two countries had grown to more than US$120 billion with Japan enjoying a sizable surplus that was responsible for much of the country's economic growth—even as China became the world's largest exporter to Japan. By 2005, China was Japan's largest trading partner, replacing the U.S. with Japanese exports to China in 2004 valued at US$74 billion and total Japanese **investment** in China reaching US$32 billion. More than one million Chinese work in Japanese factories and the PRC has become a major platform for production by some of Japan's largest companies, including Honda, Nissan, and Toyota, which have entered the Chinese **automobile** market, while even many of Japan's "old industries" of steel, chemicals, pulp, and construction have been given a new lease on life by China's insatiable demand for such products. The growing middle class in China has become a major source of demand for Japanese products, making the economies of the two countries increasingly complementary rather than competitive, with estimates indicating that, by 2050, the Japanese economy will be no larger than it is today while China will expand 30-fold and be six times the size of Japan. International competition for **energy** supplies will, however, continue to pit China and Japan against one another and intensify conflicts over access to oil and gas reserves along their disputed ocean boundary. Although both China and Japan have signed the **United Nations** (**UN**) Convention on the Law of the Sea, which allows coastal countries to set an economic zone 200 nautical miles from their shores, the two countries have not agreed on where their sea border lies; Japan sets the line of separation halfway between their shores, but China says the border is where the continental shelf ends, giving it a far larger zone.

Since the 1972 normalization, China–Japan relations have been strengthened by frequent mutual visits by top **leaders** of both countries and a variety of cultural and educational exchanges conducted under the terms of the 1979 Japan–China Cultural Exchange Agreement. In 1978, China and Japan formally ended their World War II hostilities by signing the Treaty of Peace and Friendship in **Beijing**. This was followed in 1982 by a visit to Japan of Chinese Premier **Zhao Ziyang**, who introduced China's "three principles" to govern bilateral relations: peace and friendship, equality and mutual benefit, and long-term stability. In 1984, a "fourth principle" of "mutual trust" was added by CCP leader **Hu Yaobang**, which led both sides to agree to establish the Twenty-First Century Committee to usher Sino–Japanese relations into the new millennium. Following the 1989 military crackdown on the second **Beijing Spring** in China, Japanese Prime Minister Toshiki Kaifu was the first leader from the Group of Seven leaders to visit the PRC in the aftermath of the violence—even as the two countries sparred over competing sovereignty claims on the Senkaku/Diaoyu islands. In 1992, the Japanese Emperor Akihito and Empress Michiko visited Beijing, where, at a welcoming ceremony, the emperor noted the "great sufferings that his country had inflicted on the people of China during the 1930s and 1940s," though subsequent statements in 1994 by a Japanese minister cast doubt on whether the 1938 Nanjing massacre had actually even occurred.

In a 1997 visit to Japan by Premier **Li Peng**, five principles for guiding the bilateral relationship were outlined including mutual respect and non-interference in each other's affairs, with China insisting to the Japanese that China could never accept any activity directly proposing or hinting at including Taiwan in the scope of Japan–U.S. security cooperation. Following the 1998 Japan–China Joint Declaration on Building a Partnership of Friendship and Cooperation for Peace and Development signed during a visit to Japan by President **Jiang Zemin**, China launched its "smile diplomacy" toward the Japanese, which, in 2000, led to an unprecedented six-day trip to Japan by Premier **Zhu Rongji**. And yet despite the mutual expression of good will produced by such policies and large-scale student and cultural exchanges, tensions in the bilateral relationship surfaced periodically over trade, historical, diplomatic, and other issues. Most serious was China's growing concern over Japan's increasingly close military ties to the U.S., including Japanese participation in research on a theater anti-missile system that the Chinese believe is aimed at China and Japanese support for continued American military assistance to Taiwan, which, in a direct challenge to China, was declared as part of Japan's "security zone" in 2004. Even as Japanese Prime Minister Junichiro Koizumi reiterated that Japan would never resort to war and would work for world peace, periodic visits to the Yakusuni Shrine by him and previous prime ministers and loose talk in some Japanese circles of abrogating Article IX of the Japanese constitution prohibiting the resort to force are constant irritants to the Chinese. At the same time, Chinese military modernization, including the testing of nuclear weapons in the mid-1990s, and development of new missile and cruise missile technologies and acquisition from **Russia** of Kilo-class submarines and Sukhoi jet fighters, are seen as a possible threat to Japan, which has openly referred to the "China threat" in internal government documents.

In November 2004, Japan's Maritime Self-Defense Forces went on alert when a nuclear-powered Chinese Navy submarine passed through Japanese territorial waters near Taiwan while Japan expressed concern over the marked increase in Chinese military spending. Another Japanese concern has been China's increasing territorial assertiveness vis-à-vis the Spratley (*Nansha*) Islands and recent clashes over the Senkaku/Diaoyu islands claimed by both China and Japan. Public opinion in both countries has fueled these clashes with more and more Japanese indicating that China cannot be trusted and Chinese opinion becoming increasingly anti-Japanese. In 1984, Chinese students marched in Beijing to oppose Japanese political and economic influence in China. From 1996 onward, frequent Chinese protests broke out over Japan's continued occupation of the Senkaku/Diaoyu islands that Japan has controlled since the end of the U.S. occupation following World War II, but which China claims as sovereign territory. Discoveries in 2003 in the northeast China city of Qiqihar of Japanese chemical weapons from World War II and demands for compensation by Chinese victims of Japanese air raids on the central Chinese city of **Chongqing** kept up the heat of public opinion leading some observers to characterize the bilateral relationship as "chilly politics, hot economics." Both Chinese and Japanese leaders and pundits stress the importance of continued cooperation and "good neighborly friendship" that are undoubtedly enhanced by the more than 150,000 Chinese students who attend Japanese universities. But contentious issues continue to arise, such as conflicts over the route of a proposed Russian oil pipeline out of Siberia and access to gas fields in the East China Sea and Chinese opposition to installing Japan as a permanent member of the UN Security Council. The two countries have acted in concert on a number of fronts including joint development of Asia's first standardized Linux Platform, launching of the Sino–Japan Industry Television Channel, joint action on ridding the East Asian region of pollutants, and mutual opposition by both countries to pleas by U.S. President George W. Bush in 2003 for China and Japan to allow their currencies to rise vis-à-vis the U.S. dollar. *See also* FOREIGN POLICY.

JIA QINQLIN (1935–). A graduate of the Shijiazhuang Industrial Management School in 1958, where he studied electric motor and appliance design, Jia Qinqlin, in 2005, headed the **United Front** Department of the **Chinese Communist Party (CCP)**. One of nine members of the Standing Committee of the CCP **Politburo**, Jia is considered the fourth most powerful leader in China behind President **Hu Jintao**, Premier **Wen Jiabao**, and internal security chief **Luo Gan**. During the 1960s, Jia worked for the First Ministry of Machine Building. During the **Cultural Revolution (1966–1976)**, he was sent to a **May Seventh Cadre School**. Jia spent a number of years in Fujian Province. From 1996 to 1999, he was a major figure in the **Beijing** CP, including the city's mayor from 1997–1999. After being promoted to the Politburo Standing Committee in 2002, Jia served as China's point man on dealing with the **Taiwan** issue and chairs the **Chinese People's Political Consultative Conference (CPPCC)**, a major United Front organization.

JIANG QING (1913–1991). The last wife of **Chinese Communist Party (CCP)** Chairman **Mao Zedong** and later the leading member of the so-called **Gang of Four**, Jiang Qing was born in Shandong Province under the name of Li Shumeng and was also known as Li Jin and Li Yunhe. In the 1930s, she was a film actress going by the name of Lan Ping in **Shanghai**, where she also joined the CCP underground. After divorcing her first husband (who, in later years, opened a Chinese restaurant in Paris), Jiang Qing traveled in 1938 to Yan'an, where she was introduced by **Kang Sheng** to Mao. Despite the reservations of the CCP Central Committee, Jiang Qing and Mao were married after the chairman secured a divorce from his second wife (who subsequently went insane). Although Mao initially promised his Party colleagues that Jiang Qing would stay out of politics even as she did work in the Ministry of Culture, Jiang became active in 1965 when **Yao Wenyuan** (a later cohort in the "Gang") directed his acid pen at the drama *Hai Rui Dismissed from Office* written by **Beijing** Vice-Mayor **Wu Han**. Yao suggested the play was a veiled attack on Mao's leadership style during the ill-fated **Great Leap Forward (1958–1960)**. During the **Cultural Revolution (1966–1976)**, Jiang Qing became the patron of the so-called "eight model plays," which were the only operas and ballets allowed to be performed. Later, she assumed a prominent role in the **Cultural Revolution Small Group** led by **Chen Boda**. In 1967–1968, she egged on **Red Guards** to launch vicious assaults on the Party and army.

With the purge of Chen Boda and the demise of **Lin Biao** in 1970–1971, Jiang's influence waned as she focused increasingly on **foreign policy**. After an alleged attempt to seize power, Jiang Qing was arrested in October 1976, along with the other members of the Gang of Four—**Zhang Chunqiao**, **Yao Wenyuan**, and **Wang Hongwen**—in the so-called October 1976 coup. Propaganda onslaughts against Jiang Qing throughout the 1980s were filled with enormous personal invective, with sly suggestions that she had used her well-honed sexual prowess to seduce Chairman Mao Zedong and subvert his revolutionary fervor. In November 1980–January 1981, Jiang Qing was put on trial along with other members of the Gang of Four and defended her actions by saying "I was Mao's mad dog. Whoever he asked me to bite, I bit." Sentenced to death (with a two-year reprieve) by a Chinese court for her role in causing the death and destruction that occurred during the Cultural Revolution and for supposedly plotting to assassinate Mao Zedong, in 1991, she committed suicide while still in prison. *See also* CINEMA AND FILM; LITERATURE AND THE ARTS.

JIANG ZEMIN (1926–). In 1989, Jiang Zemin was appointed by **Deng Xiaoping** as concurrently general secretary of the **Chinese Communist Party (CCP)**, **president of the People's Republic of China** and chairman of the Central **Military Affairs Commission (MAC)** of the CCP. Jiang served in the first two posts from 1989 to 2002 and from 1993 to 2003, respectively, and in the third from 1990 to 2004, when he retired at the age of 78, marking the first time a Chinese leader of the PRC voluntarily gave up official leadership positions. Jiang and other top **leaders** initially appointed by Deng were described as the "third generation" of leaders following **Hu Yaobang** and **Zhao Ziyang**—the "second generation"—who were unceremoniously purged before and after the second **Beijing Spring** in 1989.

Jiang Zemin is originally from an intellectual family in Yangzhou, Jiangsu Province, and joined the CCP in 1946, three years after his father, Jiang Shangqing, was killed during the **Sino–Japanese War (1937–1945)**. In 1947, Jiang earned a degree in electrical engineering from Communications (*Jiaotong*) University in **Shanghai** and, following the CCP takeover of China in 1949, he worked as an engineer in Shanghai factories and, in 1955, was sent to the **Soviet Union**, where he trained in the **Stalin** Automobile Factory in Moscow. In the late 1950s and 1960s, he was director of a number of industrial plants in Changsha (Hunan Province), Wuhan (Hubei Province), and in Shanghai. In 1971, he entered the central government in the First Ministry of Machine Building. In the 1980s, he served successively as vice-chairman of the State Commission for the Administration of Import and Export Affairs and the State Commission for the Administration of Foreign **Investment** and then vice-minister and minister of the Ministry of the Electronics Industry. In 1985, he became mayor of Shanghai and, in 1987, at the 13th National Party Congress, he became a member of the CCP **Politburo**. During the June 1989 student demonstrations in Shanghai, he averted violence, mollifying students by reading from Abraham Lincoln's Gettysburg address. Jiang was also instrumental in purging the editors of the Shanghai-based newspaper, *World Economic Herald*, which had been a beacon of liberal thought and opinion.

During Jiang Zemin's 13 years of leadership of the CCP, most of which he shared with Premier **Li Peng**, China experienced the fastest economic growth in its modern history. Jiang also navigated international diplomatic waters following the collapse of the Soviet Union. He added to the CCP's basic doctrine of **Marxism–Leninism–Mao Zedong Thought** and Deng Xiaoping Theory with his concept of the "three represents" (*sange daibiao*), which maintains that the ruling Communist Party should represent not just workers and farmers but all advanced production and cultural forces, and the "overwhelming majority of Chinese people." Contrary to Mao's emphasis on **class struggle** that divided the Chinese **population** into mutually hostile camps and targeted people of "bad" class background for perpetual political persecution, Jiang's theory sought to accommodate the emergence of an entrepreneurial capitalist class in China and promoted a politics of consensus-building not struggle. Jiang's theory of the "three represents" was enshrined in the CCP and state constitutions following his retirement. After retiring from Party and government posts in 2002, Jiang stayed on as chairman of both the Party and State Central Military Affairs Commissions from where he continued to influence military policy, such as the 2003 reduction in **People's**

Liberation Army (PLA) troop strength to 2.3 million. Even after giving up the Party and state MAC posts in 2004 and early 2005, respectively, Jiang Zemin is said to retain considerable influence on Chinese politics despite his retirement through a number of close political associates such as Vice-President **Zeng Qinglong**. Jiang has a good command of the English, Russian, and Romanian languages and is known for his love of both classical Chinese and Western music, especially Beethoven. Jiang is married to Wang Yeping and has two sons, one grandson, and one granddaughter. *See also* LEADERS.

– K –

KANG SHENG (1899–1975). Born into a family of well-off landlords, Kang Sheng was one of the most important **Chinese Communist Party (CCP)** early **leaders** involved in intelligence and security and liaison with foreign Communist parties. In the 1930s, he was an underground Party operative in **Shanghai**, where he established early links with the underground leader Li Kenong. He then went to Moscow to study Soviet security techniques and was CCP representative to the Comintern. Returning to Yan'an in 1937 with the pro-Soviet Wang Ming, Kang Sheng was reinstated as a **Politburo** member and headed the growing security apparatus, including the CCP Social Affairs Department or secret police, and was also a top official at the **Central Party School**. During the early 1940s, Kang promoted the notorious "rescue campaign" that aimed at ferreting out alleged **Kuomintang (KMT)** spies and "Trotskyites" in the CCP but which ended up purging and executing many innocent **intellectuals**, including **Wang Shiwei**, who, in 1947, was killed, apparently on Kang's order. In the late 1950s, Kang was involved with **Deng Xiaoping** in the growing dispute with the **Soviet Union** over ideological and other issues and, at the same time, strongly defended Mao's policies in the **Great Leap Forward (1958–1960)**.

Kang's political star rose considerably in 1962 with the purge of Marshal **Peng Dehuai**, when Kang was appointed to the Party Secretariat headed by Deng. During the **Cultural Revolution (1966–1976)** Kang served as a critical adviser to the radical faction of **Jiang Qing** and became a member of the Politburo Standing Committee. Kang collected art, and after his death in 1975 Kang's home in **Beijing** was converted to a hotel.

KHRUSHCHEV, NIKITA. *See* SOVIET UNION.

KOREA (NORTH AND SOUTH). Beginning with the military intervention by China in the **Korean War** in 1950, the relationship between the **People's Republic of China** (**PRC**) and the Democratic People's Republic of Korea (DPRK) was described over several decades as being as close as "lips and teeth." Without China's intervention, the North Korean regime, with its capital in Pyongyang, would have ceased to exist; thus, it was no surprise that, under the leadership of Kim Il-sung (1945–1994)—the "great leader"—followed by his son Kim Jong-il (1994 to present)—the "dear leader"— North Korea paid homage to China with monuments and shrines constructed throughout the country honoring the Chinese People's Volunteers for their central role in preserving the DPRK during the Korean War and, following the 1953 armistice, when China vied with the **Soviet Union** for North Korean support by providing the DPRK with military, economic, and political assistance. In 1961, China and the DPRK signed the Sino–Korean Treaty of Friendship, Cooperation, and Mutual Assistance, cementing their close political, economic, and military relationship.

Following the collapse of the Soviet Union in 1991, China's relations with the DPRK underwent substantial alteration as growing China–South Korean economic and political ties (solidified by the rapprochement between China and South Korea beginning in 1990) combined with a long economic depression in the DPRK and concomitant increases in Chinese aid to Pyongyang, positioned China as the country with the greatest influence over Pyongyang. From 1994 to 2000, however, relations between the two countries were virtually frozen until Kim Jong-il visited China in May 2000, just prior to his meeting with South Korea President Kim Dae-jung. In 1983, during a visit to **Shanghai**, Kim Jong-il denounced China's free-market policies as "**revisionism**," but during his 2000 and 2001 return visits, Kim reversed himself, praising the "earth-shaking" policies adopted by the **Chinese Communist Party** (**CCP**), which led North Korea in 2001 to hold a congress of the ruling North Korean Workers' Party that officially launched a "reform and opening" agenda that allowed **investment** from the South by such big companies as Daewoo and Hyundai. North Korea also promoted development in its Rajin-Song-bong Economic Zone on the banks of the Tumen River that has sought to lure Chinese and South Korean investment, which the Chinese see as a wedge to encourage its North Korean counterparts to follow the path of economic reform pursued by **Deng Xiaoping** since 1978–1979 that will undoubtedly benefit the development of China's northeastern provinces of Jilin and Liaoning bordering the DPRK. The establishment of a similar economic zone in Sinuiju was short-circuited when the North appointed a Chinese businessman, Yang Bin, as the director of the proposed zone, a man suspected of tax evasion in China, whom the Chinese subsequently arrested in 2004, putting an end to the zone's development.

With North Korean industry in a state of virtual collapse and with successive waves of natural disasters, which have devastated its agricultural production, China has been instrumental in propping up the **economy** of the DPRK, providing it with essential fuel and food aid, without which the DPRK could not survive. But while China provides 70% of the North's oil and 30% of its food aid, China has become increasingly intolerant of attempts by suffering North Korean refugees to cross the border into the PRC in search of food and work, especially into the Yanbian Korean Autonomous Prefecture that borders North Korea and whose population is 40% Korean. International **human rights** organizations estimate that by 2002, more than 300,000 North Koreans made it into China before tougher measures were taken along the border to stem the flow, including repatriation of refugees to the DPRK, where they face uncertain futures. In 2002, a number of North Korean refugees in **Beijing** sought asylum in the diplomatic compound of South Korea (including Hwang Chang-yop, secretary of the Korean Workers' Party who sought political asylum in the South Korean embassy in Beijing in 1997), which produced a confrontation between Chinese police and South Korean diplomatic personnel on embassy grounds, a clear violation of the Vienna Convention. Although China "expressed regret" over the incident and allowed the refugees transit to the South, diplomatic compounds in Beijing and other major Chinese cities have been cordoned off with barbed wire and other barriers to prevent a recurrence.

With the admission by the DPRK in 2002 that it was actively pursuing a nuclear weapons program to counteract the "hostile" actions of the **United States**, China emerged as a major mediator in attempting to defuse the issue while protecting North Korea's security concerns. Along with special envoys dispatched by China to talk directly with Kim Jong-il on the nuclear issue, Beijing was the site in 2003, 2004, and 2005 for six- and three-party talks (respectively, North and South Korea, the U.S., **Russia**, China, and **Japan**; and North Korea, the U.S. and China) that aimed at defusing the nuclear crisis that China fears could spur Japan and South Korea to develop their own nuclear capacities and destabilize Northeast Asia. Despite North Korea's decision in 2003 to withdraw from the Nuclear Nonproliferation Treaty (NPT), China blocked efforts at the **United Nations (UN)** Security Council to censure the North—even as top **leaders** of the PRC, including President **Hu Jintao**, distanced themselves from North Korea's militant rhetoric and pressured the North to reenter the NPT. The position of China is that it favors a non-nuclear Korean peninsula while emphasizing it wants "peace and stability" on its northeastern border. China also wants to "ease tension" while it supports the "sunshine" policy of South Korea, which aims to bring the North "out of its isolation" and conclude a peace treaty with the South. While rumors abounded in 2003 that China was actually planning a quick military intervention in North Korea, China refused to endorse the decision of the U.S. and its allies to intercept North Korean ships and aircraft in international waters to check on possible nuclear and missile proliferation efforts by the Pyongyang regime, especially to Pakistan.

While Beijing is undoubtedly agitated by the often obstreperous behavior of North Korea, which has led China to a buildup of regular army troops along its border with the DPRK, any potential collapse of the North Korean regime is viewed with enormous disfavor in Beijing because it might draw U.S. military forces and their South Korean ally right up to the borders of the PRC. Chinese officials have also repeatedly cast doubts on American intelligence estimates that North Korea has several workable nuclear devices and has urged the U.S. to offer "flexibility" to North Korea while China claims its influence over North Korea is limited. China is more worried that the reclusive North Korean regime might suddenly collapse and so it is better to maintain

the status quo than bring China's biggest potential enemy–the U.S.–
to its doorstep. If China reaches a conclusion that North Korea's real
intention is nuclear possession, however, it may take a hard-line
course such as suspending or even cutting off fuel and food assistance.
Tensions between the two Communist allies of several decades also
broke out in 2004 over Chinese claims that the ancient Koguryo
(*Goguryeo*) Kingdom, which once ruled part of northeastern China
along with the entire Korean Peninsula (and which Koreans believe is
the precursor of modern Korea), was, in fact, part of Chinese history.
Such a redefinition of history would, North Korean officials asserted,
allow China to lay claim to much of North Korean territory in the
event of a potential collapse of the DPRK. Such spats did not, however, prevent China from coming to the assistance of North Koreans
injured in 2004 by a massive blast at the Ryongchon rail station along
the PRC–DPRK border and by China's Southern Airlines launch of
direct flights from Shenyang to Pyongyang in 2004, supplementing its
existing Beijing–Pyongyang route.

From the end of the Korean War in 1953 to the early 1990s, China
and the Republic of South Korea (ROK) were barely on speaking
terms, especially during the period from 1960 to 1988 when South
Korea was ruled by right-wing military dictatorships. The momentous
political shift in China–South Korean relations followed the transition
to a democratic government in the ROK in 1988 and was given further impetus in 1990 when **trade** offices were established in Beijing
and Seoul, which led to an immediate expansion in trade from near
zero to US$3 billion by 1992 when the PRC and the ROK formally es-
tablished diplomatic relations. Since normalization, Sino–South Korean economic relations have quickened, with bilateral trade reaching
US$20 billion in 1996 and US$44 billion in 2003, with projections of
a US$100 billion annual trade by 2008. Machinery, electronic, audio,
and video products and chemicals constitute South Korea's major exports to China. The latter's exports to Seoul consist of fabrics, gar-
ments, machinery, and electrical products. South Korean investors
poured money into China, making the ROK the largest single source
of Foreign Direct Investment (FDI) in China in 2004 with US$6.25
billion, surpassing both **Hong Kong** and Japan, as major Korean companies, such as Samsung, employed thousands of Chinese workers in
30 factories. Much of this was concentrated in China's northeastern

provinces of Liaoning, Shandong, and Jilin—especially in the Yanbian Korean Autonomous Prefecture, which is also a major destination for South Korean tourists into China.

With the spurt in trade and political relations, South Koreans make up the largest **population** of foreigners in China, many of them students of the Chinese language, which surpassed English as the language of choice for many college-age South Koreans. Qingdao, Shandong Province in China is just a commuter flight across the Yellow Sea from Seoul and has become a "little Korea" where about 4,000 Korean companies of all sizes have set up shop. Korean companies have moved research and development units into China with considerable emphasis on promoting the two countries' information **technology** industries, especially involving Code Division Multiple Access (CDMA), in which South Korea has been a world leader since introducing commercial CDMA mobile telecommunications service in 1996. Economic ties in the more traditional heavy industrial sector have grown as South Korean steel exports to China grew rapidly and mainstream Korean companies such as Posco Steel made major investments in China's steel sector. Korean shipbuilders received a doubling of orders from China in 2004 to 470 ships, both containers and tankers, while the carmaker Hyundai announced plans to manufacture a million cars in China by 2007. Like Japan and **Taiwan**, South Korean companies have adopted an economic strategy of manufacturing only the most sophisticated components at home and then shipping them to China where less complicated parts are purchased locally at low cost and the final product assembled. **Transportation** links between the two countries have also accelerated with the rapid expansion of air traffic involving the increased flights by South Korean airlines and an alliance between Korean Air and China's Southern Airlines.

China–ROK political relations were strengthened by the 1992 normalization with major visits by their respective political leaders. Beginning with a 1992 visit to Beijing by ROK President Roh Tae-woo, the first visit to China by a South Korean president, a1994 five-day visit to Seoul by Premier **Li Peng** was followed by an unprecedented week-long visit by President **Jiang Zemin** in 1995, and a return trip to Beijing by South Korean President Roh Moo-hyun in 2003. In addition to the ongoing negotiation over North Korea's nuclear program, enhanced political ties have allowed the two countries to resolve their differences in only two weeks' time over the North Korean refugee problem and to address on a periodic basis such environmental issues as the threat to the Korean peninsula from increasingly severe waves of "yellow dust" originating in China's desert regions. Confidence building measures (CBMS) between the two countries' militaries have also been pursued including port calls for each other's naval ships and exchanges of military officers. China and South Korea jointly condemned the periodic visits by Japanese prime ministers to the controversial Yasukuni Shrine honoring Japanese war dead while the PRC and the ROK signed an extradition agreement for individuals apprehended for drug and human trafficking and, in 1993, agreed to cooperate in the development of nuclear power plants in China. South Korea acquiesced to China's demands not to allow visits to the ROK by the **Dalai Lama** and officials from Taiwan. Following the passage in the South Korean legislature of an Overseas Compatriots Law in 2001 that granted citizenship to "all Korean nationals by blood," China began an ideological education program targeted at Koreans in the Yanbian Autonomous Prefecture emphasizing to the Korean minority that "their motherland is China." *See also* FOREIGN POLICY; MINORITIES.

KOREAN WAR (1950–1953). The North Korean invasion of South **Korea** in June 1950 resulted from a decision by North Korean leader Kim Il-sung, in consultation with **Josef Stalin** and **Mao Zedong**, to invade the South. At this time, Mao was determined to promote Communist revolutions in Asia and apparently was spoiling for a fight with the **United States**. After the collapse of North Korean forces in late 1950, following the **United Nations** (UN) counterattack at Inchon, Mao, despite some hesitation and divisions among the top leadership, decided to send Chinese troops, dubbed "Chinese People's Volunteers," to rescue the North Korean regime and blunt UN attacks by forces under U.S. General Douglas MacArthur that had crossed the 38th parallel in the middle of the Korean peninsula and had approached China's border at the Yalu River.

China's involvement in the war stretched from October 1950 to the signing of an armistice in July 1953 that brought the fighting to an end. Chinese troops in Korea were commanded by General **Peng Dehuai**, the only top military commander in the Chinese army to serve in Korea. Mao's decision to enter the war was also made over considerable resistance from within the ruling **Politburo** and after Stalin had offered and then withdrawn promises of air support against UN forces. Chinese forces consisted of thousands of former **Kuomintang (KMT)** troops who had gone over to the **Chinese Communist Party (CCP)** during the **Civil War (1946–1949)** and were now sacrificed as cannon fodder in the infamous Chinese human wave assaults against UN forces. China's total losses in the war exceeded one million men, although China put its losses at a much-lower figure of around 336,000. The Korean conflict evidently stimulated the Chinese industrial and agricultural **economy** in the northeast. China agreed to the armistice after the U.S., under President Dwight Eisenhower, threatened the possible use of nuclear weapons. Thousands of Chinese prisoners were allowed to go to **Taiwan** and abroad after the signing of the armistice. Mao Zedong's eldest son, Mao Anying, was killed in a U.S. air raid during the war, and the Korean conflict provoked the U.S. to reverse its previous stand and provide military protection for the Nationalist regime on Taiwan against any prospective Chinese invasion.

KUOMINTANG (NATIONALIST PARTY) (KMT). Established in 1912, the KMT was the ruling party of the Republic of China (ROC) on mainland China from 1928 to its defeat by the Chinese Communists in the **Civil War (1946–1949)**. After fleeing to **Taiwan** (formerly known as Formosa), the KMT continued to exist as the dominant party in the ROC, located on the island some 100 km off the southeastern coast of China, where it carried out the transition from one-party dictatorship to a constitutional democracy. *Kuomintang* is the Wade-Giles Romanization, which is still used on Taiwan, for the Nationalist Party. In *pinyin*, which is used by the **People's Republic of China (PRC)**, the word is spelled *Guomindang*.

The KMT traces its origins to the anti-imperialist and anti-warlord struggle in early 20th century China. The party was established by Song Jiaoren out of a fledgling political organization known as the *Tongmeng hui* and several other smaller political parties. It was quickly outlawed, however, in the context of the struggle between Sun Yat-sen (China's first president) and the warlord Yuan Shih-k'ai to control the newly created Chinese Republic that was set up after the collapse of the Qing dynasty (1644–1911), China's last. In 1919, following his establishment of a rival government in the southern city of **Guangzhou** (**Canton**), Sun Yat-sen reorganized his secretive Chinese Revolutionary Party into a revitalized KMT to challenge the warlord-run government in China's north. Organizationally weak and lacking a financial base or substantial military support, the KMT was heavily dependent on local southern warlords for its survival.

After failing to obtain Western support, Sun looked to the new leaders of Soviet **Russia** for aid and, in 1924, announced the formation of a **United Front** with the newly created **Chinese Communist Party** (**CCP**), which had been formed in 1921 with substantial aid from the Communist International (Comintern). At this point, the KMT was reorganized along Leninist lines and, like the CCP, adopted the principles of **democratic-centralism** and began to build an army along Soviet lines. Sun Yat-sen became the "supreme leader" (*zongli*) and generalissimo of the KMT and introduced the Three Principles of the People—nationalism, people's rights, and people's livelihood—as the party's reigning ideology.

Following Sun's sudden death from illness in 1925, party leadership shifted to a young military leader named Chiang Kai-shek. Although trained in the **Soviet Union** and once referred to as the "red general," Chiang quickly imposed a more conservative ideology on the KMT and, in April 1927, carried out a systematic purge of his Communist allies, bringing an end to the First United Front that had been formally established in 1924. After successfully leading a military expedition against the warlord government in the north (known as the Northern Expedition), in 1928, Chiang established a new regime in the southern city of Nanking (Nanjing) on 10 October (celebrated to this day as National Day in the ROC and referred to as "double ten"). Despite persistent factionalism in the party, Chiang consolidated his rule by basing his power squarely on the growing military forces of the KMT and on the semifascist party organization known as the Blue Shirts. Although formal power in the KMT lay with the Central Executive Committee and the KMT Congress, in reality, Chiang exercised absolutist rule as the party's "exalted leader" (*zongcai*), a post that Chiang assumed in 1938. Throughout the 1930s and despite increasing incursions into China by the Japanese, Chiang was obsessed with destroying his Communist rivals who were held up in Jiangxi Province and then in Yan'an following the **Long March** (**1934–1935**).

But in 1936, Chiang was captured by a rival warlord and forced to join with the Communists in a Second United Front to oppose the Japanese. This fragile alliance continued with the Communists throughout the **Sino–Japanese War** (**1937–1945**), only to quickly collapse as the civil war broke out in 1946 and the KMT ultimately lost to the Communists. Although the KMT had won the support of certain elements of the Chinese **population** in the 1930s and 1940s, its increasing **corruption**, political repression of students and of **intellectuals**, and profound lack of concern for the fate of the Chinese peasantry ultimately robbed it of the necessary political support to win against the Communists. KMT policies of "one party, one leader" proved an inviting target for the Communists who, invoking the call by **Mao Zedong** in 1940 for a **New Democracy**, successfully mobilized student protests in the cities against the KMT, while winning over peasant support in the countryside with its promises of **land reform**. Defeated on the Chinese mainland, the KMT under Chiang Kai-shek fled to Taiwan and established the ROC on the island while claiming overall authority for the entire Chinese mainland.

The early years of KMT rule on Taiwan were marked by political repression of the indigenous population and increased reliance on the **United States**. In 1947, the local KMT commander in Taiwan sanctioned a wholesale massacre of native Taiwanese that effectively deprived the local population of political leadership. Following the North Korean invasion of South **Korea** in 1950, the U.S., which had originally not intended to defend the ROC on Taiwan from a possible invasion by the newly established Communist regime in **Beijing**, came to Taiwan's defense and, in effect, insulated the island from external threat through the signing of a mutual defense treaty in 1954.

Economically, Taiwan had been severely underdeveloped despite Japanese colonization since 1895. But beginning in the mid-1950s, the KMT promoted policies that dramatically transformed Taiwan into a prosperous, middle-class society. Land reform, which the KMT had abjured on the mainland, was carried out (often with considerable brutality against indigenous landlords), along with an export–oriented economic strategy that stressed foreign investment, open markets, and less state intervention in the **economy**. By the 1960s and 1970s, Taiwan emerged as a major exporter of both cash crops and industrial products, including textiles, electronic goods, and computers. Politically, however, Taiwan remained under the iron grip of one-party rule led by the aging Chiang Kai-shek. Elections that had taken place on the Chinese mainland in 1948 remained the basis for "representation" in the ROC Legislative Yuan (the nominal parliament), while real power lay with Chiang and his military supporters. Despite periodic student protests, the regime remained stable with a politically quiescent population.

In 1975, Chiang Kai-shek died and was replaced by his son Chiang Ching-kuo. Although during his youth in the Soviet Union, the young Chiang had flirted with Trotskyism, he later served his father well as head of military and internal security matters. Yet, as president, Chiang Ching-kuo emerged as a moderate reformer, allowing for a more open press and increasing democratization at the local level while nationally martial law (in effect since 1949) was formally lifted. Following Chiang Ching-kuo's death in 1988, the ROC was taken over by native Taiwanese President Lee Teng-hui, who went even further in allowing the emergence of opposition political parties and providing for elections to the parliament, local offices, and the prime minister. In 2000, the KMT lost its first election on Taiwan to a candidate from the opposition and pro-independence Democratic People's Party.

On the mainland, the splinter and pro-PRC Revolutionary Committee of the Kuomintang remains one of the many **democratic parties** in China with membership on the **Chinese People's Political Consultative Conference (CPPCC)**, where it provides consultation on cross-straits relations between China and Taiwan. *See also* TAIWAN STRAITS CRISES (1954 AND 1958).

– L –

LABOR. China's total urban and rural labor force in 2003 numbered 744 million, of which the urban-employed **population** was 256.4 million people (34.4%) and the rural-employed population was 487.9 million people (65.6%). Between 1990 and 2003, the employed population in China grew by 97 million, an average increase of 7.45 million per year with workers in the rural areas dropping from 73.7 to 65.6% and in urban areas growing from 26.3 to 34.4%. The female population employed in both urban and rural areas grew from 291 million in 1990 to 337 million in 2003, of which 42 million worked in the urban labor force, making up 38% of the total. In terms of employment structure, from 1990 to 2003 the proportion of those employed in primary industries dropped from 60.1 to 49.1%, those in the service sector (21.6%) remained about the same, and the proportion of those in tertiary industries rose from 18.5 to 29.3%. Over the same period, workers in **state-owned enterprises (SOEs)** decreased by 34.7 million from 103 to 68.76 million while the number employed by individual and private economic entities grew from 36 million to 42.7 million, which constituted 47% of the new jobs in the urban areas. New forms of employment included jobs in foreign-owned firms and factories, part-time jobs, temporary and seasonal jobs, and work on an hourly basis along with jobs with flexible working hours. More than 98 million rural laborers took up jobs outside their townships, a six-fold increase over the figure in 1990 as five million farmers left their homes annually in search of work elsewhere. **Township-village enterprises (TVEs)** located largely in the rural areas provided employment for 136 million laborers in 2003, or 27.8% of the rural work force. Eight million people were officially unemployed in China in 2003, approximately 4.3% of the workforce, although disguised unemployment, especially in bankrupt SOEs, remained very high because "laid-off" or "retired" (*xiagang*) state workers are not included in unemployment statistics.

Currently, 9 to 10 million new workers enter the Chinese urban labor force annually, making young people's potential unemployment an increasingly difficult problem as the **economy** generates about 10 million new jobs a year. Estimates are that China needs more than 24 million new jobs to absorb the 10 million new workers along with 6 million laid off from SOEs, 8 million officially unemployed, and tens of millions of un- or underemployed farmers in search of work in the cities as part of the country's growing **floating population**. The long-term effect of China's 2001 entry into the **World Trade Organization (WTO)** is likely to exacerbate unemployment figures, especially among farmers confronting cheap grain imports from abroad. On the other hand, the equally long-term effects of China's **one-child policy**, which has made the country one of the most rapidly aging populations in the world, has produced spot labor shortages in some of the coastal regions, where low wages and poor working conditions have dried up the once-unlimited supply of young workers—especially females who are coveted over males because of their reputation for better assembly work and greater docility. China's labor force is predicted to grow to 842 million by 2015 and then drop to 813 million by 2030.

China's policy toward unemployment—a recent phenomenon in a country where, for decades, the **iron rice bowl** (*tiefanwan*) guaranteed lifelong employment—is based on the principle of "workers finding their own jobs, employment through market regulation and employment promoted by the government." Public job agencies in more than 80 cities have been created to assist laborers of various types and have helped 10 million people find employment while other programs have been inaugurated to strengthen skill training for reemployment especially of workers laid off by SOEs. More than 18 million workers who were laid off from SOEs found jobs from 1998 to 2003, though for workers in their late 40s and early 50s, the prospects of reemployment are exceedingly slim. In 1999, China revamped its unemployment insurance program that was begun in the mid-1980s so that, by 2003, more than a 100 million workers throughout the country had underwritten unemployment insurance policies and 4.15 million people in that year received some form of unemployment payments. This is all part of China's "three guarantees" system promulgated in 1998, which, in addition to unemployment insurance, guarantees basic subsistence allowances for upward of three years for laid-off workers of SOEs, as well as minimum subsistence allowance for urban residents.

In 1994, China passed a Labor Law that instituted legal minimum wages and regulations governing work hours that, in 1995, were limited to a 40-hour, five-day work week in most urban areas, stipulations that are frequently violated by employers of workers producing low value-added products, such as textiles and toys slated for export; these workers' wages fall far below the minimum with no additions for overtime, and they are often required to work seven, 12-hour working days a week. Labor relations in most industries in China are governed by collective contracts covering salaries and wages and a consultation mechanism for dealing with labor disputes involving **trade unions**, the enterprise, and government authorities. Arbitration and litigation systems have also been established and are governed by the Labor Law, which also outlaws discrimination in the workplace and sets standards for rest and vacations as well as occupational safety and worker health that are often simply ignored by employers. As a result of the system of population registration (*hukou*), China still lacks a true national labor market that would allow prospective employees to search for work anywhere in the country without regard to residential restriction.

Despite calls by President **Jiang Zemin**, in 1998, for a guarantee of a minimal living standard and job creation for laid-off workers from SOEs, labor unrest, previously unknown in China prior to the 1978–1979 economic reforms, has undergone a big surge, especially since 1999 when 120,000 separate incidents were reported. Strikes, **social protests**, and outright confrontations between laid-off workers and local police and military authorities have been especially prevalent in the country's northeastern rust belt, where the effective jobless rate is upward of 20% and where cases of corrupt Party and enterprise officials absconding with enterprise funds while workers go hungry have been rife. As old industries, such as outmoded mines and textile plants close their doors, a generation of workers who were raised under the Communist ideology to believe they were the "masters" of the country now feels at the mercy of bankrupt companies and cash-poor municipalities. Under a system of factory buyouts introduced in 2001, workers laid off by enterprises receive a lump-sum calculated according to the number of years worked, which often turns out to be a paltry figure that leaves laborers in near subsistent condition. One of the most violent protests occurred in 2000, when tens of thousands of workers from China's largest nonferrous metals mine in Liaoning Province erupted in violent protest over what they perceived as the unfair and corrupt handling of the mine's bankruptcy and which required the introduction of troops to suppress the rioting. Unpaid compensation and benefits, including pensions, alleged **corruption** among Party and government officials involved in selling off state assets, and unsafe and abusive working conditions in domestic and foreign-owned plants, have all contributed to growing working-class discontent that has often taken a political track with labor activists submitting petitions of complaint to local, provincial, and even national leaders. Lawsuits in local courts have also been filed while some labor activists have attempted to establish opposition political parties to represent the interests of ordinary, manual workers.

The response by authorities to cases of social turmoil has been multifaceted, with harsh crackdowns against any attempt to turn labor unrest into a political movement by arresting and imprisoning labor leaders and banning news reports balanced by conciliatory gestures toward the majority of workers. In 2001, China ratified the **United Nations** (**UN**) International Covenant on Economic, Social, and Cultural Rights but with reservations on a key part of the document that upholds the right to establish free trade unions that are prohibited under Chinese law as all workers seeking to organize must affiliate with the state-controlled All-China Federation of Trade Unions. China is a member of the International Labour Organization (ILO) but has failed to ratify its core conventions on Freedom of Association and Protection of the Right to Organize and Collective Bargaining. In 2004, China welcomed the decision of the **United States** government not to investigate Chinese labor practices for having artificially reduced wages and production costs at the expense of American producers. International groups, such as Human Rights Watch and China Labor Watch, conduct independent investigations of labor practices in China, focusing on accusations of low pay, excessive work hours that violate China's own Labor Law, sexual harassment of female employees, and inadequate safety and health conditions in domestic and foreign-owned plants and especially among the country's large number of unsafe coal mines, where overtime work is needed to fulfill the country's voracious appetite for **energy**. In 2000, China's State Administration of Work Safety reported the deaths of 109,000 people from work-related accidents; that figure rose to 140,000 in 2002. In the wake of these statistics and other high-profile cases, including toxic poisoning from untreated chemical and industrial waste, China's State Council announced a plan in early 2004 to promote industrial safety—a month after a gas explosion near the city of **Chongqing** killed 243 people and forced the evacuation of more than 60,000 nearby residents.

China's management of labor, especially in export-oriented factories in the coastal regions, is very similar to the Japanese model of relying on company uniforms, early morning exercises, and even periodic training by the **People's Liberation Army (PLA)** to instill loyalty and disciplined work practices. With average salaries in the booming east coast cities for factory workers between US$120 and US$160 per month, Chinese producers have relied on an army of highly skilled laborers, especially young **women**, rather than expensive **technology** and machinery such as robots in industries from **automobiles** to metal casting. *See also* INDUSTRY.

"LABOR UNDER SURVEILLANCE" (*"GUANZHI LAODONG"*). After completing prison sentences or other forms of incarceration, individuals in China are subject to long-term "surveillance" by the local **Public Security Bureau** or the ubiquitous residence committees. This practice was first applied to so-called landlords, rich peasants, counterrevolutionaries, and "rightists" who managed to survive the campaigns of terror of the early 1950s. "Labor under surveillance" often lasted for years, especially for people such as landlords and rich peasants, who experienced this local oversight throughout their lives. Manual labor was considered essential for people to "reform" themselves, that is, to develop loyalty to the **Chinese Communist Party (CCP)**. *See also* "REFORM THROUGH LABOR."

LAND REFORM (1950–1952). "Land to the tiller" was a central plank in the **Chinese Communist Party (CCP)** program formulated by **Mao Zedong** in his 1940 speech entitled **"New Democracy."** After the CCP's seizure of national power in 1949, land reform was carried out over a period of three years under the guise of the 1950 Agrarian Reform Law. This redistribution of land continued the policies pursued by the CCP beginning in the 1930s during the period of the Jiangxi Soviet, when the CCP pursued perhaps its most radical land reform policies, and in the 1940s during the **Sino–Japanese War (1937–1945)** when the Communists built a base of support among the peasantry by redistributing land but with relatively moderate treatment of landlords and rich peasants. In 1949, more than 500 million peasants lived in China, with fully half of the cultivated land owned by one-tenth of the **population** and with two-thirds of the population owning less than one-fifth of the land. Large numbers of landless peasants populated the countryside and paid upward of 60% of their production in rent to the landowning classes. Still, China lacked the large estates and *latifundia* prevalent in other Third World countries, particularly Latin America.

The 1950 Agrarian Reform Law was relatively moderate in that it allowed rich peasants to retain their land and even let landlords hold land for their own use. However, under political pressure from above and in the context of the **Korean War (1950–1953)**, both rich peasants and landlords were subject to expropriation of their property by mobilized poor and middle peasants, and they were often physically abused and murdered in the "struggle meetings" and "people's tribunals" established by the CCP. By 1952, more than 110 million acres of land were redistributed to over 300 million peasants, along with farm tools and draught animals, which led the **New China News Agency (Xinhua)** to announce the virtual completion of land reform. In 1953, however, this "land to the tiller" policy was quickly reversed as peasants were pressured into "voluntarily" joining the **mutual aid teams**, followed by the lower and higher **Agricultural Producers' Cooperatives (APCs)**, and, finally, in 1958, the gigantic **people's communes**. Not until the **Agricultural Responsibility System** was introduced in the late 1970s was land in China returned to the "tiller" but without the guarantee of formal ownership because land is leased but not sold to rural inhabitants. *See also* AGRICULTURE.

LANGUAGE REFORM. Since the **May Fourth Movement (1919–1923)**, language reform has been a central political and literary concern in modern China. Led by such intellectual luminaries as **Hu Shi** and **Guo Moruo**, the Chinese written and spoken language was transformed from an elitist and exclusive medium into one more accessible to the common people. Of greatest importance to literary reformers determined to modernize politically and culturally was the creation of a popular **literature** corresponding to vernacular Chinese (*putonghua*) instead of the traditional classical language (*wenyan*). After 1949, the **Chinese Communist Party (CCP)** introduced major language reforms that followed on those initially introduced in the 1920s. In 1951, a plan was adopted to ensure universal comprehension of a standardized common language. This plan included the simplification of written Chinese characters and introduction of Romanized forms based on the Latin alphabet. At the National Conference on Reform of the Chinese Written Language in October 1955, *putonghua* or standard national language (known in the West as Mandarin and which is based on the **Beijing** dialect), was adopted as the common language for the entire country and introduced as the language of instruction in schools and the national media. By the late 1970s, *putonghua* was supposed to be used by all government, Party, and **education** organs. Throughout the urban areas, *putonghua* is generally understood by most of the **population**, even as local dialects continue to be used in everyday language and discourse.

In theory, *putonghua* is taught to China's 55 official **minorities** only at the request of the local population but implementing this policy has not been easy as only 21 of the minority languages have written scripts and only 10 are actually used in schools as use of *putonghua* has proved more pragmatic for minorities' economic and political interaction with the **Han** and their involvement in the Chinese state. In 1991, a survey of China's spoken languages indicated that among the Han majority 70% spoke Mandarin, 8.4% spoke the *Wu* or **Shanghai** dialect, 5% spoke Hunanese and Cantonese, 4% *Hakka*, and 3% Southern Fujianese (*minnan hua*). By 2005, it was estimated that barely half the country's total population could speak the official dialect as among the Han majority there were approximately 1,500 separate dialects, this despite the passage in 2001 of a National Language Law that mandated that *putonghua* be used in all mass media, government offices, and schools, and barred the overuse of dialects in movies and broadcasting. The diversity of spoken languages in China is immense; the *Wu* dialect (spoken in Shanghai) shares only about 31% lexical similarity to *putonghua*, or roughly the same as English to French. In places such as Fujian Province, there is a dense thicket of tongues that can vary every 15 km or so.

Simplified "shorthand characters" (*jiantizi*), with fewer strokes, have replaced many traditional "complex characters" (*fantizi*) in official publications and the schools. Since 1978, however, some *fantizi* have been revived. Other aspects of reform include the adding of new meanings to existing Chinese characters, thereby reducing to 4,000 the number of individual characters that an educated person needs to master. *Hanyu pinyin* Romanization was created in the late 1950s to facilitate the learning of Chinese characters. By 1979, all publications appearing in China using the Roman alphabet began to employ the *pinyin* script, this in conjunction with the spread of vernacular Chinese to minority nationalities. *Pinyin* is also the accepted form of Romanization used in most Western countries and has gradually replaced the former Wade-Giles Romanization that would render such *pinyin* terms as *xian* (county) and *guo* (state) as *hsien* and *kuo*.

LEADERS. China's current leadership in the **Chinese Communist Party (CCP)** and state constitute the "fourth generation" (*disidai*) of political leaders who were generally born in the 1930s and 1940s and whose adult lives have largely come after the Communist takeover in 1949. Their class backgrounds are very diverse, with their **education** largely in technical areas while many have considerable experience abroad. In this sense, they differ dramatically from the first and second generation of leaders whose formal education, if any, was in nontechnical areas; who were largely from rural backgrounds with considerable military experience; and often spent little to no time abroad while they lived through the throes of the **Sino–Japanese War (1937–1945)** and the **Civil War (1946–1949)**; and were, in many cases, the victims of internal political purges from the **Anti-Rightist Campaign (1957–1958)** to the **Cultural Revolution (1966–1976)**. The third generation of leaders, featuring such prominent individuals as former President **Jiang Zemin** and former Premier **Li Peng**, were transitional figures who, like their fourth-generation successors, had considerable technical backgrounds but who were born in time to experience the travails of the Civil War and post-1949 catastrophes, such as the **Great Leap Forward (1958–1960)**. Leaders from China's fourth generation are overwhelmingly from the more well-off and advanced eastern and northeastern provinces, particularly Shandong, Zhejiang, Liaoning, Anhui, and **Beijing** and **Tianjin** municipalities, with few from the interior provinces and virtually no representation among the top figures from the southwest or far western, non-**Han** regions, including China's wealthiest province of Guangdong. The pinnacle of political leadership in China is the Standing Committee of the CCP **Politburo**, the highest decision-making body of the Communist Party, which, in 2005, consisted of nine members: President **Hu Jintao**, Premier **Wen Jiabao**, **Luo Gan**, **Jia Qinglin**, Wu Bangguo (chairman of the **National People's Congress [NPC]**), Li Changcun, Wu Guanzheng (head of the **Central Discipline Inspection Commission [CDIC]**), Vice-President **Zeng Qinglong**, and

Vice-Premier Huang Ju. In addition, there are from 19 to 25 full members of the ruling Politburo from various posts in the Party along with their concurrent posts in the state and the **People's Liberation Army (PLA)**.

LEGAL SYSTEM. *See* CRIME AND THE LEGAL SYSTEM.

LEI FENG (1940–1962). Perhaps the most famous political model advanced by the **Chinese Communist Party (CCP)**, Lei Feng was a **People's Liberation Army (PLA)** soldier whose distinguishing qualities included loyalty to the Party and Chairman **Mao Zedong**. A peasant soldier from Mao's home province of Hunan, Lei Feng reportedly died in 1962 at the age of 22 while "serving the people" when he attempted to retrieve a telephone pole that had fallen into a river. Lei left behind a diary in which he idolized Chairman Mao, expressed his eternal love for the motherland, the people, and the Party, and described his own many good deeds as a humble soldier to assist the common people. Politically, the purpose of the Lei Feng campaign in the mid-1960s was to bolster the image of the PLA in its growing conflict with the Party leadership of **Liu Shaoqi** and others. Lei Feng was idealized as a "rust-proof screw" in the machinery of the revolution—a model of obedience to political authority that has been a staple feature of Chinese Communist ideology since 1949. Lei Feng was also canonized for never "forgetting the class hatred of the old society where people perished and families fell apart." Lei Feng was said to be on constant political alert and "never forgot the pain of the old society when the scars of exploitation were healed." Propaganda on Lei Feng declined from the late 1970s through the 1980s, but was revived after the June 1989 second **Beijing Spring** pro-democracy movement was crushed, though with little apparent effect.

LI BONING. A major figure in China's water resources bureaucracy, Li Boning is a primary supporter of the **Three Gorges Dam Project** the world's largest dam, which has been undergoing construction on the middle reaches of the Yangtze River since 1995 and is slated for completion in 2013. In the late 1950s, Li Boning was the deputy director of the Capital Construction Department of the Ministry of Water Resources and Electric Power. In 1978, he was identified as a vice-minister of water resources and electric power. In 1988, he was elected vice-chairman of the Economic Committee of the **Chinese People's Political Consultative Conference** (CPPCC) and in 1989 became the leading member of the Central Flood Prevention and Control Office.

LI GUIXIAN (1937–). A graduate of China's University of Science and Technology in 1959–1960, Li Guixian studied at the Mendeleyev Chemical Technological Institute in Moscow from 1960–1965. During the late 1960s and 1970s, Li worked as a researcher for the Ministry of Public Security, evidently in the field of electronics. In 1983, he was appointed to the Standing Committee of the Liaoning Province CP and from 1985 to 1986 he was first secretary of the Liaoning Party Committee and a member of the 12th to 16th **Chinese Communist Party** (CCP) Central Committee. From 1986 to 1988, Li served as secretary of the Anhui Province CP. In 1988, he became governor of the People's Bank of China. In 1993, Li was forced to resign his position at the People's Bank as a result of a financial scandal that reportedly involved the loss of several billion dollars, though he retained his position as a state councilor. By the early 2000s, Li assumed the post of vice-chairman of the **Chinese People's Political Consultative Conference** (CPPCC) and, reflecting his earlier training in the **Soviet Union**, became co-chair of the Sino–Russian Committee established in 1997 to foster a strategic partnership between the two countries. In 2003, Li was reelected as the president of the Chinese Association for International Understanding, which has ties with 250 international organizations and groups from more than 110 nations.

LI HONGLIN (1925–). A former president of the Fujian Academy of Social Sciences, Li Honglin was a constant critic of the "**personality cult**" (*geren chongbai*) read **Mao Zedong** in China and a strong advocate of political reform since the 1970s. During the 1970s, he was a deputy head of the Theoretical Bureau of the **Chinese Communist Party** (CCP) Propaganda Department until he was forced to step down for his liberal ideas. In March 1989, he joined 42 **intellectuals** in signing an open letter to the CCP leadership calling for the release of political prisoners and greater freedom in Chinese society. In July

1989, he was imprisoned, released in May 1990, and has since lived in **Hong Kong** with his son Li Shaomin, who was briefly detained during a trip to China in 2001.

LI PENG (1928–). China's premier from 1988 to 1998, Li Peng is the adopted son of **Zhou Enlai**. Li Peng was born in Sichuan Province to parents active in the **Chinese Communist Party (CCP)**, both of whom were executed by the **Kuomintang (KMT)** during the early 1930s. From 1948 to 1954, Li was trained as a power engineer in the **Soviet Union** and, from 1955 to 1979, worked in numerous positions in the Chinese power industry. In 1982, he became vice-minister of the Ministry of Water Resources and Electric Power and the same year became a member of the CCP Central Committee at the 12th National Party Congress. In 1985, he was appointed to the **Politburo**; in 1987, to its Standing Committee; and became premier in 1988. In June 1989, after debating with students involved in the second **Beijing Spring** on national television, Li reportedly issued the order approved by **Deng Xiaoping** for troops to use force against pro-democracy demonstrators on 3–4 June 1989. In the early 1990s, Li Peng led China's effort to restore its reputation in the international arena after the 1989 crackdown with visits to **India**, Europe, **Japan**, **Vietnam**, and to the **United Nations (UN)** headquarters in New York, where he met briefly with **United States** President George H. W. Bush. In May 1993, Li reportedly suffered a mild heart attack but returned to work later in the year. A strong proponent of the controversial **Three Gorges Dam Project**, Li led the successful effort to overturn previous opposition to the dam and win the approval of the **National People's Congress (NPC)** for the projected 18-year construction project. Li Peng's term as premier expired in March 1998 and he then assumed the role of chairman of the NPC Standing Committee, a position he held until his retirement from all positions in 2003.

With his son, Li Xiaopeng, ensconced as the head of the Huaneng Group, one of five independent power-generating companies created after the breakup of the State Power Corporation in 2002, Li Peng continues to wield considerable influence in China's power sector. He is a frequent visitor to **energy** development sites, such as the Zhonghai Shell South China Sea Petrochemical Project in Guangdong Province. In 2004, Li published his memoirs entitled *From*

Start-Up to Development: Li Peng's Diary on Nuclear Power and in an interview with **Seeking Truth (*Qiushi*)** magazine in the same year, Li claimed that the most controversial decisions of his career—the June 1989 crackdown against the second Beijing Spring, approval of the Three Gorges Project, and the push for construction of the nuclear power plant at Daya Bay across from **Hong Kong**—were all the ideas of the former paramount leader Deng Xiaoping.

LI RUI (1917–). Li Rui was the personal secretary of **Mao Zedong** on industrial affairs in the 1950s. In the 1950s and 1960s, Li also served as a vice-minister in the Ministry of Water Resources and Electric Power. He was purged for his support of **Peng Dehuai** at the **Lushan Plenum** and was denounced as an "anti-Party element" during the **Cultural Revolution (1966–1976)**, spending some 20 years in prison. Li Rui returned to prominence in 1979, was elected to the **Chinese Communist Party (CCP)** Central Committee in 1982, and was vice-director of the Organization Department of the CCP from 1983–1985. He led the effort to halt plans for construction of the massive **Three Gorges Dam Project** on the Yangtze River. Following the 1989 military crackdown against the second **Beijing Spring**, Li continued to oppose the dam even after the project was approved for construction in 1992, penning letters of opposition to CCP General Secretary **Jiang Zemin**. Although formally "retired," Li Rui serves as an adviser to the Energy and Resources Research Institute in China. In January 2005, Li attended the funeral of **Zhao Ziyang**, the former CCP leader who was ousted following the crackdown against the second Beijing Spring. In February 2006, Li Rui joined **Hu Jiwei** and **Zhu Houze** in penning a letter to China's current leadership protesting the shutting down of newspapers and excessive **censorship**.

LI RUIHUAN (1934–). Trained as a construction worker in the 1950s, Li Ruihuan cut his teeth during the **Great Leap Forward (1958–1960)** as a member of the young carpenters' shock brigade building the Great Hall of the People, one of the world's largest buildings located in Tiananmen Square in **Beijing**. In 1976, he was the director of the work site for the Mao Zedong Memorial Hall (*Mao Zedong jinan tang*) and, in 1979, became a model worker. In 1982, he became mayor of **Tianjin** Municipality and helped to clean up the city's notoriously polluted water supply. In 1987, he became first secretary of the Tianjin CP, as well as a member of the **Politburo**. Despite little formal education, Li Ruihuan frequently weighed in on issues of ideology and culture by attacking "wholesale Westernization" and calling on cultural workers to "serve the people and **socialism**"— especially after the June 1989 military crackdown against the second **Beijing Spring**. In the debate over the **Three Gorges Dam Project**, Li is said to have thoroughly quizzed the engineers and dam designers about the technical feasibility of the project. In 1993, Li Ruihuan was elected to chair the **Chinese People's Political Consultative Conference** (**CPPCC**) and, in the same year, praised Confucius and Confucianism as still having some validity and being worthy of study if combined with modern ideas. In 2003, despite his support for **Hu Jintao** as Party leader, Li Ruihuan was not reelected to the Politburo Standing Committee.

LI WEIHAN (1896–1984). An early associate of **Mao Zedong** in Hunan Province, Li Weihan traveled to France in 1920 for **education**, though he quickly returned to China for the founding congress of the **Chinese Communist Party** (**CCP**) in **Shanghai** in July 1921. Also known as "Luo Ming," Li became a member of the **Politburo** in 1927, but was soon thereafter denounced as a coward for attempting to terminate the ill-fated Autumn Harvest Uprising launched by the Communists against the **Kuomintang** (**KMT**). Li subsequently emerged in the early 1930s as a strong supporter of de facto Party leader Li Lisan and was an early opponent of the Russian Returned Student faction (also known as the Twenty-Eight Bolsheviks) who attacked the "Luo Ming line" as well as Mao Zedong. In Yan'an, Li headed the Communist Party School and was a top official in the Shaan–Gan–Ning Border Government. After 1949, Li became heavily involved in **minorities** and nationality issues and also helped guide the early campaigns to seize private business and establish total state control of the **economy**. Director of the **United Front** Department from 1944–1965, Li, in the late 1950s, launched attacks on "rightists" in China's eight **democratic parties**, including against his own brother. In 1964, however, Li was himself removed from his post and was later attacked by **Zhou Enlai** for "capitulationism in united front work." A frequent critic of Mao Zedong, Li Weihan emerged after 1978 as a supporter of political reform and urged **Deng Xiaoping** (whom Li had once saved from political persecution) to attack "**feudalism,**" an ideological codeword for the Party's autocratic traditions.

LI XIANNIAN (1909–1992). Born to poor peasants in Hubei Province, Li Xiannian was trained as a carpenter and then joined the Communists in the late 1920s. Rising to the top of the **Chinese Communist Party** (**CCP**) hierarchy as a military commander, Li Xiannian became a member of the CCP Central Committee in 1945 and after 1949 became mayor of Wuhan Municipality in Hubei Province and a vice-premier. Li Xiannian was made a member of the CCP **Politburo** in 1956 and became minister of finance in 1957. He continued to serve on the Politburo throughout the **Cultural Revolution** (**1966–1976**) and remained a central figure in economic and financial affairs in the 1980s. From 1983 to 1988, Li Xiannian served as **president of the People's Republic of China** and, during the 1989 second **Beijing Spring**, sided with his other semi-retired "**revolutionary elders**" (*geming yuanlao*) in supporting the use of lethal force against the pro-democracy student demonstrators.

LI XIMING (1926–). A graduate of **Qinghua University** in civil engineering and architecture, Li Ximing served as vice-minister in the Ministry of Power in the late 1970s. From 1982–1984, he was minister of urban and rural construction and environmental protection, and from 1984–1992 was first secretary of the **Beijing** Municipal Party Committee and first **political commissar** of the Beijing Military Area Command. In 1987, he was appointed to the **Politburo**, a post that he held until 1992. Following the June 1989 military crackdown on the second **Beijing Spring**, which he championed, Li Ximing's political star faded somewhat. In 1994, he became titular head of the **Three Gorges Dam Project** and, in January 2005, Li was one of the few top central **leaders** to present wreaths at the funeral of **Zhao Ziyang**, the Party head ousted after the June 1989 suppression.

LI YINING (1930–). A 1955 graduate of the Economics Department at **Beida (Peking University)**, Li Yining specialized in educational economics, comparative economics, and history of foreign economics and authored a book on the economic theories of the American economist John Kenneth Galbraith. He was a member of the Standing Committee of the Seventh **National People's Congress** (**NPC**) and was a financial adviser to the China Investment Consulting Experts Committee. In 2003–2004, Li served as a member of the Standing Committee of the **Chinese People's Political Consultative Conference** (**CPPCC**), where he acted as a senior adviser on the **economy** and continued to comment on China's need to invigorate **agriculture** and defended the emergence in China of private entrepreneurs.

"LIBERATION" (*"JIEFANG"*). The term used to refer to the seizure of political power in China by the **Chinese Communist Party** (**CCP**) in October 1949, "liberation" is also used more broadly to mean the freeing of the Chinese people from the shackles of the past: landlords, capitalists, and foreign **imperialism**. In Maoist theory, the lifting of restraints from the past was to produce a great burst of revolutionary energy and creativity that was apparent in Mao's proposal for the **Great Leap Forward** (**1958–1960**). Indeed, China's farmers genuinely referred to the 1949 Communist takeover and the redistribution of land as "liberation" while the implementation of the **Agricultural Responsibility System** in 1978–1979 was frequently referred to as the "second liberation." In everyday speech, average Chinese still casually refer to 1949 as "liberation" or the "founding of the nation" (*jianguo*).

LIN BIAO (**1907–1971**). The proclaimed "closest comrade in arms" of **Mao Zedong** during the **Cultural Revolution** (**1966–1976**) and his designated successor in the Ninth Constitution of the **Chinese Communist Party** (**CCP**), Lin Biao allegedly died in September 1971 after a purported attempt to assassinate the chairman. Lin was a major military leader during the **Civil War** (**1946–1949**), where his strategic prowess resulted in the rapid conquest of **Manchuria** from **Kuomintang** (**KMT**) forces but where, on one occasion, his siege of the northeast city of Changchun led to the deaths of several hundred thousand people, including large numbers of non-combatants. After spending considerable time for medical treatment in the **Soviet Union**, Lin, along with nine other **People's Liberation Army** (**PLA**) commanders, was promoted to "marshal" (*yuanshuai*), the highest rank in the army in 1955 and minister of defense in 1959 following the purge of **Peng Dehuai**. Lin Biao emerged as an important political figure in 1964 at a PLA Political Work Conference. In 1965, Lin issued his treatise *Long Live the Victory of the People's War* to commemorate the 20th anniversary of the War of Resistance against **Japan** and to proclaim that Communist military forces from the world's rural hinterlands in Asia, Africa, and Latin America would surround and then overwhelm the world's urban **population** in Europe and North America.

In August 1966, Lin joined Mao Zedong and **Zhou Enlai** at a gigantic rally in support of the Cultural Revolution in Tiananmen Square, where the **Red Guards** were given Mao's official imprimatur. In 1969, at the Ninth National Party Congress, Lin reached the pinnacle of his political power when he was canonized as Mao's official successor. Lin and his entourage maintained an uneasy alliance with the radical faction surrounding **Jiang Qing**, the wife of Mao Zedong. Following a political setback, in 1971, Lin allegedly joined with his notorious wife, **Ye Qun**, and his son, Lin Liguo, in a foiled assassination plot—code named **Project 571**—against Mao. The official CCP line is that soon after the assassination attempt, Lin Biao died in a plane crash in Mongolia after attempting to flee China. However, the rumor mill in China has it that he was actually poisoned by Mao Zedong at a banquet in **Beijing**. From 1971 to 1997, Lin Biao's name was excluded from any mention of China's marshals (whose official number was reduced from 10 to 9) but on the 80th anniversary of the founding of the PLA, Lin's name reappeared in official histories.

LITERATURE AND THE ARTS. Having inherited a rich classical and modern literary tradition, **Chinese Communist Party** (**CCP**) policy toward literature and the arts has, since 1949, shifted from strict adherence to Soviet-style socialist realism to the near extinction of any literary and artistic endeavor during the **Cultural Revolution** (**1966–1976**) to a marked but not total relaxation of political and ideological controls since 1978–1979. Following the principles laid down by **Mao Zedong** in May 1942 at the Yan'an Forum on Literature and Art, the post-1949 period in China witnessed strict adherence by writers and artists to Party doctrine and a narrow emphasis on the credible depiction of an external reality. The enormous power granted to such "cultural czars" as **Zhou Yang** and **Guo Moruo** was backed up by the creation of an elaborate bureaucratic and ideological apparatus for making sure writers and artists adhered to the current Party line. Set up in 1949 was the All-China Federation of Literary Circles (renamed the All-China Federation of Literary and Art Circles in 1953), which consists of over 50 national cultural groups, including the Chinese Writers' Association, Chinese Artists' Association, and China Theater Association, and served over the next several decades as the official body for all "literary and art workers." In 1950, the government established a Central Institute of Drama and a Central Conservatorium of Music while *People's Literature* was inaugurated in late 1949 as the main outlet for officially accepted short stories and poetry. In more recent years, artistic control has been exercised by the Ministry of Culture and the State Administration of Radio, Film, and Television while organizations, such as the China National Culture and Art Company, founded in 1987, has operated with greater autonomy sponsoring a number of foreign performances including tours of China by the Lincoln Center Jazz Orchestra and the American National Orchestra.

In 1955, the first campaign against an errant writer and his supporters took the form of the **Hu Feng Affair** when accusations and charges of "bourgeois and idealist thinking on literature and art" filled the intellectual airwaves. In a nod to China's rich musical and operatic tradition, the **Peking Opera** Company of China was formed in the same year, which was followed, in 1956–1957, by an outpouring of criticism directed at political authorities by writers and artists during the brief period of intellectual tolerance known as the **Hundred Flowers (1956–1957)**. The political backlash in the form of the **Anti-Rightist Campaign (1957–1958)** targeted a significant number of writers such as **Wang Meng** and Zhang Xianlang, who had pushed the envelope of political and ideological acceptability in their work, while many others may have avoided outright persecution but learned to toe the political line. Works produced in the latter half of 1956 about how "love is supreme" (*aiqing zhishang*) were subject to withering criticism as part of the large-scale campaign against humanism that dominated the late 1950s. On the other hand, politically acceptable literary works during this era included such novels as *Keep the*

Red Flag Flying and *The Song of Youth*, boilerplate tales of peasant life and love among revolutionary youth, and plays like Tian Han's *Guan Hanqing*. During and after the tumultuous **Great Leap Forward (1958–1960)**, such sterile paintings as *Soviet Experts Visit a Collective Farm* indicated the extent to which socialist realism had overtaken the Chinese art world though 1961 would witness the first staging of *Hai Rui Dismissed from Office* by **Wu Han**, which would become a subsequent target of left-wing denunciations during the early stages of the Cultural Revolution.

The literary and art world also emerged in the early 1960s as the starting point for entry into politics by **Jiang Qing**, the wife of Mao Zedong, who, in 1963, authored a circular on "Suspending the Performance of Ghost Plays," which attacked any and all traditional drama that was still performed throughout China, along with such *huaju* theatre as *Dragon Beard Ditch* and *Teahouse* by Lao She. Mao, too, entered the literary fray with the publication in 1963 by the People's Literary Press of *Poems of Chairman Mao* while such plays as *The Young Generation*, which was turned into a film, educated the post-1949 generation on how to become a good, revolutionary Communist. In 1964, the novel *Bright Sunny Skies* by the politically accommodating Hao Ran was published with its portrayal of the clever peasant named "convoluted" who outwits his neighbors in a dirt-poor, but happy rural village. In the same year, the large-scale historical poem with music and dancing titled *The East is Red* premiered in **Beijing**. This was followed, in 1965, by the launching of a volley of attacks on *Hai Rui Dismissed from Office* that led to perhaps the greatest assault on writers, artists, and musicians in any nation's history; piano teachers had their hands broken, bookstores were ransacked, and writers, such as Lao She, were driven to commit suicide. While drama was restricted to model plays and operas such as *Taking Tiger Mountain by Strategy* and *The Legend of the Red Lantern*, paintings were limited to such "spiritually uplifting" works—widely reproduced—as *Chairman Mao Goes to Anyuan*. Literary and artistic expression in China ground to a virtual halt as all creative work was subjected to the sternest political judgments and oversight as the All-China Federation of Literary and Art Circles was purged and failed to meet for more than a decade. While the public was only able to see no more than the "eight model operas" and a few ballets, such as *The White-Haired Girl* and *The Red Detachment of Women* (which dealt with Communist and revolutionary themes but also employed Western musical instruments), cracks in the literary monolith appeared in 1971 with the publication by Guo Moruo of *Li Bai and Du Fu*, the first book on classical literature since before the Cultural Revolution. This was followed in 1973 by a visit to China of the Vienna Philharmonic Orchestra, though highly ideological attacks on various art forms continued, such as the vitriolic denunciation of the classical novel *Water Margin* in 1975.

Although the death of Mao Zedong in September 1976 and the arrest of the **Gang of Four** in October are considered to have ended the Cultural Revolution, members of China's artistic circles look to March 1977 as the real end. Then, the Fifth Symphony by Beethoven (banned for the past decade) was performed in Bejing by the conductor Li Delun, who had survived the Cultural Revolution and had been a key player in the creation of the model operas. With the suppression of Western music and many other art forms lifted, popular hunger virtually exploded, with thousands of young people vying to be accepted at re-opened conservatories, including the renowned **Shanghai** Conservatory, whose conductor Li Delun had worked with the Yan'an Symphony Orchestra in the 1940s and took them on a long march from Yan'an to Beijing in 1947 playing music while the Communists redistributed land.

In the immediate aftermath of the Cultural Revolution, China's literary genre was dominated by so-called "scar" or "wound literature" (*shanghen wenxu*), so named for a short story titled *The Wounded* (*Shanghen*), written in 1978 by Lu Xinhua. Examining with a sympathetic eye the scars left by the Cultural Revolution on an entire generation of youth, it created an ethos of exposure and a pessimistic theme in Chinese literature that contrasted sharply with the "optimistic" and simplistic, heroic messages of socialist realism. The basic thematic line of "wound literature" was to depict the scars left on normal persons by the physical and mental suffering incurred during political movements inaugurated by the CCP, especially the Cultural Revolution. Initially, "wound literature" harmonized well with the CCP-directed campaign against the Gang of Four and official criticism of the excesses of the Cultural Revolution. "Wound literature" included such works as *The Class Counselor* by the Sichuan writer

Liu Xinwu, which was published in November 1977 as perhaps the very first example of the genre. Others included *A Youth Like This* by Zhang Jie, a work that was read over the Central People's Broadcasting to the entire nation. In 1978, "wound literature" expanded its message to include issues of **corruption** among **cadres**, privilege, and the insulation of the political system from popular control. It was thus quickly replaced by a more provocative and pointedly political "literature of protest" that included such works as *People or Monsters?* by **Liu Binyan** and such provocative poetry as *China You Can't Remain Silent* by Huang Xiang, the so-called Beast Poet of China. The Chinese premiere of Arthur Miller's work *Death of a Salesman* in 1983 was a high point in Chinese interaction with the international literary scene.

With more and more literary publications, such as *The Present* (*Dangdai*), hitting Chinese streets, the literary and art world seemed on a course to break from political controls until in 1981 even the reform-minded CCP leader **Hu Yaobang** warned of "**bourgeois liberalization**" and other unhealthy tendencies in the world of literature and art, a message to writers and artists that the struggle with political authorities in China was far from over. Musical scores taught to young, aspiring pianists in China still contained a heavy political content into the 1980s with such titles as *Brilliant Sunlight Shone on the Red Flag*, *Taking Over the Gun of **Lei Feng***, and *Glorious, the **People's Liberation Army***, which contained such awe-inspiring lines as "with our burning youth, we swept dark clouds aside in the sky, we regained the people's rights, the whole world is listening to the voice of New China." This was reinforced by ideological assaults on art and literature in the **Anti-Spiritual Pollution Campaign (1983–1984)** when literary and art circles were targeted by Party ideologues in order to save the threatened economic reforms leading to incarceration of literary figures such as Huang Xiang in detention centers.

Despite these episodic political intrusions, China's literary and art world in the early 2000s has been marked by considerable innovation and experimentation. This includes such dramas as a Chinese contemporary interpretation of Johann Wolfgang Von Goethe's *Faust*, *Che Guevara*, George Orwell's *Animal Farm*, and a lavish production of *Les Misérables* at the Shanghai Grand Theater. Annual music and arts festivals in Beijing and Shanghai also provide venues for various productions along with the Shanghai Art Museum, the China National Art Gallery, and the China Millennium Monument Art Gallery in Beijing, which, in 2006, fielded an exhibit of Italian Renaissance masters, including Leonardo Da Vinci, Raphael, and Titian. Continuing the long Chinese love affair with the piano, by the early 2000s, it was estimated that 38 million children practice piano in China daily, and in 2005 the New York Philharmonic announced the appointment of Xian Zhang, a graduate of the Central Conservatory of Music in Beijing, as its associate conductor. China also emerged in the early 21st century as the world's largest producer of pianos; led by the Pearl River Piano Group in Guangdong Province, which has surpassed Germany's Ritmuller and British firms such as Broadwood and Knight. Just as Mao Zedong spurred Chinese to appreciate poetry, subsequent **leaders**, such as former President **Jiang Zemin**, assisted the musical world in China by starting a craze for extravagant opera houses, including an ultramodern building of glass and steel costing US$157 million built in Shanghai, located next to CCP headquarters. In 1991, the first performance of William Shakespeare's *Taming of the Shrew* in Western operatic style was performed in the Central Opera Theatre in Beijing, which was followed in 1998 by a performance of *Turandot* in the Forbidden City, directed by **Zhang Yimou** and conducted by Zubin Mehta. Closer to home was a series of regional operas performed in 1995 and the large-scale performance *In Praise of the Motherland*, which celebrated 50 years of Communist rule in 1999. Since being established in 1952, the Beijing People's Art Theater has performed Chinese plays abroad for 20 years.

In 2000, the first Chinese writer to receive the Nobel Prize in literature was Gao Xinjian who won it for his work *Soul Mountain*, an odyssey through the Chinese countryside during the Cultural Revolution. Unfortunately, Gao had been exiled from China, become a French citizen, and saw his work snubbed during France's "Year of China" celebration in 2004 under apparent pressure from the Chinese government. While the poet Huang Xiang also emigrated abroad, other writers of notoriety managed to slug it out in China, including the "bad girl of Chinese literature," Mian Mian, who followed her salacious work of *Candy*, portraying a life of drugs and free love, with the whimsically titled *Panda Sex*. Comparing her character's perilously inactive mating habits similar to the notoriously sex-shy bear won the tacit approval of Beijing's still prudish censors. Although accomplished poets, such as Bei Dao representing the "Misty Poets" group, have also had to seek a life in exile, many young writers whose topics include tales of sex and depravity in works like *City of Fantasy* and *Flowers on the Other Side* are seen to have sold out to China's increasing culture of consumerism and popular fashion. Yet, novels with political subtexts continue to sell well in China and include such works as *Wolf Totem* (*Lang tuteng*) by Jiang Rong, a **Beida (Peking University)** professor whose work is an allegorical critique of Chinese civilization, which he calls soft and lacking in individuality and freedom. At the same time, some of the most extreme experimental art in the world has emerged from China, starting with nude paintings in December 1988 (closed January 1989) and more recently such exhibits as "It's Me," which used actual human body parts, self-mutilation, and aborted fetuses as material. By 2005, China's art market was booming with foreign auction houses, such as Christie's, vying to become the first to conduct auctions in Beijing.

Dance in China has retained its prominence since the establishment of the Beijing Dance Academy in 1954, along with the Beijing Modern Dance Company and the Guangdong Modern Dance Company, the first in China. Innovations by Chinese dance companies include the production of "Swan Lake" by the Guangdong Military Acrobatic Troupe in 2005 that involved an unconventional blend of classical ballet and traditional Chinese acrobatics. *See also* CINEMA AND FILM; MAO DUN.

LIU BINYAN (1925–). After joining the underground **Chinese Communist Party (CCP)** (*dixia dang*) in the 1940s in the city of **Tianjin**, Liu Binyan worked as a journalist with the *Beijing Youth Daily* in the early 1950s and later for the *People's Daily*. He was branded a "rightist" in 1957 for his scathing criticism of **bureaucratism** in China and sent to **labor** on a state farm. After returning to work in the early 1960s, he was denounced again during the **Cultural Revolution (1966–1976)**, not to be rehabilitated until 1979. In 1985, he was elected vice-chairman of the All-China Writers' Association but two years later, in 1987, he was expelled from the CCP on charges of "**bourgeois liberalization.**" Since 1988, he has been in exile in the

West, where he served as a Nieman Fellow in journalism at Harvard University from 1988–1989 and was denounced in November 1989 in the *People's Daily* as the "scum of the Chinese nation." In 2005, Liu was involved in a dispute over leadership of the **United States**-based Human Rights in China, of which he, along with such respected Chinese activists and **intellectuals** as **Fang Lizhi**, was a member. Liu also penned a letter to the new Chinese leadership of **Hu Jintao** and **Wen Jiabao** requesting permission to return to China even as he criticized the new leadership for making conditions in China worse than prior to their ascension. Liu's written works include *People or Monsters?* and *A Higher Kind of Loyalty*, the latter a study in the pursuit of truth in a totalitarian country. Although Liu holds former supreme leader **Deng Xiaoping** primarily responsible for the military crackdown against the second **Beijing Spring** in June 1989, he argues that China's political problems are fundamentally rooted in the shortcomings of Chinese culture and not just the dictatorship of the CCP.

LIU BOCHENG (1892–1986). Trained as an army officer at the time of the Republican Revolution that overthrew the Qing dynasty (1644–1911), Liu Bocheng was wounded several times and lost an eye; thereafter, he became known as the "one-eyed dragon." Liu began to support the Communists in the 1920s and went to the **Soviet Union** in the late 1920s for further military training. Liu commanded volunteer units during the epic **Long March (1934–1935)** and sided with **Mao Zedong** during his disputes with rival **leaders** promoted by **Josef Stalin** and the Comintern. Liu was appointed to the **Chinese Communist Party (CCP)** Central Committee in 1945 and headed the Second **Field Army** in which **Deng Xiaoping** served as **political commissar**. In 1955, Liu was one of 10 former field army commanders elevated to marshal, the highest rank in the **People's Liberation Army (PLA)**. In 1956, he became a member of the **Politburo** at the **Eighth National Party Congress**. Liu reportedly protected Deng Xiaoping during the **Cultural Revolution (1966–1976)**. He retired from public life in 1977 and, at his death in 1986, Deng Xiaoping gave the eulogy.

LIU GUOGUANG (1923–). A graduate with a vice-doctorate degree from the Moscow State Economics Institute, Liu Guoguang served as director of the Research Office of the Chinese Academy of Sciences (CAS) from 1955 to 1980. In 1980, he became deputy director of the Institute of Economics under the **Chinese Academy of Social Sciences (CASS)** and a professor at **Beida (Peking University)**. In 1981, he became deputy director of the State Statistical Bureau; in 1982, became an alternate member of the **Chinese Communist Party (CCP)** Central Committee and vice-president of CASS; and, in 1985, became director of the academy's Institute of Economics. Following his retirement, Liu remained an advisor to CASS and continued to comment on economic policy and China's economic future. In 2005, he was named as an "outstanding economist" for his role in helping China to move away from a planned to a market **economy**.

LIU HUAQING (1916–). A military veteran of the **Long March (1934–1935)** with close ties to **Deng Xiaoping**, Liu Huaqing became vice-president of China's First Naval Academy from 1952–1953 and attended a naval academy in the **Soviet Union**, returning to China in 1958. From 1961–1965, Liu was director of the Seventh Institute under the Ministry of National Defense and in 1965 became a deputy **political commissar** of the **People's Liberation Army (PLA)** Navy (PLAN). During the **Cultural Revolution (1966–1976)**, he was vice-chairman of the **Science and Technology** Commission for National Defense and a member of the Central **Cultural Revolution Small Group** for the PLA Navy. In 1968, he was attacked by **Red Guards**, along with **Nie Rongzhen**, for having purportedly established an "independent kingdom" in the Science and Technology Commission. In 1978, Liu became vice-minister of the State Science and Technology Commission and, in 1980, deputy chief of the PLA General Staff. In 1982, he was appointed commander of the Navy, and, in 1989, he became vice-chairman of the Central **Military Affairs Commission (MAC)**. In 1992, he was appointed to the Standing Committee of the **Politburo** as China's top military man and the only member of the PLA on this top policy-making body. Following his retirement, Liu Huaqing published his memoirs through the PLA Publishing House.

LIU HUAQIU (1939–). A specialist on American political affairs, Liu Huaqiu, in 1994, was a vice-minister of foreign affairs, a post he assumed in 1989 and held for nine years. Appointed to the **Chinese**

Communist Party (CCP) Central Committee in 1997, in 1998, Hua took over the Central Foreign Affairs Office of the CCP, its top **foreign policy** advisory post. In 2005, Liu retired from this position and was appointed a vice-chairman of the foreign affairs committee of the **Chinese People's Political Consultative Conference (CPPCC)**, a post reserved for retired officials. In a 2005 article appearing in the authoritative magazine *Seeking Truth (Qiushi)*, Liu praised China's foreign policy for adhering to peaceful development, strengthening friendly cooperation with all foreign countries, and accelerating global economic growth.

LIU SHAOQI (1898–1969). A native of Hunan Province and from a rich peasant family, Liu Shaoqi joined the **Chinese Communist Party (CCP)** in 1921 during a stay in the **Soviet Union**, where he studied at the University of the Toilers of the East. After organizing workers in **Shanghai** in the early 1920s, he returned to Moscow following the collapse of the First **United Front** in 1927 and after joining **Mao Zedong** in the Jiangxi Soviet, participated in the **Long March (1934–1935)**. In 1939, he authored the classic work on Party discipline entitled *How to Be a Good Communist* and frequently questioned the emerging **personality cult** (*geren chongbai*) that was developing around Mao Zedong during the Yan'an period (1935–1945) when Liu declared in 1942 that "there is no perfect leader in the world." In the 1950s, Liu emerged as the first heir apparent to Mao Zedong, who, in April 1959, Liu replaced as **People's Republic of China (PRC)** state chairman (a position later changed to **president**) and head of the National Defense Committee. Never an advocate of rapid collectivization of Chinese **agriculture**, Liu's appointment came after the political fallout over the disastrous **Great Leap Forward (1958–1960)**, though Liu continued to defend Mao's prestige following the purge of **Peng Dehuai**. Throughout the early 1960s, Liu's political star continued to rise as he headed the "first line of leadership" and, along with **Deng Xiaoping**, supported a substantial loosening of state controls on the **economy**, especially agriculture, to help China recover from the Great Leap. In the early stages of the **Cultural Revolution (1966–1976)**, Liu attempted to halt the escalating violence by **Red Guards** on college campuses by instructing CCP **work teams** to restrict criticism of teachers and educators to verbal attacks, a decision that was subsequently overturned by Mao Zedong and the Party Center. Denounced as "China's Khrushchev" and as "the number one Party person in authority taking the capitalist road," Liu was demoted in the Party hierarchy from second to eighth position in August 1966 and was ultimately replaced by **Lin Biao** as Mao's heir apparent. In October 1968, Liu Shaoqi was formally expelled from the CCP and died ignominiously in a solitary cell in 1969. Liu Shaoqi was posthumously rehabilitated in 1979; in 1982, *The Selected Works of Liu Shaoqi* was released to the public while an ancillary room in the Mao Zedong Memorial Hall in **Beijing**'s Tiananmen Square was dedicated to Liu and other **leaders** purged during the Cultural Revolution.

"LONG AND DRAGGED OUT PROJECT" (*"DIAOYU GONG-CHENG"*). This phrase refers to projects in basic capital construction that are unnecessary and are often considered contrary to the interest of the ordinary people. The term first appeared in an editorial of the *People's Daily* on 12 October 1983 entitled "The Hefty Task of Construction Banks" and has often been used in reference to the **Three Gorges Dam Project**, which, although slated to take 18 years to construct, could end up like other large dam projects, such as the Gezhouba dam located downriver on the Yangtze and which took more than twice as long as its original schedule to construct.

LONG MARCH (1934–1935). The seminal event in the pre-1949 history of the Chinese Communist movement, the Long March occurred between October 1934 and October 1935. Surrounded on three sides in its Jiangxi Province redoubt known as the Central Soviet by **Kuomintang** (**KMT**) armies led by Chiang Kai-shek, the Communists decided on a bold move of strategic retreat to save the majority of its forces from annihilation. Some 100,000 Red Army soldiers abandoned their base and headed west in a military maneuver that took them over rugged terrain of mountains and rivers in China's western provinces, including eastern portions of **Tibet**, until they reached a small Communist base established in Yan'an in the northwestern province of Shaanxi (then spelled *Shensi*). During the march, at the town of Zunyi top leaders of the **Chinese Communist Party** (**CCP**) decided in January 1935 to appoint **Mao Zedong** military commander after Mao had challenged the military leadership and doctrine of the dominant leadership group known as the Twenty-Eight Bolsheviks. Trained in Moscow and beholden to **Josef Stalin**, the Twenty-Eight Bolsheviks relied on the military advice of Comintern adviser Otto Braun. Led by Mao and the military commander **Zhu De**, the CCP thereafter entrusted military leadership to Mao and Zhu, thereby reducing Soviet influence in the Chinese Communist movement. Splits soon developed among the CCP leadership ranks, however, as the powerful General Zhang Guotao rejected Mao's decision to march toward Yan'an and instead fled to neighboring Sichuan Province, thereby dividing the Communist forces. Zhang's armies subsequently relocated in Yan'an as well, although Zhang himself fled the CCP's redoubt and quit the Communist movement altogether. From the late 1930s onward, the Long March was a central symbol of the Chinese Communist movement that CCP **leaders** believed preceded the Party's ultimate success in winning control over all of China.

LU DINGYI (1906–1996). After joining the **Chinese Communist Party (CCP)** in 1925, Lu Dingyi became active in the Communist **Youth League** and served as a propaganda **cadre** in the **People's Liberation Army (PLA)**. A veteran of the **Long March (1934–1935)**, he headed the Party's Propaganda Department on and off throughout the 1940s and 1950s. In May 1956, Lu delivered his famous speech "Let a Hundred Flowers Bloom," in which he favored greater freedom of thought and expression, a proposal later embraced by **Mao Zedong**. Lu Dingyi became a member of the Central Committee Secretariat in 1962 and became minister of culture in 1965. Branded a "counterrevolutionary" during the **Cultural Revolution (1966–1976)**, Lu was later rehabilitated in 1979 and took part in revising China's state constitution, which was approved in 1982. That same year, he became a member of the **Central Advisory Commission (CAC)**. In 1986, he wrote a celebrated article commemorating the **Hundred Flowers (1956–1957)**.

LU PING (1929–). A 1947 graduate of the Agricultural College of St. John's University in **Shanghai**, Lu Ping served in the 1950s as editor-in-chief of the magazine *China Reconstructs*. He disappeared during the **Cultural Revolution (1966–1976)** only to return to public life in 1978 as secretary-general of the State **Hong Kong** and Macao Affairs Office and as deputy secretary-general of the Basic Law Drafting Committee for Hong Kong in 1985. In 1987, he was appointed deputy director of the Hong Kong and Macao Affairs Office and director of the office from 1991 to 1997 during which time he promised that the future development of Hong Kong's democracy was entirely a matter for Hong Kong to decide and that the central government in **Beijing** would not interfere, a position that the Standing Committee of the **National People's Congress** (**NPC**) apparently overturned in 2004. In 2003, Lu Ping served as vice-chairman of the China Welfare Institute and the Shanghai **Song Qingling** Foundation.

LU YOUMEI (1934–). Trained as a hydrologist in the 1950s, Lu Youmei served as an engineer from 1956 to 1970 at the Liujia Gorge Hydropower station on the Yellow River and from 1974 to 1984 in the Ministry of Water Resources and Electric Power. In 1988, he was appointed vice-minister of Energy Resources and, in 1992, became the president of the **Three Gorges Dam Project** Development Corporation, the quasi-private organization charged with constructing the Three Gorges Dam on the Yangtze River in central China. Following his retirement in 2003, Lu Youmei remained active as a consultant on the Three Gorges Project, which is slated for completion in 2013, and was elected a member of the Chinese Academy of Engineering.

LUO GAN (1935–). China's top internal security officer, Luo Gan was trained in the Democratic Republic of Germany (East Germany) in the 1950s, where he learned fluent German and, like most current Chinese **leaders**, graduated with a technical degree, in his case, from the Freiburg Institute of Mining and Metallurgy and worked for a short time at the Leipzig Iron and Steel Plant. Upon his return to China, Luo joined the **Chinese Communist Party** (**CCP**) in 1960 and worked in the First Ministry of Machine Building in the early 1960s. Following a stint at a **May Seventh Cadre School** during the **Cultural Revolution** (**1966–1976**), he ran the Mechanical Engineering Academy and held a number of positions involving metallurgy and machine building including Director of the First Ministry of Machine Building from 1970 to 1980. Prior to his elevation to the **Politburo**, Luo was a vice-president of the All-China Federation of **Trade**

Unions, the Party Secretary of Henan Province, and a state councilor. In 2002, he was elevated to the Politburo Standing Committee. As the head security official, Luo Gan oversees the **Procuracy**, China's prosecution organ, as well as the powerful Ministry of State Security and the Judiciary and the **Public Security Bureau**. Out of his long association with former Premier **Li Peng**, Luo is reported to have played a central role in executing the military crackdown against the second **Beijing Spring** in June 1989 and is intensely opposed to any revision of the official political line on the "June 4" (*liusi*) incident.

LUO RUIQING (1906–1978). One of the earliest members of the Red Army and a senior military and political officer throughout the 1930s and 1940s, Luo Ruiqing was China's minister of public security in the 1950s. He helped establish the system of "**reform through labor**" and defended the execution of alleged "counterrevolutionaries" in the early 1950s as having been carried out to "appease the rightful indignation of the people." In 1959, Luo rose up the ranks after the purge of **Peng Dehuai** and became army chief-of-staff and was appointed to the Central **Military Affairs Commission (MAC)**. In 1965, he was replaced and became a major target in the **Cultural Revolution (1966–1976)**, during which time he sustained serious injuries at the hands of **Red Guards**. Rehabilitated in the late 1970s, in 1978, he traveled to West Germany for medical treatment, where he died, somewhat mysteriously, from a heart attack during an operation on his leg.

LUSHAN CONFERENCE (1959). This conference was the Eighth Plenum of the **Chinese Communist Party (CCP)** Eighth Central Committee that became a crucial turning point in the ill-fated policies of the **Great Leap Forward (1958–1960)**. Held in July–August 1959 at the CCP's mountaintop retreat on Mt. Lu (*Lushan*) in Jiangxi Province, the conference was marked by an unprecedented conflict between CCP Chairman **Mao Zedong** and the Minister of Defense **Peng Dehuai** over the issue of continuing the radical social and economic policies of the Great Leap. After extensive visits to the countryside where he inspected the devastating impact on the rural **economy** of the **backyard steel furnaces** and the **people's communes**, Peng Dehuai had concluded that the fundamental policies of the Leap and its guiding ideological line of **"politics takes command"** (*zhengzhi guashuai*) were flawed and needed to be reversed as soon as possible. Peng voiced his concerns somewhat elliptically in a letter delivered to Mao Zedong—the major proponent of the Leap—at the conference. Although Mao also endorsed a substantial slowdown in the ambitious policies of the Great Leap of dramatically increasing steel production and relying on the people's communes for dramatic increases in grain output, Mao denounced Peng's letter as "bourgeois" and called for extensive criticism of the defense minister and his supporters in the top leadership, such as Zhang Wentian and Huang Kecheng.

Peng Dehuai was forced to undergo **criticism and self-criticism** (*piping yu ziwo piping*) at the meeting, and even before the meeting was over a nationwide campaign against "rightism" was launched to ferret out purported supporters of Peng and other critics of the Great Leap. Although Peng lost the political battle, he won the war over policy as the Party ordered substantial reductions in the ambitious planned production targets for steel, coal, food, and cotton, thereby signaling the first significant slowdown in the frenetic effort of the Great Leap to alter radically China's economy in one fell swoop. The divisions revealed at the Lushan Conference between Mao's "leftist" policies and the "right" opposition would continue to fester throughout the 1960s and ultimately lead to Mao Zedong's dramatic attack on Party **leaders** and rank-and-file **cadres** during the **Cultural Revolution (1966–1976)**.

LUSHAN CONFERENCE (1970). This conference marked a split between **Mao Zedong** and his personally chosen successor **Lin Biao**. Mao's "closest comrade in arms" and former minister of defense, Marshal Lin Biao was named at the 1969 Ninth National Congress of the **Chinese Communist Party** (**CCP**) as Mao's constitutionally designated heir after the purge of **Liu Shaoqi**, Mao's first heir apparent, during the **Cultural Revolution (1966–1976)**. In the context of a restoration of the CCP apparatus that had largely been destroyed during the Cultural Revolution and a concomitant reduction in the influence of the **People's Liberation Army** (**PLA**), Lin Biao's cordial relationship with Mao was suddenly rent with tensions that spewed forth at this conference. Despite Mao's repeated opposition to reestablishing the largely honorific post of **president**, which had been abolished at the beginning of the Cultural Revolution with the purge of Liu Shaoqi, Lin Biao raised this issue at the conference and further irritated the chairman by promoting a theory of "innate genius" (*tiancai lun*) that Mao had also rejected. Underlying the tension between the two was Mao's growing concern with the military threat of the **Soviet Union** and the rise to prominence in the **foreign policy** arena of the more moderate **Zhou Enlai**. Intensely anti-American, Lin Biao was concerned with Zhou's proposals for rapprochement with the **United States** and did not believe that the Soviet Union was China's primary enemy—a position advocated by both Zhou and Mao. Following his political loss of face at the Lushan Conference and obvious vulnerability to Mao's lack of faith in his successor, Lin allegedly attempted an ill-fated coup d'état against Mao Zedong—code named **Project 571**—that failed and ultimately led to Lin's reported death in an air crash while trying to escape to the Soviet Union.

– M –

MANCHURIA. This is the large swath of territory in China's northeast that currently encompasses four provinces: Heilongjiang, Jilin, Liaoning, and parts of Inner Mongolia. A quarter the size of China proper yet with only one-10th the **population**, Manchuria was for centuries a frontier region of the Chinese Empire. Southernmost Manchuria was known as *Liaodong* ("East of the River") and included the Liaodong Peninsula, which had been part of ancient China since the **Han** dynasty (202 BC–AD 220). The northernmost parts of Manchuria were incorporated into China by the Qing dynasty (1644–1911) and included large areas that were subsequently ceded to **Russia**. Historically, Manchuria was the place north of the Great Wall where Chinese and "barbarians" from Siberia and nearby regions intermingled and where Chinese peasants were often subject to "barbarian" rule. The Qing dynasty, China's last, consisted of Manchu rulers from Manchuria who, like the Mongols, conquered the Chinese state and imposed a political structure that was a synthesis of Chinese and Manchu institutions and customs.

In the modern era, Manchuria has been the frequent target of foreign interests and conquests. Because it is rich in raw materials and situated strategically vis-à-vis **Korea** and **Japan**, Manchuria was a target for Russian and Japanese expansionism in the late 19th and early 20th centuries. In 1858 and 1860, the Chinese and Russians signed the Treaty of Aigun and the Treaty of Peking, respectively, which ceded vast territories to Russia and gave it permanent control over the maritime province in Manchuria between the Ussuri River and the Pacific. The Ussuri and Amur rivers in Manchuria were established as the formal borders between China and Russia.

Following the 1895 Sino–Japanese War, won by Japan, Russian influence in the region peaked in 1898 when Russia was granted a 25-year lease over the Liaodong Peninsula and construction began on the strategic Chinese Eastern and the South Manchurian railways, linking the western and eastern and northern and southern sections, respectively, of Manchuria. The Chinese city of Lüshun was renamed Port Arthur, and a large Russian presence was established in Harbin, largely at the expense of the indigenous Manchus. In return, Russia aided China in its confrontation with Japan over the issue of control of Korea.

In 1905, Russian expansion into Manchuria was halted by the Japanese defeat of Russian forces during the Russo–Japanese War and as Japanese forces entered Manchuria for the first time. The September 1905 Treaty of Portsmouth, mediated by the **United States**, restored Chinese sovereignty over Manchuria, but enhanced the Japanese presence in the region by giving Japan control of the South Manchurian Railway as far north as the city of Changchun. Japanese interests in Manchuria grew exponentially, especially after it annexed Korea in 1910.

Confronting an increasingly assertive and nationalistic China after the rise of the **Kuomintang** (**KMT**) in 1927, the Japanese military in Manchuria (known as the Kwangtung Army) engineered the "Mukden Incident" in September 1931 and launched an all-out military occupation of the region. In 1932, Japan announced the establishment of an independent nation named Manchukuo under the titular authority of the last Qing emperor, the Manchu ruler Aisin-Gioro Puyi (1906–1967). A puppet state, Manchukuo, under the effective control of the Japanese army, stressed industrialization, railway and hydropower construction, and heavy capital investment, as well as dictatorial control over the population. It was from Manchuria that the Japanese attacked China proper in 1937.

The Cairo Declaration issued by the Allies in 1943 during World War II explicitly promised that Manchuria would be returned to China upon defeat of the Japanese Empire. However, the 1945 Yalta Agreement called for reestablishing Russian leases on the Manchurian cities of Port Arthur and Dairen and for partially restoring Russian rights over the Chinese Eastern and the South Manchurian railways, which had been forfeited after the 1905 Russo–Japanese War. Chinese sovereignty over the area was reaffirmed in anticipation of protests from the Chinese Nationalist government, which had not been invited to the Yalta Conference. **Stalin**, however, promised that Chiang Kai-shek and the Nationalists would be asked to organize the civil administration in the areas in Manchuria under Soviet occupation.

In August 1945, Soviet forces entered Manchuria in great strength and virtually retook the region. New "democratic unions" consisting of resistance fighters against the Japanese under the supervision of the Russians were formed to assume control of the local government. From late August to September 1945, Chinese Nationalist forces with American assistance attempted to enter Manchuria by sea and air but were effectively blocked by Soviet troops. In the interim, the Chinese Communists seeped into the region from their bases in north China and established effective control over many strategic points, including several ports and airfields, and seized large stocks of Japanese weaponry. When the Soviet forces finally evacuated Manchuria in early 1946, the Chinese Communists controlled key communication lines and strategic positions.

During the ensuing **Civil War (1946–1949)**, Manchuria emerged as a major strategic area in the conflict between the Nationalists and the Communists. After the defeat of the Nationalists in 1949, Russia retained its interests and privileges under a treaty signed between China and the USSR in February 1950. These were subsequently ceded back to China after the death of Josef Stalin in 1953.

MAO DUN (1896–1981). A renown novelist, and literary and art critic, who after 1949 became China's minister of culture. Originally named Shen Yanbing, Mao Dun was born into a gentry family, and later attended the preparatory college of **Beida** (**Peking University**). In 1916, he began working at the Commercial Press, first as a proof-reader, then as a translator and editor. In 1920, as an emerging prom-ising young writer, Shen Yanbing (as he was still known) founded the Literary Study Society, together with his writer friends Ye Shengtao, Xu Yishan, and others. The society emphasized realist **literature** and literature with a social purpose. From 1921 to 1923, Shen was the ed-itor of the *Short Story Monthly*, one of the most influential literary publications at the time. After teaching for a short period at a girls' school under the control of the **Chinese Communist Party** (**CCP**), he joined the left-wing **Kuomintang** (**KMT**) under Wang Jingwei in Chungking (**Chongqing**). But after the KMT purge of the Commu-nists in 1927, he went to **Shanghai** and devoted most of his time to creative writing. At this time, he started using the pen name "Mao Dun" in order to hide his identity.

Between September 1927 and June 1928, Mao Dun completed his famous trilogy *Eclipse* composed of *Disillusion*, *Vacillation*, and *Pursuit*. The trilogy describes the life of revolutionary youth, deca-dent bourgeoisie, and **intellectuals** during the KMT-led Northern Ex-pedition era (1926–1927). Although Mao Dun was a founding mem-ber of the League of Left-Wing Writers in 1930, he did not receive national recognition until the publication of his novel *Twilight* in 1933. An insightful and in-depth study of the complex life of Shang-hai during the Depression in the 1930s, *Twilight* portrays the ruth-lessness and exploitation of capitalist society and confirms the Com-munist notion that capitalism was a cul-de-sac for China. In 1936, Mao Dun joined Lu Xun, **Hu Feng**, and other writers to form the Chinese Literary Workers Association that advocated a people's lit-erature for the national revolutionary struggle. He also produced sev-eral great short stories during this period, including *Spring Silkworm* and *The Lin Family Shop*.

In May 1940, Mao Dun headed for Yan'an where he lectured at the Lu Xun Institute. In 1941, he left for **Hong Kong** via Chungking, where he published another novel, *Putrefaction*, which expresses sympathy for the Communist enterprise and opposition to the KMT. Afterward, he worked under **Guo Moruo** on the cultural committee of the political training board of the National Military Council. Fol-lowing the **Sino–Japanese War** (**1937–1945**), Mao Dun and his wife toured the **Soviet Union** in 1947. Upon their return in 1948, Mao Dun founded the pro-Communist *Fiction Monthly* in Hong Kong.

After the Communist takeover in 1949, Mao Dun returned to **Beijing** and was subsequently elected vice-chairman of the All-China Federation of Literary Circles (renamed the All-China Federation of Literary and Art Circles in 1953) under Guo Moruo. In 1954, Mao Dun was appointed minister of culture, and was later elected as deputy to the First **National People's Congress (NPC)**. During the **Hundred Flowers Campaign (1956–1957)**, Mao Dun attacked the conformity of the Communist literary community and, as a result, he was subsequently removed from his position as minister of culture and, like other intellectuals, suffered during the **Cultural Revolution (1966–1976)**.

With the downfall of the radical **Gang of Four** in 1976, Mao Dun reemerged as a vice-chairman of the **Chinese People's Political Consultative Conference (CPPCC)**, and in 1979, he was reelected chairman of the Writers Association. He died at the age of 85 on 27 March 1981.

MAO YUANXIN (1939–). Born in Hunan Province, Mao Yuanxin was a nephew of **Mao Zedong**. He first studied in the **Soviet Union** and in 1959 became a student at the Harbin Military Engineering Academy, where he joined the **Chinese Communist Party (CCP)**. In 1964, Mao Yuanxin became a lecturer at the Harbin Academy and during the **Cultural Revolution (1966–1976)**, he rose to prominence as director of the Shenyang Municipal **People's Liberation Army (PLA)** Infantry School and **political commissar** of the Shenyang Military Region. Mao Yuanxin also served as Party secretary of Liaoning Province and a special liaison to Mao Zedong. In October 1976, after the death of Mao Zedong, Mao Yuanxin was relieved of all of his formal positions in the PLA and CCP. In 2004, Mao Yuanxin's reminiscences entitled *Eight Years of Political Life* was banned from publication by the Office of the Central Propaganda Department of the CCP because it reputedly contained various "instructions," "exhortations," and "comments" by Mao Zedong that had never been made public while publication of the book was declared to be harmful to the state and to Mao Yuanxin himself.

MAO ZEDONG (1893–1976). Chairman of the **Chinese Communist Party (CCP)** from 1938 until his death in September 1976, Mao Zedong was the paramount leader of the Chinese Communist revolution. He was born in Shaoshan, Hunan Province, into a rich peasant family and received a traditional primary **education**. Later, he ran away from home to attend middle school. In 1911, he was enrolled in what was soon to become the Hunan First Normal School. With the help of a friend, he established the New People's Study Society, which subsequently became the core of the CCP in Hunan. After graduation, Mao worked as a library assistant at **Beida (Peking University)**, where he became involved with other activist students and was influenced by Beida professor and co-founder of the CCP, Li Dazhao. During the **May Fourth Movement (1919–1923)**, Mao helped set up a Hunan student organization while two of Mao's journals—*Hsiang (Xiang) River Review* and *New Hunan*—were shut down by the authorities. After becoming involved in a student strike targeted at the Hunan governor, Mao was compelled to flee Hunan, so he traveled to **Beijing** and **Shanghai**, where he met Chen Duxiu, the leading intellectual who later became the first general secretary of the CCP. Mao was able to return to Hunan in 1920 and became head of the primary school that was attached to the Hunan First Normal School. Mao married Yang Kaihui and also opened a radical bookstore. Later, after the arrival of Comintern agent Gregory Voitinsky in China, Mao organized a Communist cell and a Socialist **Youth League** branch in Changsha, Hunan.

In July 1921, on a boat in a lake located in Shanghai, Mao participated in the First National Congress of the CCP, which then consisted of 60 members. At the Third National Party Congress, held in **Guangzhou (Canton)** in 1923, Mao was elected to the CCP Central Committee for the first time. During the first **Kuomintang (KMT)–CCP United Front (1924–1927)**, Mao was given several positions in the KMT. In 1926, Mao became director of the sixth class of the Peasant Movement Training Institute in Guangzhou. In December of that year, he promoted the importance of the peasant issue and called for intensified revolutionary action. In March 1927, Mao wrote a report that advocated harnessing peasant discontent as the great social force of the revolution just as the KMT–CCP First United Front fell apart following Chiang Kai-shek's coup against the CCP in

Shanghai. This experience confirmed Mao's belief that "political power grows out of the barrel of a gun" (*qiangganzi limian chu zhengquan*). After the failure of the Autumn Harvest Uprising in September–October 1927, Mao led some of the survivors of the movement to the mountains between Hunan and Jiangxi provinces. In April 1928, Mao's troops were joined by reinforcements led by **Zhu De** at Jinggangshan. Following the establishment of the Chinese Soviet Republic in late 1931, although Mao held two top positions in the government and the military, he lacked influence in the Party, which at that time was manipulated by the Twenty-Eight Bolsheviks who had trained in the USSR. By the time the Chinese Soviet Republic collapsed during Chiang Kai-shek's final encirclement campaigns, Mao had lost all of his authority within the CCP.

At the Zunyi Conference in 1935, Mao reassumed control over Communist military forces, and, in 1938, he was made chairman (*zhuxi*) of the CCP. After the arduous **Long March (1934–1935)** of more than 6,000 Chinese *li* (*li*=one half kilometer), Mao and his forces established a base in Yan'an. During the 1942–1944 **Rectification Campaign**, Mao consolidated his political authority, and he promulgated his **personality cult (*geren chongbai*)** in 1943. At the 1945 Seventh National Party Congress, Mao defeated the Twenty-Eight Bolshevik faction and advocated the Sinicization of Marxist–Leninist ideology to meet the circumstances and needs of the Communist revolution in China. Mao abandoned his second wife, He Zizhen, whom he had married in 1931 after his first wife was murdered by the KMT. His third marriage was to an actress from Shanghai named Lan Ping, whom Mao called **Jiang Qing**. By the time the Japanese were defeated in China in 1945, the CCP had vastly expanded its power in China. However, because Mao's troops were outnumbered by KMT forces, Mao initially favored cooperation with the KMT. Nonetheless, the diametrically opposed differences between the two parties finally triggered the **Civil War** that lasted from 1946–1949. On 1 October 1949, Mao, as the newly appointed chairman of the Central People's Government, proclaimed the establishment of the **People's Republic of China (PRC)**. In February 1950, Mao signed the Sino–Soviet Treaty of Friendship, Alliance, and Mutual Assistance in Moscow, despite ill treatment during his first visit abroad to the **Soviet Union** by **Josef Stalin**.

The initial politics of Mao's regime followed the mild prescriptions laid out in 1940 in his speech on the **New Democracy**. Mao was instrumental, however, in convincing Stalin to sanction the North Korean attack on South **Korea**, thereby igniting the **Korean War (1950–1953)**. China's decision to enter the war in October 1950 was made by Mao himself, after offers of Soviet military assistance in the form of air support were initially made and then withdrawn by Stalin. Throughout the 1950s, Mao's China was under the strong influence of the Soviet Union and, until Josef Stalin's death in 1953, the policies of the Soviet leader. During the succession crisis in the Soviet Union, Mao supported Gregori Malenkov, who ultimately lost out to Nikita Khrushchev. Although Mao's initial relations with Khrushchev were warm, the two **leaders** gradually became embroiled in a mutual animosity that ultimately led to the Sino–Soviet Conflict. Domestically, Mao resisted family-planning policies and denounced advocates of these policies, such as Ma Yinchu, which led to a huge spike in China's **population** growth.

Beginning in 1955, Mao generally supported the radical reorganization of Chinese **agriculture** and against the advice of top Party leaders initiated the **Hundred Flowers (1956–1957)** followed by the equally divisive **Anti-Rightist Campaign (1957–1958)**. All of these movements brought much suffering to China's **intellectuals** and alienated them from the Party. In 1958, Mao switched gears and initiated the **Great Leap Forward (1958–1960)**, which ended in a human tragedy that involved upward of 30 million deaths in one of the largest famines in human history. Although China gradually recovered from the post-Leap depression, Mao viewed the situation with great apprehension and grew more alienated from the intellectuals, who resented and ridiculed him. In 1962, Mao insisted on the need for **class struggle** in the countryside. He initiated the **Cultural Revolution (1966–1976)**, at the beginning of which Mao displayed his flare for the dramatic by taking a swim in the Yangtze River at the age of 69. Aimed at eliminating all opposition to his policies in the CCP, the Cultural Revolution lasted for 10 years, during which Mao was elevated to nearly "god" status in the CCP and in Chinese society.

In the 1970s, Mao ended the diplomatic isolation of China by sanctioning contacts with the **United States** that led to the establishment of diplomatic relations between the two countries. Domestically, Mao engineered the return of **Deng Xiaoping** in 1973 to run the CCP, but acquiesced in Deng's second purge in 1976 following the **April Fifth Movement**. Estranged for years from his wife, Jiang Qing, Mao apparently resisted any attempts by Madame Mao to gain control of the CCP and publicly criticized her factional tendencies.

Mao Zedong died in September 1976 at the age of 82. Despite his request for cremation, his successors followed their counterparts in the Soviet Union, **Vietnam**, and North Korea by deciding to preserve the corpse of their great leader, which was placed in a crystal sarcophagus, where it has been on public display for 27 years in the Mao Zedong Memorial Hall in Tiananmen Square in central Beijing. The **Resolution on Certain Questions in the History of Our Party since the Establishment of the People's Republic of China** passed in June 1981 evaluated Mao's contributions to the Chinese revolution, but made note of some of his shortcomings in his later years. In the 1990s and into the early 2000s, the Maoist revival—or "Mao Craze"—in China filled the ideological vacuum created by the 1989 military crackdown against the second **Beijing Spring**. Along with the writer **Ba Jin**, a group of exiled Chinese intellectuals in 2003 called on Chinese authorities to remove Mao's corpse from the Memorial Hall in time for the 2008 Beijing Olympics and to convert the mausoleum to a museum of the Cultural Revolution and to remove Mao's portrait from the entrance gate to the Forbidden City.

MAO ZEDONG THOUGHT STUDY CLASSES. Organized in response to the 7 May 1966 letter issued by **Mao Zedong** to **Lin Biao** in which the Party chairman urged Lin to "turn the whole country into a great school of Mao Zedong Thought," Mao Zedong Thought Study Classes were an integral part of the **May Seventh Cadre Schools**. Set up during the **Cultural Revolution (1966–1976)**, these classes became centers for **cadres** to practice **criticism and self-criticism** (*piping yu ziwo piping*). After the death of Mao Zedong and criticism of elements of his leadership by post-Mao **leaders** in the 1981 document **Resolutions on Certain Questions in the History of Our Party since the Establishment of the People's Republic of China**, these study classes declined in importance but were by no means eliminated as students in secondary and university **education** continued to have mandated Mao study.

MARRIAGE LAW. Since 1949, China has formally enacted two marriage laws. The first was promulgated in May 1950 by the newly formed Central People's Government and remained in force for 30 years. The second marriage law was adopted in September 1980 by the Third Session of the Fifth **National People's Congress** (**NPC**) and as of 2007 remains in force.

The 1950 Marriage Law attempted to deal with iniquities in relationships between men and **women** and husband and wife that had been part of Chinese tradition for centuries. This was reflected in Article One of the law, which affirmed that "the arbitrary and compulsory feudal marriage system, which is based on the superiority of men over women and which ignores the children's interests shall be abolished." The law went on to outlaw such traditional practices as bigamy, concubines, child betrothal, interference with the remarriage of widows, and the exaction of money or gifts in connection with marriage. Instead, the law called for marriage to be consummated by a "contract" based upon the willingness of the two parties in which both husband and wife could retain their family name and could inherit each other's property. The right to divorce, initiated by either party, was also written into the law, though with some restrictions.

Children were also granted certain rights under the new law, such as that of inheriting property. There were also obligations on the part of parents regarding the rearing and educating of children. Infanticide was strictly forbidden and was declared a "criminal act." Among the restrictions included were a minimum age for marriage (male 20 years, female 18 years); prohibition to marry if one party is sexually impotent; and a stipulation that "the husband shall not apply for a divorce when his wife is with child." It was also declared that divorce could only be granted upon mediation by local government authorities at the subdistrict level of the People's Government, a process that was obligated by the law as a means of seeking reconciliation. In practice, divorces initiated by the wife resulted in the government requiring efforts at reconciliation, while divorces initiated by the husband were more often granted outright. Application of the law was allowed a certain degree of flexibility in areas populated by **minorities** with unconventional marriage practices.

The 1980 Marriage Law was promulgated largely in response to changes in China's demographic situation. Unlike the 1950 law, the new legislation required couples to practice family planning and abide by the country's official **one-child policy**. It also increased the legal age for marriage to 22 years for the male and 20 years for the woman. Both husband and wife were also given the freedom to engage in productive work, and longstanding requirements for a health certificate and a letter from one's employer confirming that a person was single—both considered annoying by marrying couples—were dropped. Provision of ID cards and residence files along with a statement signed by both parties that they are single is the only legal requirement for marriage. Other prohibitions and enumerated rights included in the 1950 law were repeated in the 1980 version, such as the outlawing of bigamy, "mercenary marriages," and the rights of children following a divorce that can now proceed without permission from employers. In the 1980 law, the mother was given preference in custody battles when they involved a child undergoing breast-feeding. Reflecting recent social changes in China, children born out of wedlock were accorded the same rights as children of married couples. The 1950 law was declared null and void as a result of the new 1980 legislation. Further changes in regulations governing marriage were introduced in the 1990s when the Ministry of Education issued a code that prohibited college students from getting married. But this regulation was superseded in 2003 by removing the ban on students still on a university campus.

MARXISM–LENINISM–MAO ZEDONG THOUGHT. This constituted the major components of China's official ideology that provided the guiding principles for the **Chinese Communist Party (CCP)** and the Chinese state. From Marxism, the Chinese took "historical materialism" (the theory that the mode of production determines the social and political structure of any society), "**class struggle**" (the idea that human history is the history of violent struggles between social classes), and "dialectical materialism" (the view that fundamental contradictions between property systems and modes of production generate the dynamic for fundamental social and political change), plus a vision for a final Communist utopia. From Lenin, China borrowed his theory of **imperialism**, which professed that class struggle had reached an international level of conflict between capitalist imperialist states and the proletariat in Third World nations.

Lenin's theory of the Party as the "vanguard of the proletariat" and **democratic-centralism** are also centerpieces of Chinese Communist ideology.

Mao Zedong Thought is laid out in the five volumes of his *Selected Works* and contains such innovative notions as the peasantry forming the basis of the socialist revolution (undoubtedly a heretical thought to Marx, who preached that the proletariat was the vanguard revolutionary class), the "**mass line**," the emphasis on the integration of theory and practice, and the concepts of "contradictions" (*maodun*) and "**uninterrupted revolution**" (*buduan geming*). In the CCP Central Committee 1981 **Resolutions on Certain Questions in the History of Our Party since the Establishment of the People's Republic of China**, some of Mao Zedong's policies and decisions were criticized, but Mao Zedong Thought was deemed to be "a correct theory" that had been collectively formulated by Mao and other top CCP **leaders**. To "negate entirely Mao Zedong Thought," it was declared in 1978, would cause China to revert to pre-1949 conditions.

"MASS LINE" ("*QUNZHONG LUXIAN*"). A staple feature of **Mao Zedong** Thought is that the masses of workers and peasants in China should be relied on by the **Chinese Communist Party** (**CCP**) to achieve its revolutionary goals. Theoretically, this conflicted with Lenin's more authoritarian notion that the "spontaneity" of the general **population** could not be trusted and would derail the ultimate goals of the revolution. In Lenin's view, workers were burdened by a "**trade union** mentality" that fixated concerns on bread and butter issues at the expense of the more historically significant goal of building **socialism**. Russian peasants in this formulation were even more ideologically "backward," concerned solely with narrow goals of acquiring land and bread. For Lenin, the revolutionary intelligentsia of Communist Party members alone sparked the drive toward socialism.

Mao's "mass line" concept was fundamentally different from that of Lenin, though the Chinese leader did not reject the critical role of the Party, nor did he impart to the worker and peasant masses anything remotely comparable to political sovereignty. Instead, the "mass line" meant that "in all practical work of our Party, all correct leadership is necessarily 'from the masses, to the masses'." The Party would be successful if it were to incorporate the views of the masses into its political formulations and policy positions, and were to test these policies out among the masses. Of course, **Mao Zedong** provided no institutional mechanisms either for transmitting popular views to the CCP, or for ensuring that the Party sought popular endorsement. The "mass line" consisted of moral and political guidance from the top **leaders** to Party **cadres** that certainly was not followed in many cases when popular dissatisfaction and real human suffering, such as that which occurred in the **Great Leap Forward (1958–1960)**, apparently had little or no impact on CCP policies and decisions.

MAY FOURTH MOVEMENT (1919–1923). The **Chinese Communist Party (CCP)** traces its origins to this student protest movement that broke out in **Beijing** in spring 1919. Inspired by the principles of self-determination promoted at the Versailles conference by **United States** President Woodrow Wilson, the Chinese had hoped to win back the territories controlled by foreign powers. Instead, territorial concessions in China's Shandong Province were taken from Germany, as a result of its defeat in World War I, and transferred to **Japan**, which had been an ally of the victorious Western powers. The acceptance of this decision by the Chinese government infuriated students, **intellectuals**, and some workers, who organized major street protests. The movement quickly expanded into a demand for fundamental "democratic and scientific" changes in Chinese society. Exhibiting a profound cultural iconoclasm, **leaders** of the May Fourth Movement, such as Chen Duxiu, a **Beida (Peking University)** professor, advocated totalistic changes in Chinese government, society, and culture. This included calls for **language reform** by transforming the country's written language from its classical origins into a more colloquial form and access to broader **education** for the **population**. University and popular journals flourished during the late 1910s and early 1920s such as *New Youth (Xin Qingnian)* as the general level of public opinion increased. In the midst of the May Fourth Movement, the CCP was organized in 1921 by Chen Duxiu and many other veterans of the May Fourth Movement.

MAY SEVENTH CADRE SCHOOLS. Established in the 1960s on the basis of a letter written by **Mao Zedong** to **Lin Biao** on 7 May 1966, these schools were assigned the task of sending Party and government **cadres** to the countryside to engage in manual **labor**. In reality, they were no different from the draconian labor reform camps that the **Chinese Communist Party (CCP)** had set up to incarcerate political criminals and other people designated by the regime as socially and politically undesirable. In the Maoist perspective, CCP cadres had spent too much time in their offices shuffling papers, where they remained aloof from the interests of the workers and peasants whose interests the CCP theoretically promoted by "building **socialism**." The first such "schools" were set up in the northeast, often on farms in remote areas where cadres performed menial tasks and grew their own food. These experiences were to counter the pervasive tendency among cadres toward "**bureaucratism**" that had, in the Maoist view, infected the CCP and all Chinese government organizations. Altogether, three million officials and cadres spent varying amounts of time at such "schools" while they retained their official positions and salaries. After a few weeks or months, they returned to their official duties. The May Seventh Cadre Schools were abolished sometime in the 1970s.

MAY SIXTEENTH CIRCULAR (*WUYILIU TONGZHI*). Issued on 16 May 1966 by the **Chinese Communist Party (CCP)** Central Committee, this document revoked the "February Outline" and disbanded the first Central **Cultural Revolution Small Group** that had been established by **Beijing** mayor and veteran CCP leader **Peng Zhen** to carry out Mao's initial calls for a "cultural revolution." To Mao's consternation, Peng and his Cultural Revolution Group had tried to limit the issues of the "cultural revolution" to literary matters among a small group of Chinese **intellectuals**. This circular represented Mao's attempt to expand the revolution to major political issues involving the structure of the state, the course of CCP policies, and the composition of the leadership. A new Central Cultural Revolution Small Group was set up to report directly to the Standing Committee of the **Politburo** that was under Mao's control. **Ultra-leftist** organizations during the Cultural Revolution were called "May 16 Corps" to legitimize their radical political objectives.

MEDIA. *See* BROADCASTING AND TELEVISION; CENSORSHIP; *PEOPLE'S DAILY.*

MEETINGS TO RECOLLECT PAST BITTERNESS. The Chinese Communist government constantly emphasized in its propaganda the great contrasts between the "past bitterness" of the general **population** prior to the Communist takeover in 1949 and the "present happiness" of the people after 1949. This message was institutionalized in mass meetings held throughout the Maoist era (1949–1976) at which older workers and peasants with vivid memories of the past would recall to younger audiences the sufferings that they had endured under the previous **Kuomintang (KMT)** regime. These descriptions were often supplemented by such activities as the preparation of meals for the young people composed of extremely scant fare, such as wild fruits and plant roots, which was similar to the meals that many of the poor had depended on for sustenance before 1949. This "class **education**" aimed at presenting stark contrasts between the KMT past and the Communist present. Not all such meetings were successful, however, as some politically naïve workers and peasants contrasted the Communist present to the KMT past in unfavorable terms. "The food was really good back then [i.e., prior to 1949]" was how some peasants described the past to young students, to the obvious consternation of **Chinese Communist Party (CCP)** propagandists.

MILITARY AFFAIRS COMMISSION (MAC). This body is directly under the authority of the **Politburo** of the **Chinese Communist Party (CCP)** and is charged with maintaining Communist Party control over the **People's Liberation Army (PLA)**. In addition to the Party Central Military Affairs Commission, there is a companion State Military Affairs Commission that in theory is under the authority of the Standing Committee of the **National People's Congress (NPC)**, a state body separate from the CCP. In reality, these two organizations are "two names of the same group of people" as their membership is virtually identical with the same chairmen and vice-chairman, both civilians. The primary function of the MAC is to appoint and remove military personnel, especially the commanders of the key military regions of which there are seven. The size of the MAC ranges from 10 to 20 members, and includes the minister of defense—who was for many years a relatively low-ranking officer exercising little real authority over the PLA—and the heads of the General Staff Headquarters, the General Logistics Department, the General Armaments Department, and the General Political Department, which oversees the system of **political commissars** in the military who, under a separate chain of command, ensure loyalty to the CCP and the civilian government and are responsible for the political **education** of PLA troops, a tradition that dates back to the 1930s when the Revolutionary Military Committee headed by **Mao Zedong** performed this role. The military and Party **leaders** on the MAC all serve on either the Politburo and/or the Central Committee of the CCP. The chairman of the MAC is China's commander-in-chief and serves the same five-year duration as that of every Party Congress and NPC.

Historically, the chairman was also CCP chairman (later general secretary), but this was not the case from 1978 to 1989 when **Deng Xiaoping** headed the MAC despite not holding the Party's top position. Deng's effort to install his first designated successor, **Hu Yaobang**, as chairman of the MAC failed and helped precipitate Hu's fall from power in 1987. **Jiang Zemin** assumed both the Party and State MAC chairmanship in 1989 and 1990, respectively, while he also served concurrently as CCP general secretary, thereby reestablishing the previous tradition initially introduced by Mao Zedong. Following his retirement from Party positions in 2002, Jiang, like Deng Xiaoping before him, remained chairman of the MAC, where, until his retirement in September 2004, he maintained crucial control of China's armed forces.

The MAC includes a Standing Committee composed of the vice-chairmen (traditionally, the minister of defense, concurrently) and the PLA chief-of-staff. Signaling a new concept in the development of China's national defense and responding to basic changes in the conduct of modern warfare, the MAC, in 2004, was fundamentally altered in its composition by the inclusion of the director of the PLA General Armament Department, commanders of the PLA Air Force (PLAAF) and Navy (PLAN), and commander of the Second Artillery Corps, which commands China's increasingly significant strategic rocket forces. In 2004, the MAC was composed of 11 members from all the major components of the PLA and, beginning in September, was chaired by **Hu Jintao**, who had served as a vice-chairman since 1999 and, after being appointed CCP general secretary and **president**

of the People's Republic of China, inherited the position of MAC chairman in 2004 while the post of vice-chairman previously held by Hu was assumed by Xu Caihou, the head of the PLA General Political Department. Hu Jintao has indicated continuity in military policy lines developed under his predecessors by urging the whole army to uphold "Deng Xiaoping Theory" and Jiang Zemin's concept of the "Three Represents" while also emphasizing the important role of CCP control of the country's armed forces. Approval of the MAC chairman is needed to move an entire Group Army, as evidently occurred during the June 1989 military crackdown against the second **Beijing Spring**. Following the publication of a White Paper titled "China's National Defense in 2004," the MAC also signed off on a policy of significantly upgrading the technical and educational development of China's armed forces and indicated its approval of the tough stand taken by the CCP against any move toward independence by **Taiwan**. *See also* GOVERNMENT STRUCTURE; RUSSIA; UNITED STATES.

MILITARY REGIONS. *See* PEOPLE'S LIBERATION ARMY (PLA).

MINISTRY OF FOREIGN ECONOMIC RELATIONS AND TRADE (MOFERT). Established in 1982, MOFERT was created by merging the Ministry of Foreign Trade with the Foreign Investment Control Commission and the Import-Export Commission. It was designed to coordinate policy in both **trade and investment** from foreign sources, including joint ventures, and to gain greater control over China's growing economic relations with the outside world. This involves the establishment of a licensing system for both imports and exports, the imposition of export duties to curb the export of goods in short supply, and the setting up of offices at China's major trading ports. MOFERT also played a role in mapping out China's overall economic strategy in its foreign economic relations. The ministry was reorganized in a 1998 reform of the state structure into the State Economic and Trade Commission and the Ministry of Foreign Trade and Economic Cooperation. *See also* ECONOMY; FOREIGN POLICY; GOVERNMENT STRUCTURE.

MINORITIES (*SHAOSHU MINZU*). Some 104 million people in China belong to the 55 officially recognized minority groups that, in

2004, constituted 8.41% of the country's total **population**. The largest of the minority groups are the *Zhuang* (13 million) in the Guangxi Autonomous Region in the southwest; Chinese Muslims or *Hui* (seven million) and Uygurs (six million) in the Xinjiang Autonomous Region in the northwest; Mongols (three million) in Inner Mongolia; and Tibetans (four million) in **Tibet** (*Xizang*). Others include the *Yi*, *Miao*, Manchus, and Koreans, totaling approximately 16 million. Minorities constitute a majority of the population in Tibet and Inner Mongolia; they inhabit more than 90% of China's strategic border areas and 64% of the entire territory of the **People's Republic of China** (**PRC**).

During China's imperial era from the Qin dynasty (221–207 BC) to the Qing (1644–1911), a policy of "rule by custom" was adopted toward ethnic minorities in which political unification of the empire was maintained while non-**Han** ethnicities were allowed to preserve their own social systems, languages, and cultures. Immediately after 1949, central policy toward minorities in China relied heavily on coercive measures to re-incorporate minority areas, such as Tibet and Xinjiang, into China and to suppress local efforts at independence, such as the East Turkestan Movement in Xinjiang. In 1952, the Chinese government issued the "Program for the Implementation of Regional Autonomy of the PRC," which included provisions for the establishment of autonomous regions and areas that, in 1954, were formally incorporated into China's first state constitution by the **National People's Congress** (**NPC**). This was followed, in 1955, by the establishment of the Xinjiang–Uygur Autonomous Region in western China, the Guangxi–Zhuang Autonomous Region in 1958 in the southwest, and the Tibetan Autonomous Region in 1965. Minorities were also granted limited self-governance and considerable freedom to practice their indigenous cultures, including the use of their native languages, by the 1984 Law on Regional Ethnic Autonomy, which was amended in 2001. By 2003, China had established 155 ethnic autonomous areas, of which five were autonomous regions, 30 autonomous prefectures, and 120 autonomous counties (known in Inner Mongolia as banners) with central policy on minorities implemented by the State Commission of Ethnic Affairs.

During periods of political upheaval in China, numerous assaults and persecutions against minority peoples were carried out during the

Anti-Rightist Campaign (1957–1958), the **Great Leap Forward** (**1958–1959**), and especially in the **Cultural Revolution** (1966–1976), when the center imposed tighter controls on minority areas and extended political campaigns to the local level. Minority political **leaders**, such as **Ulanfu** of Inner Mongolia, were accused of "local nationalism" and purged, while minority cultural artifacts, such as temples and religious shrines, were wantonly destroyed, particularly by **Red Guards** during the Cultural Revolution. Minorities were also forced, contrary to past policies, to reorganize their social and economic systems along the "socialist" lines dictated by **Beijing**. Central policies such as "planting grain everywhere" were imposed, for instance, in Tibet, with catastrophic consequences because the area's climatic conditions were ill-suited to this policy. Radical political campaigns also involved imposing restrictions on the use of minority languages, reversing the emphasis on bilingual **education** that had dominated government policy in the early 1950s.

Beginning in 1976, Beijing relaxed its policies toward minorities, including its policies on native languages, and even encouraged minority elites to join the **Chinese Communist Party** (**CCP**) and become delegates to the NPC. Previously persecuted minority leaders, such as Ulanfu, were rehabilitated and restored to high-level positions as even greater flexibility was allowed with the passage in 1993 of Regulations on the Administrative Work of Ethnic Townships that led to the creation of over 1,100 such areas for minorities living in compact communities that did not qualify for autonomous prefecture, county, or region status. Particular emphasis was given to the Central government's role in promoting the **economy** of minority areas that had begun in 1955 with the Subsidy for Ethnic Minority Areas and continued in 1964 with the establishment of the Stand-by Fund for Ethnic Minority Areas. Since the inauguration of economic reforms in 1978–1979, minority areas in the interior fell increasingly behind their more economically advanced Han counterpart as only 5% of Foreign Direct Investment (FDI) was made in minority areas with the bulk going to the vibrant coastal areas overwhelmingly populated by the Han. Following a 1992 speech by Party General Secretary **Jiang Zemin** at the First Central Nationalities Work Conference, the Chinese government increased subsidies and special appropriations to minority areas and provided for preferential treatment for ethnic minorities in such fields as investment, **banking and finance**, and employment. Special projects directed at minority areas were also begun such as the grand strategy for the development of China's western regions announced in 2000 while annual growth rates of over 9% were recorded for all minority areas that by 2003 reportedly contributed one trillion *yuan* to the national Gross Domestic Product (GDP). In such regions as Tibet, however, much of this economic activity, especially the huge infrastructure projects of highways and hydroelectric projects, overwhelmingly benefited Han migrants into the region over the local population that remained largely in remote and very poor rural areas.

According to a White Paper published in 2004, respect for and a guarantee of freedom of **religion** have also been pursued; in it, the Chinese boasted that 1,700 Buddhist sites conducted religious activities in Tibet along with over 26,000 mosques in Xinjiang and in the Ningxia-Hui Autonomous Region. Not only are important meetings of the CCP, NPC, and **Chinese People's Political Consultative Conference (CPPCC)** provided with simultaneous translation and documents in the Mongolian, Tibetan, Uygur, Kazak, Korean, *Yi*, and *Zhuang* languages, but the White Paper also claimed that software has been developed for several of these minority languages. Much emphasis was also given in the 2004 White Paper to the protection of environmentally fragile and historical sites in minority areas that have been included in the 29 UNESCO World Cultural and Natural Heritage sites located in China, even as the government touts such undoubtedly disruptive projects as "asphalt roads to every county in Western China" and "outlet highways for impoverished counties" that have led to massive construction projects in such pristine areas as the karst mountains of Guilin along the Li River.

The status of minorities in China in recent years is, according to exile groups and **human rights** organizations, somewhat less sanguine than is represented in official Chinese documents such as the 2004 White Paper. Despite government claims on increasing numbers of minorities serving as state and Party **cadres** in minority regions, a massive influx of Han migrants to Xinjiang, Tibet, and into other autonomous regions has occurred in the last decade, where they exercise a near monopoly over money, authority, and power and secure most of the new jobs and housing. The Chinese government has also imposed an increasingly coercive control over the cultural, social, and political life of the most unassimilated minorities, especially in Central Asia, where the Chinese crackdown since 11 September 2001 has been carried out in the name of its own "war on terrorism" against a supposedly small number of extremist groups associated with the East Turkistan Islamic Movement that China claims, without verification, is linked to Osama bin Laden's Al-Qaida. In Xinjiang, scores of mosques have been razed in the name of reconstruction and people arrested on charges of separatism, which makes them subject to execution. Koranic schools have also been closed down and civil servants and teachers have reportedly been forbidden to pray in public because Islamic education is said to be unavailable in schools while foreign Muslims are prohibited from meeting with local imams (religious leaders).

In 1989 and 1990, major disturbances broke out among ethnic Muslims, the first in response to publication of a book entitled *Sexual Customs* that reportedly insulted Islam and the second when a supposed "armed counterrevolutionary rebellion" occurred in a Kirghiz Autonomous Prefecture in Xinjiang. This was followed, in 1993, by an explosion in Kaxgar, Xinjiang, attributed to a separatist group and large-scale riots against Han Chinese shops by Uygurs shouting independence slogans in 1997 in Yining, Xinjiang. On the very day of the memorial service for **Deng Xiaoping** on 25 February 1997, bombs exploded on buses in Ürümqi, the capital of Xinjiang killing nine people, which was followed a month later by bomb blasts on buses in Beijing attributed to a Uygur separatist group. While a heavy crackdown by the central Chinese government has prevented a recurrence of such violence, inter-ethnic tension has periodically broken out between *Hui* Muslim minorities and both Han and Tibetan populations in Qinghai Province and other areas where the three major cultural and social traditions intersect and where the general absence of intermarriage has prevented the creation of a Chinese version of the melting pot. While most of these disputes are over local matters involving land and petty conflicts, others are more serious, such as the armed conflict that broke out in the April 1990 "holy war" in the city of Kashgar. In 2004, China released Xinjiang's best-known political prisoner, Ms. Rebiya Kadeer, even as it tightened controls on religious worship, assembly, and artistic expression among the Autonomous Region's eight million Muslims. China also worked through the **Shanghai** Cooperation Organization, founded in 2001, which includes **Russia**, Kazakhstan, Kyrgyzstan, Tajikistan, and Uzbekistan, to ensure regional security. A rapid deployment force of the **People's Liberation Army** (**PLA**) is based in western China to put down any potential trouble in Xinjiang or Tibet.

"MOVEMENT TO RESIST U.S. AGGRESSION AND AID KOREA." (*"KANGMEI, YUANCHAO"*). The **Korean War** commenced in June 1950 with the North Korean invasion of South **Korea**. The so-called Chinese People's Volunteers intervened on the side of North Korean forces in October 1950. The "Movement to Resist U.S. Aggression and Aid Korea" aimed at mobilizing domestic support—material and psychological—for the Chinese war effort in Korea. Supplies of food and clothing were gathered for troops at the front, while an intense anti-American campaign was whipped up among the **population**. Americans who had stayed behind in China after the Communist takeover in 1949 and had, up until the war, lived in relative freedom, were rounded up, imprisoned, and, in many cases, accused of spying. The movement helped solidify the linkage between the **Chinese Communist Party** (**CCP**) and Chinese nationalism and came to an end after the Korean armistice in July 1953. The last of Chinese People's Volunteers were not withdrawn from North Korea until 1958. Chinese children were reared on this campaign, learning to sing songs with lyrics stressing the need to "eventually defeat the ambitious American imperial wolves."

"MUTUAL AID TEAMS" (*"HUZHU ZU"*). The most rudimentary form of mutual cooperation in the Chinese countryside, the Mutual Aid Teams (MATs) were first experimented with by the **Chinese Communist Party** (**CCP**) in the 1940s in the "liberated" areas of northwest China. After 1949, the formation of MATs throughout the Chinese countryside constituted the first stage in the reorganization of rural production. By late 1952, 40% of all rural households were organized into teams. In 1955, MATs were replaced by the **Agricultural Producers' Cooperatives** (**APCs**).

Mutual Aid Teams were implemented throughout China after the promulgation of the Decision on Mutual Aid and Cooperation in

Agriculture in 1951 by the Central Committee of the CCP. Theoretically, peasant participation in the MATs was voluntary, but considerable political pressure was brought to bear by rural Party **cadres** on individual peasant households to participate. One type was the temporary MATs, which were organized on a seasonal basis (sowing and harvest) and were generally quite small, constituting less than 10 peasant households that worked on individually owned land that had been distributed during the **land reform (1950–1952). Labor**, tools, and draught animals were shared, but with no transfer of ownership or control. Another type was the year-round, fixed Mutual Aid Teams, which were organized on a larger scale, generally comprising from 10 to 30 peasant households. **Work points** were allocated and tools and draught animals were subject to common ownership. Agricultural production was carried out in the fixed MATs, along with sideline production and a rudimentary division of labor for technical work, though land ownership was left essentially untouched for everyone except the landlords. A third type of MATs was, in effect, a lower form of the APCs, involving the pooling of shares of land and labor. The move to APCs began to be implemented in 1953 with the promulgation of the Decision on the Development of APCs by the CCP as MATs were effectively abandoned for a higher form of "socialized" agriculture.

– N –

NATIONAL PEOPLE'S CONGRESS (NPC). The highest government and legislative organ in the **People's Republic of China (PRC)**, the NPC has constitutional powers similar to legislative bodies in other nations, yet without much real authority because this still lies with the **Chinese Communist Party (CCP)**. The body is unicameral and, in 2004, had 2,979 members indirectly elected for a five-year term. Since 1949, 10 NPCs have been convened, the first in 1954, which elected **Mao Zedong** as chairman of the PRC (a position later changed to **president**) and **Liu Shaoqi** as chairman of the NPC Standing Committee and **Zhou Enlai** as the premier of the State Council. In subsequent years, three NPCs came at four-year intervals between 1954 and 1964, and five at five-year intervals from 1975 to

2005. During much of the **Cultural Revolution (1966–1976)** and in the midst of the **Lin Biao** affair, the NPC did not meet, and seven years transpired between the Fourth NPC in 1975 and the Fifth in 1982. The number of delegates to the NPC has varied from 1,200 in the 1950s to around 2,000 in the 1980s and 1990s when the Sixth through the Eighth NPC were convened. At the 10th NPC held in 2004, nearly 3,000 delegates attended the session, including 133 private businessmen whose recruitment into the legislative body had been encouraged by President **Jiang Zemin** and who apparently pressed the NPC to pass a constitutional amendment protecting private property. Overall representation to the NPC is malapportioned, with a ratio of one delegate to every one million rural residents and one delegate to every 130,000 urban residents.

Full NPC sessions meet for a period of about two weeks usually immediately following the meeting of the **Chinese People's Political Consultative Conference (CPPCC)**. These sessions are devoted to work reports presented by various state officials, which are discussed, and formally approved by votes of the delegates. Four different state constitutions have been approved by NPC, the first in 1954, the second in 1975 at the end of the Cultural Revolution, the third in 1978, and the fourth and current constitution in 1982. The NPC has the power to amend the constitution (with most amendments proposed by the Standing Committee, the executive body of the NPC), to enact and amend basic statutes, and to pass a budget. During the two-week sessions of the full NPC, regional groups of delegates meet and engage often in real policy debates, though most NPC sessions are noted for their strict formality and rubber-stamping of government reports. An internal CCP document leaked by a Chinese reporter in the early 1990s indicated that all NPC decisions are cleared ahead of time by top Party **leaders**, all of whom sit in major government and NPC positions. Many delegates "elected" to the NPC are model workers and peasants with little legislative experience or acumen.

Yet in the early 1980s, intense debate among delegates was allowed—apparently at the behest of **Deng Xiaoping**—as part of the reform of the political structure. In April 1992, for example, 30% of the delegates refused to vote in favor of a resolution authorizing construction of the controversial **Three Gorges Dam Project**. At the Eighth NPC in March 1993, 11% of the delegates voted "no" or abstained in the reelection of **Li Peng** as state premier, obviously in reaction to Li's role in the 1989 military crackdown on the second **Beijing Spring**. Substantial numbers of "no" and "abstain" votes have also been cast against the work report of China's Chief Justice of the Supreme Court citing the inability of the courts and the **Procuracy** to stem official **corruption**, which many delegates and citizens consider China's number one problem. Extended press conferences by political leaders during NPC sessions have also been introduced along with provisions that grant delegates greater ability to put forward proposals and motions for consideration by the NPC and the Standing Committee and that have opened up Standing Committee deliberations to observers, though the impact of such practices on actual policy making remains unclear. During all NPC sessions in **Beijing**, thousands of police officers are dispatched around the Great Hall of the People where the delegates meet to seal off streets and sidewalks so as to prevent **human rights** activists, relatives of individuals killed or injured during the military crackdown against the second Beijing Spring, and petitioners from the provinces with various grievances from disrupting the session as all such people are subject to detention and are steered to the State Bureau for Letters and Calls under the State Council.

Elected theoretically by the NPC, the Standing Committee meets regularly when the full NPC is out of session and exercises extensive powers for an executive organ. These include the power to enact and amend statutes other than those that must be enacted by the full NPC, interpret the constitution and statutes, and annul administrative rules and regulations. The Standing Committee can also reorganize the formal state structure and is the source of most amendments to the constitution. The Standing Committee has also frequently served as a rostrum to propagate major Party initiatives as most members also hold high positions in the CCP. Throughout the 1980s, NPC Standing Committee Chairman **Peng Zhen** espoused his conservative views as he is said to have reportedly blocked an effort by reformers to pass a law granting full authority to factory managers, which would have undermined the authority of Party secretaries in the industrial sector. In effect, the Standing Committee of the NPC was used to block further political reforms within the CCP. **Qiao Shi**, a strong advocate of greater legalization in China's political culture, was appointed chairman of the Standing Committee in 1993 but later lost his position in apparent disagreement with President **Jiang Zemin** and was replaced in 1998 by Li Peng. In 2004–2005, the chairman of the Standing Committee was Wu Bangguo, a top economic policymaker who graduated with a degree in electronics from **Qinghua University**, the alma mater of many "fourth generation" Chinese leaders.

Theoretically, the NPC exercises authority over the entire state apparatus in China. This includes the courts, the State Council, and the various state ministries, the state Central **Military Affairs Commission (MAC)**, and the Procuracy. Provincial, autonomous region, municipality, county, district, and township people's congresses are also subordinate to the NPC, to which these bodies send delegates. The NPC also maintains a Legislative Affairs Office whose functions include clarifying and safeguarding the integrity of the mini-constitution known as the Basic Law of **Hong Kong**.

In 2004 and 2005, the NPC responded to CCP policies and emerging social, economic, and political problems with a number of reforms. Amendments to the 1982 constitution included expanding the formal powers of the **president of the People's Republic of China** from the largely symbolic role of "receiving foreign diplomatic representatives" to "engaging in activities involving State affairs." Limited protection of private property and guarantee of human rights were also included while government power was also enhanced and given more flexibility with authority granted to declare a "state of emergency" instead of proclaiming "martial law," though the latter can be included in the former. The phrase "all builders of **socialism**" was included in the description of the "broad **united front**" led by the CCP in the constitution's Preamble, indicating a more inclusive definition of the Chinese state and replacing the emphasis on **class struggle** that had characterized the Maoist era (1949–1976). The NPC also adjusted to the demands of China's increasingly sophisticated and free market **economy** by revising its Securities Investment Fund Law and committed itself to addressing issues of food security and rural poverty, enforcing the **Trade Union** Law, and reforming the financial system. Calls were also issued by individual NPC delegates to protect brand names and intellectual property of China's indigenous products and to pass an anti-corruption law and institute independent investigators to report directly to the NPC. To the consternation of many residents of Hong Kong and **Taiwan**, the Standing

Committee of the NPC in 2004 gave Beijing veto powers over any proposed political reforms in Hong Kong while the full NPC adopted an anti-secession law in March 2005 to prevent the secession of **Taiwan** from China. *See also* GOVERNMENT STRUCTURE; STATE COUNCIL.

NATIONALIST PARTY. *See* KUOMINTANG (NATIONALIST PARTY) (KMT).

NEIBU **MATERIALS.** *See* "INTERNAL MATERIALS."

"NEW AUTHORITARIANISM" (*"XIN QUANWEIZHUYI"*). This theory propounded in the mid- to late 1980s by supporters of then **Chinese Communist Party (CCP)** General Secretary **Zhao Ziyang**, professed that the modernization of a backward country, such as China, inevitably must pass through a phase when the political system must be centered around a strong, authoritarian leader who serves as the motivating force for change, rather than following a democratic path. Reform and modernization in China require a politically powerful person, such as the kind who has emerged in the East Asian countries of Singapore under Lee Kuan Yew or **Taiwan** under Chiang Ching-kuo. The new authoritarianism did not emphasize the body politic, but the strong leader who is able to lead a country to realize its modernization smoothly by firmly establishing a free market and an institutionalized structure of legally protected property rights. Only with accumulated power and the use of autocratic authority can such changes be carried out. Similar to Western doctrines of "enlightened despotism" espoused in the 18th century, this theory largely disappeared from the Chinese media after the purge of Zhao Ziyang following the 1989 military crackdown on the second **Beijing Spring**.

NEW CHINA NEWS AGENCY (XINHUA). Started in 1931 as the Red China News Agency, China's national news agency was renamed *Xinhua* (literally "New China") in 1937 and since 1949 has operated under the direct authority of the State Council. One of two news agencies in China, the other being the China News Service, Xinhua is responsible for releasing Party and state documents and important news to the country through 33 bureaus (one for each province and the military) while also gathering and distributing news dispatches through its more than 100 foreign bureaus. Employing more than 10,000 people, Xinhua is a major news source for China's major newspapers, such as *People's Daily*. The Xinhua branch in **Hong Kong** operated as the de facto representative of the Chinese government in the former British colony until its reversion to China on 1 July 1997. Like the other major central-level news sources in the **People's Republic of China (PRC)**, Xinhua is a part of the state-run media and functions as a mouthpiece of the **Chinese Communist Party (CCP)** and the Chinese central government running articles and stories subject to **censorship** (*shencha*) that rarely challenge government policy, directly or even elliptically.

Xinhua has a complete news coverage and release system that features multiple channels, functions, and tiers. At home, it releases various types of news items on a daily basis to newspapers, radio and TV stations at the county, prefecture and provincial levels, as well as to evening newspapers and specialized newspapers. Overseas, it releases around-the-clock news in seven languages (Chinese, English, French, Spanish, Russian, Arabic, and Portuguese) and a wealth of economic information to Chinese and foreign clients, along with nearly 100 news photos a day. With its huge news and information user network at home and abroad, Xinhua has cooperation agreements on news exchanges with news agencies or media organizations in nearly 100 countries while the Xinhua Audio and Video Center, established in 1993, provides a variety of news programs and special programs for TV stations. Xinhua currently publishes nearly 40 types of newspapers and magazines, such as *Xinhua Daily Telegraph*, the *News Bulletin*, *Reference News* (daily), *Economic Information Daily*, *China Securities* (daily), *Sports Express*, *Outlook* (weekly), *Chinese Reporters* (monthly), and the *China Yearbook* (in Chinese and English versions). Also published is *China Comment*, the magazine with the largest circulation in China. Xinhua Publishing House, which is attached to the news agency, publishes annually 400 kinds of books focusing on current affairs and politics. In recent years, Xinhua has modernized its communications **technology** through a satellite communications and transmission network and has introduced computerized information processing systems covering text editing, photo processing, news communications, economic information, and data indexing. Its news communications system takes Beijing as the center, and Hong Kong, New York, Paris, and London as transmission centers, while it also maintains connections to the **Internet** through an online news website at www.chinaview.cn. Xinhua's operational businesses have steadily expanded through a variety of affiliated organizations including the China Economic Information Service, China News Development Co., China National United Advertising Corporation, China Photo Service, Global Public Relations Co., and the Hangzhou International Public Relations Co. Xinhua also runs the News Research Institute, the World Questions Research Center, and the China School of Journalism, each of which is engaged in journalism research and professional training. In 1996, Xinhua was authorized by the Chinese government to set up a special office to take charge of managing economic information released in China by foreign news agencies and their subsidiaries.

Despite its close association with the Chinese government, the advent of the Internet in the early 2000s opened up to Chinese journalists potentially new sources of information that did not cohere with Party dictates and, which, in 2003, led to a joint disciplinary and ideological campaign among the major state media—*People's Daily*, *Enlightenment Daily*, *Economic Daily*, **Seeking Truth (Qiushi)**, and Central Radio and Television—to promote Communist Party ideology and "Marxist news values." This was aimed at countering outside influences and reestablishing tight control over all media, which, despite dramatic economic reforms in China begun in 1978–1979, remain virtually the same from the Yan'an era (1935–1945), when the CCP established hegemony over **intellectuals** and journalists and imposed a rigorous regime of official censorship. In February 2006, a former deputy head of Xinhua, Li Pu, jointed **Hu Jiwei**, **Li Rui**, and **Zhu Houze** in protesting excessive censorship and the closing of newspapers. *See also* BROADCASTING AND TELEVISION; INTERNAL MATERIALS.

NEW DEMOCRACY. The political program for China outlined by **Mao Zedong** in a speech by the same name in January 1940 during the **Sino–Japanese War** (**1937–1945**) in which Mao declared that the ongoing Chinese revolution "was part of the world revolution" that aimed at changing the colonial, semi-colonial, and feudal form of Chinese society into an independent country. Reflecting the alliance between the **Chinese Communist Party (CCP)** and the **Kuomintang (KMT)** in the Second **United Front**, the speech was moderate in tone and in its political proposals, with appeals directed to China's "bourgeois-democratic" forces and promises of their "proper representation" in a system of government based on elections and universal suffrage. Capitalist property, Mao also promised, would not be confiscated, nor would capitalist production be restrained. Land would be redistributed from landlord to peasant under a program of "land to the tiller." Overall, China under the "New Democracy" would have neither a bourgeois nor proletarian dictatorship. Mao's speech on "New Democracy" is in the *Selected Works of Mao Zedong*, Volume II and is frequently cited by dissident Chinese **intellectuals** to challenge the CCP dictatorship that, they claim, has violated the basic principles of the "new democracy" since 1949.

NIE RONGZHEN (1899–1992). A participant in the **May Fourth Movement (1919–1923)** who in the 1920s was a natural science student in Belgium and the **Soviet Union**, Nie Rongzhen served under **Lin Biao** during the **Long March (1934–1935)**. In 1945, Nie was elected to the **Chinese Communist Party (CCP)** Central Committee and in 1949 participated in the "**liberation**" *(jiefang)* of **Beijing**. In the early 1950s, he was acting chief-of-staff of the **People's Liberation Army (PLA)** and was promoted in 1955 as one of China's 10 marshals, the highest military rank in the PLA. He was also a vice-chairman of the National Defense Council and became chairman of the **Science and Technology** Commission in 1958. He was a member of the **Politburo** from 1966–1969 and from 1977–1985. During the **Cultural Revolution (1966–1976)**, which Nie survived intact, he was instrumental in developing China's **atomic bomb** and in insulating the nuclear and missile program from interruption by **Red Guards**. In 1983, Nie was elected vice-chairman of the Central **Military Affairs Commission (MAC)** and helped inaugurate China's **space program.** In 1985, he resigned from all his posts and, following his death in 1992, Nie was buried, along with 500 other people involved in the space program, in a cemetery near the Jiuquan Satellite Launch Center in northwest Gansu Province.

NIE YUANZI (1921–). Born in Henan Province, Nie Yuanzi joined the **Chinese Communist Party (CCP)** in 1938. After 1949, she worked for several years for the Harbin Municipal government. In 1964, she was appointed secretary of the Party branch in the philosophy department at **Beida (Peking University).** On 22 May 1966, during the early phases of the **Cultural Revolution (1966–1976),** Nie and six others put up a **big-character poster** denouncing the university's Party committee as "members of a black gang" for suppressing the student movement. Putting out a call to "firmly, thoroughly, cleanly and totally eliminate any ox-ghosts and snake-demons" (terms of opprobrium taken from an ancient poem), the poster was broadcast nationwide on 1 June 1966 by the Central People's Radio Station and was singled out for praise by **Mao Zedong.** This event effectively inaugurated the Cultural Revolution on many college campuses and middle schools in **Beijing** that quickly degenerated into wanton violence by Red Guards against teachers, educational authorities, and just about anyone casually labeled as a "bad" person. During the Cultural Revolution, Nie would hold the following positions: director of the Leading Group of the Capital University and Middle School **Red Guards;** member of the New Beida Commune; and deputy director of the Beijing **Revolutionary Committee.** At the 1969 Ninth CCP National Party Congress, she became an alternate member of the Central Committee, but subsequently lost this position and her Party membership after falling out of political favor. In 1983, Nie was sentenced to 17 years in prison for "instigating counterrevolutionary crimes" and was deprived of her political rights.

NIXON VISIT (1972). *See* UNITED STATES.

– O –

OCTOBER SIXTH COUP (1976). *See* JIANG QING (1913–1991).

"ON CONTRADICTIONS" (*"MAODUN LUN"*). The concept of "contradictions" (*maodun*) is central to **Mao Zedong** Thought. In an August 1937 speech, Mao laid out his basic notions of contradictions in which he asserted that "internal contradiction" was present "in every single thing" and that this explained all motion and development. Conflict and change were normal aspects of any society and so perfect harmony and consensus, as in traditional Confucian society, were unattainable. In 1957, Mao elaborated on this theory in a speech titled "On the Correct Handling of Contradictions among the People" in which he postulated that neither **socialism** nor even communism would end the contradictions between social classes that produced **class struggle**. Mao also referred to two kinds of contradictions: "antagonistic contradiction" between "ourselves and the enemy" and "non-antagonistic contradictions" among the people, including the workers, the peasants, and the other revolutionary classes. According to Mao, "antagonistic contradictions" should be dealt with harshly, but "non-antagonistic contradictions" could be handled with greater moderation. Mao's political purpose in espousing this theory in 1957 was to negate the efforts within the **Soviet Union** and also among some **leaders** of the **Chinese Communist Party** (**CCP**) to terminate class struggle and to justify his assaults on political opponents in the CCP, ultimately leading to the **Anti-Rightist Campaign** (**1957–1958**) and the **Cultural Revolution** (**1966–1976**).

"ON TEN MAJOR RELATIONSHIPS" (*"SHIDA GUANXI"*). In a speech delivered in April 1956, **Chinese Communist Party** (**CCP**) Chairman **Mao Zedong** espoused perhaps his most moderate views on economic and social development in China. Contrary to the one-sided approach to economic development that he would later articulate during the **Great Leap Forward** (**1958–1960**) with its emphasis on grandiose schemes and crash programs, "On Ten Major Relationships" outlined a model of development stressing a balance between heavy and light **industry**, coastal and inland industries, economic construction and national defense, and the interests of the state, the cooperatives, and the individual. Politically, the speech also called for an equalization of interests between the Center and the localities, between revolution and counterrevolution, between Party and non-Party people, and between right and wrong inside and outside the CCP. Socially, Mao stressed the importance of equilibrium between the interests of the **Han** ethnic majority and the various **minorities** and, internationally, he called for a balanced approach to China's relations with the outside world. Proponents of moderate policies in

China would constantly cite this speech, which was not officially published in the **People's Republic of China** (**PRC**) until after Mao's death in 1976, as justification in Maoist terms for their proposals.

ONE-CHILD POLICY. The "one child per family" program has been the centerpiece of China's family planning and **population** control campaign since it was introduced in 1979. Urban and township couples who have only one child receive benefits in the form of monthly subsidies of five *yuan* for the child until the age of 14, free child health care, subsidized school fees, and preferential housing allocation and are awarded a Certificate of Honor for Single-Child Parents. Couples who have more than one child (except for those with legal exemptions) may be forced to pay a "social compensation" fine of up to 15% or more of a person's annual salary, and be denied promotion or even continued employment in one's place of work. There are no incentives for parents to remain childless, though aging families who have practiced the one-child policy are provided cash payments by the Chinese government, pension insurance, and cheaper medical services. The policy was adopted nationwide after extensive experimentation as a response to the expected rise in China's overall birthrate due to the "baby boom" from 1962 to 1970 and is enforced by the State Population and Family Planning Commission. The policy is credited with reducing the number of expected births from 1979 to 2005 by upward to 200 million with the average number of children per family dropping from 5.8 in the 1970s to 1.8 in 2005. The population drop is also credited with contributing an extra 2% of the annual Gross Domestic Product (GDP) growth and boosting **labor** productivity by 1.5% annually.

It is estimated that one-fifth of all Chinese families have one child (approximately 35 million families), almost all of whom live in the urban areas since families in rural areas were, beginning in the late 1980s, allowed to have two children and where enforcing population control policy has persistently confronted enormous political and social resistance. Difficulties in enforcing the policy stem from the fear by parents that one child, especially if it is a female, will not be sufficient to provide for them in old age because China still lacks a comprehensive social security system. Widespread preference for male offspring is another reason for the difficulties in enforcing the policy and has led to a highly skewed sex ratio in China where 119 boys are born for every 100 girls, which is far above the world average of 106 males for every 100 females, although it is not dramatically different from **India** and South **Korea**, where no such policy exists. The ratio is most imbalanced in the highly rural and generally poor provinces/autonomous regions of Fujian, Shaanxi, Guangxi, Hunan, Anhui, Hubei, Guangdong, and Hainan Island.

In the mid-1980s, the then State Family Planning Commission announced the first official relaxation in the enforcement of the policy as farmers with "special economic difficulties" were allowed to have a second child at an appropriate interval following the birth of the first child. Ethnic **minorities** and couples in which both the husband and wife are single children can also legally have a second child. Further relaxation was instituted in the late 1990s and early 2000s as spouses who are both only children can have a second child along with divorced parents who remarry. Charges that the policy has encouraged female infanticide and coerced abortions have led to central government efforts to crack down on such practices that are illegal under Chinese law, including the use of free ultrasound examinations to determine the sex of the fetus and free late-term abortions. In 2002, a new Family Planning Law was adopted that aimed at standardizing birth control policies and reducing **corruption** and coercion while the government has set the goal of lowering the sex ratio to normal by 2010 through a Care for Girls pilot program that pays and insures pensions to rural families who bear young girls and provides free **education** to poor parents of girls. Some cities where the sex imbalance is highly skewed (e.g., Guiyang, Guizhou Province, 129 boys to 100 girls) have gone so far as to outlaw abortions after the 14th week of pregnancy. China has also allowed for foreign adoption of orphans— mostly girls—who, in the past, were often discarded or left in an orphanage's "dying rooms," where the unwanted babies were allowed to waste away. Despite such revelations and criticisms from **human rights** advocates, in 1988, the **United Nations (UN)** Population Crisis Committee rated China's family planning policy as "excellent" while the UN Family Planning Agency cites the lack of conclusive evidence of coercive or involuntary policies in China. Many Chinese who have fled the country have cited the one-child policy as the reason for their escape, while individuals who enforced the policy have been denied asylum in Canada and other countries that consider forced abortion and sterilization as crimes against humanity.

After three decades, the impact of the one-child policy on Chinese society has been profound. In addition to the skewed sex ratio, the policy is blamed for producing an entire generation of spoiled and self-centered children. Indulged by fawning parents, grandparents, and aunts, these "little emperors" and "little suns" (*xiao taiyang*, a term **Jiang Qing** had also used to describe **Red Guards** during the **Cultural Revolution**), frequently suffer from various problems of obesity to "uncivil," anti-social behavior. As the only offspring and sole hope for the family, these children have often been driven mercilessly to succeed in school. During the 2002–2003 **SARS** crisis in **Beijing** and other cities, these children were sheltered at home for weeks on end during the shutdown of schools; as adolescents and adults, they have pursued a lifestyle of high consumption and a general lack of interest in permanent relationships. By 2020, it is estimated that the number of men in China who cannot find spouses, especially in the countryside, will reach 40 million, thereby creating enormous social pressure for sex trafficking into the country and perhaps a surge in violent, criminal activity that comes with the disappearance of the family for such a large segment of the population who are known in China as "bare branches." On the other hand, as the relative numbers of **women** has declined, their role in the household has increased with improved employment and economic prospects. The number of people 60 and older is also slated to increase dramatically from 11% in 2004 to 20% in 2025 as the long-term demographic effects of the one-child policy take hold and leave the country with a shrinking pool of high-rate taxpayers to support an increasingly elderly population in need of **health care** and other amenities.

Because China's total fertility rate has reached 1.8, which is below the natural replacement rate, pressure to relax the one-child policy is likely to grow. Limited relaxation of one-child restrictions in cities such as **Shanghai**, where the birth rate has reached an all-time low have not, however, produced a rush of applications from parents wanting to expand their families as the high cost of bringing up a child, including education that is no longer free, and the greater competition for jobs, limit second-child families to the better-off and more well-educated couples.

"ONE COUNTRY, TWO SYSTEMS." This is the guiding concept promulgated by the **Chinese Communist Party (CCP)** leadership to incorporate **Hong Kong**, Macao, and **Taiwan** into the **People's Republic of China (PRC)**. While mainland China will remain "socialist," these territories will be allowed to retain their "capitalist" social and economic systems as Special Administrative Regions (SAR) for a considerable period of time after "reunification with the motherland." In this way, the process of incorporation will be less disruptive. The concept was first introduced by **Deng Xiaoping** in 1982 in proposals made to Great Britain to reunify Hong Kong after 1997 so that the two diametrically opposed social systems of the PRC and the British colony could coexist under one sovereign government. In the Sino–British Joint Declaration on the Question of Hong Kong initialed by the PRC and Great Britain in 1984, China declared that "the current social and economic system in Hong Kong will remain unchanged, as will the lifestyle. Rights and freedoms, including those of the individual, of speech, the press, assembly, association, travel, movement, correspondence, strike, choice, occupation, academic research, and religious belief will be ensured by law in the Hong Kong Special Administrative Region." Private property and ownership of enterprises were also guaranteed. But because the PRC retains the power to appoint the chief executive of the Hong Kong Special Administrative Region and given that China altered the makeup of the local democratically elected Legislative Council in Hong Kong (LEGCO), there is concern that Hong Kong's autonomy will not be respected; that an authoritarian system will be gradually imposed on the colony and that **corruption**, which is endemic on the mainland, will infect Hong Kong's highly professional administrative organs and police.

The PRC has offered the same concept of "one country, two systems" as a model of reunification to Taiwan, but under the **Kuomintang (KMT)** the government initially asserted that mainland China must first abandon its one-party Communist dictatorship and respect the Three Principles of the People advocated by Sun Yat-sen, though, in recent years, KMT politicians have taken a more moderate line on the issue of reunification. In its contacts and negotiations with the **Dalai Lama**, Chinese officials have explicitly rejected the concept of "one country, two systems" for **Tibet** on the grounds that this territory, unlike Hong Kong and Taiwan, was never under the colonial control of foreign powers with their radically different economic and political legacies.

"ONE DIVIDES INTO TWO" (*"YIFENWEIER"*). This philosophical concept became a hot-button polemical issue during the **Cultural Revolution (1966–1976)** that gained enormous political significance. "One divides into two" was defended against the opposite philosophical concept that "two merge into one." The former was defended by the radical political forces to provide a "scientific," philosophical basis for "**uninterrupted revolution**" (*buduan geming*) and for the supposed political struggle between the bourgeoisie and proletariat. In the pseudo-scientific terminology of Marxist–Leninist philosophy, Chinese radical **intellectuals** proclaimed that "one divides into two" was the essence of the "law of the unity of opposites," which was a "fundamental law of the universe." Applied to the political realm, it promised unending struggle as the necessary basis for progress in human history. "Two merge into one," the radicals claimed, provided the philosophical basis for class reconciliation, class cooperation, and the elimination of **class struggle**—"bourgeois" and "revisionist" viewpoints that purportedly indicated the presence of "**capitalist roaders**" (*zouzipai*) in the **Chinese Communist Party** (**CCP**). This polemical and philosophical debate essentially ended with the demise of the Cultural Revolution in 1976 and the death of **Mao Zedong** in the same year. *See also* "REVISIONISM."

ONE-MAN MANAGEMENT. *See* STATE-OWNED ENTERPRISES (SOEs).

"OPEN-DOOR POLICY" (*"KAIFANG ZHENGCE"*). A fundamental tenet of the economic reforms initiated by **Deng Xiaoping** in 1978–1979, this policy aims primarily at opening China's **economy** to foreign **trade and investment** and the import of advanced **technology**. The essence of the open door (a term also used for the **United States** mid-19th century policy toward China) has been the **Special Economic Zones** (**SEZs**) and joint ventures. In 1992, a total of 40,000 foreign investment agreements were signed with China, totaling more than US$58 billion in investment pledges and US$16 billion in actual investments. In 1994 alone, China approved US$82 billion in foreign investments, with US$34 billion in actual investments. **Hong Kong** and Macao rank first in actual investment, South **Korea** second, followed by **Taiwan**, **Japan**, and the U.S. Cumulative Foreign Direct Investment (FDI) at the end of 2001 amounted to US$395.47 billion. In 2003, China replaced the U.S. as the largest worldwide recipient of FDI, taking in US$53 billion.

The open-door policy directly contradicted the autarkic policy of economic **self-reliance** (*zili gengsheng*) favored by **Mao Zedong** that China has all but abandoned since 1978–1979, though not without some resistance among conservative hard-line factions in the **Chinese Communist Party** (**CCP**) who feared economic dependence and the erosion of socialist ideology. Indeed, foreign investment and increased interaction with the outside world, such as student exchanges, have brought an invasion of non-Communist ideological and cultural influences that the CCP has periodically condemned in its flare for organic metaphors as "flies and germs." Periodic campaigns aimed at eliminating foreign influences, such as the **Anti-Spiritual Pollution Campaign** (**1983–1984**) and the Anti-**bourgeois Liberalization** Campaign (1987–1988), have come and gone with little apparent effect on China's youth. Despite such corrosive influences, however, China's top leadership shows little inclination to reverse the fundamentals of the open-door as throughout the 1990s and early 2000s the integration of the Chinese **economy** into the international global economy proceeded at a rapid clip.

ORGANIZATION DEPARTMENT. *See* CHINESE COMMUNIST PARTY (CCP).

– P –

"PAPER TIGER" (*"ZHI LAOHU"*). This is a term of opprobrium and contempt first used by **Mao Zedong** in 1946 to deride the military power of the **United States**. The Chinese defined the term as "things that possess a fierce appearance but are in essence very weak and hollow." In terms of the U.S., the Chinese suggested for many years thereafter in virulent and polemical propaganda that the U.S. possession of nuclear weapons and other modern military **technology** gave it an appearance of being "fierce," but, in reality, the capitalist system made America fundamentally "weak and hollow." In his classic statement on the issue Mao Zedong proclaimed: "The **atomic bomb** is a paper tiger that the U.S. reactionaries use to scare people. It looks terrible, but in fact it is not. Of course, the atom bomb is a weapon of mass slaughter, but the outcome of a war is decided by the people, not by one or two new types of weapons." Mao went on to claim that this was true for all "reactionaries, domestic and international." The term generally ceased to be used after the 1972 visit to China by U.S. President Richard Nixon.

PARTY CONGRESS. *See* CHINESE COMMUNIST PARTY (CCP).

"PARTY CORE GROUPS" (*"DANG HEXIN XIAOZU"*). *See* CHINESE COMMUNIST PARTY (CCP).

"PEACEFUL EVOLUTION" (*"HEPING YANBIAN"*). This notion was disseminated by hard-line critics of "**bourgeois liberalization**" in the **Chinese Communist Party** (**CCP**) who criticized Western countries, particularly the **United States**, for its alleged campaign to undermine the Communist dictatorship and replace it with a Western-style parliamentary system. The term was originally used by U.S. Secretary of State John Foster Dulles in the 1950s to explain the American strategy of countering Communist influence in Central and Latin America. In China, the concept was introduced following the military crackdown against the 1989 second **Beijing Spring** when **Jiang Zemin** warned of the dangers posed by peaceful evolution promoted by "international forces trying to undermine the socialist system in China." This was followed in a 1991 document entitled "The Struggle between Peaceful Evolution and Counter Peaceful Evolution is a **Class Struggle** in the World Arena," in which the Chinese government singled out the administration of U.S. President George H.W. Bush for criticism because the president had in many public statements suggested that **trade** and cultural ties with China would gradually bring about a transition to a more liberal, democratic society. Foreign residents of China, who, in the early 1990s, parodied the phrase by holding a "peaceful evolution barbecue" were given warnings by Chinese state authorities. Since then, the term has been generally dropped from official government statements and documents as China has emphasized its "peaceful rising" in the world community.

PEKING OPERA. The primary regional opera in China, Peking opera assumed its present form about 200 years ago during the Qing dynasty (1644–1911). Like all traditional Chinese theater, it combines music, singing, dancing, dialogue, acrobatics, and martial arts. Acting in Peking opera is highly symbolic, with little scenery or stage props. The music is made up of orchestral and percussion instruments, mainly drums and gongs along with the **Beijing** "fiddle" (*jinghu*) and "second fiddle" (*erhu*) while the vocal part is both spoken and sung. Spoken dialogue consists of the recitative and Beijing colloquial speech, the former by serious characters and the latter by young females and clowns. The music is taken from folk tunes from Hubei and Anhui provinces and from older opera forms from the south. The faces of the characters are usually painted with red indicating a good character, black an evil one, and a face with white spots indicating a humorous role. There are more than 2,000 Peking operas, including such famous repertoires as *Gathering of Heroes, At the Crossroads*, and *Farewell My Concubine*.

During the **Cultural Revolution (1966–1976)**, performances of Peking Opera were restricted to the so-called "eight model plays," which actually numbered more than eight and consisted of both operas and ballets and contained exclusively Communist or revolutionary themes. Created under the patronage and supervision of **Jiang Qing**, the wife of **Mao Zedong**, they were produced by the China Beijing Opera House and included: *The Legend of the Red Lantern, Shajia Hamlet, Taking Tiger Mountain by Strategy, Azalea Mountain, The Harbor, Sweeping White Tiger Regiment, Song of Dragon River, Warfare on the Plain, Panshiwan*, and *Red Detachment of Women*. The first three were the most popular while the last was also a ballet. In the last two decades, more traditional Peking Operas have been restaged and have experienced something of a revival, especially among the elderly. In 1995, the First Peking Opera Arts Festival was held in **Tianjin**; in 1999, a major performance of traditional and modern Peking Operas took place in the leadership compound of

Zhongnanhai attended by **Jiang Zemin**, **Zhu Rongji**, and **Hu Jintao** and nearly 1,000 guests. *See also* LITERATURE AND THE ARTS.

PENG DEHUAI (1898–1974). Born in 1898 in Hunan Province, Peng Dehuai emerged as one of the top military figures in the **Chinese Communist Party (CCP)**. It is said that at the age of 11, Peng's father fired a gun at his young son who showed his steely nerves by not flinching. Peng soon left his family and joined local military forces. In 1919, he was profoundly influenced by the writings of Sun Yat-sen and the liberal ideas of the **May Fourth Movement (1919–1923)**. Peng joined the CCP in the late 1920s and emerged as one of the foremost military figures in the Communist movement, commanding CCP forces in a major battle with the Japanese in 1940 and leading the First **Field Army** during the **Civil War (1946–1949)**. Peng then commanded Chinese forces during the **Korean War (1950–1953)**, where his troops fought the American forces to a standstill, but with extremely heavy losses on the Chinese side, including the son of **Mao Zedong**. Peng Dehuai was originally reluctant to commit Chinese forces to the Korean conflict, yet ended up being the sole top Chinese military officer to serve in the field during this risky venture.

A strong supporter of a professional military in China, Peng in the mid-1950s helped introduce ranks and he became one of 10 marshals, the highest rank in the **People's Liberation Army (PLA)**. Peng's letter to Mao Zedong in August 1959 raising questions about economic policy during the **Great Leap Forward (1958–1960)** led to his purge. Efforts to rehabilitate Peng in the early 1960s provoked Mao's wrath; during the **Cultural Revolution (1966–1976)**, Peng was denounced and paraded through the streets by **Red Guards** and beaten with sticks, breaking two ribs. Peng died in 1974 in obscurity and was rehabilitated four years later in 1978. In 1988, a commemorative stamp on the anniversary of Peng's 90th birthday was issued along with a film on his military career.

PENG ZHEN (1902–1997). Born of destitute peasants, Peng Zhen joined the **Chinese Communist Party (CCP)** in 1923 and served as a **political commissar** in the Eighth Route Army. In 1945, he became a member of the CCP Central Committee and the **Politburo** and from 1954 to 1966 was mayor of **Beijing**. He was the first Politburo member to be purged in the **Cultural Revolution (1966–1976)** but reappeared in 1979 as Director of the Commission for Legal Affairs of the **National People's Congress (NPC)** Standing Committee and was reappointed to the Central Committee and Politburo. From 1983 to 1988, he was chairman of the Standing Committee of the NPC. He resigned from all posts in 1987 but as one of the **"revolutionary elders"** (*geming yuanlao*) of the CCP, he reportedly played a major role in 1989 in sanctioning the military crackdown on pro-democracy demonstrations during the second **Beijing Spring**.

PEOPLE'S BANK OF CHINA. *See* BANKING AND FINANCE.

"PEOPLE'S COMMUNES" (*"RENMIN GONGSHE"***).** Promoted primarily by **Chinese Communist Party (CCP)** Chairman Mao Zedong, the people's communes consisted of very large-scale organization of rural production in the Chinese countryside that encompassed several villages as a single production unit. Officially, the formation of people's communes was authorized by the Central Committee of the CCP in August 1958 at the Beidaihe Conference after the establishment of the first people's commune known as the Sputnik Federated Cooperative in April in Henan Province. After some experimentation, a nationwide campaign to establish communes was begun in December 1958 with more than 26,000 established nationwide. Organizationally, the people's communes amalgamated the more numerous production brigades and became the top level of the three-tier organization (commune, brigade, and team) in the countryside. In this sense, the communes represented a significant centralization of authority and organization in the countryside. However, because the communes took over much power from the central government's Ministry of Agriculture, the communes also signified a decentralization of authority from urban-based bureaucracies to the countryside.

The people's communes integrated the income and production of several villages in an unprecedented reorganization of the Chinese countryside that Mao Zedong declared to be the basis for China's route to "communism." By early 1959, more than 99% of the rural **population** was organized into communes, the largest of which numbered over 100,000 members. Unwieldy organizations, the communes took over the traditional managerial functions of the "townships," which are also referred to in the countryside as "administrative villages" (*xiang*) and were generally dominated by the commune Party branch committee that quickly assumed control over production decisions and the allocation of income. The communes ran the disastrous **backyard steel furnace** campaign and implemented many of the radical decisions by **Mao Zedong** to transform agricultural production, such as the close planting of paddy rice, which also proved to be disastrous. At the height of the **Great Leap Forward** (**1958–1960**), communes ran canteens in which peasants ate collectively and were offered free supplies of food and other staples and services. The local **people's militia** was based in the communes, which also established schools and collective nurseries as a means of achieving the "**liberation**" (*jiefang*) of rural **women**. With Mao's dictum that "**politics takes command**" (*zhengzhi guashuai*) pervading CCP propaganda in the communes, the emphasis was on non-material incentives for peasants to increase production. The sharing of **labor** between villages within one communal structure was also emphasized as a way to increase agricultural production.

By 1960, it was apparent to top CCP **leaders**, including Mao Zedong that the communes had contributed to a growing crisis in **agriculture**. Excessive devotion to backyard steel production and ill-advised agricultural measures led to a dramatic falloff in total grain production that, along with enormous waste, necessitated a radical retrenchment by the top leadership. Without completely dismantling the communes, in 1960, the CCP ordered that decisions regarding production and income allocation be returned first to the production brigade (generally a single village) and then to the production team (a subunit of a single village). The "egalitarianism" in the communes was thereby abandoned and material incentives were reintroduced into the rural **economy**. The three-tier structure, with the commune at the highest level, remained, however, but authority was significantly decentralized, with only small rural factories remaining under the control of the commune administration. The 1978–1979 agricultural reform essentially ended the role of the communes, which, in 1983, were effectively replaced as administrative organs by the reestablishment of township governments while land was contracted directly to individual farmer households for up to 30 years.

PEOPLE'S CONGRESSES. *See* GOVERNMENT STRUCTURE; NATIONAL PEOPLE'S CONGRESS (NPC).

PEOPLE'S DAILY (RENMIN RIBAO). The mouthpiece of the Central Committee of the **Chinese Communist Party (CCP)**, *People's Daily* is controlled by the Propaganda Department (renamed Publicity Department) of the Central Committee. Editorials and commentaries appearing in the paper represent the policy position of the central leadership and constitute the **basic line of the Party**. *People's Daily* "commentaries" *(pinglun)* constitute the main subject for weekly political study sessions that have been conducted in China since 1949 and that are directed by the ubiquitous "Party core groups" *(dang hexin xiaozu)* that exist in virtually all public institutions. Other media, including provincial and local newspapers, are obliged to reproduce authoritative *People's Daily* editorials and commentaries. Thus, this paper plays a major role in shaping public opinion and outlining the parameters of acceptable political discourse.

In March 1949, even before the official establishment of the **People's Republic of China (PRC)**, the offices of *People's Daily* were moved to Beiping (soon renamed **Beijing**), which was quickly reestablished as the official capital of the nation. Throughout the years, the most important editorials or commentaries of *People's Daily* appeared on the newspaper's front page including major proclamations on the inauguration of the **Great Leap Forward (1958–1960)** and the **Cultural Revolution (1966–1976)**. These include the infamous 1 June 1966 editorial entitled "Fiercely Sweep Away All the Ox-Ghosts and Snake-Demons," the 1 August editorial quoting from the letter of 7 May issued by **Mao Zedong** to **Lin Biao**, which led to the outbreak of **Red Guard** violence, and the 26 April 1989 editorial "It Is Necessary to Take a Clear-Cut Stand against Disturbances," which preceded the military crackdown on the second **Beijing Spring**. In 2005, the circulation of the paper was approximately seven to nine million copies and was read by virtually all important Party and government personnel. An editorial board runs the newspaper, though all major editorials and commentaries are subject to **censorship** *(shencha)* by the CCP's newly renamed Publicity Department and top Party **leaders**. Mao Zedong and subsequent Chinese leaders used the newspaper to make authoritative comments on political developments and trends, and to issue commands to the CCP apparatus. Leader-authored articles have also been used to circumvent opposition within the CCP and to appeal directly to public opinion, a tactic Mao Zedong employed during the Cultural Revolution. Editors of the *People's Daily* have often been placed in precarious positions as their decisions regarding the publication of certain articles and/or editorials can bring them political difficulties and lead to the loss of their jobs, as occurred with **Deng Tuo**, **Wang Ruoshui**, and **Hu Jiwei**. In the aftermath of the death of Mao Zedong in 1976, *People's Daily* declared that the former chairman of the CCP had made great mistakes and that the Cultural Revolution was a great disaster. In 1984, the newspaper called for the study of the general laws and methodology of Marxism but deplored the regarding of the ideology as dogma and declared that it did not solve all problems.

People's Daily has traditionally published carefully screened letters from common citizens and since the late 1990s has run selective advertisements from commercial firms. For years, distribution of the newspaper was guaranteed by mandatory subscriptions to CCP and government-run newspapers, a practice that, in 2003, was dropped, making *People's Daily* more dependent on the market as its circulation quickly dropped to four million. In 2004, *People's Daily*, along with *Enlightenment Daily* and *Economic Daily*—China's three leading national newspapers—announced that they would no longer publish paid reports lavishing praise on local governments in special columns, this in response to public distaste for such "image advertisement." Economic profit and social benefit are the twin goals of the newspaper, though it continues to hold to the government line by censoring stories and altering text, as occurred in early 2004, when the paper's editors doctored the "full text" of a speech given by visiting **United States** Vice-President Dick Cheney whose references to North **Korea** as a "rogue state" and support for individual rights to freedom of thought, expression, and belief were excised from the official text. *People's Daily* maintains a website (www.people.com.cn) with articles translated into English. *See also* CENSORSHIP.

"PEOPLE'S LIBERATION ARMY" (PLA) ("*RENMIN JIEFANG JUN*"). The military organization of the **People's Republic of China (PRC)**, the PLA in 2005 numbered about 2.5 million men and women, making it the largest army, in terms of sheer numbers, in the world. The PLA is organized into the Ground Force (1.2 million men), the Navy (PLAN, which includes naval infantry and aviation), the Air Force (PLAAF), the Second Artillery Corps (the strategic missile force founded in 1966 and consisting of 120,000 personnel), and the People's Armed Police (*renmin wuzhuang jingcha budui*) or PAP, internal security troops nominally subordinate to the Ministry of Public Security but included by China as part of the armed forces and considered an adjunct to the PLA in wartime. Overall, the PLA has 14,000 tanks, 14,500 artillery pieces, 15–30 ICBMs, 80–100 medium-range missiles, 500 short-range missiles, 3,400 aircraft, 453 military helicopters, 70 submarines, 18 destroyers, and 35 frigates. In 2005, official military expenditures were US$30 billion with annual increases of more than 15% since the late 1990s. Including off-budget spending on foreign weapons purchases, on nuclear weapons, and subsidies to defense and defense-related industries, actual spending is estimated at US$50 to US$70 billion (2.8% of GDP), making the Chinese military budget the third largest in the world after the **United States** and **Russia**.

China is presently engaged in a major military modernization process that has not only expanded expenditures on its Ground Force, Navy, Air Force, and Second Artillery Corps components but also includes major weapons and communication systems purchased from abroad, including a US$20 billion purchase from Russia in the 1990s, and stepped-up research on asymmetrical cyber warfare. Beginning in the late 1980s, military cooperation between the PLA and American and European militaries was inaugurated but was put on hold after the military crackdown against the 1989 second **Beijing Spring**, in which PLA forces played a crucial role. By 2004, limited joint operations with French, Russian, and Central Asian nations were conducted by elements of the PLA though the European and American ban on weapons sales to China remained in place. China has also devoted limited military resources to international peacekeeping efforts in Africa while it has conducted online air defense exercises and large-scale inter-service military exercises that mock a possible invasion of **Taiwan**.

The PLA traces its origins to 1927, when, on 1 August (now celebrated in China as Army Day), a ragtag military force of about 30,000 soldiers was organized by **Zhou Enlai**, **Zhu De**, and other Communist **leaders** who had broken off from the **Kuomintang (KMT)**. When the **Chinese Communist Party (CCP)** was formally established in 1921, the Communists abjured the formation of independent military forces in accord with the First **United Front (1924–1927)** formed with the KMT. This decision, which was imposed on the Chinese Communists by the **Soviet Union** via the Comintern, proved disastrous when, in April 1927, the Nationalists, under the leadership of Chiang Kai-shek, turned on their erstwhile Communist "allies" and nearly wiped out the entire CCP organization in China's urban areas, especially in **Guangzhou (Canton)** and **Shanghai**. The Chinese Workers and Peasants Revolutionary Army was formed in 1927 by Zhou Enlai and Zhu De and became the Communist Red Army. It quickly expanded into a formidable military force that, by the early 1930s, numbered 80,000 soldiers, who were holed up in the mountain redoubt of the Jiangxi Soviet. During the **Long March (1934–1935)**, command of the Red Army was assumed by **Mao Zedong** at the Zunyi Conference.

During the **Sino–Japanese War (1937–1945)**, a Second United Front was established with the Nationalists, formally merging Communist and Nationalist military forces. The main force of the Red Army in North China became known as the Eighth Route Army while the scattered Communist units in the South were formed into the New Fourth Army. After the war, these two military forces merged into the PLA, which, in less than four years, was able to defeat its Nationalist rival, despite the latter's vast superiority in numbers and weaponry, supplied primarily by the U.S. Theoretically one army, the PLA was organized into several **field armies (*yezhan jun*)** that operated as nearly independent units in discrete territorial regions of the country and were the origins of the post-1949 system of military regions. These included the First Field Army in the northwest region under the command of **Peng Dehuai**; the Second Field Army in the southwest region under **Liu Bocheng**; the Third Field Army in east China under Chen Yi; the Fourth Field Army in the central and southern regions under **Lin Biao**; and the Fifth Field Army in the north and northeast under **Nie Rongzhen** that was later placed under the direct command of the General Headquarters of the PLA. The formal designation of the Communist military forces as the PLA occurred in

1948, although some military units had adopted this appellation in 1945–1946.

During the **Civil War (1946–1949)**, a close relationship was established between the field army commands and the civil authorities established by the Communists through the organization of military control commissions that took over the local administration from the defeated Nationalists. The commanding military officer for any particular locality headed the military control commission and concurrently held the top spot in the civil administration overseeing economic enterprises, schools, and other institutions. At the regional level, six military regions (later expanded to eleven and then reduced to seven) were established for the entire country to complement the six major administrative regions through which the CCP managed Chinese society in the early 1950s. Although military control of the country formally ended in 1953, the close linkage between the field armies, the military regions, and the state and Party organization has since been maintained as various political leaders have depended on support from key military leaders and field armies to rise to prominence. In 1955, 10 former field commanders of the PLA were promoted to "marshal" (*yuanshuai*), the highest rank in the armed forces: Liu Bocheng, Zhu De, **Ye Jianying**, Peng Dehuai, Luo Ronghuan, Xu Xiangqian, Nie Rongzhen, Chen Yi (who would later become China's foreign minister), He Long, and Lin Biao, who would be dropped from the list from 1971 to 1997. He Long, a former brigand and minor warlord, and Peng Dehuai would both be purged and would not survive the **Cultural Revolution (1966–1976)**.

During the 1950s, the PLA was transformed from a peasant army into a more modern one with the assistance of the Soviet Red Army, which helped China develop an Air Force composed of the J-4 aircraft (a copy of the MiG-15) and the J-5, J-6, and J-7 (copies of the MiG-17, MiG-19, and MiG-21, respectively) and the Xi'an H-6 bomber, a licensed copy of the Soviet Tu-16 Badger. In addition to the reoccupation of **Tibet** in 1950, the major military operations of the PLA were its involvement against American forces in the **Korean War (1950–1953)** and air operations against Nationalist forces during the **Taiwan Straits Crises (1954 and 1958)**, when, during the 1958 conflict, it suffered 14:1 loses at the hands of the superior

American-trained Nationalist air arm. There was also the short-lived **Sino–Indian War (1962)** when Chinese forces prevailed over their South Asian neighbor. As a result of the outbreak of the Sino–Soviet Conflict in 1960, China's Air Force suffered tremendously, which spurred the country to develop an indigenous Chinese aircraft design that led to the J-8. In 1969, PLA units engaged elements of the Soviet Army on the northern border near the Ussuri River; in 1979, the PLA fought the forces of **Vietnam** in the Sino–Vietnamese War. Following the declaration by **Deng Xiaoping** and Zhou Enlai that called for establishment of a professional military force as part of the "**Four Modernizations**," the PLA, from 1978 on, demobilized millions of men and women and was transformed from a land-based power centered on a vast ground force to a smaller, more mobile high-tech military, capable of mounting defensive operations beyond its borders, especially in any conflict with Nationalist and/or American forces over Taiwan.

Authority over the military is concentrated in the central **government structure**. From 1935 to his death in 1976, Mao Zedong was the unquestioned commander of the PLA. Advocating the principle that "the Party commands the gun," Mao as CCP chairman never assumed military rank, unlike his Nationalist counterpart Chiang Kai-shek, who was referred to as the "generalissimo" and often appeared in military garb. In a society that assigned low social status to the military profession, this abjuring of a formal military position strengthened Mao's political authority and undoubtedly provided an advantage over such political competitors as Marshal Lin Biao. China's other two prominent political leaders since 1949, Zhou Enlai and Deng Xiaoping, also disavowed military rank as did their successors **Jiang Zemin** and **Hu Jintao**, neither of whom had military experience. Mao's personal control over the military was evident throughout his reign as CCP chairman from the abolition of ranks in 1965 to his personal order in 1968 for the PLA to intervene in the internecine conflict of the Cultural Revolution to bring an end to factional violence and **Red Guard** terror.

In the mid-1970s, a more formal structure of military authority in China was established. The commander-in-chief of the PLA is the chairman of the Central **Military Affairs Commission** (**MAC**), a Party organ that is theoretically appointed by the CCP National Party

Congress but which actually enjoys a great deal of autonomy from both the CCP Central Committee and **Politburo**. Also, a State Central Military Commission was established by the state constitution in 1982, which is nominally subordinate to the **National People's Congress** (**NPC**) but which has little real authority over the PLA. In 1995, Jiang Zemin was MAC chairman as well as general secretary of the CCP and **president of the People's Republic of China** and was succeeded as MAC chairman by Hu Jintao in September 2004, the last post Jiang relinquished prior to his full retirement. The size of the MAC ranges from 10 to 20 members, and includes the minister of defense—who traditionally was a relatively low-ranking officer exercising little real authority over the PLA—and the heads of the General Staff Headquarters, the General Logistics Department, the General Armaments Department, and the General Political Department that oversees the system of **political commissars** in the military who under a separate chain of command ensure loyalty to the CCP and the civilian government. The chairmen and vice-chairmen of the MAC are civilians while the minister of defense is the administrative head of the PLA who oversees the PLA General Headquarters in **Beijing**. This body coordinates and executes combat operations of the various service arms and has a general logistics and procurement service. The General Staff Headquarters maintains direct control over the service arms and various engineering corps. Operationally, to move a Group Army requires the signature of the chairman of the MAC; to move a division requires the permission of the General Staff Headquarters and the MAC; a regiment, the regional Party committee; a battalion, an army-level Party committee; and a company, the division Party committee.

At the regional level, military personnel are organized in seven military regions (MR), each encompassing several provinces. Military personnel are generally assigned on a permanent basis to a region, which, in turn, is divided into military districts. The seven MRs are Beijing (the capital), Shenyang (the northeast), Jinan–Wuhan (central), Nanjing–Fuzhou (south), Guangzhou (southeast), Kunming–Chengdu (southwest), and Lanzhou–Inner Mongolia (northwest). Because of their geopolitical and strategic importance, Beijing, Shenyang, and Lanzhou–Inner Mongolia are the most important. The Beijing Garrison Division (*weishuqu*) includes four divisions, two of which protect the capital city, and two mechanized divisions that guard the capital's suburbs. Increasingly seen as obsolete for 21st-century warfare, the system of military regions may be drastically altered in the next several years.

The main force units in the PLA in the late 1990s consisted of approximately 24 group armies incorporating a total of from 75 to 90 divisions, a reduction from the 1980s when there were 35 group armies composed of around 164 divisions, many of which were undermanned and received less training often participating in productive **labor**. After a reduction in total force levels by 500,000 in 1996, a major reorganization of the PLA order of battle was carried out in line with a 1998 "White Paper on National Defense" that included the transfer of a large number of second-line divisions to the People's Armed Police (PAP), which since 1983 has assumed internal police and border responsibilities. Under the new system, a main force group army typically includes 46,300 troops organized in up to four divisions, including infantry, armor, artillery, air defense, airborne, and air support elements. The armored divisions have three regiments and 240 main battle tanks but generally lack mechanized infantry support. Approximately 16 army corps (out of a total of 38) are under the direct control of the MAC and can be deployed anywhere in the country by direct orders from Beijing. There are also regional divisions and regiments, consisting of approximately 800,000 personnel, and a **people's militia**. The Central Guard Regiment (*zhongyang jingwei tuan*), also known as the 8341 Unit, is responsible for protecting the CCP leadership.

The power projection of the PLA is limited though this capability has been strengthened in recent years by heavy investments and purchase of foreign weapons plus the development of a moderate intercontinental and theater ballistic missile capacity along with the acquisition from Russia of a multiple independently targeted reentry vehicle capability in 1996. Advanced weapons systems acquired from the late 1990s onward include from Russia Sovremenny-class destroyers (which include the lethal Moskit ship-to-ship missile—NATO designation "Sunburn SS-N-22," which at Mach 3 and carrying a 200-kg conventional warhead can overwhelm any ship defense, including those of the U.S. Navy) and eight Kilo-class submarines. China is also currently building four new destroyers including two

"Aegis" Type 052C class guided missile destroyers, its own *Song*-class diesel-electric subs (including a new stealth design), and, in 2004, launched a new class of nuclear submarines armed with nuclear missiles capable of striking across the Pacific Ocean. There are also the *Luda*-and *Luhu*-class destroyers, the *Jiangwei*-class frigates, guided missile boats and amphibious warfare ships. The PLA Navy pales in comparison to the U.S. Navy and is being transformed from its traditional role of coastal defense centered on patrol, surveillance, and torpedo boats to a major naval force capable of operating anywhere in the western Pacific and cruising for lengthy periods in the South China Sea. According to American military observers, however, China's Navy and nuclear forces lack the system integration and utilization of combat information systems so necessary to fight against advanced militaries like that of the U.S. and are still heavily dependent on foreign-made equipment. To upgrade the Air Force, China has purchased 76 Russian Sukhoi Su-27 Flankers (a heavy tactical fighter known as the J-11) and 70 Sukhoi-30 MKK aircraft, a multi-role strike platform. While the mainstay of the PLA Air Force remains the 1960s-vintage J-7 fighter, the PLA is also building an indigenous aerospace and military industry at Chengdu and Xi'an aircraft facilities with its production of the J-10 (comparable to a U.S. F-16), the Xi'an JH-7A strike aircraft, and the FC-1/JF-17. China is also developing its own tanker aircraft modeled on the Russian TU-16 Badger and a next generation XXJ fighter.

Under the Second Artillery Corps or Strategic Rocket Forces, China's 15–30 ICBMs are solid fuel and capable of striking the U.S. while its medium- and short-range missiles are also solid fuel and include air-launched cruise missiles largely aimed at Taiwan and at U.S. aircraft carriers. The ICBMs with the largest throw weight consist of around 18–20 *Dong Feng* ("East Wind")-5's equipped with a nuclear warhead of four to five megatons and a range of approximately 12,000 km, along with approximately 10 Dong Feng-4s (CSS-3) with a three megaton reentry vehicle. In recent years, China has test-fired the Dong Feng-31, a road mobile SCUD missile with a range also of approximately 12,000 km, which with multiple reentry vehicles and multiple independently targeted reentry vehicles can reach any city in the U.S. Overall, China's number of operational ICBMs has not dramatically changed in over a decade and sit unfueled in their silos while their nuclear warheads are kept in secure storage. The Strategic Rocket Forces are also not linked to systems in space for detection of an enemy's incoming missiles and the execution of an immediate, complex coordinated nuclear strike is evidently not contemplated. China also possesses 50–100 Dong Feng 3s (CSS-2) and Dong Feng-21s (CSS-5) medium range missiles (MRBMs) that are theater weapons equipped with three megaton and 600-km warheads. China's submarine-launched ballistic missile (SLBM) known as the *Julang* ("Great Wave")-2 is capable of carrying only one warhead on the single sub China has so far constructed that can carry up to 16 missiles. The Second Artillery Corps is headquartered in Qinghe, a suburb of Beijing and maintains seven missile bases each with three missile brigades. The 80302 Unit is in Huangshan, Anhui Province, and is the most important unit for conducting possible strikes against Taiwan while the 80304 Unit in Luoyang, Henan Province, maintains the DF-5 missiles aimed at the U.S. China's estimated stockpile of plutonium is put at 1.7–2.8 tons, enough to arm about 400–900 nuclear warheads indicating that the PLA continues to follow the doctrine of **Nie Rongzhen** of maintaining "the minimum means of reprisal." As a signatory to the Comprehensive Test Ban Treaty, China is prohibited from developing new warhead designs and, in 1990, ceased its production of fissile material. China also does not apparently arm its relatively aging aircraft with nuclear weapons and there is no deployment of tactical nuclear weapons as its short-range ballistic missiles are evidently all conventionally armed.

The PLA Ground Force deploys tanks that range from the Type-80 series or modified Russian T-54 to the next generation tank touted as Type-99 with a 125-mm smoothbore gun and laser rangefinder. Other mainstay Ground Force equipment includes the Type-92 armored personnel carrier, Type-89 122-mm howitzer and Type-83 152-mm China-made howitzer, Type-89 missile launch rockets, PLZ-45 rocket launcher, and FM-80 and Red Flag-61 surface-to-air missiles (SAMs). The PRC became a major arms exporter during the 1980s often through PLA-front companies such as China North Industries Corporation (NORINCO), while participation of the PLA in nonmilitary related commercial activities, such as real estate and running domestic airlines, that had begun in the 1950s and 1960s was terminated in the 1990s and early 2000s. The PLA is still involved, however, in such domestic programs as supporting the work of development in China's western regions of Xinjiang and Qinghai provinces. Research and training support for the PLA comes from a number of institutions including its military academy, the National Defense University, the Chinese Commission on Science, Technology, and Industry for National Defense, the Academy of Military Sciences, the China Ordnance Corporation, the Missile Research Academy (established in 1956 by **Qian Xuesen**), and in conjunction with **Qinghua University** the Institute of Air Force Armament. China's plans for carrying out asymmetrical warfare (including hacking websites, targeting financial institutions, and assassinating key political and economic figures) against potentially superior enemies such as the U.S. (which remains two decades ahead in **technology**) were outlined in a 2000 book titled *Unrestricted Warfare*, which discusses information warfare technology and has been translated into English by the American Central Intelligence Agency (CIA). While many American and Asian analysts previously believed that China could not develop a credible threat to the U.S. before 2010 or 2015, by 2005 that date was moved up to 2006 and certainly by 2012.

The political history of the PLA since 1949 has been a turbulent one. Following China's participation in the Korean War, Minister of Defense Peng Dehuai, who had commanded China's forces during the war, pushed for major military modernization and professionalism. Peng's demise after the **Great Leap Forward (1958–1960)**, however, led to the rise of Lin Biao, who increased the political role of the army and inaugurated a campaign for the entire nation to emulate the PLA, all at the behest of Mao Zedong. PLA heroes, such as **Lei Feng**, and model PLA units like the Good Eighth Company of Nanjing Road served as national paragons of the political virtues of "self-sacrifice," resistance to bourgeois urban life, and the importance of the "primacy of politics." The politicization of the army reached its zenith in 1965 with the abolition of ranks and insignia, as the army became the symbol of the masses purportedly waging "**class struggle**" under the direct command of Mao Zedong and Lin Biao. During the Cultural Revolution, military officers assumed key positions of authority in the Party and state bureaucracies, and emerged as the dominant force in the **Revolutionary Committees**. Military resources were also made available to Red Guards in their attacks on the Party and its leadership. By 1967–1968, however, Mao was forced to order in the military to put down the factional violence and to establish a modicum of law and order, which the PLA did, in some cases, with brutal efficiency. In effect, the PLA took control of the country as military officers assumed supervision of economic, financial, educational, media, and the **Public Security Bureau**. The political influence of the military peaked at the 1969 Ninth National Party Congress, which designated Lin Biao as Mao's "successor" and which witnessed the appointment of military men to 43% of the seats on the CCP Central Committee. In terms of military doctrine, the PLA during the Cultural Revolution adhered to Lin Biao's vision of "people's war" in which guerrilla units with mass popular support could defeat superior "imperialist" forces—a policy that Communist forces followed in the early days of the Vietnam War.

The Lin Biao affair in 1971—also known as **Project 571**—brought a rapid end to the army's dominant political role. The PLA central command was subject to a massive purge of Lin's supporters from his Fourth Field Army. The role of the PLA came to be defined primarily as a military one as the number of military officers on the CCP Central Committee and **Politburo** were drastically reduced. In 1973, an unprecedented transfer of commanders of the crucial military regions was carried out, though 30% of the 11th Central Committee elected in 1977 still consisted of military men. The continued political influence of the PLA reflected its crucial role in carrying out the arrest of **Jiang Qing** and the radical **Gang of Four** in 1976 following the death of Mao Zedong along with the deployment of PLA units from the 27th Army and People's Armed Police to put down the second **Beijing Spring** in June 1989.

Throughout the 1980s and 1990s, the focus of central Party policies has been to reduce the political role of the PLA, to reestablish military professionalism, and to engage in a major modernization of the force structure. As a former PLA chief-of-staff, Deng Xiaoping commanded great respect in the military. In 1980, he personally appointed 10 of the then 11 military region commanders and, in 1985, effected a reduction in military regions from 11 to 7. Elected chairman of the MAC in 1982, Deng became the commander-in-chief of the PLA, even though he refused the top position in the CCP and made military modernization the last of the Four Modernizations. This involved streamlining the military command structure below the MAC, improving officer training and **education**, and modernizing weaponry, including strategic weapons. Fragmented command structures over air, navy, armored, and other units were consolidated under the dual authority of the military regions and their service headquarters in Beijing, especially after the PLA suffered embarrassing military reverses in its 1979 war against Vietnam. In 2004, the PLA announced a plan to simplify its administration with a system of "two down, one in," where two retiring deputy posts are replaced with only one new incumbent.

In the mid-1980s, China also purchased military hardware from the U.S., under a six-year agreement that involved equipment for jet fighters and modern equipment from Western European countries such as West Germany. Yet throughout the 1980s, China's military expenditures were reduced by 25% from a high of US$14.3 billion in 1979 as the CCP directed critical resources to civilian economic development. Following the intervention of the PLA in the military crackdown against the second Beijing Spring in 1989, however, defense outlays have increased dramatically especially on a larger navy and strategic weapons. China's military forces remain significantly inferior to comparable armies of developed states, however, while domestically, the PLA continues to suffer from the taint of killing civilians during the 1989 pro-democracy demonstrations.

In 2005, China's top military leaders were Xu Caihou (1943–), Cao Gangchuan (1935–), Guo Boxiong (1942–), and Liang Guanglie (1940–). Xu Caihou graduated from the Harbin Institute of Military Engineering with a specialty in electronics and served in the northeast Shenyang Military Region and received additional training at the PLA Institute of Political Sciences. Director of the *Liberation Army Daily*, the PLA newspaper, Xu has headed the all-important PLA General Political Department since 2002 and sits on the Secretariat of the CCP Central Committee. Born in 1935, General Cao Gangchuan joined the PLA in 1954 and graduated from the USSR's Advanced Military Engineering School of the Soviet Artillery Corps where he mastered the Russian language. With considerable experience in the PLA General Logistics Department, Cao served on the PLA Headquarters of the General Staff and from 1992 to 1996 was deputy chief of the General Staff of the PLA. He was a state councilor and director of the Commission of Science, Technology, and Industry for National Defense from 1996 to 1998. In 2005, Cao served as a full member on the CCP Politburo and held the rank equivalent to a lieutenant general. He is a central figure in the rapid modernization of China's weapons program, which he believes is necessary to counter an increasingly hostile U.S. General Guo Boxiong is one of the few top leaders in China from an interior province, Shaanxi, and serves as a vice-chairman of the Central Military Affairs Commission and a full member of the CCP Politburo. A military officer with considerable combat training experience with the 19th Army of the PLA ground force, Guo headed this unit from 1983 to 1985 and was appointed deputy commander of the Beijing Military Area Command in 1993. General Guo also headed the Lanzhou Military Region from 1997 to 1999 and was appointed to the Central Military Affairs Commission in 1999 and a member of the Politburo in 2002. Liang Guanglie, chief of the general staff of the PLA in 2005, was, for many years, associated with the First Army of the PLA ground force and headed the Wuhan Military Area Command in the 1970s. The only top leader in China from Sichuan Province, Liang headed the Beijing Military Area Command in 1993 and, from 1997 to 1999, was commander of the Shenyang Military Area Command before being appointed chief of the general staff in 2002 and a member of the Central Military Affairs Commission in 2003. *See also* ATOMIC BOMB.

PEOPLE'S MILITIA. The **Chinese Communist Party (CCP)** has historically emphasized the creation of local armed forces to operate in coordination with regular military units. The people's militia played a major role in supporting military operations of the CCP during the Communist struggle for power before 1949. After the CCP takeover, local armed forces were organized throughout the country to maintain social order and to assist the regular armed forces in mobilizations, for example, during the **Korean War (1950–1953)**. During the **Great Leap Forward (1958–1960)**, the people's militia was expanded and joined with the **people's communes** as part of the general militarization of society that accompanied the Great Leap. During the **Cultural Revolution (1966–1976)**, local armed forces often became involved in the intense factional struggles of **Red Guards**

and were intimately involved in carrying out political violence, murder, and even cannibalism. During the latter part of the Cultural Revolution, local armed forces largely disintegrated as the regular army, the **People's Liberation Army** (**PLA**), imposed its control over Chinese society. Since the advancement of economic reforms in 1978–1979, the people's militia has largely disappeared, as the Chinese government has focused on more conventional military and police forces.

PEOPLE'S REPUBLIC OF CHINA (PRC). The formal name of the Chinese Communist state since its establishment on 1 October 1949, the PRC is officially described in the 1982 state constitution—China's last—as a "socialist state under the people's democratic dictatorship led by the working class and based on an alliance of workers and peasants." The capital city is **Beijing** while the PRC is headed by a **president** whose official powers involve "engaging in activities involving state affairs" and who is appointed by the highest state organ, the **National People's Congress** (**NPC**). The office of the president was reestablished in the 1982 state constitution after it had been deleted from the 1975 and 1978 state constitutions. From 1993 to 2003, the president of the PRC was **Jiang Zemin** who following his retirement was replaced by **Hu Jintao** who like Jiang serves concurrently as general secretary of the **Chinese Communist Party** (**CCP**) and chairman of both the Party and State Central **Military Affairs Commission** (**MAC**). Citizens of the PRC are said to enjoy "freedom of speech, of the press, of assembly, of association, and of demonstration"; in reality, such "freedoms" are severely curtailed by the demand enumerated in the same document that all citizens abide by the **Four Cardinal Principles** of absolute loyalty to the CCP. The national anthem of the People's Republic of China was proclaimed in 1949 as the *March of the Volunteers*, which was authored by Tian Han, a famous modern writer and set to music composed by Nie Er. The song was originally written in 1935 as the theme song for a film called *Sons and Daughters of the Storm* and urged people to join the National Resistance Movement against the Japanese in World War II with such lines as "Arise, ye who refuse to be slaves! With our flesh and blood, let us build our new Great Wall!" During the **Cultural Revolution (1966–1976)**, the song *The East is Red*, a paean to **Mao**

Zedong, became the de facto national anthem. Following the end of the Cultural Revolution, the NPC restored the *March of the Volunteers* as the national anthem but its lyrics were changed until 1982 when the original lyrics were restored and the song was formally incorporated into the state constitution as China's national anthem. The Chinese national flag was created by Zeng Liangsong, the secretary of the **Shanghai** Modern Economics Agency, and consists of five gold stars resting in the upper left corner of the flag on a red background. The red color stands for the revolution while the gold color of the stars signifies the dawn of a new era. The five stars grouped together symbolize the unity of the Chinese people under the leadership of the CCP. The Chinese national emblem, which hangs above the entrance to the Great Hall of the People, has at its center Tiananmen or "the Gate of Heavenly Peace," which stands at the entrance to the Forbidden City, today's Palace Museum. On the emblem, the gate is illuminated by the five stars from the national flag. As on the flag, the five stars here also symbolize the unity of the Chinese people under the leadership of the CCP. Stalks of grain, representing the peasant **population**, surround the gate while below it there is a cogwheel, a symbol of the working class.

Internationally, the PRC is recognized by most nations in the world, though a few states still maintain formal diplomatic links with the Republic of China (ROC) on **Taiwan**. Since 1971, the PRC has held a seat on the Security Council of the **United Nations** (**UN**) and, in January 1979, formal diplomatic relations were established with the **United States**. In 1999, the 50th anniversary of the founding of the PRC was celebrated in Beijing by a large-scale parade of military, economic, and cultural displays, the first in many years, and a performance of Chinese poems from the Tang (618–905 AD) and Song (960–1126 AD) dynasties in honor of China's traditional culture. National day on 1 October is also a day when many couples in China marry.

"PERSONAL DOSSIERS" (*"DANG'AN"*). These are files maintained on all members of the "**basic unit**" (*jiben danwei*) system, the honeycomb-like matrix of organization in China's urban and rural areas. Defined geographically and functionally (by work), these basic units rely on the personal dossiers as part of an elaborate system to exercise comprehensive control over all members. Files include relevant facts about a person's personal history, including cases of "erroneous" behavior and political dissent, and, up until recently, were crucial in determining an individual's ability to advance in the organization and/or to receive permission to marry, have children, or to divorce. Entries into the files are controlled by the unit head and are under the direct control of the unit personnel department. Personnel files accompany an individual when transferred from one unit to another. Various proposals were aired during the 1980s by **Zhao Ziyang** to reduce or even eliminate the *dang'an*, but to no avail. As economic reform and the **open-door policy** have made China a more liberal and open society, however, the importance of the personal dossiers in influencing people's lives have weakened—especially over personal decisions involving marriage and child-bearing but they still exist for most urban residents.

PERSONALITY CULT (*GEREN CHONGBAI*). All of China's Communist **leaders** have, in theory, opposed the personality cult as a "decadent heritage left over from the long period of human history." In reality, **Mao Zedong** and **Deng Xiaoping** both promoted elaborate praise and even worship of their person to serve their own political ends. In the Communist world, personality cults began with Vladimir Lenin and **Josef Stalin**, who were effusively praised by the official press in the **Soviet Union** and China for their "genius." Stalin, in particular, was lavished with such praise. This model was adopted in China in the mid-1940s when the cult of Mao Zedong began. Although some **Chinese Communist Party** (**CCP**) leaders, such as **Zhu De** and **Liu Shaoqi**, expressed reservations about the personality cult, "Chairman Mao" became the focus of leadership idolization in China from 1943 onward. The **Korean War (1950–1953)** and the **Great Leap Forward (1958–1960)** were two tense periods of national crisis during which Mao's leadership role was heavily emphasized and his person was accorded great stature, often on a par with both Lenin and Stalin in the international Communist pantheon.

The height of the Maoist personality cult came during the **Cultural Revolution (1966–1976)**, when Mao was praised as "the greatest genius of the present age" and his "little red book" of sayings, *Quotations from Chairman Mao* was accorded the status of Communist canon. **Red Guards** expressed fanatical admiration for Mao and different Red Guard factions fought bloody pitched battles over competing claims of loyalty to the "chairman" and his "sayings"; among the common people, there was a pervasive belief in Mao as a "god." The cult was reinforced at a mass level by pervasive pictures and statutes of Mao throughout China, as well as the production of eight billion Mao badges that came in 50,000 individual types. Although Mao expressed criticisms of the personality cult during the Cultural Revolution in a letter to his wife, **Jiang Qing**, such fanatical promotion of Mao's stature as the "great helmsman" in China did not subside until his death in 1976, when many in China felt "the sky had fallen." In the 1981 **Resolution on Certain Questions in the History of Our Party since the Establishment of the People's Republic of China**, CCP leaders criticized the excesses of the Mao cult, although without disavowing the important historical role that Mao had played in CCP history. Excessive publicity of a leader's image was also reigned in as no more badges were produced for any of the country's leaders. Deng Xiaoping joined in this criticism, but, beginning in 1978, Deng promoted his own mini-cult with the publication of his *Selected Works* and an emphasis on "Deng Xiaoping Theory," which was subsequently incorporated into the Party constitution.

The personality cult in both the Soviet Union and China has been characterized by leaders claiming authority in all realms of human behavior—politics, economics, military, art, and culture. Like Stalin and Mao Zedong, Deng Xiaoping continued this tradition by issuing statements and releasing writings on virtually all of these topics, which Party members and Chinese people were urged to "study." But unlike the Maoist years in China, social receptivity to the personality cult in China had faded, as witnessed during the 1989 second **Beijing Spring** pro-democracy movement when Deng and other **leaders** were subjected to popular ridicule and criticism in a manner that would have never occurred during Mao's lifetime. Upon his ascension to power in 2002, CCP General Secretary **Hu Jintao** expressed open opposition to personality cults and asserted that, by abolishing the system of lifelong tenure in office for leaders and by establishing an awareness of the rule of law, China would avoid the centralized personal power and patriarchy that gave rise to earlier personality cults.

In 2003, on the 110th anniversary of the birth of Mao Zedong, an updated version of the personality cult emerged, with new hip-hop songs, films, books, and concerts praising Mao's leadership, as the image of the "great helmsman" was reconfigured into that of a management guru whose pragmatic leadership style motivated subordinates and dealt with various types of crises. With people expressing continued "worship" for Mao, his durability as a commanding figure in China and the inherent appeal of the personality cult persists as a counter to China's increasingly dog-eat-dog and highly inegalitarian social environment. This reverence is undoubtedly reinforced by the preservation of Mao's body in a crystal sarcophagus in the Mao Zedong Memorial Hall located in Beijing's Tiananmen Square, which, since its opening in 1977, has been visited by 138 million people.

"PLANNED PURCHASE AND SUPPLY" (*"TONGGOU TONG-XIAO"*). Beginning in the 1950s, important commodities in the Chinese **economy** were subject to unified purchasing and marketing by state-run trading companies. This was applied especially to **agriculture** products, such as grain (rice and wheat), edible oils, cotton, and cotton cloth. The system was expanded in the mid- and late 1950s to virtually all commodities in the Chinese economy. The state was the sole purchaser and supplier of these commodities that were then rationed to the urban and rural **population**. The system involved setting quotas for each farm household based upon its requirements of food, seed, and fodder, as well as based upon the demand from grain deficit areas in the country. Private trading in these products was banned as planned purchase and supply ensured adequate stocks of essential products and maintained staple grains and oils at very low prices. Taxes, in kind, were also charged to peasant producers who consistently received very low prices for their products.

After the 1978–1979 economic reform and the introduction of the **Agricultural Responsibility System**, greater flexibility in production and sale of some non-essential commodities was allowed. But fear of inflation and radical shifts in production led the **Chinese Communist Party** (**CCP**) leadership to maintain planned purchase and supply over essential grain and edible oil production. Private trading occurs but rigid price and administrative controls are still in place on staples. The prices for farm commodities paid to rural producers have increased, but the state still prevents the emergence of a true free market in all farm commodities. Price increases for grains are often offset by increases in wages for the urban population, thereby contributing to some inflationary pressure in the post-1978 Chinese economy, especially during the 1990s. Radical proposals for price reforms and for the dismantling of the system of planned purchase and supply, initially supported by **Deng Xiaoping**, were proposed in 1988. But panic buying in China's cities led to a quick termination of this reform. The state continues to maintain a monopoly over acquisition of agricultural commodities through the bureaucratically bloated Supply and Marketing Cooperatives that since 1978 have had to adjust their role to an increased market environment.

POLICE. *See* PUBLIC SECURITY BUREAU.

"POLISH DISEASE" (*"BOLAN BIBING"*). The phrase was coined by Chinese **leaders** to express their fear of a repetition in China of the social and political changes in 1989 that led to the collapse of the Communist regime in Poland. Such fears that events in Poland would influence Chinese politics trace their history to 1956 when popular demonstrations in the Polish city of Poznan (and also in Hungary) spooked Chinese leaders and provoked major domestic policy changes, such as the **Hundred Flowers (1956–1957)** and the **Anti-Rightist Campaign (1957–1958)**. In 1980, China's domestic political situation was once again affected by developments in Poland. Initially, Chinese leaders supported the Polish resistance against the domination of the **Soviet Union** and their demands for internal reforms. But after hard-line **leaders** in China warned of serious domestic consequences if political and economic reforms were enacted in China, the situation in Poland was interpreted in graver tones, provoking **Deng Xiaoping** to retreat from his proto-democratic reform program outlined in August 1980. Fears that reforms in prices and enterprise management would unleash serious inflationary pressures and lead to massive unemployment haunted China's leaders. Their greatest fear was that a Chinese version of Solidarity or a Chinese Lech Walesa would emerge. Thus **Chinese Communist Party (CCP)** leaders during the 1989 second **Beijing Spring** were especially harsh in crushing the embryonic workers' movement and persecuting its leader, **Han Dongfang**.

POLITBURO (*ZHENGZHIJU*). The top policy-making body in the **Chinese Communist Party (CCP)**, the Politburo is formally an executive arm of the Central Committee, which meets periodically between Central Committee meetings or plenums. The Politburo's membership varies from year to year, but generally consists of around 12 to 20 top **leaders** from the CCP, the government, and the **People's Liberation Army (PLA)**. It is generally believed that the full Politburo meets approximately once a week to consider major policy issues. In theory, it is responsible to the Central Committee for its membership and policies. In reality, the Politburo controls the makeup of the Central Committee and determines its policy decisions. There are both full and alternate members of the Politburo, with the former exercising voting power, while the latter do not. The inner workings of the Politburo are generally unknown to the outside world; it is not even known for sure whether formal votes are taken or whether it operates according to consensus building.

During the Maoist period, especially from the late 1950s onward, Chairman **Mao Zedong** generally refrained from attending Politburo meetings, thus considerably reducing its authority in the CCP. Since the death of Mao Zedong in 1976, CCP leaders have attempted to increase the institutional importance of the Politburo, though at times its role has been overshadowed by the Party Secretariat, which was also revived after 1978. The crucial role of **Deng Xiaoping** in China's politics, although from 1989 to 1997 he was nominally retired, indicated that the Politburo, like other CCP institutions, remained relatively weak in the face of Deng's enormous personal authority. The Standing Committee of the Politburo is an even smaller executive body that over the years has varied in size from five to nine members. It apparently meets several times a week and on some occasion takes formal votes, such as when the decision was made to crack down on the 1989 second **Beijing Spring** pro-democracy movement.

Few changes in the functioning of the Politburo were made during the leadership reign of CCP leader **Jiang Zemin**, but, in 2003, new General Secretary **Hu Jintao**, announced plans for the Politburo to make a formal work report to the Central Committee as a measure aimed at making the executive body more accountable. In 2004, there were 24 members of the Politburo and nine members of its powerful

Standing Committee, including Hu Jintao (general secretary), Huang Ju (vice-premier), **Jia Qinglin**, Li Changchun, **Luo Gan**, Wang Lequan, **Wen Jiabao** (premier), Wu Bangguo (chair, **National People's Congress**), and **Zeng Qinglong** (CCP Secretariat and vice-president).

POLITICAL COMMISSAR (*ZHENGZHI WENYUAN*). This is part of a system to ensure Communist Party control over the military. It was first introduced in **Russia** during the Civil War between the Bolsheviks and the Whites and was adopted in China in the 1920s. Political commissars were installed in the Chinese military down to the company level, where they conducted propaganda work and ensured **Chinese Communist Party (CCP)** control over the disparate military forces. After 1949, the political commissar system was retained and remained a central component of the CCP apparatus of control over the **People's Liberation Army (PLA)**. The terms "political teachers" and "political instructors" are also used to refer to these positions. The political commissar is considered second in command and must generally countersign the orders of military commanders. The system of political commissars is controlled from the top by the General Political Department of the PLA. Supporters of greater military professionalism have periodically argued for a loosening of political controls, as occurred during the 1950s and again in the 1980s. During the late 1950s and during the **Cultural Revolution (1966–1976)**, the political role of the army in China was emphasized by **Mao Zedong** and greatly strengthened the authority of the political commissars. Since 1978, the political commissar system has been retained but with greater authority flowing to military commanders. The 1989 second **Beijing Spring**, however, reinvigorated the role of the political commissars, especially after the loyalty of the PLA to the Communist regime was questioned by the disaffection of some military commanders and by their refusal to carry out orders to fire on protestors during the pro-democracy demonstrations.

Under **Jiang Zemin** who headed the Central **Military Affairs Commission (MAC)** from 1989 to 2004, little change was effected in the system of political commissars. But following the transfer of authority from Jiang to his successor, **Hu Jintao**, a major reshuffling of political commissars occurred with the appointment of Peng Xiao-feng (son of a famous Red Army General killed in the **Sino–Japanese War**) to become the political commissar of the Second Artillery Corps or Strategic Rocket Forces while the Deputy Political Commissar was summarily dismissed. Changes rarely seen were also carried out in the PLA Air Force, the **Beijing** Military Region, and the People's Armed Police (PAP).

POLITICAL STUDY GROUPS. *See* MAO ZEDONG THOUGHT STUDY CLASSES.

"POLITICS TAKES COMMAND" (*"ZHENGZHI GUASHUAI"*). This is perhaps the most famous phrase uttered by Chairman **Mao Zedong** of the **Chinese Communist Party** (**CCP**) indicating his central belief that "politics is the commander, the soul." During the **Great Leap Forward (1958–1960)** and the **Cultural Revolution (1966–1976)**, "politics takes command" became the watchword of the Maoist model for the transformation of Chinese society and culture. In the Maoist vision, assuming a correct political standpoint could work miracles in the **economy** and society. Peasants during the Great Leap Forward were glorified for taking the correct political standpoint of adhering to Mao Zedong Thought to make enormous strides in production that later proved false. Organizationally, "politics takes command" meant that the Party branch was given total authority in the **people's communes** and in the management of **state-owned enterprises** (**SOEs**). The same was true at the provincial and central levels of government where the CCP assumed a greater role in running the country.

During the Cultural Revolution, however, "politics takes command" was used to challenge the authority of Party bureaucrats. Mao mobilized **Red Guards** and other non-CCP personages to rid the Party of his ideological and political enemies. At this time, "politics takes command" entailed adhering to Mao Zedong Thought to revolutionize society through constant turmoil and political struggle, in contrast with the ideas of Mao's revisionist critics, such as **Liu Shaoqi**, who purportedly advocated putting "economics in command."

The winding down of the Cultural Revolution and the emergence of the economic reforms in 1978–1979 brought an end to "politics takes command" as the centerpiece of CCP propaganda. The phrase is no longer used, essentially disappearing with the death of Mao in 1976. In its place, the post-1978 leadership has emphasized the role of economic forces and incentives mobilizing the Chinese people to increase national wealth by acting on the principle that "to get rich is glorious" (*facai guangrong*).

"POOR AND BLANK" (*"YIQIONG ERBAI"*). This term was used by **Mao Zedong** to describe the general character of the Chinese people. The overwhelming poverty of the Chinese people gave rise to desire for change and for action, and that, Mao argued, was good because it produced revolutionary fervor. The Chinese people were "blank" in that they were comparable to a "blank sheet of paper, free from any mark," on which the "freshest and most beautiful characters can be written. . . ." In this sense, Mao believed that the very ignorance of the Chinese people (literacy rates in the 1940s when the Communists achieved power were very low) would allow the **Chinese Communist Party** (**CCP**) to mold the **population** into a compliant popular support base for the Communists. The people generally had no preconceived opposition to the CCP and that made revolutionary change possible. The exception, of course, were the **intellectuals** whose admiration for the West and for political principles of liberalism and freedom of thought made them targets of CCP **"thought reform"** (*sixiang gaizao*).

POPULATION. In 2005, the population of the **People's Republic of China** (**PRC**) was 1.3 billion, making it the most populated nation on earth and the most people ever to live under the control of one central government in the history of the world. In 1949, when the **Chinese Communist Party** (**CCP**) came to power, China's population stood at 541 million with a male/female ratio of 51.96:48.04 and an urban:rural ratio of 10.6:89.4 percent. Throughout the 1950s, China experienced rapid population growth as the end to the **Civil War** (**1946–1949**) combined with the absence of any population control policy, which was ardently opposed by **Mao Zedong**, led to the total population's expansion in 1959 to 672 million for an annual growth rate in excess of 2% a year. Following the disastrous **Great Leap Forward** (**1958–1960**), China's population shrank in 1960 and 1961 to 662 and 658 million people, respectively, as the country suffered one of the worst famines in human history. By 1962, renewed population growth brought the total back up to 672 million. By 1980, when China announced its adoption of the **one-child policy** of population control, the total number of people in the PRC was 987 million with an urban:rural ratio of 19.4 to 80.6%. From 1980 to 2005, the population continued to grow but at reduced rates, reaching the one billion mark by 1982, and 1.2 billion in 1995 (five years earlier than authorities had planned). On 6 January 2005, Zhang Yichi, a baby boy born in **Beijing**, was crowned the 1.3 billionth citizen of the PRC. The male:female ratio in 1998 was 50.98:49.02 while the urban:rural ratio in 1999 was 30.9:69.1. Since joining the **United Nations (UN)** in 1971, China has participated in the UN-organized World Population Conference, where, in 1974, the Chinese representative attacked the Malthusian theory of population explosion as a fallacy. In 1983, China's minister in charge of the then State Family Planning Commission was one of the first two winners of the UN population awards.

Since 1949, the Chinese government has conducted five major censuses, the first in 1953, followed by additional censuses in 1964, 1982, 1990, and 2000, with smaller sample surveys conducted in 1987 and 1995. Population planners foresee the total population growing to 1.4 billion by 2010 and expect the population to peak in 2025 at 1.48 billion as the country strives to reduce its growth rate to 1.5% in the near term. Survey data indicates that in 1988 16% of babies born were not registered with authorities nationwide, 2.35% of all births in urban areas and 31.85% in the countryside. China's most populated provinces in 2000 were Henan (92 million), Shandong (90 million), Guangdong (86 million), Sichuan (83 million), and Jiangsu (74 million) while the least populated were **Tibet** (2.6 million), Qinghai (5.1 million), Ningxia (5.6 million), and Hainan Island (7.8 million), indicating a wide variation in population density for the country. China's largest urban areas in 1998 were **Shanghai** (9.5 million, a figure that, in 2003, had grown to 13.5 million), **Beijing** (7.3 million), **Chongqing** (6.14 million), and **Tianjin** (5.26 million), figures that represent the non-agricultural portions of the urban population since most large metropolitan areas in China known as *shi* incorporate substantial amount of countryside including large numbers of farmers with rural registration *hukou* who are excluded from these figures. Altogether, China has 166 cities with populations over one million (compared to nine in the U.S.) as its urban population continues to grow at 2.5% a year, one of the fastest rates in the world. The smallest city in China is Lhasa, Tibet, with a mere 120,000 people, followed by Haikou, Hainan Island (420,000), Yinchuan, Ningxia (510,000), and Xining, Qinghai (680,000).

The age structure of China's population is skewed to the younger years, with the 1995 sample census showing 17.9% of the population at nine years or younger, 42.85% of the population at 24 years and younger with the period of the most rapid growth for the young occurring from 1953 to 1964, a rate that has since fallen off. China's elderly population has also grown with people aged 65 and over expanding 4.9% between 1991 and 1995 to produce 6.69% of the total population with the overwhelming percentage made up of **women**. In 1949, life expectancy in China was 35 years; by 1996, it was put at 70.8 years, compared to 77 years in the United Kingdom and 62 years in **India**. *See also* "FLOATING POPULATION"; HEALTH CARE.

"PRACTICE IS THE SOLE CRITERION OF TRUTH" (*"SHI-JIAN SHI JIANYAN ZHENLI DE BIAOZHUN"*). The title of an article published on 12 May 1978 in the *People's Daily*, this phrase provided the ideological basis for the pragmatism of **Deng Xiaoping** in inaugurating bold economic reforms. The central premise of the article was that dogma could not be blindly accepted, but should be revised according to experience and practice. Truth can only be judged according to the objective yardstick of social and scientific practice, not on its own terms. Truth was no longer a matter of propping up the authority of an old or new leader. Nor must one avoid ideological "forbidden zones" and adhere to outworn dogmas. Rather, people should "seek truth from facts"—a saying once voiced by **Mao Zedong** himself that, this article argued, was in fundamental accord with the basic tenets of Marxism. In so doing one could "emancipate the mind" and adopt a more pragmatic approach to solve social and economic problems. Ideologically, "practice is the sole criterion of truth" served as an intellectual counterweight in 1978 to the **"two whatevers"** (*liangge fanshi*) supported by the leftist faction that called for blind loyalty to Mao's every word. Politically, the "practice criterion" mobilized support among **intellectuals** for the reformist policies of **Hu Yaobang** and his patron Deng Xiaoping that ultimately triumphed at the December 1978 **Third Plenum of the 11th Central Committee** of the **Chinese Communist Party (CCP)**.

PRESIDENT OF THE PEOPLE'S REPUBLIC OF CHINA. Formal head of state in the **People's Republic of China (PRC)**, the president of China in 2005 was **Hu Jintao**, who, in 2003, had succeeded **Jiang Zemin**. This position (also previously known as state chairman) was established by the 1954 state constitution, and was initially held by **Mao Zedong**. In the midst of the controversy surrounding the **Great Leap Forward (1958–1960)**, Mao relinquished the position to his designated successor at that time, **Liu Shaoqi**. Mao Zedong abolished the presidency in the 1975 state constitution in reaction to the purge of Liu during the **Cultural Revolution (1966–1976)**. Efforts by **Lin Biao** to reestablish the position in the 1970s contributed to his political downfall. It was not until 1982 that the presidency was reestablished by Articles 79–81 of the new state constitution—China's fourth—which also created a position of vice-president. Since then the presidency has been held by **Li Xiannian** (1983–1988), **Yang Shangkun** (1988–1993), **Jiang Zemin** (1993–2003), and **Hu Jintao** (2003–).

The president is formally elected by the **National People's Congress (NPC)** for no more than two consecutive five-year terms that coincide with NPC sessions. As head of state, the president receives foreign diplomatic representatives on behalf of the PRC and implements decisions of the Standing Committee of the NPC in ratifying and abrogating treaties with foreign states. The president also promulgates NPC statutes, and formally appoints and/or removes the premier, vice-premier, state councilors, and ministers in charge of the state ministries and commissions. Although originally lacking much real power, the role of the office was somewhat enhanced by the newly assigned official power to "engage in activities involving state affairs." The holder of this office and the vice-president are generally top-ranking members of the **Chinese Communist Party (CCP)** leadership and sit on major decision-making organs such as the **Politburo**. *See also* GOVERNMENT STRUCTURE; LEADERS.

"PRINCE'S FACTION" (*"TAIZI DANG"*). This is a term for politically influential offspring of senior Chinese political and military **leaders** who rely on family ties to get key policy-making positions in the Party and/or state-run **economy** where they can reap enormous economic rewards, often through **corruption**. Examples include: **Chen Yuan** and Chen Weihua, the son and daughter, respectively, of China's longtime economic czar, **Chen Yun**; Wang Jun, son of the **People's Liberation Army** (**PLA**) leader and arch conservative, **Wang Zhen**; Deng Zhifang, second son of **Deng Xiaoping**; He Ping, son-in-law of Deng Xiaoping; and Li Xiaopeng, son of former Premier **Li Peng** and head of the Huaneng Group, one of China's five power-generating companies. During the 1989 crisis surrounding the second **Beijing Spring**, it is said that the politically conservative members of the "prince's faction" favored a military crackdown out of fear that a political victory by the democratic movement would rob them of their positions, influence, and fat contracts with foreign investors. In 1998, China broke up many of the central ministries that for three decades controlled the **economy**, allowing members of the "prince's faction" to emerge as key players in semi-private corporations, such as Huaneng, where they exercise enormous economic and political influence.

PROCURACY. A unique feature of China's **legal system**, the Procuracy parallels the organization of the court system in China and serves as both prosecuting attorney and public defender. In addition, the Procuracy monitors and reviews the government bureaucracy and the courts to provide, in theory, a legal restraint on the government. In reality, the Procuracy is just another arm of the state bureaucracy that serves the interests of the **Chinese Communist Party** (**CCP**) dictatorship. The procurator authorizes the arrest of criminals and so-called "counterrevolutionaries" as charged by the **Public Security Bureau**—China's national and local police. The Procuracy operates under the authority of the **National People's Congress** (**NPC**) and is headed by the Supreme People's Procuratorate, which supervises subordinate bodies of the Procuracy down to the local levels. The Procuracy in China today is similar to the censorate that existed in traditional China from the Yuan dynasty (1264–1368 AD) onward, and to the Procuracy in the former **Soviet Union**, as well as to the system of ombudsmen in continental European legal systems. Prior to the **Cultural Revolution (1966–1976)**, the functions of the Procuracy were exercised by the Public Security Bureau, which, through its extrajudicial powers of "administrative detention" can still bypass the Procuracy and even the courts. In 2005, the head of the Procuracy was Jia Chunwang (1938–), a graduate of the Engineering Physics Department of **Qinghua University**, who was appointed in 2003, following years of work in the **Beijing** CP organization, the ministry of state security and as head of the People's Armed Police (PAP).

"PRODUCTION BRIGADE" (*"SHENGCHAN DADUI"*). Also referred to as higher **Agricultural Producers' Cooperatives (APCs)**, the production brigades were a middle level of collective ownership within the three-tiered system of rural production organization established after 1958. Equivalent to the "natural village" (*cun*), the brigade generally consisted of from 20 to 40 households and represented a higher form of collective ownership than the **production team**. After the disastrous **Great Leap Forward (1958–1960)**, essential decision-making authority over land and **labor** reverted to the teams; thus the brigades, like the **people's communes**, became something of an organizational shell. The only exceptions were "model" production brigades, such as the **Dazhai Brigade**, which was touted in the 1960s as an advanced form of collective agricultural production that, however, never effectively replaced the teams on a wide-scale basis.

"PRODUCTION TEAM" (*"SHENGCHAN DUI"*). Also referred to as lower **Agricultural Producers' Cooperatives (APCs)**, the production teams were the lowest level of collective ownership within the three-tiered system of rural production organization established after 1958. Production teams—also referred to as "small groups" (*xiaozu*) and "small production brigades"—were an intra-village work unit that generally consisted of seven to eight households to which land, **labor**, implements, and draught animals were allotted. Financial accounting and allocation of **work points** to determine the distribution of income was carried out at this basic level from the end of the **Great Leap Forward (1958–1960)** onward in most areas of the country until the entire system was essentially dismantled, beginning in 1978–1979, by the inauguration of the **Agricultural Responsibility System**. *See also* "PEOPLE'S COMMUNES."

"PROJECT 571." This was the purported title of the alleged plan by **Lin Biao**, the commander of the **People's Liberation Army (PLA)** and designated successor to **Mao Zedong**, to assassinate the Chairman in 1971. It has been said that "571," which in Chinese is rendered as *wuqiyi*, can also mean "armed uprising." As it turned out, the plot involved only Lin, **Ye Qun**, his wife, and Lin Liguo, his son, and a few dozen supporters. After failing to assassinate Mao, Lin and his entourage tried to flee China by air. Their plane crashed in Mongolia en route to the **Soviet Union**, where Lin had hoped to gain refuge. There is some doubt as to whether Lin Biao died in the crash or was actually murdered earlier in **Beijing**. PLA historians have called for a full reevaluation of Lin Biao based on their belief that, in fact, he never attempted to assassinate Mao.

PROVINCIALISM. This term has been used to describe the problems of China's powerful regions in their constant conflict with the central authority in **Beijing**. It denotes the centrifugal forces that are constantly at play in Chinese politics. The existence of regional political, economic, and social forces that tend to pull away from the center may be explained, to a large extent, by the vast size of the country (China is slightly smaller geographically than the **United States**), and by the many cultures represented in China's different regions among both the dominant **Han** and the **minorities**. The major regions include the north, south, central, east, west, and portions of Inner Mongolia, Xinjiang, and **Tibet** (*Xizang*). Each of these regions is an entity dominated by unique features of climate, soil composition, and variations in the spoken (and at times written) language.

Centrifugal tendencies have increased since the 1978–1979 economic reforms as the central government has allowed greater flexibility over economic (but not political) issues at the regional and local levels. The 1984 decision on economic structural reform, for instance, encouraged lateral economic relations between economic regions, thereby undermining the center's control via vertically organized state ministries. The most significant aspect of provincialism has been the increasing tensions between Beijing and the various regions over the remittance of taxes to the central authorities. Increased power at the regional level has made for less rigidly centralized economic structures, but has also revived fears of warlordism and national disunity reminiscent of the 1930s.

The greatest fear of both **Chinese Communist Party (CCP)** officials and even liberal political dissidents is the increasing forces of separatism among China's minority population of Uygurs and Tibetans who, in the 1980s and early 1990s, engaged in sometimes violent opposition to rule from Beijing. Tensions have also emerged between relatively backward inland regions, such as Sichuan Province, and the more prosperous coastal areas that have benefited enormously under the economic reforms of **Deng Xiaoping**. Some economic regions have even sought to establish their own economic autarky by economic blockades of goods from the more economically developed areas so as to protect their local industries. Countering the forces of provincialism is the increasing national and international integration of the Chinese **economy**, which is reflected in government policies that ensure equity treatment for all economic actors—domestic or foreign—in the market place as required by **World Trade Organization (WTO)** rules and prohibit discrimination by local governments against outsiders.

PUBLIC SECURITY BUREAU (*GONG'AN JU*). Public security organs constitute China's national police force to maintain domestic law and order and to protect the dictatorship of the **Chinese Communist Party (CCP)**. Every town and district in major cities in China has a public security branch (*gong'an fenju*), subordinate to a public security bureau (*gong'an ju*), which, in turn, is subordinate to the Ministry of Public Security (*gong'an bu*) based in **Beijing**. This ministry combines the tasks of domestic law and order, border police, and internal security and includes the People's Armed Police (*renmin wuzhuang jingcha budui*), a separate police force that was split off from the **People's Liberation Army (PLA)** in 1983 and that consists of more than half a million men. There is also a Ministry of State Security (*guojia anquan bu*)—located in the same buildings in Beijing as the Ministry of Public Security—that functions like the Central Intelligence Agency (CIA) in the **United States** and is responsible for collecting foreign intelligence and engaging in counterintelligence.

Public security organs and the People's Armed Police have, at times, operated as arms of local Communist Party organizations, of which all police personnel are members.

The role of the public security organs is to investigate crimes and arrest suspected criminals, and to engage in the surveillance of Chinese citizens and foreigners. Since the late 1950s, public security units in China have had the authority to issue sentences in criminal cases, especially against political enemies of the CCP, and to incarcerate those victims in **labor** reform camps for interminable periods under the procedure known as "administrative detention" (*juliu*). During the **Cultural Revolution (1966–1976)**, however, public security personnel were restricted from interfering and halting student violence by the August 1966 Central Committee "Regulation of Strictly Restraining from Sending Out Police to Oppress the Revolutionary Student Movement." Full police powers were gradually restored in the late 1960s and early 1970s while in 1978, under the rubric of "socialist legality" promoted by constitutional and legal reformists, some modest limits in the state constitution and subsequent statutes were imposed on police along with the authority of prosecution in courts and the **Procuracy**. Further efforts by reformist-minded **leaders** in China led by **Hu Yaobang** to reduce police abuse in the mid-1980s and to create a police force and **legal system** independent of the CCP were stalled as the police, like judges, are answerable to various CCP-run "adjudication committees" and "political and law committees" that in many cases effectively dictate arrests, trials, and sentencing. Arbitrary arrests and detentions also increased as China confronted major **crime** waves and dealt with participants in the 1986 and 1989 pro-democracy movements.

From the 1990s onward, efforts were made to have the police become better at doing basic, non-political everyday investigative work involving modern skills of policing. Public security organs have also been made more responsive and accountable to the public by granting individuals the right to sue public security bureaus for errors in accusing specific individuals of crimes (which, in China, are published at the local level in annals issues by local public security bureaus) and for discrimination by urban police forces against migrant populations making up the country's huge **floating population**. New rules have been issued by the Ministry of Public Security establishing for the first time that evidence obtained by torture, threats, or other illegal means cannot be used in court cases and that long-term illegal detentions of suspects must cease.

Cases of **corruption**, fraud, and involvement in organized crime by police officials have also been given prominence in the press while heads of local public security bureaus have attended radio phone-in programs especially in areas recording dramatic rises in criminal activity. In many urban areas of China, such as Shenzhen and **Guangzhou (Canton)**, rising crime rates have led to popular demands, not uncommon in other countries, for more police officers on the streets and for a greater commitment of government resources to investigating crimes including payment to people who provide information useful to investigations. Police have come under particular scrutiny and pressure to solve the increasing number of cases involving child abductions and even serial killings that victims' relatives attribute in part to police corruption and/or negligence. Growing street crime involving everything from petty theft to assault have led public security organs to build a high-tech police force, including the installation of electronic security cameras in high-profile public places in major cities. A number of urban areas in China, such as the central Chinese city of Wuhan, have gone high-tech by purchasing helicopters to increase police mobility. In the run-up to the 2008 Olympic Games in Beijing, police are being trained in English to deal with the expected influx of non-Chinese speaking tourists. As police appear increasingly incapable of solving crimes, private detectives have opened shop in China along with private security forces to assist individuals, companies, and even government bodies to solve cases and put down **social protests**.

– Q

QIAN JIAJU (1910–). A graduate of the Department of Economics of **Beida (Peking University)** in the 1930s, Qian Jiaju remained in China after the Communist takeover in 1949 as a leading figure in the **Chinese People's Political Consultative Conference (CPPCC)** and in the China Democratic League, one of the eight largely powerless

democratic parties in the **People's Republic of China** (**PRC**). In the **Hundred Flowers** (**1956–1957**), Qian criticized political interference by the **Chinese Communist Party** (**CCP**) in **science and technology**. In 1967, he was branded as a follower of **Liu Shaoqi**. He reappeared in 1981 as a member of the Democratic League and the CPPCC. He became a major critic of the docile role played by **National People's Congress** (**NPC**) delegates selected from the ranks of "model" workers and peasants who lacked legislative ability or acumen. Qian was also a major critic of the proposed gigantic **Three Gorges Dam Project** that was formally approved in April 1992 by the NPC. A strong supporter of the *perestroika* reforms advocated in the USSR by Mikhail Gorbachev, Qian vehemently criticized the economic austerity measures of Premier **Li Peng** in 1988–1989.

QIAN QICHEN (1928–). From 1988 to 1998, Qian Qichen was China's minister of foreign affairs. Born in **Shanghai**, Qian joined the **Chinese Communist Party** (**CCP**) in 1942 during the **Sino–Japanese War** (**1937–1945**) and was active in the Chinese Communist **Youth League** (**CYL**). After studying in Moscow, Qian served in the Chinese embassy in the city and, in 1963, returned to China to work in the Ministry of **Education** in charge of students studying abroad. From 1972 to 1974, Qian returned to the USSR and, from 1974 to 1976, was ambassador to Guinea. From 1977 to 1982, he was director of the Information Department of the Ministry of Foreign Affairs and, from 1982 to 1988, was a vice-minister of foreign affairs. Qian also served as a state councilor from 1991 to 2000 and a vice-premier during the same period while he also sat on the **Politburo** from 1987 to 2000. In 1999, Qian Qichen was appointed dean of the School of International Studies at **Beida** (**Peking University**).

QIAN WEICHANG (1912–). A member of the commission that drafted the Basic Law of the **Hong Kong** Special Administrative Region, Qian Weichang earned a Ph.D. in applied mathematics in the **United States** and once worked at the Jet Propulsion Laboratory at Cal Tech. In the 1950s, he returned to China and became a dean and then vice-president at **Qinghua University** and a member of the Chinese Academy of Sciences (CAS). In June 1957, during the **Hundred**

Flowers campaign, he joined **Qian Jiaju** to criticize **Chinese Communist Party (CCP)** policy on **science and technology** in an article in the *Enlightenment Daily*, which they coauthored. He was relieved of all posts in 1958 for suggesting that layman should not be permitted to set guidelines for experts. He was rehabilitated in 1960, but purged again during the **Cultural Revolution (1966–1976)**. He returned in the 1980s and developed a new coding system for computerizing Chinese-language characters while he also served as a vice-chairman on the **Chinese People's Political Consultative Conference (CPPCC)** as a member of the China Democratic League, one of China's eight largely powerless **democratic parties**.

QIAN XUESEN (1911–). Considered the father of China's **space program**, Qian Xuesen was born in Hangzhou, Zhejiang Province, and graduated in 1934 from the Mechanical Engineering Department of Communications (*Jiaotong*) University in **Shanghai**. He subsequently enrolled in **Qinghua University** before traveling to the **United States** where he studied rocket research at the Massachusetts Institute of Technology (MIT). In 1939, Qian earned a Ph.D. in aerospace engineering and mathematics at the California Institute of Technology and, during World War II, joined the U.S. Air Force, achieving the rank of colonel. He worked as the director of the Rocket Section of the U.S. National Defense Scientific Advisory Board. After a brief visit to Shanghai after the war, Qian returned to the U.S. to become a professor at Cal Tech and director of the Jet Propulsion Laboratory. Accused of harboring Communist sympathies, in 1950, Qian was stripped of his security clearance and was kept under virtual house arrest for five years.

Qian returned to China in 1955 in a negotiated exchange for American pilots shot down by the Chinese during the **Korean War (1950–1953)** and immediately submitted proposals for a space and rocketry program to the State Council. He founded the Institute of Mechanics under the Chinese Academy of Sciences (CAS), where he helped develop China's ballistic missile program and the country's first man-made earth-orbiting satellite, which was launched in 1970 on the CSS-3 intercontinental ballistic missile, which was later renamed *Long March One*. Qian also presided over experiments for placing an **atomic bomb** on short-range missiles, and in 1991 he received the "State Scientist of Outstanding Contribution" award, the highest honor that can be bestowed on a scientist in China.

Qian has always denied the spying allegations made against him by the American authorities and has lived to witness China's first successful launching of a man in orbit, which occurred in 2003. During the **Cultural Revolution** (**1966–1976**), Qian remained in favor because of his scientific prominence and served on the Commission of Science, Technology, and Industry for National Defense. *See also* WANG GANCHANG.

QIAN ZHENGYING (**1923–**). Born in the **United States**, Qian Zhengying returned with her family to China, where she studied civil engineering and, in 1941, joined the **Chinese Communist Party** (**CCP**). From 1958 to 1974, she served as vice-minister in the Ministry of Water Resources and Electric Power and was a member of the Grand Canal Commission and the Huai River Harnessing Commission. In 1973, she was elected to the CCP Central Committee. From 1975 to 1988, she served as minister of water resources and electric power and, in 1988, became minister of water resources (following the division of water resources and electric power into two separate ministries), where she strongly supported construction of the **Three Gorges Dam Project**. Following her retirement, Qian became an academician of the Chinese Academy of Engineering and a vice-chairman of the **Chinese People's Political Consultative Conference** (**CPPCC**) where she continues to consult with the Chinese government on water-use policies and problems especially in the arid northwest, which was the subject of a two-year research study on sustainable development involving 300 scientists.

QIAO SHI (**1924–**). Leader of the **Shanghai** underground student movement in the 1940s, in the 1950s, and early 1960s Qiao Shi worked in the Communist **Youth League** and in the steel industry. In 1982, he was appointed director of the International Liaison Department of the **Chinese Communist Party** (**CCP**). In 1984, he became a director of the CCP Organization Department and in 1985 became a member of the **Politburo** and the Party Secretariat and in 1987 was elevated to the Politburo Standing Committee, the top policy-making body of the CCP. In 1989, he became president of the **Central Party**

School and visited Romania, where he praised the great socialist successes of the government of Nicolae Ceauşescu two weeks before its collapse. During the 1989 second **Beijing Spring**, Qiao Shi reportedly went along, reluctantly, with the decision by **Deng Xiaoping** and **Li Peng** to deploy force against pro-democracy demonstrators in **Beijing** and other cities. Despite his senior position as China's intelligence chief, Qiao Shi was relieved of his post as head of the **National People's Congress** (**NPC**) in 1998 as a result of political differences with the more junior but recently promoted **Jiang Zemin**.

QIGONG. Part of China's rich tradition of non-Western medicine, *qigong* is a health regimen that involves both breathing exercises and meditation and is said to have great healing powers. Masters of *qigong* can allegedly cut gold and crack jade, defeat others in combat, leap onto roofs, and vault over walls. It is related to studies of the *Book of Changes* (*Ijing*), fortune-telling, divination, psychic arts, and Chinese geomancy (*fengshui*). Practitioners of *qigong* believe that there are gods and spirits in the heavens, and that all people have souls. The world is neither physical nor conceptual but is composed of the "Way" (*dao*) and elements known as the "vital energy" or *qi*. Operating on this level, people can directly perceive the world and master it. From 50 to 100 million people in China practice *qigong*, including many of China's elderly **leaders** who look to its healing powers to keep them fit and who encouraged the dissemination of *Falun Gong* (also known as *Falun Dafa*) from its inception in 1992 to 1994.

By 1996, *Falun Gong* was the fastest-growing spiritual practice in China, led by its founder Li Hongzhi, who was allowed to lecture in every major city in China. Following a mass demonstration outside **Chinese Communist Party** (**CCP**) headquarters at Zhongnanhai in **Beijing** in April 1999, a full-bore campaign against *Falun Gong* and local *qigong* associations was inaugurated; the practice was condemned as "superstitious," and members were said to belong to a "cult." Acting on orders reputedly issued by **Jiang Zemin**, police moved to repress the movement that was declared illegal as some 1,000 members reportedly died while in state custody and many more were committed to detention camps where cases of torture have been reported. Further protests by *Falun Gong* members were broken up by police in 2000, and the **National People's Congress** (**NPC**)

Standing Committee adopted a "Decision on Banning Heretical Cult Organizations and Punishing Cult Activities." *Falun Gong* is practiced in 60 countries worldwide; its leader, Li Hongzhi, now resides in the **United States**.

QIN DYNASTY (221–207 BC). *See* ANTI-LIN [BIAO], ANTI-CONFUCIUS CAMPAIGN (1973–1975).

QINGHUA UNIVERSITY. One of the top three universities in China, Qinghua was established in 1908 with funds remitted back to China from the indemnity paid to the **United States** by China after the defeat of the Boxer Rebellion by foreign armies in 1900. From the 1920s through the early 1940s, Qinghua was, for many years, a liberal arts school modeled on American universities that consistently attempted to achieve autonomy from the **Kuomintang** (**KMT**) government. After the Communist takeover in 1949, the liberal arts were largely abolished as institutional autonomy was totally eliminated. The university became a polytechnic institution that is often referred to as the "MIT of China" where many of the physicists and scientists involved in China's construction of an **atomic bomb**, such as **Wang Ganchang**, were trained. Qinghua University was a major battle ground during the **Cultural Revolution** (**1966–1976**) as one of the first **big character posters** (*dazibao*) was written by **Red Guards** from a middle school attached to the university and which "pledged to fight to the death to defend the dictatorship of the proletariat and **Mao Zedong** Thought." The school was also the scene, in August 1966, of vicious attacks on teachers by students organized into "dog-beating teams" and later by pitched battles between armed Red Guard factions that fought a "100-day war." Like many universities and high schools during this period, Qinghua periodically shut down as its students were sent down to the countryside. From 1976 onward, the university was reestablished along its previous polytechnic lines. Regular entrance procedures were also reinstituted to replace the highly politicized criteria employed for admission during the Cultural Revolution. Many of China's top scientists such as **Qian Xuesen** earned their degrees from Qinghua as the university has also served as the training ground for nuclear physicists from allied nations of the **People's Republic of China** (**PRC**), such as the Democratic Republic of **Korea** (i.e., North Korea). Among its graduates are prominent political **leaders**, such as **Hu Jintao, Li Ximing, Qian Weichang**, and **Zhu Rongji**.

As a major center for research and training in high **technology**, Qinghua has established cooperative relationships with the Chinese military, such as its liaison with the **People's Liberation Army (PLA)** Institute of Air Force Armament, which is devoted to the development of new military equipment. It has joined in the development of new energy-saving transport, such as the first fuel cell fleet of buses for China's urban areas. Qinghua has also established ties with a number of foreign institutions, such as Yale University, and multinational corporations, such as British Petroleum, in research on the **environment** and sustainable development as well as development of clean **energy**. In 2000, students attending Qinghua were authorized to take a leave of absence from the university to start their own businesses, a program that has quickly spread to other major universities in China.

QUOTATIONS FROM CHAIRMAN MAO (MAO ZHUXI YULU). This small book of Mao sayings became the "bible" of **Red Guards** during the **Cultural Revolution (1966–1976)**. First compiled in 1964 by the General Political Department of the **People's Liberation Army (PLA)**, the *Quotations*, also known as the "little red book," was first distributed for "study" to every soldier. This reflected the political role of **Lin Biao**, who, in 1960, after replacing **Peng Dehuai** as China's minister of defense, advocated that "everyone must study Chairman Mao's writings." The book was published for general distribution in 1966 in **Shanghai** and contained more than 400 quotations taken from Mao's writings in the *Selected Works of Mao Zedong*. During the Cultural Revolution, more than one billion copies of the *Quotations* were distributed to Red Guards, creating a virtual paper shortage in the country. By the late 1960s, the *Quotations* became required reading for nearly the entire **population** of the country. The subjects covered included Mao's wisdom on studying, discipline, **self-reliance** (*zili gengsheng*), "revolutionary heroism," and even how to grow tomatoes. Children reared during the Cultural Revolution were taught to wave the "little red book" with their hands as they cried out: "Chairman Mao is the reddest sun in our hearts." After the Cultural Revolution ended in 1976, the *Quotations* virtually disappeared from view in China and rapidly became a collector's item for visiting foreigners and Chinese alike.

– R –

RAIDI (1938–). One of the highest-ranking members of the **Chinese Communist Party** (**CCP**) from the **population** of **minorities** in China, Raidi is a Tibetan who graduated from the CCP-run Central Nationalities Institute in **Beijing**, a major institutional training ground for minorities willing to serve the interests of the Communist government. A long-time member of the **Tibet** (**Xizang**) Autonomous Region CP, Raidi is probably the highest-ranking Tibetan in the Chinese government who, in 1985, became the deputy secretary of the Tibet CP and chairman of the Standing Committee of the Autonomous Region People's Congress. By 2005, Raidi, who like many members of minorities in China goes by one name, served as a vice-chairman of the Standing Committee of the **National People's Congress** (**NPC**), where he has met with a variety of foreign dignitaries from their nations' parliamentary bodies.

"REBEL FACTION" (*"ZAOFANPAI"***).** The most radical faction of **Red Guards** in the **Cultural Revolution** (**1966–1976**), the Rebel Faction was made up primarily of individuals whose parents and relatives had been deposed under the **Chinese Communist Party** (**CCP**) regime. These included many temporary and contract workers who lacked secure employment, youths who had been rusticated to rural areas and had surreptitiously returned to the cities, students from **Five Black Categories** background, various social derelicts and criminal elements, and even some CCP members and demobilized soldiers who had run afoul of their superiors. With many axes to grind and bearing harsh grudges against the CCP establishment, members of the *zaofanpai* engaged in the most severe and often-violent attacks on Party **cadres** and just about anyone chosen for retribution. This largely cohered with **Mao Zedong**'s purpose of purging the CCP of its mainstream membership and installing a new "revolutionary" generation of **leaders**. *Zaofanpai* and the more conservative factions of the Red Guards engaged in intense internecine struggle and conflicts that severely disrupted urban life in China, until, in 1968, Mao ordered most Red Guards to the countryside, effectively terminating their central role in the Cultural Revolution. Members of the *zaofanpai* were later singled out for retribution during the criticism of the so-called **Gang of Four** in the late 1970s that followed the purge of Mao Zedong's widow, **Jiang Qing**, and her radical followers in China.

"RECTIFICATION CAMPAIGNS" (*"ZHENGFENG YUNDONG"*). Campaigns of political "study" and "investigation" in China, rectification was periodically employed by the **Chinese Communist Party (CCP)** leadership to achieve ideological orthodoxy, unification of the Party, mass compliance to central policies, and the elevation of **Mao Zedong** to supreme leadership. The first such "rectification" occurred in 1942–1944 when alleged political opponents of the chairman were weeded out of the CCP along with free-thinking **intellectuals**, such as **Wang Shiwei**, who were vilified and, in Wang's case, ultimately executed. The major purpose of this and subsequent "rectification" campaigns, however, was to boost the authority and **personality cult (*geren chongbai*)** of Mao Zedong. Thus, for the first time in CCP history, Mao's writings in 1942–1944 became a major source for **cadres** "political study" and discussion in political study groups. **Criticism and self-criticism (*piping yu ziwo piping*)** by errant cadres was also employed as a central component of the "rectification" that undoubtedly increased the ideological unity of the Party in China, but at the expense of greater intimidation and fear among Party cadres and especially intellectuals and artists. The same type of campaign occurred in the **Anti-Rightist Campaign (1957–1958)**.

"RED AND EXPERT" (*"HONG YU ZHUAN"*). This was a major job requirement for the millions of Party **cadres** in China during the era of **Mao Zedong** (1949–1976). The idea was to ensure that Party workers were both politically pure and professionally competent as one at the expense of the other could erode the authority of the **Chinese Communist Party (CCP)**. A Party cadre who was politically suspect but professionally competent was a threat to the ideological purity of the CCP, while a Party cadre who was politically loyal but professionally incompetent could alienate the **population** through poor leadership and flawed decision making. Party cadres were thus chided to avoid "'becoming expert before one becomes red' and of 'becoming expert without having to become red.'"

This standard was first promulgated in 1957 after **intellectuals** had criticized the CCP during the liberal **Hundred Flowers (1956–1957)** for promoting people into positions of authority on the basis of political loyalty rather than merit. This reflected the fact that many Party members espoused the proper political attitudes but without developing the professional skills necessary for the CCP to carry out its goals of administering the **economy** and managing institutions such as schools, **health care** facilities, and the military. During the **Cultural Revolution (1966–1976)**, radical political forces associated with Mao's wife, **Jiang Qing**, emphasized only the political dimension (that is, "redness"). Conservative groups associated with **Liu Shaoqi** and **Deng Xiaoping**, tended, on the other hand, to concentrate on the professional competence of Party cadres. Since 1978, the "red and expert" criterion has largely been dropped from CCP propaganda, though political loyalty to the regime is still an important factor in judging a Party cadre's status in the CCP.

RED FLAG (HONGQI). The major theoretical publication of the Central Committee of the **Chinese Communist Party (CCP)**, *Red Flag* was published monthly from 1958 to 1979, and then bi-monthly from 1980 until its termination in 1988. When inaugurated in 1958 at the start of the **Great Leap Forward (1958–1960)**, *Red Flag* was edited by **Chen Boda** and replaced the magazine *Study (Xuexi)*. Along with *People's Daily* and *Liberation Army Daily*, *Red Flag* was a major publication in the **People's Republic of China (PRC)** with a national circulation of about nine million and often joined the other two major papers in publishing important joint editorials. During the **Cultural Revolution (1966–1976)**, *Red Flag* was generally an outlet for the radical faction and published their most important political and ideological articles often under pseudonyms, including the famous 1965 article by **Lin Biao** entitled "Long Live People's War," in which the **People's Liberation Army (PLA)** leader and Mao confidante declared that the rural areas of the world (poor countries) would surround and defeat the urban areas (rich countries) by waging guerilla war. Chen Boda served as editor-in-chief of *Red Flag* until his purge in 1970. During the post-Mao era, *Red Flag* was headed by, among others, Xiong Fu who promoted the leftist concept of the **"two whatevers"** (*liangge fanshi*) and generally resisted any liberal reform campaign. In 1978, Xiong refused to publish commentary on the topic of **"practice is the sole criterion of truth"** that was used to attack leftist dogma. Instead, he supported efforts of the hard-line, conservative faction led by **Deng Liqun** and **Chen Yun** to turn back political and economic reform. In 1988, *Red Flag* was terminated and replaced by *Seeking Truth* (*Qiushi*), which remains the major theoretical organ of the CCP.

"RED GUARDS" (*"HONG WEIBING"*). A major political force during the **Cultural Revolution (1966–1976)**, the Red Guards were composed of university, high, and middle school students, and even elementary pupils. The first Red Guard unit was formed in July–August 1966 at the Middle School attached to **Qinghua University** in **Beijing**, where they attacked and beat the principal and vice-principal. Membership in Red Guard organizations was initially restricted to young people from **Five Red Categories** while students from such families as clerks or office workers joined so-called "Red Periphery" or "Red Allied Force" organizations that played a supportive role. Formed in Beijing and other major cities, the Red Guards were given strong support by **Chinese Communist Party (CCP)** Chairman **Mao Zedong** who sanctioned their role of waging battle against the established apparatus of Party and government in China. Mao first reviewed the Red Guards at a mass rally in August 1966 and donned his own "red armband," worn by all Red Guards, that declared his support for their organization in "revolutionizing" Chinese society and guaranteeing "revolutionary successors." The rites performed by Red Guards in promoting the **personality cult** (*geren chongbai*) of Mao Zedong included wearing a Mao badge, carrying the "little red book" *Quotations from Chairman Mao*, singing the songs of Mao's quotations, shouting "Long Live Chairman Mao" (*Mao Zhuxi wansui*), and taking part in huge rallies and parades.

From 1966 to 1968, Red Guard groups rampaged through China's cities attacking Party and government personnel, **intellectuals**, and teachers, and, under the banner of destroying the **"four olds"** (*sijiu*), they pillaged vestiges of China's traditional culture, such as religious temples and museums, including several thousand temples in **Tibet**. As the Red Guards became increasingly factionalized in 1967–1968, pitched battles between competing groups broke out on China's university campuses, such as Qinghua University, where a "100-day war" ensued with many casualties. The increasing violence and social and economic disruption led Mao to order the **People's Liberation Army** (**PLA**) to bring Red Guard violence under control. By late 1968, most Red Guards had been sent to the countryside for "further revolutionary training." There, the groups were disbanded and many Red Guards ended up feeling deeply disillusioned. Memoirs by former Red Guards include *Blood Red Sunset* by Ma Bo. *See also* BIBLIOGRAPHY.

"REFORM THROUGH LABOR" (**"*LAODONG GAIZAO*"**). This is a form of punishment in China also known as "*laogai*" that is frequently applied to criminals who have been sentenced for commission of a **crime**, often a political one. In jails or labor reform camps, prisoners are subject to different degrees of supervision and management in an effort to make them into "new men" by virtue of enforced manual labor. This system was initiated soon after the **Chinese Communist Party** (**CCP**) took power in 1949 and was justified by CCP Chairman **Mao Zedong** so as to ensure that prisoners did not "eat without working." The system of labor reform camps in China is very large and the number of labor reform prisoners may now number in the millions, though not all are political prisoners. These camps are economic enterprises that produce goods for the domestic and international markets. Sale of Chinese prison-made goods in the United States became a major source of tension in **United States**–China relations in the 1990s. Since the inauguration of economic reform policies in 1978–1979, the labor reform system has been maintained intact with very few changes even as international **human rights** groups criticize the operation of the system and charge Chinese authorities with torture and other inhumane treatment.

RELIGION. As a Communist country since 1949, China has suppressed and/or subjected to intense state control the free exercise of religion. From the beginning of economic reforms in 1978–1979, however, religious practice has been more open with less (though not unknown) persecution of religious practitioners. Prior to the Communist takeover, the vast majority of Chinese practiced a combination of Buddhism, Daoism, and ancestor worship. China also had practicing Christians, and among its **population** of 90 million **minorities** there exist a variety of religions, such as Islam among the Muslim (or *Hui* people who migrated over the centuries to China from Persia) and Lamaism (a branch of Buddhism) in **Tibet**. From 1949 to 1978, religious practice in China was severely constrained and subject to outright persecution during periods of political radicalism, such as the **Cultural Revolution (1966–1976)**. Although Buddhism was denounced as "evil" and normal Buddhist services across the country were prevented, Lamaist monks and monasteries in Tibet during this era were particularly hard hit by rampaging **Red Guards** as upward of 10,000 monasteries in the autonomous region were destroyed during a 10-year period.

Christians were also subject to persecution throughout the history of the **People's Republic of China** (**PRC**), beginning in the 1950s with the inauguration of the "Three Selfs Movement," which required Chinese Christians to cut all ties with foreigners that led to the expulsion and imprisonment of foreign missionaries. Chinese Catholics, such as Archbishop Dominic Tang Yiming, who refused to renounce ties to the Vatican and join the state-affiliated Patriotic Association of Catholics, were subject to years of imprisonment and persecution and were only released in the 1980s, usually because of illness. Beginning with the break in diplomatic relations between China and the Holy See in 1951, the Chinese government consistently denounced ties between Chinese Catholics and the Vatican as a violation of state sovereignty and periodically arrested Chinese church officials, such as the Bishop of **Shanghai**, who, in 1960, was sentenced to life imprisonment. The Vatican, in turn, issued its 1958 encyclical *Ad Apostolorum Principis*, in which it condemned the Church of the China Patriotic Catholic Association and declared its appointed bishops invalid. In 2001, the Chinese government was outraged when Pope John Paul II canonized 120 Catholic Chinese as martyrs on 1 October, China's national day. In 2004–2005, however, indirect discussions between representatives of the PRC and the Vatican on establishing normal ties were inaugurated.

The major organizations recognized by the government as "patriotic" religious associations are the China Patriotic Catholic Association, the Buddhist Association of China, the Daoist Association of China, the Islamic Association of China, and the Three-Self Protestant Movement, which brings all Protestant denominations under one organizational umbrella. Government policies and guidelines on religious affairs are formulated and implemented by the State Administration for Religious Affairs, which operates under the State Council. Since 1978–1979, the Chinese government has tolerated the open practice of Christianity and other religions with the number of Chinese Catholics (*Tianzhujiao*) worshipping at state-approved churches numbering five million while Protestants (*Xinjiao*) grew from three million in 1982 to 16 million in 2005. Unofficial estimates put the number of Christians in China as high as 50–100 million (including 12–20 million Catholics, according to the Vatican) while churches in such cities as **Beijing** are generally packed on Sundays. The number of people practicing Buddhism was estimated in 2003 at 100 million with 10,000 temples scattered throughout the country, along with 34 academies (the largest recently constructed in Yangzhou, Jiangsu Province) and a nationwide contingent of 200,000 monks and nuns. Courses in Buddhism and other religions are offered at Chinese universities, along with institutes for the "scientific study" of religion at the **Chinese Academy of Social Sciences (CASS)** and other research centers. The first ever international Buddhist cultural festival in China was also held in 2004 at Mt. Wutai, a Buddhist sanctum located in Shanxi Province, where there are 47 temples and more than 3,000 monks and nuns. Individuals who practice outside the state-affiliated organizations, especially members of the so-called underground or "home" churches, are, however, still subject to persecution and often accused of such nebulous crimes as "inciting the gathering of state secrets."

Chinese government policy statements toward religion began with the 1954 document "Summary of Principal Experiences Concerning Work Performed by the Party among Ethnic Minorities" while, in 1957, a conference of the officially sanctioned China Catholic Patriotic Association recognized the pope's authority in religious matters but not over political issues. This was followed in 1982 by the **Chinese Communist Party (CCP)** Central Committee's "Basic Viewpoint and Policy on the Religious Question" and by regulations issued in 1994 by the State Council on the management of sites for religious activities and on foreign nationals' religious activities in China. In 2005, new "Provisions on Religious Affairs" outlined somewhat clearer procedures for registering religious groups and institutions that cover everything from how licensed religious organizations can accept religious donations and claim tax exemptions to procedures for enrollment of foreign students. The new rules also declare that citizens have the right to provide religious **education** for their children (though, in many areas of China, churchgoers must be 18 years old) but the rules also call for criminal charges against anyone who compels citizens to believe or not believe in any religion. Ideologically, recent official CCP pronouncements have declared a "separation of politics and religion" as the official Party line while Chinese **leaders**, such as CCP former General Secretary **Jiang Zemin**, have gone on record as declaring the mutual adaptation of religion with socialist society. This more-tolerant atmosphere was evident from 1990 onward when theological colleges in China began to graduate nuns but was somewhat counteracted beginning in 1999 with a government crackdown against the *Falun Gong* spiritual group that was part of a larger effort led by a state agency known as the 610 Office to wipe out illegal religious groups that were denounced in official media as "evil cults" engaged in "feudalistic superstition." Many "illegal" temples and churches have been shut down and even demolished in a campaign that also targeted Turkic-speaking Muslims in western China.

While leaders of the officially sanctioned organizations declare a "golden age" for current religious practice in China, underground religious leaders suggest that religious freedom in China actually declined from 2003 to 2005 with a growing number of arrests and imprisonment of religious leaders and worshippers. This is especially true in rural areas, where sects and cults led by charismatic leaders thrive in the midst of widespread official **corruption** and a collapse in state-sponsored **health care** and social services and where the void left by the erosion of Communist ideology has often been filled by religion. Growing violence among competing sects, such as the Christian Three Grades of Servants and the Eastern Lighting (now both banned but which claim several million members in China's interior) and their charismatic leaders who often claim divine powers and, in some cases, claim to be a reincarnation of Jesus Christ, has raised concern among government authorities. Religious activity in the countryside is not banned but with cumbersome registration requirements and periodic harassment, established religious institutions find it difficult to operate there because most state-sponsored churches are located in urban areas. With offerings of social services and millenarian appeals reminiscent of the mid-19th-century *Taipings* who almost brought down the Qing dynasty (1644–1911), the apocalyptic and often anti-Communist sects are seen as a possible threat to CCP political power. *See also QIGONG*; SOCIAL PROTESTS.

"RESOLUTION ON CERTAIN QUESTIONS IN THE HISTORY OF OUR PARTY SINCE THE ESTABLISHMENT OF THE PEOPLE'S REPUBLIC OF CHINA." Issued by the Sixth Plenum of the 11th National Party Congress in June 1981, this official **Chinese Communist Party** (**CCP**) document condemned **Mao Zedong** for his "mistakes" in expanding the **Anti-Rightist Campaign** (**1957–1958**) to large numbers of **intellectuals**, in launching the catastrophic **Great Leap Forward** (**1958–1960**), in purging Marshal **Peng Dehuai**, and in instigating the **Cultural Revolution** (**1966–1976**). The document also repudiated the theory of "continuing the revolution under the dictatorship of the proletariat," which had served as the ideological underpinning for the Cultural Revolution and other radical leftist policies. The Resolution claimed that Mao Zedong's leadership had degenerated from the late 1950s onward into an increasingly "despotic" and "patriarchal" style and that Mao's **"personality cult"** (***geren chongbai***) robbed the CCP of its "revolutionary tradition" of "collective leadership" (*jiti lingdao*). The document was reportedly toned down in its criticism of Mao by the personal intervention of **Deng Xiaoping**, who made sure that Mao's leadership was defined as overwhelmingly "correct." Mao Zedong Thought was also reinterpreted to fit the goals of modernization pursued by the post-1978 CCP leadership. Overall, this document was much less critical of Mao Zedong than was the scathing denunciation of **Josef Stalin** by Nikita Khrushchev in his "secret speech" at the 1956 20th Congress of the Communist Party of the **Soviet Union** (**CPSU**).

"RESTRICTION OF BOURGEOIS RIGHTS" (*"XIANZHI ZICHANJIEJI FAQUAN"*). In the mid-1970s, just a year before the death of **Mao Zedong**, pressure was building from reformist elements who had been recently rehabilitated in the **Chinese Communist Party** (**CCP**), primarily **Deng Xiaoping**, to change dramatically the course of China's development. The **Cultural Revolution (1966–1976)** had viciously attacked all vestiges of "capitalism" in China and had purged from the Party prominent **leaders**, such as **Liu Shaoqi**, who had wanted greater attention to economic problems. China's **economy** was stagnating and individuals were prohibited from owning just about any private property, thereby destroying any individual incentive for accumulating wealth. As the reaction against the political radicalism and anti-development thrust of the Cultural Revolution began to build in the mid-1970s, radical forces composing the **Gang of Four** mobilized the propaganda machine under their control to attack all "bourgeois rights." These "rights" referred to exchanges of commodities with money, ownership of property, and determination of wages according to work performed. **Zhang Chunqiao**, a prominent radical and member of the Gang of Four, published a major article in *Red Flag*, the major theoretical journal of the CCP, on the need to create the necessary "ideological weapons" against "bourgeois rights" and to employ the "dictatorship of the proletariat" to ensure that "bourgeois rights" not reappear. Mao Zedong also weighed in by calling for the elimination of the differences between workers and peasants, town and country, and mental and menial **labor**—the ultimate goals of Communism. After having reappeared in late 1973 and promoted China's turn toward economic and technological development, Deng Xiaoping was purged again in April 1976 and thus the campaign against "bourgeois rights" intensified. The death of Mao Zedong in September 1976 and the arrest of the Gang of Four in October 1976 ended the criticism of "bourgeois rights" per se and led to the promotion of significant economic reforms in which money and commodities were exchanged and wage scales more generally reflected the quality of work. Criticism of **"bourgeois liberalization"**—code words in China for political reform—did, however, continue throughout the 1980s and 1990s.

"REVERSAL OF VERDICTS" (*"PINGFAN"*). A judicial-political term, also translated as "rehabilitation," it means to correct a legal case or alter a political judgment that had been decided improperly and to compensate individuals whose cases were handled incorrectly or who have been sentenced or executed unjustly. Historically, the term precedes the Communist period and has its roots in the ancient **Han** dynasty (202 BC–220 AD). After 1949, it was used in the case of individuals whom the Communists had wrongly persecuted during the **Anti-Counter-revolutionary Campaigns** in the early and mid-1950s. Writing in 1957, **Mao Zedong** admitted to "mistakes in the work of suppressing counterrevolutionaries" and insisted that steps were taken to correct them. Nevertheless, during the relative freedom of the **Hundred Flowers**, (**1956–1957**), non-Communist members called for the establishment of an independent organ of the government to investigate the wrongful persecution of innocent people, but to no avail. **Chinese Communist Party** (**CCP**) members purged during the 1950s and 1960s, especially during the **Cultural Revolution** (**1966–1976**), were themselves "rehabilitated" after 1978. These mass "rehabilitations" of many top **leaders**, including **Yang Shangkun** and **Bo Yibo**, were pushed by CCP leader **Hu Yaobang** against considerable political resistance from remnant leftist forces in the CCP. Many **intellectuals** persecuted by the CCP, such as **Wang Shiwei**, were also rehabilitated posthumously. But some CCP leaders from the past (especially those purged in the power struggles of the 1930s and 1940s) and many intellectuals persecuted by the Communists during the **Anti-Rightist Campaign** (**1957–1958**) and other campaigns, such as the journalist and writer Chu Anping, have not to this day been rehabilitated.

"REVISIONISM" (*"XIUZHENGZHUYI"*). In Marxist–Leninist ideology, "revisionism" refers to negating the "basic principles of Marxism and its universal truths" by self-proclaimed Marxist–Leninists. They are heretics who by willfully distorting the meaning of Marxism–Leninism have undermined the pursuit of revolutionary goals. Historically, the first revisionist was Eduard Bernstein, who, in the late 19th century, suggested that **socialism** could be achieved through a process of evolution instead of revolution, with Marxist parties working through, rather than against, parliamentary bodies. For this, Bernstein was roundly condemned by Lenin and other defenders of Marxist orthodoxy. After World War II, the newly established Communist-controlled country of Yugoslavia was denounced by the **Soviet Union** as "revisionist" for its anti-Stalinist positions and more liberal approaches to political and economic questions. In China's eyes, the Soviet Union itself became "revisionist" under the leadership of Nikita Khrushchev and his brand of Communism that stressed economic and technical achievements over ideological orthodoxy. And within China, **Liu Shaoqi** and other top **leaders** of the **Chinese Communist Party** (**CCP**) were labeled as "revisionist" for their purported opposition to Maoist policies. Since the 1978–1979 economic reforms, the term revisionism has largely been dropped from official Chinese political rhetoric.

REVOLUTIONARY COMMITTEES. Established during the **Cultural Revolution** (**1966–1976**) to replace the regular **Chinese Communist Party** (**CCP**) organizational structure, these committees proved to be very unwieldy and were dismantled as administrative bodies in the late 1970s. The first Revolutionary Committee was set up in 1967 in China's northeast province of Heilongjiang by local **Red Guard** groups. It comprised a "three-in-one combination" of "mass revolutionary rebel groups" that was mostly composed of Red Guard organizations; representatives from the **People's Liberation Army** (**PLA**) and **people's militia**; and Maoist revolutionary **cadres** from the former Party and government bureaucracies. By 1968, virtually every province and autonomous region in China had established a Revolutionary Committee. Below the provincial level, revolutionary committees were organized throughout the country in schools and universities, factories, **people's communes**, and government offices, where they were to provide for mass input into China's political process. In reality, it was the PLA that effectively ran most Revolutionary Committees and turned them into the organized arms of radical political **leaders** in **Beijing**. Under the leadership of **Lin Biao**, the PLA generally sided with the leftist forces. But once Lin fell from power in 1971, the PLA took a decidedly conservative direction and thus ceased supporting the radical goals of the Revolutionary Committees. At the same time, the regular Party committee structure of the CCP was gradually reestablished with Mao's blessings in provinces and lower levels in China's political structure, thereby effectively negating the Revolutionary Committees. After the arrest of the **Gang of Four** in October 1976, the Revolutionary Committees were reduced to administrative arms of local People's Congresses. The return of **Deng Xiaoping** and the beginning of economic reforms in 1978–1979 led to the formal abolition of Revolutionary Committees in 1979.

"REVOLUTIONARY ELDERS" (*"GEMING YUANLAO"*). This is a reference to those senior Party **leaders**, such as **Peng Zhen, Song Renqiong, Song Ping**, and Madame **Deng Yingchao** (wife of **Zhou Enlai**), whose long service in the **Chinese Communist Party (CCP)** and enormous personal status was transferred into considerable political influence with or without formal position. Many of these "elders" were nominally retired in China but continued to wield substantial influence on major political and economic decisions of the CCP, such as the June 1989 military crackdown on the second **Beijing Spring** where, like a Greek Chorus, they stood behind the decision by **Deng Xiaoping**, perhaps the most famous (and influential) "revolutionary elder," to deploy force against young pro-democracy student demonstrators.

RIGHTISTS. *See* ANTI-RIGHTIST CAMPAIGN (1957–1958).

RIVER ELEGY (HESHANG). A six-part documentary produced in 1988 for Central China Television (CCTV) by a group of academics, writers, and TV directors, *River Elegy* was written by Su Xiaokang, an ex-**Red Guard** and Wang Luxiang, a university lecturer, and directed by a 26-year-old named Xia Jun. The work weaves together a number of cultural, historical, and political themes that question the country's obsession with such national icons as the Great Wall and the dragon, and urged the Chinese people to break out of the interminable cycle of disasters and cultural stagnation that the authors tied to the cult of the Yellow River. Comparing China's "old civilization" to the "silt accumulated on the bed of the Yellow River," *River Elegy* called for the creation of an industrial society and further opening to the "blue water" civilizations of the West so as to infuse the country with the dynamism necessary to transform its backward culture. In this sense, *River Elegy* was reminiscent of themes espoused in the **May Fourth Movement (1919–1923)** that led to the establishment of the **Chinese Communist Party (CCP)** in 1921. Combining interviews of leading reform **intellectuals** with footage from the **Great Leap Forward (1958–1960)** and the **Cultural Revolution (1966–1976)**, the film equated Maoism and the Communist state with traditional culture and the dynastic state—both of which had brought huge disasters to the country. The traditional inland world view rooted in China's peasant society and embodied in Confucian and Maoist orthodoxies needed, the film suggested, to be supplanted by an outward-oriented society, linked to the rest of the world by commerce, **trade**, and a cosmopolitan world view.

Popular response to the series was overwhelming. Estimates are that more than 200 million Chinese viewed it and many thousands also purchased copies of the script or wrote letters of comment to the TV studio. But because *River Elegy* had violated many cultural and political proscriptions and had vilified such historical icons as the Great Wall, the Yellow River, and the dragon (a symbol of the emperor and fertility in China), it came under intense pressure from hard-line CCP **leaders**, such as Vice-President **Wang Zhen**. Supportive of the reform faction led by CCP General Secretary **Zhao Ziyang** who was deposed during the 1989 second **Beijing Spring**, *River Elegy* was ultimately banned. In 1990, the CCP responded to the film with its own documentary titled *On the Road: A Century of Marxism*, which lauded the accomplishments of the CCP and praised Marxism–Leninism and the leadership of **Deng Xiaoping**. *See also* CINEMA AND FILM.

RONG YIREN (1916–2005). Born in Wuxi, Jiangsu Province to one of China's richest families, Rong Yiren graduated from St. John's University in **Shanghai** in 1937. Upon the "**liberation**" (*jiefang*) of China in 1949, Rong remained in the country as one of the "red capitalists" heading two family firms in the cotton and flour mill industries. Even as most of his family fled abroad, Rong served in several official posts including mayor of Shanghai from 1957 to 1959 and vice-minister of the Textile Industry. During the **Cultural Revolution (1966–1976)**, his family companies were confiscated, and he was beaten, denounced, and made to work menial jobs. Rong survived and emerged as a managing director of the Bank of China and chairman of the Board of Directors of the **China International Trust**

and Investment Corporation (CITIC), a position he assumed on the personal orders of **Deng Xiaoping**. As the company grew into a global conglomerate with diverse holdings in airlines, **banking and finance**, and real estate, Rong became one of China's richest men; his son, Rong Zhijian (Larry Yung), was put in charge of CITIC's **Hong Kong** subsidiary where his accumulated wealth of over US$1 billion made him China's richest man in 2004. In 1987, Rong Yiren was appointed honorary chairman of China's National Committee for Pacific Economic Cooperation. Despite Rong's support of **Zhao Ziyang** and the second **Beijing Spring**, Rong was appointed vice-president of China in 1993, replacing the retiring **Wang Zhen** and served until 1998.

RUI XINGWEN (1927–2005). A native of Jiangsu Province, Rui Xingwen joined the **Chinese Communist Party (CCP)** in 1945 and served in a variety of posts in China's heavy industrial and chemical **industry** and, in 1984, was appointed deputy director of the State Planning Commission and minister of urban and rural construction. Appointed secretary of the **Shanghai** CP in 1985, Rui was elected to the Central Secretariat in 1987 and, in 1988, became deputy chief of the leading group of the CCP on propaganda and ideology. Despite his well-known alliance with General Secretary **Zhao Ziyang**, who was deposed after the 1989 military crackdown against the second **Beijing Spring**, Rui Xingwen survived politically and, in 1991, was reappointed as deputy director of the State Planning Commission and later served as a member of the Standing Committee of the **Chinese People's Political Consultative Conference (CPPCC)**.

RUSSIA. The establishment of the Russian Federation in 1993, following the disintegration of the **Soviet Union** in 1991 witnessed a continuation in the "normalization" of its relations with China that had begun in 1989 after 32 years of belligerency during the Sino–Soviet Conflict. Normalization entailed Russian–Chinese cooperation and joint action on a number of political, military, economic, and environmental issues though some areas of contention remain between the two nations that share the longest border in the world (4,300 km). Despite their very different political systems, with Russia making the transition to democracy and China maintaining its system of one-party Communist autocracy, the two countries share a number of areas of common ground in the international and domestic arenas that have been addressed in frequent visits by their respective presidents, premiers, and foreign ministers and by exchanges at meetings such as the **Shanghai** Cooperation Organization that consists of China, Russia, Kazakhstan, Kyrgyzstan, Uzbekistan, and Tajikistan. Expressing their common devotion to international friendship and cooperation, the two countries announced in 1993 a Sino–Russo ministry-to-ministry defense cooperation agreement while, in 1994, the two countries signed an official treaty on the prevention through joint military exercises of "dangerous military activities" along their respective borders whose demarcation and resolution of border guard issues was finalized by a series of agreements in 1991, 1994, and 1995, followed, in 2004, by the "Supplementary Agreement on the Eastern Section of China–Russia Boundary Line," which completed the delimitation that had been negotiated over a period of 40 years.

Following a 1992 visit to China by then Russian President Boris Yeltsin, in which the two countries expressed their mutual friendship, in 1996, Russia and China entered into a "strategic cooperative partnership" and, along with Kazakhstan, Kyrgyzstan, and Tajikistan, agreed on a series of military confidence-building measures (CBMs), along their respective borders. This was followed in 1997 by an agreement among the same group of nations to engage in troop limitations and armament reductions. Following further border agreements between China and Russia in 1997 during a trip by President **Jiang Zemin** to Moscow and a second trip to **Beijing** by Boris Yeltsin in the same year, the two sides agreed on a view of the world as multi-polarized and emphasized partnership between the two countries as most outstanding border issues were resolved. In 2001, the two countries signed a Good-Neighborly Treaty of Friendship and Cooperation, which committed them to principles of mutual respect of each other's territorial integrity, non-aggression, and non-interference in each other's internal affairs. As part of their mutual pledge to peaceful coexistence, the two countries declared a mutual "no-first-use" policy on nuclear weapons and called for any and all disputes to be settled in line with stipulations in the **United Nations** (**UN**) charter. Russia pledged to respect the **People's Republic of China** (**PRC**) as the sole legal government of China and declared that **Taiwan** is an inalienable part of China, while China reciprocated by declaring the Russian campaign against breakaway Chechnya as a purely internal affair. China supported Russian opposition to the expansion of the North Atlantic Treaty Organization (NATO) toward its borders and agreed on opposition to a **United States**-planned anti-ballistic missile defense shield (including a theater missile defense) and the deployment of nuclear or any major weapons in space.

Following the 11 September 2001 attacks in the U.S., China and Russia pledged to promote strategic cooperation to fight terrorism and agreed to strengthen cooperation in the field of security and international issues that has led to a series of joint security exercises. Both countries vehemently opposed the U.S.-led invasion of Iraq and looked to closer ties, especially on military matters, to counter the increasing presence of U.S. forces in the Central Asian arena. **Hu Jintao's** first trip abroad as China's **president** in 2003 was to Moscow, where, in meetings with Russian President Vladimir Putin, the two **leaders** renewed the Sino–Russo "strategic cooperative partnership" and called for a multi-polar world in which relations among nations are "democratized" and the UN plays a key role in the settlement of international conflicts. Both Russia and China pledged their opposition to the development of nuclear weapons by North **Korea**, but they both blocked a UN Security Council statement in 2003 condemning North Korea and pledged to safeguard existing arms control and disarmament treaties, such as the Comprehensive Nuclear Test Ban Treaty that the U.S. has refused to sign.

Since 1990, China has been a major buyer of Russian weaponry, which has included more than 100 Russian fighter jets, such as the SU-27 and the SU-30 MKK (with licenses from Russia to build both models in China), diesel submarines, air-defense systems, and guided-missile destroyers with possible sale to China of a Russian-made aircraft carrier. Russian air-to-air missiles—the R-77—were test-launched by Chinese aircraft in 2002, and the two countries negotiated the sales of the third batch of Tor-M1 surface-to-air missiles (SAMs) to China, along with additional submarines armed with the Klub long-range, anti-ship missile. China has also obtained the Russian-designed 3M-82 Moskit ship-to-ship missile (NATO designation "Sunburn SS-N-22"), which at speeds of MACH 3 and with a capacity to carry a 200-kg warhead up to a range of 145 km has no known defense by the

U.S. Navy because the missile was explicitly designed to defeat the U.S. Aegis battle-management system. China and Russia have also set up cooperative efforts at cyber-attack capability aimed at disrupting an enemy's command center and even its economic infrastructure and have joined in upgrading the "Benthal satellite," a deep-sea submarine carrier robot with potential military applications.

Normalization of relations between Russia and China has also led to growth in bilateral **trade and investment** and various technological and educational exchanges. During the 1990s, annual bilateral trade between the two countries averaged around US$6 billion, but, with annual growth rates of 20%, that figure had swelled to nearly US$16 billion by 2003, as China imported substantial amounts of Russian oil, along with nuclear power, space, and electronic goods. Russia, in turn, purchased Chinese mechanical, communications, and electronic technologies. In 2003, it was agreed that Russia would export 4.5 to 5.5 million tons of oil to China over a three-year period with the amount to rise in 2006 to 15 million tons annually largely by rail but with some to be transported along a 2,500-mile pipeline from Angarsk near Lake Baikal in eastern Siberia to China's **Daqing oilfield**, though, in 2005, this project had yet to be finalized because of a competing plan to terminate the pipeline in the Russian Pacific port of Nakhodka for trans-shipment to **Japan**. Russia also agreed to construct nuclear reactors in China for the second phase of the Tianwan nuclear power plant in eastern China and the Lianyungang nuclear power station in Jiangsu Province while an agreement was signed between Russia's GazProm and China's state-owned National Petroleum Corporation in 2004 to develop Russian natural gas resources for Chinese use. Russia is China's eighth largest trade partner with the two countries' entry into the **World Trade Organization** (**WTO**) likely to enhance their economic relationship that, in 2010, is slated to reach US$60–$80 billion enhanced by the establishment of free trade zones on their respective borders. Russia also maintains trade with **Taiwan** to China's consternation but has promised major investment in China's Western Region Development Plan while China has also expressed interest in the development of Siberia and the Russian Far East. Chinese investment in Russia has also come in real estate, **agriculture**, and color TV production facilities by Chinese companies while, beginning in 2001, the two countries conducted a financial forum to further bilateral financial cooperation between their respective **banking and finance** systems.

That a majority of Russian politicians, business leaders, and journalists in 2000 viewed China as a more reliable partner than the U.S. helps advance the two nations' ties forward, though periodic trade disputes have broken out over synthetic rubber imports into China from Russia and heightened Russian tariffs on Chinese commodities involved in "irregular trade." On issues involving the **environment**, Russia and China have established cooperative ventures to control tree felling along their border areas as both nations expressed support for the Kyoto Protocol, which China joined in 2001 and the Russian parliament ratified in 2005. Scientific and technological exchanges were advanced by the establishment of such centers as the Sino–Russian Science and Technology Center in the Chinese municipality of Shenyang, Liaoning Province, which is slated to concentrate on research into aeronautics and astronautics, bio-engineering, **energy**, new materials, laser technology, and environmental sciences. *See also* FOREIGN POLICY.

– S –

SARS. Severe Acute Respiratory Syndrome (SARS) is a lethal coronavirus that apparently jumped from wildlife to humans, causing atypical pneumonia. It first appeared in southern China in Guangdong Province in November 2002 and quickly spread to **Hong Kong** and **Beijing** and to other nations in Asia, including Singapore, and to Canada. From 2002 to 2004, 5,329 infections occurred in China with 349 deaths. Initially, Chinese officials in the Ministry of Health and at local levels covered up the extent and danger of the virus until a semi-retired surgeon at the prestigious No. 301 Military Hospital named Jiang Yanyong reported that there were far more SARS patients than the health authorities had reported. Dr. Jiang's revelations resulted in China's international condemnation and ultimately led to the resignations of the minister of health and the mayor of Beijing. Accurate information on the spread of the disease was also conveyed throughout the country by the widespread use of text messaging among cell phone and **Internet** users that effectively bypassed state-controlled media. Beginning in April 2003, China admitted to the earlier coverup and began to confront the virus head-on. Led by the straight-talking and tough new minister of health and vice-premier, **Wu Yi**, a series of measures were adopted to gain comprehensive information on the extent of the epidemic and to break the chain of human-to-human transmission of the virus. A national task force was created to combat SARS with supervision teams sent to infected provinces and regions to coordinate anti-SARS efforts while all local health departments were ordered to include information on the virus's spread to the national disease report management system.

Particularly hard hit by the virus were the cities of Beijing and **Guangzhou (Canton)**, although cases of SARS were also reported in 23 of the country's 31 provinces and autonomous regions, including such remote regions of China's interior as Inner Mongolia. During the height of the SARS epidemic in Beijing, the city was virtually shut down as anyone displaying SARS symptoms—high fever, chills, and dry cough—was quarantined. In addition to closing down the city's school system and places of entertainment for several weeks to restrict close human contact, vast segments of the capital's **population**, especially children, were subject to constant monitoring of body temperature and 4,000 people were forcibly quarantined. Although the number of patients admitted to hospitals in Beijing and Guangzhou was staggering, emergency measures, such as the canceling of the May Day holiday and major restrictions on travel and the massive mobilization of **health care** personnel, along with the construction in only one-week's time of a special hospital for SARS patients outside Beijing by the **People's Liberation Army (PLA)**, helped stem the spread of the virus. Emergency measures were also taken to interrupt the suspected animal-to-human transmission of the disease, including the massive killing of civet cats in Guangzhou's wild game markets where raccoon dogs and hog badgers were also exterminated by health authorities over the objections of local sellers of these rare delicacies that are favored in southern Chinese cuisine. Individuals who violated quarantines in China and/or knowingly spread the disease were dealt with by harsh penalties, including long-term imprisonment and even the threat of execution. Although a few cases were reported, in late 2003 and 2004, of individuals working in laboratories and health care facilities, SARS has been effectively contained by an elaborate system of early detection, isolation of suspected cases, contact tracing, and international reporting, which has won China plaudits from the World Health Organization (WHO). In June 2004, a reagent kit to detect SARS was developed and sold in China, and human trials on an experimental SARS vaccine were also begun under the auspices of China's State Food and Drug Supervision Administration.

Despite China's apparent success in stemming SARS, this disease, like HIV/**AIDS**, revealed enormous weaknesses in China's public health care system, especially in rural areas, as local clinics lacked sufficient supplies, such as surgical masks and latex gloves, while antibiotics necessary to fight the disease remained too expensive for the poorest rural dwellers. While the government offered free drugs to anyone displaying SARS symptoms, interruption of the virus in rural areas was often accomplished by draconian quarantine measures, such as blocking off entire villages from contact with the outside world and subjecting all travelers and migrants to temperature screening and disinfectant spraying. Suspected SARS patients were, like their HIV/AIDS-infected counterparts, subject to widespread discrimination and surveillance, with rewards offered by many municipalities to anyone "turning in" an infected individual. Modern methods of spreading information and combating rumors were employed, including the establishment of 24-hour SARS hotlines in many cities and the use of infra-red scanners at airports to check the body temperature of inbound and outbound passengers. Regulations on wildlife **trade** in China were tightened, and major research projects tracing the virus were begun. The **People's Republic of China** (**PRC**) also joined in an international effort to coordinate control of the disease. The economic impact of SARS amounted to billions of dollars in lost revenue from travel, tourism, and trade, but the overall effect on the Chinese **economy** was short-term. The last SARS cases reported were in April 2004, when the WHO declared an end to the SARS outbreak in China.

SATELLITE PARTIES. *See* DEMOCRATIC PARTIES.

SCIENCE AND TECHNOLOGY. From the 1st to the 13th centuries, China was a center of scientific innovation that witnessed the Four

Great Inventions of the compass, gunpowder, papermaking, and printing; Chinese astronomers were among the first in the world to observe supernovas. For a variety of reasons that are still not fully explained, scientific innovation slowed to a halt; by the 20th century, few scientific or technical innovations were developed in China. Coming to power in 1949, the **Chinese Communist Party (CCP)** was committed to building up the country's scientific and technical base as the foundation for a modern **economy** and military power. From the 1950s through the 1970s, China reorganized its scientific establishment along Soviet lines with its emphasis on a bureaucratic rather than professional principle of organization, the separation of research from production, and the establishment of specialized research institutes. In the 1949 **Common Program**, development of the natural sciences was given top priority as the newly formed Chinese Academy of Sciences (CAS) was designated to adjust scientific research to meet the requirements of the productive sector of the economy. With large numbers of Chinese scientists trained in the **Soviet Union**, a Joint Commission for Cooperation in Science and Technology was set up by the two countries in 1954 but floundered after the outbreak of the Sino–Soviet Conflict in the early 1960s.

Scientists who used the brief period of free expression during the **Hundred Flowers (1956–1957)** to air complaints about political interference in scientific work were criticized during the subsequent **Anti-Rightist Campaign (1957–1958)** as all scientists were encouraged to be both "**red and expert**." With attacks on large numbers of scientists during the **Cultural Revolution (1966–1976)**, China's scientific establishment and capacity for technical innovation were all but shut down as individual scientists were singled out as "counterrevolutionaries" and entire staffs of research institutes underwent "**transfer to lower levels**" (*xiafang*) to the countryside where they engaged in manual **labor**. Scientific journals also ceased publication and subscriptions to foreign journals were allowed to lapse as Chinese scientists were effectively cut off from the outside world for 10 years with the only progress occurring in nuclear weapons development and fusion research that as major military projects remained largely untouched by the political turmoil. In the early 1970s, a revival of science was attempted but with emphasis on mass participation, eradication of distinctions between scientists and workers, and concentration on immediate practical problems in **agriculture, industry**, and earthquake prediction that produced very few real accomplishments.

In the early and mid-1970s, China began a fundamental reorganization and redefinition of its scientific and technological goals as modernization of the science and technology sectors were included in the **Four Modernizations** laid out by **Zhou Enlai** and **Deng Xiaoping**. With the arrest of the radical faction known as the **Gang of Four** in 1976, their often ill-trained supporters in newly opened research institutes and universities were quickly replaced by professionally qualified personnel, and the news media began to refer to scientists and technicians as part of society's "productive forces." In 1978, a National Science Conference was held in **Beijing** attended by over 6,000 scientists and administrators and top Chinese **leaders** as a rapid and ambitious plan of scientific development was incorporated into a draft Eight-Year Plan for the Development of Science and Technology, which, in 1981, was scaled back as renewed emphasis was given to the application of science to practical problems and the training of a new generation of scientists and engineers. By 1985–1986, China had more than eight million personnel working on science in research institutes, **state-owned enterprises** (SOEs), and government offices with 350,000 designated as "research personnel" many of whom had studied abroad, especially in the **United States.**

By far, the greatest employers of scientists in the 1980s were still the more than 10,000 research institutes that were directed and funded by various central and regional government authorities and whose research tasks were often set by higher-level administrators as part of an overall research plan. Organized into five major subsystems with little lateral contact or communication, the major research institutes remained the Chinese Academy of Sciences (CAS), which was originally modeled on the Soviet Academy of Sciences and managed 120 separate research institutes scattered across the country employing 40,000 scientific personnel. Formally subordinate to the State Science and Technology Development Commission (reorganized in 1998), CAS reports directly to the State Council and oversees such institutions as the Chinese University of Science and Technology in Hefei, Anhui Province, where, in 2005, plans were announced to create China's first "science city" modeled on Silicon Valley in the

United States. For years, the many research institutes embedded in major ministries, such as electronics, coal, and railway, were overseen by the State Science and Technology Commission. Military-related research organs have some of the best-trained scientific and technological personnel in China and have been supervised by the Commission of Science, Technology, and Industry for National Defense (created in 1982) while they operate in comparative isolation from the civilian economy.

Since the advent of the economic reforms in 1978–1979, some limited changes in China's organization of science and technology have occurred to address such perennial problems as the lack of coordination among scientific fields, lack of communication between research and production units, duplication of research, and maldistribution of personnel. While the military crackdown against the second **Beijing Spring** in June 1989 led to the exile of such prominent Chinese scientists as the astrophysicist **Fang Lizhi,** the scientific community benefited from a major decision in 1995 to increase spending on research and development to the equivalent of 1.5% of Gross Domestic Product (GDP) as scientific personnel were encouraged to move out of their isolated institutes into private enterprises. New funding organizations have been set up, including the National Science Foundation of China, which grants peer-reviewed awards along with the Ministry of Science and Technology, while, in 1992, the then Science and Technology Development Commission issued a document approved by the State Council entitled "State Medium and Long-Term Science and Technology Development Program," which set a general goal of achieving the level of technology reached by developed countries by 2020. Beginning in 1993, China initiated its own Genome Project headquartered in **Shanghai**; at the international level, China has participated in Global Change and Warming research projects, the International Thermonuclear Experimental Reactor (ITER), which will be built in France as a pilot project for electricity-producing fusion power plants, and it renewed the China–U.S. Science and Technology Agreement.

From 1998 to 2004, the Chinese Academy of Sciences conducted 122 key national projects on basic research while China has also announced its support for stem cell research and has engaged in an aggressive campaign to lure Chinese students studying abroad and foreign scientists to the **People's Republic of China** (**PRC**). Among the major scientific and technological breakthroughs in the past 20 years in China are development of a new supercomputer that went on line in 1992; the successful trial flight of a supersonic unmanned plane in 1995; the world's first synthesis and identification of the new nuclide americium (Am)-235 in 1996; the world's first replication of a human ear from the body of an animal through extrinsic cell reproduction in 1997; the birth of China's first test-tube twins in 1998; genetic modification of food and insect-resistant crops in 1999; cloning of neural deafness genes in 1999 and of a female goat in 2000; development of advanced ocean wave power systems for stable electricity flow; experimentation on fuel cell and hybrid **automobiles**; explorations of the structure of evolution of the universe by high-resolution simulations of galaxy formation; navigation to the Arctic Ocean by a scientific research vessel to study interaction of the sea, ice, and the atmosphere and their impact on the climate; and continued work on developing an inhibitor of the **SARS** virus.

These and other accomplishments in the scientific and technical fields undoubtedly reflect the commitment of central leaders, many trained in the sciences and technology such as President **Hu Jintao** (engineering) and Premier **Wen Jiabao** (geology) to accelerate science and technology development. In terms of the innovativeness of Chinese research papers in 2005, as measured by the number of citations, Chinese scientists performed well in the fields of mathematics, materials science, chemistry, and engineering, but with dramatically fewer citations in agriculture and life sciences. China's share in world patents is even smaller than its share in research papers. *See also* ATOMIC BOMB; EDUCATION; SPACE PROGRAM.

SECRETARIAT OF THE CCP. *See* CHINESE COMMUNIST PARTY (CCP).

SEEKING TRUTH (QIUSHI). Established in May 1988, *Seeking Truth* replaced ***Red Flag (Hongqi)*** as the primary theoretical and ideological journal of the **Chinese Communist Party** (**CCP**). Unlike *Red Flag*, *Seeking Truth* does not operate under the direct authority of the Central Committee but is managed by the **Central Party School**. Although initially set up to promulgate theories and ideas related to China's political and economic reform and opening to the outside world, the magazine has served the interests of the CCP in countering excessively liberal opinion—especially since the military crackdown against the second **Beijing Spring** in 1989. This role was evident in articles in 2003 that called for a "discipline campaign" for journalists whose increasing reliance on sources outside direct CCP control, such as off the **Internet**, was seen as violating the official propaganda line that calls on all journalists to abide by the "Marxist conception of news."

Along with other official media, such as the *People's Daily*, *Enlightenment Daily*, the **New China News Agency** (**Xinhua**), *Economic Daily*, Central People's Radio Station, and China Central Television (CCTV), *Seeking Truth* formed a "self-discipline pact" that was also supposedly aimed at eliminating the phenomena of paid news stories, occasional fraudulent news reports, the spreading of vulgarity, and bad advertisements, all of which have recently infected central-level journalism in China. Articles hailing the "innovative spirit" and "important thinking" of the theory of "Three Represents" (on the importance of the CCP modernizing the nation by representing the demands for the development of advanced social productive forces, the direction of advanced culture, and the fundamental interests of the greatest majority of people) espoused by former CCP General Secretary **Jiang Zemin** and reaffirmed by current General Secretary **Hu Jintao** indicate that *Seeking Truth* continues its primary role of upholding and defending the political power and policies of the CCP. Similar articles in 2005 by China's top security official, **Luo Gan,** calling for a crackdown on "hostile forces" that threaten the country's security in areas such as **Tibet** and Xinjiang and on the "favorable situation" in the world for the **foreign policy** of the **People's Republic of China** (**PRC**) indicate that newspapers and journals such as *Seeking Truth* continue to carry out the politically obedient role that was originally assigned to the press during the CCP's period of revolutionary struggle in Yan'an (1935–1945).

Yet, on occasion the magazine has run articles that appear as somewhat elliptical challenges to the effects of central government policies. A series of articles in 2005 lauding the economic ideas of former conservative economic czar **Chen Yun** that stressed his emphasis on solving the problems of a low-income workforce, imbalanced development, and impoverished farmers could be read as a not-so-subtle critique of policies pursued since the economic reforms of 1978–1979, which Chen originally opposed and which have produced increasing gaps between the wealthy urban areas and the increasingly destitute countryside. Even more provocative was an article in 2003 by a researcher from the **Chinese Academy of Social Sciences (CASS)**, which advocated that the Chinese people should have greater democratic involvement in the running of the country according to law and in an orderly way, though the entire piece was couched in terminology and references to decisions of the CCP 16th National Party Congress held in 2004. *Seeking Truth* is also a frequent outlet for articles by retired senior **leaders**, such as one of the pieces on Chen Yun that was authored by CCP elder **Song Ping** and a 2005 article on China's role in world affairs by veteran Chinese diplomat **Liu Huaqiu**.

"SELF-RELIANCE" ("*ZILI GENGSHENG*"). This phrase was first used by **Mao Zedong** in 1945 just prior to the outbreak of the **Civil War (1946–1949)** with the **Kuomintang (KMT)**. Mao rejected any dependence on foreign aid and declared that the **Chinese Communist Party (CCP)** would rely on its own army and people to achieve its political goals. Significant military support for the Chinese Communists was not provided by the **Soviet Union**, which limited its material aid to the Chinese to outmoded Japanese weaponry captured at the end of World War II in China's northeast. Thus the CCP largely won the Civil War with weapons captured from the KMT and originally supplied by the **United States**, which helped solidify the concept of "self-reliance" among top CCP military and political **leaders**.

In 1960, when in the midst of the Sino–Soviet Conflict the **Soviet Union** withdrew its technical experts from China and terminated work on 156 different industrial and related projects, Mao reiterated China's determination to be "self-reliant." In effect, this translated into considerable international isolation on China's part from most of the world as it pursued an autarkic strategy of economic growth without external debt that lasted until the "opening up" that began in the early 1970s with the visit to China of U.S. President Richard Nixon. During this period from the early 1960s to the 1970s, China generally avoided formal contacts or strategic alliances with other nations, all of which changed after 1978 as the **People's Republic of China**

(**PRC**) under the rubric of the **open-door policy** pursued a policy of engagement with the global **economy** and established a series of bilateral and multilateral agreements with countries of interest such as **Russia** and the U.S.

"SETTLING ACCOUNTS" ("*QINGSUAN*"). This term has its origins in financial transactions and obligations in Chinese society where at the end of the lunar year people with debts and other binding promises "settle accounts" and clear the books. Politically, the term became a metaphor for seeking revenge against political enemies from the various campaigns and movements, particularly the **Cultural Revolution (1966–1976)**. Since revenge carried a momentum of its own, efforts were made to prohibit the mutual recriminations and antagonisms that "settling accounts" entailed well into the 1980s. At one time, the term could not be used by ordinary people, for instance at restaurants where it means to "pay the check."

SHANGHAI. Located at the eastern end of the Yangtze River delta, *Shanghai* (literally "on the sea") is China's second largest urban area with a total **population** in 2003 estimated at 20 million residents, of which 13.5 million are considered permanent and registered, four million permanent and unregistered, and three million part of the country's **floating population**. Shanghai municipality (*Shanghai shi*) is over 6,000 km² in size and has produced national political figures from **Zhang Chunqiao** during the **Cultural Revolution (1966–1976)** to former **Chinese Communist Party** (**CCP**) General Secretary **Jiang Zemin** and Premier **Zhu Rongji**, both of whom served as the city's mayor from 1985 to 1989 and 1987 to 1990, respectively. The Party secretary of the Shanghai CP in 2005 was Chen Liangyu (1946–) from Zhejiang Province who trained as an engineer and from 1968 to 1970 served as a **People's Liberation Army** (**PLA**) soldier while the mayor was Han Zheng. Other city luminaries include Huang Ju, a former Party secretary and mayor of the city who, in 2005, was a member of the CCP **Politburo** Standing Committee.

Shanghai emerged as a bustling port city during the Song dynasty (960–1279 AD) and, in 1553, it was encompassed by construction of a city wall, which, in imperial China, marked the beginning of a recognized urban area. Shanghai played little role in imperial Chinese history as unlike **Beijing** or nearby Hangzhou, the city never served as an imperial capital but from the late 19th and early 20th centuries on, it emerged as a major industrial and shipping center with substantial commercial links to the West. Opened up by unequal treaties with Great Britain and France, major parts of Shanghai were divided up into concession areas that were reserved for foreign residents and made largely off-limits to most Chinese. Jewish merchants from Iraq, Syria, and **Russia** settled in the city during the 1930s while foreign-owned textile and chemical firms were built along Suzhou Creek, which meanders through the city. Shanghai also became a center of vice, drugs, and prostitution, which earned it the title in Western countries of "The Whore of Asia" along with other less derogatory titles, including "The Paris of the East" and "Queen of the Orient." Shanghai had China's first banks (1848), streetlights (1882), running water (1884), telephones (1881) and its first **automobiles** (1901) and tram (1908). Bombed mercilessly by the Japanese from the air and nearby warships during the **Sino–Japanese War** (**1937–1945**), Shanghai was occupied by Japanese forces until the end of the war. During the ensuing **Civil War** (**1946–1949**), the city was liberated by Communist armies in May 1949.

During the period of central economic planning from 1954 to 1978, the city became a major site of huge **state-owned enterprises** (**SOEs**) producing textiles, handbags, and Forever Bicycles and providing 70 to 80% of the entire tax revenue collected by the central government. With the economic reforms inaugurated in 1978–1979, many of the old SOEs were shuttered and laid off hundreds of thousands of workers but with the construction of new industrial facilities, such as the massive **Baoshan Iron and Steel Complex**, the growth of the port of Shanghai into the largest such facility in Northeast Asia (replacing Pusan, South **Korea**), and infusion of foreign investment into the city's Zhangjiang High-Tech Zone and Xinzhuang Industrial Park, the city quickly rebounded with an unemployment rate in 2004 of just 5% and an **economy** that generates 400,000 new jobs annually. In addition to 8,000 SOEs still operating in the metallurgical, shipbuilding, light **industry**, and petrochemical sector, the city has attracted a number of foreign companies including Nokia, Intel, NEC, Motorola, Siemens, Texas Instruments, and the **Taiwan** laptop maker Tech Front. Foreign automakers, such as Volkswagen and General Motors, also have major operations in Shanghai, along with 1,000 firms from Taiwan as the city's huge pool of industrial **labor** and numerous colleges and technical institutes have proved a major lure making the city one of the most cosmopolitan in China with upward to 100,000 foreign residents, 20,000 of them Japanese. The Pudong Development Zone in the northeast part of the city, which was constructed out of rural marshland and was open to foreign **investment** in 1990, is now home to some of China's largest domestic and foreign institutions of **banking and finance**, making the city the financial capital of the country, especially in the aftermath of the handover of **Hong Kong** to China in 1997. In 2003, the Gross Domestic Product (GDP) of Shanghai came to 625 billion *yuan* and following **Guangzhou (Canton)**, Shanghai residents in 2004 enjoyed the second highest disposable income in China of 14,867 *yuan* (US$1,858).

Along with the economic boom has come a series of classic urban problems including overcrowded streets and subways and an overheated real estate market that is fueled by a substantial influx of international capital that has driven average real estate prices sky high with apartments in the downtown area selling for as much as US$300,000, far beyond the reach of the average Shanghai resident. Despite plans drawn up in the early 1980s for Shanghai to avoid unmanageable traffic and congestion, the lure of automobiles to affluent Shanghai residents have led the city to pass the two million car mark, which was predicted not to occur until 2020. With 500 km of subway track, plans call for an additional 160 km to ease traffic congestion with 70 to 80% of the city's increased air pollution coming from automobiles. Shanghai is also the location of the world's fastest train, a magnetic levitation vehicle that zips from downtown to the airport in 10 minutes but which, like much of the non-auto urban transport in the city, including the subway, is underutilized. Among the city's 4,000 skyscrapers (double the number that are in New York with plans for an additional 1,000 by the end of the decade) is the world's tallest hotel, the 88-story Grand Hyatt, complete with the world's highest swimming pool and longest laundry chute. Pudong is the site of the metallic Jin Mao skyscraper, the third-tallest building in the world, and the partially constructed World Financial Center, which, at 101 storics, will be the tallest building in the world, along with the Pearl TV Tower, which appears as a space needle with a satellite dish. Shanghai's varied **architecture** is the product of such prominent international designers as John Portman, Sir Norman Foster, Michael Graves, and Meinhard von Gerkan and domestic designers from the Shanghai Architectural Institute.

Like many other major metropolitan areas in China, Shanghai also suffers from periodic electricity shortages that hopefully will be alleviated in the future by construction of the **Three Gorges Dam Project** on the Yangtze River in central China. Since the 1960s, rising sea levels and subsidence of Shanghai (exacerbated by over-pumping of ground water) has led to corrective efforts by city officials, including construction of hundreds of kilometers of flood walls and a proposed dam on the city's main river, the Huangpu, to stem sinking that once reached 100 mm a year but has dropped to 10 mm and which has also caused substantial loss of coastline.

In 2004, city authorities announced plans to restore and protect the residential district of *Waitan* or the Bund (which earned the nickname "Shanghai's Vienna") that during World War II had housed nearly 30,000 Jews who had fled Germany and Austria for the peaceful refuge offered by wartime Shanghai. Shanghai is also trying to preserve its famous "stone gate" (*shikumen*)-style residential row houses with interior courtyards built by the British during the colonial era that, at one time, housed 80% of the population but which have been demolished in great numbers to make way for new high-rises. In 1999, Shanghai began publication of the country's first truly English-language newspaper, *Shanghai Daily*, while, in recent years, the city has also hosted the Shanghai Open Tennis tournament played on hard courts at its Xian Xia Stadium. In 2010, Shanghai will host the World Expo on a 1,300-acre site of riverfront land, from which 50,000 residents will be relocated, along with more than 270 factories, including the country's largest shipyard. Among many of Shanghai's cultural contributions that marry Eastern and Western styles is the *cheongsam*, a high-cut, tight-fitting dress that first appeared in 1910, but was banned during the Maoist era (1949–1976) and since the 1980s has reappeared. Native Shanghainese speak the *Wu* dialect, which shares only about 31% lexical similarity to the national language, *putonghua*. Although it is said that Beijing residents "can talk about anything," Shanghainese, it is commonly believed, "can do anything."

SHANGHAI COMMUNIQUÉ (1972). This was the first official joint document that began the normalization of relations between the **United States** and the **People's Republic of China** (**PRC**). The process ended in 1979 when the U.S. and China fully normalized diplomatic relations and exchanged ambassadors.

The Shanghai Communiqué was issued during President Richard Nixon's path-breaking trip to China in February 1972. It effectively signaled the recognition of China's Communist government after more than 20 years of U.S. refusal to accept the **Chinese Communist Party** (**CCP**) regime as the legitimate government of China. The text of the communiqué was not agreed upon until President Nixon's historic trip had nearly ended with his visit to the city of **Shanghai**, hence the title "Shanghai Communiqué." In the document, the U.S. accepted the principle of "one China" by acknowledging that "all Chinese on either side of the **Taiwan** Strait maintain there is but one China and that Taiwan is a part of China." Both China and the U.S. agreed to disagree on whether force could legitimately be used by the Communist government to reincorporate Taiwan into China. In effect, the Shanghai Communiqué allowed the U.S. and China to proceed with normal relations without really solving the knotty Taiwan issue. Ultimately, with full diplomatic recognition between the U.S. and China, the U.S. dropped its mutual defense treaty with Taiwan and ended diplomatic relations with the island. But the passage of the Taiwan Relations Act in 1979 perpetuated U.S. defense commitments in the absence of a formal treaty. U.S. and China differences over how to incorporate Taiwan back into China remain as the Chinese insist they have the right to resort to force, while the U.S. rejects this position. The Shanghai Communiqué also committed both countries to avoid seeking "hegemony," that is domination, in East Asia, though differences remained in how the U.S. and China perceived the evolving triangular relationship between China, the U.S., and the **Soviet Union**.

SHENZHEN. *See* SPECIAL ECONOMIC ZONES (SEZs).

SINO–INDIAN WAR (1962). This was a short but intense conflict between Chinese and Indian troops involving disputed claims over border lands in the Himalayas of **Tibet** and northern **India**. Focus of the conflict was competing claims over the Aksai Chin (Ladakh) territories and conflicts regarding the McMahon "line of actual control" (LAC) that had been established by British colonial authorities in 1914 as the territorial boundary between India and China but rejected by the latter. After weeks of parrying and thrusts by military units on both sides, the Chinese **People's Liberation Army** (**PLA**) attacked in force in October and November 1962 and drove Indian Army units south of the McMahon Line, thereby establishing undisputed Chinese control over 3,750 mi^2 of territory claimed by China, in the east near the Himalayan state of Bhutan and, in the West, near the border with Burma (now Myanmar). Once the fighting receded in late November, China declared a unilateral cease-fire and withdrew its forces (except for border police units) fully 20 km behind the old, disputed frontier. Indian forces lost more than 3,000 men with indeterminate casualties on the Chinese side. The conflict came in the midst of the **United States**–Soviet confrontation in the Cuban Missile Crisis and after years of growing tension in Sino–Indian affairs following the Tibetan revolt in 1959, which led the **Dalai Lama** to flee Tibet for refuge in India. India's close ties with the USSR from the 1950s to the 1990s and its increasingly cordial relations with the U.S. beginning in the late 1950s also helped provoke the outbreak of the Sino–Indian war. A final negotiated settlement of the border issue has never been achieved.

SINO–JAPANESE WAR (1937–1945). The war between China and **Japan** began on 7 July 1937 and ended with the **United States** defeat of the Japanese Empire in 1945. The Chinese–Japanese conflict grew out of a long period of intensifying conflict between the two nations that began with China's unification in 1928 under the **Kuomintang** (**KMT**) Nationalist government. In the 1930s, Japan expanded its control over **Manchuria** that at the time was outside Nationalist control and established the puppet state of Manchukuo in 1932 under the titular authority of Aisin-Gioro Puyi, the last emperor of the Qing dynasty (1644–1911) and a Manchu. Japan then proceeded to gain control over four northern provinces in China proper in 1936 through the use of puppet troops and Chinese political **leaders** opposed to the Nationalist regime of Chiang Kai-shek. War erupted after the infamous 1937 Marco Polo Bridge Incident when an exchange of gunfire between Japanese and Chinese troops just outside Beiping (**Beijing**) served as a pretext for Japan to commence a full-scale invasion of China, though technically war was not formally declared between the two countries until 7 December 1941. Japanese forces quickly overran huge parts of China in 1937 and 1938, forcing Chiang Kai-shek's armies to retreat to the inland city of Chungking (**Chongqing**) in Sichuan Province, trading space for time. In the interim, the Japanese captured the Nationalist capital city of Nanking (Nanjing) and carried out systematic murder of 100,000 civilians in the notorious of Rape of Nanking. All major coastal cities in China came under Japanese control through a series of puppet regimes as Chinese casualties approached 500,000. In 1939, after a failed Chinese counteroffensive, the war bogged down with the Japanese occupying huge stretches of China with more than two million troops. After the U.S. entry into the war, America provided crucial assistance to Nationalist forces while contacts were made with Communist forces holed up in Yan'an, where the **Chinese Communist Party** (**CCP**) successfully mobilized peasant resistance to the Japanese in the vast countryside. By 1945, CCP armies numbered almost one million and Communist-run border governments effectively controlled 50 million people, thereby giving the Communists a distinct advantage in the post–World War II **Civil War** (**1946–1949**). In contrast, the Nationalists emerged from the war with poor morale and weakened popular support that proved fatal in the ensuing struggle with the CCP. The Sino–Japanese War, in effect, fundamentally altered the political landscape in China.

SINO–SOVIET TREATY OF FRIENDSHIP, ALLIANCE, AND MUTUAL ASSISTANCE (1950). Signed by **Chinese Communist Party** (**CCP**) Chairman **Mao Zedong** and Soviet leader **Josef Stalin**, this treaty formally established an alliance between the new Communist government of China and the **Soviet Union**. Stalin was initially reluctant to sign the treaty because he suspected the new Communist government in China would be similar to the Communist regime in Yugoslavia under Marshal Josef Tito, which had broken with Stalin in 1948. It took the outbreak of the **Korean War** in 1950 to convince the Soviet leader of China's true Communist credentials that ultimately led Stalin to sign on. Although the treaty was supposed to remain in force for 30 years, it was effectively dead by the early 1960s when the Sino–Soviet Conflict arose. Formally, the treaty was not terminated until China announced its withdrawal in 1979.

The focus of the treaty was purportedly on preventing a reemergence of Japanese fascism in East Asia. In addition to its military goals, the treaty also called for economic and cultural ties between China and the Soviet Union that flourished until 1960. In 1964, China formally accused the Soviet Union of having violated terms of the treaty when the USSR withdrew more than 1,000 technical experts working in China in 1960 and canceled 156 industrial and scientific projects that were never completed. This Sino–Soviet Treaty of Friendship, Allianc,e and Mutual Assistance should be differentiated from the Sino–Soviet Treaty of Friendship and Alliance that was signed in 1945 with the **Kuomintang** (**KMT**) and which defined the Soviet position in immediate post-war China.

"SLAUGHTERING TEN THOUSAND ERRONEOUSLY RATHER THAN LETTING ONE GUILTY ESCAPE" (*"NINGKE CUOSHA YIWAN, BUKE FANGUO YIGE"*). A phrase popular during the **Cultural Revolution** (**1966–1976**) and generally followed by **Red Guards** who were willing to murder innocent individuals just to ensure that people purportedly "guilty" of political crimes would not escape. This notion has been prominent throughout the history of the **Chinese Communist Party** (**CCP**) and blocked any effort to introduce the "assumption of innocence" into the Chinese legal code. Legally, people charged with a crime in China are assumed to be guilty and the result is that, without adequate due process of law, many innocents have indeed been "slaughtered" to ensure that a "guilty" one does not escape. This includes people incarcerated in prison and the large number of people executed in China, a country that employs the death penalty gratuitously for hundreds of **crimes**.

SNOW, EDGAR (1905–1972). Perhaps the most famous American journalist to visit China, Edgar Snow is most remembered for his interviews conducted with **Chinese Communist Party** (**CCP**) Chairman **Mao Zedong** in the late 1930s in the Communist redoubt of Yan'an. Snow's accounts of talks with Mao and his visit to Yan'an in the late 1930s are contained in his best-known work, *Red Star over China*. Snow also worked in China for the Chinese Industrial Cooperative Movement, along with **Rewi Alley**, and established a magazine advocating democracy for China that was closed down by the Japanese occupation force in northern China in 1939. Snow left China in 1941 for the **United States**. After World War II, the McCarthy hearings led Snow and his wife to move to Switzerland. In the 1960s and again in 1970, Snow made return visits to China, where he acted as a liaison between the Chinese and American governments in reestablishing diplomatic contacts that ultimately led to the visit to China in 1972 by President Richard Nixon. Edgar Snow died of cancer the very week in February 1972 when President Nixon visited **Beijing**.

SOCIAL PROTESTS. During the Maoist era (1949–1976), social discontent and unease were channeled into mass campaigns such as the **Cultural Revolution (1966–1976)** that often targeted local and even high-level officials. Since the end of mass campaigns and especially with the inauguration of economic reforms in 1978–1979, Chinese citizens suffering social grievances and resentment have increasingly resorted to various forms of social protest that have often resulted in violence. While the primary cause of the increasing discontent is the growing gap between rich and poor in China that, in 2004, was one of the largest in the world, specific cases of strikes, demonstrations, violent confrontations with police and officials, and highly staged suicides by aggrieved parties stem from a variety of economic, social, and political sources that the Chinese government finds increasingly difficult to control. The first major violent outburst occurred in 1992–1993 in mass protests in Sichuan Province against increased taxes and exactions for local infrastructure projects that culminated in attacks on property and violent clashes between government officials and villagers that required intervention of provincial police. Even as the central government issued circulars urging **Chinese Communist Party (CCP)** authorities and governments at all levels to lighten the burden on farmers, in the tradition of "officials driving the people to rebel" (*guanbi minfan*), outbursts of social unrest were sparked largely by charges of **corruption**, high unemployment, and excessive taxation. Concentrated primarily in the countryside but also in some urban areas, these short but intense uprisings continued into the late 1990s and early 2000s, with one of the largest protests occurring in 1999 by 5,000 farmers in Daolin Township, Hunan Province.

In 2004, local disturbances and cases of social protest in China numbered about 74,000, a seven-fold increase over 1993 when some 10,000 incidents were reported. A total of three million people were involved in protests ranging from a few hundred people to several thousand, sometimes resulting in casualties, such as had occurred in the southern town of Dongzhou in 2005, when more than 20 people were killed by paramilitary forces. And although the outbreaks generally remain localized, with little evidence of nationwide leadership or coordination, the advent of the **Internet** and text messaging have allowed for greater exchange of information and online circulation of petitions that have begun to cross provincial and regional lines even as the official media largely ignore all but the most dramatic incidents. In the tradition of "benevolent" government practiced in China since the imperial era, the response of officials to such protestors has often entailed a combination of payoffs to the rank-and-file, isolation and arrests of **leaders**, and promises of future improvement but with little attempt to institutionalize the political and legal reforms for resolving conflicts in a systematic and non-confrontational manner as no formal dialogue between Chinese citizens and the one-party state yet exists.

In rural areas, most of the protests occur when farmers are cheated out of their land by corrupt local officials often acting in cahoots with developers who make deals without consulting the local **population** and offer little-to-no compensation as China's farmers are still prohibited from owning land. In China's rush to modernization since 1978–1979, 40 million farmers have been displaced, in many cases, by giant hydroelectric projects, such as the Three Gate Gorge (*Sanmenxia*) dam built in the 1960s on the Yellow River in Henan Province that spurred one of the first cases of long-term organized protests by displaced farmers who confronted **People's Liberation Army (PLA)** troops in open battles throughout the 1980s. More recent cases of confrontation between authorities and displaced persons came in late 2004 in Sichuan Province, where tens of thousands of villagers from the Hanyuan Reservoir area staged a series of protests over their forced relocation to make way for the Pubugou Dam. More than 10,000 soldiers were deployed against the protestors, who, at one point, surrounded and detained for several hours the provincial Party secretary. In all, several villagers and two police officers were reported killed. Because China has plans to build additional large-scale hydroelectric stations and large-scale power plants over the next several years, more such outbreaks are likely as farmers are relocated onto marginal lands, where their capacity to make a livelihood is seriously undermined.

Social protests in China's urban areas have largely come in the form of strikes, demonstrations, and even riots largely by workers laid-off from **state-owned enterprises** (**SOEs**) and/or individuals, many from the **floating population**, whose wages are in arrears and/or who suffer from inadequate **health care** and paltry pension payments. Since the early 1990s, and especially following the 1997 15th National Party Congress, some 60 million employees of SOEs have been laid off with many forced to "retire" (*xiagang*), which, according to the Ministry of Public Security, provoked the number of worker protests to grow "like a violent wind." Even as China, on average, created 10 million new jobs annually, in many cities in the northeast rust belt, where shutdowns of SOEs have had a major impact on local employment, violent confrontations between workers and authorities have broken out. The worst cases occurred in 2004 among 30,000 people in Qiqihar, Heilongjiang Province, 7,000 workers in Xianyang Municipality, Shaanxi Province, 100,000 coal miners in Huainan, Anhui Province, 80,000 workers in Wanzhou outside **Chongqing**, and 3,000 employees of a PLA-owned plant in Luzhou, Sichuan, who faced termination as a result of "restructuring." Yet, even the most prosperous areas, such as the Shenzhen **Special Economic Zone** (**SEZ**), were hit by similar protests, when, in October 2004, 3,000 employees of an electronics factory disrupted traffic in the entire city to protest low wages and harsh working conditions.

Other major issues that have provoked protests include residents attempting to shut down highly polluting factories as occurred in two cities in 2004 and 2005 in Zhejiang Province; private tradesmen protesting abuses by tax collectors; students in **Tibet** protesting officials' failure to provide jobs to graduates; urban residents taking to the streets and blocking traffic to protest official corruption and waste; retired soldiers of the PLA taking advantage of the officially sanctioned anti-**Japan** demonstrations in Beijing in 2005 to complain about inadequate retirement and social security benefits; investors sitting in at government offices to protest local authorities' involvement in an oil-privatization scheme that caused massive financial losses; workers in **Hong Kong**–owned textile plants in Guangdong going on strike to protest arbitrary pay reductions; and pitched battles between ethnic **minorities** and **Han** over a variety of sometimes minor disputes. All these and others have fueled a level of social unrest that even official news media in China have warned could lead to a "contradictions-stricken age" of chaos.

The response, in the 1990s, to these outbreaks by General Secretary **Jiang Zemin** was to call for "rule by virtue" as the solution to growing instability even as his policies strongly favored urban areas. The new leadership of General Secretary **Hu Jintao** and Premier **Wen Jiabao** called for a more serious attempt to address problems of income inequality, though their advocacy of a "harmonious society" probably does little to assuage aggrieved citizens who, with an increasing "consciousness of rights" and reliance on modern **technology**, have engaged in higher levels of interaction. Proposals to do away with the long-standing Communist system of "petitioning" (*shangfang*) that has its roots in the imperial era could scrap the only channel available to people to air their grievances, though few such petitions (two out of every 1,000) ever warrant any official response. Along with proposals by major urban areas, such as Chongqing to limit land transfers, the capacity of a new breed of social activists and lawyers in China to organize lawsuits on behalf of aggrieved parties provides one relatively new legal outlet. For those unaware or unable to afford such avenues, their individual actions of protests remain the only alternatives. *See also* ENVIRONMENT.

SOCIALISM (*SHEHUIZHUYI*). In orthodox Marxist terms, the creation of a socialist society in which private property is abolished and the state begins to wither away, presupposes certain historically necessary changes, namely capitalist formation and the full development of an industrialized society. An abundance of material goods, creation of sophisticated **technology**, and emergence of a complex division of labor defined by Karl Marx as the preconditions for socialism did not exist in China in 1949. The failure of previous regimes in China to overcome the country's economic backwardness and underdevelopment created the basis for the Communists' rise to power, but it also denied them the foundations on which to begin the transition to Communism. Thus the **Chinese Communist Party**

(**CCP**) faced a severe dilemma: forsake the socialization of the means of production and employ capitalist measures to create the necessary social base for a socialist system; or, rely on a state machine to eliminate "prematurely" private property and take over the tasks of industrialization and technological revolution to create the very foundations that Marx described. During the era of **Mao Zedong** (1949–1976), the first strategy was chosen as any sign of "capitalism" was crushed by the CCP while a powerful state bureaucracy emerged to organize and develop the **economy** toward full industrialization. Since the economic reforms of 1978–1979, however, the regime under **Deng Xiaoping** and subsequent **leaders** has recognized the critical importance of China's backwardness. Whereas in the **Great Leap Forward** (**1958–1960**), Mao Zedong trumpeted the beginning of China's "transition to Communism," Deng's regime declared that since the 1950s the country has been in the "primary stage of socialism," a historical stage that makes greater reliance on capitalist forces more ideologically acceptable and which is slated to last at least a century until "socialist modernization" is fully achieved. The **People's Republic of China** (**PRC**) is now said to have "socialism with Chinese characteristics," that is a mixture of market economy with state-run industries. With income disparities growing and private wealth on the rise, however, it is difficult to predict the future character of socialism in China. *See also* "SOCIALIST SPIRITUAL CIVILIZATION."

SOCIALIST EDUCATION MOVEMENT (1962–1966). Also known as the "four cleans" (*siqing*), this mass movement was a harbinger of the **Cultural Revolution** (**1966–1976**) and was designed to eliminate **corruption** primarily in rural Party and government organizations. Fraud in the handling of accounts and determination of **work points** for peasants, and mismanagement of state-owned warehouses and assets, were the original targets of the campaign. In 1965, the movement was expanded to "purification" of politics and economics and rectification of ideology among Party members. The fundamental contradiction in Chinese society was declared to be that between "**socialism** and capitalism," which eclipsed the previous emphasis on low-level corruption and venality in the rural administrative apparatus. During the Cultural Revolution, **Liu Shaoqi** was accused of restricting the target of the Socialist Education Movement to corruption and ignoring the more fundamental conflict between "socialism and capitalism" in the Party. As the "number one **capitalist roader** (*zouzipai*) in the **Chinese Communist Party (CCP)**," Liu was vilified for obstructing **Mao Zedong** in his goal of carrying out a broader attack on ideological deviants in the CCP. Thus, the Socialist Education Movement was expanded and directly led to the widespread purges and political struggles of the Cultural Revolution.

"SOCIALIST SPIRITUAL CIVILIZATION." In order to counteract the threat to its legitimacy by contact with the outside world, the **Chinese Communist Party (CCP)**, in the early 1980s, launched a campaign to "build socialist spiritual civilization." Communist thinking, ideals, beliefs, morality, and discipline were to be cultivated in official propaganda and educational curricula as a counterweight to the "material civilization" associated with Western society and a modern **economy**. Radical leftists in the CCP attempted to use this campaign to block all reform efforts and undermine **Deng Xiaoping's** plan to depoliticize **education** and encourage professional training. Building "socialist spiritual civilization" was also directed at combating the attraction to Western culture by the young and the spreading enchantment among the general **population** to **"always thinking of money"** (*yiqie xiang qian kan*) and the enjoyment of consumer goods. Communist ideological principles were declared to be the "core" of "socialist spiritual civilization" that distinguished China from the West. In this sense, this campaign was reminiscent of the effort in the late 19th century to distinguish Chinese "essence" (*ti*) from Western "utility" (*yong*). In 1986, reformist forces led by **Hu Yaobang** severely restricted this campaign and prevented it from expanding into a general assault on the reform program.

SONG PING (1917–). Song Ping studied in the 1940s in Yan'an at the **Central Party School** and the Institute of Marxism–Leninism. In the late 1950s, he became vice-minister of the State Planning Commission and during the 1960s was put in charge of defense construction projects for inland areas, the so-called **Third Front**. He was active in the **Cultural Revolution (1966–1976)** in Gansu Province and, in 1976, read a eulogy to **Mao Zedong** following the chairman's death.

In 1983, he became a state councilor and minister of the State Planning Commission and in 1987 assumed the directorship of the **Chinese Communist Party** (**CCP**) Organization Department, where, in 1988, he opposed the creation of a professional civil service as proposed by General Secretary **Zhao Ziyang**. In June 1989, as a member of the CCP conservative faction, which supported the military crackdown against the second **Beijing Spring**, Song became a member of the **Politburo** Standing Committee but was dropped from that body at the 1992 First Plenum of the 14th CCP Central Committee along with other elderly members including **Wan Li**, **Yang Shangkun**, and **Yao Yilin**. Along with **Song Renqiong** and Madame **Deng Yingchao**, Song Ping was long considered one of China's prominent "**revolutionary elders**" (*geming yuanlao*) who exercised considerable influence from behind the scenes. In 2005, Song Ping published an article in *Seeking Truth* (*Qiushi*), which lauded the conservative economic ideas of **Chen Yun** and elliptically criticized economic policies that had produced enormous income gaps between urban and rural residents and led to the impoverishment of many farmers, policies that Chen Yun had previously opposed.

SONG [SOONG] QINGLING (1893–1981). Wife of Sun Yat-sen and later a vice-chairman and honorary **president of the People's Republic of China**, Song Qingling was born in **Shanghai** and attended school in the **United States**, receiving her B.A. in 1913 at Wesleyan College for Women in Georgia. Upon returning to China, Song became secretary to Dr. Sun Yat-sen, leader of the Chinese Republican Revolution. Song and Dr. Sun married in **Japan** in 1914 over her father's strong opposition to their union. During the Second Revolution in 1917, Sun and Song moved their base to **Guangzhou** (**Canton**) in southern China to join up with Chen Chiung-ming, the local warlord. The conflict between Chen and Sun over expansion into the Guangdong region and over the larger issue of national unification led Chen to stage a mutiny on 16 June 1922. The arduous escape, which resulted in a miscarriage for the young bride, turned Song into a national heroine.

During their 10-year marriage, Song remained supportive of Sun's political ideals that unfortunately were disrupted by Sun's sudden death on 25 March 1925. The assassination of Nationalist leader and

Sun confidante Liao Zhongkai in 1925 and the purges of Communists and other left-wing elements in the **Kuomintang (KMT)** before the Northern Expedition in 1926–1927 convinced Song that she should carry the banner of her late husband. At the Second National Congress of the KMT in 1926, Song was elected to the Central Executive Committee and was re-elected at every subsequent congress until 1945. In 1927, Song openly opposed her sister Song Meiling's marriage to Chiang Kai-shek, the KMT leader and reputed heir to Sun Yat-sen's political legacy. This led Song Qingling to join Teng Yen-ta, a general who had turned against Chiang, to form a Third Force as an alternative to the KMT and the **Chinese Communist Party (CCP)**. After the outbreak of the **Sino–Japanese War** in 1937, Song moved to **Hong Kong**, where she founded the China Defense League in 1938 to channel medical relief to Communist bases in the hinterland. She was considered a Communist by most Westerners, although she was not a Party member.

In September 1949, Song Qingling was invited to Beiping (subsequently renamed **Beijing**) as a delegate to the newly formed **Chinese People's Political Consultative Conference (CPPCC)** legislative body, which announced the formation of the PRC on 1 October 1949. Song became one of three non-Communist vice-chairmen of the government and during the years until her death in 1981, she was offered many other posts as she continued with welfare work and led frequent delegations abroad. During the **Cultural Revolution (1966–1976)**, Song was labeled as a "bourgeois liberal" and her house was stormed by **Red Guards**, but she was rescued by the personal intervention of **Zhou Enlai**. Stricken by leukemia in 1960, Song, despite her weakened state, lived nearly 20 more years, and, shortly before her death, she joined the CCP. The only sister to survive her, Song Meiling (Madame Chiang Kai-shek) refused to attend her funeral. The Song Qingling Foundation was established in 1983 for undertakings in culture, **education**, and **science** for young people.

SONG RENQIONG (1909–2005). Born in Hunan Province, Song Renqiong was a graduate of the **Kuomintang (KMT)** Whampoa Military Academy in the 1920s and, after joining with the **Chinese Communist Party (CCP)**, he took part in the **Long March (1934–1935)**. A close associate of **Liu Bocheng**, Song organized so-called Death Corps in Shanxi Province in 1942; in 1945, he was elected to the CCP Central Committee. In the early 1950s, Song served in Southwest China regional government and, in 1954, returned to **Beijing**, where he became a member of the National Defense Council. In the early 1960s, Song became deputy secretary-in-chief of the Central Committee and minister of the Third Ministry of Machine Building, a key part of China's military industrial infrastructure. Throughout the **Cultural Revolution (1966–1976)**, Song was repeatedly attacked by **Red Guards** but returned in 1979 to become director of the CCP Organization Department. In 1982, he was elected to the **Politburo**. In 1985, he resigned to join the **Central Advisory Commission (CAC)**, a political half-way house to retirement. Song was long considered one of China's "eight immortals," a phrase borrowed from Chinese folklore and similar to "**revolutionary elders**" (*geming yuanlao*), which has been used to describe elderly members of the CCP, including most notably **Deng Xiaoping**, who, in the 1980s, did not hold top official positions but nevertheless set policy from behind the scenes.

SOUTH-TO-NORTH WATER DIVERSION PROJECT. First proposed in 1952 by **Chinese Communist Party (CCP)** Chairman **Mao Zedong** and finally inaugurated in 2002, the South-to-North Water Diversion Project is the largest such water conservancy scheme in the world for transferring upward of 45 billion m^3 of water from China's water-rich south to the parched north, including the cities of **Beijing** and **Tianjin**. The project consists of three separate diversion canals— an eastern, central, and western route—all more than 1,000 km in length that will draw water from the lower, middle, and upper reaches of the Yangtze River, including the reservoir created by the construction of the massive **Three Gorges Dam Project**, diverting it to the valleys of the Yellow, Huai, and Hai rivers where one-third of the country's farmland, grain output, and GDP are produced. Work began on the eastern line in 2002 running from Jiangsu Province along the Yangtze River and using the 1,400-year-old Grand Canal as its main body. In 2003, the central canal was begun and will take water from the Danjiangkou Reservoir, which was built in 1958 in Hubei Province, transferring it to the large cities of Beijing, Tianjin, Shijiazhuang (Hebei Province), and Zhengzhou (Henan Province). The western line, which will cut through high mountains near **Tibet** to link the Yangtze River with the headwaters of the Yellow River, is still in the planning stages and will not be completed until 2050. The project is expected to cost 486 billion *yuan* (US$59 billion), twice the cost of the Three Gorges Dam Project, and is to be financed by a combination of central government allocations, bank loans, and monies from China's water fund.

In 2004, a nine-bank consortium was established to coordinate the financing led by the State Development Bank and involving China's four main commercial institutions of **banking and finance**—China Construction Bank, Bank of China, Agricultural Bank of China, and the Industrial and Commercial Bank of China—along with the privately owned Minsheng Bank. Planning and oversight of the project is in the hands of the South-to-North Water Diversion Construction Commission, which is attached to the State Council and takes full responsibility for fund raising, construction, operation management, loan repayment, and insured value while operating separate from local governments in order to reduce the level of **corruption** that has plagued such large capital infrastructure projects in China in the past. The transferred water will be sold to local waterworks via corporations set up by the Commission. The project will require the relocation of upward of 400,000 people in seven provinces and municipalities during construction of the three lines, which will be carried out under "Provisional Methods for Land Requisition Compensation and Residents Relocation" promulgated in 2005. There are also concerns with the impact on the **environment** from pollution of the diverted water from agricultural, industrial, and urban areas along the diversion routes so much so that one-third of the project's entire cost is earmarked for 379 separate pollution-control and water treatment projects. The impact on land use, possible regional climatic variations, and agricultural productivity along the planned routes has also been the subject of a joint China–Italian project known as the Sustainable Water Integrated Management of the South-to-North Water Diversion Project East Route that was launched in 2004. The fate of cultural relics and antiquities in the construction zone poses problems similar to those in the building of the Three Gorges Dam Project. However, with water shortages worsening in North China, especially Beijing, due to severe droughts in the early 2000s, the project has been put on a fast-track for completion of the eastern and central lines in six to eight years and is already reportedly strapped by financial difficulties and environmental problems. *See also* SOCIAL PROTESTS.

SOVIET UNION. Relations between the **Chinese Communist Party** (**CCP**) and the Soviet Union ranged from military alliance and cooperation in the international Communist movement to confrontation and outright hostility that in 1969 brought China and the USSR to the brink of war. Prior to the ascension to power of the CCP in 1949, Soviet leader **Josef Stalin**, after maintaining diplomatic relations with the Republic of China (ROC) for years, advised CCP Chairman **Mao Zedong** not to attempt to seize power but to negotiate with his **Kuomintang** (**KMT**) rivals. Following the victory of the CCP during the **Civil War** (**1946–1949**) in which Soviet assistance to its Chinese Communist brethren was paltry, Mao Zedong traveled to Moscow for a two-month visit in late 1949 and early 1950, where he secured low-interest Soviet loans of US$300 million, a 30-year military alliance against **Japan**, and an agreement to the Treaty of Friendship, Alliance, and Mutual Assistance. Despite his rather cool relations with the Soviet leader, Mao Zedong acknowledged Stalin as leader of the international Communist movement while the **People's Republic of China** (**PRC**) and the USSR allied in the **Korean War** (**1950–1953**).

In the immediate aftermath of the death of Stalin in 1953, relations remained cordial as Stalin's successor, Nikita Khrushchev, visited China in 1954 and promised to remove all troops from the area around the port of Lüshun, held over since the end of World War II. Although Mao did not openly dissent from Khrushchev's 1956 De-Stalinization speech (also known as the Secret Speech) delivered to the 20th Congress of the Communist Party of the Soviet Union (CPSU), which contained a scathing critique of the enormous "crimes of the Stalin era," Mao hinted that the speech reeked of "**revisionism**." Nevertheless, following the outbreak of the **Hungarian Revolution** (**1956**), China expressed strong support for the "leading role" of the USSR in the international Communist movement and denounced the reformist efforts of the Hungarian CP and its intellectual supporters among the Petofi Club. From 1956 to 1958, the conflict remained essentially submerged in inter-Party statements as China would denounce Marshal Tito of Yugoslavia as a surrogate of Khrushchev and the USSR and the Russians would respond by attacking Enver Hoxha of Albania (China's lone ally in Eastern Europe) as a surrogate for Mao Zedong. In 1958, in the second of two **Taiwan Straits Crises**, China expected full-scale Soviet support that was not forthcoming as the USSR was undoubtedly concerned with the reckless behavior of its Chinese counterparts in provoking a military confrontation with the **United States** and the ROC on **Taiwan**—a confrontation the Chinese would ultimately lose. Even as Khrushchev accused China of warmongering, China's concern with the direction of Soviet assistance and support mushroomed in 1959 when the USSR sided with **India** in its growing border conflict with China. The coup d' grace came in the decision by the Soviet Union in 1959 to terminate the recently signed defense accord with China in which the Russians had apparently offered the Chinese technical assistance in constructing an **atomic bomb**. A short visit to China in 1959 by Khrushchev after his trip to the U.S. (which coincided with the 10th anniversary celebrations of the PRC) failed to assuage the Chinese who accused the Soviet Union of siding with the U.S. Khrushchev also angered the Chinese by denouncing the **Great Leap Forward** (**1958–1960**), saying that the transition to Communism could not be achieved in such a rapid and slipshod manner, even though some Russians evidently sympathized with this strain of Chinese idealism.

The outbreak of the Sino–Soviet Conflict occurred with the public rupture in Chinese–Soviet relations in 1960 at a Congress of the Romania Communist Party in June, where Khrushchev openly attacked the Chinese representative **Peng Zhen**. This was followed by another clash in November 1960 at a conference of 81 Communist parties in Moscow that was largely papered over by a final, vaguely worded resolution—even as the Chinese denounced the ideological errors of the Russian leadership in a *Red Flag* article titled "Long Live Leninism." Conflict arose again in 1961 at the 22nd Party Congress of the Communist Party of the Soviet Union, as the USSR severed relations with Albania and decided to end all economic and military support to the PRC, including the termination of 156 scientific and industrial projects and the withdrawal from China of more than 1,000 technical personnel, who left the country with blueprints in hand. Although the Soviet Union supported India during the brief **Sino–Indian War** (**1962**), Mao criticized Khrushchev for backing down during the October 1962 Cuban Missile Crisis. The signing of the Nuclear Test Ban Treaty between the U.S. and the USSR in 1963 convinced the Chinese that the Soviet leadership was hopelessly revisionist and had surrendered in its holy war against **imperialism**, even as joint Sino–Soviet talks were held in Moscow in 1963 to resolve their bilateral differences. Khrushchev criticized China's overly aggressive policies as leading to a possible nuclear war; in 1964, Mao claimed that a counter-revolution had occurred in the Soviet Union. Despite a high-level meeting in 1965 between Soviet Premier Aleksei Kosygin and Mao Zedong and **Liu Shaoqi** in **Beijing**, Party-to-Party relations were broken off with both sides issuing public condemnation of the other—"Proposal Concerning the General Line of the International Communist Movement" by China and the Soviet response in the form of an "Open Letter of the CPSU." Chinese accusations against Soviet revisionism would continue even as the Russians, along with the Chinese, provided substantial aid to the North Vietnamese Communists in their war with the U.S. military. China condemned the Soviet August 1968 invasion of Czechoslovakia. From March to June 1969, armed clashes between Chinese and Soviet forces occurred on both the western and eastern borders, which almost led to outright war as the two countries sparred over control of the uninhabited Damansky (*Zhenbao*) Island on the Ussuri River. Despite another hastily arranged meeting at the Beijing airport between **Zhou Enlai** and Soviet Premier Kosygin, by 1970, China was openly warning of nuclear war with the USSR and undertook civil defense efforts in its major cities, such as Beijing, where a vast network of tunnels and facilities was built in the "underground city" (*dixia cheng*) to shelter the **population** during a possible nuclear exchange. The **Lin Biao** Affair in 1971 further complicated the relationship but, fortunately, cooler heads ultimately prevailed and both sides reverted to rhetorical conflicts, though significant military forces were maintained by the two countries on their mutual border well into the 1980s.

A brief thaw in Sino–Soviet relations occurred in the mid-1970s as China sought out Soviet views on the border issue. In 1980, negotiations between the two sides were carried out after China formally ended its 1950 alliance with Moscow. These talks achieved little success however as China demanded the Soviet Union remove "three obstacles" to normalizing relations: a Soviet pullout from **Afghanistan**; withdrawal of Soviet support for the North Vietnamese occupation of **Cambodia**; and reduction of Soviet troops along the Sino–Soviet border. In a major speech in March 1982, Soviet President Leonid Brezhnev appealed for better Sino–Soviet relations "on the basis of mutual respect for each other's interests and non-interference in each other's affairs" and in September called for a normalization of relations as his top priority. A visit to Moscow by Chinese Premier **Li Peng** in 1985 led to an agreement with Soviet Party General Secretary Mikhail Gorbachev for major improvements in Sino–Soviet relations, which apparently allowed both countries to downplay an armed border clash in July 1986. Following a 1988 visit to the Soviet Union by Chinese Foreign Minister **Qian Qichen**, Soviet leader Mikhail Gorbachev visited Beijing in May 1989 and agreed with **Deng Xiaoping** to full normalization as both countries agreed to halt military aid to the contending parties in **Cambodia** as North Vietnamese troops withdrew. This effectively ended the Sino–Soviet conflict as relations between the two states consistently improved since the collapse of the USSR and the establishment of its successor the Russian Federation under Boris Yeltsin and his successor Vladimir Putin. *See also* FOREIGN POLICY; RUSSIA.

SPACE PROGRAM. China's space program began in 1956 when, despite the country's enormous poverty, it opened the Number Five Institute of Missile and Rocket Research attached to the Ministry of Defense. The primary force behind the space program for the next 30 years was **Qian Xuesen**, an American-trained rocket engineer, formerly attached to the Jet Propulsion Laboratory in California, who was expelled from the **United States** in 1955 on charges of being a Communist sympathizer, and Zhao Jiuzhang, who initiated development of China's first satellite. In 1957, the Chinese government announced the "Mission 581" program, which aimed at making satellite launches and, in 1958, carried out construction of the Jiuquan Satellite Launch Center in Gansu Province, where most of the country's space launches and tests have since been conducted. In 1960, China developed its first rocket, aided by Russian scientists, the first in the

"Long March" (*Changzheng*) series that would ultimately number 12 different rockets. China's first successful launch of a vehicle came in 1964, when tubes containing albino rats and white mice were lifted by Long March 1 to an altitude of 70 km. In 1966, the Taiyuan Satellite Launch Center situated in Shanxi Province near the Gobi Desert was established and put into operation in 1968 and is believed to be an ideal site for launching solar-synchronous satellites. On 24 April 1970, China became the fifth country in the world to send a satellite into orbit when the "East is Red" (*Dongfang hong*) vehicle was lifted into space on a Long March rocket and remained in orbit for 26 days transmitting the revolutionary song by the same name. China approved "Project 714" to develop the *Shuguang* manned spacecraft for launch in 1973, but cancelled the entire program one year later.

During the political turmoil surrounding the later stages of the **Cultural Revolution (1966–1976)**, China's space program largely ground to a halt but was revived in the mid- to late 1970s and early 1980s with the accession to power of **Deng Xiaoping**. The recovery of a remote sensing satellite from orbit in 1975 was a major breakthrough that led to hints in the Chinese press, in 1979, that China was planning a manned space flight. Although this effort was apparently halted by fiscal constraints and technological setbacks, in 1980, China successfully launched its first carrier rocket to the Pacific Ocean. In 1984, a third launch site was constructed at Xichang in southwestern Sichuan Province, which provided a capacity to place satellites in geostationary orbit. The new site also relieved pressure on the Jiuquan and Taiyuan sites, especially as China began to enter the commercial satellite launch market in 1986. In 1990, China launched Asia's first regional communications satellite, the American-made Asia-sat 1, followed by the Asia-Pacific No. 1, and the Australian-owned Optus-B3 satellites in 1994. In 1992, the State Council prodded by President **Jiang Zemin** adopted "Project 921" aimed at achieving manned space flight in the near term as Chinese officials visited Russia's space program that culminated in an agreement for China to acquire Russian space **technology** and for Chinese pilots to undergo training at the Star City launch site in **Russia** in 1997. Throughout this period, Chinese rockets incurred several failures in 1991, 1992, 1995 (when a Long March 2E rocket exploded during takeoff from Xichang, killing eight people), plus two more failures in 1996. With the assistance of U.S. firms, such as Hughes Space and Communications, the problems were ironed out. In 1994, China successfully launched small animals into space and, in 1996, recovered a satellite that had been sent into orbit for scientific and technological experiments. Two successful launches of commercial satellites occurred in 1997, one into a preordained orbit and the other in a meteorological satellite in 1999.

China's drive to put a man in space gathered momentum in 1998 with the development of the *Shenzhou* ("Divine Vessel") space vehicle, which weighs more than eight tons and is roughly modeled on the Russian Soyuz craft with a pressurized capsule for up to three people and a forward module where astronauts can work. One year later, *Shenzhou* I was launched and put into orbit by the 19-stories-high Long March 2F rocket. After circling the earth 14 times, the vessel returned and was recovered. At the same time, China began selecting and training a corps of future astronauts (known as *taikonauts* as the word *tai* in Chinese means "space") that, in 1998, was narrowed to 12 former **People's Liberation Army** (**PLA**) pilots. In 2001, *Shenzhou* II was successfully launched and returned for a hard landing in Inner Mongolia followed in 2002 by the successful launch and recovery of *Shenzhou* III, which orbited the earth 108 times. In the same year, China, whose space program was historically marked by great secrecy and which has been excluded from the International Space Station, publicly announced plans to build a space station within 15 years. And following the successful launch of *Shenzhou* IV in December 2002, the country also announced its intention of putting a man in space.

On 15 October 2003, China successfully launched the *Shenzhou* V from Jiuquan with *taikonaut* Yang Liwei on board for a flight that made 14 orbits around the globe that was followed up in October 2005 by the launch of *Shenzhou* VI with two astronauts on a five-day mission. Overall, by October 2003, China had 79 launches, of which 67 were successes, eight complete failures, and four partial failures (satellites were placed into incorrect orbits). Most of these launches were of Chinese communications, weather, remote sensing, navigation, and scientific satellites, although an unknown number undoubtedly had dual military applications. Some 27 launches in all were conducted on a commercial basis through the Great Wall Industries Corporation for foreign countries and/or companies, including the

U.S. Because virtually all communication satellites requiring commercial launch services are built in the U.S. or include U.S.-made components, U.S. export licenses must be granted to send satellites to China for launch. While the administration of President Ronald Reagan negotiated an agreement with China for commercial launches in return for the commitment of the **People's Republic of China** (**PRC**) to three **United Nations** (**UN**) treaties concerning technology protection, allegations emerged in 1997 that China had managed to obtain militarily useful information from two American companies (Loral and Hughes) following a launch failure. Since 1999, the U.S. has not issued any export licenses for commercial satellite launches, which led China to suspend its commercial operations. China has developed international cooperation arrangements with several countries, including Russia, Brazil, and the European Union, with which China is participating in the EU–ESA Galileo navigation satellite system that will simulate the American Global Positioning System. Two tracking stations exist outside the territorial boundaries of the PRC, one in the Pacific and another in Namibia, Africa.

The major organizations and companies involved in China's space program include the China National Space Administration (China's "NASA") and the China Aerospace Corporation (CASC) established in 1993 out of the former Ministry of Aerospace Industry. Five main research academies are organized under CASC: Chinese Academy of Launch Vehicle Technology, which is responsible for the design and manufacture of the Long March series of liquid propellant launch vehicles; the Chinese Academy of Space Technology, which designs and manufactures satellites, including the original "East is Red" craft in 1970; the Academy of Solid Rockets; Academy of Tactical Missile Technology; and the Academy of Cruise Missile Technology. Overall, supervision of the space program is in the hands of the State Commission of **Science**, Technology, and Industry for National Defense under the State Council. A host of smaller organizations are responsible for developing specialty payloads, such as the **Shanghai** Institute of Technological Physics for remote sensing vehicles and the Shanghai Institute of Microsystems and Information Technologies for China's *Chuangxin* small satellite. China Remote Sensing Satellite Ground Station provides commercial service of Spot, Landsat, ERS, and future ZY-1 images while the China Satellite Communications

Corporation is the country's largest satellite telecommunications company operating ChinaSat-6 and ChinaStar-1, as well as GlobalStar and ACeS services. BD Star Technologies operates the *Beidou* Navigation System and provides GPS and Glanoss services. Long March launchers are still marketed internationally by Great Wall Industries Corporation, which retains business relations with companies and institutes in Europe, Latin America, Australia, and North America. Since the 1950s, departments of aeronautics have been established in a number of Chinese universities, including Northwest Polytechnical University, which has granted 5,000 undergraduate and 600 graduate degrees in aeronautics since 1958. Altogether, China spends around US$2 billion annually on its space program, which employs tens of thousands of people involving 100 institutes with production spread across 3,000 factories.

China's future plans for its space program include six additional manned flights aboard *Shenzhou* between 2006 and 2010 and the launching of a space laboratory between 2010 and 2015. A lunar orbiter is scheduled to be launched in 2007 from Xichang with plans for a manned lunar outpost by 2020. Satellite launches will also continue at about 10 per year aimed at developing an integrated space infrastructure and satellite ground application system that harmonizes spacecraft and ground equipment and establishes independent systems of earth observation, telecommunications, and navigation and positioning systems. Within a decade China's space activities could very easily surpass those of Russia and the European Space Agency and challenge the U.S. in particular areas.

In its 2000 official "White Paper on Space Activities," China promised to "utilize outer space for peaceful purposes" and along with Russia has criticized American plans to develop a space-based anti-missile defense system while both countries have also called for multilateral and bilateral instruments to regulate international space activities. To the extent China's space program has a military application, this is apparently limited to communication satellites for linking Chinese military forces, reconnaissance satellites to provide imagery for military action, and global positioning systems to guide missiles. China is also reportedly developing high-energy lasers that could temporarily dazzle or permanently blind sensors on an enemy's sensing satellites.

SPECIAL ECONOMIC ZONES (SEZs). A central feature of the economic reforms introduced in China beginning in 1978–1979, SEZs have been established in Guangdong Province (Shenzhen, Zhuhai, and Shantou), Fujian (Xiamen), and the entire island of Hainan Province. In economic terms, the SEZs are free-**trade** and tax-exempt areas established to lure Foreign Direct Investment (FDI), **technology** transfer, and trade. Wage rates in the zones are much more flexible than in China proper and **labor** is hired on a contractual basis fundamentally at odds with the **iron rice bowl** (*tiefanwan*) that for years dominated much of industrial labor in the **state-owned enterprises** (**SOEs**) of the Chinese **economy**. Imports come into the zones tax free and considerable development has occurred in the real estate market of the largest such zone, Shenzhen, which is located near **Hong Kong**. Most of the **investment** into the export processing industries of the zones has come from Overseas Chinese, especially from Hong Kong and **Taiwan**. The zones have also helped to increase the per capita income of both Guangdong and Fujian provinces. In 2005, the Gross Domestic Product (GDP) of Shenzhen was put at 342 billion *yuan* (US$41 billion) with a per capita GDP in the city of eight million residents of US$7,162, which is dramatically higher than the national average of US$1,000.

Originally, Shenzhen was a fishing village of approximately 30,000 people and the target for development of the first SEZ in 1980, which was carried out by **cadres** of the **People's Liberation Army** (**PLA**), who resided in bamboo huts during the initial stages of construction of basic infrastructure of roads, electrical facilities, and other urban amenities. Over the course of two decades, the city's economy grew by 1,000% and even managed a 16% growth rate during the 2002–2003 **SARS** crisis. Among the many major Chinese corporations operating in Shenzhen are the Huawei Group, a manufacturer of high-tech telecommunications equipment, and the Pearl River Piano Company, which, in 2003, was the largest piano-maker in the world. During the first phases of the SEZs, there was considerable controversy in the **Chinese Communist Party** (**CCP**) as conservative political **leaders** led by **Chen Yun** opposed the zones comparing them to the foreign "concessions" that had existed in China before 1949. Overlapping the nation's 19th century treaty ports, the zones were considered by their critics as a possible entrepôt into

China of "**bourgeois liberalization**" and other nefarious influences that would gradually erode the country's socialist system. In the midst of the **Anti-Spiritual Pollution Campaign** (**1983–1984**), concern grew among foreign businessmen that the anti-Western, anti-capitalist thrust of the campaign would lead to policy reversals on the zones. The intervention of **Deng Xiaoping** to oppose conservative forces ended this threat, however, and brought quick termination to the campaign. Yet, throughout the 1980s and 1990s, the zones remained a source of controversy as some critics in China argued that their rapid development had come at the expense of other regions in China, especially interior areas, that it is claimed, effectively subsidized the rapid growth along the coastal regions. Concerns were also voiced by foreign businessmen who complained about increasing costs and bureaucratic delays in negotiating contracts. But Chinese leaders insisted that the zones would continue and plans were drawn up for creating new zones along the coast, and in the interior, such as the area surrounding the **Three Gorges Dam Project**.

Now over two decades since its development from a fishing village, Shenzhen has a skyline of towering buildings interspersed with palm trees and ever-present construction cranes as the city continues to undergo a construction boom that has spilled over into nearby towns such as Dongguang, Guangdong Province. While the city hosts high-tech firms in modern production facilities and, in 1999, was the site of the First China International High-Tech Results Fair, Shenzhen also has its share of poorly lit, poorly ventilated factories where large numbers of China's **floating population** of migrants seek employment. In 2004, complaints by workers over wages in arrears or wages lower than the government-set minimum led to a rash of petitions and **social protests** that included actions taken by 3,000 workers from an electronics factory in October, in which traffic was disrupted and 100 police deployed. Possible labor shortages have emerged because workers' interests have been so recklessly abused while concern has also emerged over Shenzhen's overbuilt real estate sector that could develop into a rapidly deflating bubble. The other major SEZ in Xiamen, Fujian Province, was hit in 2000 by a major **corruption** and smuggling scandal. So-called development zones and export processing zones have also been set up in many Chinese cities, such as Dalian in the northeast, but without all the financial incentives to FDI provided by the SEZs.

SPIRITUAL POLLUTION. *See* ANTISPIRITUAL POLLUTION CAMPAIGN (1983–1984).

STALIN, JOSEF. China's relations with and views of the great Soviet leader have been mixed. In 1935, **Mao Zedong** emerged as the top leader in the **Chinese Communist Party (CCP)** by supplanting the Twenty-Eight Bolsheviks, a group of young Chinese Communists, led by Wang Ming, who had been trained at Moscow's Sun Yat-sen University to do Josef Stalin's bidding in China. Mao's victory over Stalin's men in China was finalized during the 1942–1944 **rectification campaign** that effectively undermined the waning authority of Wang Ming. After 1949, China adopted policies on collectivization of **agriculture** and industrialization that also varied from boilerplate Stalinist methods. Mao also intimated in the 1950s that Stalin had hurt the Chinese revolution, and that if the CCP had followed his orders, it would have been destroyed. Yet, officially China's **leaders**, led by Mao Zedong, praised Stalin both before and after his death. In 1939, on the occasion of Stalin's 60th birthday, Mao hailed Stalin as "the savior of all the oppressed" and on his 70th birthday Mao declared "Comrade Stalin to be the 'teacher and friend of mankind' and of the Chinese people." At Stalin's death in 1953, Mao lamented the passing of "the greatest genius of the present age." Following Nikita Khrushchev's "secret speech" at the 1956 20th Congress of the Communist Party of the Soviet Union (CPSU) in which he criticized Stalin, the Chinese issued an editorial titled "On the Historical Experience of the Dictatorship of the Proletariat," which recognized Stalin's "mistakes" but reiterated his enormous achievements for the international Communist movement.

Privately, the Chinese were outraged that the new Soviet leader had decided to launch criticisms against Stalin without first consulting the Chinese leadership. "Stalin did not belong to Moscow," a Chinese official is quoted as saying at the time, "Stalin belonged to all of us." Following the **Hungarian Revolution (1956)**, which broke out in reaction in part to Khrushchev's attack on Stalin, the Chinese, in December 1956, issued a second editorial titled "More on the Historical Experiences of the Dictatorship of the Proletariat," which evaluated Stalin in an even more favorable light. Soviet criticisms of Stalin for "placing himself above the Party" and for fostering a **personality**

cult (*geren chongbai*) were especially sensitive in China where Mao could be accused of the same deviations from Leninist norms. Thus, from 1956 to the death of Mao Zedong in 1976, Stalin was officially revered in China as a "great Marxist–Leninist revolutionary" who deserved recognition and praise, despite his unfortunate "mistakes." Since 1978, less has been said about Stalin officially in China, though no comprehensive denunciation comparable to Khrushchev's "secret speech" has been issued.

STANDING COMMITTEE. *See* POLITBURO.

STATE COUNCIL. *See* GOVERNMENT STRUCTURE.

STATE-OWNED ENTERPRISES (SOEs). The centerpiece of China's Soviet-style planned **economy** adopted in the early 1950s, state-owned enterprises (SOEs) numbered 45,000 firms in 1978, along with more than 300,000 mostly small-scale, collectively run enterprises run by county, township, and village governments. The most important SOEs were approximately 2,500 large-scale enterprises (defined as employing more than 1,000 workers), which operated under the direct authority of the central plan governed by the State Planning Commission and controlled by vertically organized, functional ministries that distributed supplies to enterprises from central government agencies and handed over their production for unified allocation. By the late 1970s, these enterprises employed 45 million members of the urban **labor** force and were responsible for one-half of the country's industrial output, tax revenue, and exports with iron and steel and machine-building consuming one-third of total **investment** in industrial capital construction. Enterprise managers were evaluated and promoted according to their success in meeting output quotas while enterprises had virtually no responsibility to market their own products or procure their own inputs, though the plan never covered 100% of an enterprise's needs, thereby forcing managers to secure some of their own materials. Under the principle of the **iron rice bowl** (*tiefanwan*) workers were guaranteed virtually life-time employment including such amenities as housing, **health care**, **education**, and pensions. The income of managers and workers was not linked to the performance of the enterprise as Chinese managers, unlike their counterparts in the **Soviet Union**, rarely received bonuses while workers received infrequent pay raises largely according to seniority along with strong doses of moral incentives and labor emulation campaigns. During the frequent political campaigns that roiled China, such as the **Anti-Rightist Campaign (1957–1958)** and especially the **Great Leap Forward (1958–1960)** when **Chinese Communist Party (CCP)** Chairman **Mao Zedong** insisted that "politics takes command" (*zhengzhi guashuai*) the economic performance of enterprises was often undermined as poorly trained Party secretaries took over leadership from the more technically qualified managers. Industrial inefficiency of SOEs during the central planning era also stemmed from several endemic institutional problems: poor information flowing from managers to central planners; the difficulty of making good investment decisions without rational prices; the lack of managerial incentive to undertake technological innovations; the presence of monopolistic firms that faced little to no domestic or foreign competition; and the lack of managerial incentives to meet customer demand by improving the quality or variety of product lines. Efficiency was also undermined by the rigidity of central plans and by such illicit mechanisms as stockpiling materials and labor to ensure against uncertainties in the supply system.

Beginning in the 1980s, the Chinese government began a systematic effort at a structural and economic reform of the SOEs whose numbers had swelled by the thousands and the work force had grown to over 80 million workers with some enterprises, such as the giant **Baoshan Iron and Steel Complex** in **Shanghai** employing over 200,000 workers. Over the course of the next 20 years, this reform policy proceeded through three separate stages: the tax-for-profits and management contract system from 1983 to 1985, followed by the management responsibility and internal contract system that began in 1985, and the shareholding system inaugurated in the 1990s. The large-scale industrial enterprises were the focus of reforms that aimed at decentralizing decision-making authority out of central ministries into the hands of state-owned companies organized along modern corporate lines, reducing the role of the CCP in the economy, reforming the price system, and altering the tax structure. These reforms proceeded from a 1978 report to the State Council by **Hu Qiaomu** titled "Act in Accord with Economic Laws, Step up the

Four Modernizations" in which the highly politicized and ideologically driven model of industrial organization and development based on the model of the **Daqing oilfield** was criticized while Chinese economists were encouraged to study management techniques of capitalist **industry** abroad. This report did not, however, challenge the fundamentals of the Chinese system of state planning, namely that planners rather than the market establish prices and economic goals.

At the Wuxi Conference in April 1979, proposals were made to integrate the state economic plan and the market and to give greater decision-making authority to individual enterprises freeing them from their close integration with the state bureaucracy. Criticisms of the state planning system were also aired for its over-concentration of authority that effectively stifled managerial initiative and innovation and led to a one-sided emphasis by enterprises on output value and a neglect of costs and efficiency, resulting in huge wastes of resources and labor. Prices of processed goods were too high and those of basic industrial goods and **energy** were too low. Thus, a new system was proposed to bring about an "organic" integration of plan and market and reliance on the "law of value" to establish prices. Enterprises needed to have greater flexibility to establish horizontal ties with other producers and to break the limitations of vertical, ministerial branch systems and of local government controls, both of which kept enterprises in dependent positions. In this way, enterprises that had protected themselves from arbitrary outside controls by almost totally self-sufficient (and highly inefficient) operations would establish networks of supplies and would contract work to make for a more efficient state sector. The state plan would not be mandatory but serve only as a guide to production and pricing. Some Chinese economists even went so far as to suggest that ownership of enterprises be shifted from the state to collective (but not private) hands.

In 1981, the leadership structure in state enterprises was also adjusted, giving greater stress to the role of industrial managers over enterprise Party committees, but without fundamentally altering the CCP committee system. In 1984, a State Council decision advanced enterprise reform by authorizing experimental reforms in Guangdong Province and Shanghai, where enterprises were given control over their profits and losses after paying various state taxes, which were established through a contract between the enterprise and the state authorities (i.e., the tax-for-profits and management contract system). Wages were linked to profits, and enterprises were given authority to hire their own laborers, buy materials on the market, and set prices according to demand, while funds were established at the enterprise level for reinvestment purposes. A "factory responsibility system" was also adopted through which enterprises were allowed to retain profits above a certain quota. Small-scale state enterprises in the retail, service, and repair sectors were leased out and large-scale state-owned enterprises not engaged in vital production were allowed to form joint-stock companies.

As a result of these reforms, output rose dramatically in the mid-1980s, contributing to rapid inflation that ultimately led to government cutbacks and restrictions and the reinstitution of price controls in key sectors. Party **cadres** and bureaucrats also often took advantage of the new two-tiered pricing system (low, subsidized state-set prices of goods and high market prices), thus leading to an explosion in **corruption** and "official profiteering" (*guandao*).

In October 1984, at the Third Plenum of the 12th CCP Central Committee, the decision on the "Structural Reform of the Economy" fundamentally altered relations between the Party and enterprises by replacing the Party committee system in factories with a "managerial responsibility system" (*yichang zhizhang*). But such experimentation occurred on only a small scale in a few enterprises. However, in 1986, there were proposals that the enterprise Party committees no longer be subordinate to Party committees in the relevant state ministries but, instead, be subordinate to territorial Party committees (city districts or residential Party committees), thereby breaking the longstanding vertical connection to **Beijing**. This change was more apparent than real, however, as Party secretaries familiar with production and exercising capable leadership were simply switched to the position of industrial manager. By 1989, the new managerial system was established in most of the large and medium enterprises employing more than 1,000 workers. In order to gain the support of labor, increases in salaries, bonuses, and wages were enacted, thereby dramatically fueling the inflation that contributed to the 1989 second **Beijing Spring** and that after the 1989 crisis provoked the government to adopt severe austerity measures.

With state-run factories still reluctant to fire or lay off workers and with increasing overhead costs, losses and debts at these industrial facilities rose substantially, leading the central bank to issue loans and lines of credit to tide over the firms. Austerity measures were eased from 1993 onward, but the prospect of huge losses in the industrial sector and massive bankruptcies have generally prevented any further moves toward fundamental enterprise reform; even in the new share-holding system adopted in the 1990s the state remains the major actor. By 1995, despite huge losses, the state-owned sector in China was actually expanding as a **Chinese People's Political Consultative Conference** (**CPPCC**) decision in 1999 on "Major Issues Concerning the Reform and Development of State-Owned Enterprises" called for the continuing reform of SOEs but with the government retaining its dominant control over important industries. This apparently stiffened resistance to the kind of privatization measures that China must adopt in accordance with its 2001 ascension to the **World Trade Organization** (**WTO**).

Throughout the 1980s and 1990s, SOEs went through a series of reform efforts, including instituting the contract operational responsibility system and establishing a modern corporate structure consisting of joint stock companies with a regularized corporate legal person consisting of boards of directors and share-holding systems organized into major industrial groups and subsidiaries. The major laws governing this reform process were the 1984 "Provisional Regulations on the Enlargement of Autonomy of State Industrial Enterprises," which allowed SOEs to make price setting, output sales, and input purchases; the 1988 Bankruptcy Law; the 1992 "Enterprise Bill of Rights," which guaranteed non-interference in enterprise affairs by the state; and the 1993 Company Law, which established the legal framework for the formation of corporate organizations. In 1996, total loses by SOEs equaled 1% of the Gross domestic Product (GDP) while top political **leaders**, such as Premier **Zhu Rongji**, declared a complete victory in turning around the often very inefficient and bloated state-owned sector in 1998. With only a small percentage of shares in SOEs publicly traded on China's two **stock markets** in Shanghai and Shenzhen, the state still carries out the basic share-holding function while the fundamental structure of SOEs remained unchanged as most continued to operate under the direct authority of intrusive and often economically inefficient government supervision. By 2003, the number of SOEs in China totaled nearly 160,000 separate companies and constituted as much as two-thirds of the entire **economy**. Achievements in the reform of the state-owned sector included closing down nearly one-half of all such companies, especially those with long-term prospects of losses and involvement in so-called "debt chains," from which the enterprises could never escape. From 1980 to 2001, employment at SOEs fell from 67% to just 16.5% of the workforce (39.5 million) as 27 million redundant workers were laid off. According to the government, many of these workers were able to find new jobs especially in the expanding private sector, which grew over the same time period to 15% of the workforce (36.6 million workers). Organizationally, 85% of state-owned firms have realized multi-level property rights as overall profits in the state sector grew from 84 billion *yuan* (US$10 billion) in 1992 to 220 billion *yuan* (US$27 billion) in 2002 though profit margins are less sizeable compared to the non-state sector largely because of the higher circulation tax rates and higher capital intensity of SOEs. The formation of the State-Owned Assets Supervision and Administration Commission to guide state-owned enterprise reform and management in 2003 (taking over responsibilities of the former State Economic and Trade Commission and the Work Committee of Enterprises of the CCP) also gave rise to a flurry of corporate mergers and acquisitions that produced 11 Chinese firms, which, in 2002, entered the global top-500 list of companies.

Persistent problems in the state-owned sector made enterprise reform a priority of both the 1997 15th and the 2002 16th National Party Congresses. Issues addressed included enterprises taking on financial burdens inherited from the old socialist system of providing social services to present and past employees that constituted on average 40% of enterprise costs. Of equal concern was the pervasive lack of senior managers and qualified technicians and inadequate marketing and product innovation that left many Chinese firms at a disadvantage when compared to transnational corporations. China's backward corporate tax structure was also considered an obstacle to further reform along with the absence of a clear-cut quitting mechanism for eliminating inefficient and poorly run firms from the market and the inability of enterprises to shed auxiliary units. Asset stripping by enterprise managers remains a serious problem along with reliance on "soft" budgets that lead to bail-outs of money-losing firms by entrenched administrative officials who are overwhelmingly concerned with the possibility of **social protests** by laid-off employees. Efforts have also been made to reduce the share of Chinese government ownership of state-owned firms and to increase investment from foreign capital, especially into labor-intensive industries. "Provisional Regulations on Supervision and Management of State-Owned Assets" passed in 2003 provided guidelines for the investment of state-owned assets on behalf of the central government, which, once again, aimed at reducing direct government intervention in enterprises and separating state ownership from management along with handling the relations between the rights and interests of investors (shareholders' rights) and the property rights of enterprises as legal persons. While the Chinese state is still committed to building up large state-owned enterprises for the foreseeable future, it is relinquishing control of small and medium-sized companies that will increasingly operate on their own. The system of public ownership is to remain the centerpiece of China's enterprise system into the near future though efforts are in place to encourage greater development of the private sector and to reduce the high proportion of processing industry and common service industry in the state-owned economy where workers face quota increases and speed-ups, longer working hours, new controls over labor attendance, and use of monetary sanctions and penalties to control labor. *See also* BANKING AND FINANCE; GOVERNMENT STRUCTURE.

STATE PLANNING COMMISSION. *See* GOVERNMENT STRUCTURE.

STOCK MARKETS. China's first "stock market" (*zhengquan jiaoyisuo*) opened in 1904 in the foreign concession of the International Settlement in **Shanghai** and listed exclusively foreign companies involved primarily in **banking and finance**, the rubber trade, and dog-racing. In 1941, the market closed in the face of the Japanese occupation and remained so after the Communist takeover in 1949 and throughout the period of Soviet central planning (1953–1978) and into the early years of the economic reforms begun in 1978–1979. With **state-owned enterprises** (**SOEs**) increasingly starved for funds, two stock exchanges were opened in Shanghai and the Shenzhen **Special Economic Zone** (**SEZ**) in 1990, first as purely local exchanges that, in 1996, were converted to national markets. Operating under the Securities Law of the **People's Republic of China** (**PRC**) with oversight by the China Securities Regulatory Commission, the two markets offer publicly traded shares, which are approved for sale by the State Council Securities Management Department for companies with capitalization over US$90 million that have been in business for three years and make 25% of their shares available for trade. The majority of listed companies serve as small arms of giant enterprises controlled by the state and offer "Individual Person Shares" (*geren gu*), which make up approximately one-third of all company shares. The other two-thirds consist of "State Shares" (*guojia gu*) and "Legal Person Shares" (*faren gu*), both of which are non-tradable and are held by the Ministry of Finance and other investing SOEs, respectively. Similar to stock markets in other developing countries, China segmented its stock offerings into separate categories of shares: Class A shares denominated in Chinese **currency** for domestic buyers; Class B shares denominated in international currencies for foreign investors (which carry no ownership rights and were made available to domestic buyers in 2001); and Class H shares of companies listed on the **Hong Kong** stock market and denominated in the Hong Kong dollar. Class A shares outnumber B and H shares by a ratio of 5-to-1 while both A and B shares are entitled to the same rights and obligations under Chinese law. The two have also traded at significantly different prices, with substantial discounting of Class B shares that is attributed to different sets of **investment** opportunities available to domestic versus foreign investors and their risk tolerance. Foreign investors require a higher rate of return to adjust for country-specific risks in China, namely the political risk, exchange rate risk, interest rate risk, and market risk with the political risk as the most important component.

During the 1990s, the Chinese stock markets showed substantial and sustained growth as shares reached artificially high levels with an average price-earnings (P/E) ratio of 40 compared to 10 to 20 in more developed world stock markets. Large numbers of accounts were opened by small investors but with a significant percentage holding few if any stocks as most were for the express purpose of entering

Initial Public Offering (IPO) lotteries that ensured 100% returns by selling shares on the first day of trading. With plans to compete with Hong Kong's Hang Seng Index, the Shanghai market established a blue chip composite index in 1995, followed in 2003 by a stock exchange 100 index and the possibility of stock index futures. By 2001, the Chinese markets ranked 20th in the world after Brazil and Finland with total capitalization equal to about 30% of Gross Domestic Product (GDP), compared to 300% for the Hang Seng. Since 2001, fully one-half of the two markets' capitalization has been lost and, in 2005, was valued at US$573 billion consisting of 1,200 listed companies and with a daily capacity of 20 million trades while financial management companies operating with "privately raised funds" (*simu ji-jin*) emerged as the largest holder of stocks. Along with a series of securities fraud cases, investor confidence was dampened by a sense that the Chinese markets were beset by inside deals and shoddy governance whereby share prices were manipulated by the government to serve the interests of favored firms. Sustained losses and problematic accounting in many SOEs also contributed to the downturn in the markets along with the continued prohibition against listings by private enterprises though so-called backdoor listings have become commonplace. The poor performance of the stock markets raised the possibility in 2005 of a US$15 billion bailout by government banks of the exchanges but without any move toward fundamental reform. *See also* GOVERNMENT STRUCTURE.

"STRUGGLE BETWEEN TWO LINES" (*"LIANGTIAO LUXIAN DE DOUZHENG"*). An ideologically charged notion propagated by Maoists in China and many outside observers that major factional divisions in China in the 1950s and 1960s were between moderate and radical elites and their respective policy "lines." In this model, which saw policy under constant contention between these two basic factions, **Mao Zedong** played a key role, sometimes siding with the moderate line but more often joining the radicals to attack and purge his "moderate" opponents, especially during the **Cultural Revolution (1966–1976)**. The leftist line included support for socialist **agriculture** and **industry**, ideological purity, "**uninterrupted revolution (*buduan geming*)**," militant nationalism, and opposition to Soviet "**revisionism**" and American "**imperialism**." The moderate line involved relying on limited market mechanisms, ideological pragmatism, an end to **class struggle**, and greater accommodation with domestic and international forces, including the **United States**.

STRUGGLE SESSIONS. Individuals and groups targeted for "**thought reform**" (*sixiang gaizao*) and/or political criticism were grilled, interrogated, and often physically abused in sessions that could last for days. The general purpose of such sessions that during the **Cultural Revolution (1966–1976)** even involved top **leaders** of the **Chinese Communist Party (CCP)** was to extort "confessions" and wear down the individual's resistance to pressure. Accused of being a "rightist" or "**capitalist roader**" (*zouzipai*), the targets of these struggle sessions were cajoled and pressured to admit to their "crimes," admissions that had to be made again and again. During the Cultural Revolution, struggle sessions became veritable witch hunts in which vigilante **Red Guards** acted as prosecutors and often as executioners. Since 1978, struggle sessions have generally disappeared from the Chinese political landscape, though some revival evidently followed the military crackdown against the second **Beijing Spring** in June 1989.

SU SHAOZHI (1923–). An economist by training, Su Shaozhi was one of China's leading Marxist theorists and proponents of reform who, in the mid-1980s, headed the Institute of Marxism–Leninism at the **Chinese Academy of Social Sciences (CASS)** and the Theory Department at *People's Daily*. In December 1988, Su attended a forum to commemorate the decade of reform where he defended the liberal advocate **Wang Ruoshui** and attacked conservative ideologues such as **Hu Qiaomu**. In February 1989, Su signed an open letter calling for the release of political prisoners in China and, along with **Fang Lizhi**, carried out the New Enlightenment Movement while also protesting the shutting down of the *World Economic Herald* in **Shanghai**. He fled China after the June 1989 crackdown against the second **Beijing Spring** and has since held several university posts in the **United States** and heads the Princeton China Initiative while he has also pled the cases of Chinese dissidents in Australia.

SUN CHANGJIANG. Trained as a philosopher, Sun Changjiang was once deputy-director of the Theory Research Department of the

Central Party School. He authored the article "Practice is the Sole Criterion of Truth" published in May 1978 that helped inaugurate the era of economic reform and prompted liberal advocates to call for major political reforms. When, in 1982, **Wang Zhen** replaced **Hu Yaobang** as president of the Central Party School, the Theory Research Department was dismantled and Sun was ousted from the Party School and became a faculty member at the **Beijing** Teacher's College. Sun subsequently became the editor-in-chief of the *Science and Technology Daily* (*Keji ribao*), a post from which he was ousted following the 4 June 1989 military crackdown against the second **Beijing Spring**. In a 1997 interview, Sun offered a bleak assessment of Chinese aspirations for democracy by saying "the common people don't know what democracy is because their **education** level is so low" and he even castigated China's college students for not caring about democracy.

– T –

TAIWAN. The relations between the Republic of China (ROC) on Taiwan and the **People's Republic of China** (**PRC**) have ranged from military conflict and confrontation during the period from 1949 to the 1970s to increasing **trade** relations in the 1980s and preliminary political contacts in the 1990s and early 2000s but with the threat of force against the island from the mainland a constant part of their political interaction. In 1945, China regained sovereignty from **Japan** over Taiwan (formerly known as Formosa) and following the defeat of Nationalist forces on the mainland the **Kuomintang** (**KMT**) fled to Taiwan in 1948–1949. The Chinese Communists planned an invasion across the Taiwan Straits to finish the **Civil War** (**1946–1949**) but intervention by the **United States** following the June 1950 North Korean invasion of South **Korea** provided Taiwan with a defensive shield provided primarily by the U.S. Navy's Seventh Fleet. During the **Taiwan Straits Crises** (**1954 and 1958**), Communist and Nationalist forces engaged in combat largely to contest control over the offshore islands of Quemoy (*Jinmen*) and Matsu, which, in 1955, the U.S. committed itself to defend. The refusal of **Beijing** to formally renounce the potential use of force against Taiwan prevented Washington from withdrawing its military shield and effectively prevented any resolution of the Taiwan issue as periodic shelling of the islands from mainland batteries continued until the two sides came to an uneasy truce in the 1980s. For years in the mid-1950s, Beijing made periodic but unsuccessful offers to the ROC leader Chiang Kai-shek for a resolution of the conflict.

The establishment of contacts in 1971 and then formal ties between the U.S. and China in 1979 brought an end to the representation of the ROC in the **United Nations** (**UN**) and a break in U.S.–ROC diplomatic and formal military ties. The 1979 Taiwan Relations Act, however, maintained a U.S. military commitment to the island as the U.S. continued to press China for a "peaceful settlement" of the Taiwan–PRC conflict, even as it recognized in the **Shanghai Communiqué** that Taiwan was part of China.

Internationally, the PRC staked its political claims to Taiwan by requiring all nations with which it established diplomatic relations to drop recognition of the ROC on Taiwan and that Taiwan be excluded from any international body of which the PRC is a member—from the Asia–Pacific Economic Cooperation (APEC) to the **Association of Southeast Asian Nations** (**ASEAN**) + 3 (10 Southeast Asian states plus China, Japan, and South Korea) to the World Health Organization (WHO) and to the UN, where China has blocked every attempt by Taiwan to regain its membership under the title "Republic of China." Domestically, the PRC strengthened this claim by maintaining representation of Taiwan on the **National People's Congress** (**NPC**), staffing a Taiwan Affairs Office in the central government, and, in 2005, passing an anti-secession law that was targeted directly at Taiwan. Real decision-making power on the Taiwan issue was put in the hands of the leading small group on Taiwan affairs that consisted of top Party and government **leaders**. In 1981, China unveiled a more flexible policy toward Taiwan by proposing a nine-point program, including economic and cultural exchanges, official and unofficial contacts between officials on both sides of the straits, and a general reduction in military tensions near the offshore islands. According to Beijing's plan known as **"one country, two systems,"** Taiwan would ultimately become a Special Administrative Region (SAR) of the PRC (similar to **Hong Kong** after 1997), with a distinct economic and political system and with a high degree of autonomy.

Taiwan would be represented in international affairs by the central government in Beijing, though Taiwan would be allowed to retain its own military forces and separate **legal system**. Negotiations on the final status of Taiwan would be carried out between the Communist and Nationalist parties on an equal basis.

After democratic changes were introduced into Taiwan's political structure in the late 1970s by Chiang Ching-kuo (son of Chiang Kai-shek) and the emergence after Chiang Ching-kuo's death of a Taiwan-born president, Lee Teng-hui, the government of Taiwan accepted and then promoted exchanges with the mainland. In 1993, China's vice-minister for sports arrived in Taipei, the most senior official to travel to Taiwan since 1949; at the same time, China issued a White Paper entitled "The Taiwan Question and the Reunification of China," which argued in favor of a peaceful reunification of Taiwan into the mainland. Relations were further enhanced by visits of Taiwan residents to the PRC that began in 1987 and, by 2005, numbered more than 17 million people. China reciprocated in 2005 by allowing mainlanders to visit Taiwan. Joint participation by Taiwanese and Chinese athletes in Olympic events was also agreed upon as both sides established organizations (on the ROC side, Taiwan Straits Exchange Foundation [SEF], and on the PRC side, the Association for Relations across the Taiwan Straits [ARATS]) to address common problems in the waters of the Taiwan Straits, such as fishing rights and human trafficking. Formal contacts were not initiated, however, as Taiwan continued to adhere to its policy enunciated in 1979 by Chiang Ching-kuo of "three no's"—no [formal] contact, no negotiation, and no compromise. Taipei, backed by Washington, also refused to agree to direct postal and **transportation** linkages while Beijing still refused to issue a no-force pledge. China also opposed Taiwan's adoption of its "flexible diplomacy," under which Taiwan would, if possible, establish formal diplomatic relations with nations that simultaneously recognized the PRC and the ROC, or upgrade unofficial relations with nations that formally recognized the PRC but desired increased economic ties with Taiwan, which, in the 1980s, became one of the world's largest holders of foreign exchange reserves.

Increased sentiment for independence on Taiwan brought on by political liberalization and the emergence of the avowedly pro-independence Democratic Progressive Party (DPP) has also concerned

China. The military crackdown in June 1989 against the second **Beijing Spring** severely undermined popular support on Taiwan for eventual reunification with China and apparently strengthened pro-independence sentiment. In 1995, PRC President **Jiang Zemin** outlined eight points to govern cross-straits relations, including an official end to the state of hostility and peaceful reunification. However, during the 1996 campaign on Taiwan for president, won by Lee Teng-hui, China fired four M9 surface-to-surface missiles into the Taiwan Straits as the U.S. dispatched elements of the Seventh Fleet into the area. Efforts at reducing tensions were renewed in 1998, including a visit to the mainland by the head of Taiwan's SEF who met with President Jiang. Tensions arose anew, however, in 1999 when President Lee referred to relations between Taiwan and the mainland as "state-to-state." Prior to the 2000 presidential election on Taiwan, won by DPP leader Chen Shui-bian, China called for a timetable and urgent preparations for early cross-strait reunification and issued another White Paper that departed from the "peaceful reunification" themes of the previous document and threatened the use of force, a position reiterated by Chinese Premier **Zhu Rongji** who warned that "if the Taiwan independence forces achieve power it could trigger a war between the two sides of the straits."

Efforts continued, however, to ease tensions and consisted of limited direct exchanges between Taiwan's offshore islands and selected Chinese seaports along with indirect charter flights during the Chinese New Year. Chen Shui-bian's narrow reelection in 2004 was followed by more conciliatory gestures when the first direct charter flights were allowed in five decades over the Lunar New Year. But as Chen raised the possibility of submitting an amendment to Taiwan's constitution, which aimed at eventual independence for the island, tensions escalated again with spokesmen for China suggesting that the use of force "may become unavoidable" and that any attempt by Taiwan to become independent would constitute the biggest threat to security in the Asia–Pacific region and would be "smashed." Even as Chen softened his tone and promised that his administration would not hold a referendum on Taiwan's status as long as Beijing did not attack, both sides raised the ante by conducting high-profile war games, with the **People's Liberation Army** (**PLA**) simulating an amphibious assault on an offshore island similar in contours to Taiwan and with the vice-chairman of China's Central **Military Affairs Commission** (**MAC**) stressing the importance of preparing for war should events lead to the separation of Taiwan from China. In March 2006, President Chen scrapped the Guidelines for National Unification and the National Unification Council all the while insisting that "Taiwan has no intention of changing the status quo" in cross-straits relations.

The position of the KMT toward Taiwan-mainland relations has shifted dramatically since it became Taiwan's largest opposition party in 2000. In late 2003, the KMT announced its intention of introducing resolutions in the parliament calling for the status quo to be maintained of an independent sovereign Republic of China and that mainland China should gradually withdraw its missiles targeting Taiwan, this in opposition to the plan of President Chen Shui-bian to initiate a "defensive referendum" to protect Taiwan's sovereignty. During the 2004 election campaign, the KMT, led by Lien Chan, joined in an alliance with the People First Party and the New Party in favoring a less confrontational approach toward the PRC by promising, if elected, to travel to mainland China in person for a "journey of peace" on the basis of the 1992 "consensus" between Taiwan and mainland China leaders stipulating that there is only one China. In late December 2004 during parliamentary elections, the KMT-led coalition won a two-seat majority in the Taiwan legislature, which effectively prevented Chen Shui-bian and the DPP from giving Taiwan the formal trappings of an independent state. A final bill passed by the Taiwan legislature and supported by the KMT bars any referenda on changing the flag of Taiwan or changing the island's official name from the Republic of China to the "Republic of Taiwan," and makes it extremely hard to hold a referendum to amend the Constitution to include the goal of independence. In May 2005, KMT leader Lien Chan took the unprecedented move of traveling to the mainland for a meeting with President **Hu Jintao**—the first contact between the CCP and KMT in 60 years—where the two leaders' handshake was broadcast on live mainland TV while both leaders called for resolving the Taiwan issue under the formula of "two sides, one China," a reworking of language that seemed to offer some room for negotiation. At the same time, China promised to sign a formal peace agreement with Taiwan, establish military-to-military ties, and allow Taiwan to join some international bodies, such as the WHO, in exchange for the island's acceptance of the "one China" principle. This was followed by another high-profile visit to Beijing by James Song, leader of the People First Party, Taiwan's second-largest opposition party and a supporter of eventual reunification. The KMT endorsed expanding the three "mini links" of direct trade, transport, and postal services between the mainland and Quemoy and Matsu to Taiwan proper. Yet, even as Hu Jintao called on Taiwan's president to accept the principle of "two sides, one China," Chen Shui bian insisted that only Taiwan's 23 million people could decide on any change in the island's status. Although China began to refer to Taiwan in more hard-line terms as "sacred territory" (*shensheng*), Taiwan's national examinations and school curriculum increasingly emphasized a unique "Taiwanese" identity based on the South Minnan (*Minnan hua*) dialect, which had previously been banned under KMT rule but now fills the island's TV and airwaves.

On the military front, Taiwan has claimed that 800 short- and medium-range missiles would be aimed by China at the island by 2006, along with 200 or so cruise missiles that Taiwan has asked Chinese leaders to remove. Military spending by the ROC in 2001 made up 17% of the national budget (versus 7.5% for China) as the island strengthened its defenses with U.S.-made PAC-2 anti-missile systems to protect the populous Taipei area. Taiwan also test-fired an AIM-120 advanced air-to-air missile bought from the U.S. to counteract the Russian-built AA-12 Adder missiles, which is part of the PLA arsenal.

Trade between Taiwan and the PRC was initially limited to indirect exchanges via Hong Kong but, by 1988, grew to more than US$3 billion. **Investment** in the mainland **economy** by Taiwanese corporations also expanded to more than a US$1 billion by the end of the 1980s with more than 30,000 Taiwan factories operating largely in coastal provinces employing three million workers. The killings of 24 Taiwanese tourists in 1994 strained economic relations as Taiwan investors lost some of their enthusiasm for the Chinese market and cut back on mainland investments, at least temporarily. Relations gradually improved and trade ties recovered as Taiwan, in 1995, called for talks between Taipei and Beijing on common problems and issues. In 1996, China National Offshore Oil Company (CNOOC) and Taiwan's

China Petroleum Corporation signed an oil agreement, while in 2002 Taiwan Semiconductor Manufacturing Corporation applied for permission to construct an advanced eight-inch wafer plant in **Shanghai**. By 2004, the mainland was Taiwan's largest export market with Taiwanese investment in China amounting to US$160 billion as much of China's high-tech exports originated in Taiwanese-run factories.

TAIWAN STRAITS CRISES (1954 AND 1958). On two occasions, the **Taiwan** Straits were the site of a military confrontation between the mainland and the **Kuomintang** (**KMT**)-controlled island. The first occurred in 1954 and was followed four years later by the more serious confrontation that came after a breakdown in Sino–U.S. talks that had been periodically conducted in Warsaw, Poland, since their inauguration in 1955. With an apparent view to begin the reconquest of Taiwan, the Chinese Communists, in August 1958, launched artillery and air force attacks against the islands of Quemoy (*Jinmen*) and Matsu, two small islands off China's coast that were vital to Taiwan's strategic defense. In reaction, the **United States** deployed air force and naval units into the region and backed up its forces with strong statements of defense of Taiwan by President Dwight Eisenhower and Secretary of State John Foster Dulles. Air combat over the straits between **People's Liberation Army** (**PLA**) fighter aircraft and American-built planes of the Chinese Nationalist Air Force resulted in heavy losses for the Communist side. After the apparent refusal of the **Soviet Union** to actively aid China in its confrontation, China's **leaders**, in September, beat a hasty retreat and promised to renew the Warsaw Talks. As a result of China's "irresponsible" behavior during this crisis, the Soviet leadership apparently decided to renege on its promise to share nuclear secrets with the Chinese, contributing further to the emerging Sino–Soviet Conflict. *See also* FOREIGN POLICY.

TAN ZHENLIN (1902–1983). A earlier follower of **Mao Zedong** in the **Chinese Communist Party** (**CCP**), Tan Zhenlin participated in the 1927 Autumn Harvest uprising and became a **political commissar** during the **Sino–Japanese War** (**1937–1945**) in the Communist New Fourth Army. A vice-premier of the State Council, Tan, in 1956, was appointed to the CCP Central Committee and became a vice-chairman of the State Planning Commission. In 1967, he promoted the so-called **February Adverse Current** that attempted to terminate the **Cultural Revolution (1966–1976)** and outlaw the **Red Guards**. He was purged and then reappeared in 1973 and was reappointed to the Central Committee.

TANGSHAN EARTHQUAKE. Occurring on 28 July 1976 at 3:00 A.M. and registering 7.8 on the Richter scale, the earthquake in and around the city of Tangshan in eastern China was the third most destructive in recorded history. Out of the city's one million inhabitants, it is believed that 242,000 people were killed and 160,000 injured. After the quake, it took 12 hours for China's **leaders** in **Beijing**, 160 km to the northwest, to discover that the city had been nearly destroyed. Troops mobilized for relief operations piled the dead into deep mine pits outside the city as the country's leadership forbade any foreign aid. More than a decade was required to rebuild the city as other major urban centers took responsibility for restoring individual neighborhoods. In Chinese history, natural disasters were said to foretell great political changes; at this time, China was embroiled in a major power struggle because of the impending death of **Mao Zedong**. As the Chinese press derided old superstitions by proclaiming that "an earthquake was only an earthquake," Mao died two months later, opening the way for the major economic and political changes inaugurated by **Deng Xiaoping** in 1978–1979. By the 1990s and early 2000s, Tangshan had been completely rebuilt and resumed its role as a major industrial city and center of foreign **investment**. Other major earthquakes in China include one in 1975 in the Haicheng–Yingkou region of Liaoning Province and a 1998 quake at Jiashi in the Xinjiang Autonomous Region.

TAO ZHU (1906–1969). Joining the **Chinese Communist Party (CCP)** in 1930, Tao Zhu emerged as a major regional leader in China from the southern province of Guangdong. Associated with **Li Xiannian**, Tao was appointed chairman of the Wuhan Municipal Military Control Commission after the Chinese Communist seizure of power in 1949. In 1953, he became vice-chairman of the People's Government of Guangdong Province and, in 1955, was appointed the provincial governor. In 1956, he became a member of the CCP Central Committee and until 1957 was identified as the first Party secretary of

Guangdong. In 1961, Tao was made the first Party secretary of the Central-South Bureau of the CCP and, in 1962, became **political commissar** of the **Guangzhou (Canton)** Military Region. In 1965, he became a vice-premier of the Chinese Government and, in 1966, headed the Propaganda Department of the CCP and was appointed to the **Politburo**. During the **Cultural Revolution (1966–1976)**, he was branded as a "counterrevolutionary revisionist" and purged. Tao Zhu died ignominiously in 1969 at the hand of **Red Guards**.

TECHNOLOGY. *See* SCIENCE AND TECHNOLOGY.

TERRORISM. *See* FOREIGN POLICY; MINORITIES.

"THEORY OF BEING 'DOCILE TOOLS'" (*"XUNFU GONGJU LUN"*). A fundamental concept on the role of the individual in the **Chinese Communist Party (CCP)** and the **Chinese Communist** revolution, this theory was most fully articulated by Liu Shaoqi and essentially instructed CCP members to rid themselves of personal interests or aspirations. Party members, Liu Shaoqi argued, should "serve as a docile tool and a tool easy to control." During the **Cultural Revolution (1966–1976)**, Liu's theory was pilloried by Party radicals for purportedly "regarding the masses as 'beasts of burden' and 'slaves.'" In addition, Liu was criticized for having "distorted the relationship between the Party leadership and rank-and-file members as one between man and tool, between slave-owner and slave, a relationship of absolute obedience." The fundamental flaw in this theory was that it forced Party members to obey that which is "wrong," even though the Leninist concept of democratic-centralism, with its emphasis on obedience to higher authority, was a centerpiece of CCP doctrine. Party members, it was claimed, had been turned into "mindless machines" and forced to "forsake the principle of struggle for the sake of organization and obedience." In its place, the radicals sanctioned the principle of "to rebel is justified" (*zaofan youli*), which led to chaos and the near disintegration of the CCP and which, since 1978, has been disavowed by the CCP leadership.

THEORY OF THREE WORLDS (*SANGE SHIJIE LUN*). A theory propounded by **Mao Zedong** and **Deng Xiaoping** in the early 1970s, it replaced previous Chinese pronouncements on the state of global and international relations. According to this formulation, the "social-ist camp" was no longer in existence because the **Soviet Union** had completed degenerated into "social **imperialism**." The two super-powers—the **United States** and the Soviet Union—were equated as members of the First World, joined together in an insatiable campaign to exploit and oppress the many poor nations of the Third World. The Second World comprised European and other equally developed na-tions, also joined in the exploitation of the Third World but were them-selves exploited by the giant superpowers. China was a member of the Third World and had assumed the role of an international proletariat, a revolutionary force opposed to colonialism, imperialism, and "social imperialism," China's appellation for the Soviet Union under Leonid Brezhnev. In 1974, Deng Xiaoping expostulated on his Three Worlds Theory in a speech to the **United Nations** (**UN**); in 1977, the *People's Daily* extolled the theory as a "major contribution to Marxism–Lenin-ism." From the 1980s onward, and especially following the collapse of the USSR, China focused more on world peace and economic de-velopment, while it refused to join such Third World organizations as OPEC or the Group of 24, a gathering of poorer nations in the Inter-national Monetary Fund (IMF).

THIRD FRONT. A 17-year effort that was launched mostly in prepara-tion for possible wars in the 1960s, China's Third Front program in-volved a huge effort to relocate hundreds of factories and institutes in the Chinese interior where the **Chinese Communist Party** (**CCP**) had waged its struggle against the Japanese during the **Sino–Japan-ese War** (**1937–1945**). The rationale for the grandiose project was the belief of CCP Chairman **Mao Zedong** that any attack from foreign en-emies, including the **Soviet Union** or the **United States**, would most likely come along the coast and that China's strategy would be to "re-treat to the hinterland" where it would be less susceptible to attack and could carry on production in a war of attrition, thereby trapping the enemy in a vast terrain, where it would be surrounded by "oceans of people's war." Begun in 1964 during a volatile international situation, industrial bases were built in remote areas of southwestern and west-ern China, including **energy**, aviation, and electronic plants, along with major heavy industrial facilities, such as the Panzhihua Iron and

Steel plant in Sichuan Province. In the warlike atmosphere that the involvement of the military inevitably entailed at this time, the normal and routine functions of China's **economy** were turned upside down as the sites for the dismantled plants were often selected by military staff by simply drawing circles somewhere on a map.

With the advent of China's economic reforms in 1978–1979, Third Front facilities became quickly outmoded as a result of the high cost of their operations in the interior and the enormous expense of building and maintaining the communication, energy, and **transportation** infrastructure (especially railways). In 1983, the Chinese government inaugurated a program to relocate and transform the facilities as a number of obsolete factories were shut down while more economically and technologically competitive facilities were moved to urban areas, where production was converted from military to civilian use. Costs of the conversion came to 20 billion *yuan* (US$2.4 billion), most of which was raised by the individual enterprises while much of the supporting infrastructure of the project is no longer functioning. In December 2003, a symposium was held in **Beijing** to mark the 20th anniversary of the Third Front.

THIRD PLENUM OF THE 11TH CCP CENTRAL COMMITTEE (1978). The watershed meeting in December 1978 that launched China on the path to economic and limited political reform. Preceded by a Central Work Conference at which major policy initiatives were announced by **Deng Xiaoping**, the Third Plenum of the 11th Central Committee marked the return of Deng Xiaoping as China's paramount leader and the political eclipse of **Hua Guofeng**, the designated successor of **Mao Zedong**, and such Mao flunkies as **Chen Yonggui**. Politically, the plenum announced the end of mass campaigns and a "reversal of verdicts" (*pingfan*) on the Tiananmen Incident known as the **April Fifth Movement (1976)**, and announced plans for a full evaluation of Mao Zedong's leadership—warts and all. Economically, the plenum called for a shift in the primary work of the Communist Party to socialist modernization but without the grandiose plans for a "Foreign Leap Forward" that had been previously advocated by Hua Guofeng. Instead, the plenum adopted the **Chen Yun** approach to "balanced development" and sanctioned radical liberalization of the policy on **agriculture** while beginning the dismantling of the **people's communes'** and other Maoist innovations in the countryside. Following the plenum, major leadership changes were announced as **Hu Yaobang** was elevated to chairman (the last) of the Party and **Hu Qiaomu** and **Yao Yilin** to Party deputy secretaries. A formal investigation was also announced of Mao's former police chief, the deceased **Kang Sheng**, while the leftist leader and top police official, **Wang Dongxing**, was dismissed.

"THOUGHT REFORM" (*"SIXIANG GAIZAO"*). In 1951, **Mao Zedong** referred to "thought reform" (*sixiang gaizao*, which is also translated as "ideological remolding") as "one of the important prerequisites for our country to realize thoroughly democratic reform in all respects. . . ." For the victims of this intense process, primarily Chinese **intellectuals**, artists, and some Americans who were imprisoned in China after 1949, the experience was described as classic "brainwashing." Among Chinese intellectuals, the strong appeal of liberalism and intellectual and artistic freedom made them frequent targets of thought-reform efforts, which were orchestrated by the **Chinese Communist Party** (CCP). Interrogations, the writing of "confessions," incarceration, and torture were all used to remold the "thoughts" of intellectuals who did not support the CCP nor accept the Marxist–Leninist–Maoist worldview. As a Chinese-style inquisition, "thought reform" peaked in China during the **Anti-Rightist Campaign (1957–1958)** and during the **Cultural Revolution (1966–1976)**. Yet, even after the beginning of the reforms in 1978–1979, intellectuals, writers, and artists have come under periodic assault for their renewed beliefs in liberalism and general intellectual and academic freedom. The **Anti-Spiritual Pollution Campaign (1983–1984)** and the post-1989 Anti-**Bourgeois Liberalization** Campaign renewed these very intense criticisms of intellectuals, though psychological and physical pressure like that of the 1950s and 1960s has been generally avoided.

"THREE-ANTIS CAMPAIGN" (*"SANFAN YUNDONG"*). This was one of the first mass political movements initiated by the **Chinese Communist Party** (CCP) in 1952. The official purpose was to oppose **corruption**, waste, and bureaucracy in the Party and state organs. **Mao Zedong** labeled such problems in China as "the poisonous residue of the old society" that needed to be "washed clean." All CCP members were forced to re-register and those determined to be "corrupt and degenerate" were targeted for expulsion or even more severe punishment. Most CCP members were spared harsh treatment, especially if they "confessed" to their purported transgressions, but a small minority were viciously attacked and, in many cases, executed. Criticisms were often during huge public rallies, where transgressors were first "tried" and immediately afterward taken out and shot. These "negative examples" were used in the Three-Antis and other similar campaigns to frighten the majority into compliance with central demands for greater discipline and obedience to Party policies. The campaign began with the issuance of policy documents, which became the basis for **"criticism and self-criticism"** (*piping yu ziwopiping*) and attacks on the targeted few. It ended in late 1952.

THREE BITTER YEARS. *See* "GREAT LEAP FORWARD" (1958–1960).

"THREE CATEGORIES OF PERSONS" (*"SANZHONGREN"*). These people, during the **Cultural Revolution** (1966–1976), had headed the violent **Rebel Faction** (*zaofanpai*), who engaged in fighting, and/or committed acts of "smashing and looting." They were singled out for criticism and separation from the **Chinese Communist Party** (**CCP**) in the aftermath of the arrest of **Mao Zedong's** widow, **Jiang Qing**, and the launching of the anti–**Gang of Four** campaign in the late 1970s. In effect, the appellation was often arbitrarily assigned to just about anyone who the regime wanted to push aside. This even included advocates of liberal political reforms whose experiences during the Cultural Revolution had convinced them of China's need to undergo the kind of broad-based liberalization that led them to be singled out for attack by conservative political **leaders**, who were intent on stalling the reform program initiated in 1978–1979.

"THREE FAMILY VILLAGE." The newspaper column "Notes from a Three Family Village" (*Sanjia cunzha ji*) was published from 1961 to 1964 in the **Beijing** Party Committee journal, *Frontline* (*Qianxian*) and authored pseudonymously by **Deng Tuo**, Liao Mosha, and **Wu Han**. As an opening shot in the **Cultural Revolution (1966–1976)**, this column and another, titled "Evening Chats at Yanshan," were vehemently criticized by the leftwing polemicist **Yao Wenyuan** as "poisonous arrows," resulting in the purge of their authors and the ultimate suicide of Deng Tuo. The thrust of both columns was mild and often indirect criticism of socialist China, its leadership (including **Mao Zedong**), especially lower-level **cadres** in the **Chinese Communist Party** (**CCP**). Published in the aftermath of the **Great Leap Forward** (**1958–1960**) and during the Three Bitter Years (1960–1962) of widespread rural famine, the "Notes" and "Evening Chats" criticized the policy failures of the Leap and lampooned arrogant and brazen **leaders** who had neglected the people's interests. In the tradition of classical Confucian literati, Deng Tuo reminded the Party leadership of the fine traditions in Chinese classical statecraft, especially famine relief, and called on Party leaders from top to bottom to exercise self-discipline and traditional "benevolence." The importance of individual cultural enjoyment and an appreciation for the past and a cosmopolitan attitude in cultivating proper behavior were also primary themes. Deng Tuo's approach was elitist and somewhat paternalistic, but also expressed concern that the CCP serve the public good and not squander its hard-won legitimacy by reckless policies and arrogant leadership.

Two years after their termination, these columns were viciously attacked by leftist proponents of the Cultural Revolution, most notably by Yao Wenyuan in his May 1966 *People's Daily* diatribe titled "Criticizing the 'Three Family Village'—The Reactionary Nature of 'Evening Chats at Yanshan' and 'Notes from a Three Family Village.'" After the Cultural Revolution, the columns and their authors were "rehabilitated" in such articles as the 1979 piece "It Is No Crime to Criticize Idealism, It Is Meritorious to Propagandize Materialism—Refuting Yao Wenyuan's False Charges in Criticizing 'Evening Chats at Yanshan' and 'Notes from a Three Family Village.'"

THREE GORGES DAM PROJECT. Planned as the largest hydropower project in the world, the Three Gorges dam, when completed in 2013, will be 2,300 m wide, 185 m high, with a 483-m long spillway and 22 sluice gates on the surface and below with 23 bottom outlets to pass sediment. At its peak, the dam—with 26 turbines provided by the foreign firms of Swiss-based Alstom Ltd. and Voith-Siemens Hydro Power Generation Co. and domestic producers

Sichuan-Dongfang Electric Co. and Harbin Electric—will have an installed capacity of 18,000 megawatts (a fraction of China's total generating capacity of 350,000 megawatts) and be able to produce 84.7 billion kWh of electric power a year that will be offered at 0.25 *yuan* per kWh, compared to the current average in China of 0.29 *yuan* per kWh. Construction of the project is underway on the Yangtze River in the scenic Three Gorges (*sanxia*) area and will take 18 years from its inauguration in 1994 to complete at a projected cost of 160 billion *yuan* (US$20 billion), much of which has come in the form of corporate bonds. Major domestic investors in the project include Huaneng Power International Inc., China National Nuclear Corp., China National Petroleum Corp, the Gezhouba Construction Group, and the Changjiang (Yangtze) Institute of Survey, Planning, Design, and Research with **China International Trust and Investment Corporation** (**CITIC**) Securities Co. serving as the underwriter.

It is claimed that when completed the dam will help prevent downstream flooding that cost more than 500,000 lives in the 20th century. The huge reservoir that will form behind the dam will cover 632 km^2 encompassing two cities, 11 counties, 140 towns, and 1,300 villages requiring the displacement of 1.3 million people, the largest number in world history whose resettlement is often to such far-off places as the Xinjiang Autonomous Region and Jiangsu Province and is slated to cost four billion *yuan* (US$482 million). Critics in China and outside the country argue that the dam will fundamentally alter the ecology of the river valley and because of sedimentation and other problems it will never produce the intended electrical output, nor provide adequate flood control.

The dam was first proposed in 1919 as part of the "Plan to Develop Industry" promulgated by Sun Yat-sen and was championed in 1944 by the American hydrologist John Savage. After 1949, top **leaders** of the **Chinese Communist Party** (**CCP**), including **Mao Zedong**, periodically discussed the feasibility of the project, especially in the aftermath of devastating floods that hit the Yangtze River valley in 1954, but it was consistently rejected or put on hold as leaders cited unresolved technical problems and costs. In 1957, critics of the project, such as **Li Rui**, were labeled as "rightists," but despite the role of the dam as a symbol of the drive by the CCP to conquer nature, construction was constantly postponed because of economic and political turmoil involving the **Great Leap Forward (1958–1960)** and the **Cultural Revolution (1966–1976)**. Recommendations to construct the dam were revived in 1985, but construction was postponed at a key **National People's Congress (NPC)** meeting in March 1989 that followed domestic and foreign opposition to its construction. Following the military crackdown in 1989 against the second **Beijing Spring**, many Three Gorges Dam opponents were removed from power. Critics, such as the journalist **Dai Qing**, were incarcerated while dam supporters, such as Premier **Li Peng**, were now in a position to push for its approval. Construction was finally authorized at an April 1992 NPC meeting while preliminary work began in 1993, headed by the Committee on the Construction of the Three Gorges Project under the State Council. Foreign financing of the dam has been sparse because the World Bank and other such international lending institutions oppose its construction, as do many environmental groups, such as Probe International in Canada.

Construction and operation of the dam is in the hands of the Three Gorges Project Corporation, a ministry-level **state-owned enterprise (SOE)** and parent of the China Yangtze Electric Power Corporation with IPO stock offering on the **stock exchange** in **Shanghai**. From 1993 to 1997, during the first stages of construction, the project relied overwhelmingly on state **investment** and state bank loans with major financing of 35 billion *yuan* (US$4.23 billion) coming from the China Development Bank. During the second stage, which spanned from 1998 to 2003, social funds became increasingly important as 19 billion *yuan* of bonds were issued to the public along with borrowing from commercial loans. The third stage of construction covers 2004 to 2009 and when completed 26 generators each with a generating capacity of 700,000 kWh will be installed. Construction has proceeded on schedule as the reservoir behind the dam began filling in June 2003 and is to proceed in four steps from a depth of 82.28 m to 135, 156 and finally 185 m, submerging 98,800 ha (350,000 *mu*) of land, including much valuable river valley farmland and houses. Except for the most prominent temples and relics located along the river that have been moved, an enormous numbers of unexcavated historical and archaeological sites dating back to the third century BC will also be permanently submerged.

Dam officials claim that the impounded reservoir of water behind the dam has produced no major change in water quality, in good part as a result of the construction of 19 sewage treatment plants in and around the Three Gorges area. Other voices inside and outside the Chinese government, however, paint a very different picture of the 600-km-long reservoir as a giant cesspool fed by **Third Front** industrial facilities upriver that dump pollutants such as heavy metals from paper, steel, textile, and chemical plants untreated into the river. As the river waters are stilled by the creation of the reservoir, the spread of parasitic worms dangerous to humans and a jump in E. coli, the bacterial marker of sewage contamination, have already been registered. In 2004, 51 out of 147 polluting projects that should have been treated remained untouched while 206 out of 304 highly polluting companies expected to be closed were still operating.

Dam officials claim that the build-up of silt behind the structure that some fear will clog **Chongqing** harbor in less than 10 years is "under control" as about 40% of the sediment flowing into the reservoir at the dam site has been washed away, thereby avoiding the rapid accumulation of silt that has effectively rendered the Three Gate Gorge (*Sanmenxia*) dam built in the 1960s on the Yellow River all but inoperable. In 2004, the five-level ship lock constructed at the Three Gorges officially opened after a year's worth of operational testing allowing 10,000-ton vessels to traverse the reservoir up to Chongqing. In 2004, the number of people slated to be relocated was revised upward with no specific figure given and some of the construction work had to be redone as cracks appeared in the façade of the concrete structure that is 40 stories high. Upon completion of the dam, the reservoir will impound 3.93 billion m^3 of water with a flood storage capacity of 22.15 billion m^3 in a river with an annual volume of 453 billion m^3. China also announced that it had stationed "anti-terror troops" from the People's Armed Police (PAP) to defend the dam from a "clearly rising threat from the **United States** and **Japan**" and perhaps **Taiwan**. Along with complaints by relocatees of enormous **corruption** in the disbursement (or lack of it) of compensation funds, several high profile cases of fraud surrounding the project have surfaced, including the prosecution and execution of a central figure in a large-scale embezzlement scheme in 2000. Other major dam projects planned for the Yangtze River would inundate

Tiger Leaping Gorge in western China, one of the deepest and most spectacular gorges in the world. *See also* ARCHAEOLOGY; ENERGY.

THREE RED BANNERS. This refers to the various campaigns in the late 1950s in China to dramatically accelerate the country's economic growth and political transformation. The first "banner" was the General Line for Socialist Construction that **Mao Zedong** initiated in 1957. It called for "going all out, aiming high, and achieving greater, faster, better and more economical results in building **socialism**." In practical terms, this meant China should move as quickly as possible to the construction of a modern industrial and agricultural base. The second "banner" was the **Great Leap Forward (1958–1960)**, which involved an attempt to carry out a huge expansion of agricultural and industrial production. The goals were to "overtake" Great Britain in 15 years and the **United States** in 20 years through the construction of **backyard steel furnaces** and massive water conservancy projects. The third "banner" was the **people's commune**, the massive rural production organizations that were designed to dramatically increase both agricultural and industrial production in the countryside and cities. The disastrous results of the Great Leap in 1960 brought an end to the Three Red Banners, though, in the early 1960s, Mao Zedong tried to build support for yet another leap, an effort that ultimately failed and that led to his attacks on the Party leadership during the **Cultural Revolution (1966–1976)**.

TIANANMEN MASSACRE (1989). *See* BEIJING SPRING.

TIANANMEN SQUARE INCIDENT (1976). *See* APRIL FIFTH MOVEMENT (1976).

TIAN JIAYING (1922–1966). Born in Chengdu, Sichuan Province, Tian Jiaying (originally named Zeng Zhengchang) traveled to Yan'an in Shaanxi Province to join the **Chinese Communist Party (CCP)** where at age 26 he lectured on popular history to Party **cadres** and was picked by **Mao Zedong** to serve as his secretary, a position he held for the next 18 years. In 1955, Tian Jiaying was formally appointed to the Staff Office for the Chairman of the **People's Republic**

of China (PRC) and continued with his hobby of collecting written script by historically important figures from the Qing dynasty (1644–1911). Tian played the role of an indispensable assistant to Mao by helping to build his library and finding without delay the provenance of the little-known quotations Mao would embed in his poems or historical characters to which the chairman would often allude. Tian committed suicide during the **Cultural Revolution (1966–1976)** reportedly because of his split with Mao Zedong on many economic and political issues, including the ambitious but ultimately destructive policies of the **Great Leap Forward (1958–1960)**. In line with his expressed wishes, Tian's family donated many of his Qing scripts to the Museum of Chinese History.

TIAN JIYUN (1929–). From Guizhou Province in China's southwest, Tian Jiyun in the early 1950s joined the **Chinese Communist Party (CCP)** as head of a **land reform** team and, in the 1970s, after the **Cultural Revolution (1966–1976)** became a financial expert in Sichuan Province. In 1981, he became an official in the State Council and, in 1982, was appointed to the CCP Central Committee and a vice-premier the next year. In 1985, he was elected to the **Politburo** and Party Secretariat and, in 1987, became a member of the Politburo Standing Committee. In September 1989, he was put in charge of breaking up and merging companies and firms and served as a vice-chairman of the **National People's Congress (NPC)** but was sidelined in the aftermath of the military crackdown against the second **Beijing Spring** in June 1989. Following his forced retirement from the Politburo in 2002, Tian Jiyun was one of the few former top **leaders** who, in 2005, dared to lay a wreath at the funeral of former CCP General Secretary **Zhao Ziyang** after calling on the CCP Central Committee to hold a farewell ceremony commensurate with Zhao's former positions.

TIANJIN. One of four provincial-level municipalities in China, Tianjin Municipality (*Tianjin shi*) like **Beijing**, **Shanghai**, and **Chongqing** is under the direct authority of the central government in China and is the third largest urban area in the country. Rendered as *Tientsin* under Wade-Giles Romanization, the municipality is divided into 18 county-level divisions including 15 districts (*qu*) and three counties (*xian*) with a total **population** in 2004 of 10.24 million of which 9.3 held the Tianjin urban registration (*hukou*) and 5.6 million lived in the urban areas of the municipality and 3.8 in rural enclaves. Located in the northeastern part of the North China Plain, along the Hai River with ports on Bohai Gulf, Tianjin also borders Hebei Province and Beijing Municipality.

The development of the city traces its origins to the Sui dynasty (581–618 AD) when the opening of the South-to-North Grand Canal prompted the area's development as a trading center that was originally called *Zhigu* ("straight port") but was renamed *Tianjin* ("heavenly ford") in the 15th century to commemorate the fording of the Hai River by the emperor-to-be Yongle of the Ming dynasty (1368–1644). During the 19th century, Tianjin was one of the many ports in China forcibly open to foreign **trade** by the unequal treaties signed in the aftermath of the Opium Wars with the British and French. Large swaths of the old city center became self-contained foreign concessions leaving the city with a rich combination of Chinese and Western **architecture** that, in recent years, municipal authorities have tried to preserve even as much of the city has undergone substantial renewal and reconstruction since 1994. During World War II, Tianjin fell to the Japanese in July 1937 and in 1945 became a base to American forces until 1947, when the American contingent was forced to evacuate the city in the aftermath of a series of rapes of young women by American soldiers. During the **Civil War (1946–1949)**, armies of the **Chinese Communist Party (CCP)** captured the city in January 1949. From 1958 to 1967, Tianjin lost its municipality status and was designated the capital of Hebei Province.

Long a center of trade and commerce via its seaport and proximity to the Grand Canal and Beijing, Tianjin's **economy** is a major industrial base in north China with an output marginally larger than the capital in industries ranging from petrochemicals, textiles, **automobile** manufacturing, and metal working, along with oil production from the nearby Dagang District oilfield. Wheat, rice, and maize are the most important crops grown in its rural enclaves with substantial fishing along the coast. Following the inauguration of the economic reforms in 1978–1979, Tianjin lagged behind other urban areas as its economic base remained wedded to increasingly inefficient and indebted **state-owned enterprises (SOEs)** with little in the way of private sector

investment and development. The creation in 1984 of the Tianjin Economic and Development Area (TEDA) lying just east of the city proper and the creation of a special economic region around the nearby Bohai Gulf in 1986 were both designed to pull in foreign capital, which, in the last several years, has run at about US$2 billion annually, with major investments by such companies as Motorola at an industrial complex that produces 20 million handset phones a year. Tianjin is also the selected site for the German High-Tech Industrial Park that began construction in 2004 and will include a College of Application of **Science and Technology** to be administered by the German Vocational Education Commission.

In 2004, Tianjin produced 293 billion *yuan* of Gross Domestic Product (GDP) for a per capita GDP of 31,600 *yuan* with urban and rural per capital income of 11,467 and 6,525 *yuan*, respectively. Although Tianjin was the first city in China to have a railway station (1888) and its own city-wide bus system (1904), the city's subway, which was constructed in 1970, was shut down in 2001 for reconstruction and has reopened. An elevated commuter rail system connecting the downtown area with TEDA opened in 2004 while the city plans to build five expressways to solve its severe traffic congestion problems. The Binhai International Airport serving Tianjin is the site of China's first privately run airline, Okay Airways, which began operations in early 2005. A former Soviet aircraft carrier, the Kiev, was purchased by a local Tianjin tourist firm and is now the center of a theme park built in the city. Since 2003, the mayor of Tianjin has been **Dai Xiaolong**, the former governor of the People's Bank of China.

Noted for its local snacks of *goubuli* (so delectable "even a dog wouldn't touch it"), *baozi* or steamed buns, *mahua* twisted dough sticks, and *erduoyan* fired rice cakes, Tianjin is also known for producing China's most famous practitioners of comic cross talk (*xiangsheng*). Tianjiners are often referred to as *weizuizi* roughly translated as "Tianjin mouth" because of their somewhat stereotypical reputation of being loud and prone to argument. Tianjin and Nankai universities are the city's most famous and prestigious institutions of higher **education** directly administered by the Ministry of Education in Beijing, while 15 other universities, including two medical universities, are administered by the Tianjin municipal government.

TIBET (*XIZANG*). Situated in the southwest part of China, Tibet is known as the "roof of the world" with an average elevation of more than 4,000 m. Site of the Himalayas and Mount Everest, Tibet is home to the Lamaist religion, a branch of Mahayana Buddhism, and was once the site of more than 13,000 monasteries, many of which were destroyed by rampaging **Red Guards** during the **Cultural Revolution (1966–1976)**. Tibet's major religious sites, such as the Jokhang temple in the capital city of Lhasa and the Drepung monastery (which formerly housed 10,000 monks), are periodically opened by Chinese authorities but often closed down for long periods of time. Continued training of Tibetan lamas (monks) has also been a constant source of tension between Tibet's religious elite and **Chinese Communist Party** (**CCP**) authorities. In 1994, the Chinese government ordered that monastery and temple construction (and reconstruction) must stop while an absolute cap has been placed on the number of monks and nuns to be trained. Foreign travel to Tibet has also been periodically restricted in recent years during political flare ups, though a 15-year campaign to promote tourism into the region began in 2003.

Historically, Tibet was an independent kingdom in the seventh century, encompassing an empire that stretched into significant parts of China proper, **Russia**, and Inner Mongolia. By the 13th century, Tibet was incorporated into the Chinese Empire, but with Chinese control limited under the principle of "rule by custom" to external affairs while Tibetans remained sovereign on domestic matters, an arrangement that lasted until the end of the Qing dynasty (1644–1911). Following a British invasion of the territory in 1904 and the collapse of the Qing in 1911, Tibet declared its independence from the new Republic of China (ROC) but the territory was quickly carved up by the 1913 Simla Conference convened in **India** that consisted of China, Tibet, and Great Britain. An inner part of Tibet was made into a southwestern province of China, while an outer part was granted full autonomy. China, however, refused to ratify the treaty. In 1950, Chinese Communist forces entered Tibet to reclaim the territory and terminate the 1911 Tibetan declaration of independence. After some resistance, the Tibetans capitulated and the 1951 "Agreement of the Central People's Government and the Local Government of Tibet on Measures for the Liberation of Tibet" was signed in which China recognized Tibet's autonomy but asserted full sovereign powers.

In 1952, the **Dalai Lama** was appointed chairman of the Preparatory Committee for the Tibetan Autonomous Region that was granted power to govern the domestic affairs of the territory. In 1959, conflict broke out once again as Tibetans protested the presence of Chinese military garrisons whom they feared were about to kidnap the Dalai Lama and whose refusal to suppress the uprising brought an immediate Chinese military response that forced the Dalai Lama to flee the country and seek refuge in northern India, where he lives with approximately 10,000 Tibetans to this day. The International Commission of Jurists in the same year noted that "deliberate violations of fundamental **human rights** had taken place in Tibet." In 1960, the **United Nations** (**UN**) addressed the issue of Tibet but only in terms of the issue of human rights, not sovereignty. In 1965, regional autonomy for Tibet was implemented by its official designation as an Autonomous Region with large swaths of "greater" Tibet—Amdo and Kham—incorporated into Qinghai, Sichuan, Yunnan, and Gansu provinces. In 1984, the **People's Republic of China** (**PRC**) passed the "Law of the People's Republic of China on Regional Ethnic Autonomy" that specified the policy guidelines for autonomous regions while between 1984 and 2001 four forums on government work in Tibet were convened.

During the reform era beginning in China in 1978–1979, the issue of Tibet has influenced Chinese domestic and international politics. Throughout the 1980s, CCP **leaders** pushed a number of "liberalizing" policies, such as increasing the number of Tibetan natives in the government of the region and withdrawing **Han** officials from the capital city of Lhasa. Increases in central government **investment** were also implemented along with tax exemptions for Tibetan farm animals and recognition of the right of Tibetans (unlike Chinese farmers) to own private land as Tibetans were encouraged to shift from **agriculture** to animal husbandry with the benefit of interest-free loans from the People's Bank of China. One of 55 officially recognized nationalities or **minorities** in China, Tibetans were also exempted from the **one-child policy**. The Tibetan New Year, the *Shoton* (Yogurt) Festival, and other traditional holidays are recognized by the government of the Tibetan Autonomous Region, where the official work week is 35 hours, five fewer than the national statutory work week. Still, the Chinese have yet to appoint a Tibetan to the top Party post in the region, which, in 2003, was held by a member of the Han ethnicity Guo Jinlong (and was previously held by the current president and CCP General Secretary **Hu Jintao**), though the governor in 2003 was a Tibetan named Jampa Phunstsok. Riots have also periodically broken out, the most serious occurring in 1989 when 30 people were killed and China imposed martial law that lasted until May 1990, which was followed by further disturbances in 1993 when large-scale demonstrations were carried out in the name of independence. The issue of human rights in Tibet has influenced relations between China and the **United States**. In 1992, the Human Rights Commission of the UN took up the question, though ultimately the commission accepted a European proposal to end the debate. Negotiations between representatives of the Dalai Lama and the Chinese government have been ongoing since 1993, with Tibetan envoys visiting China in 2002 and 2003. The highest-ranking Tibetan in the CCP is **Raidi**, who, in 2005, was a vice-chairman of the **National People's Congress** (**NPC**) Standing Committee.

From 1965 to 2003, the GDP of Tibet increased from 327 million *yuan* to more than 18 billion *yuan* with per capita income of its 2.62 million people (the least populated province in China) growing from 241 *yuan* to 6,874 *yuan* (50% of the national average) largely because of very substantial investments in the autonomous region by the central government. This includes the construction of a 1,230-km railway link between Qinghai Province and Tibet that began in 2001 and was completed as the world's highest railway in October 2005 at a cost of 26 billion *yuan*. For 17 consecutive years, Tibet has raised a bumper harvest despite its harsh natural conditions with major crops consisting of highland barley, wheat, potatoes, peas, and rapeseed. The state sector in Tibet employs 150,000 people, including 100,000 ethnic Tibetans, and controls 90% of the **economy**, the largest in China after **Shanghai**, with much state spending in Tibet focused on construction of new roads, airports, and power grids, including the Yamzho Yumco hydropower station, which began operations in 1997. During an inspection tour of Tibet in 1990, President **Jiang Zemin** urged the need to accelerate economic development and yet most average Tibetans live off stagnant occupations, such as carpet making, herding, mining, and forestry, that leave the average income of rural Tibetans at only 1,600 *yuan*.

In 2005, the foreign **trade** of Tibet amounted to US$253 million as southern Tibetan cities, such as Tsetang, the region's third largest, have experienced a boom with new buildings rising as Chinese Han migrants continue to move in producing what some fear is an erosion of Tibet's unique, highly insular culture. Intermarriage between Tibetans and Han have reduced ethnic tensions somewhat while the **education** level of average Tibetans has been improved dramatically as the construction of over 1,000 schools of various types has reduced the illiteracy rate to less than 30%. Equal attention in schools is paid to the Tibetan and Chinese languages and all relevant government documents are produced in both scripts. The average life span in Tibet has grown from 36 to 67 years while the infant death rate has declined from 20 to 0.661%, which doubled the Tibetan **population** from 1953 to 2003. More than one million tourists visited Tibet in 2003 for mountaineering, expeditions, and pilgrimages, contributing to 6% of the autonomous region's Gross Domestic Product (GDP) while exhibits, such as the 1999 Shining Pearl of the Snowlands in **Beijing** featured Tibetan history and culture, along with performances in the capital in the same year of the *Qomolangma* or Tibetan-style music and dance.

Nonetheless, books or articles on Tibet considered excessively sympathetic to the Dalai Lama or Tibetan culture are periodically banned and, in 2004, international advocacy organs for Tibet, such as the International Campaign for Tibet, claimed that Chinese authorities were strengthening measures to control Buddhist worship in Tibet that amounted to a "second Cultural Revolution." Although negotiations between representatives of the Dalai Lama and the Chinese government are ongoing, in 2003, a drill by police, paramilitary, and military units in Tibet was carried out in the name of "counterterrorism" against "infiltration and terrorist activities in the area by Dalai Lama 'separatist' forces backed by the West." The Dalai Lama has repeatedly appealed to Chinese authorities to allow him to return to Tibet, where he believes he can make Tibetans calm, but China has responded with demands that he end all "separatist" activities and it continues to arrest monks on such charges as painting a Tibetan flag and/or possessing photographs of the exiled leader. The **"one country, two systems"** formula established by China for **Hong Kong**, Macao, and **Taiwan** is considered by the PRC as totally inappropriate for Tibet because, unlike these other areas, it was never under colonial rule. *See also* RELIGION; SOCIAL PROTESTS; TRANS-PORTATION.

"TO REBEL IS JUSTIFIED" (*"ZAOFAN YOULI"*). The signature slogan chanted by **Red Guards** during the **Cultural Revolution (1966–1976)** to justify attacks on **Chinese Communist Party (CCP)** members and top **leaders**, such as **Liu Shaoq**, this phrase was specifically directed at negating all rules and regulations in schools, work units, and Party and government organizations that inhibited "revolutionary" action. The slogan was given legitimacy in 1967 by the theoretical journal *Red Flag* that was under the control of the radical faction of the **Gang of Four** associated with **Jiang Qing**. Restraints on the activities of Red Guards were removed and, throughout 1967 and early 1968, Red Guards rampaged throughout China's urban areas and in minority areas such as **Tibet** wreaking great destruction. By 1968, however, **Mao Zedong** decided to end the increasing violence and many Red Guards were sent into the countryside for long sojourns.

TOWNSHIP VILLAGE ENTERPRISES (TVEs). A product of the **Agricultural Responsibility System** inaugurated in 1978–1979, rural township village enterprises have grown at rapid rates soaking up surplus rural **labor** (estimated at 200 million workers nationwide) freed by the abolition of socialist **agriculture**. Owned and operated by local governments at the level of townships (*xiang*) and villages (*cun*) (the administrative successors to the former **people's communes** and brigades) and by individual households or groups of households, these enterprises have become a mainstay of China's **economy**, especially in rural areas. From 1984 to 2004, the gross value of goods produced by these enterprises rose from 170 billion *yuan* (US$29 billion) to four trillion *yuan* (US$500 billion) or about 30% of China's GDP of which 1.7 trillion *yuan* of goods were produced for export. Their total employment in the same period grew from 50 million to 138 million workers with two million more workers, mostly farmers, added annually. Initially concentrated in the southeast in the Pearl River Delta and Guangdong Province, TVEs have also become major fixtures in recent years of the rural economy in the Yangtze River delta, which embraces **Shanghai** Municipality and Jiangsu and Zhejiang provinces, and in the Bohai Gulf–rim area of **Beijing** and **Tianjin** municipalities and Shandong and Liaoning provinces.

Approximately 70% of the enterprises are industrial, producing machinery, building materials, and textiles, 15% in construction (particularly housing construction, which has boomed in China's rural areas since 1978), and 8% in services. In recent years, TVEs engaged in mining, and heavily polluting industries have been reduced in number while those in services, processing of farm produce, and **technology**-intensive industries have increased. Most TVEs operate outside the state planning mechanism relying on the market to acquire materials and selling their output through private and collective channels. Tax evasion and **corruption** have been constant charges levied against these enterprises by Chinese government authorities who oversee the TVEs through the Township Enterprises Bureau under the Ministry of Agriculture. TVEs have also been faulted for substandard production of such articles as fireworks that led to a spate of explosions at ill-equipped firework facilities, which, in 2004, killed more than 200 people. Other problems besetting TVEs include the impending competition of imports as a result of China's 2001 entry into the **World Trade Organization** (**WTO**), the slow growth of TVEs in China's more backward western regions, blind investment and duplicated construction, and the gradual drying up of the abundant bank loans that in the 1980s and 1990s produced the rapid growth of TVEs.

TRADE AND INVESTMENT. In 2005, China's total trade came to US$1.4 trillion, the third largest in the world, with US$762 billion in exports and US$660 billion in imports, a nearly five-fold increase from 1995 when China's total trade was US$289 billion. China's major trade partners were in order of value: **Japan**, the **United States**, South **Korea**, Germany, Singapore, Malaysia, **Russia**, and the Netherlands. China's largest trade surplus (US$170 billion) was with the U.S., double the 1999 figure, while its total foreign exchange reserves came to US$795 billion, double the 2003 level. Of the five busiest ports in the world, three are in China with the port of **Shanghai** surpassing Pusan, South Korea, as the world's largest. Although Foreign Direct Investment (FDI) in China stalled after the military crackdown against the second **Beijing Spring** in June 1989, it quickly recovered and from 1992 to 2002, the cumulative value of FDI in China came to US$350 billion as China replaced the U.S. in 2003 as the world's largest recipient of FDI netting US$53 billion, US$10 billion from Japan.

During the period of Soviet-style central planning and the dominance of the Maoist ideal of **self-reliance** (*zili gengsheng*), China's total trade outside the Soviet bloc was minimal with virtually no FDI entering the country as capital accumulation depended almost completely on the expropriation of wealth from the countryside under a price scissors policy in which agricultural products were appropriated at below market value and industrial goods were fixed at relatively high prices. But with the inauguration of the economic reforms in 1978–1979 that included the **open-door policy**, China engaged the world trading system and welcomed FDI. While all trade and investment is carried out under the guise of the Chinese state, a number of laws were passed to clarify and guarantee the legal status of foreign trade and investment interests. These included the 1979 Equity Joint Venture Law, which sanctioned joint Sino–Foreign enterprises and offered foreign firms and individuals legal protection for investment projects; amendments to the State constitution in 1982 and 1988, which recognized the right of foreigners to "invest in China and to enter various forms of economic cooperation with Chinese enterprises"; the 1982 Civil Procedure Law, which explicitly afforded foreigners the right to sue in Chinese courts; the 1985 Foreign Economic Contract Law, which regulates all contracts involving a foreign and domestic party; and the 1994 Foreign Trade Law, which consolidated all previous legal enactments involving foreign trade. Wholly owned foreign enterprises were sanctioned in 1986 while, in 1990, the Chinese government eliminated the 30-year time restriction on the establishment of joint ventures and also allowed foreign partners to become chairs of joint venture boards.

Along with these domestic legal changes, China signed on to major international agreements and treaties that have a direct bearing on foreign trade and investment: The first was the Paris Convention for the Protection of Industrial Property signed in 1984; the New York Convention on the Recognition and Enforcement of Foreign Arbitral Awards signed in 1987; the **United Nations** Convention on Contracts for the International Sale of Goods (Vienna Convention) and the Hague Convention on the Service of Documents Abroad both signed in 1991; and the Berne Convention on Protection of Literary and Artistic Works, which China joined in 1992. In addition, China entered into numerous bilateral trade agreements with other nations, including an Agricultural Cooperation Agreement with the U.S. in 1999 that lifted longstanding Chinese prohibitions against importation of citrus, grain, beef, and poultry. Contrary to American practice, China has agreed that if there is a conflict between Chinese domestic legislation and the provision of an international agreement, the international provision takes precedence unless China has specifically reserved the right to apply its own law. A member since 1991 of the Asia–Pacific Economic Cooperation (APEC), which is devoted to enhancing trade among countries bordering on the Pacific, China ascended to the **World Trade Organization** (**WTO**) in 2001 with requirements to lower tariffs on agricultural products from 31 to 14% and on industrial products from 25 to 9%, both by 2004. Following a surge of Chinese textile exports in 2005 to the U.S. after the end of international textile quotas, China and the U.S. agreed to limits on clothing exports for the next three years.

China's trade and investment regime has a number of unique characteristics. First, a substantial amount of China's trade is conducted by foreign-invested enterprises. In 2003, foreign firms conducted 56.2% of China's imports and 54.8% of China's exports. To a very large extent, China's trade is quite heavily dependent on enterprises from other economies. Because of the involvement of foreign-invested enterprises in China's exports this implies that foreign firms, including U.S. firms, directly benefit from the explosive growth of China's trade with the rest of the world. In 2002, the rate of return for U.S. multinationals in computer and electronic products was estimated at 21.2%. Second, a large amount of China's trade is first shipped to **Hong Kong** and then reexported. In 2003, 28.3% of Chinese exports to the world were reexported via Hong Kong, while 21.9% of Chinese imports from the world were first sent to Hong Kong before being reexported into China. Third, China's trade and Foreign Direct Investment (FDI) are geographically concentrated. In 2003, Guangdong's imports accounted for 31.7% of China's total imports, while Guangdong's exports accounted for 34.9% of China's total exports. Most of the FDI into China still flows to the east and coastal areas, primarily Shanghai, Jiangsu, Zhejiang, Fujian, Shandong, Guangdong, Hainan, **Beijing**, **Tianjin**, Hebei, Liaoning, and Guangxi, which overall received 89.5% of realized FDI in 2002. Fourth, a large percentage of China's trade is related to processing and assembly. In 2003, 55.2% of China's exports were processed exports, while 39.5% of China's imports were processed imports. On average, the domestic value-added of Chinese exports is still relatively modest. In 1995, US$1 worth of aggregate Chinese export to the U.S. induced a direct domestic value-added of US$0.19. Fifth, according to China's Custom Statistics, in 2003, China exported US$110.3 billion (25.2% of China's total exports) of high-**technology** products and imported US$119.3 billion (28.9% of total imports) of high-technology goods. This partly reflects the fact that, in certain industries, China is now a part of the global supply chain network and is engaged in both importing and exporting of various components and parts. Sixth, most recent FDI into China is not via joint ventures but is going instead to wholly foreign-owned enterprises.

Among the problems that have beset foreign trade and investment with China is the protection of intellectual property rights. In 1982, China enacted its first modern intellectual property law, a Trademark Law, which was amended in 1983 to permit the registration of service marks. This was followed by Patent and Copyright laws, respectively, in 1985 and 1990, and an Unfair Competition Law in 1993 that forbids unauthorized use of commercial names and false and misleading claims about a product. In addition to these laws, China has entered into several Memoranda of Understanding with the U.S. concerning measures to be taken for the better protection of intellectual property. While the content of these measures compare favorably with the intellectual property laws of most modern commercial nations, major concern has focused more on the lack of enforcement in China particularly by provincial and local authorities who have often ignored exhortations from the central government to clamp down on illicit production of computer software, movies, and music.

A second problem concerns the impact of decentralization in authority and decision making in China since 1978–1979 on negotiations over trade and investment. In the past, almost all of China's economic activity was in the hands of a relatively few large Chinese national companies, each with a headquarters and numerous branches, which legally constituted a single business entity. But that situation has undergone enormous changes as what once previously large conglomerates have since the 1980s been broken up into numerous independent operating entities, each responsible for its own profits and losses. Previously a national company might be held ultimately responsible for an export contract entered into by a provincial branch while now what looks like a provincial branch of a national company, though retaining the former national company's name, may, in fact, be an independent legal entity with exclusive responsibility for its contractual commitments. With information and records on Chinese business concerns often in disarray, foreigners often find it impossible to establish the exact legal status of a Chinese business entity with which they propose to deal, that is whether it is an independent entity or a branch, and whether it has authorization to engage in foreign trade.

Third is the issue of China's commodity inspection system that, despite the creation of a Commodity Inspection Bureau, lacks exact standards subject to full transparency. Where disputes over inspection decisions and other trade- and investment-related matters arise, China put in place a system for the arbitration of international trade disputes in 1988 with the establishment of the China International Economic and Trade Arbitration Commission (CIETAC). This tribunal is authorized to handle all international trade disputes, which, in recent years, have grown in number, making it one of the busiest arbitration tribunals in the world. In 1995, a new Arbitration Law was enacted that broadened the scope of disputes that may be submitted to arbitration and set tight time limits on the rendering of awards. It also allows arbitration to continue even when the underlying contract is found to be invalid. Bowing to China's demand that large import agreements for anything from **automobiles** to computer software be accompanied by technology transfer and lured by persistent low wages, many multinationals have resorted to buying or investing in factories in China to supply the Chinese market instead of exporting the same goods every year, thereby reducing total trade volume.

TRADE UNIONS. The All-China Federation of Trade Unions is the sole **labor** organization in China, one of the many "mass" organizations in the Chinese Communist **government structure**. The Federation exercises leadership over unions throughout the country as a "transmission belt" for implementing central Party and government policy toward labor. The Federation is composed of the All-China Labor Congress and the Executive Committee of the All-China Federation of Trade Unions produced by the congress. There is a chairman, vice-chairmen, and members with day-to-day work handled by the Secretariat of the Federation. In 1983, 72 million workers were members of the Federation and by 1998 that number had grown to 90 million. With the enrollment of large numbers of migrant workers who are part of China's vast **floating population**, by 2003, the Federation had a membership of 134 million organized into 1.7 million local branches in the state, collective, and private sectors of the **economy**. The supreme leading body of the Federation is the national congress, which meets every five years and its executive committee, which is elected at the congress subject to **Chinese Communist Party** (**CCP**) approval. Fourteen national congresses have been held, the last in 2003. The Federation was headed in 2005 by Wang Zhaoguo, who is also a vice-chairman of the **National People's Congress** (**NPC**) and a member of the CCP **Politburo**. All Chinese and foreign companies with more than 100 employees are required by law to open a branch of the national union, a rule that is widely ignored or undermined by the reluctance of local governments to organize union branches in foreign-owned firms for fear of alienating their owners or by the practice of putting enterprise managers in charge of the union. The Federation maintains active relations with the International Labour Organization (ILO) that, after a long hiatus, were resumed in 1983 and with unions of various political stripes in over 130 countries and regions.

Communist interest in organizing labor unions began immediately after the establishment of the CCP in 1921. In 1922, the First All-China Labor Congress was convened in **Guangzhou** (**Canton**) in southern China and in 1925 the All-China Federation of Trade Unions was established as a CCP "front" organization at the time of the May 30th anti-imperialist mass movement. Membership in the Federation peaked in early 1927 at two million organized workers. Following the April 1927 anti-Communist coup launched by Chiang Kai-shek, the Federation was forced underground and, from 1927 to 1949, waged a struggle against the **Kuomintang (KMT)** in the urban areas. Membership in the Federation dropped precipitously and did not recover until the 1940s, when anti-Japanese sentiment and the CCP–KMT Second **United Front** provided a political opening for leftwing labor activity.

After the establishment of the **People's Republic of China (PRC)** in 1949, the Federation was restored and took as its main task the propagandizing and political **education** of the Chinese working class under the rubric of the Trade Union Law of the PRC promulgated in 1950. A political and administrative "transmission belt" for the CCP, the Federation encompassed all industrial workers and its local organs as membership grew from 10 million in 1953 to 16 million in 1957. The Federation propagandized workers in the policies and **basic line of the Party**. During the **Hundred Flowers Campaign (1956–1957)** strikes and other working class political activity broke out in **Shanghai** and other cities indicating that CCP control of the working class was far from solid. During the **Cultural Revolution (1966–1976)**, the Federation was essentially gutted as workers joined in various **Red Guard** factions and the **leaders** of the Federation were disgraced and purged. By 1978, however, the organization was revived and membership grew to more than 61 million. During the 1989 second **Beijing Spring** pro-democracy movement, the head of the Federation, **Zhu Houze**, threatened to call a general strike to back up student demands for political reforms. A rank-and-file worker, **Han Dongfang**, challenged the Federation by setting up an alternative labor organization, claiming the Federation was a mouthpiece for the CCP leadership. Following the military crackdown on 4 June 1989, Zhu Houze was sacked and Han Dongfang was arrested. Since 1994, there have been periodic work slowdowns, strikes, and industrial violence as part of a general pattern of rising **social protests** in China as worker have responded to a number of grievances, most notably large-scale lay-offs from **state-owned enterprises (SOEs)**, inadequate **health care**, and pension and wage payments held in arrears sometimes for months or even years, and abuses at the hands of employers—private and state—and their hired thugs. Opposition has also risen against the common practice in domestic and foreign-owned firms of putting enterprise managers in charge of the union branch, who rarely, if ever, meet with workers, a practice that, at least formally, was outlawed in 2003 by the Method for Implementing the PRC Trade Union Law. Other complaints include the failure of the government to enforce minimum wage laws and regulations on overtime and on workplace safety.

The more active role of the Federation in protecting labor interests and ensuring workplace safety after a series of major industrial and coal mine disasters resulted in a major change in its constitution when in 2003 at the 14th National Congress an amendment was approved, making protection of labor union members' legal rights the organization's essential responsibility. The same congress also added a provision stipulating that union members could keep and transfer their membership when moving from one work place to another, thereby protecting a legal basis for migrant workers to join the Federation. In the past, the union only accepted workers with an urban household registration (*hukou*). Addressing the increasing problem of unemployment among workers, especially those laid off from SOEs, local branches of the Federation have set up reemployment bases throughout the country that offer workers assistance in job searches and short-term financial help. With more and more workers employed in private or foreign-funded enterprises, many local branches of the Federation have cast aside their traditional role as a "toothless" management-controlled body dedicated to preventing conflict and have, instead, become a more assertive advocate for workers' interests, such as retrieving back-pay and supervising employer adherence to the Law on Work Safety passed in 2002.

Draft election rules drawn up in 2003 are to allow a popular vote for branch chairmen and shop leaders, which have already been carried out on an experimental basis in the coastal provinces to ensure greater accountability of unions to workers' interests, though many of these elected leaders are reportedly ignored by higher-ups in the Federation when they try to communicate worker concerns. Bowing to pressure from the Federation, the American retail giant Wal-Mart, which in 2004 had 39 stores with 20,000 employees in China, agreed to permit unions to be set up in its stores if employees requested it, this after the Federation threatened to sue it, along with other foreign companies, such as Dell and Eastman Kodak, for their no-union policy, which is considered a violation of China's 1994 Labor Law.

"TRANSFER TO LOWER LEVELS" (*"XIAFANG"*). Fear of "**bureaucratism**" and insulation of government and **Chinese Communist**

Party (CCP) officials from the Chinese people led to periodic transfer of personnel to lower-level organizations and even to the countryside, where they engaged in manual **labor**. At the height of the **Cultural Revolution (1966–1976)**, even top Party **leaders** were "sent down" and some did not survive the ordeal. Non-government **intellectuals** and urban youth were also periodically "sent down," especially from 1968 onward when violence among **Red Guard** factions in the cities led **Mao Zedong** to order "educated young people" to hinterland rural areas for "re-education by the poor and lower-middle peasants." Many urban youth languished in the countryside for decades and, after marrying a local, they lost their all-important urban household registration (*hukou*). By the mid- to late 1970s, most urban youth had returned to the cities and many re-entered colleges and universities. Since 1978, the CCP has not generally employed *xiafang* of government personnel as an administrative tool for fighting "bureaucratism."

TRANSPORTATION. China's transportation sector consists of all conventional modes: inter-city and urban rail and subway systems; roadways and bridges; inland water, coastal and ocean shipping; and air transport. Throughout the history of the **People's Republic of China (PRC)** in both the Maoist era (1949–1976) of Soviet-style central planning and the era of economic reform beginning in 1978–1979, transportation has been a major factor in the country's national **economy** with heavy reliance on the rail network for the bulk of freight and passenger travel. In recent years, the greatest increases in transport volume have come from the growth of privately owned vehicles and a domestic **automobile industry**, with the rapid expansion of civil aviation and maritime shipping also contributing to China's growing transportation sector.

China's railway network is organized around two trunk lines, north-to-south with **Beijing** as its hub and west-to-east with Zhengzhou, Henan Province as the hub. The former consists of the Beijing–**Guangzhou (Canton)**, Beijing–**Shanghai**, Beijing–Kowloon, and Beijing–Harbin lines and the latter of the Liangyungang–Lanzhou and Lanzhou–Ürümqi lines with extensions into the newly independent nation of Kazakhstan, through which Asia is linked to Europe. New railway lines were also built in mountainous areas in southwestern China, mainly the Chengdu–**Chongqing**, Baoji–Chengdu,

Chengdu–Kunming, and Nanning–Kunming lines along with the recently completed Turpan–Kashi railway in the Xinjiang Autonomous Region. From 1949 to 1978, the economic emphasis on rapid heavy industrialization led to a transportation development strategy that relied on railways as the primary mode of inter-city transportation with freight, especially coal, taking up the overwhelming proportion of transportation volume with very little passenger service as China adhered to a rigid internal passport system that severely restrained individual travel.

On coming to power in 1949, the **Chinese Communist Party (CCP)** inherited approximately 23,000 km of rail line (half inoperable) from the period of construction that began with China's first railroad in Hebei Province built in 1876 during the later stages of the Qing dynasty (1644–1911) and continuing through the Nationalist era (1912–1949). Much of the network was concentrated in the central and northeastern coastal regions and the southwest and had been financed and owned by foreign interests, especially those from **Russia** and **Japan** who resided in **Manchuria**. Beginning in 1950, the CCP inaugurated a moderate railway construction program that between 1950 and 1985 added approximately 30,000 km to the network along with repair and upgrading of existing lines. In addition to the completion of the long-projected Longhai railway connecting Jiangsu Province with Lanzhou (the capital of Gansu Province), major lines were constructed in some of the most difficult terrain of the country including the Baotou–Lanzhou line, which passes through the Tengri Dessert, and the Baoji–Chengdu and Chengdu–Kunming lines that traverse rugged mountainous regions in the southwest where the emphasis on the defensive role of these routes as part of China's **Third Front** strategy led to the construction of bridges and tunnels (991 and 427, respectively, along the 1,000-km Chengdu–Kunming line) at great human cost with little immediate economic payback. Running along the rough Yunnan–Guizhou plateau, one of the most geologically unstable regions in the entire country, the Chengdu–Kunming line was constructed during the 1960s in record time as the centerpiece of the Third Front's grand "anti-**imperialism**, anti-revisionism, and anti-counter-revolution battle plan." "As long as the Chengdu–Kunming railway remains unfinished,"

Mao Zedong is said to have uttered, "I shall not sleep well." With this one line uttered from the all-powerful CCP chairman, the project quickly became top priority for the military construction gangs. Many of the lines constructed for the Third Front duplicated existing but more militarily vulnerable lines, resulting in enormous waste of resources as the heavy cost of maintaining these lines over the years often far exceeding their original cost of construction. The Zhicheng–Liuzhou line was built in the mountains of western Hunan Province as a parallel alternate route to the Beijing–Guangzhou line purely out of military necessity. Major rail lines were also constructed in China's rich forestry and mineral regions, particularly in the northeast, along with international rail links, such as the 1954 Beijing–Moscow line. Ancillary projects also included major bridges over the Yangtze River at Wuhan and Nanjing, which were completed in 1957 and 1968, respectively, the latter despite strong objections by foreign consultants on its engineering feasibility.

Throughout this period, operation of the rail lines was under the total control of the central government's Ministry of Railways (MOR), which, with three million employees, was one of the country's largest **state-owned enterprises** (**SOEs**). In addition to providing rail transport services, the MOR carried out a large variety of non-rail transport activities including manufacture of rolling stock (that up until 1988 consisted of steam-driven locomotives), civil construction, running of schools and universities, along with the Chinese Academy of Railway Sciences, design and development of rolling stock, housing, hospitals, and hotels. Overall, China's investment in the rail system during the Maoist era (1949–1976) was highly wasteful and generally inadequate to its economic needs because major construction projects were often driven by military and political considerations, such as the Third Front, leaving the country with an overtaxed rail infrastructure that has yet to be remedied. At the same time, modern highways and civil aviation were all but ignored while other forms of transport were also generally neglected as an economic development goal.

In the post-1978 reform era, increasing the capacity of China's rail network was designated a top priority. By 2005, China had 68,000 km of track with double-tracking and electrification upgrades for both the north–south and west–east trunk lines, along with many of its crucial branch lines. China's railroads remain heavily used and are the primary single mode of long-distance freight transport, especially for the shipment of coal from Shanxi and other western provinces to the coastal regions. Overall rail use for freight transportation has, however, declined in recent years from 58% in 1975 to 36% in 1995 while road transport grew during the same years from 3 to 13%. Inland river and ocean transport combined increased from 35 to 49% of total freight transport while passenger traffic on roads (bus and automobile) has surpassed the rail system, though passenger trains still average a 150% load factor, carrying half again as many people as there are seats, a figure that expands to 200% during high-use holidays. Construction of highways has averaged 10,000 km a year since 1978 while China has continued to build railways in often remote and poverty-stricken areas, such as the Nanning–Kunming line, which was described as "China's largest relief project of the 1990s." More economically viable lines include the completion in just three years time of the Beijing–Kowloon (**Hong Kong**) line that is part of the main north–south trunk line. Expansion of railway electrification, which in 2000 constituted 25% of all rail lines, and double-tracking continued, along with high-profile inner-city lines, particularly the high-speed magnetic levitation (maglev) train built by a German firm as the world's first commercial service linking downtown Shanghai with the city's international airport, a distance of 30 km. Beijing, **Tianjin**, Shanghai, and Guangzhou have operating subway lines while in 2001, 20 cities in China announced plans to build subways and light rails.

Reorganization of the rail administrative structure, which has long been overseen by the powerful Ministry of Railways, includes plans to separate railway administration between northern and southern regions, to close down underutilized stations and freight depots, to form quasi-corporate entities to manage railway sectors outside transport (e.g., real estate, production of rolling stock, and material sales), and to issue bonds to domestic and foreign investors to finance future projects. Five-year contracts have been signed between the MOR and 14 individual rail bureaus that were given responsibility for their profits and losses. Production and maintenance of modern locomotives has also made an important contribution to larger rail capacity with increased output of electric and diesel locomotives to replace steam-powered ones as the last steam locomotive factory in the city of Datong was closed in 1988. By 1995, 54% of all locomotives in operation were diesel, 29% steam, and 17% electric while, in the same year, the 2,536-km Beijing–Kowloon (Hong Kong) line was completed. This was followed by the 900-km electrified single-track Nanning–Kunming railway in 1997 and by completion of the 1,451-km South Xinjiang railroad project in 1999. Introduction of such modern features as containerization, the purchase of high-speed bullet trains that will run on 12,000 km of high-speed rail, and a joint rail-sea system with Japan indicate the high priority the Chinese government has assigned to improving the country's rail network. China is also committed to reducing the number of rail accidents such as the 1988 derailment on the Kunming–Shanghai express, which resulted in the loss of 90 lives. But with user fees and tariffs still extremely low—a legacy of the Soviet-era planning system—and the high cost of **investment** and land acquisition, the enormous bottlenecks that plague the entire rail system—freight and passenger—are not likely to disappear in the near term while vast swaths of the nation still lack rail service entirely. China's railway construction plans are often fraught with political controversy, such as the planned Golmud–Lhasa rail line over 1,000 km from Qinghai Province into **Tibet**, which was completed in October 2005 and inaugurated service on 1 July 2006.

The most dramatic development in China's transportation sector in recent years has been the explosive growth in the automobile industry, along with other forms of motorized transport, including buses, trucks, and other heavy vehicles. In 1949, one-third of the counties in China had no roads because roadway and highway construction received low priority throughout the Maoist era, with a few modest exceptions, such as the construction of the country's longest highway bridge over the Yellow River in 1972. With 890,000 km of roads in 1978, major construction projects were begun in the post-1978 reform era, including the first motorway between the northeast cities of Shenyang and Dalian (375 km) and the first inter-provincial motorway between Beijing and Tianjin. This was followed by expressways from Changchun to Siping (Jilin Province), the Taiyuan to Pingding expressway (Shanxi Province), the Guilin to Liuzhou expressway (Guangxi Autonomous Region), the Hohhot to Baotou expressway (Inner Mongolia), and the Ji'nan–Taian expressway, which completed the linking of Beijing by expressway with both Shanghai and Fuzhou (Fujian Province) and brought the total length of expressways in China in 1999 to 10,300 km. Class II and above roads (paved and unpaved) still make up the vast bulk of China's antiquated road network that, although linking all regions and ports of the country, leave 20% of its villages without any road access. Modern ring roads have been built in Beijing, Tianjin, and other relatively wealthy urban centers and are also planned for interior cities, such as Ürümqi, Xinjiang Autonomous Region, while the world's largest cable-stayed bridge (7,658 m), spanning the Huangpu River in Shanghai, opened to traffic in 1993. From 1980 to 1993, the share of passenger road transport grew from 32 to 47% while freight volume grew from 6.5 to 13.3%, which dramatically increased China's demand for oil, making it a net oil importer. Plans call for building 45 road transportation hubs nationwide from 2001–2010 and includes seven major north-south highways. Total highway mileage in China is expected to overtake the American Interstate system, the world's largest, sometime around 2020.

With its 110,000 km of navigable rivers and canals (including the world-renowned Grand Canal linking Beijing and Hangzhou), China has relied for centuries on its inland water system for freight and passenger transportation. By far the most heavily traveled waterway is the Yangtze River (China's "golden waterway"), which, with its 6,000 km of navigable waterways, carries 70% of the freight and passenger transport that, in 1998, amounted to 1,940 billion tons/km and 12 billion persons/km, respectively, for the entire country. Including other major navigable rivers, such as the Heilong ("Black Dragon") River in the northeast and the Pearl River in the Southeast, China has 70 major inland river ports, of which Nanjing is the largest with an annual capacity of 40 million tons. The more than 85,000 dams constructed in China are generally an obstacle to inland shipping, though some, like the **Three Gorges Dam Project** on the Yangtze's middle reaches, create reservoirs that will reportedly enhance river navigation.

On its coasts, China has 20 major harbors with one billion tons annual capacity. Shanghai harbor ranks as the world's largest trading facility with an annual capacity of over 100 million tons while Dalian, Qinhuangdao, Tianjin, Qingdao, Ningbo, and Guangzhou all exceed

50 million tons capacity. Coastal shipping lines mainly transport coal, grain, and sundry goods across two major navigable zones, the north and the south with Shanghai and Dalian as their respective centers. During the 1960s, China's maritime fleet had fewer than 30 ships; by 1986, China ranked ninth in the world, with more than 600 ships and a total tonnage of 16 million, including modern roll-on and roll-off ships, container ships, oil tankers, refrigerator ships, and large bulk carriers. China's international shipping annually exceeds 100 million tons of goods. In 2004, the country was ranked fourth in the world in ship construction and has an extensive maritime training system including Dalian Maritime University, the country's largest such facility, which operates under the Ministry of Communications. Since 1975, river and coastal **trade** has grown an average of 10% per year, although, in some inland areas, the deterioration of the river system (most notably the Yellow River) has led to net reductions in usage.

In 2003, as part of the reform program, port administration in China was decentralized with local governments restricted to the role of supervision and coordination while port companies, many joint ventures with foreign firms, were held responsible for port operation and expansion. This was in response to the poor management and limited offloading facilities that plagued China's ports in the 1980s, when, in the midst of the early trade boom, as many as 500 ships a day waited out of port. China's current international arrangements on shipping include its involvement in the Tumen River Area Development Program in conjunction with Russia, a project that is designed to create a new trade and transport route between the west coast of the **United States** and northeast China via ports in Russia's Far East. Agreements have also been signed with Myanmar, **Cambodia**, Laos, and **Vietnam** to develop river, as well as highway and railway, transportation linkages. The China Ocean Shipping Company (COSCO) has established a major strategic presence in Southeast Asia, especially Singapore, while it also maintains close ties to the Chinese **People's Liberation Army** (**PLA**). China relies on a large fleet of river and ocean ferries for passenger traffic, which have also had safety problems including the 1999 sinking of the *Dashun* in the Yellow Sea off Shandong Province in which 280 people died, the worst maritime disaster in PRC history.

Between 1949 and 1978, China invested several billion *yuan* to construct and upgrade its civil airports laying the foundation for civil aviation in the country. At the end of 1998, China had 140 civil airports of which 80 could accommodate such aircraft as Boeing-777s and Airbus-340s while eight could handle the larger Boeing-747s, including those China began buying from the U.S. in 1972. The total length of civil air routes in 1998 was 1.5 million km, a 10-fold increase over 1978. The country's civil air fleet in 1994 consisted of 175 aircraft, 150 of which were purchased from Boeing between 1972 and 1993, replacing the aging fleet of Soviet-made aircraft that had a dismal safety record. Major airline accidents in China occurred beginning in 1988 with the largest loss of life coming in a 1992 crash in Guangzhou when 141 people were killed. Domestic airlines radiate from Beijing to all provinces, autonomous regions, and centrally administered municipalities and to major tourist and border areas while international routes fly to 57 major cities though permanent direct air links to **Taiwan** have still not been established. In 2005, China negotiated major aircraft purchases from Boeing and Europe's Airbus with prospects that the latter would build an assembly plant in China. By 2023, China is expected to be flying more than 2,800 aircraft making it the biggest commercial aviation market in the world after the U.S.

Beginning in the 1950s, China's civil aviation was operated by the General Administration of Civil Aviation (CAAC), which operated under the Ministry of Communications with functions comparable to the Federal Aviation Agency (FAA) in the U.S. This included operation of China's only international and domestic airline that was also known as CAAC, which inaugurated service between Beijing and New York in 1981. Later renamed Air China, it continues to dominate China's domestic and international routes with 70 aircraft and suffered its first fatal international crash in South **Korea** in April 2002. In the mid-1980s, regional airlines—passenger and freight—were set up under the aegis of CAAC numbering 28 separate airlines, including China Southern Airlines operating out of Guangzhou with total passengers numbering 80 million in 2004. In 2000, China merged 10 of its airlines into three large groups: Air China, China Eastern, and China Southern as the country produced its first passenger aircraft, the MA-60. Flight schedules and times in China still remain erratic with often very long check-in times and even longer journeys to and from the airport. Security at Chinese airports has been stepped up as several flights in China in recent years have been hijacked; generally overworked flight attendants complain of unruly passengers, who, on occasion, have tried to open the emergency hatches in mid-flight! Unless China can dramatically increase the number of air crews it trains and improve air traffic management, future growth of aviation may be hampered. *See also* ECONOMY; ENERGY; ENVIRONMENT.

"TWO WHATEVERS" (*"LIANGGE FANSHI"*). In the aftermath of the death of **Chinese Communist Party** (**CCP**) Chairman **Mao Zedong** in 1976, a fierce struggle broke out among contending **leaders** to inherit the mantle of Mao's leadership and gain control of the Chinese Communist state and Party apparatus. Appointed by Mao as his successor, **Hua Guofeng** tried to secure his legitimacy in the CCP and resist any backsliding from radical Maoist policies by asserting the political principle that "Whatever policies Chairman Mao had decided, we shall resolutely defend; whatever instructions he issued, we shall steadfastly obey." Pegged as the "two whatevers," this slogan became the clarion call of Hua and the various leftist political leaders who had tied their star to Mao and resisted the return of more moderate CCP leaders, especially **Deng Xiaoping**. As a riposte, the ever-creative Deng suggested in 1977 that the "two whatevers" had damaged Mao Zedong Thought and that Mao himself would never have agreed with the idea. "The 'two whatevers' are unacceptable," Deng retorted and, in its place, he suggested that "we should use genuine Mao Zedong Thought taken as an integral whole to guide the Party"—a formulation that allowed much greater flexibility in policy formation and ideological creativity by the post-Mao leadership. With Hua Guofeng's political defeat at the hands of Deng Xiaoping at the December 1978 **Third Plenum of the 11th Central Committee of the** CCP, reference to the "two whatevers" disappeared from China's political landscape, along with most radical leftist leaders.

– U –

ULANFU (1906–1988). Born in 1906 in rural Inner Mongolia, Ulanfu and his brother attended the Beiping (**Beijing**) Mongolian–Tibetan School in 1922. In the spring of 1924, Ulanfu became a member of the Chinese Communist **Youth League (CYL)**. In the following year, he joined the **Chinese Communist Party (CCP)**. Ulanfu and his brother then went to Moscow, where Ulanfu entered Sun Yat-sen University and became acquainted with his classmate, Wang Ruofei, who later became Ulanfu's superior in underground Party work. Ulanfu returned to China in 1930, joined the underground, and barely escaped arrest when Wang Ruofei was himself arrested and incarcerated. In 1932, when Japanese forces in China threatened the northern Chinese provinces of Jehol and Chahar (which were subsequently abolished), Ulanfu became involved in organizing Mongol anti-Japanese guerrilla forces. After the Xi'an incident in 1936 and the outbreak of the **Sino–Japanese War (1937–1945)**, Ulanfu served in the Pai Haifeng–Suiyuan Mongolian Peace Preservation Corps as a **political commissar**. In 1941, he fled to the Communist redoubt in Yan'an and became head of the Nationalities' Institute of the Anti-Japanese Military and Political University under Gao Gang. In 1944, Ulanfu became the chairman of the Suiyuan Border Region government.

In September 1949, Ulanfu was appointed to the Standing Committee of the Preparatory Committee of the **Chinese People's Political Consultative Conference (CPPCC)**. In October, he became a member of the Central People's Government Council, which served as the chief executive body of the **People's Republic of China (PRC)** until 1954. In 1952, Suiyuan was incorporated to form the Suiyuan Inner Mongolia Military District where Ulanfu held the top positions becoming chairman of the Suiyuan People's Government. In 1956, he became one of the top CCP **leaders** when he was elected to full membership in the Central Committee after the **Eighth Party Congress (1956)** and became an alternate member of the **Politburo**.

In 1967, during the **Cultural Revolution (1966–1976)**, Ulanfu was attacked and deposed by the CCP army that entered Inner Mongolia. He was rehabilitated in 1973 and was elected to the CCP 10th Central Committee in the same year. In 1977, he was appointed head of the CCP **United Front** Department and a member of the 11th Central Committee, as well as a member of the Politburo in the same year. In 1978, Ulanfu became the vice-chairman of the Standing Committee of the Fifth CPPCC; in 1982, he was reelected to the Politiburo at the 12th CCP National Congress. In 1983, Ulanfu was reelected as the vice-chairman of the PRC and died five years later in 1988.

"ULTRA-LEFTISM" (*"JIZUO"*). This was a catch-all term used in the late 1960s to attack radical elements in the **Cultural Revolution (1966–1976)**. From 1966 to early 1967, **Chinese Communist Party (CCP)** Chairman **Mao Zedong**, the primary instigator of the Cultural Revolution, had seemingly thrown his entire support to the extreme left in its attacks on top Party **leaders** and the CCP apparatus. But, in spring 1967, as **Red Guards** began to target military commanders and the **People's Liberation Army (PLA)**, plus the Ministry of Foreign Affairs headed by **Zhou Enlai**, the tide began to turn against the extreme left as Mao gradually withdrew his support and came down on the side of order and stability in the country that had been threatened by the far left. Red Guard assaults on the Foreign Ministry and on the offices of the CCP Central Committee only heightened concern that the Cultural Revolution was spinning out of control.

At this point, Mao sanctioned criticism of "ultra-leftists," who were accused of attempting to "overthrow the proletarian headquarters of Mao Zedong" and "seizing state power." Fiery political leaders whom Mao and his wife, **Jiang Qing**, had recently embraced were now singled out for attack. This included Wang Li, Guan Feng, and Qi Benyu, leftist polemicists who had stoked the ideological fires of the Cultural Revolution. Lower-level "ultra-leftists" were singled out for public execution. In the Orwellian language of the Cultural Revolution, "ultra-leftists" were now described as "ultra-left in form, but ultra-right in essence," a suggestion that, all along, these activists had been anti-Communist and opposed to Chairman Mao. The attack on "ultra-leftism" turned into a permanent purge of the leaders responsible for the Cultural Revolution, except Mao Zedong, and even involved leftwing army leaders, such as Yang Chengwu, who was accused of plotting against Mao Zedong by promoting an extreme version of the **personality cult** (*genren chongbai*). The attacks against "ultra-leftists" as political "swindlers" continued with the purge of **Chen Boda**, the **Lin Biao** affair in 1971, the purge of Jiang Qing and the **Gang of Four** in 1976–1977, and the general reversal of the policies of the Cultural Revolution throughout the 1980s.

"UNINTERRUPTED REVOLUTION" (*"BUDUAN GEMING"*). This is a central concept in Chinese Communist ideology that was heavily promoted during the reign of **Mao Zedong**, especially during the **Cultural Revolution (1966–1976)**. Also known as "continuous revolution," the term required that Chinese society be maintained in a constant state of turmoil and political struggle to insure the "ultimate liberation of the working class and the people as a whole." Mao Zedong was especially fearful that China, like the **Soviet Union**, would gradually stabilize around a highly centralized political structure that would concentrate solely on economic and technical developments managed by a professional class and with little input by the masses of workers and peasants. "Uninterrupted revolution" would inoculate China against this kind of **"revisionism"** and prevent any subsiding of the purported revolutionary fervor of the masses. The Cultural Revolution was perhaps the best example of this theory put into practice. Since 1978, the Cultural Revolution has been officially condemned in China and the idea of "uninterrupted revolution" effectively dropped in theory and practice.

UNITED FRONT. A centerpiece of **Chinese Communist Party (CCP)** strategy inherited from the dictates of Soviet leader Vladimir Lenin and the Comintern in the early 1920s, united front refers to alliances between the CCP and its natural constituency of workers and poor peasants with classes and political parties that are periodically defined as collaborators in the revolutionary struggle. During the pre-1949 period, two formal united fronts were established with the **Kuomintang (KMT)** in 1924–1927 and 1936–1945 to combat common enemies, in the first case northern warlords, and, in the second, the Japanese. In each instance, CCP **leaders** developed the appropriate ideological rationales that justified these political arrangements and created a United Front Department in the CCP apparatus. After 1949, united front policies involved periodic CCP efforts to build alliances with non-proletarian social elements, particularly merchants and "bourgeois" **intellectuals**. These policies were undermined and even assaulted during radical phases of CCP rule such as during the **Three-Antis Campaign** in the 1950s and the **Cultural Revolution (1966–1976)**, when, in contrast to the emphasis on "unity" characteristic of generic united front strategy, **"class struggle"** was the dominant ideological theme. As CCP leaders increasingly stressed the inclusion of broader groups into the Chinese state, in 1992, CCP General Secretary **Jiang Zemin** expanded united front work to include respect for religious beliefs and cultural differences among **minorities**. The continued existence of the **democratic parties** and the **Chinese People's Political Consultative Conference** (**CPPCC**) are all part of united front strategy, which, in 2005, was the portfolio of **Politburo** Standing Committee member **Jia Qinglin**. *See also* NEW DEMOCRACY.

UNITED NATIONS (UN). From "**liberation**" in October 1949 to its official reentry into the United Nations in 1971, the **People's Republic of China** (**PRC**) was effectively cut off from involvement in the world body as the "China seat" on the Security Council was held by the government of the Republic of China (ROC) on **Taiwan**. During this period, China was sometimes the target of UN action, such as the 1951 embargo on the exportation of strategic equipment to China that coincided with its entry as an enemy of the UN-sanctioned police action in the **Korean War** (**1950–1953**). Yet, China consistently insisted that it had a right to sit at the UN and often joined other Third World **leaders**, such as President Sukarno of Indonesia, in making that demand. However, China did not refrain from criticizing ongoing UN actions, such as the world body's role in 1962 in the central African country of the Congo, where China apparently had political and economic interests that were at odds with those of the **United States**. During this period, especially in the **Cultural Revolution** (**1966–1976**), the UN was often condemned by China as an "instrument" of U.S. **imperialism** and a vehicle for American advancement of "neo-colonialism" because it was Washington that consistently blocked China's entry into the world body. China's hopes for entry in the early 1960s, when it was garnering increased support from Asian, Latin American, and African UN members, was dealt a serious blow when the General Assembly decided for the first time that the question of China's entry was an "important question" that required a two-thirds vote. The UN decision to adopt a resolution on **Tibet**, albeit mildly worded, further antagonized China's relations with the world body. Throughout the 1960s, China insisted that its entry come at the expense of the ROC and that Taiwan not be allowed to remain in the UN under the rubric of a "two Chinas" policy.

The decision in 1970–1971 by Washington to fundamentally alter its relationship with **Beijing** led to China's entry into the UN and the ouster of the ROC from the Security Council and the General Assembly. Resolution 2758 adopted at the 26th UN General Assembly in 1971 stipulated that the representative of the PRC government is China's sole legitimate representative. Upon joining the UN General Assembly and seated as one of five permanent members of the Security Council, China gradually entered all 45 UN organs, specialized agencies, and commissions, beginning with the United Nations Educational, Scientific, and Cultural Organization (UNESCO) in 1971. This included the UN Development Program (UNDP), UN Conference on Trade and Development (UNCTAD), and the UN **Human Rights** Commission (UNHRC). The PRC also participated in special sessions of the UN General Assembly, such as the 1982 Second Special Session on Disarmament, where Chinese Foreign Minister Huang Hua put forth the PRC position. In the 1970s, China pursued a relatively belligerent tone in the world body, condemning Russian proposals for a collective security pact in Asia and championing the political and economic interests of developing countries. On issues the Chinese found repugnant to their interests or values, China generally refrained from participation and simply abstained on votes involving, for example, UN peacekeeping. Yet, China did not challenge the basic organizational structure of the UN and generally paid its contributions to the world body.

During the 1980s, the Chinese shifted their strategy somewhat and adopted positions on various issues confronting the world body in terms of how it affected the **Soviet Union**, China's major nemesis in world affairs. China's actions on the Angolan Civil War, for example, seemed to be guided by the principle that "We must oppose everything the enemy defends and defend everything the enemy opposes." After the 1989 reconciliation between the USSR and China, however, China moderated its tone and took a more active part in the consultative-consensual process of Security Council decision making, tolerating peacekeeping efforts of the UN and refraining from vetoing such UN-sanctioned operations as the 1991 war against Iraq (Resolution 678) on which China abstained. On most issues brought before the Security Council, which are incompatible with its principles while actually not affecting its national interests, China rarely exercises the veto but chooses instead to abstain. China has, however, been willing to veto resolutions brought before the council when the issue of Taiwan is a major concern, such as its 1990 veto of peace-keeping operations in Guatemala and Macedonia, to punish those countries for their favorable policies toward Taiwan. In 2002, China made it clear that along with **Russia** and France it opposed any attempt by the U.S. and Great Britain to seek a second resolution authorizing the use of force against Iraq. China did, however, participate in the International Conference on Iraq in 2004 as it supports the stabilization and reconstruction process. Beginning with its first dispatch of military observers in 1990 to a UN peacekeeping operation to **Cambodia**, China has sent over 3,500 military personnel to 13 UN peacekeeping operations including East Timor in 1998 and, more recently, to the Democratic Republic of Congo. In 1995, China hosted the Fourth UN World Conference on **Women** in Beijing, which adopted a Platform for Action drafted by 189 participating countries.

On the issue of human rights, in 1988, China signed the global covenant against the use of torture and, in 1993, participated in the UN World Conference on Human Rights held in Vienna. While endorsing the UN's commitment to human rights, China also expressed opposition to those countries that "impose their values" on others. The PRC signed the final Vienna document that paid lip service to the universality of human rights but left the implementation to individual countries and also reaffirmed the right to development and other collective rights. In March 1994, a draft resolution criticizing the PRC before the UNHRC, consisting of 53 UN member states, was tabled. In this resolution that was narrowly defeated, the PRC was criticized for its treatment of dissidents, reports of torture, arbitrary arrests, unfair trials, and the situation in Tibet. Since 1990, China has successfully defeated all U.S.-led attempts to put China on the agenda of the UN human rights session on 11 separate occasions, including the last effort in April 2004, when most European nations supported the U.S. while countries, such as the Republic of **Korea**, Mexico, and Argentina—all of which have growing economic ties with China—abstained as China pointed to controversial American actions in Iraq involving alleged torture to successfully defeat the American-led effort. After 10 years of negotiation, China, in 2005, allowed the UN special rapporteur on torture into the country though it challenged an initial summary of the investigation, which accused Chinese police, prison guards, and other judicial officials of relying on torture to extract confessions and eliminate "deviant behavior" and called on China to allow the development of an independent judiciary and legal protections for criminals and suspects.

As for related issues of international law, China has generally accepted the sovereignty-centered principle of the Westphalian legal order in opposing any major extension of international legal authority, though its support for many UN resolutions, such as the solution to the crisis in Cambodia indicates implied acceptance of a strengthened international legal regime. In the specialized agencies of the Food and Agricultural Organization (FAO), World Health Organization (WHO), International Civil Aviation Organization (ICAO), etc., China has taken a low-profile role, avoiding extensive involvement in the technical minutia of decision making as its delegates often continue to infuriate and amuse other nations' representatives. In 2004, China's permanent representative to the UN was Wang Guangya, a former vice-minister of foreign affairs, who expressed strong support for the UN Millennium Development Goals that had been established in 2000. From 2001 to 2005, the UN Development Assistance Framework for China was implemented which was devoted to carrying out sustainable development and poverty elimination. Backed by large-scale **social protests** and on-line petitions in China posted on the **Internet**, the PRC has opposed the ascension of **Japan** to a permanent seat on the Security Council as long as Japanese prime ministers continue to visit the Yakasuni Shrine with its interred Class-A war criminals, and the country allows school textbooks and other media to downplay and whitewash Japan's aggression toward China in World War II. *See also* FOREIGN POLICY.

UNITED STATES. Since 1949, relations between the United States and the **People's Republic of China** (**PRC**) have varied from outright hostility and conflict to relatively friendly political and economic ties. During the Chinese **Civil War** (**1946–1949**), the U.S. through the mission of Secretary of State George C. Marshall attempted to mediate the conflict between the **Kuomintang** (**KMT**) and the Communists, but ultimately failed. Although U.S. aid, under the administration of President Harry Truman, to the KMT during the civil conflict was limited, **Mao Zedong** and the Chinese Communists identified the U.S. as a major ally of its domestic enemy. On the eve of the Communist victory, Mao declared in his essay "On the People's Democratic Dictatorship" that China would "lean to one side" in its foreign policy and align with the **Soviet Union**. Several months later Mao traveled to Moscow after which the two countries would sign a Treaty of Friendship, Alliance, and Mutual Assistance in 1950. In August 1949, the U.S. State Department published a White Paper entitled "United States Relations with China" as Washington initially left open the possibility of immediate recognition of the PRC after its formal establishment on 1 October 1949 as the American ambassador remained in Nanking (the KMT national capital) waiting for a gesture of goodwill from the new Communist leadership (during World War II American military and State Department personnel had established informal ties with the Communist **leaders** in Yan'an via the Dixie Mission and, thus, some basis of mutual trust and reconciliation was thought to exist). But mistrust and indignation quickly surfaced as the new government in **Beijing** subjected American corporations to rough treatment, seized U.S. consular buildings, arrested U.S. consul Angus Ward on espionage charges, and persecuted Christian missionaries, while the U.S. showed continuing sympathy for Chiang Kai-shek and his plight. Unlike its European allies, such as Great Britain, the U.S. did not recognize the new regime but maintained formal diplomatic ties with the Republic of China (ROC) on **Taiwan**. The outbreak of the **Korean War** in June 1950 led the U.S. to establish a defensive perimeter in the Taiwan Straits deploying the Seventh Fleet, while in China many American students and missionaries who had remained behind after the withdrawal of the U.S. diplomatic mission were arrested and imprisoned on charges of "spying." The Chinese intervention in the Korean conflict in October 1950 brought the military forces of the PRC and the U.S.—operating under a **United Nations (UN)** mandate—into direct conflict until the Korean Armistice was signed in 1953.

Throughout the 1950s and 1960s, China and the U.S. maintained their mutual hostility, though some informal contacts and efforts at altering their relations occurred. At the 1954 Geneva Conference terminating the first Indochina War, Chinese Foreign Minister **Zhou Enlai** offered his hand in friendship to U.S. Secretary of State John Foster Dulles but was refused even as Chinese delegates to the conference met with their U.S. counterparts on six occasions. At the

1955 **Bandung Conference of Afro–Asian States** in Indonesia, China offered to open formal negotiations with the U.S. to produce a comprehensive détente in East Asia and in the Taiwan Straits. But with irreconcilable divisions over the Taiwan question, no such meetings were ever convened as the U.S. insisted that China first renounce the use of force against Taiwan, something Beijing was unwilling to do. The Formosa Resolution passed by the U.S. Congress in 1955 extended American protection to Taiwan's offshore islands of Quemoy (*Jinmen*) and Matsu while the U.S. government formally declared that the legal status of Taiwan remained officially unresolved despite the decision of the 1943 Cairo Conference to return the island to Chinese sovereignty. After China provoked a crisis in 1955 over Quemoy, the two countries decided to initiate contacts at the ambassadorial level in Geneva and, later, in Warsaw that went on for 15 years and involved 136 meetings. Ostensibly, these meetings focused on outstanding issues left over from the Chinese Civil War and the Korean War, namely the fate of 80 Americans still held in China and 3,000 Chinese students in the U.S. Although periodically suspended, the Geneva and Warsaw encounters provided the U.S. and China with a venue to discuss a range of political, economic, and military issues dividing the two nations that lasted until 1970. Yet, with U.S. Secretary of State Dulles under President Dwight Eisenhower committed to an unrelenting anti-Communism that continued into the administrations of John F. Kennedy and Lyndon Johnson, full rapprochement between the U.S. and China remained virtually impossible.

Conflicts involving the two sides, such as the **Taiwan Straits Crises (1954 and 1958)** only exacerbated this mutual hostility. The U.S. built up its anti-Communist alliance in East and Southeast Asia through military ties with **Japan** and South **Korea** and defensive alliances largely aimed at China, such as the Southeast Asia Treaty Organization (SEATO). In the same period, China remained nominally aligned with the Soviet Union, the main worldwide antagonist of the U.S. The U.S. was among many countries that condemned China for suppressing the 1959 uprising in **Tibet** while China, in turn, accused the U.S. Central Intelligence Agency (CIA) of directly assisting the Tibetans in mounting the rebellion. A visit to Taiwan in 1960 by U.S. President Eisenhower was protested in China with anti-American propaganda that spread agitation throughout China's major cities and towns. Chinese proposals for bilateral talks on Taiwan, the establishment of a nuclear-free zone in Asia, and mutual exchange of journalists went nowhere as China took every opportunity to denounce the actions of the U.S., going so far as to direct personal insults at both presidents Eisenhower and Kennedy.

Hostility in U.S.–China relations continued throughout the mid- and late 1960s inflamed by American involvement in the **Vietnam** War (1965–1973). China feared the establishment of a permanent American military presence in Vietnam and Thailand, but the U.S. considered the Vietnamese Communists a direct extension of Chinese military and political power. China's vitriolic denunciation of "U.S. **imperialism**" as a **"paper tiger"** was aimed at mobilizing support for the Chinese position in the Third World, including Latin America. China even weighed in on domestic American affairs with impassioned declarations by Mao Zedong supporting American blacks in the civil rights struggle. America was the symbol of the much-hated capitalism and its powerful presence in East Asia thwarted the restoration of Chinese hegemony that had existed for more than two millennia. The U.S. also protected the KMT regime on Taiwan and blocked China's "rightful" place on the Security Council in the UN. Direct confrontation between the U.S. and China was avoided however, as potentially explosive conflicts over U.S. violations of Chinese air space near Vietnam were dealt with rhetorically rather than by actual combat.

From 1966 to 1969, Chinese **foreign policy** was effectively paralyzed by the radical politics and internecine conflicts of the early stages of the **Cultural Revolution (1966–1976)**, though China now directed its animosity at both the U.S. and the Soviet Union, as both countries were accused of dividing up the world into bipolar spheres of influence. In 1969, however, the U.S. and China began to seriously prepare for negotiations as Washington partially lifted its **trade** embargo against China, but because of domestic complications in both countries and the impact of international events, especially the U.S.-led invasion of **Cambodia**, the reconciliation did not really begin until 1970. Despite continued tensions over Southeast Asia and blustering comments on "world revolution" by Mao Zedong, the U.S. under President Richard Nixon took the initiative by permitting American citizens to visit the PRC. As American troops began their withdrawal from Vietnam and China became more concerned with threats from the Soviet Union, the U.S. and China finally agreed to break the diplomatic ice after a 1971 visit to China of an American ping pong team that was quickly followed by two secret visits to Beijing by National Security Adviser Henry Kissinger in the summer, which produced an agreement for a formal trip to China by the American president in February 1972. This relatively cordial visit by the U.S. president, which was given enormous news coverage by the American press, led to a mutual declaration by both sides in the **Shanghai Communiqué**, on the central issue of Taiwan, in which the U.S. "acknowledg[ed]" that the island was part of China and called for a "peaceful settlement" of the issue.

Liaison offices were quickly established in both capitals while the U.S. withdrew its opposition to the PRC taking over the China seat in the UN and acquiesced to Taiwan's ouster from the world body. Scientific and trade ties were established and, after President Nixon's resignation, President Gerald Ford visited the PRC in 1975. The Communist takeover in Vietnam in 1975 did not produce any visible increase in U.S.–China tensions, but instead raised Chinese anxieties over growing Vietnamese "hegemony" in Southeast Asia. The U.S. and China agreed to coordinate their policies on Cambodia and shared concerns about Soviet expansionism, though the U.S. in hopes of solidifying a Soviet–American détente, resisted Chinese efforts to enlist Washington in a broad anti-Soviet alliance. In December 1978, the U.S. and China agreed to establish formal diplomatic relations as the U.S. broke its formal diplomatic ties with Taiwan and announced its intention to terminate the mutual defense treaty within a year. Passage in 1979 of the Taiwan Relations Act, however, maintained American commitments to the island redoubt of the Nationalists and allowed the U.S. to continue limited sales of "defensive" arms to the ROC. In 1979, **Deng Xiaoping**, the architect of China's economic reforms, visited the U.S. and received tacit American approval of his plans to invade Vietnam. U.S. President Jimmy Carter also granted China Most Favored Nation (MFN) trade status that was subject to annual Congressional review and authorized formal military-to-military contacts, and intelligence sharing, though China requested (and did not receive) permission to purchase U.S. arms.

In the early 1980s, U.S.–China relations went through a short period of tension and disillusionment as the newly elected U.S. President

Ronald Reagan campaigned on a promise to upgrade U.S. relations with Taiwan. This dramatic turn for the worse in relations was also caused by increased Chinese textile exports to the U.S., restrictions on American **technology** transfer to China, potential sales of U.S. aircraft to Taiwan, and defections by Chinese citizens to the U.S. Resolution of some of these issues in 1982, however, improved Sino–American ties as Washington promised an eventual end to arms sales to Taiwan, though without providing a timetable. This was followed in 1984 by President Reagan's trip to the PRC when agreements were reached on co-production of military technology, a new textile accord, and dramatic increases in scholarly exchanges between U.S. and Chinese researchers. A visit to the U.S. by PRC Premier **Zhao Ziyang** followed by President **Li Xiannian** won China's commitment to enforce nonproliferation of nuclear weapons to Third World countries, while the U.S. liberalized its technology export controls to China and agreed to sell high-technology electronic aviation equipment as trade between the two countries expanded rapidly in the mid-1980s. By 1987–1988, however, new tensions emerged over apparent violations by China of its pledge on nonproliferation of nuclear technology as evidence emerged of Chinese sales to Pakistan and China's sale of Silkworm missiles to Iran via North Korea and intermediate range ballistic missiles (IRBMs) to Saudi Arabia that posed a direct threat to Israel. A visit to the U.S. by the **Dalai Lama** in 1987, when he denounced China's policies in the autonomous region and called for Tibet to be designated a "zone of peace" were followed by disturbances in its capital city of Lhasa.

The year 1989 proved to be a watershed in U.S.–China relations involving the issue of **human rights**. In February 1989, during a visit to China by U.S. President George H. W. Bush, Chinese police forcibly detained the famous dissident, astrophysicist **Fang Lizhi**, preventing him from attending a reception at the U.S. embassy. Then, in June 1989, the military crackdown on the second **Beijing Spring** by the **People's Liberation Army** (**PLA**) produced severe condemnations of the Chinese government from the U.S. and the imposition of a variety of political and economic sanctions, including termination of high-level diplomatic exchanges and an end to formal military-to-military relations. President Bush refused to lift China's MFN status, though he committed the U.S. government to allowing Chinese students to remain indefinitely in the U.S. out of fear of retribution if they returned to China. President Bush also provided safe haven in the U.S. embassy in **Beijing** for Fang Lizhi. However, the Bush administration also quickly backtracked on its sanction package by authorizing secret visits to Beijing by high-level U.S. officials and allowing the sale of Boeing aircraft to China to go forward along with a US$10 million loan from the U.S. Export–Import Bank to the China National Offshore Oil Corporation (CNOOC). In 1990, the U.S. won China's tacit support for its tough line against Iraq in the UN, this despite reports that China had supplied Saddam Hussein with substantial military supplies, including nuclear technology, after the start of the Persian Gulf War. In addition to conflicts over human rights and a growing U.S. trade deficit with China, persistent reports of Chinese missile sales and even chemical weapons' materials (later proved false) to the Middle East inflamed the Sino–American relationship throughout the early 1990s, though President Bush denounced any move to "isolate" China through tougher actions.

President Bill Clinton came to office promising a tougher stand on the human rights issue, but after one year of little response from Beijing, the Clinton administration decided to de-link the MFN debate and human rights altogether. A policy of "active engagement" was pursued with China that produced little improvement in the human rights situation in the PRC but did lead to the 1992 Sino–American Memorandum of Understanding on U.S. access to Chinese markets. During the 1993 Asia–Pacific Economic Cooperation (APEC) forum, President **Jiang Zemin** met with President Clinton and two years later a major trade agreement on protection of intellectual property rights in China was signed, even as the U.S. trade deficit with China soared to over US$30 billion a year. In the same year, Washington supported China's entry into the **World Trade Organization (WTO)** but tensions quickly reemerged when the U.S. announced its decision to permit Taiwan President Lee Teng-hui to pay a "private visit" to the U.S., which China claimed violated the basic principles of the three China-U.S. joint communiqués. An agreement by the U.S. to sell Taiwan surface-to-air Stinger missiles, American accusations of persistent violations of intellectual property rights infringements by China, and Chinese counteraccusations in 1996 at the UN against U.S. meddling in Chinese domestic affairs with its "Radio Free Asia" broadcasts all stirred the diplomatic pot. The first official state visit by President Jiang Zemin in 1997 smoothed things over again as the two countries promoted exchanges and cooperation in such fields as politics, economics, **science**, environmental protection, and judiciary while a return visit by President Clinton in 1998 provided the U.S. with a chance to restate its firm commitment to a "one China" policy. Despite a visit to the U.S. by Premier **Zhu Rongji** in 1999, the accidental bombing of the Chinese embassy in Belgrade during NATO operations against Yugoslavia and the issuance of the Cox Report by the U.S. House of Representatives, which accused China of stealing U.S. nuclear technology, followed by the arrest of the Chinese–American scientist Lee Wen-ho, who was thought to have leaked key American nuclear information to China (and was later exonerated), all fueled new tensions in the U.S.–China relationship. This occurred even as President Clinton argued strongly against efforts to "contain" China or initiate a new "cold war" and offered China financial compensation for the Belgrade bombings.

The tension in Sino–American relations continued into the early 2000s as the U.S. put forth proposals expressing concerns about human rights in China and both sides bristled over the April 2001 collision between a U.S. spy plane and a PLA fighter aircraft whose pilot died as a result. Following the 11 September 2001 terrorist attacks in the U.S., China declared its support for a global war on terrorism as the U.S. granted China permanent MFN status in December 2001, following President George W. Bush's visit to **Shanghai** for an APEC meeting.

Current issues in Sino–American relations include the problem of the ballooning U.S. trade deficit with China that rose from US$10 billion in 1985 to US$164 billion in 2004, as Chinese exports to the U.S. exceeded imports by nearly six to one. The American trade deficit with China is now larger than with any other country or with the entire European Union while China has also become the second largest foreign creditor after Japan of the U.S., holding more than US$600 billion in Treasury securities and other dollar-denominated instruments. This growing imbalance has led Washington to pressure China to drop the *yuan*-to-dollar peg, which Beijing altered in July 2005 by pegging the *yuan* to a basket of currencies, allowing for a small appreciation of 2%. The U.S. has also called on China to uphold intellectual property rights that deny enormous revenues to American software, film, DVD, and music producers. In early 2005, the U.S. reimposed a number of tariffs and quotas on Chinese imports, including color television sets, furniture, and especially textiles and garments as Chinese exports into the U.S. surged after the formal end of global textile quotas on 1 January 2005 with predictions that China would soon control 75% of the U.S. textile market. The overall American reaction to China is muted, however, by the reliance of the Chinese on joint ventures with major American multinationals, such as Dell Computer, Goldman Sachs, Morgan Stanley, Nike, and Wal-Mart, which look to operations in the PRC for future growth potential.

In return, China has threatened to raise tariffs on imports from the U.S. while noting that U.S. exports to the PRC, including scrap steel, of which China is now the largest importer from the U.S. had jumped by over 50% in 2004 over 2003. China has relaxed controls on the import of automobiles and **automobile** parts and will allow foreign car makers, such as General Motors, to start making car loans to Chinese auto buyers. China also called on the U.S. to help balance trade between the two countries by allowing the import of nuclear technology and techniques into China that have been long barred by U.S. law and it criticized growing protectionism in the U.S. and American abuse of WTO anti-dumping rules for its own benefit. The American **labor** union, the AFL-CIO, countered by arguing that the illegal repression of workers' rights in China translated into a 43% cost advantage for China, leading the union to file an unusual trade complaint in 2004 that called on the Bush administration to punish China. Although the U.S. has lost 2.7 million manufacturing jobs to China since 2000, many American companies shifted production from the U.S. to the PRC for sale in China or in the global **economy**. The Chinese firm Lenovo purchased IBM's personal computer business while offers were also tendered for the appliance-maker Maytag (abandoned in 2005), and the American-owned oil company Unocal, which after provoking a strong negative reaction among members of the U.S. Congress, was also abandoned.

On non-economic matters, China reiterated its policy on Taiwan in 2004 during a visit by U.S. National Security Advisor Condoleezza Rice and called on the U.S. to end its sales of advanced weapons to the island while warning that China would not "sit idly by" if foreign forces supported Taiwan independence. The U.S., in turn, reaffirmed its commitment under the Taiwan Relations Act to defend the island and sent an unprecedented seven aircraft carriers and their strike groups into waters off the Chinese coast in summer 2004, which immediately prompted Beijing to strengthen its military capacity in the region and to issue an informal warning against the U.S. in 2005 that any military interference on the side of Taiwan would provoke the PRC to use nuclear weapons, the second time since 1995 China has issued such a threat, which brought an immediate U.S. rebuke and was subsequently revoked. Although both the U.S. and China reiterated their commitment to a nuclear weapons-free Korean peninsula and to conduct the six-party talks on North Korea, which includes **Russia**, South Korea, and Japan, the PRC questioned American intelligence estimates on reputed progress in the North Korean nuclear program and warned that its own influence over the North Koreans was limited. China also urged the U.S. to be more flexible in the next round of talks, which began in summer 2005, voicing frustration over the lack of progress in resolving the nuclear crisis. During another visit to China in early 2005, U.S. Secretary of State Condoleezza Rice joined President **Hu Jintao** in asserting that the two countries have a "very strong relationship" and that disputes will be resolved "in a mutually respectful manner," including the Taiwan issue, which Hu described as the key to the sound and steady development of Sino–American ties.

Although some observers in the U.S. believe the two countries are in the early stages of a second Cold War as a result of the increasing economic, political, and military muscle of the PRC, which is winning it considerable support throughout Asia, Chinese observers consistently denounce the "China threat" as groundless. Many top leaders in China apparently believe the U.S. will not tolerate China as a world power even in Asia, while others believe accommodations and a condominium with the U.S. can be achieved and that the continued presence of the U.S. in Asia is a force for stability. Public opinion in China is said to be highly nationalistic and frequently anti-American and there is widespread criticism of supposed government softness in dealing with the U.S. and Japan. Still, in 2005, following a visit to China by U.S. Secretary of Defense Donald H. Rumsfeld, the two countries moved to revitalize military-to-military dialogue, with both sides pursuing the creation of an emergency telephone link between their two militaries to prevent misunderstandings and miscommunication. *See also* AFGHANISTAN; FOREIGN POLICY.

USSURI RIVER. *See* MANCHURIA; SOVIET UNION.

UYGUR PEOPLE. *See* MINORITIES.

– V –

VIETNAM. Since 1949, China's relations with the Democratic Republic of Vietnam have ranged from alliance to outright hostility and military conflict to grudgingly tolerable bilateral relations. **Beijing** and Hanoi established diplomatic relations in 1950—even as the Vietminh (the Vietnamese nationalists/Communists) were still fighting the French, which led to the French defeat in 1954 at the decisive battle of Dien Bien Fu in which Chinese military advisers, such as **Wei Guoqing**, actively participated. During the subsequent Geneva Conference that formally ended the First Indochina War, China pressured its Vietnamese counterparts into accepting the negotiated agreement despite Vietnamese Communist reservations concerning the creation of a South Vietnamese regime subject to American influence. From 1954 to 1958, China, in keeping with the "spirit" of accommodation expressed at the1955 **Bandung Conference of Afro–Asian States**, pursued this moderate line in its relations with Vietnam, but, in 1958, China took a slightly more aggressive posture by supporting North Vietnamese opposition to American military aid to South Vietnam and, in 1963, China and the Democratic Republic of Vietnam signed a joint statement that called for struggle against **imperialism** headed by the **United States**. Relations between China and Vietnam consisted mainly of economic and commercial ties as China granted North Vietnam substantial loans (in rubles) and technical aid for the North's economic development projects as China seemed less concerned with supporting the struggle of the South Vietnamese Communist movement (Vietcong) than with opposing the transformation of South Vietnam into an American "colony" and military base from which the U.S. could threaten China.

After the inauguration of American bombing of North Vietnam following the August 1964 Gulf of Tonkin incident, which China denounced (accurately) as a fabrication, the **People's Republic of China (PRC)** called for a reconvening of the Geneva conference and declared that aggression against Vietnam was equivalent to aggression against China and established a permanent delegation to the South Vietnamese Communist political arm, the National Liberation Front. As the military conflict in Vietnam in 1966–1967 heated up, China provided strong support for the Vietnamese Communists including the dispatch of 320,000 troops between 1965 and 1969 to assist in construction and air defense. Both **Mao Zedong** and **Lin Biao** evidently opposed direct Chinese intervention in the armed conflict. China officially recognized the Provisional Revolutionary Government of the Republic of South Vietnam—the Vietcong's political front organization—created in June 1969 and provided Vietnam with increased economic and military aid. It also now opposed the convening of a new Geneva conference, ignored the Paris talks between the U.S. and Vietnam, and denounced purported Soviet–American "collusion" in the international arena, even as increasing internecine conflict of the **Cultural Revolution (1966–1976)** led to disruptions in the delivery of Soviet and Chinese military supplies to Vietnam. Ho Chi Minh's death in 1969 brought the Chinese and Vietnamese leadership closer together, at least temporarily, but these ties were quickly strained by the sudden rapprochement between China and the U.S. as a result of the initiatives in 1971 and 1972 by U.S. President Richard Nixon. The 1973 Paris Accords ending U.S. involvement in Indochina was hailed by the Chinese as a continuation of the "Geneva spirit" of 1954.

However, the attack in 1975 launched by North Vietnamese forces against the South evidently received no encouragement or direct aid from China. By 1978, tension between the two countries erupted as China accused Vietnam of persecuting Chinese residents in Vietnam and ceased all economic and technical aid recalling its experts while armed clashes between Chinese and Vietnamese forces erupted at Friendship Pass on their mutual border. China condemned the Soviet–Vietnamese Treaty of Friendship and Cooperation signed in late 1978 as a threat to peace and security in the Asia–Pacific region and, following Vietnam's assault on **Cambodia** in December 1978, declared that Vietnam needed to be punished. In February 1979, China launched attacks into Vietnam and by March seized the Vietnamese city of Langson and began an immediate withdrawal as Chinese forces suffered over 20,000 killed, sometimes self-inflicted, this the result of poor inter-unit coordination and communications that demonstrated serious flaws in the technological capacity of the **People's Liberation Army** (**PLA**). Following China's withdrawal from Vietnamese territory, the conflict over border issues continued to flare up as China and Vietnam both claimed the Spratly (*Nansha*) and Paracel (*Xisha*) islands located off the coasts of Vietnam and China's Hainan Island. By 1983, however, the two Communist countries decided to maintain an uneasy but relatively peaceful relationship that was fostered by mutual state visits by top **leaders** and economic agreements, which reduced tensions and created greater normalcy in their relations. But even as Vietnam announced the withdrawal of its forces from Cambodia in July 1988, continuing disputes over the Spratly and Paracel islands led to renewed clashes.

Following a visit to **Beijing** by Vice-Chairman Vo Nguyen Giap in 1990 for the opening of the Asian Games, the first visit of a senior Vietnamese leader to China in more than a decade, relations between the two countries began to thaw and, one year later, in 1991, led to the re-normalization of diplomatic relations. This was followed by a trip to Vietnam by Premier **Li Peng**, the first Chinese premier to do so since 1971, as both sides agreed to seek a negotiated settlement over the Spratly Islands and a non-binding agreement by the **Association of Southeast Asian Nations** (**ASEAN**) (of which Vietnam is a member) forbidding construction on the uninhabited Spratly and Paracel islands to prevent territorial disputes from escalating. In 1993, Vietnamese President Le Duc Anh met with President **Jiang Zemin**, the first such presidential visit since 1955, and the two countries signed an agreement on the basic principles for the settlement of border territory disputes, which was followed, in 1994, by a commitment to resolve disputes over the Tonkin (*Beibu*) Gulf (a self-enclosed sea, which is surrounded by land territories of China's Hainan Island and Vietnam, where massive reserves of oil and gas are believed to exist). Although China denounced a 1996 decision by Vietnam to grant oil companies the right to engage in oil exploration around the Spratly Islands, after a series of mutual visits by top leaders and intense negotiations in

2000, China and Vietnam initialed an agreement on the Delimitation of the Territorial Sea, Exclusive Economic Zone, and Continental Shelf of the Two Countries in Beibu Gulf along with an Agreement on Fishery Cooperation in Beibu Gulf. Visits to China, in 2002, by the general secretary of the Vietnam Communist Party and a return visit to Vietnam by PRC President **Jiang Zemin** led to further assertions of friendship and cooperation backed by a growth in bilateral trade from US$30 million to US$5 billion in 2004 and a host of joint construction projects, including exploration of oil and gas in the disputed South China Sea area with the participation of the Philippines, which is a third claimant to the territories. Additional agreements on demarcating the land border between Vietnam and China were reached in 2003 as tourist **trade** between the countries soared to more than one million Chinese visiting Vietnam and 700,000 Vietnamese touring China, which was facilitated by the establishment of air links between China Southern Airlines and **Shanghai** Airlines to Ho Chi Minh City (the former Saigon) in 2002 and 2005. *See also* FOREIGN POLICY.

VILLAGE-LEVEL ELECTIONS. In 1987, China's **National People's Congress** (**NPC**) passed the Organic Law of the Villager Committees of the **People's Republic of China** (**PRC**) requiring "village committees" (*cunmin weiyuanhui*) to implement democratic administration and subjecting them to fiscal accountability. The concept of self-governance for China's 700,000 villages, ranging in size from a few hundred to a few thousand residents, emerged from the political and economic chaos brought on by the **Cultural Revolution** (**1966–1976**) to promote stability and prosperity by allowing village residents to choose their own **leaders** and to assist the local branch of the **Chinese Communist Party** (**CCP**) to implement unpopular policies such as tax collection and family planning. While official government data indicate that competitive elections are held in at least 80% of villages, other estimates put the figure as low as 10%. Under the law, all adult registered villagers have the right to vote and stand for election to the Village Committee with a 50% turnout of registered voters required to validate the results. The Village Committee consists of three to seven members, including a chair, one or more vice-chairs, and regular members who serve three-year terms, and serve as the executive arm of the village assembly, which is a body of all villagers 18 years and older that reviews the committee's annual report and charter. The major task of the Village Committee, which operates on the principle of majority rule, is to manage and allocate village lands and collective property and mobilize support for cooperative economic production and village production.

Organizationally, the Village Committee is not formally under the leadership of the local CP branch or state organs and is subject only to government "guidance, support, and assistance." Administration of the Organic Law is in the hands of the Ministry of Civil Affairs and has received substantial international support from the Ford and Asia Foundations, Carter Center, and International Republican Institute and several European governments. While local CP leaders have, in many cases, resisted full implementation of the law by attempting, sometimes successfully, to install Party **cadres** in the Village Committees, the law is designed to ensure an open and competitive election process involving direct nominations by individuals, multiple candidates, secret ballots, and a public count of the votes. In a number of high-profile cases, local villagers unhappy with CP branch decisions and **corruption** have demanded and won the backing of authorities at the township level—the lowest rung in the formal central **government structure**—to prevent the thwarting of elections by local officials with some villagers refusing to pay taxes or engaging in **social protests** to make their demands heard. Although an elected village head was, for the first time in PRC history, voted out of office in Heilongjiang Province in 1999, cases have also been reported of widespread subversion of the election process by intimidation, illegal disqualification of candidates, rigged results, and outright police interference.

In agricultural villages, where most income is generated inside the village, the elected committees are much more likely to exercise real power. But in villages where much of the economic activity takes place outside the village, the Party branch retains its strength, especially where the Party secretary is one of the key entrepreneurial leaders. In some villages, the election process has led to a restructuring of the local CP branch with villagers in one Shanxi Province county voting for local CP branch leaders and pilot programs for election of township CP secretaries by rank-and-file Party members, which were legitimized by the decision of the 2002 16th National Party Congress to promote greater "inner-Party democracy." In 2000, Village Committee elections in Fujian Province were preceded by open primaries (referred to as "sea elections" [*haixuan*]) while direct election of the township leader, who is normally appointed by the township CP, was experimented with in Sichuan, Hubei, Guangdong, and Shanxi provinces—even though the process is technically illegal. In other villages, however, the village committees have all but ceased to operate and, in some cases, have been replaced by the Maoist practice of mass meetings.

In urban areas, experiments in direct elections to "local residents' committees" (*chengshi jumin weiyuanhui*) patterned after the Organic Law were also introduced in 1999 with the Ministry of Civil Affairs selecting 20 cities for a pilot program involving 5,000 committees that are to employ more open procedures for staffing of these bodies, which date back to 1954 and are normally appointed by the local CP branch. More open nomination and candidate selection for urban people's congresses have also begun. The procedures are, however, much more opaque than the Village Committee elections, with the relevant Party organization still retaining considerable control over the official candidate list of people's congresses through gerrymandering of districts and outright intimidation, though a few high-profile cases of self-nominated candidates winning a seat have occurred in **Beijing** and other cities. At the provincial level, in 1999, the Guangdong Provincial People's Congress held a legislative hearing open to the public, which allowed citizens the right to speak on and oppose legislation. Experiments in open elections have also occurred at the grassroots level of **trade unions** and in the **All-China Federation of Women**. The commitment of the national leadership to expand democratic elections remains unclear with President **Hu Jintao** calling, in 2003, for an increase in public participation and democratic decision making but without endorsing explicit reforms such as nationwide expansion of township direct elections. In 2005, China is slated to have 300,000 village committee elections in 18 provinces.

– W –

WAN LI (1916–). Wan Li fought with Communist forces throughout the 1930s and 1940s. After 1949, he assumed various positions in the

Beijing Party and government organizations. Branded, during the **Cultural Revolution** (**1966–1976**), as a follower of **Liu Shaoqi**, Wan Li reappeared in 1971 only to be dismissed, along with **Deng Xiaoping**, after the **April Fifth Movement** (**1976**). In the late 1970s, Wan Li reappeared again and assumed a position in Anhui Province, where radical changes in agricultural policy that effectively dismantled the old system of **people's communes** were carried out with Wan's apparent blessing. In 1982, Wan was appointed to the **Politburo** and assumed the role of acting premier during the foreign travel of Premier **Zhao Ziyang**. In 1988, he became the chairman of the **National People's Congress** (**NPC**) Standing Committee. In 1989, during the second **Beijing Spring** pro-democracy demonstrations, Wan cut short his visit to the **United States** and Canada and returned to China where he reportedly voiced initial support of Zhao Ziyang's proposal to deal with the student protests according to the principles of "democracy and law," which Deng Xiaoping personally overruled. During the 1992 NPC session that passed a resolution approving construction of the **Three Gorges Dam Project**, Wan, despite his credentials as a reformer, summarily cut off debate and effectively prevented dam opponents from mobilizing opposition among NPC delegates. Following the death of **Zhao Ziyang** in January 2005, Wan Li joined with other Party elders, such as **Tian Jiyun**, to promote a proper ceremony and burial for the former general secretary.

WANG DONGXING (**1916–).** A member of various guard units in the 1930s for top **leaders** of the **Chinese Communist Party** (**CCP**), Wang Dongxing, in 1949, became director of the Security Office of the Central CCP Secretariat. In the same year, he accompanied **Mao Zedong** to Moscow as his personal bodyguard and was also appointed as deputy director of the Eighth Bureau, Ministry of Public Security. In 1955, Wang became vice-minister of public security; in 1958, he was appointed vice-governor of Jiangxi Province. In 1960, he became vice-minister of public security and was a leading figure in China's security forces. During the **Cultural Revolution** (**1966–1976**), he was appointed director of the General Office of the CCP Central Committee and became a member of the CCP Central Committee in 1969 at the Ninth National Party Congress. In 1973, he was promoted to the **Politburo** and, in 1977, became a vice-chairman of the CCP and member of the Politburo Standing Committee. As commander of the security forces in **Beijing**, Wang played a key role in arresting the **Gang of Four**. In February 1980, he was removed from all Party and state posts but, in 1982, was made an alternate member of the Central Committee. In 1985, he joined the **Central Advisory Commission (CAC)** and nominally retired. Since the late 1980s, he has been under house arrest in Beijing.

WANG GANCHANG (1907–). A graduate in physics from **Qinghua University** in 1929 and Berlin University in 1934, Wang Ganchang also studied at the University of California in 1948 and returned to China where he became a member of the September Third Society (*Jiusan*), one of China's largely powerless **democratic parties**. From 1953 to 1958, Wang was deputy director of the Physics Institute of the Chinese Academy of Sciences (CAS) and helped organize a research team at the Joint Soviet Nuclear Research Center Physics Institute in Dubna, **Soviet Union**. Wang worked on the restriction of nuclear fusion through laser inertia and was a major scientist involved in the development of the **atomic bomb** in China in 1964 and its hydrogen bomb in 1967. Like the rocket scientist **Qian Xuesen**, Wang went unscathed in the **Cultural Revolution (1966–1976)**; in 1978, became deputy director of the Atomic Energy Institute of the CAS; and, from 1979 to 1982, served as a vice-minister of the Second Ministry of Machine Building, which was a major sector of military production for the **People's Liberation Army (PLA)**. Wang also served as member of the **National People's Congress (NPC)** Standing Committee from 1978 to 1988; from 1984 to 2000, he was honorary president of the Society of Nuclear Physics.

WANG HONGWEN (1935?–1992). Wang Hongwen rose during the **Cultural Revolution (1966–1976)** from a low-level **labor** leader in **Shanghai** to the heir-apparent of **Mao Zedong**, before being purged in 1976 as a member of the notorious **Gang of Four**. Very little is known of him before his emergence in politics during the Cultural Revolution. According to one source, Wang was born in 1935 to a poor peasant family in northern Jiangsu Province but another source records that he was born in the northeastern province of Liaoning in 1932. As a young man in his late teens or early twenties, Wang joined the "Chinese People's Volunteers" during the **Korean War** (**1950–1953**), when he reportedly became a member of the **Chinese Communist Party** (**CCP**). At the end of the war, Wang was assigned as a worker to the No. 17 National Cotton Mill Factory in Shanghai, a major facility under the direct control of the Ministry of Textile Industries. Very soon, Wang became a member of the personnel office in the factory and a workshop Party committee secretary.

In June 1966, Wang was a key figure in stirring up the "revolutionary" wave in the No. 17 Cotton Mill in response to Mao Zedong's May 16th Circular that targeted the "enemies" of the Cultural Revolution. Wang was also active in writing **big-character posters** (*dazibao*) denouncing the Party secretary at the factory. This bold action by Wang was later singled out by Mao as the first significant big-character poster of the Cultural Revolution in Shanghai. Wang expanded his attacks and targeted **cadres** holding high-level ranks: Chen Pixian, First Party Secretary of Shanghai and Cao Diqiu, Mayor of Shanghai. When the Maoist faction began to take control of **Beijing**, Wang and others traveled to the capital and were warmly received by the **Central Cultural Revolution Small Group** headed by **Jiang Qing**, and Mao Zedong himself.

Back in Shanghai in September 1966, Wang organized the Shanghai Workers Revolutionary Rebels General Headquarters (SWRRGH) and further expanded his attacks, which, in one incident, resulted in bloodshed. **Zhang Chunqiao** was sent by the CCP Central Committee to mediate the matter and ended up giving official recognition to Wang's organization in the name of the Central Cultural Revolution Small Group. From that point on, the SWRRGH became the mainstay of the Cultural Revolution in south and central-south China as Wang became the vice-chairman of the Shanghai **Revolutionary Committee** and chairman of the No.17 Cotton Mill Revolutionary Committee. In January 1971, Wang became secretary of the reconstructed Shanghai Municipal Party Secretariat whose first secretary was Zhang Chunqiao and second secretary was **Yao Wenyuan**. In August 1973, Wang became vice-chairman of the presidium of the CCP 10th National Party Congress. He was elected a member of the 10th CCP Central Committee and became a member of the **Politburo**. For a brief time in the mid-1970s, he reportedly controlled access to the increasingly ill Mao Zedong. Wang was also a vice-chairman of the Central

Military Affairs Commission (MAC) in the post-Cultural Revolution CCP. Despite Wang's high positions, his function in the post-Cultural Revolution era was slim. On October 1976, Wang, along with Jiang Qing, Zhang Chunqiao, and Yao Wenyuan, was arrested and together they were incarcerated as the Gang of Four and put on public trial in 1980 while purged from the Party permanently. At the trial, Wang confessed his errors and was given a relatively light sentence. Wang died of liver cancer in 1992.

WANG MENG (1934–). The son of a philosophy professor, Wang Meng joined the Communist **Youth League** in 1949 when he was a Middle School student and began to study political science. In 1958, Wang Meng published his first major novel, titled *The Young Newcomer in the Organization Department*, which portrayed the clash between young, idealistic revolutionaries with older, entrenched bureaucrats and almost immediately subjected Wang to accusations as a "rightist" during the **Anti-Rightist Campaign (1957–1958)**. Forced to work as a laborer, Wang remained virtually silent for 20 years, especially after being exiled to the Xinjiang Autonomous Region in China's far northwest, where he lived with Uygur **minorities** and mastered their language. In 1978, Wang was rehabilitated and returned to **Beijing**, where he published his novella *Butterfly (Hudie)*, for which he was awarded a national prize. In 1982, Wang was identified as the vice-president of the China PEN Center and was elected as an alternate member of the **Chinese Communist Party (CCP)** Central Committee by the 12th National Party Congress. In 1983, Wang Meng became editor-in-chief of *People's Literature (Renmin wenxue)* and a vice-chairman of the All-China Writers' Association. In 1986, he was appointed minister of culture and, in 1987, became editor-in-chief of *Chinese Literature*. Following the military crackdown on the second **Beijing Spring** in June 1989, Wang was relieved of his post as minister of culture and subject to increasing political criticism. *The Works of Wang Meng* were published in China in 1993 as Wang continued to write, although his most important output had come in his early career. *See also* LITERATURE AND THE ARTS.

WANG RUOSHUI (1926–2002). Trained as a Marxist philosopher and for a short time an editor at the *People's Daily*, Wang Ruoshui in

1946–1948 studied at **Beida** (**Peking University**) and then traveled to the Communist "liberated" areas in north China. In the 1950s, he worked for the **Beijing** Municipal Party Committee and in the Theory Department of *People's Daily*. He took part in the 1950s in the criticisms of **Hu Shi** and Liang Shuming and, in 1960–1962, was involved in the ideological polemics on "the identity of thought and existence." He became famous in 1963 for his essay "The Philosophy of the Table," which argued against the notion that ideas simply reflect in a mechanical way pre-existing realities, a piece that won Wang praise from **Chinese Communist Party** (**CCP**) Chairman **Mao Zedong**. In the late 1970s, Wang wrote on alienation in a socialist society and, in 1979, criticized the **personality cult** (*geren chongbai*) of Mao Zedong. After he composed an essay entitled "A Defense of Humanism," he was ordered by the CCP Propaganda Department to compose an attack on the concept and was subsequently dismissed from his position at *People's Daily* and later expelled from the Party. In February 1989, Wang signed a letter to CCP **leaders** calling for political liberalization. Visiting the **United States** in May 1989 during the outbreak of the second **Beijing Spring** pro-democracy movement, he returned to China to participate in the demonstrations. After temporarily locating in the West, in 1994, Wang returned to China and, in February 1995, joined 11 other **intellectuals** in petitioning the central government for a radical change in political structure toward a constitutional democracy and an end to official **corruption**. In 1999, he wrote the Preface to the Chinese edition of Raya Dunayevskaya's work entitled *Marxism and Freedom* and remained a Marxist committed to the principles of **human rights**, free speech, and the rule of law.

WANG RUOWANG (1917–2001). After joining the **Chinese Communist Party** (**CCP**) during the **Sino–Japanese War** (**1937–1945**), Wang Ruowang traveled to Yan'an, where he became involved with a wall newspaper called *Light Cavalry* (*Qingqidui*) that exposed the darker sides of the CCP. As a result, he was exiled to a remote area in Shandong Province by chief of the secret police, **Kang Sheng**. Rehabilitated, he became a journalist in post-1949 China and was branded a "rightist" in 1957 for writing several "critical essays" (*zawen*) during the **Hundred Flowers** (**1956–1957**). Rehabilitated once more, in 1962, he launched into more criticisms of the CCP for its policies during the **Great Leap Forward (1958–1960)** and was singled out for attack by **Shanghai** Party boss Ke Qingshi, an event that evidently contributed to the death of Wang's wife. Jailed in 1966 as a "counterrevolutionary," Wang was rehabilitated for a third time in 1979. At the height of the "wound literature" describing the human suffering brought on by the **Cultural Revolution (1966–1976)**, Wang wrote *Hunger Trilogy*. This largely autobiographical account portrays prison conditions as relatively more humane under the Nationalist regime of the **Kuomintang (KMT)** in comparison to the Communist period. A Party member for 50 years, Wang was expelled from the CCP in 1987. In 1989, he supported the second **Beijing Spring** pro-democracy demonstrations and was imprisoned for more than a year from 1989 to 1990. *See also* LITERATURE AND THE ARTS.

WANG SHIWEI (1908–1947). One of the first **intellectuals** to be persecuted and executed by the **Chinese Communist Party (CCP)** during the Yan'an **Rectification Campaign**, Wang Shiwei was born in Henan Province to a scholar's family. He attended a preparatory school for study in the **United States** in Henan, where he acquired a basic knowledge of English. Poverty stricken, Wang Shiwei sought a low-level position in the **Kuomintang (KMT)** headquarters in Nanking (Nanjing). In 1937, after the start of the **Sino–Japanese War (1937–1945)**, Wang went to Yan'an and became involved in translating the works of Marx and Lenin into Chinese. During the Yan'an Rectification, he published a series of critical essays entitled *Wild Lilies*. In 1942, Wang was wrongly accused of several crimes: "counterrevolutionary," "Trotskyite spy," "hidden KMT spy," and "member of the Five-Member Anti-Party Gang," and was subsequently executed. Following the 1978 **Third Plenum of the 11th CCP Central Committee**, the Party Organization Department rendered a decision in February 1982 that denied the existence of the so-called "Five Member Anti-Party Gang" and as a result an official "**reversal of verdicts**" (*pingfan*) on Wang was posthumously issued.

WANG ZHEN (1908–1993). Born to poor peasants, Wang Zhen attended only three years of elementary school until forced to work on the railway. Wang joined the **Chinese Communist Party (CCP)** in

1927 and, two weeks after their marriage, his wife was executed by the **Kuomintang** (**KMT**). After fighting under CCP General He Long, Wang became commander of the Yan'an garrison in the 1940s and was appointed by **Mao Zedong** to oversee the **Rectification Campaign** directed primarily against outspoken **intellectuals**, including **Wang Shiwei**, who was executed on He Long's orders. After 1949, Wang Zhen was stationed in the Xinjiang Autonomous Region, where, with **Deng Liqun**, he helped put down local Muslim resistance to Chinese Communist control. In 1956, he was appointed minister of state farms and reclamation and became a member of the CCP Central Committee. Wang retained his posts throughout the **Cultural Revolution** (1966–1976) and, in 1978, became a member of the **Politburo** and the Central **Military Affairs Commission** (**MAC**). From 1982 to 1987, Wang headed the **Central Party School** and in 1988 became the vice-president of China. Known as the "big cannon," Wang Zhen is said to have strongly supported the use of force against pro-democracy demonstrations during the 1989 second **Beijing Spring** and evidently rode in a **People's Liberation Army** (**PLA**) tank during the operation.

WEI GUOQING (1913–1989). A member of the Zhuang **minorities** from southwestern China, Wei Guoqing (old name Bangkuan) took part in a local farmers self-defense army in 1927 and the 1929 Baise Uprising. In 1931, he joined the **Chinese Communist Party** (**CCP**) and rose through the military hierarchy in the Third Field Army of **Peng Dehuai**. Following the "**liberation**" (*jiefang*) in 1949, he assisted the Vietnamese Communists in their 1954 defeat of the French at the battle of Dien Bien Phu where he directed Chinese-supplied artillery. Wei returned to China and became Party secretary in his home province of Guangxi in China's southwest. In 1966, Wei became the **political commissar** of the **Guangzhou (Canton)** Military Region and survived through the **Cultural Revolution (1966–1976)**, though sometimes criticized by **Red Guards**. In the late 1960s and early 1970s, he headed the **Revolutionary Committee** in Guangxi Province, where Wei evidently tolerated massive violence committed against the Zhuang that degenerated into politically driven cannibalism. Nevertheless, Wei was appointed to the **Politburo** in 1973 and from 1977 to 1982 became director of the General Political Department of the

People's Liberation Army (PLA). In 1985, he resigned his Party posts. *See also* VIETNAM; ZHENG YI (1947–).

WEI JINGSHENG (1950–). China's most prominent dissident, Wei Jingsheng is from an Anhui Province **cadre** family and was trained as an electrician. During the **Cultural Revolution (1966–1976)**, he was a **Red Guard** and also imprisoned. In 1979, at *Xidan* **Democracy Wall** in **Beijing**, Wei called on **Deng Xiaoping** to initiate a "**Fifth Modernization**" of democracy and **human rights**, arguing that Deng's **Four Modernizations** stressing economic development and scientific and military modernization were insufficient for China's overall development. Wei was arrested in October 1979 on charges of being a "counterrevolutionary" and for revealing "state secrets" to a foreigner and sentenced to 15 years imprisonment, often in solitary confinement. Wei was released in 1993 and was reincarcerated in 1994; finally, under American pressure, he was allowed to leave China for the **United States**, where he has since resided. In 2005, Wei was nominated for the Nobel Peace Prize and continues to speak out against the abuse of human rights in China and has opposed policies of Western nations, such as the possibility of the European Union lifting its arms embargo on China, which was imposed in the aftermath of the military crackdown against the second **Beijing Spring**.

WEN JIABAO (1942–). The premier and head of the State Council in China since 2003, Wen Jiabao graduated from the **Beijing** Geology Institute in 1965 with an advanced degree from the same institute in 1968. He served as a vice-minister of geology and mineral resources and took the lead in the reform of **state-owned enterprises (SOEs)** by introducing corporate models of organization to replace the strict hierarchical organization of ministries and production facilities that was characteristic of the Soviet-style planning system, which dominated the Chinese **economy** from 1953 to 1978–1979. In the late 1980s, Wen Jiabao was the director of the General Office of the **Chinese Communist Party (CCP)** Central Committee and, in 1992, became a member of the Party Secretariat and secretary of the Work Committee of Departments under the Central Committee. A member of the **Politburo** since 1997, and a vice-premier from 1998 to 2002,

Wen Jiabao was elevated to the nine-member Politburo Standing Committee in 2002 and made premier in 2003.

"WHAT I SAY IS WHAT COUNTS" (*"YIYANTANG"*). This phrase appeared in **Chinese Communist Party (CCP)** documents and speeches by top **leaders** that periodically criticized the tendency of some Party and government officials to engage in arbitrary action. It was held to be inconsistent with the principles of **democratic-centralism** that theoretically guarantee discussion of issues and "collective leadership" (*jiti lingdao*) within the CCP. During the Maoist era, it was also apparently used by detractors of **Mao Zedong** within the CCP and the Party's propaganda organizations as an elliptical way to criticize the all-too-frequent tendency of the chairman to make arbitrary decisions on crucial national issues, such as **agriculture** and the **Great Leap Forward (1958–1960)**. Rather than criticizing Mao face to face—a virtual impossibility in China that carried enormous risks—such phrases as *yiyantang* focused on Mao Zedong's arbitrary leadership that some CCP leaders believed robbed them of their legitimate role in the Party's top decision-making bodies and that often led to economic, financial, and political disasters. Since 1978, the phrase has reappeared in official and unofficial propaganda in China and perhaps was aimed at the tendency of **Deng Xiaoping** to also act as the CCP patriarch. Following the military crackdown against the second **Beijing Spring** in June 1989—which Deng Xiaoping is said to have personally ordered with the support of key military officials, thereby overriding the apparent decision of the **Politburo** Standing Committee to deal with student protests according to the principles of "democracy and law"—calls were once again issued by deposed leaders, such as **Bao Tong**, to rid the CCP of "one-man politics" and strengthen the role of institutional procedures and law.

WHATEVERIST FACTION. *See* "TWO WHATEVERS."

"WHITE-HAIRED GIRL" (*"BAIMAO NÜ"*). A revolutionary ballet that was composed by **He Jingzhi** in the 1940s, the *White-Haired Girl* was promoted by **Jiang Qing** during the **Cultural Revolution (1966–1976)** as one of the so-called "eight model operas." Inspired by the socialist realist traditions of Soviet art under **Josef Stalin**, the ballet combined military drill, folk steps, clutched weapons, and clenched fists as major motifs. The story line focused on a girl from a poor peasant family whose young lover goes off to join the **Chinese Communist Party** (**CCP**) Eighth Route Army. After her father commits suicide rather than submit to the oppression of the local landlord, the girl flees into the mountains, where, because of lack of salt in her diet, her hair turns white. The story ends when the girl is reunited with her young lover, who, with his contingent of Communist soldiers, discovers her mountain redoubt. *See also* LITERATURE AND THE ARTS.

WOMEN. Improving the status of women in Chinese society was a major policy goal for the **Chinese Communist Party** (**CCP**) on its accession to power in 1949. Throughout his revolutionary career, **Mao Zedong** had made the overthrow of patriarchal authority in China a primary target of the revolution as he proclaimed that women "hold up half the sky." From the Communist point of view, women had been subject to a long history of mistreatment by husbands, employers, and officials, including such insidious practices as concubinage, footbinding, female infanticide, forced prostitution, and slavery, all of which needed immediate eradication. This commitment was clearly indicated in 1949, when the first National Women's Congress was held in March—even before the official establishment of the **People's Republic of China** (**PRC**) on 1 October 1949. In 1950, one of the first acts of the Chinese government was to pass the **Marriage Law**, which granted women the right to divorce and to own property and established minimum ages for marriage. In 1980, the minimum ages were revised, setting a marital age for men at 22 and women at 20. While the CCP promoted a number of policies to enhance the status of women in China, it, too, would engage in practices that often fell back into the traditional mode of placing women in an inferior position.

In addition to its promulgation of the Marriage Law, a number of other policies were formulated to favor the economic, political, and social position of women. During the **land reform (1950–1952)**, rural women received land just like their male counterparts because Mao Zedong viewed women as a "vast reserve of **labor** power" for the country's work force. Women were also moved into the urban labor force. By 1957, more than three million women were employed as workers and staff, a 5.5 fold increase over 1949. With the CCP-led campaign to wipe out prostitution and close down brothels, women were major targets of the government's literacy campaign, which, by 1958, had led to 16 million women learning how to read. Women were also granted the right to vote under the Electoral Law of the PRC, which helped to account for women making up 12% of the deputies to the **National People's Congress** (NPC) in the 1960s and 1970s and 10% of representatives to the **Chinese People's Political Consultative Conference** (CPPCC) whose vice-chairman was Ms. **Song Qingling**, the widow of Sun Yat-sen. Top **leaders** of the CCP, especially members of the all-powerful **Politburo**, were almost all exclusively male until the emergence of **Jiang Qing**, Mao Zedong's wife, during the **Cultural Revolution (1966–1976)**.

From the late 1950s to the advent of economic reforms in 1978–1979, sexual differences in China were muted as women and men alike wore the same blue or gray jackets, except women were required either to wear their hair in braids or have a very short cut. And even as women moved increasingly into professional positions, such as doctors, engineers, and factory managers, the CCP stuck to social conservative notions of females as primarily child bearers and managers of the household. Traditional social models, such as the "**Five Good Women**" (*wuhao funü*), were reinforced by Mao Zedong's call in the 1950s for women to bear many children to replenish the loss of an estimated 30 million people during the **Sino–Japanese War (1937–1945)** and the **Civil War (1946–1949)**. Women workers in China were granted paid maternity leave, and new laws guaranteed equal pay for equal work, although, in reality, Chinese women wage earners still fall short of their male counterparts; at home, women were primarily responsible for securing basic necessities that were subject to government rationing. During the height of the anti-**Gang of Four** campaign that followed upon Mao Zedong's death in 1976, Jiang Qing was subject to merciless attacks on her character, many of which carried male chauvinistic and anti-feminist themes, suggesting that she had used her sexual prowess to lure the chairman away from his proper revolutionary, political duties. The fact that Mao made a practice of surrounding himself in later years with young females also indicated the role of women in the higher echelons of power in China had not been fundamentally altered.

Since the advent of economic reforms in 1978–1979, the position of women in Chinese society has continued to progress in many respects while some of the gains of the 1949–1978 period have been lost. Whereas in 1950 less than 20% of young girls in China attended elementary school, by 1990, that figure had grown to 96%, and over 110 million women have attained literacy since 1949. The proportion of females in middle schools, colleges, and postgraduate schools in 1992 was 43%, 34%, and 25%, respectively, while women made up 10% of Ph.D. recipients in the same year. Women made up 40% of scientists and technicians in 2002, though the number of women engineers has undergone a recent decline. Nationwide, women composed about 44% of all teachers, historically a pure male preserve. One-third of all faculty members at **Beida (Peking University)**, one of China's most prestigious institutions of higher **education**, are women, although overall women constitute only about one-third of all university students in China. In the medical profession, where great strides for women were made from 1949 onward, women make up the bulk of maternity and childcare medical professionals, who constitute 55% of all medical workers in the country. At the village level, women officials are usually assigned to family planning, which, because of widespread resistance to the **one-child policy**, is one of the most unpopular jobs in China, especially in the countryside. In terms of total national employment, women constitute 50% of all laborers in the countryside, 22% in **industry**, and 28% in the service sector, altogether constituting 45% of the national work force (approximately 330 million women), which is higher than the average world rate. Nearly 200,000 women have senior professional titles.

China's labor market is still segregated by gender, however, with males concentrated in occupations, such as managers, drivers, and technicians, with women in sales, clerical work, and personal services and shop-floor production in light industry. The gender wage gap in China is substantial as women in 1999 earned about 70% of men's pay in the urban sector and 59% in the rural sector, a drop in relative rates from 10 years earlier. Gender wage gaps are larger in the private sector than in the **state-owned enterprises (SOEs)**— even though women accounted for 39% of the self-employed and 35% of the owners of private and individual businesses in 1996. Women have less access to formal credit than their male counterparts, work on average one hour longer than men a day, and constitute 53% of the urban unemployed with slightly lower probability of finding a new job. Gender discrimination is even more pervasive in the rural than urban sector with the advent of **township village enterprises (TVEs)** in the countryside increasing the gender wage gap with outright discrimination against women more likely to occur in the private than state-owned sector. Although males outnumber females by two-to-one among China's migrant **floating population**, the proportion of female migrants is growing with an average age of 25–26 for women versus 28–29 for men. Retirement age in China is still unequal with women civil servants required to retire at age 55 (with reduced income) five years earlier than men, a situation that the **All-China Federation of Women** promised to change at its Ninth Congress in 2003. Some employers in China still specify "men only" for certain occupations and require that female applicants be "young and attractive." Pornography has spread throughout China, especially via the **Internet**, while human trafficking of women sold as brides to the highest bidder in remote towns with few females has reemerged, along with increased rates of female infanticide, often motivated by economic reasons.

Socially, Chinese women in the post-1978 era have become more assertive in certain realms while suffering setbacks in others. During the 1950s, China experienced a wave of divorces, mostly inaugurated by husbands wanting to break arranged marriages in their villages. By the 1990s, the tables turned a bit, with more and more women initiating divorce proceedings citing unfaithful and/or unaffectionate and sometimes even violent husbands. Although low by American standards, where half of all marriages end in divorce, China's divorce rate in 2005 of 19% is five times the 1979 rate. In large cities, such as **Beijing**, it has skyrocketed to 60%. In addition to looking for professions and outlets other than the family for personal satisfaction, Chinese women seemed more inclined to seek romance and sexual pleasure as central features of the marriage bond, replacing the traditional satisfaction with a steady marriage and secure income. China has experienced an explosion in marriage consultant services, women's research centers, and hotlines that previously were virtually unknown in the very puritanical and tight lipped society of the pre-reform period, when wives were forbidden by husbands from even talking to another man. China is also experiencing a wave of "flash marriages" followed by "flash divorces" with young couples marrying in the morning, arguing at midday, and divorcing in the afternoon. Although women in China are more willing to seek outside help for such traumas as domestic violence, others have resorted to force, including murder, to deal with abusive husbands; half of incoming female criminals in recent years are jailed for violent crimes. The first rules in China to make it explicitly illegal for Chinese men to beat up their wives were not passed until 1996 by Changsha Municipality in the Hunan Province. Women remain at a distinct disadvantage in divorce court, where they are often unable to get their fair share of common assets, which are often concealed by duplicitous husbands.

For the single or recently divorced woman in China, dating services and websites offering "Chinese women seriously seeking long-term relationships with gentlemen around the world" have sprouted up throughout the country. Young Chinese girls, especially from remote rural areas, such as Yunnan Province, have also become part of the international sex trade and industry to **Japan**, Thailand, and other sex industry hotspots. With each economic downturn in China, such as in 1998, increasing numbers of young girls drop out of school and become prostitutes. The suicide rate of Chinese women outpaces that of men by 25%, and suicide among young rural women constituting the number one cause of death in the countryside. Sexual abuse of young women is also rampant in the prison-like environments of large-scale factories in China's coastal south where females constitute the overwhelming percentage of the work force. In a 2005 amendment to the Law on the Protection of the Rights of Women and Children in China, sexual harassment was made illegal for the first time; a survey found that 86% of women respondents claimed to have been victims of such practices in the workplace or elsewhere, including sleazy mobile phone messages and e-mails. China also launched a project aimed at improving girls and young women's abilities to avoid becoming victims of human trafficking when seeking jobs, especially females from rural areas in the provinces of Henan, Anhui, and Hunan, where large numbers of migrants originate, including girls and young women, who are often deceived or lured into sexual exploitation or other unacceptable forms of labor, which may account for the rise of women HIV/**AIDS** carriers in the country in recent years. Increasingly stressful lives and longer working hours have also caused an increase in health problems among women, including a sizable increase in the occurrence of breast cancer in cities such as Beijing.

With the massive expansion of wealth in China, newly rich, married males have resumed old traditions of concubinage, installing a stable of young women in expensive "concubine villages" where they are indulged in costly habits. Young, unmarried women, in turn, have resorted to refusing marriage to any suitor with an inadequate bank account, a practice that has contributed to the drop in China's marriage rate from 2.08 people getting married for every 100 in 1981 to 1.26 in 2003. Unmarried Chinese women are apparently engaging in pre-marital sex with greater frequency (with some then seeking surgical repair of their hymen prior to marriage) while a slew of lifestyle magazines and Internet sites promote visions of female beauty that have led to a rash of cosmetic surgery—often in preparation for equally innumerable beauty pageants (known as "Miss contests"), which have mushroomed since 2003 when China hosted the Miss World pageant. While the Women's Federation has responded by calling on the government to impose limits on local government involvement in such contests and restrict media coverage, such concerns did not prevent the launching of a "Chinese new girl" project, along with the national "Super Girl" contest that was modeled on American Idol and reportedly attracted 400 million television viewers. Teenage girl readers have also become the target of numerous new publications, such as the **Taiwan**-based magazine, *Women of China*.

In 2000, women in China had a life expectancy of 73, near the standards of the developed world, although in contrast to the past, breast cancer in 2003 became the biggest killer of Chinese women. Chinese women have excelled in international sports, including in the Olympics and, more recently, in professional tennis, often more than their male counterparts. Women have also entered such previously male preserves as the **People's Liberation Army** (**PLA**) special military police, astronauts, and private detectives. At the same time, China continues to promote "model" women, especially on International Working Women's Day (8 March), as "pace setters" and "national exemplary workers" committed to "building a well-off society," language more reminiscent of the Soviet-style era of the 1950s and 1960s.

China's political scene is still largely a male preserve with all nine current members of the **Politburo** Standing Committee being men; the only top female leaders in China's post-1949 history were Jiang Qing and **Ye Qun** (the wife of **Lin Biao**) whose political roles lived and died with their prominent husbands. In 2005, there were four women among top CCP and government leaders (one minister out of 29 on the State Council) and 20 women working as vice-ministers in the ministries and commissions. The percentage of women in the 198-member Central Committee of the CCP dropped to 2.5%, an all-time low in the Party's history, from a high of 10% in 1973 during the Maoist era. The most prominent woman in the Chinese government is State Councilor **Wu Yi**, China's "iron lady" and former trade minister who ran the Ministry of Health during the 2002–2003 **SARS** crisis. In 56 years of CCP rule, only three women have headed a province, which includes the current governor of Qinghai Province in China's northwest. Women account for just 1% of the mayors in China while, overall, women make up 36% of the country's total number of **cadres** in government departments at various levels and institutions and enterprises. Fourteen percent of total CCP membership is female while women constitute less than 1% of top officials at the village level, a drop from 5% in the1990s. Within the **National People's Congress** (**NPC**), women constitute 20% of all deputies—a figure that has not changed since 1978—although eight women served as vice-chairmen between 1954 and 1993. In 1992, China passed the Law of the PRC on the Protection of Women's Rights and Interests that aimed at achieving equality of Chinese women in all walks of life, especially as the country underwent major transformations brought on by economic reform. In 2005, this law was amended to require each village Party committee in China to include at least one woman while the law governing **village-level elections** in China requires an "appropriate number" of women to sit on the semi-independent village committees. Women were also called upon in 2005 by the Women's Federation in their capacity as the wives of officials to implore their husbands to avoid **corruption**.

"WOMEN WITH BOUND FEET" (*"XIAOJUE NÜREN"***).** This phrase was used by **Mao Zedong** during a critical 31 July 1955 conference of **Chinese Communist Party** (**CCP**) secretaries of provincial, municipal, and autonomous region Party committees. Incensed that the pace of agricultural cooperativization was too slow and that newly formed coops were being dismantled in parts of the country, Mao launched attacks against what he saw as foot-draggers on the issue of agricultural cooperativization among top **leaders** whom Mao likened to "women with bound feet." While Mao proclaimed in his report that a "new upsurge in the socialist mass movement is imminent throughout the countryside," he vociferously claimed that "some of our comrades are tottering along like women with bound feet and constantly complaining, 'You're going too fast.'" In the chairman's view, rural society was ready for the "socialist upsurge"; only Party **cadres** were holding it back. In reality, many top leaders, such as **Liu Shaoqi**, had genuine concerns about the impact on food production and general morale in the countryside of an excessively fast pace of cooperativization that they had dubbed "rash advance" (*maojin*). Famines in Zhejiang Province and peasant protests against the formation of the cooperatives, following by only a few years CCP promises of land ownership during the **land reform (1950–1952)**, evidently provoked these social dislocations that some top leaders took as a warning signal to halt or at least slow down cooperativization. In the face of Mao's severe and very politically effective condemnations, opposition to rapid cooperativization quickly dissolved. Mao's July 1955 démarche thus had its intended effect as plans previously approved by central bodies for a slow pace were cast aside and Mao's more ambitious targets were adopted.

WORK POINTS (*GONGFEN*). These were the centerpiece of the system for allocating income in agricultural coops prior to the 1978–1979 agricultural reforms. Peasants earned work points for certain tasks with the harder and more physically demanding **labor** carrying greater value. The system generally favored men over **women** as the latter were generally relegated to performing more menial tasks that carried fewer work points. Actual income earned by the individual was based on total accumulated income of the cooperative (i.e., the **production team**) as the greater annual income of the coop increased the value of the total accumulated work points for each laborer. Cooperative members wanting to make a bigger income had to earn more points and each member had to do their best to increase the total income of the coop. Actual income to be distributed was determined after deducting production expenses and monies for reserve and welfare funds along with paid-out dividends on the land. **Corruption** in computation of points and allocation of monies to production team **leaders** and staff led to widespread discontent with the system in rural areas and contributed to the emergence of the **Agricultural Responsibility System** in the late 1970s. Suppression of individual and family interests in the work point system to that of the collective also undermined incentives for work.

WORK TEAMS (*GONGZUO DUI***).** These are groups of Party **cadres** organized by **Chinese Communist Party** (**CCP**) authorities to carry out specific objectives or political movements. Work teams were generally sent to lower levels of the Party and organizations at the grassroots to expedite and lead a particular political movement, such as the 1952 **Three-Antis Campaign**, the **Socialist Education Movement** (**1962–1966**), and the **Cultural Revolution** (**1966–1976**). Under the guise of "correcting" political views, the teams in fact operated as a sort of judge and jury in dealing with purported ideological and political crimes. Work teams forced confessions and publicly denounced offenders and exacerbated political and ideological divisions that sprouted up in any particular work unit. The teams generally disbanded after the movement or work was completed and cadres returned to their regular duties and functions. During the Socialist Education Movement, work teams were initially deployed to the lower levels by **Liu Shaoqi** to operate on a clandestine basis and to engage in confidential interviews with willing informants hostile to the local leadership. Liu also ordered work teams into schools and universities to alter school curriculum and to restrain any violence perpetrated by **Red Guards** in the early stages of the Cultural Revolution in June and July 1966. With the withdrawal of work teams from many of **Beijing's** educational institutions and a countermand of Liu's restraining order, violence against teachers and educational administrators broke out marking the beginning of the most violent phase of the Cultural Revolution. Twenty years later, work teams were also deployed in the run up to the 1989 second **Beijing Spring** to stifle dissent among Party and government organs, especially in the media.

WORLD ECONOMIC HERALD (SHIJIE JINGJI DAOBAO). A beacon of liberal opinion in Shanghai throughout the 1980s, this newspaper was founded in 1980 by Qin Benli, a veteran journalist and high-ranking Party cadre who had previously edited the *Wenhui Daily* in **Shanghai** and had been denounced as a "rightist" in 1957. Published jointly by the Chinese World Economists' Association and the Shanghai Academy of Social Sciences, the *World Economic Herald* started from scratch with no public funding and was initially concerned solely with international economics, but gradually expanded coverage to domestic political issues. With a circulation that ultimately reached 300,000 readers—thereby freeing it from stringent government regulations—the paper became known for its bold style of "hitting line balls," a phrase taken from China's national game of ping pong that, in effect, meant writing stories that bordered on the politically impermissible. Unlike other media in China, the *World Economic Herald* was able to avoid direct Party censorship because its sponsor was not a local Party committee— the situation with most newspapers in China—but two academic associations. The editor in chief of *World Economic Herald*, Qin Benli, was also protected by his close association with **Chinese Communist Party** (**CCP**) reformers, including General Secretary **Zhao Ziyang**. The paper was also independent of government subsidies, depending on advertising and subscribers for financial support. Zhu Xingqing, a very intelligent journalist who was not a Party member but who had made no political mistakes, was appointed as the deputy editor-in-chief.

Throughout the 1980s, the paper published articles by many reform advocates on topics such as separating the Party and government in China (a major reform proposal aired by Zhao Ziyang since the early 1960s), introducing the rule of law, and integrating China into the world **economy**. At various times after publishing particularly provocative articles, the office and personnel of the *World Economic Herald* were visited by CCP **work teams**, but somehow the newspaper managed to survive because of its support from the Party center. During the 1989 second **Beijing Spring**, however, the paper finally ended up being shut down after it published a compilation of articles by prominent reformers, such as **Dai Qing**, on the fate of former Party Chairman **Hu Yaobang**, whose death in April 1989 had sparked the crisis. Qin Benli died two years later and many *World Economic Herald* reporters were imprisoned or went into exile.

WORLD TRADE ORGANIZATION (WTO). On 10 November 2001, at the WTO Ministerial Conference in Doha, Qatar, an agreement on the terms of accession of the **People's Republic of China (PRC)** into the WTO was reached and on 11 December 2001 China became the organization's 143rd member. China's accession followed 15 years of negotiations that had begun in 1986 when the PRC applied for re-admission to the WTO's predecessor, the General Agreement on Tariffs and Trade (GATT) of which China (under **Kuomintang** rule) had been a founding member. Like all WTO accession negotiations, over the years China and a Working Party of the GATT focused on three basic aspects: information on China's **trade** regime; bilateral negotiations with individual WTO members, especially the **United States** and the European Union, regarding market access concessions and commitment in the goods and services area; and multilateral negotiations with Working Party members on the rules that would govern trade with China. At the time of its accession, China was the seventh leading exporter and eighth largest importer of merchandise trade and the 12th leading exporter and 10th leading importer of commercial services in the world.

With its accession to the WTO, China committed itself to implementing significant changes in its **trade** regime at all levels of government and to instituting systematic reforms that would facilitate business dealings with the global **economy**, especially in the area of transparency, predictability, and fairness. In addition, China assumed the obligations of more than 20 existing multilateral WTO agreements with only minimal periods of transition where necessary. China was required to provide non-discriminatory treatment to all WTO members under "national treatment" principles whereby equal treatment is given to all trading partners and there is no discrimination between domestic and foreign products or services. Dual pricing practices were also eliminated as well as differences in treatment accorded to goods produced in China in comparison to those produced for export. Trade liberalization commitments include substantial tariff reductions on industrial and agricultural goods and elimination of non-tariff barriers (NTBs) and other institutional and legal obstacles to foreign entry into China's growing service sector of the economy. China also consented to the creation of special China-specific safeguard mechanisms to protect businesses, farmers, and workers of existing WTO members.

China's ministries and agencies in the central and lower level **government structure** will gradually transition out of their old role of directing and controlling enterprises that existed under the previous central planning system and increasingly focus on the implementation and enforcement of laws, regulations, and other measures to help promote the smooth functioning of markets. Under the principle of transparency, all these laws, regulations, and other measures at all levels of government in China relating to trade in goods and services will be translated into one or more of the WTO languages (English, French, and Spanish) and before implementation of these laws and regulations China will provide a reasonable period of public comment to the appropriate government authorities. Uniform implementation and administering of the law is required under WTO rules as well as the establishment of tribunals for the review of all administrative actions relevant to the implementation of laws and regulations related to trade in goods and services.

In the industrial sector, China agreed to reduce tariffs from a base average of 25% (in 1997) to 9% with a range from zero to 47% with some of the highest rates (38%) applied to **automobiles** and related products. China also agreed to participate in the Information **Technology** Agreement, which requires the elimination of tariffs on computers, semiconductors, and other information technology products by, in China's case, 2005 and to the Agreement on Textiles and Clothing with all its rights and obligations. Average Chinese tariffs on textiles and apparel will drop from 35% to averages of 11% in 2005. Quotas on textiles were eliminated for all WTO members on 1 January 2005 but with a safeguard mechanism in place until 2008 that the U.S. quickly invoked in May 2005 following a 1,000% surge in Chinese textile imports. In conjunction with the Chemical Tariff Harmonization Agreement, China will implement reduced tariffs on two-thirds of the 1,100 products covered in the agreement and by 2006 will reduce tariffs on automobiles from 80–100% to 25% and auto parts from a base average of 23% down to 9.5%. Tendering requirements for non-governmental purchases of construction equipment have been eliminated with tariffs on scientific, pharmaceutical, and agricultural equipment reduced from an average of 11% to 5.5%. Tariffs in the wood and paper sectors are reduced from a 1997 average of 18 and 15–25%, respectively, down to 5 and 7.5%, respectively.

In the agricultural sector, China committed to reduce tariffs from a 1997 average of 31% to 14% over a period of five years. Consistent with WTO rules, China will not provide export subsidies and will institute an 8.5% cap for trade-and-production-distorting domestic subsidies that are lower than the cap permitted under WTO to developing countries. China also lifted long-standing bans on the importation of agricultural goods, such as corn, wheat, citrus products, and meat, and it must implement tariff-rate quotas that provide significant market access for bulk goods such as grains, soy oil, and cotton. Import monopolies maintained by State trading enterprises on agricultural goods, such as wheat, rice, and corn, were eliminated while non-State trading enterprises were granted the right to import such goods.

In the service sector, China committed to the General Agreement on Trade in Services (GATS) of the WTO, which provides a legal framework for addressing market access and national treatment limitations affecting trade and investment in services. Entry into WTO requires a substantial opening of a broad range of services through the elimination of many existing limitations on market access at all levels of government, such as in **banking and finance**, insurance, telecommunications, and professional services. New licenses to foreign banks must be granted solely on prudential criteria with no quantitative limits on the number of licenses or restrictions, while immediately upon accession foreign banks will be able to conduct foreign **currency** business with Chinese enterprises and individuals throughout the country. New licenses to foreign insurance businesses are also based solely on prudential criteria with foreign life insurers permitted to hold 50% equity in joint ventures. Among the services that foreign telecommunications companies—previously restricted to equipment sales—can provide include joint ventures with 25% equity in mobile voice and data services and 30% equity in joint ventures in electronic mail, voice mail, and online information. Having accepted key principles from the WTO Agreement on Basic Telecommunications Services, China must separate the regulatory and operating functions of its Ministry of Information Industry, which has both regulated telecommunications and operated the China Telecom monopoly. Upon accession, wholly Chinese-invested enterprises were to have full trading rights subject to certain minimum registered capital requirements that will be gradually decreased during a three-year transition period. All foreign-invested enterprises were also to have the right to distribute and provide related services for goods that they make in China.

China accepted the Code of Good Practice of the WTO that obligates the country to review existing technical regulations, standards, and conformity assessment procedures and harmonize them with international norms. In accordance with Trade-Related Investment Measures (TRIMs), China also agreed to eliminate export performance, local content and foreign exchange balancing requirements from its laws, regulations, and other measures. China is also obligated to WTO agreements related to the protection of foreign intellectual property rights under Trade-Related Intellectual Property Rights (TRIPs), including those related to patents, trademarks, trade secrets, integrated circuits, and copyrights. Import licensing, rules of origin, and customs valuation must also be harmonized with international standards so as not to act as a trade barrier. Enforcement of these agreements is in the hands of a Transitional Review Mechanism that will operate annually until 2009 and require China to provide detailed information on its implementation efforts and give all WTO members the opportunity to raise questions. Anti-dumping provisions and textile safeguards were also instituted and will remain in effect from seven to 15 years as China-specific safeguard mechanisms, which were designed to prevent injury to other WTO members. In 2001, just prior to its WTO accession, China produced new patent, copyright, and trademark laws with appropriate implementing regulations, though criminal enforcement in China remains a serious problem.

Since China's accession to the WTO, progress and problems have emerged in the country's move toward integration into the global economy. Tariff reductions occurred satisfactorily with China lowering tariffs on some goods ahead of the WTO schedule while the country also moved speedily to issue revised legislation and regulations to meet its yearly requirements. China also revoked preferential tax policies enjoyed by 20 border-trade products, an important step toward treating products imported through normal and border trade equally. Problem areas included concerns by the U.S. and other WTO members that China continues to use export subsidies for corn and perhaps cotton and, more importantly, China lacks sufficient transparency involving provisions for public comment and disclosure by appropriate bodies of their respective analyses and decision-making processes that entails adoption, revision, and outright repeal of many laws and regulations. Serious problems have also arisen over China's backtracking on investment provisions in the country's agricultural bio-technology sector as well as administration of China's Tariff-Rate Quota System (TRQS) for bulk agricultural commodities. There were also unreasonably high capital requirements to establish banking, insurance, and telecom branches, and accusations of arbitrary application of sanitary and phytosanitary measures and inspection requirements on imported goods. Lack of an independent telecom regulator raised concerns about China's commitment to effective intellectual property rights protection. In 2004, the U.S. filed the first complaint against China in the WTO over tax rebates for domestic semiconductor manufacturers and unfair application of the Value-Added Tax (VAT) to foreign importers. With China's agreement to stop providing VAT rebates to domestic producers, this case was settled in 2005 but with high levels of piracy of copyrighted American-produced material (including music, films, and software) in China, the U.S. weighed bringing a second formal complaint against China.

In 2004, China's State Intellectual Property Office launched a nationwide campaign to boost intellectual property awareness among the general **population**, though national policy guidelines are often openly flaunted by local governments at the provincial level and below. China also created a number of new bureaucratic entities to administer and conform to WTO rules and standards, including the General Administration of Quality Supervision, Inspection, and Quarantine. Within five years, 70% of China's national standards will be based on international norms. Despite China's accession to the WTO Agreement on Technical Barriers to Trade, intense high-level engagement was necessary to resolve a dispute over China's decision to implement its own mandatory standards for encryption over Wireless Local Area Networks (WLANs). Entry into China's growing insurance industry occurred with the announcement by American International Group (AIG) that it planned to buy a 10% share in China's largest non-life insurer, PICC Property and Casualty, while Star China, a wholly owned subsidiary of Rupert Murdoch's News Corporation, was set up in China as a wholly foreign-owned advertising company. China has consistently criticized the U.S. and other nations of abusing anti-dumping and other rules of the WTO to gain unfair advantage. The PRC has also waged a campaign to lower the profile of **Taiwan** in the WTO, which it joined in 2002, with proposals to change the title of Taiwan's mission from "permanent mission" to something like the **Hong Kong** or Macao Economic and Trade Office, which does not imply sovereignty of a state. With increasing foreign competition in China's domestic market spurred by WTO entry, some of China's biggest companies are being forced to adopt global strategies, which include setting up overseas operations, acquiring foreign assets, and transforming such local firms as Amoi and Panda Systems into widely known multinational corporations and brand names. This strategy has also included efforts by Chinese companies to take over well-known foreign brands, such as the acquisition of IBM's personal computer business by the Chinese computer maker Lenovo. The closing of factories and mines in China as a result of increased imports and foreign competition has also provoked a series of **social protests**, such as the riot by 20,000 workers at a recently shuttered molybdenum mine in Liaoning Province. *See also* AGRICULTURE; FOREIGN POLICY; INDUSTRY; TRANSPORTATION.

WOUND LITERATURE. *See* LITERATURE AND THE ARTS.

WU GUOGUANG. A young member of a think tank operated by General Secretary **Zhao Ziyang** and a journalist at *People's Daily*, Wu Guoguang fled China following the military crackdown against the second **Beijing Spring** and enrolled as a graduate student in the **United States** at Princeton University. After receiving his Ph.D., Wu became a professor at Chinese University in **Hong Kong**, where he is a frequent commentator on Chinese politics and **foreign policy**.

WU HAN (1909–1969). Son of a poor peasant, Wu Han became a worker–student and graduated from China's prestigious **Qinghua University** in 1934; one year later, he was appointed a professor of history. In 1948, he joined the Communist movement and, in 1950, was appointed vice-mayor of **Beijing**. In 1953, he was appointed chairman of the Democratic League, one of China's eight **democratic parties**, and, in 1954, he became a member of the **National People's Congress** (**NPC**) representing Beijing. In 1955, Wu Han became a member of the Department of Philosophy and Social Sciences of the Chinese Academy of Sciences (CAS) and, in 1964, he became president of the Beijing Television University. Criticism of Wu Han's play, *Hai Rui Dismissed from Office*, launched the beginning of the **Cultural Revolution (1966–1976)**. In 1966, Wu Han was subject to "struggle" at the hands of **Red Guards** and, in 1969, he died during their frenzied attack on **intellectuals**. Wu Han's play was "rehabilitated" in 1978 at a forum of writers in Beijing. Wu Han also authored many books on the history of the Ming (1368–1644 AD) and Yuan (1206–1333 AD) dynasties.

WU YI (1938–). One of the most powerful **women** among top **leaders** in China, Wu Yi is from a prominent family of **intellectuals** and has considerable experience in **industry**, having attended the **Beijing** Petroleum College and worked in the Lanzhou Oil Refinery in Gansu Province. This was followed by nearly 20 years of work as a technician, chief engineer, and then deputy manager of major oil refineries and petrochemical facilities. Minister of Foreign Trade and Economic Cooperation in 1998, she was appointed a state councilor and was made an alternate member of the **Politburo**. Known as China's "iron lady" for her commanding leadership style, Wu Yi was appointed as a concurrent minister of health during the 2002–2003 **SARS** crisis and is credited for bringing the transmission of the virus under quick control. Wu Yi has also been involved in sensitive negotiations with the **United States** and **Japan** on a variety of international economic and political issues.

WU ZUGUANG (1917–). One of China's premier war-time dramatists and author of more than 40 plays and film scripts, Wu Zuguang was labeled as a "rightist" in the **Anti-Rightist Campaign (1957–1958)** and sent to northeast China for physical labor. He returned in 1960, only to be sent back to the countryside in 1966, where he remained for 10 years. In 1980, his play, *Itinerant Players*, was performed in **Tianjin**, but Wu was once again criticized as a "bourgeois liberal" in

1987. In spring 1989, Wu joined other **intellectuals** in signing a petition to the **Chinese Communist Party (CCP)** leadership calling for greater political freedom. Following the military crackdown against the second **Beijing Spring** in June, Wu was barred from speaking about the need for a reassessment of the "June 4" (*liusi*) incident at a meeting of the **Chinese People's Political Consultative Conference (CPPCC)**. *See also* LITERATURE AND THE ARTS.

WU'ER KAIXI (1968–). A former undergraduate student at **Beijing** Teachers University, Wu'er Kaixi emerged as the charismatic leader of the 1989 second **Beijing Spring** pro-democracy movement. Following the military crackdown in Beijing, he was listed as one of the 21 activists slated for arrest by the Chinese government. A member of the Uygur **minorities**, Wu'er Kaixi won his fame as a member of the student team, who, dressed in pajamas during a hospital stay in the middle of a hunger strike, carried out a dialogue with Premier **Li Peng** at a nationally televised meeting in May 1989. After the crackdown on 4 June 1989, Wu'er Kaixi managed to escape China via **Hong Kong** with the help of some underground organizations and became a founding member of the **Front for a Democratic China**. After living in the **United States** and attending Harvard University for a brief stint, Wu'er Kaixi moved to **Taiwan**, where he runs his own talk show.

WUHAN INCIDENT (JULY 1967). During the peak of the **Cultural Revolution (1966–1976)**, political and military forces in the central China city of Wuhan were at a point of near civil war. A group in Wuhan known as the "Million Heroic Army" was a defender of the existing power structure in the city and had engaged in open-pitched battles with **Red Guards** and other radical organizations. Central **leaders** sent from **Beijing** to resolve the dispute were arrested by the city leadership upon their arrival. They were only released after the personal intervention of **Zhou Enlai** and the deployment of central military forces to the area. Wuhan city leaders were themselves arrested and incarcerated and the "Million Heroic Army" was disbanded. The Wuhan Incident demonstrated to the central government that the Cultural Revolution was pushing China to the edge of civil war and had to be restrained, which, in fact, occurred in 1968.

– X –

XIA FANG. See "TRANSFER TO LOWER LEVELS."

"*XIA HAI*." Literally meaning "going to the sea," this phrase was popular in China throughout the 1980s and 1990s and was applied to young entrepreneurs who traveled to southern China, especially Guangdong Province, to make their fortunes in the booming **economy**. This group included people from all walks of life, **intellectuals**, workers, professionals, and even formerly imprisoned political dissidents. The long-range effect is to perhaps create in China a stable middle class similar to that which has emerged in the Newly Industrialized States of East Asia, such as South **Korea** and **Taiwan**.

XIA YAN (1900–). Educated in **Japan**, Xia Yan joined with Lu Xun in 1930 to establish the League of Left-Wing Writers. Xia translated a number of works into Chinese, such as Maxim Gorky's *Mother*, and wrote such film scripts as *Fascist Germs*. In 1949, he became deputy-director of the Propaganda Department of the **Chinese Communist Party** (**CCP**) East China Bureau and in 1954 vice-minister of culture. In 1965, he was labeled as "bourgeois" for his film script *Lin's Shop*, which was based on a short novel by **Mao Dun**, and was also accused of serving as an "agent" of **Liu Shaoqi** in literary and art circles. After the **Cultural Revolution (1966–1976)**, Xia reappeared in 1977 and became minister of culture until the early 1980s. In 1980, he was elected vice-president of the Chinese PEN Center and in 1990 president of the Society for Japan Studies. *See also* LITERATURE AND THE ARTS.

XU WEICHENG (1930–). A member of the Communist **Youth League**, Xu Weicheng served in the late 1950s and early 1960s as an editor of *Youth News* in **Shanghai**. During the **Cultural Revolution (1966–1976)**, he was reportedly a member of the radical **Rebel Faction** (*zaofanpai*) of **Red Guards** and a protégé of the radical leftist **Gang of Four**. In the early 1980s, he became a member of the **Beijing** Party Organization and, in 1987, launched frenzied attacks in *Beijing Daily* on **intellectuals** as part of the overall onslaught against "**bourgeois liberalization**." During the second **Beijing Spring**, Xu apparently had a hand in crafting the 26 April 1989 *People's Daily* editorial (based on comments by **Deng Xiaoping**) that condemned the pro-democracy movement as a "planned conspiracy and disturbance." In 1990, he was elevated to deputy-director of the **Chinese Communist Party** (CCP) Propaganda Department. In the early 2000s, he headed the National Commission for Poverty Relief through Cultural Activities.

– Y –

YAN JIAQI (1942–). A vice-president of China's Political Science Society, Yan Jiaqi was trained in the 1950s as an applied mathematician and later studied philosophy. In the mid-1980s, Yan served in the Office of Political Reform and helped shape the proposals of General Secretary **Zhao Ziyang** to develop a modern professional civil service in China and to eliminate the life-long tenure of political **leaders**. After giving speeches in Tiananmen Square during the 1989 second **Beijing Spring** pro-democracy demonstrations, Yan fled China and in Paris helped found the **Front for a Democratic China**. He currently resides in New York.

YAN MINGFU (1931–). A graduate of the Harbin Foreign Languages Institute, Yan Mingfu became a **cadre** in the General Office of the **Chinese Communist Party** (CCP) in the late 1950s before disappearing during the **Cultural Revolution (1966–1976)**. In 1985, he reappeared and became director of the **United Front** Department of the CCP Central Committee and a member of the CCP Secretariat. He was purged following the 4 June 1989 military crackdown on the second **Beijing Spring** for his failed attempt to resolve the crisis over the pro-democracy student movement without the use of force, but returned to government service in the early 1990s, where he served as vice-chairman of the **Chinese People's Political Consultative Conference (CPPCC)**.

YAN'AN WAY. This is a reference to the political and economic policies formulated by the Chinese Communists during the period from 1936 to 1945, when the Central leadership was headquartered in the small provincial town of Yan'an in northwest Shaanxi (then Shensi) Province that also served as the capital of the **Chinese Communist Party (CCP)** Shaan-Gan-Ning Border Government. After the CCP seized power in 1949, the "Yan'an Way" gained enormous symbolic significance for the CCP that was exploited by **Mao Zedong** and later **Deng Xiaoping** in imposing their vision on the Party and Chinese society in general. The heart of the "Yan'an Way" was the **mass line** propagated by Mao Zedong for fostering close cooperation and a spirit of egalitarianism between Party and government **cadres** and the peasantry that constituted the bulk of the **population** in areas controlled by the CCP. The "Yan'an Way" was also associated with the tradition of CCP-led **rectification campaigns** and the advent of Mao Zedong Thought as the dominant ideology in the CCP. Most importantly, Yan'an came to symbolize the selflessness and willingness on the part of CCP **leaders** and cadres to sacrifice for national goals, a legacy that was subsequently invoked by Party leaders from 1949–1995 to combat increasing arrogance and **bureaucratism** among the leadership and rank-and-file of the Party. Considered part of the "golden age" of the CCP, since the 1950s the town has become and remains a major site for domestic and international tourists. The "myth" of the "Yan'an Way" was punctured, however, by the memory of the CCP intellectual **Wang Shiwei**, who, as a staff translator in Yan'an during the 1940s, had criticized perks and privileges among the CCP leaders that ultimately led to his purge and eventual execution.

YANG BAIBING (1920–). A full general in the **People's Liberation Army (PLA)**, Yang Baibing was a key figure in the late 1970s and early 1980s in the strategic **Beijing** Military Region, where he served as **political commissar** until 1987. Yang joined the **Chinese Communist Party (CCP)** in 1938 and served in the Eighth Route Army during the **Sino–Japanese War (1937–1945)** and also served in the subsequent **Civil War (1946–1949)**. From the 1950s to the 1970s, Yang served in various military posts in China's southwest and in 1979 joined the senior ranks in the Beijing Military Area Command. At the November 1987 13th National Party Congress, Yang was appointed director of the PLA General Political Department, the key central organ responsible for maintaining loyalty among the troops to the CCP and, in 1988, was promoted to the rank of general when he also became a member of the Central **Military Affairs Commission (MAC)**. Along with his half-brother President **Yang Shangkun**, Yang Baibing played a prominent role in suppressing the second **Beijing Spring** in June 1989. In November 1989, he was appointed to the Secretariat of the CCP Central Committee and became secretary general of the Military Commission. In 1992, he failed to be re-nominated for that position at the 14th National Party Congress, and, in 1997, was dropped from the **Politburo**. This loss of status of both Yang Baibing and Yang Shangkun apparently reflected concerns by China's paramount leader **Deng Xiaoping** over the rising power of the "Yang family clique."

YANG SHANGKUN (1907–1998). Yang Shangkun was a member of the Twenty-Eight Bolsheviks trained in Moscow in the late 1920s and, in the 1940s, headed a drama troupe performing propaganda plays for Communist troops. In 1945, he became head of the General Office of the **Chinese Communist Party (CCP)**, a post he held until the **Cultural Revolution (1966–1976)**. He became a member of the Central Committee in 1956 but fell out of favor with **Mao Zedong** in the early 1960s, reportedly after bugging the residence of the chairman (a fact apparently discovered by one of Mao's many mistresses). In 1966, he was branded a "counterrevolutionary" and did not reappear until 1978. In 1982, he was appointed to the **Politburo** and became permanent vice-chairman of the Central **Military Affairs Commission (MAC)** and, in 1988, became **president of the People's Republic of China**. During this period, Yang and his half brother, **Yang Baibing**, became known as the "Yang family clique" for their influence in the military. During the 1989 second **Beijing Spring** pro-democracy movement, Yang Shangkun was reportedly instrumental in helping to convince **Deng Xiaoping** to support the declaration of martial law that ultimately led to the deployment of force against the demonstrations. Despite this crucial role, Yang Shangkun and his brother both lost their positions at the October 1992 14th National Party Congress allegedly after Deng Xiaoping found out their plans to place all the blame for the military crackdown on Deng following his death. In an interview in 1998, Yang Shangkun agreed that the decision to send soldiers against demonstrators had been a mistake that would eventually be redressed.

YAO WENYUAN (1931–). Born in Zhejiang Province, Yao Wenyuan is the son of the leftist writer Yao Pengzi. As a middle school student in 1948 in **Shanghai**, he joined the **Chinese Communist Party** (**CCP**). After the Communists takeover of Shanghai, Yao became a resident correspondent for the *Literary Gazette*, the official publication of the All-China's Writers' Association. Yao emerged as a young and fierce literary critic during the 1955 leftist-inspired campaign of denunciation and criticism that became known as the **Hu Feng Affair**. As an arduous contributor to *Wenhui Daily* and *Liberation Army Daily*, Yao finally caught the attention of **Mao Zedong** in 1957. Around 1963, Yao, together with **Zhang Chunqiao**, became close allies of Mao's wife and resident radical, **Jiang Qing**. In 1965, publication of Yao's article titled "On the New Historical Play *Hai Rui Dismissed from Office*" eventually led to the downfall of **Peng Zhen**, the then mayor of **Beijing**. At the Ninth National Party Congress in April 1969, Yao was elected a member of the **Politburo** and in Spring 1976, Yao joined with Zhang Chunqiao and Jiang Qing in starting a nationwide media campaign against **Deng Xiaoping** in an effort to hold on to the policies and practices of the fading **Cultural Revolution** (**1966–1976**). Yao was arrested in October 1976, a month after the death of Mao Zedong, and, together with the other three members of the **Gang of Four**, was put on public trial for crimes committed during the Cultural Revolution. Yao was sentenced to 18 years in prison and, in 1996, was released and allowed to return to his home in Shanghai as the only surviving member of the radical leftist faction.

YAO YILIN (1917–1994). Trained in chemistry and as a teacher, Yao Yilin led armed uprisings in eastern China in the 1940s. After 1949, he became vice-minister of commerce and negotiated **trade** agreements with the **Soviet Union**. In 1958, he was appointed to the Bureau of Finance and Commerce under the State Council and, in 1960, minister of commerce. Criticized in the **Cultural Revolution** (**1966–1976**) as a "three anti-element of the **Peng Zhen** clique," he returned in 1973 and became involved in foreign trade issues and, in 1977, became a member of the **Chinese Communist Party** (**CCP**) Central Committee. In 1980, he became director of the State Planning Commission, a member of the leading group on finance and economics headed by **Zhao Ziyang**, and, in 1985, was appointed to the

Standing Committee of the **Politburo**. In 1988, he served as acting premier during the absence of Premier **Li Peng** and was also chairman of the State **Three Gorges Dam Project** Examination Committee. A member of the Standing Committee of the Politburo during the 1989 second **Beijing Spring** pro-democracy movement, Yao reportedly sided with such hardliners as **Li Peng** in the decision to deploy lethal force against the student demonstrations. Yao Yilin is buried in the Babaoshan Revolutionary Cemetery outside **Beijing** in an area reserved for top CCP **leaders**.

YE JIANYING (1887–1992). Born in a family of wealthy merchants, Ye Jianying was an instructor at the **Kuomintang (KMT)** Whampoa Military Academy and, in 1927, joined the **Chinese Communist Party (CCP)**. He studied military science in Moscow and participated in the **Long March (1934–1935)**, when he sided with Zhang Guotao, the major nemesis of **Mao Zedong**. In 1945, Ye became a member of the Central Committee and, after 1949, was appointed vice-chairman of the National Defense Council. In 1955, he was promoted along with nine other field army commanders to marshal, the highest rank in the **People's Liberation Army (PLA)** and, in 1966, was appointed to the **Politburo**. In 1967, he became vice-chairman of the Central **Military Affairs Commission (MAC)** and, in 1973, was appointed to the Standing Committee of the Politburo. In 1975, he became minister of national defense and, in 1979, Ye proposed the crucial Conference on Guidelines in Theory Work that promoted liberal political reforms. After the death of **Mao Zedong** in 1976, Ye, along with Marshal Xu Xiangqian, was the main military force behind the coup d'etat by then Chairman **Hua Guofeng** to arrest **Jiang Qing** and the **Gang of Four**. In 1985, Ye, who was the godfather of the liberal journalist **Dai Qing**, resigned from all his posts.

YE QUN (1917–1971). Born in Fujian Province on China's eastern coast, Ye Qun was the wife of **Lin Biao**, who, at the 1969 Ninth National Party Congress, was officially designated as the successor to **Mao Zedong**. Ye Qun began her political career in the 1935 December Ninth Student Movement and later traveled to the **Chinese Communist Party (CCP)** redoubt in Yan'an. During the **Cultural Revolution (1966–1976)**, Ye Qun was involved as a member of Lin Biao's personal organization that allegedly sought to seize power from Mao Zedong. After 1967, Ye held several important positions in the Central Committee: deputy-director of the All-Military Cultural Revolution Group; director of the Lin Biao Office; and member of the CCP Military Commission Work Group. Following the Ninth Congress, Ye Qun was promoted into the CCP Central Committee and became a member of the **Politburo**. After Lin Biao's effort to seize power during the 1970 Second Plenum of the CCP had failed, Ye Qun allegedly joined her husband in organizing an attempted coup against Mao Zedong. The purported assassination attempt against Mao failed in September 1971 and Ye joined her husband and her son, Lin Liguo, in trying to flee China by plane, but all were killed when the plane crashed in Mongolia. On 20 August 1973, the CCP Central Committee formally removed the Party membership of Ye Qun, posthumously.

YE WENFU. A poet and a member of the military, Ye Wenfu became famous for his poem titled "General You Shouldn't Have Done This," in which he criticized a **People's Liberation Army** (**PLA**) general for using his authority to expand his house that displaced a children's kindergarten. Ye's speech at **Beijing** Teachers' University that was warmly welcomed by students, offended the university Party committee and the Beijing Municipal government, which singled Ye out as a typical case of "**bourgeois liberalization**." Ye was also personally criticized by **Deng Xiaoping** for the same "erroneous tendency" of self-enrichment at public expense.

YOUTH LEAGUE (CYL). The major "mass" organization for Chinese youth, the Communist Youth League (CYL) is described as a "big school for organizing youth in learning the ideas of communism, an assistant to and the reserve force of the **Chinese Communist Party** (**CCP**)." The nucleus of the All-China Federation of Youth, the CYL is reserved for youth from the ages of 14 to 28 and is an absolute must for anyone wanting to "join the CCP" (*rudang*). The CYL is also responsible for guiding the activities of the Young Pioneers, an organization for children under the age of 15. In 2005, CYL membership stood at 72 million, the largest youth organization in the world, organized into 203,000 committees and 2.5 million branches at the grassroots level and was chaired by Zhou Qiang, a post once held by **Hu Qili** and President **Hu Jintao**, who both used the position to rise to prominence in the CCP.

The Communist Youth League was founded in China in 1920, before the establishment of the CCP, and was first called the Socialist Youth League of China. The first Congress was held in 1922 in the southern city of **Guangzhou (Canton)**, a major base of Chinese Communist support. In 1925, it took the name of Communist Youth League of China and, in 1935, the CYL was deeply involved in organizing opposition to Japanese **imperialism**. Throughout the war, the CYL acted as a patriotic "front" organization for mobilizing Chinese youth of all political persuasions against the Japanese occupation forces. In 1946, the organization was renamed the New Democratic Youth League in accordance with the call by **Mao Zedong** for the creation of a **New Democracy** in the Chinese state. This organization was formally inaugurated in 1949 and did not change its title to Communist Youth League until 1957 after the official completion of the "socialist transformation" of the country. The major purpose of the CYL as a "transmission belt" of the CCP is to educate Chinese youth in the Communist spirit and "unite all youth to participate in socialist construction and create conditions for the realization of communism."

In recent years, the CYL has reiterated the standard phrases of China's top **leaders**, such as the concept of "three represents" (that the ruling Communist Party should represent not just workers and peasants but all advanced production and cultural forces, and the "overwhelming majority of Chinese people") promoted by **Deng Xiaoping** and **Jiang Zemin** and the "two musts" ("comrades must be taught to remain modest, prudent, and free from arrogance and must preserve the style of plain living and hard struggle") put forth by Hu Jintao. The CYL National Congress is the highest leading organ of the CYL with a Central Committee and Standing Committee akin to the organizational structure of the CCP and, like the Party, has a national congress in **Beijing** every five years. From 1957 to 1964, the CYL was chaired by **Hu Yaobang** who fostered a liberal atmosphere of democracy and openness that anticipated his plans for political reform in the late 1970s, when he was elevated to CCP chairman and then general secretary. During the 1989 second **Beijing Spring** pro-democracy movement, student activists condemned the CYL for its ideological and administrative dependence on the CCP, prompting efforts to organize alternative youth groups that were quickly quashed by central authorities.

Throughout the 1990s and early 2000s, the CYL shifted its function from the near unilateral political preaching and supervision of young students to providing a range of social services to young people. This included assisting students in entering high school and taking examinations for college and addressing increasing problems of youth unemployment and drug addiction. Helping young people find jobs is described as the number one priority of the CYL in China's increasingly market-oriented **economy**, which has involved launching CYL websites (www.gradnet.edu.cn and www.chinajc.com), where employment opportunities for recent college grads and job fairs are listed. The CYL has also arranged for business start-up loans for young people and has drawn into its membership many young entrepreneurs and CEOs, including Chen Tianqiao, known as "the Chinese Bill Gates" for his highly successful online games company ("Legendary" and "*Chuangqi*"), which made him a billionaire at age 30. Other CYL projects include Project Hope, a national charity program aimed at assisting poor school-age children in rural areas in receiving primary **education** (where high fees and rural work demands have led to high drop-out rates), and a number of entertainment projects for youth, such as carnivals, "idol" contests, and a joint effort with the Disney Company to introduce Chinese youth to the pleasures of Mickey Mouse (dubbed by Western journalists as the "Mickey Mao" project).

On a more serious note, since the 1980s the CYL has organized a Department of Teenagers' Rights Protection to help abused young people and has used its major press organ, *China Youth Daily*, to feature the cases of underprivileged young people who have confronted exploitation as members of China's huge migrant labor force, the **floating population**, or who have been detained for no reason at detention centers. CYL branches and members were part of the vast mobilization carried out by Chinese authorities to halt the 2002–2003 **SARS** crisis while university students have also been mobilized by the CYL to volunteer for work in China's backward western regions as part of the Western Region Development Plan promoted by the CCP from the late 1990s onward. The CYL has also been authorized to set up branches in the country's growing number of private colleges and universities and has launched a campaign in advance of the 2008 Olympics in Beijing to avoid the embarrassment of improper and salacious English employed in official city signs and ads on buildings (e.g., "massage the house").

For years, the *China Youth Daily* had a reputation in China for spirited reporting that tested the limits of **censorship** (*shencha*) imposed by the propaganda organs of the CCP. Reports in 2003 appearing in the newspaper and its tabloid subsidiary, *Youth Reference*, exposed cases of official **corruption** and abuse of power that, in turn, led to tension between the top leadership of the Youth League, which is subservient to the political demands of its superiors in the CCP, and young, idealistic reporters who take their role as journalists seeking out the truth seriously. The *China Youth Daily* (circulation 730,000) was one of the first national newspapers to run articles and editorials criticizing an official abuse of power in the Shenzhen **Special Economic Zone** (**SEZ**) and was the only major newspaper to cover the ill-behavior of Chinese soccer fans who demonstrated intense anti-Japanese sentiment at a 2004 match in **Chongqing**. In February 2006, a publication of the Youth League entitled *Freezing Point* was shutdown in reaction to its consistently provocative articles of news and public opinion, though it was later reopened.

YU GUANGYUAN (1915–). A veteran of the anti-Japanese 1935 December Ninth Movement, Yu Guangyuan joined the **Chinese Communist Party** (**CCP**) just prior to the Japanese invasion of China in 1937. In the 1950s, Yu became actively involved in developing China's scientific establishment, especially in the field of physics, and the philosophy of natural science. During the **Anti-Rightist Campaign** (**1957–1958**), he launched attacks against other philosophers; in 1962, he became a professor at **Beida** (**Peking University**). In 1967, he was branded a "counterrevolutionary" and sent to a **May Seventh Cadre School** and purged from the Party but then returned to become a senior member of the Party Research Office of the State Council, a deputy president of the **Chinese Academy of Social Sciences** (**CASS**), and in 1977 a vice-minister of the then State Science and Technology Commission. In the early 1980s, Yu headed a number of societies dealing with economic development and was elected to the presidium of the Chinese Academy of Sciences (CAS). The intellectual mentor of **Yan Jiaqi**, Yu became president of the Society for the Study of **Marxism–Leninism–Mao Zedong Thought** in 1988. After the military crackdown on the second **Beijing Spring** in June 1989, the *Beijing Daily* criticized Yu for "negating the people's democratic dictatorship." At age 83, Yu wrote a book translated in the West as *Deng Xiaoping Shakes the World: An Eyewitness Account of China's Party Conference and the Third Plenum (November–December 1978)*, which described the key debates held during the 34-day Party Work Conference, which inaugurated China's economic reforms and were formally approved by the **Third Plenum of the 11th Central Committee**. Yu is president of the Pacific Society of China and the chief editor of the *Pacific Journal* and an advisor to the Institute of American and Chinese Culture.

YU HAOCHENG. A vice-president of the Chinese Political Science Society in 1982 and a legal and constitutional expert, Yu Haocheng also headed the Masses (*Qunzhong*) publishing house run by the Ministry of Public Security. In February 1982, he signed a petition calling for greater freedoms and release of political prisoners and was put on the Ministry of Public Security's wanted list in June 1989 for his role in the second **Beijing Spring** pro-democracy demonstrations.

– Z –

ZENG QINGLONG (1939–). The vice-president of China and one of nine members of the **Politburo** Standing Committee of the **Chinese Communist Party** (**CCP**) in 2005, Zeng Qinglong is a long-time protégé of former President **Jiang Zemin**. Son of a revolutionary era army commander and with a brother who is a senior military leader, Zeng Qinglong graduated from the **Beijing** Institute of Technology in 1963 and served for two years in the **People's Liberation Army** (**PLA**). He then served in various posts relevant to China's defense industries, as well as petroleum, **energy**, and economic planning and, in 1984, assumed important posts in the **Shanghai** CP, becoming part of the political network headed by Jiang Zemin. In 1989, Zeng was promoted to the central government becoming director of the General

Office of the CCP Central Committee in 1993 and director of the critical Organization Department of the CCP in 1999. In 2002, he was promoted to the Politburo Standing Committee. Zeng also sits on the crucial Secretariat of the CCP Central Committee, which controls appointments throughout the vast CCP apparatus giving him day-to-day control of the Party's organizational affairs. Along with General Secretary **Hu Jintao**, Zeng has pursued a harsh line against so-called "liberal elements" in China, particularly among the media. He has also taken a great interest in ties with the **United States** and has courted influence among China's rising class of wealthy entrepreneurs. He was also one of the few contemporary Chinese **leaders** to visit the ailing **Zhao Ziyang** prior to the former general secretary's death in 2005, overseeing arrangements for Zhao's funeral.

ZHANG CHUNQIAO (1917–2005). Born in Shandong Province, Zhang Chunqiao joined the **Chinese Communist Party (CCP)** at the age of 21 and became a guerrilla fighter during the 1940s. In the early 1950s, Zhang was managing director of the newspaper *Liberation Daily* in **Shanghai** and made his mark with an influential article entitled "On Exercising All-Round Dictatorship over the Bourgeoisie," in which he railed against the possibility of a capitalist "restoration" in China. In 1959, Zhang was appointed to the **Politburo** of the Shanghai Municipal Party Committee and director of its Propaganda Department. In 1966, he became deputy-head of the Central **Cultural Revolution Small Group** and helped initiate demonstrations by the radical **Rebel Faction** (*zaofanpai*) of the **Red Guards**, whom he urged to go after **Liu Shaoqi**: "Go after them. Make them odious. Do not do it halfway," Zhang is reported to have told Red Guards at **Qinghua University** at the height of the radical frenzy in 1968. When municipal authorities in Shanghai tried to curb the wave of protests among students and factory workers, Zhang acting on the behalf of **Mao Zedong** declared that all commercial, industrial, and government offices had the right to establish mass organizations. Zhang held a series of mass meetings to humiliate the Shanghai Party leadership, whom he accused of "economism" for giving in to workers' demands for better pay. Zhang headed the Shanghai People's Commune that later became the Shanghai **Revolutionary Committee** and, in 1969, became a member of the CCP Central Committee and the **Politburo.** Delegated to welcome **United States** President Richard Nixon during his 1972 trip to China, Zhang was considered by Mao as his possible successor but was apparently angered by Zhang's close association with **Jiang Qing,** from whom Mao had grown distant. In 1973, Zhang was elevated to the Standing Committee of the Politburo; in 1975, he became second vice-premier and director of the **People's Liberation Army (PLA)** General Political Department. Following the death of Mao Zedong in September 1976, Zhang was arrested in October as a member of the **Gang of Four** and in 1981, along with Jiang Qing, was unrepentant at his trial and was sentenced to death with a two-year reprieve. With his sentence later commuted to life, Zhang was finally released in 2002 for medical reasons.

ZHANG YIMOU (1951–). Born in Xi'an in Shaanxi Province, Zhang Yimou is perhaps China's greatest living film director. During the **Cultural Revolution (1966–1976),** Zhang worked in the countryside and in a factory; in 1978, he entered the **Beijing** Film Academy. In the early 1980s, Zhang did the photography for *Yellow Earth* and played the hero Wang Quan in the film version of *The Old Well* by China's greatest living novelist, **Zheng Yi.** Zhang also directed *Red Sorghum,* which won the Golden Bear award at the 1988 Berlin Film Festival. In the early 1990s, Zhang directed *Raise the Red Lantern, Judou* (which received the American Oscar nomination for Best Foreign Film in 1990) and *The Story of Qiu Ju.* In 1999, Zhang won the Golden Lion award at the Venice Film Festival for his film *Not One Less* about a female teacher who brought fame and fortune to a backward village; in 2000, he received an award at the Berlin Film Festival for *The Road Home.* He also directed the Hollywood-style big-budget film *Hero,* which idolized the efforts by the emperor Qin Shihuang to unite China in 221 BC. *See also* CINEMA AND FILM.

ZHAO ZIYANG (1919–2005). Born to a landlord family in a county in Henan Province where large numbers of Chinese Jews resided, Zhao Ziyang attended middle school (where he changed his name from Zhao Xiuye) and then joined the China **Youth League** in 1932 and the **Chinese Communist Party (CCP)** in 1938. During the 1940s, he worked in rural areas; after 1949, he worked in the Central

South China Sub-bureau of the CCP Central Committee. In 1955, he became deputy-secretary of the Guangdong Party Committee and, in the early 1960s, proposed a system of countervailing powers in the CCP. Dismissed as a supporter of **Liu Shaoqi** in 1966 at the start of the **Cultural Revolution (1966–1976)**, Zhao was paraded through the streets by **Red Guards**. Rehabilitated at the behest of **Zhou Enlai**, Zhao reappeared in 1971 becoming secretary of the Guangdong Party Committee; in 1975, he became secretary of the Sichuan Party Committee, where he authorized experiments in the reorganization of **agriculture** away from the giant **people's communes** established during the **Great Leap Forward (1958–1960)**.

Elevated in 1979 to the **Politburo** during the inauguration of the economic reforms, Zhao was appointed premier in September 1980 and signed the Sino–British Joint Declaration on the Question of **Hong Kong** in 1984. Following the dismissal of **Hu Yaobang** in early 1987, he became CCP general secretary and a vice-chairman of the Central **Military Affairs Commission (MAC)**, which remained under the effective control of **Deng Xiaoping**, China's paramount leader. During the second **Beijing Spring** in 1989, Zhao called for restraint and wanted a peaceful end to the student demonstrations in accord with "democracy and law" but he was overruled by Deng who authorized the publication of the provocative 26 April editorial in *People's Daily* and the ultimate use of force against the students on 3–4 June 1989. Zhao vehemently opposed the declaration of martial law and penned a letter of resignation but was dismissed from the Politburo and all other posts and put under house arrest for supposedly "splitting the Party." Retaining his Party membership, in 1997, Zhao was rumored to have written the 15th National Party Congress suggesting a reappraisal of the "June 4" (*liusi*) incident and renewed this call during a 1998 visit to China by **United States** President Bill Clinton. Zhao's death at age 85 in January 2005 created a conundrum for the new CCP leadership, who initially banned extensive news reports about his passing, over whether to conduct a state funeral for a leader who had not been officially rehabilitated. Bowing to pressure from Party elders, such as **Wan Li** and **Tian Jiyun**, Zhao Ziyang's funeral was held at Babaoshan Revolutionary Cemetery outside Beijing, where his remains were buried in a plot reserved for top Party **leaders**.

ZHENG YI (1947–). Born in Sichuan Province, Zheng Yi is one of China's greatest contemporary writers. During the **Cultural Revolution (1966–1976)**, Zheng Yi was forced to work in the countryside in a mountainous region of Shanxi Province, where he learned carpentry and then worked in a coal mine. After 1978, he studied in the Chinese Department of Shanxi Normal College and began to publish short stories and plays, including his most famous, *The Old Well*. In the mid-1980s, Zheng Yi traveled to Guangxi Province, where he did an extensive investigation of officially sanctioned cannibalism during the Cultural Revolution among one of China's largest **minorities**, the Zhuang, in the province's rural areas. He later published a book titled *Scarlet Memorial*, which documented these events and revealed the role of local **Chinese Communist Party** (**CCP**) officials in the killing. After the 1989 military crackdown against the second **Beijing Spring**, Zheng Yi fled to the **United States**, where he now lives and has authored a book on China's **environment** entitled *China's Ecological Winter*. See also LITERATURE AND THE ARTS; WEI GUOQING (1913–).

ZHOU ENLAI (1898–1976). Born in Jiangsu Province, Zhou Enlai was raised by his uncle and an adopted mother in **Shanghai** and later studied at Nankai Middle School and Waseda University in Tokyo, **Japan**. The **May Fourth Movement (1919–1923)** brought Zhou back to China, where he got involved in political action, including the establishment of the Awakening Society that became a nucleus of the **Chinese Communist Party** (**CCP**) established in 1921. Zhou formally became a member of the CCP in 1922 and, afterward, traveled to England, Belgium, and Germany.

In 1924, Zhou returned to China and held important political positions in **Guangzhou** (**Canton**), including head of the political department at the **Kuomintang** (**KMT**) Whampoa Military Academy, a training facility for revolutionary soldiers. Zhou was removed from his KMT posts in 1926 after the clash between the CCP and KMT. After the CCP's military arm took control of Wuhan, Hubei Province, in late 1926, Zhou became head of the new Military Department of the CCP. At the April–May Fifth National Party Congress, Zhou was elected a member of the Central Committee and its **Politburo**. In mid-1928, he participated in the Sixth National Party Congress held in

Moscow and emerged as a CCP leader second only to Li Lisan. Zhou returned to China in late 1928 and targeted Li Lisan as the scapegoat for the Chinese Red Army's failure to hold the city of Changsha in Hunan Province during a failed military uprising. In 1931, Zhou joined **Mao Zedong** and **Zhu De** in the Jiangxi Soviet and held important political and military positions in the Chinese Soviet Republic. Zhou gained international attention when he successfully negotiated the release of Chiang Kai-shek during the Xi'an Incident in 1936 and the agreement to establish the Second **United Front**.

With the establishment of the **People's Republic of China** (**PRC**) in 1949, Zhou was appointed as the premier of the Government Administrative Council, a temporary governing body, and minister of foreign affairs. Beginning in 1954, he led China's efforts to be recognized internationally with trips to Europe and Asia, including a visit to **India**, where, with Prime Minister Jawaharlal Nehru, a joint communiqué was issued, committing the two countries to the Five Principles of Peaceful Coexistence. In the same year, Zhou also played an important role as China's representative to the 1954 Geneva Conference on Indochina, where China was one of the signatories to the Final Declaration, which the **United States** refused to sign. Zhou continued his high profile in international affairs by heading the Chinese delegation in 1955 to the **Bandung Conference of Afro–Asian States** in Indonesia, which was attended by 29 nonaligned countries and where Zhou stressed China's commitment to peaceful coexistence and neutrality, this despite its alliance with the **Soviet Union**. In 1958, Zhou was replaced as foreign minister by Chen Yi, though he continued to exert substantial influence over the **foreign policy** of the PRC. This included Zhou's high-profile role in the growing Sino–Soviet Conflict, in China's opening to Africa in 1964 when Zhou accompanied Foreign Minister Chen Yi on a multination tour, and in the opening to the U.S. in 1971–1972.

In domestic politics, Zhou Enlai was appointed premier of the newly established State Council in 1954, where he generally supported the strategy of balanced economic growth incorporated in the First **Five Year Plan**. During the **Great Leap Forward (1958–1960)** and the **Cultural Revolution (1966–1976)**, Zhou's role was controversial in that he appeared to support the radical leftist line of Mao Zedong and his wife **Jiang Qing** by appearing with Mao Zedong and

Lin Biao at the 18 August 1966 giant rally in support of the Cultural Revolution. At the same time, however, Zhou reportedly saved a number of prominent CCP **cadres** and **intellectuals** from persecution and ordered the **People's Liberation Army** (**PLA**) to protect from **Red Guard** violence the most important historical and cultural sites in China, such as the Forbidden City in central **Beijing**. Zhou played a major role in ending the crisis surrounding the **Wuhan Incident** (**July 1967**) and helped bring a quick end to **Lin Biao** in 1971. At the 10th National Party Congress in 1973, Zhou read the official version of the Lin Biao Affair and was elevated to the number two leader in China but was indirectly attacked by **Jiang Qing** and the **Gang of Four** in the **Anti-Lin [Biao], Anti-Confucius Campaign** (**1973–1975**). During the run-up to the reestablishment of economic and diplomatic relations with the U.S., Zhou held secret talks in July 1971 with National Security adviser Dr. Henry Kissinger and issued the formal invitation to President Richard Nixon for his 1972 visit.

Zhou died of cancer in 1976 at the age of 78, but prior to his death, he made **Deng Xiaoping** his expected successor. Riots in Tiananmen Square on 5 April 1976 by mourners who were prevented from memorializing Zhou Enlai signaled major shifts in China's internal politics and became known as the **April Fifth Movement**. In 1981, the People's Press of China published volume I of the *Selected Works of Zhou Enlai* followed by a final volume in 1984 and a 1989 volume entitled *Biography of Zhou Enlai*. Zhou was also featured in a 1990 documentary film on his life. But in a posthumous and highly critical book published in **Hong Kong** entitled *Zhou Enlai's Later Years* by a former senior researcher in the CCP Central Documents Office, Zhou, contrary to popular belief, was depicted as a tragic, backroom schemer and a puppet of Mao Zedong, who only protected people after first checking with Mao, his wife Jiang Qing, and Lin Biao. The book, which has been banned in China, also charges Mao with denying Zhou **health care** that could have lengthened his life.

ZHOU YANG (1907–1989). Zhou Yang in 1930 was secretary of the League of Left-Wing Writers in **Shanghai** and, during the **Sino–Japanese War** (**1937–1945**), defended the concept of "literature of national defense" in controversies with **Ba Jin** and other writers. In the early 1950s, Zhou joined in the literary persecution campaign known as the **Hu Feng Affair** by denouncing the writer Hu Feng as a "counterrevolutionary." During the **Cultural Revolution (1966–1976)**, Zhou Yang was himself branded a "three-anti element" and publicly denounced, along with the famous journalist **Lu Dingyi**. But Zhou reappeared in 1977 as an adviser to the **Chinese Academy of Social Sciences (CASS)**, a vice-chairman of the All-China Writers' Association, and, until 1982, a deputy director of the CCP Propaganda Department.

ZHU DE (1886–1976). One of the founders of the Red Army and the top military leader of the **Chinese Communist Party (CCP)** during the **Civil War (1946–1949)**, Zhu De was born in Sichuan Province to a family of tenant farmers. A member of Sun Yat-sen's revolutionary organization, the *Tongmeng hui* and the secret society known as the *Gelaohui*, Zhu participated in the 1911 Republican Revolution and was a member of the **Kuomintang (KMT)**. He also joined the CCP in the early 1920s during the First **United Front** and traveled to Europe attending lectures at the University of Göttingen in Germany, where he became acquainted with Marxism. After returning to China, Zhu played a major role in the 1927 Northern Expedition directed by Chiang Kai-shek against northern warlords and, in August 1927, participated in the aborted Nanchang Uprising orchestrated by the CCP. In 1928, Zhu forged a cooperative relationship with **Mao Zedong** that would last throughout the period of the Chinese Soviets and Yan'an when the team of "Zhu–Mao" was considered the combined leadership of the Communist movement in China. In 1934, Zhu became a member of the CCP **Politburo** and was made the commander-in-chief of the **Long March (1934–1935)**, of the Eighth Route Army, and on 1 October 1949 of the **People's Liberation Army (PLA)**. One of ten marshals—the highest military rank in the PLA—in 1954 Zhu relinquished his command of the PLA and in 1959 was appointed a member of the Standing Committee of the **National People's Congress (NPC)**. During the 1960s and 1970s, Zhu stayed clear of politics, though he was attacked during the **Cultural Revolution (1966–1976)** for allegedly having questioned the **personality cult (*geren chongbai*)** of Mao Zedong. In 1983, *The Selected Works of Zhu De* was published posthumously by the People's Press.

ZHU HOUZE (1931–). In the 1950s and early 1960s, Zhu Houze was involved in Communist **Youth League** work in Guiyang, Guizhou Province. After being sent down to the countryside during the **Cultural Revolution (1966–1976)**, he became secretary of the Guizhou Party Committee and director of the **Chinese Communist Party (CCP)** Propaganda Department in 1985. In 1987, he was relieved of this post and became deputy-director of the Rural Development Center under the State Council. In 1988, he became secretary of the All-China Federation of **Trade Unions** until purged after the fall of General Secretary **Zhao Ziyang**. In 2003, Zhu Houze took part in a conference on constitutional reform in Qingdao, Shandong Province, that broached the issue of reevaluating the official position on the June 1989 second **Beijing Spring**. He was immediately reprimanded for agreeing that the constitution should be free from all ideology in what was considered a direct slap at then CCP General Secretary **Jiang Zemin**, who was being promoted as a "great man" of China. In February 2006, Zhu joined **Li Rui** and **Hu Jiwei** in penning a letter to CCP leaders decrying the shutdown of major newspapers and criticizing excessive **censorship** (*shencha*).

ZHU MUZHI (1916–). Director of the **New China News Agency (Xinhua)** in the 1950s, Zhu Muzhi became a member in the 1960s of the China Journalist Association. After the **Cultural Revolution (1966–1976)**, he became a member of the **Chinese Communist Party (CCP)** Central Committee in 1973; in 1977, became a deputy-director of the CCP Propaganda Department; and, in 1978, became a member of the **Central Discipline Inspection Commission (CDIC)**. From 1982 to 1986, he was minister of culture; in 1988, he became a member of the leading group on propaganda and ideology under the Central Committee. Appointed honorary president of the China Society for **Human Rights** Studies, Zhu consistently defended the military crackdown against the second **Beijing Spring** that he described to foreign journalists as a "rebellion" by "flies and mosquitoes" while dismissing complaints from family members of relatives killed in the suppression by what he describes as "stray bullets."

ZHU RONGJI (1928–). Zhu Rongji graduated from the Electric Motor Engine Department of **Qinghua University** with a major in electrical engineering, joining the **Chinese Communist Party (CCP)** in 1949. After a stint at the Northeast China Ministry of Industries, Zhu worked at the State Planning Commission from 1952 to 1958, when he became deputy director of the minister's office. Critical of China's economic policy, in 1958, he was labeled a "rightist," which resulted in a five-year period of **labor** in the countryside. Returning to the State Planning Commission, where he worked until 1969 as a teacher at a school for **cadres** and an engineer, Zhu was forced to undergo another "re-education" from 1970 to 1975 at a **May Seventh Cadre School** during the **Cultural Revolution (1966–1976)**. Zhu was rehabilitated in the late 1970s and then worked in the Ministry of Petroleum. In 1983, he was appointed as vice-minister of the State Economic Commission and, from 1987 to 1990, served as the mayor of **Shanghai**, where he oversaw the opening up of the Pudong Development Zone and also served as a member of the CCP Central Committee. Following a stint at the **China International Trust and Investment Corporation (CITIC)**, he became a vice-premier in 1991, when he launched a drive to solve the enormous problems of "debt chains" of **state-owned enterprises (SOEs)** and, in 1993, became a member of the **Politburo**. As governor of China's central bank, the People's Bank of China, from 1993 to 1995, he was put in charge of cooling down the Chinese **economy** and taming hyperinflation by relying on a mixture of monetary and fiscal interventions, along with some high-handed administrative measures.

Zhu Rongji was the driving force behind the streamlining of the Shanghai economy and gave high priority to completion of Pudong, as well as favoring development of the entire Yangtze River delta, which became a major outlet for **Taiwan** investors. In 1997, Zhu became a member of the Politburo Standing Committee and, in 1998, was appointed premier, where he served as China's reputed "economic czar" until his retirement in 2003. Confronted by the 1997–1998 Asian financial crisis, Zhu vowed that China would not devalue its **currency** and embarked on an expansionary fiscal policy with massive government spending on fixed-asset investment. Zhu also encouraged foreign participation and **technology** imports for large state infrastructure projects, especially in China's crucial **energy** sector. Despite his early work in China's northeast industrial heartland, Zhu led a major dismantling of the region's command economy and a restructuring of SOEs along corporate lines that led to substantial layoffs (4.35 million workers in 2003) and factory closings, along with pension defaults of 10 billion *yuan*. In 1999, Zhu was the first premier to visit the **United States** in 15 years and personally intervened to salvage negotiations between American and Chinese officials on a number of crucial **trade** issues involving China's accession to the **World Trade Organization (WTO)**. Zhu also attended several **Association of Southeast Asian Nations (ASEAN)** plus three summits in the 1990s, where he took the lead in offering Chinese advice on the scope and direction of cooperation among East Asian nations. Since his retirement in 2003, Zhu has reportedly avoided public appearances and has become enamored of Tang dynasty poetry.

ZHUANG PEOPLE. *See* MINORITIES.

ZOU JIAHUA (1926–). Born in **Shanghai** and a graduate of the Moscow Engineering Institute, Zou Jiahua joined the New Fourth Army of the **People's Liberation Army (PLA)** in 1944 and the **Chinese Communist Party (CCP)** in 1945. In the 1950s and 1960s, he served as a director of a machine tool plant in Shenyang Municipality and then worked in the First Ministry of Machine Building followed by positions in the Office of National Defense Industry; Commission of Science, **Technology**, and Industry for National Defense; and the State Machine-Building Industry Commission. In 1977, he was elected to the 11th CCP Central Committee; in 1985, he became minister of ordnance industry, and, in 1989, he headed the State Development and Reform Commission. In 1991, Zou was made a vice-premier; from 1992 to 1997, he was a member of the CCP **Politburo** and a member of the **National People's Congress (NPC)**. From 1998 to 2003, he served as a vice-chairman of the Ninth NPC and served on the Macao SAR Preparatory Committee.

Bibliography

A wealth of English-language materials on the People's Republic of China is available. Included in this bibliography are major books by university and commercial publishers and a listing of major journals, newspapers, and websites that are available on the Internet. These include translations of Chinese-language newspapers and radio transmissions provided by various outlets of the Foreign Broadcast Information Service (FBIS), the United States Department of Commerce. Chinese-language books published in the PRC, Hong Kong, and Taiwan are increasingly available in the United States through specialized commercial outlets and research libraries at major universities, however they are not included here except for those that have been translated into English. Several commercial publishers in the United States specialize in publishing books on contemporary China and Chinese-language translations, such as EastBridge Press, M. E. Sharpe, Westview, and Lynne Rienner Press as more and more Chinese authors have made their works available for non-Chinese consumption.

The bibliography is arranged topically and begins with a comprehensive list of reference materials. Travel guides and accounts have been generally excluded, while literature, poetry, and films are limited to works available in English and/or with English subtitles. Major Chinese literary works and *belles lettres* published since economic and social reforms began in China in 1978–1979 are quite rich with some of the most outstanding works included below. Chinese-language films from the mainland are also generally available on DVD collections at bookstores and media outlets in major Chinatowns in the United States and Canada. English- and Chinese-language sources on contemporary China have also flourished since 1978–1979 mainly because of greater openness in China and increased access to Chinese society and sources by outside researchers that were generally unavailable during the 1949 to 1976 period of China's general isolation from the outside world. Many works on China have been published in Europe, especially in France, and in Japan, but, with the exception of the English-language works, most of which were published in Great Britain, these are generally not listed here. Online sources on the Internet inside and outside the PRC are listed in a separate section at the end of the Bibliography.

Major libraries of English- and Chinese-language works on China are organized into the Council on East Asian Libraries and exist at the following institutions: Starr East Asian Library, Columbia University; Wason Collection, Cornell University; Fairbank Center Library, Harvard University; Asian Reading Room, Library of Congress; East Asian Library, Princeton University; Hoover Institution East Asian Collection, Stanford University; Center for Chinese Studies Library, University of California, Berkeley; East Asian Library, University of California, Los Angeles; East Asian Collection, University of Chicago; The Asia Library, University of Michigan; East Asian Library, University of Washington; and East Asian Library, Yale University. Major documentary collections on the Cultural Revolution and U.S. National Intelligence Estimates on China from 1948–1978 are also available on DVD. U.S. government collections include the *C.I.A. World Fact Book, Records of Hearings before the U.S.–China Security Review Commission of the United States Congress,* and reports of the Joint Economic Committee on China of the United States Congress. Contemporary Chinese works in translation are available in a series of journals—*Chinese Law and Government, The Chinese Economy, Contemporary Chinese Thought,* and *Chinese Studies in History*—published by M. E. Sharpe. Highly recommended and readable works listed below are noted with an *, while works for beginners are labeled with a + and films by a ^.

Since the late 1970s, most English language titles with Chinese names and terminology employ *Hanyu pinyin* spelling, while previously published works use Wade-Giles (i.e., "Deng Xiaoping" and "Mao Zedong" in the former and "Teng Hsiao-p'ing" and "Mao Tsetung" in the latter).

The bibliography is categorized as follows:

PART 1: REFERENCE WORKS AND JOURNALS, MAP COLLECTIONS, YEARBOOKS, AND FILMS

Asian Survey. Berkeley: University of California, 1961.

Bartke, Wolfgang. *Atlas of China*. 1st ed. Beijing: Foreign Languages Press, 1989.

*———. *Who's Who in the People's Republic of China*. Armonk, N. Y.: M. E. Sharpe, 1981.

*———. *Who's Who in the People's Republic of China*. 2nd and 3rd eds. Munich: K. G. Saur, 1987 and 1991.

Blunden, Caroline, and Mark Elvin. *Cultural Atlas of China*. New York: Facts on File, 1983.

Boorman, Howard L., ed. *Biographical Dictionary of Republican China*. New York: Columbia University Press, 1967–1979, 56 vols.

Chaffee, Frederic H., et al. *Area Handbook for Communist China*. Washington, D. C.: United States Government Printing Office, 1967.

Chan Ming K., and S.H. Lo. *Historical Dictionary of Hong Kong SAR and Macao SAR*. Lanham, Md.: Scarecrow, 2006.

Cheng, Peter. *A Chronology of the People's Republic of China from October 1, 1949*. Totowa, N. J.: Rowman & Littlefield, 1972.

———. *A Chronology of the People's Republic: 1970–1979*. Metuchen, N. J.: Scarecrow, 1986.

^*The Challenge From Asia: China and the Pacific Rim.* Videorecording. Princeton: Films for the Humanities, 1989.

China Briefing. Boulder, Colo.: Westview, 1980–1996; Armonk, N. Y.: M. E. Sharpe, 1997–2000.

China Business Review. Washington: U.S.-China Business Council, 1977–.

China Directory in Pinyin and Chinese. Tokyo: Radiopress, 1978–1991.

China, Facts and Figures Annual. Gulf Breeze, Fla.: Academic International Press, 1978–1993.

China, Financial Sector Policies and Institutional Development. Washington, D. C.: World Bank, 1990.

China Journal. Canberra: Contemporary China Centre, Australia National University, 1996–. formerly *Australian Journal of Chinese Affairs, 1979–1995.*

China Official Yearbook. Hong Kong: Dragon Pearl Publications Ltd., 1983–.

China Report: Agriculture. Arlington, Va.: Foreign Broadcast Information Service, 1979–1987.

China Report: Economic Affairs. Arlington, Va.: Foreign Broadcast Information Service, 1979–1987.

China Report: Plant and Installation Data. Arlington, Va.: Foreign Broadcast Information Service, 1978–1985.

China Report: Political, Sociological, and Military Affairs. Arlington, Va.: Foreign Broadcast Information Service, 1979–1994.

China Report: Science and Technology. Arlington, Va.: Foreign Broadcast Information Service, 1979–1996.

China Statistical Yearbook. State Statistical Bureau, PRC, 1981–.

^*China, The Mandate of Heaven.* Video-recording. Ambrose Video Publishing, 1991.

Daily Report: PRC. Springfield, Va.: Foreign Broadcast Information Service, United States Department of Commerce.

*Davis, Edward. *Encyclopedia of Contemporary Chinese Culture.* London: Routledge, 2005.

Hero, Videorecording, Miramax, 2004.

Hinton, Harold C., ed. *The People's Republic of China: A Handbook.* Boulder, Colo.: Westview, 1979.

———, ed. *The People's Republic of China, 1949–1979: A Documentary Survey.* Wilmington, Del.: Scholarly Resources, 1980. 5 vols.

Hook, Brian, ed. *The Cambridge Encyclopedia of China.* 2d ed., Cambridge: Cambridge University Press, 1982.

Hsieh Chiao-min. *Atlas of China.* New York: McGraw-Hill, 1973.

Johnson, Graham E., and Glen D. Peterson. *Historical Dictionary of Guangzhou (Canton) and Guangdong.* Lanham, Md.: Scarecrow, 1999.

Johnston, Douglas, and Chiu Hungdah, eds. *Agreements of the People's Republic of China, 1949–1967.* Cambridge, Mass.: Harvard University Press, 1968.

Joint Publication Research Service: China. Washington, D. C.: United States Department of Commerce.

^*Ju Dou*. Video-recording. Miramax Films, 1990.

Klein, Donald W., and Anne B. Clark. *Biographic Dictionary of Chinese Communism, 1921–1965*. Cambridge, Mass.: Harvard University Press, 1971. 2 vols.

Leung, Edwin Pak-wah. *Historical Dictionary of Revolutionary China, 1839–1976*. Lanham, Md: Scarecrow, 2002.

^Li Yang. *Blind Shaft (Mang Jing)*. Kino International Release (Chinese with English Subtitles).

Liu, William T., ed. *China: Social Statistics*. New York: Praeger, 1989.

^Long Bow Group, Inc. *The Gate of Heavenly Peace: The Epic and Explosive Documentary on the Events Leading Up to the Tiananmen Square Uprisings*. Video-recording. Directed by Carma Hinton and Richard Gordon. Produced by Peter Kovler, USA, 1995.

*/+Mackerras, Colin. *The New Cambridge Handbook of Contemporary China*. Cambridge: Cambridge University Press, 2001.

*/+——, Donald H. McMillen, and Andrew Watson. *Dictionary of the Politics of the People's Republic of China*. London and New York: Routledge, 1998.

New China News Agency. *People's Republic of China Yearbook*. Hong Kong: Economic & Information Agency, 1981–.

Ni Zhen. *Memoirs from the Beijing Film Academy: The Genesis of China's Fifth Generation*. Chris Berry, trans. Durham, N. C.: Duke University Press, 2002.

Pacific Affairs. Vancouver: University of British Columbia, 1928– .

Peking Review. Beijing: Peking Review, 1958–1978.

^Perry, Ellen. *Great Wall across the Yangtze*. PBS Films, 1999.

Population Census Office of the State Council, ed. *The Population Atlas of China*. Oxford: Oxford University Press, 1987.

^*Red Sorghum*. Video-recording. New York: New Yorker Films, 1991.

Sivin, Nathan, ed. *The Contemporary Atlas of China*. Boston: Houghton-Mifflin, 1988.

Sorich, Richard. *Documents on Contemporary China, 1949–1975: A Research Collection*. Greenwich, Conn.: Johnson Associates, 1976.

Tanis, Norman E., et al., comp. *China in Books: A Basic Bibliography in Western Languages*. Greenwich, Conn.: JAI Press, 1979.

The China Quarterly. London: Contemporary China Institute of the School of Oriental and African Studies, 1960– .

Tibet Information Network, Human Rights Watch/Asia. *Cutting off the Serpent's Head: Tightening Control in Tibet, 1994–1995*. New York: Human Rights Watch, 1996.

Tregear, Thomas R. *China: A Geographical Survey*. New York: Wiley, 1980.

Twitchett, Dennis, and John King Fairbank, eds. *The Cambridge History of China*. Cambridge: Cambridge University Press, 1978– .

United States Central Intelligence Agency. *World Fact Book* (www.cia.gov).

United States Government. *Directory of Chinese Government Officials*. 1963–1991.

Wang, Richard T. *Area Bibliography of China*. Lanham, Md.: Scarecrow, 1997.

Who's Who in Communist China. Hong Kong: Union Research Institute, 1970, 2 volumes.

PART 2: GENERAL WORKS: BOOKS AND ARTICLES

Biographies and Memoirs

Benton, Gregor, et al. "Mao: The Unknown Story—An Assessment," *The China Journal*, no. 55 (January 2006): 85–139.

Breslin, Shaun. *Mao*. London: Addison Wesley Longman, 1998.

Bryan, John, and Robert Pack. *The Claws of the Dragon: Kang Sheng, the Evil Genius behind Mao and His Legacy of Terror in People's China*. New York: Simon & Schuster, 1991.

Jung Chang, and Jon Halliday. *Mao: The Unknown Story*. New York: Knopf, 2005.

Chi Hsin. *Teng Hsiao-p'ing: A Political Biography*. Hong Kong: Cosmos Books, 1978.

Dai Qing. *Tiananmen Follies: Prison Memoirs and Other Writings*. Nancy Yang Liu, Peter Rand, and Lawrence R. Sullivan, trans. Norwalk, Conn.: EastBridge Press, 2004.

Evans, Richard. *Deng Xiaoping and the Making of Modern China*. New York: Viking, 1994.

Franz, Uli. *Deng Xiaoping*. Boston: Harcourt Brace Jovanovich, 1988.

Goldstein, Melvyn, William Siebensschuh, and Tashi Tsering. *The Struggle for Modern Tibet: The Autobiography of Tashi Tsering*. Armonk, N. Y.: M. E. Sharpe, 1997.

Goodman, David S. *Deng Xiaoping and the Chinese Revolution: A Political Biography*. London: Routledge, 1994.

*Li Zhisui, with Anne Thurston. *The Private Life of Chairman Mao: The Memoirs of Mao's Personal Physician*. New York: Random House, 1994.

Lynch, Michael. *Mao*. London: Routledge, 2004.

+Ma Yan. *The Diary of Ma Yan: The Struggles and Hopes of a Chinese Schoolgirl*. New York: Harper Collins, 2005.

MacFarquhar, Roderick, Timothy Cheek, and Eugene Wu, eds. *The Secret Speeches of Chairman Mao: From the Hundred Flowers to the Great Leap Forward*. Cambridge, Mass.: Council on East Asian Studies, Harvard University, 1989.

Pye, Lucian. *Mao Tse-tung: The Man in the Leader*. New York: Basic Books, 1976.

*Rand, Peter. *China Hands: The Adventures and Ordeals of the American Journalists Who Joined Forces with the Great Chinese Revolution*. New York: Simon & Schuster, 1995.

Rice, Edwin. *Mao's Way*. Berkeley and Los Angeles: University of California Press, 1972.

Ruan Ming. *Deng Xiaoping: Chronicle of an Empire*. Nancy Yang Liu, Peter Rand, and Lawrence R. Sullivan, trans. Boulder, Colo.: Westview, 1994.

Salisbury, Harrison E. *The New Emperors: China in the Era of Mao and Deng*. New York: Avon, 1993.

*Schram, Stuart R. *The Thought of Mao Tse-tung*. Cambridge: Cambridge University Press, 1989.

———, ed. *Mao's Road to Power: Revolutionary Writings, 1912–1949*. Armonk, N. Y.: M. E. Sharpe, 1992–1995. 3 vols.

———, ed. *Chairman Mao Talks to the People: Talks and Letters: 1956–1971*. New York: Pantheon Books, 1974.

———. *The Political Thought of Mao Tse-tung*. New York: Praeger, 1963.

Schrift, Melissa. *Biography of a Chairman Mao Badge: The Creation and Mass Consumption of a Personality Cult*. East Brunswick: Rutgers University Press, 2001.

Selected Works of Deng Xiaoping. Beijing: Foreign Languages Press, 1984, 1992, 1994. 3 vols.

Selected Works of Mao Tse-tung. Beijing: Foreign Languages Press, 1965, 1977. 5 vols.

Shambaugh, David, ed. *Deng Xiaoping: Portrait of a Chinese Statesman*. Oxford: Clarendon Press, 1995.

———. *The Making of a Premier: Zhao Ziyang's Provincial Career*. Boulder, Colo.: Westview, 1984.

Shao Kuo-kang. *Zhou Enlai and the Foundations of Chinese Foreign Policy*. New York: St. Martin's Press, 1996.

Spence, Jonathan D. *Mao Zedong*. New York: Viking, 1999.

Teiwes, Frederick C., and Warren Sun. *The Tragedy of Lin Biao: Riding the Tiger during the Cultural Revolution, 1966–1971*. London: Hurst, 1996.

*Terrill, Ross. *Madame Mao: The White Boned Demon, A Biography of Madame Mao Zedong*. New York: Simon & Schuster, 1992.

———. *Mao: A Biography*. New York: Harper & Row, 1980.

Wilson, Dick, ed. *Mao Tse-tung in the Scales of History.* Cambridge: Cambridge University Press, 1977.

Witke, Roxane. *Comrade Chiang Ch'ing.* Boston: Little, Brown & Co., 1977.

Wu, Harry, and Carolyn Wakeman. *Bitter Winds: A Memoir of My Years in China's Gulag.* New York: John Wiley & Sons, 1994.

Yan Jiaqi. *Toward a Democratic China: The Intellectual Autobiography of Yan Jiaqi.* David S.K. Hong, Denis C. Mair, trans. Honolulu: University of Hawai'i Press, 1992.

Yang, Benjamin. *Deng: A Political Biography.* Armonk, N. Y.: M. E. Sharpe, 1998.

Yang Zhongmei. *Hu Yaobang: A Chinese Biography.* William A. Wycoff, trans. Armonk. N. Y: M. E. Sharpe, 1988.

The Cultural Revolution

Ahn, Byungjoon. *Chinese Politics and the Cultural Revolution.* Seattle: University of Washington Press, 1976.

Bao Ruo-wang (Jean Pasqualini), and Rudolph Chelminski. *Prisoner of Mao.* New York: Coward, McCann, and Geoghegan, 1973.

Cheek, Timothy. *Propaganda and Culture in Mao's China: Deng Tuo and the Intelligensia.* Oxford: Clarendon Press, 1997.

+Chen Jo-hsi. *The Execution of Mayor Yin and Other Stories from the Great Proletarian Cultural Revolution.* Bloomington: Indiana University Press, 1978.

Chen Xuezhao. *Surviving the Storm: A Memoir.* Ti Hua and Caroline Greene, trans. Armonk. N. Y.: M. E. Sharpe, 1990.

+Cheng Nien. *Life and Death in Shanghai.* New York: Grove Press, 1986.

Dittmer, Lowell. *Liu Shao-ch'i and the Chinese Cultural Revolution: The Politics of Mass Criticism.* Berkeley and Los Angeles: University of California Press, 1974.

Domes, Jurgen. *China after the Cultural Revolution: Politics Between Two Party Congresses.* Berkeley and Los Angeles: University of California Press, 1977.

Fan Shen. *Gang of One: Memoirs of a Red Guard.* Lincoln: University of Nebraska Press, 2004.

Feng Jicai. *Voices from the Whirlwind: An Oral History of the Chinese Cultural Revolution.* New York: Pantheon Books, 1991.

*Gao Yuan. *Born Red: A Chronicle of the Cultural Revolution.* Stanford, Calif.: Stanford University Press, 1987.

Hinton, William. *Hundred Day War: The Cultural Revolution at Tsinghua University.* New York: Monthly Review Press, 1972.

+Jiang Jili. *Red Scarf Girl: A Memoir of the Cultural Revolution.* New York: HarperCollins, 1997.

Jin Qiu. *The Culture of Power: The Lin Biao Incident in the Cultural Revolution*. Stanford, Calif.: Stanford University Press, 1999.

Joseph, William A., Christine P. W. Wong, and David Zweig, eds. *New Perspectives on the Cultural Revolution*. Cambridge, Mass.: Harvard University Press, 1991.

Ken Ling. *Revenge of Heaven*. New York: Putnam, 1972.

Lee Hong Yong. *The Politics of the Cultural Revolution: A Case Study*. Berkeley and Los Angeles: University of California Press, 1978.

Liang Heng, and Judith Shapiro. *After the Nightmare: A Survivor of the Cultural Revolution Reports on China Today*. New York: Alfred A. Knopf, 1986.

Lu Xinhua. *The Wounded: New Stories of the Cultural Revolution, 1977–78*. Geremie Barmé and Beneett Lee, trans. Hong Kong: Joint Publishing Co., 1979.

+Ma Bo. *Blood Red Sunset: A Memoir of the Chinese Cultural Revolution*. Howard Goldblatt, trans. New York: Viking, 1995.

Ma Jisen. *The Cultural Revolution in the Foreign Ministry of China*. Hong Kong: The Chinese University Press, 2004.

MacFarquhar, Roderick. *The Origins of the Cultural Revolution*, 3 vols. New York: Oxford and Columbia University Press, 1974, 1983, and 1997.

Perry, Elizabeth J., and Li Xun. *Proletarian Power: Shanghai in the Cultural Revolution*. Boulder, Colo.: Westview, 1997.

Pusey, James R. *Wu Han: Attacking the Present through the Past*. Cambridge, Mass.: East Asian Research Center, Harvard University, 1969.

Rae Yang, *Spider Eaters*. Berkeley: University of California Press, 1997.

Rosen, Stanley. *Red Guard Factionalism and the Cultural Revolution in Guangzhou*. Boulder, Colo. Westview, 1982.

Schram, Stuart R., ed. *Authority, Participation and Cultural Change in China*. Cambridge: Cambridge University Press, 1973.

Schoenhals, Michael, ed. *China's Cultural Revolution, 1966–1969: Not a Dinner Party*. Armonk, N. Y.: M. E. Sharpe, 1996.

Song Yongyi, and Sun Dajin. *The Cultural Revolution: A Bibliography, 1966–1996*. Eugene Wu, ed. Cambridge, Mass.: Harvard University Press, 1998.

——, et al., eds. *The Chinese Cultural Revolution Database* CD-ROM. Hong Kong: The Chinese University Press, 2002.

Thurston, Anne. *Enemies of the People*. New York: Knopf, 1987.

Tsou Tang. *The Cultural Revolution and Post-Mao Reforms: A Historical Perspective*. Chicago: University of Chicago Press, 1986.

Wang Shaoguang. *The Failure of Charisma: The Cultural Revolution in Wuhan*. New York: Oxford University Press, 1995.

*Wang Youqin, "Student Attacks against Teachers: The Revolution of 1966." Retrieved from www.cnd.org/CR/english/articles/violence.htm (July 2005).

Wen Chihua. *The Red Mirror: Children of China's Cultural Revolution*. Boulder, Colo.: Westview, 1995.

White, Lynn T., III. *Policies of Chaos: The Organizational Causes of Violence in China's Cultural Revolution*. Princeton, N. J.: Princeton University Press, 1989.

Xing Lu. *Rhetoric of the Chinese Cultural Revolution: The Impact on Chinese Thought, Culture, and Communication*. Columbia: University of South Carolina Press, 2004.

Yang Xiguang, and Susan McFadden. *Captive Spirits: Prisoners of the Cultural Revolution*. Hong Kong: Oxford University Press, 1997.

Zang Xiaowei. *Children of the Cultural Revolution: Family Life and Political Behavior in Mao's China*. Boulder, Colo.: Westview, 2000.

+Zhang Ange. *Red Land, Yellow River: A Story from the Cultural Revolution*. Toronto: Groundwood Books, 2004.

Democracy Movements and Human Rights

Amnesty International. *People's Republic of China: Torture, a Growing Scourge in China, Time for Action*. London: International Secretariat, 2001.

——. *People's Republic of China: Nine Years after Tiananmen: Still a "Counterrevolutionary Riot"?* New York: Amnesty International, 1998.

——. *China, No One Is Safe: Political Repression and Abuse of Power in the 1990s*. New York: Amnesty International, 1996.

——. *China: The Massacre of June 1989 and Its Aftermath*. London: Amnesty International, 1990.

——. *People's Republic of China: Preliminary Findings on Killings of Unarmed Civilians: Arbitrary Arrests and Summary Executions Since June 3, 1989*. New York: Amnesty International, 1989.

——. *China: Torture and Ill-treatment of Prisoners*. London, Amnesty International,

——. *Violations of Human Rights: Prisoners of Conscience and the Death Penalty in the People's Republic of China*. London: Amnesty International, 1984.

——. *Political Imprisonment in the People's Republic of China*. London: Amnesty International, 1978.

Angle, Stephen C. *Human Rights and Chinese Thought: A Cross-Cultural Inquiry*. Cambridge: Cambridge University Press, 2002.

——, and Marina Svensson. *The Chinese Human Rights Reader: Documents and Commentary, 1900–2000*. Armonk, N. Y.: M. E. Sharpe, 2001.

*Barmé, Geremie, and John Minford, eds. *Seeds of Fire: Chinese Voices of Conscience*. Hong Kong: Far Eastern Economic Review, Ltd., 1986.

———, and Linda Javin, eds. *New Ghosts, Old Dreams*. New York: Times Books, 1992.

Benton, Gregor, and Alan Hunter, eds. *Wild Lily, Prairie Fire: China's Road to Democracy, Yan'an to Tian'anmen, 1972–1989*. Princeton, N. J.: Princeton University Press, 1995.

Black, George, and Robin Munro. *Black Hands of Beijing: Lives in Defense of China's Democracy*. New York: John Wiley, 1993.

Calhoun, Craig. *Neither Gods nor Emperors: Students and the Struggle for Democracy in China*. Berkeley and Los Angeles: University of California Press, 1994.

Che Muqi. *Beijing Turmoil: More Than Meets the Eye*. Beijing: Foreign Languages Press, 1990.

Chen Erjin. *China: Crossroads Socialism: An Unofficial Manifesto for Proletarian Democracy*. Robin Munro, trans. London: Verso, 1984.

China Rights Forum: *The Journal of Human Rights in China*. New York: Human Rights in China, 1989–.

Cohen, Jerome Alan. *The Criminal Process in the People's Republic of China 1949–1963: An Introduction*. Cambridge, Mass.: Harvard University Press, 1968.

———, R. Randle Edwards, and Fu-mei Chang Chen, eds. *Essays on China's Legal Tradition*. Princeton, N. J.: Princeton University Press, 1980.

Davis, Michael C., ed. *Human Rights and Chinese Values: Legal, Philosophical, and Political Perspectives*. Hong Kong: Oxford University Press, 1995.

*De Bary, William Theodore, and Tu Weiming. *Confucianism and Human Rights*. New York: Columbia University Press, 1998.

Des Forges, Roger V., Ning Luo, and Wu Yen-bo, eds. *Chinese Democracy and the Crisis of 1989: Chinese and American Reflections*. Albany: State University of New York Press, 1993.

Edwards, R. Randle, Louis Henkin, and Andrew J. Nathan, eds. *Human Rights in Contemporary China*. New York: Columbia University Press, 1986.

+Fang Lizhi. *Bringing Down the Great Wall: Writings on Science, Culture and Democracy in China*. James H. Williams, trans. New York: Alfred A. Knopf, 1991.

Feigon, Lee. *China Rising: The Meaning of Tiananmen*. Chicago: Ivan Dee, 1990.

Friedman, Edward. *National Identity and Democratic Prospects in Socialist China*. Armonk. N. Y.: M. E. Sharpe, 1995.

Gilley, Bruce. *China's Democratic Future: How It Will Happen and Where It Will Lead*. New York: Columbia University Press, 2004.

Goldman, Merle. *Sowing the Seeds of Democracy in China: Political Reform in the Deng Xiaoping Era*. Cambridge, Mass.: Harvard University Press, 1994.

———. *China's Intellectuals: Advise and Dissent*. Cambridge, Mass.: Harvard University Press, 1981.

———. *Literary Dissent in Communist China*. Cambridge, Mass.: Harvard University Press, 1967.

Han Minzhu, ed. *Cries for Democracy: Writings and Speeches from the 1989 Chinese Democracy Movement*. Princeton N. J.: Princeton University Press, 1990.

He Baogang. *The Democratic Implications of Civil Society in China*. Basingstoke: Macmillan, 1997.

———. *The Democratization of China*. London: Routledge, 1996.

———, and Guo Yingjie. *Nationalism, National Identity and Democratization in China*. Aldershot, UK: Ashgate, 2000.

Hicks, George, ed. *The Broken Mirror: China after Tiananmen*. Chicago: St. James Press, 1990.

Hu Shao-hua. *Explaining Chinese Democratization*. Westport: Praeger, 2000.

Kent, Ann. *China, the United Nations, and Human Rights: The Limits of Compliance*. Philadelphia: University of Pennsylvania Press, 1999.

Kirby, William C. *Realms of Freedom in Modern China*. Stanford, Calif.: Stanford University Press, 2004.

McCormick, Barrett L. *Political Reform in Post-Mao China: Democracy and Bureaucracy in a Leninist State*. Berkeley and Los Angeles: University of California Press, 1990.

Nathan, Andrew J. *Chinese Democracy*. New York: Alfred A. Knopf, 1985.

———. *China's Crisis: Dilemmas of Reform and Prospects for Democracy*. New York: Columbia University Press, 1990.

Ogden, Suzanne, Kathleen Hartford, Lawrence R. Sullivan, and David Zweig, eds. *China's Search for Democracy: The Student and the Mass Movement of 1989*. Armonk, N. Y.: M. E. Sharpe, 1992.

Oksenberg, Michel, Marc Lambert, and Lawrence R. Sullivan, eds. *Beijing Spring, 1989, Confrontation and Conflict: The Basic Documents*. Armonk, N. Y.: M. E. Sharpe, 1990.

Pieke, Frank N. *The Ordinary and the Extraordinary: An Anthropological Study of Chinese Reform and the 1989 People's Movement in Beijing*. London: Kegan Paul International, 1996.

Saich, Tony, ed. *The Chinese People's Movement: Perspectives on Spring 1989*. Armonk, N. Y.: M. E. Sharpe, 1990.

*/+Schell, Orville. *Discos and Democracy: China in the Throes of Reform*. New York: Pantheon, 1988.

———. *Mandate of Heaven: A New Generation of Entrepreneurs, Dissidents, Bohemians, and Technocrats Lays Claim to China's Future*. New York: Simon & Schuster, 1994.

Seymour, James D., ed. *The Fifth Modernization: China's Human Rights Movement, 1978–1979*. Stanfordville, N. Y.: Human Rights Publishing Group, 1980.

Simmie, Scott, and Bob Nixon. *Tiananmen Square: An Eyewitness Account of the Chinese People's Passionate Quest for Democracy*. Toronto: Douglas and McIntyre, 1989.

Svensson, Marina. *Debating Human Rights in China: A Conceptual and Political History*. Lanham, Md.: Rowman & Littlefield, 2002.

Unger, Jonathan, ed. *The Pro-Democracy Protests in China: Reports from the Provinces*. Armonk, N. Y.: M. E. Sharpe, 1991.

Van Ness, Peter, ed. *Debating Human Rights: Critical Essays from the United States and Asia*. London: Routledge, 1999.

Wasserstrom, Jeffrey N., and Elizabeth J. Perry, eds. *Popular Protest and Political Culture in Modern China*. 2nd ed. Boulder, Colo.: Westview, 1994.

Williams, Philip F., and Wu Yenna. *The Great Wall of Confinement: The Chinese Prison Camp through Contemporary Fiction and Reportage*. Berkeley: University of California Press, 2004.

Wu, Harry. *Laogai: The Chinese Gulag*. Boulder, Colo.: Westview, 1992.

Yan Jiaqi. *Toward a Democratic China: The Intellectual Autobiography of Yan Jiaqi*. Honolulu: University of Hawai'i Press, 1992.

Yi Mu, and Mark V. Thompson. *Crisis at Tiananmen: Reform and Reality in Modern China*. San Francisco: China Books and Periodicals, 1989.

*Zhang Liang (compiler). *The Tiananmen Papers*. Andrew J. Nathan and Perry Link, eds. New York: Public Affairs Press, 2001.

Zheng Yongjian. *Will China Become Democratic? Elite, Class and Regime Transition*. Singapore: Eastern Universities Press, 2004.

Domestic and International Economics

Andors, Stephen. *China's Industrial Revolution: Politics, Planning and Management, 1949 to the Present*. New York: Pantheon Books, 1977.

Asian Research Service. *China's Agricultural Economy*. Hong Kong: Asian Research Service, 1985.

——. *China's Railway Network*. Hong Kong: Asian Research Service, 1984.

——. *China's Coal Mining Industry*. Hong Kong: Asian Research Service, 1984.

——. *China's Hydrocarbon Potential*. Hong Kong: Asian Research Service, 1984.

Ash, Robert. "The Agricultural Sector in China: Performance and Policy Dilemmas during the 1990s." *The China Quarterly*, no. 131 (September 1992): 545–76.

Bhalla, A.S., and Qiu Shufang. *The Employment Impact of China's WTO Accession*. London: Routledge/Curzon, 2004.

Barnett, A. Doak. *China's Economy in Global Perspective*. Washington, D. C.: The Brookings Institution, 1981.

Bartke, Wolfgang. *The Economic Aid of the People's Republic of China to Developing and Socialist Countries.* Munich: K. G. Saur, 1989.

Baum, Richard, ed. *China's Four Modernizations: The New Technological Revolution.* Boulder, Colo.: Westview, 1980.

*Becker, Jasper. *Hungry Ghosts: China's Secret Famine.* London: John Murray, 1996.

Bian Yanjie. *Work and Inequality in Urban China.* Albany: State University Press of New York, 1994.

Bramall, Chris. *Sources of Chinese Economic Growth, 1978–1996.* Oxford: Oxford University Press, 2000.

Breslin, Shaun. *China in the 1980s: Centre-Province Relations in a Reforming Socialist State.* Basingstoke: Macmillan, 1996.

Brown, Colin G., Scott A. Waldron, and John W. Longworth. *Modernizing China's Industries: Lessons from Wool and Wool Textiles.* Cheltenham: Edward Elgar, 2005.

Brown, David H., and Alasdair MacBean, eds. *Challenge for China's Economic Development: An Enterprise Perspective.* London: Routledge, 2005.

Byrd, William A., ed. *Chinese Industrial Firms Under Reforms.* New York: Oxford University Press, 1993.

Cao Tianyu. *The Chinese Model of Modern Development.* London: Routledge, 2005.

Chai, Joseph, C. H. *China: Transition to a Market Economy.* Oxford: Clarendon Press, 1997.

Chen Jian. *Corporate Governance in China.* New York: Routledge/Curzon: 2005.

Chen Hongyi. *The Institutional Transition of China's Township and Village Enterprises: Market Liberalization, Contractual Form, Innovation, and Privatization.* Aldershot, UK: Ashgate, 2000.

Cheung, Peter T. Y., et al., eds. *Provincial Strategies of Economic Reform in Post-Mao China: Leadership, Politics, and Implementation.* Armonk, N. Y.: M. E. Sharpe, 1998.

Chen Chien-hsun, and Shih Hui-tzu. *High-Tech Industries in China.* Cheltenham: Edward Elgar, 2005.

———. *Banking and Insurance in the New China: Competition and the Challenge of Accession to the WTO.* Cheltenham: Edward Elgar, 2004.

China and the WTO: Compliance and Monitoring: Hearing before the U.S.–China Economic and Security Review Commission, 108th Congress, 2nd Session, February 5, 2004. Washington, D. C.

China's Economy Looks toward the Year 2000. 2 vols. Washington, D. C.: United States Government Printing Office, 1986.

China's Industrial, Investment, and Exchange Rate Policies: Impact on the United States: Hearing before the U.S.–China Economic and Security Re-

view Commission, 108th Congress, 1st Session. Washington, D. C.: September 25, 2003.

Chow, Nelson, W. S. *Socialist Welfare with Chinese Characteristics: The Reform of the Social Security System in China*. Hong Kong: Centre of Asian Studies, University of Hong Kong, 2000.

De Keijzer, Arne. *China: Business Strategies for the '90s*. Berkeley: Pacific View Press, 1979.

DeGlopper, Donald R. *Lukang: Commerce and Community in a Chinese City*. Albany: The State University of New York Press, 1995.

Ding Lu and Chee Kong Wong. *China's Telecommunications Market: Entering a New Competitive Age*. Cheltenham: Edward Elgar, 2003.

———, and Tang Zhimin. *State Intervention and Business in China: The Role of Preferential Policy*. Cheltenham: Edward Elgar, 1997.

———, James Wen, and Zhou Huizhong. *China's Economic Globalization through the WTO*. Aldershot, UK: Ashgate, 2003.

Ding X. L. "The Illicit Asset Stripping of Chinese State Firms." *The China Journal*, no. 43 (January: 2000): 1–29.

Dirlik, Arif. *After the Revolution: Waking to Global Capitalism*. Hanover: Wesleyan University Press, 1994.

*Donnithorne, Audrey. *China's Economic System*. New York: Praeger, 1967.

Draguhn, Werner, and Robert Ash, eds. *China's Economic Security*. Surrey: Curzon, Richmond, 1999.

Drysdale, Peter, and Song Ligang, eds. *China's Entry to the WTO: Strategic Issues and Quantitative Assessments*. London: Routledge, 2000.

Duckett, Jane. *The Entrepreneurial State in China: Real Estate and Commerce Departments in Reform Era Tianjin*. London: Routledge, 1998.

Eckstein, Alexander. *Communist China's Economic Growth and Foreign Trade: Implications for U.S. Policy*. New York: McGraw-Hill, 1966.

Feng Chen. "Subsistence Crises, Managerial Corruption and Labour Protests in China." *The China Journal*, no. 44 (July 2000): 41–64.

Feuerwerker, Albert. *China's Early Industrialization*. Cambridge, Mass.: Harvard University Press, 1958.

*Fewsmith, Joseph. *Dilemmas of Reform in China: Political Conflict and Economic Debate*. Armonk, N. Y.: M. E. Sharpe, 1994.

Findlay, Christopher, Andrew Watson, and Harry X. Wu, eds. *Rural Enterprises in China*. New York: St. Martin's, 1994.

Fishman, Ted C. *China, Inc.: How the Rise of the Next Superpower Challenges America and the World*. New York: Simon & Schuster, 2005.

Frazier, Mark W. *The Making of the Chinese Industrial Workplace: State, Revolution, and Labor Management*. Cambridge: Cambridge University Press, 2002.

———. "China's Pension Reform and Its Discontents." *The China Journal*, no. 51 (January 2004): 97–114.

Fung Hung-Gay, and Kevin H. Zhang, eds. *Financial Markets and Foreign Direct Investment in Greater China*. Armonk, N. Y.: M. E. Sharpe, 2002.

Garnaut, Ross, et al. *Private Enterprise in China*. Canberra: Asia Pacific Press, 2001.

*Gore, Lance. *Market Communism: The Institutional Foundations of China's Post-Mao Hyper-Growth*. Hong Kong: Oxford University Press, 1998.

———. "The Communist Legacy in Post-Mao Economic Growth." *The China Journal*, no. 41 (January 1999): 25–55.

Granick, David. *Chinese State Enterprises: A Regional Property Rights Analysis*. Chicago: University of Chicago Press, 1990.

Gu Shulin. *China's Industrial Technology, Market Reform and Organizational Change*. London: Routledge, 1999.

Harwit, Eric. *China's Automobile Industry: Policies, Problems, and Prospects*. Armonk, N. Y.: M. E. Sharpe, 1995.

Hay, Donald, et al. *Economic Reform and State-Owned Enterprises in China, 1979–1987*. Oxford: Clarendon Press, 1994.

He Qinglian. "China's Descent into a Quagmire." Nancy Yang Liu and Lawrence R. Sullivan, trans. *The Chinese Economy*, I–IV. Armonk, N. Y.: M. E. Sharpe, May/June 2000; January/February 2002.

Hinton, William. *The Great Reversal: The Privatization of China, 1978–1989*. New York: Monthly Review Press, 1990.

Holtz, Carsten A. *The Role of Central Banking in China's Economic Reforms*. Ithaca: Cornell University Press, 1993.

Howe, Christopher. *China's Economy: A Basic Guide*. New York: Basic Books, 1978.

———, ed. *Shanghai: Revolution and Development in an Asian Metropolis*. Cambridge: Cambridge University Press, 1981.

Howe, Jude. *China Opens Its Doors: The Politics of Economic Transition*. Boulder, Colo.: Lynne Rienner, 1993.

Huang Yasheng. *Inflation and Investment Controls in China: The Political Economy of Central-Local Relations During the Reform Era*. Cambridge: Cambridge University Press, 1996.

Huang Yiping. *China's Last Steps across the River: Enterprise and Banking Reforms*. Canberra: Asia Pacific Press, 2001.

Jae Ho Chung, ed. *Cities in China: Recipes for Economic Development in the Reform Era*. London: Routledge, 1999.

Joint Economic Committee, Congress of the United States. *China's Economic Future: Challenges to U.S. Policy*. Armonk, N. Y.: M. E. Sharpe, 1997.

Kennedy, Scott. "The Price of Competition: Pricing Policies and the Struggle to Define China's Economic System." *The China Journal*, no. 49 (January 2003): 1–30.

*Lardy, Nicholas R. *Integrating China into the Global Economy*. Washington D. C.: Brookings Institution Press, 2002.

——. *China in the World Economy*. Washington D. C.: Institute for International Economics, 1994.

——. *Foreign Trade and Economic Reform in China, 1978–1990*. Cambridge: Cambridge University Press, 1992.

——. *Agriculture in China's Modern Economic Development*. Cambridge: Cambridge University Press, 1983.

——. *Economic Growth and Distribution in China*. Cambridge: Cambridge University Press, 1978.

——. "Redefining U.S.–China Economic Relations." *National Bureau of Asian and Soviet Research*, NBR Analysis Series Paper, No. 5, 1991.

——, and Kenneth Lieberthal, eds. *Chen Yun's Strategy for China's Development*. Armonk, N. Y.: M. E. Sharpe, 1983.

Laurenceson, James, and Joseph C.H. Chai. *Financial Reform and Economic Development in China*. Cheltenham: Edward Elgar, 2003.

Lee Keun. *Chinese Firms and the State in Transition: Property Rights and Agency Problems in the Reform Era*. Armonk, N. Y.: M. E. Sharpe, 1992.

Lee, Peter, N. S. "Enterprise Autonomy in Post-Mao China: A Case Study of Policy-Making, 1978–83." *The China Quarterly*, no. 105 (March 1986).

——. *Industrial Management and Economic Reform in China, 1949–1984*. New York: Oxford University Press, 1987.

Lee Tae-Woo, Michael Roe, Richard Gray, and Mingnan Shen, eds. *Shipping in China*. Aldershot, UK: Ashgate, 2002.

Lew, Alan A., and Lawrence Yu. *Tourism in China: Geographic, Political, and Economic Perspectives*. Boulder, Colo.: Westview, 1995.

Liew Leong. *The Chinese Economy in Transition from Plan to Market*. Cheltenham, UK: Edward Elgar, 1997.

Lim, Edwin. *China: Long-Term Development Issues and Options*. Baltimore: Johns Hopkins University Press, for the World Bank, 1985.

Lin, Justin Yifu, Cai Fang, and Li Zhou. *The China Miracle: Development Strategy and Economic Reform*. Hong Kong: Chinese University Press, 1996.

——. *State-owned Enterprise Reform in China*. Hong Kong: The Chinese University Press, 2001.

Liu Xiuwu, R. *Jumping into the Sea: From Academics to Entrepreneurs in South China*. Lanham, Md.: Rowman & Littlefield, 2001.

Lloyd, Peter, and Zhang Xiaoguang, eds. *Models of the Chinese Economy*. Cheltenham: Edward Elgar, 2001.

Lo Dic. *Market and Institutional Regulation in Chinese Industrialization*. London: Macmillan, 1997.

*Lu Qiwen. *China's Leap into the Information Age: Innovation and Organization in the Computer Industry*. New York: Oxford University Press, 2000.

Lyons, Thomas P. *Economic Integration and Planning in Maoist China*. New York: Columbia University Press, 1987.

Mann, Jim. *Beijing Jeep: The Short Unhappy Romance of American Business in China*. New York: Simon & Schuster, 1989.

Marton, Andrew M. *China's Spatial Economic Development: Restless Landscapes in the Lower Yangze Delta*. London: Routledge, 2000.

McClain, Charles, and Cheng Hang-sheng. "China's Trade and Foreign Investment Law." Paper presented to the San Francisco Conference, March 24–25, 1995, Federal Reserve Bank of San Francisco.

Moore, Thomas G. *China in the World Market: Chinese Industry and International Sources of Reform in the Post-Mao Era*. Cambridge: Cambridge University Press, 2002.

Moser, Michael, ed. *Foreign Trade, Investment and the Law in the People's Republic of China*. Oxford: Oxford University Press, 1984.

Naughton, Barry. *Growing Out of the Plan: Chinese Economic Reform, 1978–93*. Cambridge: Cambridge University Press, 1995.

Nolan, Peter. *The Political Economy of Collective Farms: An Analysis of China's Post-Mao Rural Reforms*. Boulder, Colo.: Westview, 1988.

———, and Dong Fureng, eds. *Market Forces in China, Competition, and Small Business: The Wenzhou Debate:* London: Zed Books, 1989.

Oi, Jean C. "Patterns of Corporate Restructuring in China: Political Constraints on Privatization." *The China Journal*, no. 53 (January 2005): 115–44.

———, *Rural China Takes Off: Institutional Foundations of Economic Reform*. Berkeley: University of California Press, 1999.

——— and Andrew Walder, eds. *Property Rights and Economic Reform in China*. Stanford, Calif.: Stanford University Press, 1999.

O'Leary, Greg, ed. *Adjusting to Capitalism: Chinese Workers and the State*. Armonk, N. Y.: M. E. Sharpe, 1997.

Overholt, William H. *The Rise of China: How Economic Reform Is Creating a New Superpower*. New York: W. W. Norton, 1993.

Park Jung-Dong. *The Special Economic Zones of China and Their Impact on Its Economic Development*. Westport, Conn.: Praeger, 1997.

Pearson, Margaret. *China's New Business Elite: The Political Consequences of Economic Reform*. Berkeley: University of California Press, 1997.

———. *Joint Ventures in the People's Republic of China: The Control of Foreign Direct Investment under Socialism*. Princeton, N. J.: Princeton University Press, 1991.

Perkins, Dwight. *China: Asia's Next Economic Giant?* Seattle: University of Washington Press, 1986.

———. *Market Control and Planning in Communist China*. Cambridge, Mass.: Harvard University Press, 1966.

Perry, Elizabeth, and Christine Wong, eds. *The Political Economy of Reform in Post-Mao China*. Cambridge, Mass.: Harvard University Press, 1985.

Potter, Pitman B. *The Economic Contract Law of China: Legitimation and Contract Autonomy in the People's Republic of China*. Seattle: University of Washington Press, 1992.

Qi Luo. *China's Industrial Reform and Open-Door Policy 1980–1997: A Case Study from Xiamen*. Aldershot, UK: Ashgate, 2001.

Qian Wenbao. *Rural-Urban Migration and its Impact on Economic Development in China*. Aldershot, UK: Ashgate, 1996.

Rawski, Thomas G. *Economic Growth and Employment in China*. Oxford: Oxford University Press, 1979.

Reuvid, Jonathan, and Li Yong. *Doing Business with China*. Sterling, Va.: Kogan Page, 2003.

"*Res Publica*: Essays," *The Chinese Economy*. Armonk, N. Y.: M. E. Sharpe, July–August, 1999.

Reynolds, Bruce, ed. *Reform in China, Challenges and Choices*. Armonk, N. Y.: M. E. Sharpe, 1987.

Richman, Barry M. *Industrial Society in Communist China*. New York: Random House, 1969.

Riskin, Carl. *China's Political Economy: The Quest for Development since 1949*. Oxford: Oxford University Press, 1987.

*————, Zhao Renwei, and Li Shi, eds. *China's Retreat from Equality*. Armonk, N. Y.: M. E. Sharpe, 2001.

————, and Azizur Rahman Khan. *Inequality and Poverty in China in the Age of Globalization*. New York: Oxford University Press, 2001.

Rosen, Daniel H. *Behind the Open Door: Foreign Enterprises in the Chinese Marketplace*. Washington D. C.: Institute for International Economics, 1999.

Rui Huaichuan. *Globalization, Transition, and Development in China: The Case of the Coal Industry*. London: Routledge/Curzon: 2005.

Selden, Mark. *The Political Economy of Chinese Development*. Armonk, N. Y.: M. E. Sharpe, 1992.

Shih Chih-yu. *State and Society in China's Political Economy: The Cultural Dynamics of Socialist Reform*. Boulder, Colo.: Lynne Rienner, 1995.

Shirk, Susan L. *The Political Logic of Economic Reform in China*. Berkeley and Los Angeles: University of California Press, 1993.

Smyth, Russell, On-Kit Tam, Malcolm Warner, and Cherrie Jiuhua, eds. *China's Business Reforms: Institutional Challenges in a Globalized Economy*. London: Routledge/Curzon, 2005.

So, Alvin, ed. *China's Developmental Miracle: Origins, Transformations, and Challenges*. Armonk, N. Y.: M. E. Sharpe, 2003.

Solinger, Dorothy J. "Chinese Urban Jobs and the WTO." *The China Journal*, no. 49 (January 2003): 61–88.

——. *Chinese Business under Socialism: The Politics of Domestic Commerce, 1949–1980*. Berkeley and Los Angeles: University of California Press, 1984.

——. *China's Transition from Socialism: Statist Legacies and Market Reforms, 1980–1990*. Armonk, N. Y.: M. E. Sharpe, 1993.

Stavis, Benedict. *Making Green Revolution: The Politics of Agricultural Development in China*. Ithaca: Rural Development Monograph, No. 1, Cornell University Press, 1974.

——. *The Politics of Agricultural Mechanization in China*. Ithaca: Cornell University Press, 1978.

*Steinfield, Edward S. *Forging Reform in China: The Fate of State-Owned Industry*. Cambridge: Cambridge University Press, 1998.

Tam On-Kit. *The Development of Corporate Governance in China*. Cheltenham: Edward Elgar, 1999.

Tang Jie. *Managers and Mandarins in Contemporary China: The Building of an International Business Alliance*. London: Routledge, 2005.

Tang Wenfang, and William Parish. *Chinese Urban Life Under Reform: The Changing Social Contract*. Cambridge: Cambridge University Press, 2000.

Tidrick, Gene, and Jiyuan Chen, eds. *China's Industrial Reform*. Oxford: Oxford University Press, 1987.

Tisdell, Clement A., and Joseph C. H. Chai, eds. *China's Economic Growth and Transition: Macroeconomic, Environmental and Social/Regional Dimensions*. Commack, N. Y.: Nova Science Publishers, 1997.

Tomba, Luigi. *Paradoxes of Labor Reform: Chinese Labor Theory and Practice from Socialism to Market*. London: Routledge/Curzon, 2002.

Tong, Donald D. *The Heart of Economic Reform: China's Banking Reform and State Enterprise Restructuring*. Hampshire, UK: Ashgate, 2002.

Tong, James. "Fiscal Reform, Elite Turnover, and Central-Provincial Relations in Post-Mao China." *Australian Journal of Chinese Affairs*, 22 (July 1989).

Tsai, Kellee S. *Back-Alley Banking: Private Entrepreneurs in China*. Ithaca: Cornell University Press, 2002.

Vermeer, Eduard B., Frank N. Pieke, and Woei Lien Chong, eds. *Cooperative and Collective in China's Rural Development Between State and Private Sectors*. Armonk, N. Y.: M. E. Sharpe, 1998.

Unger, Jonathan, and Anita Chan. "Inheritors of the Boom: Private Enterprise and the Role of Local Government in a Rural South China Township." *The China Journal*, no. 42 (July 1999): 45–76.

Walder, Andrew G., ed. *China's Transitional Economy*. Oxford: Oxford University Press, 1996.

*——. *Communist Neo-Traditionalism: Work and Authority in Chinese Industry*. Berkeley and Los Angeles: University of California Press, 1986.

——. "Wage Reform and the Web of Factory Interests." *The China Quarterly*, no. 109 (March 1987).

Wang Feiling. *From Family to Market: Labor Allocation in Contemporary China*. Lanham Md.: Rowman & Littlefield, 1998.

Wang Hongying. *Weak State, Strong Networks: The Institutional Dynamics of Foreign Direct Investment in China*. New York: Oxford University Press, 2001.

Wang Gungwu, and John Wong, eds. *China's Political Economy*. Singapore: Singapore University Press, 1998.

Wang Liming and John Davies. *China's Grain Economy: The Challenge of Feeding More than a Billion*. Aldershot, UK: Ashgate, 2000.

Wang, N. T. *China's Modernization and Transnational Corporations*. Lexington, Mass.: Lexington Books, 1984.

*Wang Shaoguang, and Hu Angang. *The Political Economy of Uneven Development: The Case of China*. Armonk, N. Y.: M. E. Sharpe, 1999.

Waters, Harry J. *China's Economic Development, Strategies for the 21st Century*. Westport, Conn.: Quorum Books, 1997.

Webber, Michael, et al., eds. *China's Transition to a Global Economy*. Basingstoke: Palgrave Macmillan, 2002.

White, Gordon. *Riding the Tiger: The Politics of Economic Reform in Post-Mao China*. London: Macmillan, 1993.

Wolf, Charles Jr., et al. *Fault Lines in China's Economic Terrain*. Santa Monica; RAND, 2003.

Wong, Christine, P. W. *Financing Local Government in the People's Republic of China*. Hong Kong: Oxford University Press, 1997.

——. "Between Plan and Market: The Role of the Local Sector in Post-Mao China." *Journal of Comparative Economics*, no. 3 (1987).

——. "The Economics of Shortage and Problems of Reform in Chinese Industry." *Journal of Comparative Economics* 10, 4 (1986).

Wong, John, and Lu Ding. *China's Economy into the New Century: Structural Issues and Problems*. Singapore: Singapore University Press, 2002.

Woodward, Kim. *The International Energy Relations of China*. Stanford, Calif.: Stanford University Press, 1980.

World Bank. *China Updating Economic Memorandum: Managing Rapid Growth and Transition*. Washington, D. C.: World Bank, 1993.

——. *China: Between Plan and Market*. Washington, D. C.: World Bank, 1990.

Wu Jinglian, et al. "Strategic Plans for Economic Reform of China's Industrial Sector," Nancy Yang Liu and Lawrence R. Sullivan, trans. *The Chinese Economy*. Armonk, N. Y.: M. E. Sharpe, January–February 1997.

Xing You-tien. *Making Capitalism in China: The Taiwan Connection*. Oxford: Oxford University Press, 1998.

Xu Xiaoping. *China's Financial System under Transition*. New York: St. Martin's, 1998.

*Xu Yichong. *Power China: Reforming the Electric Power Industry in China*. Aldershot, UK: Ashgate, 2002.

Yabuki, Susumu. *China's New Political Economy: The Giant Awakes*. Boulder, Colo.: Westview, 1995.

Yan Sun. *Corruption and Market in Contemporary China*. Ithaca, N. Y.: Cornell University Press, 2004.

Yang Xueye with Ding Zijiang. "Chinese Renaissance: The Reemergence of a Private Economy in China." Nancy Yang Liu and Lawrence R. Sullivan, trans. *The Chinese Economy*. Armonk, N. Y.: M. E. Sharpe, I–III, January/February, 1998–September/October, 1998.

Yeung Y. K., and David K. Y. Chu. *Fujian: A Coastal Province in Transition and Transformation*. Hong Kong: The Chinese University Press, 2000.

Yeung Yue-man, and Shen Jian-fa. *Developing China's West: A Critical Path to Balanced National Development*. Hong Kong: The Chinese University Press, 2004.

——, and David K.Y. Chu, eds. *Guangdong: Survey of a Province Undergoing Rapid Change*. Hong Kong: The Chinese University Press, 1998.

——, and Hu Xuwei, eds. *China's Coastal Cities: Catalysts for Modernization*. Honolulu: University of Hawai'i Press, 1991.

Yi Gang. *Money Banking, and Financial Markets in China*. Boulder, Colo.: Westview, 1994.

Yin, Jason Z., Lin Shuanglin, and David F. Gates. *Social Security Reform: Options for China*. Singapore: World Scientific Publishing, 2000.

Zhao Minghua, and Theo Nichols. "Management Control of Labour in State-Owned Enterprises: Cases from the Textile Industry." *The China Journal*, no. 36 (July 1996): 1–25.

Zhou Ji. *China's Enterprise Reform: Changing State/Society Relations after Mao*. London: Routledge, 1998.

Young, Susan. *Private Business and Economic Reform in China*. Armonk, N. Y.: M. E. Sharpe, 1995.

Zhang Jian. *Government and Markets in China: A Local Perspective*. New York: Nova Science Publishers, 2003.

Zhang Weiwei. *Ideology and Economic Reform under Deng Xiaoping, 1978–1993*. London: Kegan Paul International, 1996.

Zheng Yongnian. *Globalization and State Transformation in China*. Cambridge: Cambridge University Press, 2004.

Education, Political Socialization, and Youth

Agelasto, Michael, and Bob Adamson, eds. *Higher Education in Post-Mao China*. Hong Kong: Hong Kong University Press, 1998.

Asian Research Service. *China's Human Resources*. Hong Kong: Asian Research Service, 1984.

*Chan, Anita. *Children of Mao: Personality Development & Political Activism in the Red Guard Generation*. Seattle: University of Washington Press, 1985.

Cherrington, Ruth. *Deng's Revolution: Young Intellectuals in 1980s China*. London: Macmillan, 1997.

Du Ruqing. *Chinese Higher Education: A Decade of Reform and Development (1978–1988)*. London: Macmillan, 1992.

Epstein, Irving, ed. *Chinese Education: Problems, Policies, and Prospects*. New York: Garland, 1991.

Farrer, James. *Opening Up: Youth Sex Culture and Market Reforms in Shanghai*. Chicago: The University of Chicago Press, 2002.

Hayhoe, Ruth, ed. *Education and Modernization: The Chinese Experience*. Oxford: Pergamon Press, 1992.

Jiang Yarong and David Ashley. *Mao's Children in the New China: Voices from the Red Guard Generation*. London: Routledge, 2000.

Jing Jun, ed. *Feeding China's Little Emperors: Food, Children and Social Change*. Cambridge: Cambridge University Press, 2000.

Kinney, Anne Behnke. *Chinese Views of Childhood*. Honolulu: University of Hawai'i, 1995.

Kohrmann, Matthew. *Bodies of Difference: Experiences of Disability and Institutional Advocacy in the Making of Modern China*. Berkeley: University of California Press, 2005.

Lau Sing. *Growing Up the Chinese Way: Chinese Child and Adolescent Development*. Hong Kong: The Chinese University Press, 1996.

*Link, Perry, et al., eds. *Popular Culture: Unofficial Culture in a Globalizing Society*. Lanham, Md.: Rowman & Littlefield, 2002.

Orleans, Leo. *Chinese Students in America: Policies, Issues, and Numbers*. Washington, D. C.: National Academy Press, 1988.

Pepper, Suzanne. *China's Education Reform in the 1980s: Policies, Issues, and Historical Perspectives*. Berkeley: Institute of East Asian Studies, University of California, 1990.

——. *Radicalism and Education Reform in 20th Century China*. Cambridge: Cambridge University Press, 1996.

Peterson, Glen. *The Power of Words: Literacy and Revolution in South China, 1949–1995*. Vancouver: University of British Columbia Press, 1997.

Schoenhals, Martin. *The Paradox of Power in a People's Republic of China Middle School*. Armonk, N. Y.: M. E. Sharpe, 1993.

Seeberg, Vilma. *The Rhetoric and Reality of Mass Education in Mao's China*. Lewiston: Edwin Mellen Press, 2000.

Seybolt, Peter J. (compiler). *Revolutionary Education in China: Documents and Commentary*. White Plains, N. Y.: International Arts & Sciences Press, 1973.

—— and Gregory Kuei-ke Chiang, eds. *Language Reform in China: Documents and Commentary*. White Plains, N. Y.: M. E. Sharpe, 1979.

Stafford, Charles. *The Roads of Chinese Childhood: Learning and Identification in Angang*. New York: Cambridge University Press, 1995.

Sun Lung-Kee. *The Chinese National Character: From Nationhood to Individuality*. Armonk, N. Y.: M. E. Sharpe, 2002.

Unger, Jonathan. *Education under Mao: Class and Competition in Canton Schools, 1960–1980*. New York: Columbia University Press, 1982.

Wang Jing. *High Culture Fever: Politics, Aesthetics, and Ideology in Deng's China*. Berkeley: University of California Press, 1996.

Xu Luo. *Searching for Life's Meaning: Changes and Tensions in the Worldviews of Chinese Youth in the 1980s*. Ann Arbor: University of Michigan Press, 2002.

Environment

Coggins, Chris. *The Tiger and the Pangolin: Nature, Culture, and Conservation in China*. Honolulu: University of Hawai'i Press, 2003.

*Dai Qing. *The River Dragon Has Come: The Three Gorges Dam and the Fate of the Yangtze River*. Yi Ming, trans. Armonk, N. Y.: M. E. Sharpe, 1997.

——. *Yangtze! Yangtze!: Debate over the Three Gorges Project*. Nancy Yang Liu, et al., trans. London and Toronto: Earthscan Publications and Probe International, 1994.

*/+Economy, Elizabeth C. *The River Runs Black: The Environmental Challenge to China's Future*. Ithaca, N. Y.: Cornell University Press, 2004.

Edmonds, Richard Louis. *Patterns of China's Lost Harmony: A Survey of the Country's Environmental Degradation and Protection*. London: Routledge, 1994.

*He Bochuan. *China on the Edge: The Crisis of Ecology and Development*. San Francisco: China Books and Periodicals, Inc., 1991.

Ho, Peter. "Mao's War against Nature? The Environmental Impact of the Grain-First Campaign in China." *The China Journal*, no. 50 (July 2003): 37–60.

Luk Shiu-Hung, and Joseph Whitney, eds. *Megaproject: A Case Study of China's Three Gorges Project*. Armonk, N. Y.: M. E. Sharpe, 1993.

*Ma Jun. *China's Water Crisis: Zhongguo shui weiji*. Nancy Yang Liu and Lawrence R. Sullivan, trans. Norwalk, Conn: EastBridge, 2004.

Ma Xiaoying, and Leonarad Ortolano. *Environmental Regulation in China: Institutions, Enforcement and Compliance*. Lanham, Md.: Rowman & Littlefield, 2000.

McElroy, Michael, et al., eds. *Energizing China: Reconciling Environmental Protection and Economic Growth*. Cambridge, Mass.: Harvard University Press, 1998.

Nickum, James E., ed. *Water Management Organization in the People's Republic of China*. Armonk, N. Y.: M. E. Sharpe, 1981.

Richardson, S. D. *Forests and Forestry in China*. Washington, D. C.: Island Press, 1990.

Ross, Lester. *Environmental Policy in China*. Bloomington: Indiana University Press, 1988.

Rozelle, Scott, et al. *China from Afforestation to Poverty Alleviation and Natural Forest Management*. Washington D. C.: World Bank, 2000.

Ryder, Grainne. *Damming the Three Gorges: What Dam-Builders Don't Want You to Know*. Toronto: Probe International, 1990.

Shaller, George. *The Last Panda*. Chicago: University of Chicago Press, 1993.

*Shapiro, Judith. *Mao's War against Nature: Politics and the Environment in Revolutionary China*. Cambridge: Cambridge University Press, 2000.

*Smil, Vaclav. *China's Past, China's Future: Energy, Food, Environment*. London: Routledge/Curzon, 2004.

———. *China's Environmental Crisis: An Inquiry into the Limits of National Development*. Armonk, N. Y.: M. E. Sharpe, 1993.

———. *The Bad Earth: Environmental Degradation in China*. Armonk, N. Y.: M. E. Sharpe, 1984.

Van Slyke, Lyman P. *Yangtze: Nature, History, and the River*. Reading, Mass.: Addison-Wesley, 1988.

Winchester, Simon. *The River at the Center of the World: A Journey Up the Yangtze and Back in Chinese Time*. New York: Henry Holt, 1996.

Zhang Zhongxiang. *The Economics of Energy Policy in China: Implications for Global Climate Change*. Cheltenham: Edward Elgar, 1998.

Foreign Relations, Military Affairs, and International Law and Organization History

Allen, Kenneth et al. *China's Air Force Enters the 21st Century*. Santa Monica: RAND, 1995.

Atlantic Council and National Committee on U.S.–China Relations. *United States and China Relations at a Crossroads*. Washington, D. C. and New York: Atlantic Council and National Committee on U.S.–China Relations, 1993.

Austin, Greg, and Stuart Harris. *Japan and Greater China: Political Economy and Military Power in the Asian Century*. London: Hurst, 2001.

———. *China's Ocean Frontier: International Law, Military Force and National Development*. Sydney: Allen and Unwin, 1998.

——— ed. *Missile Diplomacy and Taiwan's Future: Innovations in Politics and Military Power*. Canberra: Australian National University, 1997.

Brahm, Laurence J. *China as No. 1, The New Superpower Takes Centre Stage*. Singapore: Butterworth-Heinemann Asia, 1996.

Barnett, A. Doak. *The Making of Foreign Policy in China: Structure and Process*. Boulder, Colo.: Westview, 1985.

Barnouin, Barbara, and Yu Changgen. *Chinese Foreign Policy during the Cultural Revolution*. London: Kegan Paul, 1998.

Brömmelhörster, Jorn, and John Frankenstein, eds. *Mixed Motives, Uncertain Outcomes: Defense Conversion in China*. Boulder, Colo.: Lynne Rienner, 1997.

Chan, Gerald. *Chinese Perspectives on International Relations: A Framework for Analysis*. New York: St. Martin's, 1999.

Chang, Gordon. *Friends and Enemies: The United States, China, and the Soviet Union, 1948–1972*. Stanford, Calif.: Stanford University Press, 1990.

Chase, Michael, Kevin Pollpeter, and James Mulvenon. *Shanghaied? The Economic and Political Implications of the Flow of Information Technology and Investment across the Taiwan Strait*. Santa Monica: RAND, 2004.

Chen Jian. *Mao's China and the Cold War*. Chapel Hill: University of North Carolina Press, 2001.

——. *The China Challenge in the Twenty-First Century: Implications for U.S. Foreign Policy*. Washington, D. C.: U.S. Institute of Peace, 1998.

——. *China's Road to the Korean War: The Making of the Sino-American Confrontation*. New York: Columbia University Press, 1994.

Ching, Frank. *Hong Kong and China: For Better or for Worse*. New York: Asia Society and Foreign Policy Association, 1985.

Chiou C. L., and Leong G. Liew. *Uncertain Future: Taiwan–Hong Kong–China Relations after Hong Kong's Return to Chinese Sovereignty*. Aldershot, UK: Ashgate, 2000.

Christensen, Thomas J. *Useful Adversaries: Grand Strategy, Domestic Mobilization, and Sino-American Conflict*. Princeton, N. J.: Princeton University Press, 1996.

Clough, Ralph N. *Cooperation or Conflict in the Taiwan Strait?* Lanham, Md.: Rowman & Littlefield, 1999.

*/+Clubb, O. Edmund. *China and Russia: The Great Game*. New York: Columbia University Press, 1971.

Cohen, Jerome Alan, and Hungdah Chiu. *People's China and International Law*. Princeton, N. J.: Princeton University Press, 1974.

Cohen, Warren I. *America's Response to China: A History of Sino-American Relations*, 3rd ed. New York: Columbia University Press, 1990.

Copper, Franklin. *China's Foreign Aid: An Instrument of Peking's Foreign Policy*. Boston: D. C. Heath, 1976.

Curley, Melissa G., and Hong Liu, eds. *China and Southeast Asia: Changing Socio-Cultural Interactions*. Hong Kong: The University of Hong Kong, 2002.

Deng Yong, and Wang Fei-ling, eds. *China Rising: Power and Motivation in Chinese Foreign Policy*. Lanham, Md.: Rowman & Littlefield, 2005.

Dreyer, June Teufel, ed. *Chinese Defense and Foreign Policy*. New York: Paragon, 1989.

+Economy, Elizabeth, and Michel Oksenberg, eds. *China Joins the World: Progress and Prospects*. New York: Council on Foreign Relations, 1999.

Elleman, Bruce A. *Modern Chinese Warfare, 1795–1989*. London: Routledge, 2001.

Ellison, Herbert J., ed. *The Sino–Soviet Conflict: A Global Perspective*. Seattle: University of Washington Press, 1982.

Fairbank, John King. *The United States and China*. 4th ed. Cambridge, Mass.: Harvard University Press, 1983.

Faust, John R., and Judith Kornberg. *China in World Politics*. Boulder, Colo.: Lynne Rienner, 1995.

Fingar, Thomas, Paul Blencoe, et al., eds. *China's Quest for Independence: Policy Evolution in the 1970s*. Boulder, Colo.: Westview, 1980.

Foot, Rosemary. *The Practice of Power: U.S. Relations with China Since 1949*. Oxford: Oxford University Press, 1995.

Franda, Marcus. *China and India Online: Information Technology Politics and Diplomacy in the World's Two Largest Nations*. Lanham, Md.: Rowman & Littlefield, 2002.

Garson, Robert. *The United States and China Since 1949: A Troubled Affair*. London: Pinter, 1994.

Garver, John W. *Protracted Contest: Sino–Indian Rivalry in the Twentieth Century*. Seattle: University of Washington Press, 2001.

——. *Face Off: China, the United States, and Taiwan's Democratization*. Seattle: University of Washington Press, 1997.

——. *Foreign Relations of the People's Republic of China*. Englewood Cliffs, N. J.: Prentice Hall, 1993.

George, Alexander. *The Chinese Communist Army in Action: The Korean War and Its Aftermath*. New York: Columbia University Press, 1967.

Gilkey, Langdon. *Shantung Compound*. San Francisco: Harper & Row, 1966.

Gittings, John. *The World and China, 1922–1972*. New York: Harper & Row, 1974.

Godwin, Paul, ed. *The Chinese Defense Establishment: Continuity and Change in the 1980s*. Boulder, Colo.: Westview, 1983.

Goncharov, Sergei N., et al. *Uncertain Partners: Stalin, Mao, and the Korean War*. Stanford, Calif.: Stanford University Press, 1993.

Goodman, David S. G., and Gerald Segal, eds. *China Rising: Nationalism and Interdependence*. London: Routledge, 1997.

Gries, Peter Hays. *China's New Nationalism: Pride, Politics, and Diplomacy*. Berkeley: University of California Press, 2004.

———. "Tears of Rage: Chinese Nationalist Reactions to the Belgrade Embassy Bombings." *The China Journal*, no. 46 (July 2001): 25–44.

Gurtov, Melvin, and Byong-Moo Hwang. *China's Security: The New Roles of the Military*. Boulder, Colo.: Lynne Rienner, 1998.

Harding, Harry. *A Fragile Relationship: The United States and China Since 1972*. Washington, D. C.: The Brookings Institution, 1992.

Harris, Stuart, and Gary Klintworth, eds. *China as a Great Power: Myths, Realities and Challenges in the Asia-Pacific Region*. Melbourne: Longman, 1995.

Harrison, Selig. *China, Oil, and Asia: Conflict Ahead?* New York: Columbia University Press, 1977.

*/+Hopkirk, Peter. *Trespassers on the Roof of the World: The Secret Exploration of Tibet*. New York: Kodansha International, 1995.

Hsiung, James C., and Samuel Kim, eds. *China in the Global Community*. New York: Praeger, 1980.

Jacobson, Harold. *China's Participation in the IMF, the World Bank, and GATT: Toward a Global Economic Order*. Ann Arbor: University of Michigan Press, 1990.

Jagchid, Sechin, and Van Jay Symons. *Peace, War, and Trade along the Great Wall: Nomadic-Chinese Interaction through Two Millennia*. Bloomington: Indiana University Press, 1989.

Jencks, Harlan W. *From Muskets to Missiles: Politics and Professionalism in the Chinese Army, 1945–1981*. Boulder, Colo.: Westview, 1982.

Joffe, Ellis. *The Chinese Army after Mao*. Cambridge, Mass.: Harvard University Press, 1987.

Johnston, Alistair Iain, and Robert S. Ross. *Engaging China: The Management of an Emerging Power*. London: Routledge, 1999.

Karl, Rebecca E. *Staging the World: Chinese Nationalism at the Turn of the Twentieth Century*. Durham, N. C.: Duke University Press, 2002.

Keith, Ronald C., ed. *China as a Rising World Power and Its Response to "Globalization."* London: Routledge, 2005.

Kim, Samuel S. *China and the World: Chinese Foreign Relations in the Post-Cold War Era*. 3rd ed. Boulder, Colo.: Westview, 1994.

———. *The Third World in Chinese World Policy*. Princeton. N. J.: Center of International Studies, 1989.

———. *China, the United Nations, and World Order*. Princeton, N. J.: Princeton University Press, 1979.

———, and Ralph W. Huenemann. *China's Open Door Policy: The Quest for Foreign Technology and Capital*. Vancouver: University of British Columbia Press, 1984.

Kleinberg, Robert. *China's "Opening" to the Outside World: The Experiment with Foreign Capitalism*. Boulder, Colo.: Westview, 1990.

Kumaraswamy, P. R., ed. *China and the Middle East*. Delhi: Sage Publications, 1999.

Lampton, David M., ed. *The Making of Chinese Foreign and Security Policy in the Era of Reform*. Stanford, Calif.: Stanford University Press, 2001.

Lewis, John Wilson, and Xue Litai. *China Builds the Bomb*. Stanford, Calif.: Stanford University Press, 1988.

———. *China's Strategic Seapower: The Politics of Force Modernization in the Nuclear Age*. Stanford, Calif.: Stanford University Press, 1994.

Lilley, James R., and David Shambaugh, eds. *China's Military Faces the Future*. Armonk, N. Y.: M. E. Sharpe, 1999.

Lilley, James R., and Wendell L. Willkie, II, eds. *Beyond MFN: Trade with China and American Interests*. Washington, D. C.: American Enterprise Institute Press, 1994.

Madsen, Richard. *China and the American Dream: A Moral Inquiry*. Berkeley and Los Angeles: University of California Press, 1995.

Maxwell, Neville. *India's China War*. London: Jonathan Cape, 1970.

Mulvenon, James C., and Richard H. Yang. *The People's Liberation Army in the Information Age*. Santa Monica: RAND, 1999.

Murray, Geoffrey. *China the Next Superpower: Dilemmas in Change and Continuity*. Richmond, Surrey: Curzon, 1998.

Myers, Ramon H., Michel Oksenberg, and David Shambaugh, eds. *Making China Policy: Lessons from the Bush and Clinton Administration*. Lanham: Rowman & Littlefield, 2001.

Nathan, Andrew J., and Robert Ross. *The Great Wall and the Empty Fortress: China's Search for Security*. New York: W. W. Norton, 1997.

Nelsen, Harvey. *The Chinese Military System: An Organizational Study of the Chinese People's Liberation Army*. Boulder, Colo.: Westview, 1977.

*Oksenberg, Michel. "A Decade of Sino–American Relations." *Foreign Affairs* 61, 1 (Fall 1982).

Pollack, Jonathan D., and Richard H. Young. *In China's Shadow: Regional Perspectives on Chinese Foreign Policy*. Santa Monica: RAND, 1998.

Puska, Susan. *People's Liberation Army after Next*. Carlisle Barracks, Pa.: U.S. Army War College, 2000.

Roberti, Mark. *The Fall of Hong Kong: China's Triumph and Britain's Betrayal*. New York: John Wiley, 1994.

Robinson, Thomas W., and David Shambaugh, eds. *Chinese Foreign Policy: Theory and Practice*. Oxford: Clarendon Press, 1994.

Ross, Robert S. *After the Cold War: Domestic Factors and U.S.-China Relations*. Armonk, N. Y.: M. E. Sharpe, 1998.

———. *Negotiating Cooperation: The United States and China, 1969–1989*. Stanford, Calif.: Stanford University Press, 1996.

——. *The Indochina Tangle: China's Vietnam Policy, 1975–1979.* New York: Columbia University Press, 1988.

——, and Jiang Changbin. *Re-examining the Cold War: U.S.–China Diplomacy 1954–1973.* Cambridge, Mass.: Harvard University Press, 2001.

Roy, Denny. *China Foreign Relations.* Oxford: Rowman & Littlefield, 1998.

Ryan, Mark A., et al. *Chinese Warfighting: The PLA Experience since 1949.* Armonk, N. Y.: M. E. Sharpe, 2003.

Scobell, Andrew. *China's Use of Military Force: Beyond the Great Wall and the Long March.* Cambridge: Cambridge University Press, 2003.

Segal, Gerald, ed. *Chinese Politics and Foreign Policy Reform.* London: Kegan Paul International, 1990.

——, and Richard H. Yang, eds. *Chinese Economic Reform: The Impact on Security.* London: Routledge, 1996.

Service, John S. *The Amerasia Papers: Some Problems in the History of U.S.–China Relations.* Berkeley: Center for Chinese Studies, University of California, 1971.

Shau Kuo-kang. *Zhou Enlai and the Foundations of Chinese Foreign Policy.* Basingstoke, UK: Macmillan, 1996.

Shambaugh, David. *Beautiful Imperialist: China Perceives America, 1972–90.* Princeton, N. J.: Princeton University Press, 1991.

Sheng Lijun. *China and Taiwan: Cross-Straits Relations under Chen Shui-bian.* Singapore: Institute of Southeast Asian Studies, 2002.

Stokes, Mark A. *China's Strategic Modernization: Implications for the United States.* Carlisle Barracks, Pa.: U.S. Army War College, 1999.

Sufott, E. Zev. *A China Diary: Towards the Establishment of China–Israel Diplomatic Relations.* London: Frank Cass & Co., 1997.

Sutter, Robert G. *China's Rise in Asia: Promises and Perils.* London: Rowman & Littlefield, 2005.

——. *Chinese Policy Priorities and Their Implications for the United States.* Lanham, Md.: Rowman & Littlefield, 2000.

——. *U.S. Policy Toward China: An Introduction to the Role of Interest Groups.* Oxford: Rowman & Littlefield, 1998.

——. *China-Watch: Toward Sino-American Reconciliation.* Baltimore: Johns Hopkins University Press, 1978.

Swaine, Michael D. *China: Domestic Change and Foreign Policy.* Santa Monica: RAND, 1995.

——. *The Military and Political Succession in China: Leadership, Institutions and Beliefs.* Santa Monica: RAND, 1992.

Tan Qingshan. *The Making of US China Policy: From Normalization to the Post-Cold War Era.* Boulder, Colo.: Lynne Rienner, 1992.

Terrill, Ross. *The New Chinese Empire: And What It Means to the World.* Sydney: The University of New South Wales, 2003.

United States-China Security Review Commission. *Hearings on Military Modernization and Cross-Strait Balance*. 108th Congress, 2nd Session. Washington, D. C.: 2004.

——. *Report to the Congress on the National Security Implications of the Economic Relationship between the United States and China*. Washington, D. C.: 2002.

Van Ness, Peter. *Revolution and Chinese Foreign Policy: Peking's Support for Wars of National Liberation*. Berkeley and Los Angeles: University of California Press, 1970.

Vogel, Ezra F., et al. *The Golden Age of the U.S.–China–Japan Triangle, 1972–1989*. Cambridge, Mass.: Harvard University Press, 2002.

Westad, Odd Arne, ed. *Brother in Arms: The Rise and Fall of the Sino–Soviet Alliance, 1945–1963*. Stanford, Calif.: Stanford University Press, 1998.

*Whiting, Allen. *The Chinese Calculus of Deterrence: India and Indochina*. Ann Arbor: University of Michigan Press, 1975.

——. *China Crosses the Yalu: The Decision to Enter the Korean War*. New York: Macmillan, 1960.

Whitson, William. *The Chinese High Command: A History of Communist Military Politics, 1927–71*. New York: Praeger, 1973.

—— ed. *The Military and Political Power in China in the 1970s*. New York: Praeger, 1972.

Wilson, Jeanne. *Strategic Partners: Russian-Chinese Relations in the Post-Soviet Era*. Armonk, N. Y.: M. E. Sharpe, 2004.

Yahuda, Michael. *China's Foreign Policy after Mao: Towards the End of Isolationism*. New York: Macmillan, 1983.

Yang, Richard H., et al. *Chinese Regionalism: The Security Dimension*. Boulder, Colo.: Westview, 1994.

Yee, Herbert, and Ian Storey, eds. *The China Threat: Perceptions, Myths and Reality*. London: Routledge, 2002.

Zagoria, Donald S. *The Sino-Soviet Conflict, 1956–1961*. New York: Atheneum, 1964.

Zhang Shuguang. *Economic Cold War: America's Embargo against China and the Sino-Soviet Alliance, 1949–1963*. Stanford, Calif.: Stanford University Press, 2001.

Zhang Yongjin. *China in International Society since 1949: Alienation and Beyond*. New York: St. Martin's, 1998.

—— and Greg Austin, eds. *Power and Responsibility in Chinese Foreign Policy*. Canberra: Asia Pacific Press, 2001.

Zheng Yongnian. *Discovering Chinese Nationalism in China: Modernization, Identity and International Relations*. Cambridge: Cambridge University Press, 1999.

Zweig, David. *Internationalizing China: Domestic Interests and Global Linkages*. Ithaca: Cornell University Press, 2002.

History

Bakken, Børge, *The Exemplary Society, Human Improvement, Social Control, and the Dangers of Modernity in China*. Oxford: Oxford University Press, 2000.

*/+Bianco, Lucien. *Origins of the Chinese Revolution, 1915–1949*. Stanford, Calif.: Stanford University Press, 1971.

Benewick, Robert, and Paul Wingrove, eds. *China in the 1990s*. London: Macmillan, 1995.

Brady, Anne-Marie. *Friend of China—The Myth of Rewi Alley*. London: Routledge/Curzon, 2003.

Bulag, Uradyn E. *The Mongols at China's Edge: History and the Politics of National Unity*. Lanham, Md.: Rowman & Littlefield, 2002.

*Chow Tse-Tsung. *The May 4th Movement: Intellectual Revolution in Modern China*. Cambridge, Mass.: Harvard University Press, 1960.

Dai Qing. "Chu Anping and the 'Party Empire.'" Nancy Yang Liu and Lawrence R. Sullivan, trans. *Chinese Studies in History*. Armonk, N. Y.: M. E. Sharpe, Summer and Fall, 2000.

Dietrich, Craig. *People's China: A Brief History*. Oxford: Oxford University Press, 1998.

+Dong, Stella. *Shanghai: The Rise and Fall of a Decadent City, 1842–1949*. New York: Harper Collins, 2001.

+Fairbank, John King. *China: A New History*. Cambridge, Mass.: Harvard University Press, 1992.

———. *China Watch*. Cambridge, Mass.: Harvard University Press, 1987.

+Fritz, Jean, and Ed Young. *China's Long March: 6,000 Miles of Danger*. New York: Putnam, 1988.

Gao, James Z. *The Communist Takeover of Hangzhou: The Transformation of City and Cadre, 1949–1954*. Honolulu: University of Hawai'i Press, 2004.

Goldman, Merle, and Leo Ou-fan Lee, eds. *An Intellectual History of Modern China*. Cambridge: Cambridge University Press, 2002.

*Isaacs, Harold R. *The Tragedy of the Chinese Revolution*. 2nd ed., Stanford, Calif.: Stanford University Press, 1961.

MacFarquhar, Roderick, and John King Fairbank, eds. *The Cambridge History of China: The People's Republic of China*. Vols. 14 and 15. Cambridge: Cambridge University Press, 1987 and 1991.

+Meisner, Maurice. *Mao's China: A History of the People's Republic*. New York: Free Press, 1977.

———. *The Deng Xiaoping Era: An Inquiry into the Fate of Chinese Socialism, 1978–1994.* New York: Hill and Wang, 1996.

Myers, James T., et al., eds. *Chinese Politics: Documents and Analysis. The Death of Mao (1976) to the Fall of Hua Guofeng.* Vol. 3, Columbia: University of South Carolina Press, 1995.

———. *Chinese Politics: Documents and Analysis. The Fall of Hua Guofeng (1980) to the Twelfth Party Congress* (1982). Vol. 4, Columbia: University of South Carolina, 1995.

Porter, Edgar A. *The People's Doctor: George Hatem and China's Revolution.* Honolulu: University of Hawai'i Press, 1997.

Saich, Tony, and Hans van de Ven, eds. *New Perspectives on the Chinese Communist Revolution.* Armonk, N. Y.: M. E. Sharpe, 1995.

———. *The Rise to Power of the Chinese Communist Party.* Armonk, N. Y.: M. E. Sharpe, 1996.

Salisbury, Harrison E. *The New Emperors: China in the Era of Mao and Deng.* Boston: Little, Brown, 1992.

Selden, Mark. *The Yenan Way in Revolutionary China.* Cambridge, Mass.: Harvard University Press, 1971.

Sinclair, Kevin. *The Yellow River: A 5,000 Year Journey Through China.* Los Angeles: Knapp Press, 1987.

Snow, Edgar. *The Long Revolution.* New York: Random House, 1972.

———. *Red Star Over China.* London: Gollancz, 1937.

Spence, Jonathan D. *The Gate of Heavenly Peace: The Chinese and Their Revolution, 1895–1980.* New York: Viking, 1981.

Wang Ban. *Illuminations from the Past: Trauma, Memory, and History in Modern China.* Stanford Calif.: Stanford University Press, 2004.

Literature and the Arts, Archaeology, Cinema, Culture, Philosophy, and Journalism

"Absolut Marxism: Articles on Superstition, Heresy, and Correct Ideology from *Propaganda Trends,*" *Chinese Studies in Philosophy.* Armonk, N. Y.: M. E. Sharpe, Fall 1996.

*Barmé, Geremie. *In the Red: On Contemporary Chinese Culture.* New York: Columbia University Press, 1999.

———. "CCP tm & Adcult PRC," *The China Journal,* no. 41 (January 1999): 1–24.

Berry, Chris, *Postsocialist Cinema in Post-Mao China: The Cultural Revolution after the Cultural* Revolution. New York: Routledge, 2004.

——— ed. *Perspectives on Chinese Cinema.* London: BFI Publishers, 1991.

Birch, Cyril, and Donald Keene. *Anthology of Chinese Literature.* New York: Grove Press, 1965–1972.

Bunnin, Nicholas, ed. "Political Philosophy and Political Reform: Liberalism and the New Left." *Contemporary Chinese Thought*. Armonk, N. Y.: M. E. Sharpe, Spring 2003.

Capon, Edmund. *Art and Archaeology in China*. South Melbourne: Macmillan, 1977.

Chang Jung. *Wild Swans: Three Daughters of China*. New York: Simon and Schuster, 1991.

Chang Kwang-chih. *The Archaeology of Ancient China*. New Haven, Conn.: Yale University Press, 1977.

Chen Fong-Ching, and Jin Guantao. *From Youthful Manuscripts to River Elegy: The Chinese Popular Cultural Movement and Political Transformation, 1979–1989*. Hong Kong: The Chinese University Press, 1997.

Chen Xiaomei. *Acting the Part: Political Theater and Popular Drama in Contemporary China*. Honolulu: University of Hawai'i Press, 2002.

Clark, Paul. *Chinese Cinema: Culture and Politics Since* 1949. Cambridge: Cambridge University Press, 1987.

Clausen, Søren, and Stig Thøgersen. *The Making of a Chinese City: History and Historiography in Harbin*. Armonk, N. Y.: M. E. Sharpe, 1995.

"Cultural Heat: Chinese Intellectual Currents." *Contemporary Chinese Thought*. Armonk, N. Y.: M. E. Sharpe, Summer 1998.

Dai Qing. *Wang Shiwei and "Wild Lilies": Rectification and Purges in the Chinese Communist Party, 1942–1944*. Nancy Yang Liu and Lawrence R. Sullivan, trans. Armonk, N. Y.: M. E. Sharpe, 1994.

———. *Piquant Essays*. Nancy Yang Liu and Lawrence R. Sullivan, trans. *Chinese Studies in Philosophy (I & II)*, Winter 1995–1996–Spring 1996.

Dai Siji. *Mr. Muo's Traveling Couch*. Ina Rilke trans. New York: Knopf, 2005.

"Demonizing China: A Critical Analysis of the U.S. Press." *Contemporary Chinese Thought*. Armonk, N. Y.: M. E. Sharpe, Winter 1998–1999.

Donald, Stephanie Hemelryk. *Little Friends: Children's Film and Media Culture in China*. Lanham, Md.: Rowman & Littlefield, 2005.

——— et al., eds. *Media in China: Consumption, Content and Crisis*. London: Routledge, 2002.

Els, Paul Van. "The Many Faces of Huang-Lao," *Contemporary Chinese Thought*. Armonk, N. Y.; M. E. Sharpe, Fall 2002.

Farquhar, Mary Ann. *Children's Literature in China: From Lu Xun to Mao Zedong*. Armonk, N. Y.: M. E. Sharpe, 1999.

Fu, Poshek. *Between Shanghai and Hong Kong: The Politics of Chinese Cinema*. Stanford, Calif.: Stanford University Press, 2003.

"Gao Ertai—The Alienated Aesthete." *Chinese Studies in Philosophy*. Armonk, N. Y.: M. E. Sharpe, Fall 1993.

Goldman, Merle, and Edward Gu. *Chinese Intellectuals: Between State and Market*. London: Routledge/Curzon, 2004.

Guo Yingjie. *Cultural Nationalism in Contemporary China: The Search for National Identity under Reform*. London: Routledge/Curzon, 2004.

*Ha Jin. *War Trash*. New York: Pantheon, 2004.

Hamrin, Carol Lee, and Timothy Cheek, eds. *China's Establishment Intellectuals*. Armonk, N. Y.: M. E. Sharpe, 1986.

Hao Zhidong. *Intellectuals at a Crossroads: The Changing Politics of China's Knowledge Workers*. Albany: State University of New York Press, 2003.

Howkins, John. *Mass Communication in China*. London: Longman, 1982.

Hsu Kai-yu, et al., ed. *Literature of the People's Republic of China*. Bloomington: Indiana University Press, 1980.

Huang Xiang. *Poetry Out of Communist China*. Andrew G. Emerson, trans. Pittsburg: Edwin Mellen Press, 2004.

"In Celebration of Blasphemy: The Strange Musings of Zhang Zhiyang." *Chinese Studies in Philosophy*. Armonk, N. Y.: M. E. Sharpe, Spring 1994.

Javin, Linda. *The Monkey and the Dragon: A True Story about Friendship, Music, Politics and Life on the Edge*. Melbourne: Text Publishing, 2001.

Jernow, Allison Liu. *"Don't Force Us to Lie": The Struggle of Chinese Journalists in the Reform Era*. New York Committee to Protect Journalists, (nd).

Kinkley, Jeffrey C. *Chinese Justice, the Fiction: Law and Literature in Modern China*. Stanford, Calif.: Stanford University Press, 2000.

——, ed. *After Mao: Chinese Literature and Society, 1978–1981*. Cambridge, Mass.: Council on East Asian Studies, Harvard University, 1985.

Kraus, Richard C. *The Party and the Arts in China: The New Politics of Culture*. Lanham, Md.: Rowman & Littlefield, 2004.

——. *Pianos and Politics in China: Middle Class Ambitions and the Struggle Over Western Music*. Oxford: Oxford University Press, 1989.

Lagerkvist, Johan, ed. "Chinese Intellectuals' Thoughts on the Internet." *Contemporary Chinese Thought*. Armonk, N. Y.: M. E. Sharpe, Winter 2003–2004.

Laing, Ellen Johnston. *The Winking Owl: Art in the People's Republic of China*. Berkeley and Los Angeles: University of California Press, 1988.

Laughlin, Charles A. *Chinese Reportage: The Aesthetics of Historical Experience*. Durham, N. C.: Duke University Press, 2002.

Lee Chin-chuan, ed. *China's Media, Media's China*. Boulder, Colo.: Westview, 1994.

Li Ji. *Anyang*. Seattle: University of Washington Press, 1977.

Li Shenzhi. "In Defense of Liberalism." *Contemporary Chinese Thought*. Armonk, N. Y.: M. E. Sharpe, Winter 2001–2002.

Liang Sicheng, and Wilma Fairbank. *A Pictorial History of Chinese Architecture: A Study of the Development of its Structural System and the Evolution of its Types*. Cambridge, Mass.: M.I.T. Press, 1984.

*/+Link, Perry. *Evening Chats in Beijing: Probing China's Predicament*. New York: W. W. Norton, 1992.

——, ed. *Stubborn Weeds: Popular and Controversial Chinese Literature after the Cultural Revolution*. Bloomington: Indiana University Press, 1983.

——, Richard Madsen, and Paul G. Pickowicz, eds. *Unofficial China: Popular Culture and Thought in the People's Republic*. Boulder, Colo.: Westview, 1989.

Liu Binyan. *People or Monsters? And Other Stories and Reportage from China after Mao*. Perry Link trans. and ed. Bloomington: Indiana University Press, 1983.

Liu Haiping, and Lowell Swortzell, eds. *Eugene O'Neill in China: An International Centenary Celebration*. New York: Greenwood Press, 1992.

Liu Jianmei. *Revolution Plus Love: Literary History, Women's Bodies, and Thematic Repetition in Twentieth Century China*. Honolulu: University of Hawai'i Press, 2003.

Lu, Sheldon H., and Emilie Yueh-yu Yeh. *Chinese-Language Film: Historiography, Poetics, Politics*. Honolulu: University of Hawai'i Press, 2005.

Lynch, Daniel C. *After the Propaganda State: Media, Politics and "Thought Work" in Reformed China*. Stanford, Calif.: Stanford University Press, 1999.

Mackerras, Colin. *The Performing Arts in Contemporary China*. Boston: Routledge and Kegan Paul, 1981.

Mackinnon, Stephen R., and Oris Friesen. *China Reporting: An Oral History of American Journalism in the 1930s & 1940s*. Berkeley and Los Angeles: University of California Press, 1987.

Martin, Helmut, and Jeffrey Kinkley, eds. *Modern Chinese Writers: Self-Portrayals*. Armonk: N. Y.: M. E. Sharpe, 1992.

McDougall, Bonnie S. *Fictional Authors, Imaginary Audiences: Modern Chinese Literature in the Twentieth Century*. Hong Kong: The Chinese University Press, 2003.

——. *Love-letters and Privacy in Modern China: The Intimate Lives of Lu Xun and Xu Guangping*. Oxford: Oxford University Press, 2002.

——, and Kam Louie. *The Literature of China in the Twentieth Century*. New York: Columbia University Press, 1998.

——, ed. *Popular Chinese Literature and Performing Arts in the People's Republic of China, 1949–1979*. Berkeley and Los Angeles: University of California Press, 1984.

Melvin, Sheila, and Jindong Cai. *Rhapsody in Red: How Western Classical Music Became Chinese*. New York: Algora, 2004.

Munro, Donald J. *The Concept of Man in Contemporary China*. Ann Arbor: University of Michigan Press, 1977.

Murck, Christian F. *Artists and Traditions: Uses of the Past in Chinese Culture*. Princeton, N. J.: The Art Museum, Princeton University Press, 1976.

+O'Connor, Jane. *The Emperor's Silent Army: Terracotta Warriors of Ancient China*. New York: Viking, 2002.

Rong Cai. *The Subject in Crisis in Contemporary Chinese Literature*. Honolulu: University of Hawai'i Press, 2004.

Schwarcz, Vera. *The Chinese Enlightenment: Intellectuals and the Legacy of the May Fourth Movement of 1919*. Berkeley and Los Angeles: University of California Press, 1986.

Schwartz, Benjamin. *Communism and China: Ideology in Flux*. Cambridge, Mass.: Harvard University Press, 1968.

———. *In Search of Wealth and Power: Yen Fu and the West*. Cambridge, Mass.: Harvard University Press, 1964.

Sickman, L. C. S., and Alexander Coburn Soper. *The Art and Architecture of China*. Baltimore: Penguin Books, 1956.

Silbergeld, Jerome. *Hitchcock with a Chinese Face: Cinematic Doubles, Oedipal Triangles, and China's Moral Voice*. Seattle: University of Washington Press, 2004.

+Simonds, Nina, Leslie Swartz, and Meilo So. *Moonbeams, Dumplings, & Dragon Boats: A Treasury of Chinese Holiday Tales, Activities, and Recipes*. San Diego: Harcourt, 2002.

Song Yongyi, et al., eds. "The Debate between the Blood Lineage Theory and Yu Luoke's 'On Family Background' during the Cultural Revolution." *Contemporary Chinese Thought*. Armonk, N. Y.: M. E. Sharpe, Summer 2004.

Song Yongyi, and Zhou Zehao. "Heterodox Thoughts during the Cultural Revolution," Parts I & II. *Contemporary Chinese Thought*. Armonk, N. Y.: M. E. Sharpe, Summer 2001 & Fall 2001.

Sun Shuyun. *Ten Thousand Miles without a Cloud*. Hammersmith: Harper Perennial, 2003.

Tang Xiaobing. *Chinese Modern: The Heroic and the Quotidian*. Durham, N. C.: Duke University Press, 2000.

Unger, Jonathan, ed. *Using the Past to Serve the Present: Historiography and Politics in Contemporary China*. Armonk, N. Y.: M. E. Sharpe, 1993.

Wagner, Rudolf G. *The Contemporary Chinese Historical Drama: Four Studies*. Berkeley and Los Angeles: University of California Press, 1990.

Wang Ruoshui. "The Anti-Spiritual Pollution Drive: A Former *People's Daily* Editor Remembers." *Chinese Studies in Philosophy*. Armonk, N. Y.: M. E. Sharpe, Summer 1996.

Wang Ruowang. *Hunger Trilogy*. Kyna Rubin, trans. Armonk, N. Y.: M. E. Sharpe, 1991.

Wu Hung. *Exhibiting Experimental Art in China*. Chicago: Smart Museum of Art and University of Chicago Press, 2001.

Yang Xiaoneng. *The Golden Age of Chinese Archaeology: Celebrated Discoveries from the People's Republic of China*. New Haven, Conn.: Yale University Press, 1968.

Zhang Yingjin. *Chinese National Cinema*. New York: Routledge/Curzon, 2004.

——. *Screening China: Critical Interventions, Cinematic Reconfigurations, and the Transnational Imaginary in Contemporary Chinese Cinema*. Ann Arbor: University of Michigan Press, 2002.

——. *The City in Modern Chinese Literature and Film: Configurations of Space, Time & Gender*. Stanford, Calif.: Stanford University Press, 1996.

Zhang Xudong, ed. *Whither China? Intellectual Politics in Contemporary China*. Durham, N. C.: Duke University Press, 2001.

Zheng Shusen, and Alice Low. *A Young Painter: The Life and Paintings of Wang Yani—China's Extraordinary Young Artist*. New York: Scholastic, 1991.

——, and Zhou Yingxiong. *China and the West: Comparative Literature Studies*. Hong Kong: Chinese University Press, 1980.

Political and Legal Affairs and Government Policy Making

Bachman, David. *Bureaucracy, Economy, and Leadership in China: The Institutional Origins of the Great Leap Forward*. Cambridge: Cambridge University Press, 1991.

——. *Chen Yun and the Chinese Political System*. Berkeley: Institute of East Asian Studies, University of California, 1985.

Bakken, Børge, ed. *Crime, Punishment, and Policing in China*. Lanham Md.: Rowman & Littlefield, 2005.

*Barmé, Geremie. *Shades of Mao: The Posthumous Cult of the Great Leader*. Armonk, N. Y.: M. E. Sharpe, 1996.

Barnett, A. Doak. *China's Far West: Four Decades of Change*. Boulder, Colo: Westview, 1993.

——. *Cadres, Bureaucracy, and Political Power in Communist China*. New York: Columbia University Press, 1967.

——, and Ralph N. Clough, eds. *Modernizing China: Post Mao Reform and Development*. Boulder, Colo.: Westview, 1986.

+Baum, Richard. *Burying Mao: Chinese Politics in the Age of Deng Xiaoping*. Princeton, N. J.: Princeton University Press, 1994.

Bennett, Gordon. *Yundong: Mass Campaigns in Chinese Communist Leadership*. Berkeley: Center for Chinese Studies, University of California, 1976.

Bo Zhiyue. *Chinese Provincial Leaders: Economic Performance and Political Mobility*. Armonk, N. Y.: M. E. Sharpe, 2002.

Brook, Timothy, and B. Michael Frolic, eds. *Civil Society in China*. Armonk, N. Y.: M. E. Sharpe, 1997.

Brown, Ronald C. *Understanding Chinese Courts and Legal Process: Law with Chinese Characteristics*. The Hague: Kluwer Law International, 1997.

Burns, John P. *The Chinese Communist Party Nomenklatura System: A Documentary Study of Party Control of Leadership Selection*. Armonk, N. Y.: M. E. Sharpe, 1989.

——. *Political Participation in Rural China*. Berkeley and Los Angeles: University of California Press, 1988.

——, and Stanley Rosen, eds. *Policy Conflicts in Post-Mao China*. Armonk, N. Y.: M. E. Sharpe, 1986.

Burton, Charles. *Political and Social Change in China Since 1978*. Westport, Conn.: Greenwood, 1990.

+Butterfield, Fox. *China: Alive in the Bitter Sea*. New York: Times Books, 1982.

Chan, Alfred L. *Mao's Crusade: Politics and Policy Implementation in China's Great Leap Forward*. Oxford: Oxford University Press, 2001.

Chang, Parris. *Power and Policy in China*. University Park: Pennsylvania State University Press, 1976.

——. "The Rise of Wang Tung-hsing: Head of China's Security Apparatus." *The China Quarterly*, no. 73 (March 1978).

Chen, Albert Hung-yee. *An Introduction to the Legal System of the People's Republic of China*. Singapore: Butterworths Asia, 1992.

Cheng, Joseph Y.S., ed. *China in the Post-Deng Era*. Hong Kong: Chinese University Press, 1998.

Cheng Li. *China's Leaders: The New Generation*. Lanham, Md.: Rowman & Littlefield, 2001.

Ch'i Hsi-Sheng. *Politics of Disillusionment: The Chinese Communist Party Under Deng Xiaoping, 1978–1989*. Armonk, N. Y.: M. E. Sharpe, 1991.

Chinoy, Mike. *China Live: Two Decades in the Heart of the Dragon*. Atlanta: Turner Publishing, 1997.

Diamond, Larry, and Ramon H. Myers, eds. *Elections and Democracy in Greater China*. New York: Oxford University Press, 2001.

Dikötter, Frank. *Crime, Punishment and the Prison in Modern China*. London: Hurst, 2002.

Ding Xueliang. *The Decline of Communism in China: Legitimacy Crisis, 1977–1989*. Cambridge: Cambridge University Press, 1994.

Dittmer, Lowell. *China under Reform*. Boulder, Colo.: Westview, 1994.

——. *China's Continuous Revolution: The Post-Liberation Epoch, 1949–1981*. Berkeley and Los Angeles: University of California Press, 1987.

*Domenach, Jean-Luc. *The Origins of the Great Leap Forward: The Case of One Chinese Province*. A. M. Berrett, trans. Boulder, Colo.: Westview, 1995.

Domes, Jurgen. *The Government and Politics of the PRC: A Time of Transition*. Boulder, Colo.: Westview, 1985.

Dreyer, June Teufel. *China's Political System: Modernization and Tradition.* Basingstoke, UK: Macmillan, 1993.

Dutton, Michael R. *Policing and Punishment in China: From Patriarchy to "the People."* Cambridge: Cambridge University Press, 1992.

Dwyer, Denis, ed. *China: The Next Decades.* Harlow: Longman Scientific and Technical, 1994.

Fang Zhu. *Gun Barrel Politics: Party-Army Relations in Mao's China.* Boulder, Colo.: Westview, 1998.

*Fewsmith, Joseph. *China since Tiananmen: The Politics of Transition.* New York: Cambridge University Press, 2001.

——. *Elite Politics in Contemporary China.* Armonk, N. Y.: M. E. Sharpe, 2001.

——. *Dilemmas of Reform in China: Political Conflict and Economic Debate.* Armonk, N. Y.: M. E. Sharpe, 1994.

Forster, Keith. *Rebellion and Factionalism in a Chinese Province: Zhejiang, 1966–1976.* Armonk, N. Y.: M. E. Sharpe, 1990.

Gilley, Bruce. "The 'End of Politics' in Beijing." *The China Journal,* no. 51 (January 2004): 115–42.

Goldman, Merle and Roderick McFarquhar, eds. *The Paradox of China's Post-Mao Reforms.* Cambridge, Mass: Harvard University Press, 1999.

Goldstein, Avery. *From Bandwagon to Balance-of-Power Politics: Structural Constraints and Politics in China, 1949–1978.* Stanford, Calif.: Stanford University Press, 1991.

Goodman, David S. G. *Centre and Province in the People's Republic of China: Sichuan and Guizhou, 1955–1965.* Cambridge: Cambridge University Press, 1986.

——, and Gerald Segal. *China Deconstructs: Politics, Trade and Regionalism.* London: Routledge, 1994.

Guillermaz, Jacques. *The Chinese Communist Party in Power, 1949–1976.* Boulder, Colo.: Westview, 1976.

Guo Xuezhi. "Dimensions of *Guanxi* in Chinese Elite Politics." *The China Journal,* no. 46 (July 2001): 69–94.

Hamrin, Carol Lee. *China and the Challenge of the Future: Changing Political Patterns.* Boulder, Colo.: Westview, 1990.

——, and Zhao Suisheng, eds. *Decision-Making in Deng's China: Perspectives from Insiders.* Armonk, N. Y.: M. E. Sharpe, 1995.

Harding, Harry. *China's Second Revolution: Reform after Mao.* Washington, D. C.: TheBrookings Institution, 1987.

——. *Organizing China: The Problem of Bureaucracy 1949–1976.* Stanford, Calif.: Stanford University Press, 1981.

Heufers, Rainer, et al. *The Impact of the Administrative Procedure Law on Legal Security in the People's Republic of China.* Beijing: Friedrich Naumann Foundation, 1996.

Hsu, Immanuel C. Y. *China without Mao*: *The Search for a New Order*. Oxford: Oxford University Press, 1982.

Hua Shiping. *Chinese Political Culture, 1989–2000*. Armonk, N. Y.: M. E. Sharpe, 2001.

+Hudson, Christopher, ed. *The China Handbook*. Chicago: Fitzroy Dearborn Publishers, 1997.

Ji Fengyuan. *Linguistic Engineering: Language and Politics in Mao's China*. Honolulu: University of Hawai'i Press, 2004.

Jia Hao and Lin Zhimin, eds. *Changing Central-Local Relations in China*: *Reform and State Capacity*. Boulder, Colo.: Westview, 1994.

Jiang Jinsong. *The National People's Congress of China*. Beijing: Foreign Languages Press, 2003.

Joseph, William A. *The Critique of Ultra-Leftism in China, 1958–1981*. Stanford, Calif.: Stanford University Press, 1984.

Kau, Michael Ying-Mao, ed. *The Lin Piao Affair: Power, Politics, and Military Coup*. White Plains, N. Y.: International Arts and Sciences Press, 1975.

———, and Susan Marsh, eds. *China in the Era of Deng Xiaoping*: *A Decade of Reform*. Armonk, N. Y.: M. E. Sharpe, 1993.

Kwong, Julia. *The Political Economy of Corruption in China*. Armonk, N. Y.: M. E. Sharpe,1997.

Ladany, Laszlo. *The Communist Party of China and Marxism, 1921–1985*: *A Self-Portrait*. Stanford, Calif.: Hoover Institution Press, 1988.

Lam, Willy Wo-Lap. *China after Deng Xiaoping: The Power Struggle in Beijing since Tiananmen*. Singapore: John Wiley & Sons, 1995.

Lampton, David M., ed. *Policy Implementation in Post-Mao China*. Berkeley and Los Angeles: University of California Press, 1987.

Lee, Peter Nan-Shong, and Carlos Wing-Hung Lo. *Remaking China's Public Management*. Westport: Quorum Books, 2001.

Lewis, John Wilson. *Leadership in Communist China*. Ithaca: Cornell University Press, 1963.

———. ed. *Party Leadership and Revolutionary Power in China*. Cambridge: Cambridge University Press, 1970.

+Leys, Simon. *Broken Images*: *Essays on Chinese Culture and Politics*. New York: St. Martin's, 1990.

———. *Chinese Shadows*. New York: Viking Press, 1977.

Lichtenstein, Peter M. *China at the Brink: The Political Economy of Reform and Retrenchment in the Post-Mao Era*. New York: Praeger, 1991.

Lieberthal, Kenneth G. *Governing China: From Revolution through Reform*. New York: W. W. Norton, 1995.

———. *Revolution and Tradition in Tientsin, 1949–52*. Stanford, Calif.: Stanford University Press, 1980.

——, and Bruce J. Dickson. *A Research Guide to Central Party and Government Meetings in China, 1949–1986.* Armonk, N. Y.: M. E. Sharpe, 1989.

——, and David M. Lampton, eds. *Bureaucracy, Politics, and Decision-Making in Post-Mao China.* Berkeley and Los Angeles: University of California Press, 1992.

*——, and Michel Oksenberg. *Policy Making in China: Leaders, Structures, and Processes.* Princeton, N. J.: Princeton University Press, 1988.

*/+Lifton, Robert Jay. *Thought Reform and the Psychology of Totalism: A Study of Brainwashing in China.* New York: W. W. Norton, 1961.

Liu, Allan P. I. *Mass Politics in the People's Republic: State and Society in Contemporary China.* Boulder, Colo.: Westview, 1996.

Liu Binyan. *China's Crisis, China's Hope: Essays from an Intellectual in Exile.* Cambridge, Mass.: Harvard University Press, 1990.

——. *A Higher Kind of Loyalty.* Zhu Hong, trans. New York: Pantheon Books, 1990.

Lo, Carlos Wing-Hung. *China's Legal Awakening: Legal Theory and Criminal Justice in Deng's Era.* Hong Kong: Hong Kong University Press, 1995.

Lü Xiaobo. *Cadres and Corruption: The Organizational Involution of the Chinese Communist Party.* Stanford, Calif.: Stanford University Press, 2000.

Lubman, Stanley B. *Bird in a Cage: Legal Reform in China after Mao.* Stanford, Calif.: Stanford University Press, 1999.

—— ed. *China's Legal Reforms.* Oxford: Oxford University Press, 1996.

MacFarquhar, Roderick, ed. *The Eras of Mao and Deng.* Cambridge: Cambridge University Press, 1997.

Mackerras, Colin, Pradeep Taneja, and Graham Young. *China Since 1978: Reform, Modernization and "Socialism with Chinese Characteristics."* Melbourne: Longman, 1998.

Manion, Melanie. *Retirement of Revolutionaries in China: Public Policies, Social Norms, Private Interests.* Princeton, N. J.: Princeton University Press, 1993.

McCormick, Barrett L., and Jonathan Unger, eds. *China after Socialism: In the Footsteps of Eastern Europe or East Asia?* Armonk, N. Y.: M. E. Sharpe, 1996.

Miles, James A. R. *The Legacy of Tiananmen: China in Disarray.* Ann Arbor: University of Michigan Press, 1996.

Nathan, Andrew J., and Bruce Gilley. *China's New Rulers: The Secret Files.* New York: New York Review of Books, 2002.

Nathan, Andrew J. with Hong Zhaohui and Steven R. Smith, eds. *Dilemmas of Reform in Jiang Zemin's China.* Boulder, Colo.: Lynne Rienner, 1999.

—— with Shi Tianjin and Helena V. S. Ho. *China's Transition.* New York: Columbia University Press, 1997.

O'Brien, Kevin J. *Reform without Liberalization: China's National People's Congress and the Politics of Institutional Change*. Cambridge: Cambridge University Press, 1990.

———, and Li Lianjiang. "Suing the Local State: Administrative Litigation in Rural China." *The China Journal*, no. 51 (January 2004): 75–96.

Ogden, Suzanne. *China's Unresolved Issues: Politics, Development, and Culture*. 3rd ed. Englewood Cliffs, N. J.: Prentice Hall, 1994.

Peerenboom, Randal. *China's Long March Toward the Rule of Law*. Cambridge: Cambridge University Press, 2002.

Potter, Pittman B., ed. *Domestic Law Reforms in Post-Mao China*. Armonk, N. Y.: M. E. Sharpe, 1994.

Pye, Lucian. *The Spirit of Chinese Politics*, new ed. Cambridge, Mass: Harvard University Press, 1992.

Sargeson, Sally, and Jian Zhang. "Re-assessing the Role of the Local State: A Case Study of Local Government Interventions in Property Rights Reform in a Hangzhou District. *The China Journal*, no. 42 (July 1999).

Schoenhals, Michael. *Doing Things with Words in Chinese Politics: Five Studies*. Berkeley: Institute of East Asian Studies, University of California, 1992.

Schurmann, Franz. *Ideology and Organization in Communist China*. Berkeley and Los Angeles: University of California Press, 1966.

Sexton, John, and Alan Hunter. *Contemporary China*. New York: St. Martin's, 1999.

Seymour, James D. *China's Satellite Parties*. Armonk, N. Y.: M. E. Sharpe, 1987.

———, and Richard Anderson. *New Ghosts, Old Ghosts: Prisons and Labor Reform Camps in China*. Armonk, N. Y.: M. E. Sharpe, 1988.

Shambaugh, David, ed. *Is China Unstable?* Armonk, N. Y.: M. E. Sharpe, 2000.

Shi Tianjian. *Political Participation in Beijing*. Cambridge, Mass. Harvard University Press, 1997.

Shirk, Susan L. *Competitive Comrades*. Berkeley and Los Angeles: University of California Press, 1982.

Shue, Vivienne. *The Reach of the State: Sketches of the Chinese Body Politic*. Stanford, Calif: Stanford University Press, 1988.

*Solomon, Richard H. *Mao's Revolution and the Chinese Political Culture*. Berkeley and Los Angeles: University of California Press, 1971.

Starr, John Bryan. *Understanding China: A Guide to China's Economy, History, and Political Structure*. New York: Hill and Wang, 1997.

Su Shaozhi, et al. *Marxism in China*. Nottingham: Spokesman, 1983.

Sullivan, Lawrence R., ed. *China since Tiananmen: Political, Economic, and Social Conflicts*. Armonk, N. Y.: M. E. Sharpe, 1995.

Tanner, Harold M. *Strike Hard! Anti-Crime Campaigns and Chinese Criminal Justice*, 1979–1985. Ithaca, N. Y.: Cornell University East Asia Program, 1999.

Tanner, Murray Scot. *The Politics of Law-Making in Post-Mao China, Institutions, Processes, and Democratic Prospects.* Oxford: Clarendon Press, 1999.

Teather, David, and Herbert Yee, eds. *China in Transition: Issues and Policies.* Basingstoke, UK: Macmillan, 1999.

Teiwes, Frederick C. *Politics and Purges in China: Rectification and the Decline of Party Norms 1950–1965.* Armonk, N. Y.: M. E. Sharpe, 1993.

———. *Politics at Mao's Court: Gao Gang and Party Factionalism in the Early 1950s.* Armonk, N. Y.: M. E. Sharpe, 1990.

——— with Warren Sun. *China's Road to Disaster: Mao, Central Politicians, and Provincial Leaders in the Unfolding of the Great Leap Forward, 1955–1959.* Armonk, N. Y.: M. E. Sharpe, 1999.

Terrill, Ross. *China in Our Time: The Epic Saga of the People's Republic from the Communist Victory to Tiananmen Square and Beyond.* New York: Simon & Schuster, 1992.

Tien Hung-mao, and Yun-han Chu. *China under Jiang Zemin.* Boulder, Colo.: Lynne Rienner, 1999.

Townsend, James. *Politics in China.* 3rd ed. Boston: Little, Brown & Co., 1986.

———. *Political Participation in Communist China.* Berkeley and Los Angeles: University of California Press, 1967.

Vogel, Ezra. *One Step Ahead in China: Guangdong under Reform.* Cambridge, Mass: Harvard University Press, 1989.

———. *Canton under Communism: Programs and Politics in a Provincial Capital, 1949–1968.* Cambridge, Mass.: Harvard University Press, 1969.

Wang, James C. F. *Contemporary Chinese Politics: An Introduction.* 6th ed. Englewood Cliffs, N. J.: Prentice Hall, 1999.

Wong Yiu-chung. *From Deng Xiaoping to Jiang Zemin: Two Decades of Political Reform in the People's Republic of China.* Lanham, Md.: University Press of America, 2005.

Womack, Brantly, ed. *Contemporary Chinese Politics in Historical Perspective.* Cambridge: Cambridge University Press, 1991.

Wong, John, and Zheng Yongnian, eds. *The Nanxun Legacy and China's Development in the Post-Deng Era.* Singapore: Singapore University Press, 2001.

Yang, Dali L. *Beyond Beijing: Liberalization and the Regions in China.* London: Routledge, 1997.

Yu Guangyuan. *Deng Xiaoping Shakes the World: An Eyewitness Account of China's Party Work Conference and the Third Plenum (November–December 1978).* Ezra Vogel and Steven I. Levine, eds. Norwalk, Conn: EastBridge Press, 2004.

Zong Hairen. *Disidai (The Fourth Generation).* New York: Mirror Books, 2002.

Population, Women, and Minorities

Amnesty International, *People's Republic of China: Gross Violations of Human Rights in the Xinjiang Uighur Autonomous Region*. New York: Amnesty International USA, 1999.

——. *Women in China: Imprisoned and Abused for Dissent*. New York: Amnesty International, 1995.

Andors, Phyllis. *The Unfinished Liberation of Chinese Women, 1949–1980*. Bloomington: Indiana University Press, 1983.

Asian Research Service, *China's Coastal Cities*. Hong Kong: Asian Research Service, 1986.

——. *China's Urban Development*. Hong Kong: Asian Research Service, 1985.

*/+Avedon, John F. *In Exile from the Land of Snows*. New York: Alfred A. Knopf, 1984.

Banister, Judith. *China's Changing Population*. Stanford, Calif.: Stanford University Press, 1987.

Barlow, Tani E., *The Question of Women in Chinese Feminism*. Durham, N. C.: Duke University Press, 2004.

—— ed. *Gender Politics in Modern China: Writing and Feminism*. Durham, N. C.: Duke University Press, 1993.

Barnett, Robert, ed. *Resistance and Reform in Tibet*. London: Hurst, 1994.

Becquelin, Nicolas. "Xinjiang in the Nineties." *The China Journal*, no. 44 (July 2000): 65–92.

Benson, Linda, and Ingvar Svanberg, eds. *China's Last Nomads: The History and Culture of China's Kazaks*. Armonk, N. Y.: M. E. Sharpe, 1998.

——. *The Kazakhs of China: Essays on an Ethnic Minority*. Stockholm: Almqvist & Wiksell International, 1988.

Bossen, Laurel. *Chinese Women and Rural Development: Sixty Years of Change in Lu Village*. Lanham, Md.: Rowman & Littlefield, 2002.

Cao Changching, and James D. Seymour, eds. *Tibet through Dissident Chinese Eyes: Essays on Self-Determination*. Armonk, N. Y.: M. E. Sharpe, 1998.

Croll, Elisabeth, ed. *The Women's Movement in China: A Selection of Readings, 1949–1973*. London: Anglo–Chinese Educational Institute, 1974.

——, Delia Davin, and Penny Kane, eds. *China's One-Child Family Policy*. New York: St. Martin's, 1985.

Dawa Norbu. *China's Tibet Policy*. Richmond, UK: Curzon, 2001.

Day, Lincoln H., and Ma Xia, eds. *Migration and Urbanization in China*. Armonk, N. Y.: M. E. Sharpe, 1994.

Dillon, Michael. *Xinjiang—China's Muslim Far Northwest*. London: Routledge/Curzon, 2004.

Donnet, Pierre-Antoine. *Tibet: Survival in Question*. Tica Broch trans., London: Zed Books, 1994.

*Dreyer, June Teufel. *China's Forty Millions: Minority Nationalities and National Integration in the People's Republic of China.* Cambridge, Mass.: Harvard University Press, 1976.

Du Ruofu, and Vincent F. Yip. *Ethnic Groups in China.* Beijing & New York: Science Press, 1993.

Evans, Harriet. *Women & Sexuality in China.* Oxford: Polity Press, 1997.

Fong, Vanessa L. *Only Hope: Coming of Age under China's One-Child Policy.* Stanford, Calif.: Stanford University Press, 2004.

Gaetano, Arianne M., and Tamara Jacka. *On the Move: Women in Rural-to-Urban Migration in Contemporary China.* New York: Columbia University Press, 2004.

Gillette, Maris Boyd. *Between Mecca and Beijing: Modernization and Consumption among Urban Chinese Muslims.* Stanford, Calif.: Stanford University Press, 2001.

Gladney, Dru C. *Dislocating China: Muslims, Minorities and Other Subaltern Subjects.* London: Hurst & Company, 2004.

———. *Muslim Chinese: Ethnic Nationalism in the People's Republic.* Cambridge, Mass: Council on East Asian Studies, Harvard University, 1991.

Goldstein, Melvyn C., Dawei Sherap, and William R. Siebenschuh. *A Tibetan Revolutionary: The Political Life and Times of Bapa Phüntso Wangye.* Berkeley: University of California Press, 2004.

Goldstein, Melvyn C. *The Snow Lion and the Dragon: China, Tibet and the Dalai Lama.* Berkeley & Los Angeles: University of California Press, 1997.

———, and Matthew T. Kapstein, eds. *Buddhism in Contemporary Tibet: Religious Revival and Cultural Identity.* Berkeley and Los Angeles: University of California Press, 1998.

*Grunfield, A. Tom. *The Making of Modern Tibet.* Armonk, N. Y.: M. E. Sharpe, 1996.

Hansen, Mette Halskov. *Lessons in Being Chinese, Minority Education and Ethnic Identity in Southwest China.* Seattle: University of Washington Press, 1999.

Harrell, Stevan, ed. *Perspectives on the Yi of Southwest China.* Berkeley: University of California Press, 2001.

Heberer, Thomas. *China and Its National Minorities: Autonomy or Assimilation?* Michael Vale, trans. Armonk, N. Y.: M. E. Sharpe, 1989.

Honig, Emily, and Gail Hershatter. *Personal Voices: Chinese Women in the 1980s.* Stanford Calif.: Stanford University Press, 1988.

Hsiung Ping-Chun et al., eds. *Chinese Women Organizing: Cadres, Feminists, Muslims, Queers.* New York: New York University Press, 2001.

Jaschok, Maria, and Suzanne Miers, eds. *Women & Chinese Patriarchy: Submission, Servitude and Escape.* Atlantic Highlands, N. J.: Zed Books, 1994.

Johnson, Kay Ann. *Women, the Family, and Peasant Revolution in China.* Chicago: University of Chicago Press, 1983.

Kaup, Katherine Palmer. *Creating the Zhuang: Ethnic Politics in China*. Boulder, Colo.: Lynne Rienner, 2000.

Kolås, Åshild, and Monika P. Thowsen. *On the Margins of Tibet: Cultural Survival on the Sino-Tibetan Frontier*. Seattle: University of Washington Press, 2005.

Laogai Research Foundation. *Better Ten Graves than One Extra Birth: China's Systematic Use of Coercion to Meet Population Quotas*. 2004.

Lee Ching Kwan. *Gender and the South China Miracle: Two Worlds of Factory Women*. Berkeley and Los Angeles: University of California Press, 1998.

Lee, Mary Jo Benton. *Ethnicity, Education, and Empowerment: How Minority Students in Southwest China Construct Identities*. Aldershot, UK: Ashgate, 2001.

Lemoine, Jacques, and Chiao Chien, eds. *The Yao of South China: Recent International Studies*. Paris: Pangu, 1991.

Litzinger, Ralph A. *Other Chinas: The Yao and the Politics of National Belonging*. Durham, N. C: Duke University Press, 2000.

*Mackerras, Colin. *China's Minority Cultures: Identities and Integration Since 1912*. Melbourne: Longman, 1995.

———. *China's Minorities: Integration and Modernization in the Twentieth Century*. Hong Kong: Oxford University Press, 1994.

Maurer-Fazio, Margaret, et al. "Inequality in the Rewards for Holding Up Half the Sky: Gender Wage Gaps in China's Urban Labour Market, 1988–1994." *The China Journal*, no. 41 (January 1999): 55–88.

McLaren, Anne. *Chinese Women: Living and Working*. London: Routledge/Curzon, 2004.

Milwertz, Cecilia Nathansen. *Accepting Population Control: Urban Chinese Women and the One-Child Policy*. Richmond, UK: Curzon, 1997.

Olivier, Bernard Vincent. *The Implementation of China's Nationality Policy in the Northeastern Provinces*. San Francisco: Mellen Research University Press, 1993.

Orleans, Leo A. *Every Fifth Child: The Population of China*. Stanford, Calif.: Stanford University Press, 1972.

Peng Xizhe. *Demographic Transition in China: Fertility Trends since the 1950s*. Oxford: Clarendon Press, 1991.

Poston, Dudley L., and David Yaukey, eds. *The Population of China*. New York: Plenum Press, 1992.

Qu Geping, and Li Jinchang. *Population and the Environment*. Jiang Baozhong and Gu Ran trans. Boulder, Colo.: Lynne Rienner, 1994.

Rudelson, Justin Jon. *Oasis Identities: Uyghur Nationalism along China's Silk Road*. New York: Columbia University Press, 1997.

Safran, William, ed. *Nationalism and Ethnoregional Identities in China*. London: Frank Cass, 1998.

Scharping, Thomas. *Birth Control in China: 1949–2000: Population Policy and Demographic Development*. London: Routledge/Curzon, 2003.

Schein, Louisa. *Minority Rules: The Miao and the Feminine in China's Cultural Politics*. Durham, N. C.: Duke University Press, 2000.

Shakya, Tsering. *The Dragon in the Land of Snows: A History of Modern Tibet since 1947*. London: Pimlico, 1999.

+Sis, Peter. *Tibet: Through the Red Box*. New York: Farrar Straus Giroux, 1998.

Solinger, Dorothy J. *Contesting Citizenship in Urban China: Peasants, Migrants, the State and the Logic of the Market*. Berkeley and Los Angeles: University of California, 1999.

Starr, S. Frederick. *Xinjiang: China's Muslim Borderland*. Armonk, N. Y.: M. E. Sharpe, 2004.

Tanner, Murray Scot. "State Coercion and the Balance of Awe: The 1983–1986 'Stern Blows' Anti-Crime Campaign." *The China Journal*, no. 44 (July 2000): 93–128.

Tapp, Nicholas. *The Hmong of China: Context, Agency, and the Imaginary*. Leiden: Brill, 2001.

Verschuur-Basse, Denyse. *Chinese Women Speak*. Westport: Praeger, 1996.

Wang, Gabe T. *China's Population: Problems, Thoughts and Policies*. Aldershot, UK: Ashgate, 1999.

Wang Jiye, and Terence H. Hull, eds. *Population and Development Planning in China*. Sydney: Allen & Unwin, 1991.

Wolf, Arthur P., and Chieh-shang Huang. *Marriage and Adoption in China: 1845–1945*. Stanford, Calif.: Stanford University Press, 1980.

Wolf, Margery. *Revolution Postponed: Women in Contemporary China*. Stanford, Calif.: Stanford University Press, 1985.

Young, Marilyn B. (compiler). *Women in China: Studies in Social Change and Feminism*. Ann Arbor: Center for Chinese Studies, University of Michigan, 1973.

*Yue Daiyun with Carolyn Wakeman. *To the Storm: The Odyssey of a Revolutionary Chinese Woman*. Berkeley and Los Angeles: University of California Press, 1985.

Yusuf, Shahid, and Wu Weiping. *The Dynamics of Urban Growth in Three Chinese Cities*. New York: Oxford University Press, 1997.

Zhang Weiguo. *Economic Reforms and Fertility Behavior: A Study of a North China Village*. London: China Library, 2002.

Rural Affairs

Bennett, Gordon. *Huadong: The Story of a Chinese People's Commune*. Boulder, Colo.: Westview, 1978.

Bernstein, Thomas. "Stalinism, Famine and Chinese Peasants—Grain Procurement during the Great Leap Forward." *Theory and Society* 13, no. 3 (1984): 339–77.

———., *Up to the Mountains and Down to the Villages: The Transfer of Youth from Urban to Rural China.* New Haven: Yale University Press, 1977.

———, and Lü Xiaobo. *Taxation without Representation in Contemporary Rural China.* Cambridge: Cambridge University Press, 2003.

Bianco, Lucien. *Peasants without Party: Grass-roots Movements in Twentieth Century China.* Armonk, N. Y.: M. E. Sharpe, 2001.

Björn, Alpermann. "The Post-Election Administration of Chinese Villages." *The China Journal*, no. 46 (July 2001): 45–68.

Blecher, Marc, and Vivienne Shue. *Tethered Deer: Government and Economy in a Chinese County.* Stanford, Calif.: Stanford University Press, 1996.

Bruun, Ole. "The *Fengshui* Resurgence in China: Conflicting Cosmologies between State and Peasantry." *The China Journal*, no. 36 (July 1996): 47–66.

Byrd, William A., and Lin Qinsong, eds. *China's Rural Industry: Structure, Development, and Reform.* Oxford: Oxford University Press, 1990.

*/+Chan, Anita, Richard Madsen, and Jonathan Unger. *Chen Village: The Recent History of a Peasant Community Under Mao and Deng.* Berkeley and Los Angeles: University of California Press, 1992.

Chen Chih-Jou Jay. *Transforming Rural China: How Local Institutions Shape Property Rights in China.* London: Routledge/Curzon, 2004.

Chen Guidi, and Wu Chuntao. *Will the Boat Sink the Water: The Life of Chinese Peasants.* trans. Zhu Hong, New York: Public Affairs, 2006.

Chung Him. *China's Rural Market: Development in the Reform Era.* Aldershot, UK: Ashgate, 2004.

Findlay, Christopher, et al. *Rural Financial Markets in China.* Canberra: Asia Pacific Press, 2003.

Friedman, Edward, Paul Pickowicz, and Mark Selden. *Chinese Village, Socialist State.* New Haven: Yale University Press, 1991.

Gao Mobo C. F. *Gao Village: A Portrait of Rural Life in Modern China.* London: Hurst, 1999.

Gilley, Bruce. *Model Rebels: The Rise and Fall of China's Richest Village.* Berkeley: University of California Press, 2001.

Guldin, Gregory Eliyu. *Farewell to Peasant China: Rural Urbanization and Social Change in the Late Twentieth Century.* Armonk, N. Y.: M. E. Sharpe, 1997.

He Liyi with Claire Annee Chik. *Mr. China's Son: A Villager's Life.* Boulder, Colo.: Westview, 1993.

Hendrischke, Hans J., and Feng Chongyi, eds. *The Political Economy of China's Provinces: Comparative and Competitive Advantages.* London: Routledge, 1999.

Hilllman, Ben. "The Rise of the Community in Rural China: Village Politics, Cultural Identity, and Religious Revival in a Hui Hamlet." *The China Journal*, no. 51 (January 2004): 53–74.

*/+Hinton, William. *Fanshen: A Documentary of Revolution in a Chinese Village*. New York: Monthly Review Press, 1966.

Ho, Peter. *Institutions in Transition: Land Ownership, Property Rights, and Social Conflict in China*. Oxford: Oxford University Press, 2005.

Ho, Samuel P. S. *Rural China in Transition: Non-Agricultural Development in Rural Jiangsu, 1978–1990*. Oxford: Clarendon Press, 1994.

Huang Shu-min. *The Spiral Road: Change in a Chinese Village through the Eyes of a Communist Party Leader*. Boulder, Colo.: Westview, 1989.

Huang Yiping. *Agricultural Reform in China: Getting Institutions Right*. Cambridge: Cambridge University Press, 1998.

Kipnis, Andrew B. "The Disturbing Educational Discipline of 'Peasants.'" *The China Journal*, no. 46 (July 2001): 1–24.

———. *Producing Guanxi: Sentiment, Self, and Subculture in a North China Village*. Durham, N. C.: Duke University Press, 1997.

Li Lianjiang. "The Two-Ballot System in Shanxi Province: Subjecting Village Party Secretaries to a Popular Vote." *The China Journal*, no. 42 (July 1999): 103–24.

Longworth, John W., et al. *Beef in China: Agribusiness Opportunities and Challenges*. St. Lucia: University of Queensland Press, 2001.

Lyons, Thomas P. *Poverty and Growth in a South China County: Anxi, Fujian, 1949–1992*. Ithaca. N. Y.: Cornell University Press, 1994.

Madsen, Richard. *Morality and Power in a Chinese Village*. Berkeley and Los Angeles: University of California Press, 1984.

Mosher, Steven W. *Broken Earth: The Rural Chinese*. New York: Free Press, 1983.

Murphy, Rachel. *How Migrant Labor Is Changing Rural China*. Cambridge: Cambridge University Press, 2002.

Oi, Jean C. *Rural China Takes Off: Institutional Foundations of Economic Reform*. Berkeley: University of California Press, 1999.

———. *State and Peasant in Contemporary China: The Political Economy of Village Government*. Berkeley and Los Angeles: University of California Press, 1989.

Parish, William L., ed. *Chinese Rural Development: The Great Transformation*. Armonk, N. Y.: M. E. Sharpe, 1985.

———, and Martin King Whyte. *Village and Family in Contemporary China*. Chicago: University of Chicago Press, 1978.

Perkins, Dwight. *Rural Small-Scale Industry in the People's Republic of China*. Berkeley and Los Angeles: University of California Press, 1977.

———, and Shahid Yusuf. *Rural Development in China*. Baltimore: Johns Hopkins University Press, 1984.

Potter, Sulamith Heins, and Jack M. Potter. *China's Peasants: The Anthropology of a Revolution.* Cambridge: Cambridge University Press, 1990.

Putterman, Louis G. *Continuity and Change in China's Rural Development: Collective and Reform Eras in Perspective.* New York: Oxford University Press, 1993.

Rozelle, Scott, et al. "The Engines of a Viable Agriculture: Advances in Biotechnology, Market Accessibility, and Land Rentals in Rural China." *The China Journal*, no. 53 (January 2005): 81–114.

Ruf, Gregory. *Cadres and Kin: Making a Socialist Village in West China, 1921–1991.* Stanford, Calif.: Stanford University Press, 1998.

Seybolt, Peter J. *Throwing the Emperor from his Horse: Portrait of a Village Leader in China, 1923–1995.* Boulder, Colo.: Westview, 1996.

Siu, Helen F. *Agents and Victims in South China: Accomplices in Rural Revolution.* New Haven: Yale University Press, 1989.

———, and Zelda Stern, eds. *Mao's Harvest: Voices from China's New Generation.* Oxford: Oxford University Press, 1983.

Skinner, G. William. "Marketing and Social Structure in Rural China." *Journal of Asian Studies* 1, no. 24, (November 1964), Part I; 2, no. 24, (February 1965), Part II; 3, no. 24, (May 1965), Part III.

Unger, Jonathan. *The Transformation of Rural China.* Armonk, N. Y.: M. E. Sharpe, 2002.

Vermeer, Eduard B., et al., eds. *Cooperative and Collective in China's Rural Development: Between State and Private Interests.* Armonk, N. Y.: M. E. Sharpe, 1998.

Walder, Andrew, ed. *Zouping in Transition: The Process of Reform in Rural North China.* Cambridge, Mass.: Harvard University Press, 1998.

Walker, Kenneth R. *Food Grain Procurement and Consumption in China.* Cambridge: Cambridge University Press, 1984.

Wang Zhonghui. *A Study of Public Policy Influences upon the Development of China's Rural Enterprises, 1978–1992.* Aldershot, UK: Ashgate, 1997.

Wedemann, Andrew H. *From Mao to Market: Rent Seeking, Local Protectionism, and Marketization in China.* Cambridge: Cambridge University Press, 2003.

White, Lynn T., III. *Unstately Power.* 3 vols. Armonk, N. Y.: M. E. Sharpe, 1998.

Whiting, Susan. *Power and Wealth in Rural China: The Political Economy of Institutional Change.* Cambridge: Cambridge University Press, 2001.

Xin Liu. *In One's Own Shadow: An Ethnographic Account of the Condition of Post-reform Rural China.* Berkeley: University of California Press, 2000.

Yan Yunxiang. *Private Life under Socialism: Love, Intimacy, and Family Change in a Chinese Village, 1949–1999.* Stanford, Calif.: Stanford University Press, 2003.

Yep, Ray. *Manager Empowerment in China: Political Implications of Rural Industrialization*. London: Routledge/Curzon, 2003.

Yeung Y. M., and K. Y. Chu. *Guangdong: Survey of a Province Undergoing Rapid Change*. Hong Kong: Chinese University Press, 1994.

Yuen Sun-pong, et al. *Marriage, Gender, and Sex in a Contemporary Chinese Village*. Yu Fong-ying, trans. Armonk, N. Y.: M. E. Sharpe, 2004.

Zhou, Kate Xiao. *How the Farmers Changed China: Power of the People*. Boulder, Colo.: Westview, 1996.

Zweig, David. *Freeing China's Farmers: Rural Restructuring in the Reform Era*. Armonk, N. Y.: M. E. Sharpe, 1997.

——. *Agrarian Radicalism in China, 1968–1981*. Cambridge, Mass.: Harvard University Press, 1989.

Science, Medicine, and Technology

Bowers, John Z., J. William Hess, and Nathan Sivin, eds. *Science and Medicine in Twentieth-Century China: Research and Education*. Ann Arbor: Center for Chinese Studies, University of Michigan, 1988.

Chen C. C. *Medicine in Rural China: A Personal Account*. Berkeley and Los Angeles: University of California Press, 1989.

Chen Junshi, and T. Colin Campbell, et al., eds. *Diet, Life Style and Mortality in China: A Study of the Characteristics of 65 Chinese Counties*. Ithaca: Cornell University Press, 1990.

Cong Cao. *China's Scientific Elite*. London: Routledge/Curzon, 2004.

*Henderson, Gail, and Myron Cohen. *The Chinese Hospital: A Chinese Work Unit*. New Haven: Yale University Press, 1984.

Hu Danian. *China and Albert Einstein: The Reception of the Physicist and His Theory in China, 1917–1979*. Cambridge, Mass.: Harvard University Press, 2005.

Hua Shiping. *Scientism and Humanism: Two Cultures in Post-Mao China (1978–1989)*. Albany: State University of New York Press, 1995.

Kleinman, Arthur. *Social Origins of Distress and Disease: Depression, Neurasthenia, and Pain in Modern China*. New Haven: Yale University Press, 1986.

Lampton, David M. *Health, Conflict, and the Chinese Political System*. Ann Arbor: Center for Chinese Studies, University of Michigan, 1974.

Li-Hua, Richard. *Technology and Knowledge Transfer in China*. Aldershot, UK: Ashgate, 2004.

Lin Tsung-Yi et al., eds. *Chinese Societies and Mental Health*. Hong Kong: Oxford University Press, 1995.

*Pearson, Veronica. *Mental Health Care in China: State Policies, Professional Services, and Family*. London: Gaskell, 1995.

Phillips, Michael R. "The Transformation of China's Mental Health Services." *The China Journal*, Issue no. 39 (January 1998), pp. 1–38.

Rosenthal, Marilyn M. *Health Care in the People's Republic of China: Moving toward Modernization*. Boulder, Colo.: Westview, 1987.

Saich, Tony. *China's Science Policy in the 80s*. Atlantic Highlands, N. J.: Humanities Press International, 1989.

*Schneider, Laurence. *Biology and Revolution in Twentieth Century China*. Lanham, Md.: Rowman & Littlefied, 2003.

*Segal, Adam. *Digital Dragon: High Technology Enterprises in China*. Ithaca: Cornell University Press, 2003.

Simon, Denis Fred, and Merle Goldman, eds. *Science and Technology in Post-Mao China*. Cambridge, Mass.: Council on East Asian Studies, Harvard University, 1989.

Suttmeier, Richard P. *Science, Technology and China's Drive for Modernization*. Stanford, Calif.: Hoover Institution Press, 1980.

———. *Research and Revolution: Science Policy and Societal Change in China*. Lexington, Mass.: Lexington Books, 1974.

World Bank. *China: The Health Sector in China*. Washington, D. C.: World Bank, 1984.

Society, Ethnicity, and Religion

Bray, David. *Social Space and Governance in Urban China: The Danwei System from Origins to Reform*. Stanford, Calif.: Stanford University Press, 2005.

Davis, Deborah, and Ezra Vogel, eds. *Chinese Society on the Eve of Tiananmen: The Impact of Reform*. Cambridge, Mass.: Harvard University Press, 1990.

———, and Stevan Harrell, eds. *Chinese Families in the Post-Mao Era*. Berkeley and Los Angeles: University of California Press, 1993.

Chen, Nancy N., et al., eds. *China Urban: Ethnographies of Contemporary Culture*. Durham, N. C.: Duke University Press, 2001.

*Dikötter Frank. *The Discourse of Race in Modern China*. Stanford, Calif.: Stanford University Press, 1992.

Dutton, Michael. *Street Life China*. Melbourne: Cambridge University Press, 1998.

Falkenheim, Victor, ed. *Citizens and Groups in Contemporary China*. Ann Arbor: Center for Chinese Studies, University of Michigan, 1992.

Fried, Morton. *Fabric of Chinese Society: A Study in the Social Life of a Chinese County Seat*. New York: Praeger, 1953.

Friedman, John. *China's Urban Transition*. Minneapolis: University of Minnesota Press, 2005.

Frolic, B. Michael. *Mao's People: Sixteen Portraits of Life in Revolutionary China*. Cambridge, Mass.: Harvard University Press, 1980.

Garside, Roger. *Coming Alive: China After Mao*. New York: McGraw-Hill, 1981.

Gold, Thomas, et al. *Social Connections in China: Institutions, Culture, and the Changing Nature of Guanxi*. Cambridge: Cambridge University Press, 2002.

Goldstein, Melvyn, and Matthew Kapstein. *Buddhism in Contemporary Tibet: Religious Revival and Cultural Identity*. Berkeley: University of California Press, 1998.

Hui Wang. *China's New Order: Society, Politics, and Economy in Transition*. Theodore Huters, ed. Cambridge, Mass.: Harvard University Press, 2003.

Kam Wing Chan. *Cities with Invisible Walls: Reinterpreting Urbanization in Post-1949 China*. Hong Kong: Oxford University Press, 1994.

Kindopp, Jason, and Carol Lee Hamrin. *God and Caesar: Policy Implications of Church–State Tensions*. Washington D. C.: Brookings Institution Press, 2004.

Kraus, Richard C. *Class Conflict in Chinese Socialism*. New York: Columbia University Press, 1981.

Kristof, Nicholas D., and Sheryl WuDunn. *China Wakes: The Struggle for the Soul of a Rising Power*. New York: Times Books, 1994.

Levy, Marion Joseph. *The Family Revolution in Modern China*. New York: Octagon Books, 1963.

Lewis, John Wilson, ed. *The City in Communist China*. Stanford, Calif.: Stanford University Press, 1971.

Liang Heng, and Judith Shapiro. *Son of the Revolution*. New York: Alfred A. Knopf, 1983.

Lily, Lee Tsai. "Cadres, Temples and Lineage Institutions, and Governance in Rural China." *The China Journal*, no. 48 (July 2002): 1–28.

Lin Zhiling, and Thomas W. Robinson, eds. *The Chinese and Their Future: Beijing, Taipei, and Hong Kong*. Washington, D. C.: American Enterprise Institute Press, 1994.

Lindbeck, John M. H., ed. *China: Management of a Revolutionary Society*. Seattle: University of Washington Press, 1971.

Liu Dalin, et al. *Sexual Behavior in Modern China*. New York: Continuum Publishing Co., 1997.

Lozada, Eriberto P. *God Aboveground: Catholic Church, Postsocialist State, and Transnational Processes*. Stanford, Calif.: Stanford University Press, 2001.

Lü Xiaobo, and Elizabeth J. Perry, eds. *Danwei: The Changing Chinese Workplace in Historical and Comparative Perspective*. Armonk, N. Y.: M. E. Sharpe, 1997.

MacInnis, Donald E. (compiler). *Religious Policy and Practice in Communist China: A Documentary History*. New York: Macmillan, 1972.

Madsen, Richard. *China's Catholics: Tragedy and Hope in an Emerging Civil Society*. Berkeley: University of California Press, 1998.

Massonnet, Philippe. *The New China: Money, Sex, and Power*. Hannah Taïeb trans. Boston: Tuttle Publishing, 1997.

Mitter, Rana. *A Bitter Revolution: China's Struggle with the Modern World*. Oxford: Oxford University Press, 2004.

Mozingo, David, and Victor Nee, eds. *State and Society in Contemporary China*. Ithaca: Cornell University Press, 1983.

Pasternak, Burton. *Marriage and Fertility in Tianjin, China: Fifty Years of Transition*. Honolulu: East West Center, University of Hawai'i, 1986.

Rosenbaum, Arthur Lewis. *State and Society in China: The Consequences of Reform*. Boulder, Colo.: Westview, 1992.

Shanor, Donald, and Constance Shanor. *China Today*. New York: St. Martin's, 1995.

Smith, Christopher J. *China: People and Places in the Land of One Billion*. Boulder, Colo.: Westview, 1990.

Tomba, Luigi. "Creating an Urban Middle Class; Social Engineering in Beijing." *The China Journal*, no. 51 (January 2004): 1–26.

Tyson, James, and Ann Tyson. *Chinese Awakenings: Life Stories from the Unofficial China*. Boulder, Colo.: Westview, 1995.

Wang Fei-ling. *Organizing through Division and Exclusion: China's Hukou System*. Stanford, Calif.: Stanford University Press, 2005.

Watson, James L., ed. *Class and Social Stratification in Post-Revolution China*. Cambridge: Cambridge University Press, 1984.

Watson, Rubie, and Patricia Ebrey, eds. *Marriage and Inequality in Chinese Society*. Berkeley and Los Angeles: University of California Press, 1991.

Whyte, Martin King. "Continuity and Change in Urban Chinese Family Life." *The China Journal*, no. 53 (January 2005): pp. 9–34.

*——. *Small Groups and Political Rituals in China*. Berkeley and Los Angeles: University of California Press, 1974.

——, and William L. Parish. *Urban Life in Contemporary China*. Chicago: University of Chicago Press, 1984.

^Yuan Zhiming. *The Cross: Jesus in China*. VCD, Documentary Film, 2004.

Zhang Xinxin, and Sang Ye. *Chinese Lives: An Oral History of Contemporary China*. New York: Pantheon, 1987.

Zheng Yi. *Scarlet Memorial*. T. P. Sym, trans. Boulder, Colo.: Westview, 1996.

PART 3: SELECTED INTERNET SITES (2003–2005)

These sites provide a wealth of current and historical data, including newspaper articles, academic papers and studies, historical documents, films, government statements, audio files, songs and music, photographs, maps, television footage, and access to online library facilities.

Almost all of the government ministries, provinces and cities, corporations, and many libraries in the People's Republic of China maintain websites; some are in English, but most are generally noninteractive. *China News Digest* (www.cnd.org) is a major assembler of sites containing photos, historical records, scholarly works, and original sources.

Asia Foundation (www.asiafoundation.org)

Asia Times (www.atimes.com)

CCTV News (www.cctv.com/english/news)

Carnegie Council on Ethics and International Affairs (www.carnegiecouncil.org)

Channel News Asia (www.channelnewsasia.com)

China Business Review (www.chinabusinessreview.com)

China Council for the Promotion of International Trade (www.ccpit.org)

China Court (www.chinacourt.org) Sponsored by the Supreme People's Court of China this website contains information on legal cases, new laws, and regulations. Chinese and English.

China Daily, Business Weekly (www.chinadaily.net)

China Digital News (http://journalism.berkeley.edu/projects/chinaadn/en)

China Education and Research Network (www.edu.cn/HomePage/english) The official web site of China's Ministry of Education.

China Elections & Governance (www.chinaelections.org/english). Operated by the Beijing Center for Policy Research and focuses on electoral reform in China.

ChinaEWeekly (www.chinaeweekly.com)

ChinaGov (www.chinagov/main/whois)

China In Brief (www.china.org)

China Infohighway Communications (www.chinatoday.com)

China Information Center (www.oservechina.net)

China Internet Information Center (www.china.org.cn/english). This is the Chinese government's authorized portal published under the China International Publishing Group and the State Council.

China Journal (Canberra) (http://rspas.anu.edu.au/ccc/journal.htm)

China Labour Bulletin (www.china-labour.org.hk/iso/)

China Labor Watch (www.chinalaborwatch.org)

China Legislative Information Network System
(www.chinalaw.gov.cn). Operated by the Legislative Affairs
Office of China's State Council, the database includes current
laws and regulations in English translation.

China News Digest (www.cnd.org)

China on Internet (www.chinaoninternet.com)

ChinaOnline (www.chinaonline.com/issues)

China Radio International (www.cri.com.cn)

ChinaSite.com (www.chinasite.com) (English and Chinese).

China Survey (www.surveyCN.com)

China through a Lens (www.china.org.cn)

China Today (www.chinatoday.com)

China WWW Virtual Library/Internet Guide for Chinese Studies
(Sinological Institute, Leiden University, Netherlands)
(sun.sino.uni-heidelberg.de/igcs/)

China Vitae (www.chinavitae.com)

Council on East Asian Libraries (www.darkwing.uoregon.edu/
~felsing/cstuff/cshelf.html)

Embassy of the People's Republic of China
(www.chinaembassy.org.in)

European Association of Sinological Libraries
(www.easl.org/libra.html)

Facts about China (www.china.com.cn)

*Fairbank Chinese History Virtual Library (www.cnd.org/fairbank)

Finding News about China (freenet.buffalo.edu/~cb863/china.html)

Freenet (www.freenet-china.org) Provides free software to help
Chinese Web users access the Internet without fear of censorship.

Hong Kong Standard (www.hkstandard.com)

Human Rights Watch (www.hrw.org)

Hytelnet (www.lingts.com/hytelnet) Links to library catalogs mostly
in Chinese of Peking University and Shanghai Communications
(*Jiaotong*) University.

Inside China Today (www.insidechina.com/china.html)

Nationmaster.com (www.nationmaster.com)

New York Public Library (www.nypl.org) with links mostly in
Chinese to Library of Chinese Academy of Sciences, National
Library of China, Peking Digital University Library, Shanghai
Library.

Pacific Forum CSIS Comparative Connections. An E-Journal on East Asian Bilateral Relations. (www.csisorg/pacfor)

People's Daily (www.people.com.cn)

South China Morning Post (www.scmp.com/news/index.idc?)

*"The Unbearable Heaviness of Industry" Photos of Chinese factory workers and miners. (www.zhouhai.com)

Tour in China (www.ihep.ac.cn/tour/china_tour.html)

*Virtual Museum of China 89 (www.cnd.org/June 4) Photos (many graphic) of casualties from 3–4 June 1989 military crackdown in Beijing and CNN Video Records link.

*Virtual Museum of the "Cultural Revolution" (www.cnd.org/CR). Contains "micro-history" materials, including personal memoirs, interviews, and discussions with witnesses to key events as well as key government documents from the era.

Voice of America: (www.voa.gov).

Wikipedia, the free encyclopedia. (http://en.wikipedia.org/wiki/Wikipedia

World Resources Institute (www.wri.org)

World Tibet Network News (www.tibet.ca)

About the Author

Lawrence R. Sullivan is an associate professor in Adelphi University, Garden City, New York, and an associate in research at the East Asian Institute, Columbia University. He received his Ph.D. in political science from the University of Michigan in 1976. He has written many articles on contemporary Chinese politics and environmental affairs. He is coauthor of *Chinese Communist Materials at the Bureau of Investigation Archives, Taiwan* (1976); coeditor of *Beijing Spring, 1989, Confrontation and Conflict: The Basic Documents* (1990); and *China's Search for Democracy: The Student and Mass Movement of 1989* (1992). He is also coeditor and cotranslator of Dai Qing, *Yangtze! Yangtze! Debate over the Three Gorges Project* (1994); Ma Jun, *China's Water Crisis* (2004); Dai Qing, *Tiananmen Follies: Prison Memoirs and Other Writings*; and editor of *China since Tiananmen: Political, Economic, and Social Conflicts* (1995).